A WORLD OF IDEAS

ESSENTIAL READINGS
FOR
COLLEGE WRITERS

ALSO WRITTEN OR EDITED
BY
LEE A. JACOBUS

Improving College Reading, Seventh Edition, 2001

Aesthetics and the Arts, 1968

Issues and Response, 1968, 1972

Developing College Reading, Fourth Edition, 1990

Seventeen from Everywhere: Short Stories from Around the World, 1971

Poems in Context (with William Moynihan), 1974

John Cleveland: A Critical Study, 1975

The Humanities through the Arts (with F. David Martin), Fifth
     Edition, 1997

The Sentence Book, Third Edition, 1989

The Paragraph and Essay Book, 1977

Sudden Apprehension: Aspects of Knowledge in Paradise Lost, 1976

Longman Anthology of American Drama, 1982

Humanities, The Evolution of Values, 1986

Writing as Thinking, 1989

The Compact Bedford Introduction to Drama, Fourth Edition, 2001

The Bedford Introduction to Drama, Fourth Edition, 2001

Shakespeare and the Dialectic of Certainty, 1992

Literature: An Introduction to Critical Reading, 1996

Literature: An Introduction to Critical Reading, Compact Edition, 2002

Substance, Style, and Strategy, 1998

SIXTH EDITION

A
WORLD OF
IDEAS

ESSENTIAL READINGS
FOR
COLLEGE WRITERS

LEE A. JACOBUS
University of Connecticut

BEDFORD/ST. MARTIN'S
Boston ◆ *New York*

For Bedford/St. Martin's

Developmental Editor: Mikola De Roo
Senior Production Editor: Harold Chester
Production Supervisor: Jennifer Wetzel
Marketing Manager: Brian Wheel
Art Director: Lucy Krikorian
Text Design: Anna George
Cover Design: Donna Lee Dennison
Cover Art: Johannes Vermeer, *The Geographer,* c. 1668–69,
    Städelsches Kunstinstitut, Frankfurt-am-Main
Composition: Pine Tree Composition, Inc.
Printing and Binding: Haddon Craftsmen, Inc.

President: Charles H. Christensen
Editorial Director: Joan E. Feinberg
Editor in Chief: Nancy Perry
Director of Marketing: Karen R. Melton
Director of Editing, Design, and Production: Marcia Cohen
Managing Editor: Erica T. Appel

Library of Congress Control Number: 00-111685

Manufactured in the United States of America.

7   6   5   4   3   2
f   e   d   c

For information, write: Bedford/St. Martin's, 75 Arlington Street, Boston, MA 02116
(617-399-4000)

ISBN: 0-312-39019-X

PREFACE

Among the pleasures of editing *A World of Ideas* are the discussions I have had with students and teachers who have used the book in their writing classes. The very first person to read the book was a recent college graduate. She told me that she had heard about many of the writers whose works are represented in the text but had never read them, and she was delighted to meet them together in this book. The most recent student to write me—five editions and nearly twenty years later—told me that the book meant a great deal to her, and her experience impelled her to wonder what originally inspired me to assemble the first edition. I explained that my teaching of first-year writing has always inclined toward ideas that serious writers and thinkers have explored and contemplated throughout the ages; early on, I could not find a composition reader that introduced students to the kinds of important thinkers whose writing I believe should be basic to everyone's education. As a result of that need, *A World of Ideas* took shape and has continued to grow and develop through six editions, attracting a wide audience of teachers and students who value the thought-provoking ideas that affect the way we interpret the world.

In preparing the sixth edition of *A World of Ideas*, I have benefited, as usual, from the suggestions of hundreds of users of earlier editions. The primary concern of both students and teachers is that the book remain centered on the tradition of important ideas and on the writers whose work has had a lasting impact on society. To that end, I have chosen writers whose ideas are central to our most important and lasting concerns. A new edition offers the opportunity to reevaluate old choices and make new ones that expand and deepen what has always been the fundamental purpose of this composition reader: to present college students in first-year writing courses with a representative sampling of important ideas examined by men and women who have shaped the way we think today.

The selections in this volume are of the highest quality. Each was chosen because it clarifies important ideas and can sustain discussion and stimulate good writing. Unlike most composition readers, *A World of Ideas* presents substantial excerpts from the work of each of its authors. The selections are presented as they originally appeared; only rarely are they edited and marked with ellipses. They average fifteen pages in length, and their arguments are presented completely as the authors wrote them. Developing a serious idea in writing takes time and a willingness to experiment. Most students are willing to read deeply into the work of important thinkers to better grasp their ideas because the knowledge yielded by the efforts is so vast and rewarding.

New in This Edition

The eight parts of the sixth edition of *A World of Ideas* — Government, Justice, Wealth and Poverty, Mind, Nature, American Culture, Faith, and Feminism — represent a wide range of thought. Perhaps the most notable additions to this edition are two new sections: American Culture, and Feminism. The American Culture section contains selections by six writers who each contemplate and explore the question "What is an American?" The range of these essays is profound and complex, as are the ideas and issues they examine. The five writers in the Feminism section each treat issues that center on justice, liberty, and equality and that pertain to modern life throughout the industrialized world. Like the authors from previous editions, these eleven writers are among the most powerful thinkers in our culture.

Of the forty-five selections (four more than in the fifth edition), twenty are new to the sixth edition, including Elizabeth Cady Stanton, Milton and Rose Friedman, Francis Crick, Rachel Carson, Richard Feynman, J. Hector St. John de Crèvecoeur, Alexis de Tocqueville, Harriet Jacobs, Frederick Jackson Turner, James Baldwin, *The Book of Job* from the Bible, Simone Weil, Mary Wollstonecraft, Carol Gilligan, and bell hooks. Some of the authors in the fifth edition appear now with new selections or translations: Aristotle, Adam Smith, Michio Kaku, Virginia Woolf, and Simone de Beauvoir. Those writers with selections that remain from the fifth edition are Lao-tzu; Niccolò Machiavelli; Jean-Jacques Rousseau; Thomas Jefferson; Hannah Arendt; Frederick Douglass; Henry David Thoreau; Martin Luther King Jr.; Karl Marx; John Kenneth Galbraith (with a revised and updated version of his essay); Robert B. Reich; Plato; Sigmund Freud; Carl Jung; Karen Horney; Howard Gardner; Francis Bacon; Charles Darwin; Stephen Jay Gould; Álvar Núñez Cabeza de Vaca; Siddhārtha Gautama; the Buddha; St. Matthew; the *Bhagavad Gītā;* the Prophet Muhammad; and Friedrich Nietzsche.

A Text for Readers and Writers

Emphasis on Critical Thinking. A *World of Ideas* has always been predicated on dialogues between students, teachers, and the texts in the book. To strengthen the emphasis of previous editions on critical thinking, reading, and writing, one of the new features in this edition is prereading questions for every selection. The content of some of the selections is challenging, and the addition of two or three prereading questions can help students in first-year writing courses overcome minor difficulties in understanding the author's meaning. These brief questions are designed to help students focus on central issues during their first reading of each selection.

The sixth edition, like previous editions, also offers a number of features that help students engage with and interact with the texts as they learn to analyze ideas and develop their own ideas in writing. The book begins with an introduction, "Evaluating Ideas: An Introduction to Critical Reading," that demonstrates a range of methods students can adopt to participate in a meaningful dialogue with each selection. This dialogue—an active, questioning approach to texts and ideas—is one of the keys to critical reading.

Because this book has always been a reader for writers, I try to emphasize ways in which the text can be read to develop ideas for writing. The best method for developing such ideas is to annotate carefully: this establishes both a dialogue with the text and a system for retrieving ideas formulated during that dialogue. In the introduction, a portion of Machiavelli's essay on "The Qualities of the Prince" is presented in annotated form, and the annotations are discussed for their usefulness in understanding this essay and in developing other annotations while reading the essays in the book.

The emphasis on critical reading is developed further in the appendix, "Writing about Ideas: An Introduction to Rhetoric." This section explains how a reader can make annotations while reading critically and then use those annotations to write effectively in response to the ideas presented in any selection in the book. The appendix relies on the annotations of the Machiavelli selection illustrated in "Evaluating Ideas: An Introduction to Critical Reading." A sample essay on Machiavelli, using all the techniques taught in the

context of reading and writing, gives students a model for writing
their own material. In addition, this section helps students understand how they can apply some of the basic rhetorical principles discussed throughout the book.

Introductions for Each Selection.   Each selection is preceded by
a detailed introduction to the life and work of the author and by comments about the primary ideas presented in the reading. The most
interesting rhetorical aspects of the selection are identified and
discussed to help students discover how rhetorical techniques can
achieve specific effects. These essays all offer useful models for writing: Douglass representing narrative; Darwin and Gould, example;
Bacon and Feynman, enumeration; Kaku, cause and effect; Machiavelli, analysis of circumstance; Turner and Woolf, analysis of quotations. These kinds of models of thought and structure are the materials of invention and arrangement that beginning writers find useful.

***"Questions for Critical Reading" and "Suggestions for Writ-
ing," Including "Connections" Questions.***   At the end of each selection is a group of discussion questions designed for use inside or
outside the classroom. Although the "Questions for Critical Reading"
focus on key issues and ideas, they can also be used to stimulate
general class discussion and critical thinking. The "Suggestions for
Writing" help students practice some of the rhetorical strategies employed by the author of a given selection. These suggestions ask for
personal responses, as well as complete essays that involve research.
A number of these assignments, labeled "Connections," promote
critical reading by requiring students to connect particular passages
in a selection with a selection by another writer, either in the same
part of the book or in another part. The variety of possible connections is intriguing—Arendt with Darwin, Jefferson with Douglass
and Rousseau, Aristotle with Beauvoir and Woolf, and many more.

Instructor's Manual.   I have prepared an extensive manual,
Resources for Teaching A WORLD OF IDEAS, that contains further background on the selections, examples from my own classroom responses to the selections, and more suggestions for classroom discussion as well as student writing assignments. Sentence outlines for
the selections—which have been carefully prepared by Carol Ver-
burg, Ellen Troutman, Ellen Darion, and Michael Hennessy—can
be photocopied and given to students. The idea for these sentence
outlines came from the phrase outlines that Darwin created to pre-
de each chapter of *On the Origin of Species.* These outlines may be
to discuss the more difficult selections and to provide addi-

tional guidance for students. At the end of the manual, brief bibliographies are provided for all forty-five authors. These bibliographies may be photocopied and distributed to students who wish to explore the primary selections in greater depth.

Acknowledgments

I am grateful to a number of people who made important suggestions for earlier editions, among them Shoshana Milgram Knapp of Virginia Polytechnic Institute and State University and Michael Hennessy of Southwest Texas State University. Among Michael Hennessy's suggestions for inclusion were the passages from Álvar Núñez Cabeza de Vaca and the Koran. I also remain grateful to Michael Bybee, now at Saint John's College in Santa Fe, for his suggestions of many fascinating pieces by Asian thinkers, all of which he has taught to his own students. Thanks to him, this edition includes Lao-tzu and Siddhārtha Gautama, the Buddha, as interpreted by Buddhist monks.

Like its predecessors, this edition is indebted to a great many creative people at Bedford/St. Martin's, whose support is invaluable. I want to thank Chuck Christensen, whose concern for the continued excellence of this book and whose close attention to detail are truly admirable. I appreciate as always the advice of Joan E. Feinberg, whose suggestions were timely and excellent. My editor, Mika De Roo, collaborated closely on this project, reading each selection we kept as well as all those we considered but did not use. Her support and advice were invaluable, and her shrewd judgment made this a better book. Nancy Perry, editor in chief, and Carla Samodulski, former executive editor, offered many useful ideas and suggestions as well, especially in the early stages of development. Karen Henry, editor and friend, kept her sharp eye on the project throughout. Harold Chester, production editor, also helped with innumerable important details and suggestions. Alice Vigliani, copyeditor, improved the prose and watched out for inconsistencies. Thanks also to some important staff members and researchers: Sandy Schechter cleared permissions, Donna Dennison designed the cover, and Alice Lundoff secured the art for the cover. In earlier editions I had help from Sarah Cornog, Rosemary Winfield, Michelle Clark, Professor Mary W. Cornog, Ellen Kuhl, Mark Reimold, Andrea Goldman, Beth Castrodale, Jonathan Burns, Mary Beth McNulty, and Beth Chapman; I felt I had a personal relationship with each of them. I want to thank Anatoly Dverin, Lyrl Ahern, and especially Bill Ogden for their wonderful portraits of the writers, which have added a special dimension to the book. I also want to thank the students—quite a few of them—who wrote to me directly about their experiences in reading the first five editions. I have attended carefully to what they told me, and I am warmed by their high regard for the materials in this book.

Earlier editions have named the hundreds of users of this book who sent their comments and encouragement. I would like to thank them again (you know who you are). In addition, the following professors were generous with criticism, praise, and detailed recommendations for the sixth edition: Raphael Allison, New York University; Wendy W. Allman, Baylor University; Jonathan Ausubel, Chaffey College; Sara-Jane Bailes, New York University; Carolyn Sue Baker, San Diego State University; James E. Barcus, Baylor University; Nancy Barta-Smith, Slippery Rock University; Mark Bayhurst, San Diego State University; N. Bender, New York University; Tara Bookataub, University of Oregon; Kathryn Broyles, Warner Southern College; Elaine Burklow, Southern Illinois University—Carbondale; Erica L. Burleigh, Johns Hopkins University; Gary Carlson, Norwalk Community College; Nadine Chapman, Whitworth College; Mark Daniel Chilton, University of Oregon; Lois A. Coleman, University of Connecticut; David Colonne, Eastern Michigan University; Robert Comeau, Union County College; William Cooper, Allan Hancock College; Lynne Crockett, New York University; Michelle Dent, New York University; Rachel Dresbeck, Portland Community College; Eugenia C. Eberhart, Southern Illinois University—Carbondale; Linda H. Elegant, Portland Community College; Cynthia Fillmore, San Diego State University; Wilma M. Finney, North Arkansas College; Hedda Fish, San Diego State University; Tania Friedel, New York University; Natalie Friedman, New York University; Ryan Friesen, Winona State University; Ronald J. Ganze, University of Oregon; Jaclyn Geller, New York University; April Gentry, Southern Illinois University—Carbondale; Joe Glaser, Western Kentucky University; Donald A. Gordon, Rocky Mountain College of Art and Design; Sara Groce, University of Oregon; Jackie Gruenwald, Southern Illinois University—Carbondale; Mara Hatfield, Southern Illinois University—Carbondale; Douglas Haynes, Southern Illinois University—Carbondale; Theodore Hendricks, Towson University; Michael Hennessy, Southwest Texas State University; June Henry, Allan Hancock College; Sarah James, Towson University; Arthur C. Johnson, Towson University; Jennifer Johnson, University of Minnesota; Margaret Faye Jones, Nashville State Tech; Steve Juenemann, University of Minnesota; Rivad A. Kaye, Davidson College; Robert Kenneth Kirby, Samford University; Deborah L. Kirkman, University of Kentucky; Shoshana Milgram Knapp, Virginia Tech; Michael Lackey,

University of St. Thomas; Allison Langdon, University of Oregon; Denise MacNeil, University of Redlands; Kellie Manning, University of Texas—Permian Basin; Donna Marsh, Syracuse University; Pam Mathis, North Arkansas College; Gerald McCarthy, San Antonio College; Todd McGowan, Southwest Texas State University; Kerri McKeand, San Diego State University; Megan Miller, Southern Illinois University—Carbondale; Paul Miller, College of Marin; Candace Montoya, University of Oregon; David Morris, San Diego State University; Ruth Newberry, Duquesne University; Stacey O. Nicklow, Southern Illinois University—Carbondale; Alexis S. Olds, Allan Hancock College; Crystal O'Neal, Southern Illinois University—Carbondale; Elizabeth Parker, Nashville State Tech; Jonna Perrillo, New York University; Justin A. Pittas-Giroux, College of Charleston; Sarah Pletz, San Antonio College; James Polchin, New York University; Miriam Heddy Pollock, New York University; Brian Price, New York University; Darren C. Reilley, University of Oregon; Ilana Simons, New York University; Ann Snodgrass, Massachusetts Institute of Technology; Robert J. Stagnaro, San Diego State University; Jennifer Stevenson, Rocky Mountain College of Art and Design; Ben Stewart, New York University; Jenny Su, New York University; Laura Tanenbaum, New York University; Marty Terrill, North Arkansas College; Deb Thornton, Utah Valley College; Stephanie Utley, Southern Illinois University—Carbondale; Allen Vogt, Carthage College; Janet White, Los Angeles Harbor Community College; Stan Wiggins, San Antonio College; Melissa Williams, San Diego State University; Sherraine Pate Williams, Southern Illinois University—Carbondale; Angela Williamson, University of Minnesota; Joyce P. Wilson, Boston University; Amanda Yesnowitz, New York University; Monica Young, New York University; Meryl Zwanger, New York University.

Gardner

CONTENTS

Preface   *v*

EVALUATING IDEAS: An Introduction to Critical Reading   *1*

PART ONE

GOVERNMENT

– 13 –

LAO-TZU   *Thoughts from the* Tao-te Ching   *19*

> *In recommending that a ruler practice judicious inactivity rather than wasteful busyness, the ancient Chinese philosopher minimizes the power of the state over the individual.*

NICCOLÒ MACHIAVELLI   The Qualities of the Prince   *35*

> *In this excerpt from the most notorious political treatise of all time, Machiavelli, a veteran of intrigue at Florence's Medici court, recommends unscrupulous tactics for the ruler who wishes to secure power for himself and stability in his domain.*

JEAN-JACQUES ROUSSEAU   The Origin of Civil Society   *53*

> *The French philosopher Rousseau speculates that members of a society forfeit individual freedoms for the greater good of all and stresses a revolutionary view — equality before the law.*

THOMAS JEFFERSON   The Declaration of Independence   75

In this primary document of modern democratic government, Jefferson justifies the right of the American colonies to dissolve their bonds with a tyrannical monarchy and to construct a free nation of independent souls in its stead.

HANNAH ARENDT   Ideology and Terror: A Novel Form
of Government   85

Arendt sees the misapplication of the principles of Karl Marx and Charles Darwin in the ideologies of terror-dominated governments in Communist Russia and fascist Germany in the mid-twentieth century.

P A R T   T W O

JUSTICE

– 105 –

ARISTOTLE   A Definition of Justice   *111*

In his Politics, *Aristotle meditates on the nature of justice and how it is perceived, especially in a democracy. For him, the concept of equality is the key to understanding justice in society.*

FREDERICK DOUGLASS   *From* Narrative of the Life
of Frederick Douglass, an American Slave   *125*

Douglass, one of the most influential nineteenth-century African Americans, reveals how an indomitable human spirit reacts to a government-sanctioned system that treats some people as chattel and denies them justice.

HENRY DAVID THOREAU   Civil Disobedience   *141*

A man who lived by his ideals of justice, Thoreau explains how and why it is not only reasonable but also sometimes essential to disobey unjust laws imposed by the state.

ELIZABETH CADY STANTON   Declaration of Sentiments
and Resolutions   169

*Stanton draws on her experience as a feminist and on Thomas
Jefferson's format to show that, one hundred years after the Declaration of Independence, half of America still waited to be freed
from tyranny.*

MARTIN LUTHER KING JR.   Letter from Birmingham Jail   179

*King, a minister and civil rights leader, advocates nonviolent
action as a means of changing the unconscionable practices of
racial segregation and of achieving justice for all.*

PART THREE

WEALTH AND POVERTY

– 201 –

ADAM SMITH   Of the Natural Progress of Opulence   207

This excerpt from the classic work on modern capitalism, The
Wealth of Nations, *explores the economic relationship between
rural areas and cities in an attempt to understand the "natural"
steps to wealth.*

KARL MARX   The Communist Manifesto   219

*Marx, the chief critic of laissez-faire capitalism, traces the de-
humanizing progress of the nineteenth-century bourgeois economic
structure and heralds its downfall at the hands of a united international proletariat.*

JOHN KENNETH GALBRAITH   The Position of Poverty   247

*Improving the plight of society's poorest members is a central re-
sponsibility for today's wealthy nations, says Galbraith, the most
widely read economist of the past four decades.*

MILTON AND ROSE FRIEDMAN   Created Equal   *261*

> *Noted conservative economists consider the Declaration of In-
> dependence's insistence that "all men are created equal." Their
> view is that equality of opportunity is essential in a democracy,
> but that equality of outcome is a denial of personal freedom.*

ROBERT B. REICH   Why the Rich Are Getting Richer
and the Poor, Poorer   *287*

> *The former secretary of labor talks about major categories of workers
> in contemporary U.S. society and the inevitable and essential changes
> occurring as the economy is altered by globalization.*

PART FOUR

MIND

– 307 –

PLATO   The Allegory of the Cave   *313*

> *Plato, the founder of Western philosophy, talks about the nature of
> perception and the limits of the human mind, emphasizing the difficul-
> ties everyone encounters in discovering the truth about appearances.*

SIGMUND FREUD   *From* The Interpretation of Dreams   *327*

> *As the founder of modern psychiatry, Freud developed extensive
> theories about the importance of dreams for the healthy mind and in
> this essay examines how dreams fulfill our unspoken waking wishes.*

CARL JUNG   The Personal and the Collective Unconscious   *341*

> *Whereas Freud examines the individual unconscious in dreams,
> Jung proposes that as a cultural group we have a collective uncon-
> scious — unconscious awarenesses and needs that transcend the
> individual and represent the needs of the group to which we belong.*

KAREN HORNEY   The Distrust between the Sexes   357

*Horney, the first major female psychoanalyst, examines Freud's
theories and other cultures to establish a theory of development
that accounts for the tangled relations between the sexes.*

HOWARD GARDNER   A Rounded Version: The Theory
of Multiple Intelligences   373

*Gardner, a contemporary psychologist, has a novel view of the
mind that proposes seven distinct forms of human intelligence—
linguistic, logical-mathematical, spatial, musical, bodily-
kinesthetic, interpersonal, and intrapersonal.*

FRANCIS CRICK   The General Nature of Consciousness   395

*The discoverer of the structure of DNA (deoxyribonucleic acid)
discusses the mystery of consciousness. Crick's approach is strictly
scientific, establishing the nature of the problem and focusing on
memory and attention.*

PART FIVE

NATURE

– 411 –

FRANCIS BACON   The Four Idols   417

*A prominent figure in philosophy and politics during the reign of
Elizabeth I, Bacon describes the obstacles that hinder human beings'
efforts to understand the world around them and the mysteries of
nature.*

CHARLES DARWIN   Natural Selection   435

*The scrupulous habits of observation that culminated in the land-
mark theory of evolution are everywhere evident in Darwin's
analysis of the ways species adapt to their environments in nature.*

RACHEL CARSON   Nature Fights Back   453

In a pioneering essay, Carson calls attention to the devastation of our environment by the indiscriminate long-term use of insecticides. In addition to other unexpected results, the very pests the chemicals were designed to kill have come back to haunt us.

STEPHEN JAY GOULD   Nonmoral Nature   471

Gould, a scientist of diverse experience, warns against assuming that the natural world mirrors our own ideas of good and evil.

MICHIO KAKU   The Mystery of Dark Matter   487

To understand why galaxies do not fly apart, physicists postulate the existence of a form of matter that makes up 90 percent of the universe but that cannot be seen or touched: dark matter. Eminent physicist Kaku explains the history of the theory of dark matter and reveals the difficulties modern physicists face in describing how the universe works.

RICHARD P. FEYNMAN   The Relation of Science and Religion   503

One of the nation's foremost nuclear physicists, Feynman considers the philosophical problem of how science and religion interact. In this inquiry over whether belief in both science and God is possible, he examines two ways in which the mind searches for truth: in terms of doubt and in terms of faith.

PART SIX

AMERICAN CULTURE

– 517 –

ÁLVAR NÚÑEZ CABEZA DE VACA   From La Relación   523

A secretary in the company of the conquistadores who landed in Florida in 1528, Cabeza de Vaca became a legendary healer. Here he describes his life in the Americas and the culture of the Avavares Indians with whom he stayed.

J. HECTOR ST. JOHN DE CRÈVECOEUR   What Is an
    American?   537

Crèvecoeur became famous for writing Letters from an American
Farmer, *a depiction of eighteenth-century colonial life. In the
letter included here, he attempted one of the first definitions of
the American, an individual that Crèvecoeur saw as transformed
from the European immigrant by independence and opportunity.*

ALEXIS DE TOCQUEVILLE   Influence of Democratic Ideas
    and Feelings on Political Society   565

*Tocqueville visited America in the early nineteenth century and
found its expression of democracy so extraordinary that he wrote*
Democracy in America, *a classic treatise on Americans and their
political institutions. In this excerpt, he considers the importance of
equality in a democratic society.*

HARRIET JACOBS (LINDA BRENT)   Free at Last   585

*Although her freedom was purchased by a kindly employer,
Harriet Jacobs despised the fact that as a nineteenth-century
American slave she was essentially a commodity. This excerpt
from her autobiography depicts painful and intolerable experiences under slavery and recounts Jacobs's difficult path to
freedom.*

FREDERICK JACKSON TURNER   *From* The Significance
    of the Frontier in American History   599

*In his landmark Turner Thesis, this renowned historian explores
how the continually shifting frontier made new demands on Americans by placing them in close contact with Native Americans and
by testing their sense of adventure and independence. For Turner,
the frontier shaped the American character and our democracy.*

JAMES BALDWIN   The American Dream
    and the American Negro   629

*One of our most distinguished modern writers, Baldwin sounds a
prescient note of warning in this 1965 essay. The prosperity of
white America, Baldwin cautions, is not shared equally by African
Americans. He predicts that until the American dream is in reach
of all, we can expect social unrest and individual bitterness.*

PART SEVEN

FAITH

– 639 –

✓SIDDHĀRTHA GAUTAMA, THE BUDDHA   Meditation:
The Path to Enlightenment   645

> *Buddhist monks, continuing in the tradition of the Buddha, who re-*
> *vealed the eightfold path of right living and self-control, describe*
> *the path to enlightenment through meditation—the technique of*
> *clearing one's mind through zazen.*

THE BIBLE   *From* The Book of Job   665

> *In one of the most beautifully written books of the Hebrew Bible,*
> *Job, a good man, suffers terrible torments because of a challenge to*
> *God. The narrative imparts the wisdom of accepting how little one*
> *ultimately knows.*

ST. MATTHEW   The Sermon on the Mount   691

> *Matthew, the tax gatherer who walked with Jesus, recorded Jesus'*
> *sermon on the mount, in which he gave his disciples the Lord's*
> *prayer and guidelines for a way of life that expressed faith in God.*

THE BHAGAVAD GĪTĀ   Meditation and Knowledge   703

> *In this Hindu poem, faith is implicit as the Lord Krishna speaks to*
> *his disciple Arjuna, explaining that the way to knowledge is through*
> *discipline and that discipline is developed through meditation.*

THE PROPHET MUHAMMAD   *From the* Koran   719

> *In this surah, or chapter, from the Koran, Allah tells Muhammad*
> *about the harsh fate of those who have no faith and are unbelievers*
> *and the bliss and reassurance of the believer whose faith carries*
> *him to the truth.*

FRIEDRICH NIETZSCHE   Apollonianism and Dionysianism   *731*

> *The nineteenth-century philosopher Nietzsche examines two op-*
> *posing psychological capacities that exist in us all—divine forces*
> *that we must learn to balance in order to live well and fully.*

SIMONE WEIL   Spiritual Autobiography   *751*

> *Written during World War II by social philosopher Simone Weil,
> this letter to her spiritual adviser reveals the depth of Weil's think-
> ing about Christianity and the intensity of her commitment to her
> own ethical principles.*

PART EIGHT

FEMINISM

– 773 –

MARY WOLLSTONECRAFT   Pernicious Effects Which Arise
from the Unnatural Distinctions Established in Society   *779*

> *In this excerpt from one of the first great works of feminism, Woll-
> stonecraft argues that the laws, property rights, and class distinc-
> tions of her day are mechanisms of control that deny women their
> liberty and demean their lives.*

VIRGINIA WOOLF   Shakespeare's Sister   *797*

> *In this excerpt from her book-length essay on the role of women in
> history and society,* A Room of One's Own, *Woolf imaginatively
> reconstructs the environment of Shakespeare's hypothetical sister
> and demonstrates how little opportunity she would have had in the
> sixteenth century.*

SIMONE DE BEAUVOIR   Woman: Myth and Reality   *817*

> *Beauvoir was a French philosopher who meditated on feminism
> and many other aspects of modern life. In this essay, she explains
> how the persistent myths about women as "the Eternal Feminine"
> distort reality and harm real women in society.*

CAROL GILLIGAN   Woman's Place in Man's Life Cycle   *835*

> *In this excerpt from her ground-breaking book,* In a Different
> Voice: Psychological Theory and Women's Development,
> *Gilligan shows how historically men have made woman the de-
> viant in society, such as Eve in the Garden of Eden. Men often
> fashion women, she suggests, out of "a masculine cloth."*

bell hooks   Black Women: Shaping Feminist Theory   *859*

> *In this stinging rebuke, bell hooks surveys the standard canon of feminist literature only to find that it presupposes a white, middle-class feminist. She sets the record straight by clarifying the needs and contributions of black women to the movement.*

WRITING ABOUT IDEAS: An Introduction to Rhetoric   *879*

INDEX OF RHETORICAL TERMS   *903*

EVALUATING IDEAS
An Introduction to Critical Reading

The selections in this book demand a careful and attentive reading. The authors, whose works have changed the way we view our world, our institutions, and ourselves, make every effort to communicate their views with clarity and style. But their views are complex and subtle, and we must train ourselves to read them sensitively, responsively, and critically. Critical reading is basic for approaching the essays in this book. Indeed, it is fundamental for approaching any reading material that deserves serious attention.

Reading critically means reading actively: questioning the premises of the argument, speculating on the ways in which evidence is used, comparing the statements of one writer with those of another, and holding an inner dialogue with the author. These skills differ from the passive reception we employ when we watch television or read lightweight materials. Being an active, participating reader makes it possible for us to derive the most from good books.

Critical reading involves most of the following processes:

- *Prereading* Developing a sense of what the piece is about and what its general purposes seem to be.

- *Annotating* Using a pencil or a pen to mark those passages that seem important enough to return to later. Annotations establish a dialogue between you and the author.

- *Questioning* Raising issues that you feel need to be taken into consideration. These may be issues that you believe the author has treated either well or badly and that you feel are important. Questioning can be part of the annotation process.

- *Reviewing* Rereading your annotations and underlinings in order to grasp the entire "picture" of what you've just read.

Sometimes writing a summary of the piece as you review makes the meaning even clearer.

- *Forming your own ideas*   Reviewing what you have read, evaluating the way that the writer presents the issues, and developing your own views on the issues. This is the final step.

THE PROCESS OF CRITICAL READING

Prereading

Before you read a particular selection, you may find it useful to turn to the beginning of the part in which it appears. There you will find an introduction discussing the broader issues and questions central to all the selections in the part that may help you to focus your thoughts and formulate your opinions as you read the essays themselves.

Begin any selection in this book by reading its headnote. Each headnote supplies historical background on the writer, sets the intellectual stage for the ideas discussed in the essay, and comments on the writer's main points. The second part of each headnote also introduces the main rhetorical or stylistic methods that the writer uses to communicate his/her thoughts. In the process of reading the headnote, you will develop an overview that helps prepare you for reading the essay.

This kind of preparation is typical of critical reading. It makes the task of reading more delightful, more useful, and much easier. A review of the headnote to Niccolò Machiavelli and part of his essay "The Qualities of the Prince" will illustrate the usefulness of such preparation. This essay appears in Part One—Government—so the content can already be expected to be concerned with styles of government. The introduction to Machiavelli provides the following points, each followed here by the number of the paragraph in which it appears:

Machiavelli was an Italian aristocrat in Renaissance Italy. (1)

Machiavelli describes the qualities necessary for a prince—that is, any ruler—to maintain power. (2)

A weak Italy was prey to the much stronger France and Spain at this time. (2)

Machiavelli recommends securing power by whatever means necessary and maintaining it. (3)

His concern for moralizing or acting out of high moral principle is not great. (3)

He supports questionable means of becoming and remaining prince. (3)

Machiavelli does not fret over the means used to achieve his ends and sometimes advocates repression, imprisonment, and torture. (3)

Machiavelli has been said to have a cynical view of human nature. (4)

His rhetorical method is to discuss both sides of an issue: cruelty and mercy, liberality and stinginess. (8)

He uses aphorisms to persuade the reader that he is saying something wise and true. (9)

With these observations in mind, the reader knows that the selection following will be concerned with governance in Renaissance Italy. The question of ends versus means is central to Machiavelli's discussion, and he does not idealize people and their general goodness. Yet because of Machiavelli's rhetorical methods, particularly his use of aphorism,[1] the reader can expect that Machiavelli's argument will be exceptionally persuasive.

Thus, as a critical reader, you will be well advised to keep track of these basic statements from the headnote. You need not accept all of them, but you should certainly be alert to the issues that will probably be central to your experience of the essay. Remember: it is just as reasonable to question the headnote as it is to question the essay itself.

Before reading the essay in detail, you might develop an overview of its meaning by scanning it quickly. In the case of "The Qualities of the Prince," note the subheadings, such as "On Those Things for Which Men, and Particularly Princes, Are Praised or Blamed." Checking each of the subheadings before you read the entire piece might provide you with a map or guide to the essay.

Each passage is preceded by two or three prereading questions. These are designed to keep two or three points in mind as you read. Each of these questions focuses your attention on an important idea or interpretation in the passage. For Machiavelli the questions are:

1. Why does Machiavelli praise skill in warfare in his opening pages? How does that skill aid a prince?
2. Is it better for a prince to be loved or to be feared?

---

[1] **aphorism** A short, pithy statement of truth.

In each case a key element in Machiavelli's argument is the center of each question. By watching for the answer to these questions you will find yourself focusing on some of the most important aspects of the passage.

Annotating and Questioning

As you read a text, your annotations establish a dialogue between you and the author. You can underline or highlight important statements that you feel help clarify the author's position. They may be statements to which you will want to refer later. Think of them as serving one overriding purpose: to make it possible for you to review the piece and understand its key points without having to reread it entirely.

Your dialogue with the author will be most visible in the margins of the essay, which is one reason the margins in this book are so generous. Take issue with key points or note your assent — the more you annotate, the more you free your imagination to develop your own ideas. My own methods involve notating both agreement and disagreement. I annotate thoroughly, so that after a quick second glance I know what the author is saying as well as what I thought of the essay when I read it closely. My annotations help me keep the major points fresh in my mind.

Annotation keeps track both of what the author says and of what our responses are. No one can reduce annotation to a formula — we all do it differently — but it is not a passive act. Reading with a pencil or a pen in hand should become second nature. Without annotations, you often have to reread entire sections of an essay to remember an argument that once was clear and understandable but after time has become part of the fabric of the prose and thus "invisible." Annotation is the conquest of the invisible; it provides a quick view of the main points.

When you annotate,

- Read with a pen or a pencil.
- Underline key sentences — for example, definitions and statements of purpose.
- Underline key words that appear often.
- Note the topic of paragraphs in the margins.
- Ask questions in the margins.
- Make notes in the margins to remind yourself to develop ideas later.

- Mark passages you might want to quote later.
- Keep track of points with which you disagree.

Some sample annotations follow, again from the second essay in the book, Niccolò Machiavelli's "The Qualities of the Prince." A sixteenth-century text in translation, *The Prince* is challenging to work with. My annotations appear in the form of underlinings and marginal comments and questions. Only the first few paragraphs appear here, but the entire essay is annotated in my copy of the book.

A Prince's Duty Concerning Military Matters

The prince's profession should be war.

A prince, therefore, must not have any other object nor any other thought, nor must he take anything as his profession but war, its institutions, and its discipline; because that is the only profession which befits one who commands; and it is of such importance that not only does it maintain those who were born princes, but many times it enables men of private station to rise to that position; and, on the other hand, it is evident that when princes have given more thought to personal luxuries than to arms, they have lost their state. And the first way to lose it is to neglect this art; and the way to acquire it is to be well versed in this art.

Examples

Francesco Sforza became Duke of Milan from being a private citizen because he was armed; his sons, since they avoided the inconveniences of arms, became private citizens after having been dukes. For, among the other bad effects it causes, being disarmed makes you despised; this is one of those infamies a prince should guard himself against, as will be treated below: for between an armed and an unarmed man there is no comparison whatsoever, and it is not reasonable for an armed man to obey an unarmed man willingly, nor that an unarmed man should be safe among armed servants; since, when the former is suspicious and the latter are contemptuous, it is impossible for them to work well together. And therefore, a prince who does not understand military matters, besides the other misfortunes already noted, cannot be esteemed by his own soldiers, nor can he trust them.

Being disarmed makes you despised. Is this true?

Training: action/mind

He must, therefore, never raise his thought from this exercise of war, and in peacetime he must train himself more than in time of war; this can be done in two ways: one by action, the other by the mind. And as far as actions are concerned, besides keeping his soldiers well disciplined and trained, he must always be out hunting, and must accustom his body to hardships in this manner; and he must

Knowledge of terrain

also learn the nature of the terrain, and know how mountains slope, how valleys open, how plains lie, and understand the nature of rivers and swamps;

Two benefits

and he should devote much attention to such activities. Such knowledge is useful in two ways: first, one learns to know one's own country and can better understand how to defend it; second, with the knowledge and experience of the terrain, one can easily comprehend the characteristics of any other terrain that it is necessary to explore for the first time; for the hills, valleys, plains, rivers, and swamps of Tuscany, for instance, have certain similarities to those of other provinces; so that by knowing the lay of the land in one province one can easily understand it in others. And a prince who lacks this ability lacks the most important quality in a leader; because this skill teaches you to find the enemy, choose a campsite, lead troops, organize them for battle, and besiege towns to your own advantage.

[There follow the examples of Philopoemon, who was always observing terrain for its military usefulness, and a recommendation that princes read histories and learn from them. Three paragraphs are omitted.]

On Those Things for Which Men, and Particularly Princes, Are Praised or Blamed

Now there remains to be examined what should be the methods and procedures of a prince in dealing with his subjects and friends. And because I know that many have written about this, I am afraid that writing about it again I shall be thought of as presumptuous, since in discussing this material I depart radically from the procedures of others. But since my intention is to write something useful for anyone who understands it, it seemed more suitable to me to search after the effectual truth of the matter rather than its imagined one. And many writers have imagined for themselves republics and principalities that have never been seen nor known to exist in reality; for there is such a gap between how one lives and how one ought to live that anyone who abandons what is done for what ought to be done learns his ruin rather than his preservation: for a man who wishes to make a vocation of being good at all times will come to ruin among so many who are not good. Hence it is necessary for a prince who wishes to maintain his position to learn how not to be good, and to use this knowledge or not to use it according to necessity.

Those who are good at all times come to ruin among those who are not good.

Prince must learn how not to be good.

Leaving aside, therefore, the imagined things concerning a prince, and taking into account those that are true, I say that all men, when they are spoken of, and particularly princes, since they are placed on a higher level, are judged by some of these qualities which bring them either blame or praise. And this is why one is considered generous, another miserly (to use a Tuscan word, since "avaricious" in our language is still used to mean one who wishes to acquire by means of theft; we call "miserly" one who excessively avoids using what he has); one is considered a giver, the other rapacious; one cruel, another merciful; one treacherous, another faithful; one effeminate and cowardly, another bold and courageous; one humane, another haughty; one lascivious, another chaste; one trustworthy, another cunning; one harsh, another lenient; one serious, another frivolous; one religious, another unbelieving; and the like. And I know that everyone will admit that it would be a very praiseworthy thing to find in a prince, of the qualities mentioned above, those that are held to be good, but since it is neither possible to have them nor to observe them all completely, because human nature does not permit it, a prince must be prudent enough to know how to escape the bad

Note the prince's reputation.

Prince must avoid reputation for the worst vices.

reputation of those vices that would lose the state for him, and must protect himself from those that will not lose it for him, if this is possible; but if he

Some vices may be needed to hold the state. True?

cannot, he need not concern himself unduly if he ignores these less serious vices. And, moreover, he need not worry about incurring the bad reputation of those vices without which it would be difficult to hold his state; since, carefully taking everything into account, one will discover that

Some virtues may end in destruction.

something which appears to be a virtue, if pursued, will end in his destruction; while some other thing which seems to be a vice, if pursued, will result in his safety and his well-being.

Reviewing

The process of review, which takes place after a careful reading, is much more useful if you have annotated and underlined the text well. To a large extent, the review process can be devoted to accounting for the primary ideas that have been uncovered by your annotations and underlinings. For example, reviewing the Machiavelli annotations shows that the following ideas are crucial to Machiavelli's thinking:

- The prince's profession should be war, so the most successful princes are probably experienced in the military.
- If they do not pay attention to military matters, princes will lose their power.
- Being disarmed makes the prince despised.
- The prince should be in constant training.
- The prince needs a sound knowledge of terrain.
- Machiavelli says he tells us what is true, not what ought to be true.
- Those who are always good will come to ruin among those who are not good.
- To remain in power, the prince must learn how not to be good.
- The prince should avoid the worst vices in order not to harm his reputation.
- To maintain power, some vices may be necessary.
- Some virtues may end in destruction.

Putting Machiavelli's ideas in this raw form does an injustice to his skill as a writer, but annotation is designed to result in such summary statements. We can see that there are some constant themes, such as the insistence that the prince be a military person. As the headnote tells us, in Machiavelli's day Italy was a group of rival city-states, and France, a larger, united nation, was invading these states one by one. Machiavelli dreamed that one powerful prince, such as his favorite, Cesare Borgia, could fight the French and save Italy. He emphasized the importance of the military because he lived in an age in which war was a constant threat.

Machiavelli anticipates the complaints of pacifists—those who argue against war—by telling us that those who remain unarmed are despised. To demonstrate his point, he gives us examples of those who lost their positions as princes because they avoided being armed. He clearly expects these examples to be persuasive.

A second important theme pervading Machiavelli's essay is his view on moral behavior. For Machiavelli, being in power is much more important than being virtuous. He is quick to admit that vice is not desirable and that the worst vices will harm the prince's reputation. But he also says that the prince need not worry about the "less serious" vices. Moreover, the prince need not worry about incurring a bad reputation by practicing vices that are necessary if he wishes to hold his state. In the same spirit, Machiavelli tells us that there are some virtues that might lead to the destruction of the prince.

Forming Your Own Ideas

One of the most important reasons for reading the texts in this book critically is to enable you to develop your own positions on issues that these writers raise. Identifying and clarifying the main ideas is only the first step; the next step in critical reading is evaluating those ideas.

For example, you might ask whether Machiavelli's ideas have any relevance for today. After all, he wrote nearly five hundred years ago and times have changed. You might feel that Machiavelli was relevant strictly during the Italian Renaissance or, alternatively, that his principles are timeless and have something to teach every age. For most people, Machiavelli is a political philosopher whose views are useful anytime and anywhere.

If you agree with the majority, then you may want to examine Machiavelli's ideas to see whether you can accept them. Consider just two of those ideas and their implications:

- Should rulers always be members of the military? Should they always be armed? Should the ruler of a nation first demonstrate competence as a military leader?

- Should rulers ignore virtue and practice vice when it is convenient?

In his commentary on government, Lao-tzu offers different advice from Machiavelli because his assumptions are that the ruler ought to respect the rights of individuals. For Lao-tzu the waging of war is an annoying, essentially wasteful activity. Machiavelli on the other hand, never questions the usefulness of war: to him, it is basic to government. As a critical reader, you can take issue with such an assumption, and in doing so you will deepen your understanding of Machiavelli.

If we were to follow Machiavelli's advice, then we would choose presidents on the basis of whether or not they had been good military leaders. Among those we would not have chosen from American history might be Thomas Jefferson, Abraham Lincoln, and Franklin Delano Roosevelt. Those who were high-ranking military men include George Washington, Ulysses S. Grant, and Dwight D. Eisenhower. If you followed Machiavelli's rhetorical technique of using examples to convince your audience, you could choose from either group to prove your case.

Of course, there are examples from other nations. It has been common since the 1930s to see certain leaders dressed in their military uniforms: Benito Mussolini (Italy), Adolf Hitler (Germany), Joseph Stalin (Russia), Idi Amin (Uganda), Muammar al-Qaddafi (Libya). These are all tyrants who have tormented their citizens and their neighbors. That gives us something to think about. Should a president dress in full military regalia all the time? Is that a good image for the ruler of a free nation to project?

Do you want a ruler, then, who is usually virtuous but embraces vice when it is necessary? This is a very difficult question to answer. When Jimmy Carter swore to the American people that he would never lie to them, many Americans were skeptical. They thought that politics was essentially a game of careful and judicious lying— at least at times. In other words, these Americans were already committed to Machiavelli's position.

These are only a few of the questions that are raised by my annotations in the few pages from Machiavelli examined here. Many other issues could be uncovered by these annotations, and many more from subsequent pages of the essay. Critical reading can be a powerful means by which to open what you read to discovery and discussion.

Once you begin a line of questioning, the ways in which you think about a passage begin expanding. You find yourself with more ideas of your own that have grown in response to those you have been reading about. Reading critically, in other words, gives you an enormous return on your investment of time. If you have the chance to investigate your responses to the assumptions and underlying premises of passages such as Machiavelli's, you will be able to refine your thinking even further. For example, if you agree with Machiavelli that rulers should be successful military leaders for whom small vices may be useful at times, and you find yourself in a position to argue with someone who feels Machiavelli is mistaken in this view, then you will have a good opportunity to evaluate the soundness of your thinking. You will have a chance to see your own assumptions and arguments tested.

In many ways, this entire book is about such opportunities. The essays that follow offer you powerful ideas from great thinkers. They invite you to participate in their thoughts, exercise your own knowledge and assumptions, and arrive at your own conclusions. Basically, that is the meaning of education.

PART ONE

GOVERNMENT

Lao-tzu
Niccolò Machiavelli
Jean-Jacques Rousseau
Thomas Jefferson
Hannah Arendt

INTRODUCTION

At the core of any idea of government is the belief that individuals need an organized allocation of authority to protect their well-being. However, throughout history the form of that allocation of authority has undergone profound shifts, and each successive type of government has inspired debates and defenses. The first civilizations in Mesopotamia and Egypt (4000–3000 B.C.) were theocracies ruled by a high priest. Gradually these political systems evolved into monarchies in which a king whose role was separate from that of the religious leaders held power. During the sixth century B.C. the Greek city-state Athens developed the first democratic system wherein male citizens (but not women or slaves) could elect a body of leaders. As these forms of government developed, so too did the concept of government as the center of law and administration. However, governments and ideas of governments (actual or ideal) have not followed a straight path. History has witnessed constant oscillations between various forms and functions of government, from tyrannies to republics. In turn, these governments and their relation to the individual citizen have been the focus of many great thinkers.

In this section, the thinkers represented have concentrated on both the role and form of government. Lao-tzu reflects on the ruler who would, by careful management, maintain a happy citizenry. Machiavelli places the survival of the prince above all other considerations of government and, unlike Lao-tzu, ignores the concerns and rights of the individual. For Machiavelli, power is the issue, and maintaining it is the sign of good government. Rousseau's emphasis on the social contract focuses on the theory that citizens voluntarily submit to governance in the hopes of gaining greater personal freedom.

Whereas governing well concerns most of these thinkers, the forms of government concern others. Thomas Jefferson struggled with the monarchical form of government, as did Rousseau before him, and envisioned a republic that would serve the people. Kings were a threatened species in eighteenth-century Europe, and with Jefferson's aid, they became extinct in the United States. Hannah Arendt was convinced that the totalitarian governments of the twentieth century were the product of new ideologies formed from misunderstanding Darwinian theories and misapplying Marxian concepts of class struggle.

Lao-tzu, whose writings provide the basis for Taoism, one of three major Chinese religions, was interested primarily in political systems. His work, the *Tao-te Ching,* has been translated loosely as "The Way of Power." One thing that becomes clear from reading his work—especially the selections presented here—is his concern for the well-being of the people in any government. He does not recommend specific forms of government (monarchic, representative, democratic) or advocate election versus the hereditary transfer of power. But he does make it clear that the success of the existing forms of government (in his era, monarchic) depends on good relations between the leader and the people. He refers to the chief of state as Master or Sage, implying that one obligation of the governor is to be wise. One expression of that wisdom is the willingness to permit things to take their natural course. His view is that the less the Master needs to do—or perhaps the less government needs to intervene—the happier the people will be.

Niccolò Machiavelli was a pragmatic man of the Renaissance in Italy. As a theoretician and as a member of the political court, he understood government from the inside and carefully examined its philosophy. Because his writings stress the importance of gaining and holding power at any cost, Machiavelli's name has become synonymous with political cunning. However, a careful reading of his work as a reflection of the instability of his time shows that his advice to wield power ruthlessly derived largely from his fear that a weak prince would lose the city-state of Florence to France or to another powerful, plundering nation. His commitment to a powerful prince is based on his view that in the long run strength will guarantee the peace and happiness of the citizen for whom independence is otherwise irrelevant. Therefore, Machiavelli generally ignores questions concerning the comfort and rights of the individual.

In contrast, Jean-Jacques Rousseau is continually concerned with the basic questions of personal freedom and liberty. A fundamental principle in "The Origin of Civil Society" is that the individual's agreement with the state is designed to increase the individual's freedoms, not to diminish them. Rousseau makes this assertion while at the same time admitting that the individual forfeits certain rights to the body politic in order to gain overall freedom. Moreover, Rousseau describes civil society as a body politic that expects its rulers—including the monarch—to behave in a way designed to benefit the people. Such a view in late eighteenth-century France was revolutionary. The ruling classes at that time treated the people with great contempt, and the monarch rarely thought of the well-being of the common people. Rousseau's advocacy of a republican form of government in which the monarch served the people was a radical view at the time and would find its ultimate expression decades later in the French Revolution.

Thomas Jefferson's views were also radical for his time. Armed with the philosophy of Rousseau and others, his Declaration of

Independence advocates the eradication of the monarch entirely. Not everyone in the colonies agreed with this view. Indeed, his political opponents, such as Alexander Hamilton and Aaron Burr, were far from certain such a view was correct. In fact, some efforts were made to install George Washington as king (he refused). In the Declaration of Independence, Jefferson reflects Rousseau's philosophy by emphasizing the right of the individual to "life, liberty, and the pursuit of happiness" and the obligation of government to serve the people by protecting those rights.

The issues of freedom, justice, and individual rights were all virtually irrelevant in the totalitarian regimes that served as the focus of Hannah Arendt's work. Arendt argued that the fascist states, especially Nazi Germany, and the communist states, especially the Soviet Union, represented a novel form of government, one in which individual rights were sacrificed for the good of "the state." In her work *The Origins of Totalitarianism,* Arendt argues that the power of totalitarian states rises from the extreme distortion of logical premises coupled with the use of terror to enforce the ideology. The result is a form of government that eclipses the tyrannical extremes Rousseau and Jefferson sought to eradicate and exceeds even Machiavelli's imaginings of absolute power.

LAO-TZU
Thoughts from the Tao-te Ching

THE AUTHOR of the *Tao-te Ching* (in English often pronounced "dow deh jing") is unknown, although the earliest texts
ascribe the work to Lao-tzu (sixth century B.C.), whose name can
be translated as "Old Master." However, nothing can be said with
certainty about Lao-tzu as a historical figure. One tradition holds
that he was named Li Erh and born in the state of Ch'u in China at
a time that would have made him a slightly older contemporary of
Confucius (551–479 B.C.). Lao-tzu was said to have worked in the
court of the Chou dynasty for most of his life. When he decided to
leave the court to pursue a life of contemplation, the keeper of the
gate urged him to write down his thoughts before he went into a
self-imposed exile. Legend has it that he wrote the *Tao-te Ching*
and then left the state of Ch'u, never to be seen again.

Lao-tzu's writings offered a basis for Taoism, a religion officially founded by Chang Tao-ling in about A.D. 150. However, the
Tao-te Ching is a philosophical document as much about good government as it is about moral behavior. The term *Tao* cannot be easily understood or easily translated. In one sense it means "the
way," but it also means "the method," as in "the way to enlightenment" or "the way to live." Some of the chapters of the *Tao-te
Ching* imply that the Tao is the allness of the universe, the ultimate
reality of existence, and perhaps even a synonym for God. The text
is marked by numerous complex ambiguities and paradoxes. It constantly urges us to look beyond ourselves, beyond our circumstances, and become one with the Tao—even though it cannot tell
us what the Tao is.

The *Tao-te Ching* has often been called a feminine treatise because it emphasizes the creative forces of the universe and fre-

---

From *Tao-te Ching*. Translated by Stephen Mitchell.

quently employs the imagery and metaphor of the womb—for example, "The Tao is called the Great Mother." The translator, Stephen Mitchell, translates some of the pronouns associated with the Master as "she," with the explanation that Chinese has no equivalent for the male- and female-gendered pronouns and that "of all the great world religions the teaching of Lao-tzu is by far the most female."

The teachings of Lao-tzu are the opposite of the materialist quest for power, dominance, authority, and wealth. Lao-tzu takes the view that possessions and wealth are leaden weights of the soul, that they are meaningless and trivial, and that the truly free and enlightened person will regard them as evil. Because of his antimaterialist view, his recommendations may seem ironic or unclear, especially when he urges politicians to adopt a practice of judicious inaction. Lao-tzu's advice to politicians is not to do nothing but to intercede only when it is a necessity and then only inconspicuously. Above all, Lao-tzu counsels avoiding useless activity: "the Master / acts without doing anything / and teaches without saying anything." Such a statement is difficult for modern westerners to comprehend, although it points to the concept of enlightenment, a state of spiritual peace and fulfillment that is central to the *Tao-te Ching*.

Lao-tzu's political philosophy minimizes the power of the state—especially the power of the state to oppress the people. Lao-tzu takes the question of the freedom of the individual into account by asserting that the wise leader will provide the people with what they need but not annoy them with promises of what they do not need. Lao-tzu argues that by keeping people unaware that they are being governed, the leader allows the people to achieve good things for themselves. As he writes, "If you want to be a great leader, / you must learn to follow the Tao. / Stop trying to control. / Let go of fixed plans and concepts, / and the world will govern itself" (Verse 57); or in contrast, "If a country is governed with repression, / the people are depressed and crafty" (Verse 58).

To our modern ears this advice may or may not sound sensible. For those who feel government can solve the problems of the people, it will seem strange and unwise. For those who believe that the less government the better, the advice will sound sane and powerful.

The Rhetoric of the *Tao-te Ching*

Traditionally, Lao-tzu is said to have written the *Tao-te Ching* as a guide for the ruling sage to follow. In other words, it is a handbook for politicians. It emphasizes the virtues that the ruler must possess, and in this sense the *Tao-te Ching* invites comparison with Machiavelli's efforts to instruct his ruler.

The visual form of the text is poetry, although the text is not metrical or image-laden. Instead of thoroughly developing his ideas, Lao-tzu uses a traditional Chinese form that resembles the aphorism, a compressed statement weighty with meaning. Virtually every statement requires thought and reflection. Thus, the act of reading becomes an act of cooperation with the text.

One way of reading the text is to explore the varieties of interpretation it will sustain. The act of analysis requires patience and willingness to examine a statement to see what lies beneath the surface. Take, for example, one of the opening statements:

> The Master leads
> by emptying people's minds
> and filling their cores,
> by weakening their ambition
> and toughening their resolve.
> He helps people lose everything
> they know, everything they desire,
> and creates confusion
> in those who think that they know.

This passage supports a number of readings. One centers on the question of the people's desire. "Emptying people's minds" implies eliminating desires that lead the people to steal or compete for power. "Weakening their ambition" implies helping people direct their powers toward the attainable and useful. Such a text is at odds with Western views that support advertisements for expensive computers, DVD players, luxury cars, and other items that generate ambition and desire in the people.

In part because the text resembles poetry, it needs to be read with attention to innuendo, subtle interpretation, and possible hidden meanings. One of the rhetorical virtues of paradox is that it forces the reader to consider several sides of an issue. The resulting confusion yields a wider range of possibilities than would arise from a self-evident statement. Through these complicated messages, Lao-tzu felt he was contributing to the spiritual enlightenment of the ruling sage, although he had no immediate hope that his message would be put into action. A modern state might have a difficult time following Lao-tzu's philosophy, but many individuals have tried to attain peace and contentment by leading lives according to its principles.

The following prereading questions may help you anticipate key issues in the discussion on Lao-tzu's "Thoughts from the *Tao-te Ching*." Keeping them in mind during your first reading of the selection should help focus your reactions.

- What is the Master's attitude toward action?

- The Tao is "the way"—how are we to understand its meaning? What does it mean to be in harmony with the Tao?

- According to Lao-tzu, why is moderation important in government?

Thoughts from the Tao-te Ching

3

If you overesteem great men,   1
people become powerless.
If you overvalue possessions,
people begin to steal.

The Master leads   2
by emptying people's minds
and filling their cores,
by weakening their ambition
and toughening their resolve.
He helps people lose everything
they know, everything they desire,
and creates confusion
in those who think that they know.

Practice not-doing,   3
and everything will fall into place.

17

When the Master governs, the people   4
are hardly aware that he exists.
Next best is a leader who is loved.
Next, one who is feared.
The worst is one who is despised.

If you don't trust the people,   5
you make them untrustworthy.

The Master doesn't talk, he acts.   6
When his work is done,
the people say, "Amazing:
we did it, all by ourselves!"

18

When the great Tao is forgotten,   7
goodness and piety appear.
When the body's intelligence declines,
cleverness and knowledge step forth.
When there is no peace in the family,
filial piety begins.
When the country falls into chaos,
patriotism is born.

19

Throw away holiness and wisdom,   8
and people will be a hundred times happier.
Throw away morality and justice,
and people will do the right thing.
Throw away industry and profit,
and there won't be any thieves.

If these three aren't enough,   9
just stay at the center of the circle
and let all things take their course.

26

The heavy is the root of the light.   10
The unmoved is the source of all movement.

Thus the Master travels all day   11
without leaving home.
However splendid the views,
she stays serenely in herself.

Why should the lord of the country   12
flit about like a fool?
If you let yourself be blown to and fro,

you lose touch with your root.
If you let restlessness move you,
you lose touch with who you are.

29

Do you want to improve the world?   13
I don't think it can be done.

The world is sacred.   14
It can't be improved.
If you tamper with it, you'll ruin it.
If you treat it like an object, you'll lose it.

There is a time for being ahead,   15
a time for being behind;
a time for being in motion,
a time for being at rest;
a time for being vigorous,
a time for being exhausted;
a time for being safe,
a time for being in danger.

The Master sees things as they are,   16
without trying to control them.
She lets them go their own way,
and resides at the center of the circle.

30

Whoever relies on the Tao in governing men   17
doesn't try to force issues
or defeat enemies by force of arms.
For every force there is a counterforce.
Violence, even well intentioned,
always rebounds upon oneself.

The Master does his job   18
and then stops.
He understands that the universe
is forever out of control,
and that trying to dominate events
goes against the current of the Tao.
Because he believes in himself,
he doesn't try to convince others.

Because he is content with himself,
he doesn't need others' approval.
Because he accepts himself,
the whole world accepts him.

31

Weapons are the tools of violence;   19
all decent men detest them.

Weapons are the tools of fear;   20
a decent man will avoid them
except in the direst necessity
and, if compelled, will use them
only with the utmost restraint.
Peace is his highest value.
If the peace has been shattered,
how can he be content?
His enemies are not demons,
but human beings like himself.
He doesn't wish them personal harm.
Nor does he rejoice in victory.
How could he rejoice in victory
and delight in the slaughter of men?

He enters a battle gravely,   21
with sorrow and with great compassion,
as if he were attending a funeral.

37

The Tao never does anything,   22
yet through it all things are done.

If powerful men and women   23
could center themselves in it,
the whole world would be transformed
by itself, in its natural rhythms.
People would be content
with their simple, everyday lives,
in harmony, and free of desire.

When there is no desire,   24
all things are at peace.

38

The Master doesn't try to be powerful;   25
thus he is truly powerful.
The ordinary man keeps reaching for power;
thus he never has enough.

The Master does nothing,   26
yet he leaves nothing undone.
The ordinary man is always doing things,
yet many more are left to be done.

The kind man does something,   27
yet something remains undone.
The just man does something,
and leaves many things to be done.
The moral man does something,
and when no one responds
he rolls up his sleeves and uses force.

When the Tao is lost, there is goodness.   28
When goodness is lost, there is morality.
When morality is lost, there is ritual.
Ritual is the husk of true faith,
the beginning of chaos.

Therefore the Master concerns himself   29
with the depths and not the surface,
with the fruit and not the flower.
He has no will of his own.
He dwells in reality,
and lets all illusions go.

46

When a country is in harmony with the Tao,   30
the factories make trucks and tractors.
When a country goes counter to the Tao,
warheads are stockpiled outside the cities.

There is no greater illusion than fear,   31
no greater wrong than preparing to defend yourself,
no greater misfortune than having an enemy.

Whoever can see through all fear   32
will always be safe.

53

The great Way is easy,
yet people prefer the side paths.
Be aware when things are out of balance.
Stay centered within the Tao.

When rich speculators prosper
while farmers lose their land;
when government officials spend money
on weapons instead of cures;
when the upper class is extravagant and irresponsible
while the poor have nowhere to turn—
all this is robbery and chaos.
It is not in keeping with the Tao.

57

If you want to be a great leader,
you must learn to follow the Tao.
Stop trying to control.
Let go of fixed plans and concepts,
and the world will govern itself.

The more prohibitions you have,
the less virtuous people will be.
The more weapons you have,
the less secure people will be.
The more subsidies you have,
the less self-reliant people will be.

Therefore the Master says:
I let go of the law,
and people become honest.
I let go of economics,
and people become prosperous.
I let go of religion,
and people become serene.
I let go of all desire for the common good,
and the good becomes common as grass.

58

If a country is governed with tolerance,
the people are comfortable and honest.

33

34

35

36

37

38

If a country is governed with repression,
the people are depressed and crafty.

When the will to power is in charge,   39
the higher the ideals, the lower the results.
Try to make people happy,
and you lay the groundwork for misery.
Try to make people moral,
and you lay the groundwork for vice.

Thus the Master is content   40
to serve as an example
and not to impose her will.
She is pointed, but doesn't pierce.
Straightforward, but supple.
Radiant, but easy on the eyes.

59

For governing a country well   41
there is nothing better than moderation.

The mark of a moderate man   42
is freedom from his own ideas.
Tolerant like the sky,
all-pervading like sunlight,
firm like a mountain,
supple like a tree in the wind,
he has no destination in view
and makes use of anything
life happens to bring his way.

Nothing is impossible for him.   43
Because he has let go,
he can care for the people's welfare
as a mother cares for her child.

60

Governing a large country   44
is like frying a small fish.
You spoil it with too much poking.

Center your country in the Tao   45
and evil will have no power.

Not that it isn't there,
but you'll be able to step out of its way.

Give evil nothing to oppose   46
and it will disappear by itself.

61

When a country obtains great power,   47
it becomes like the sea:
all streams run downward into it.
The more powerful it grows,
the greater the need for humility.
Humility means trusting the Tao,
thus never needing to be defensive.

A great nation is like a great man: 48
When he makes a mistake, he realizes it.
Having realized it, he admits it.
Having admitted it, he corrects it.
He considers those who point out his faults
as his most benevolent teachers.
He thinks of his enemy
as the shadow that he himself casts.

If a nation is centered in the Tao,   49
if it nourishes its own people
and doesn't meddle in the affairs of others,
it will be a light to all nations in the world.

65

The ancient Masters   50
didn't try to educate the people,
but kindly taught them to not-know.

When they think that they know the answers,   51
people are difficult to guide.
When they know that they don't know,
people can find their own way.

If you want to learn how to govern,   52
avoid being clever or rich.
The simplest pattern is the clearest.
Content with an ordinary life,

you can show all people the way
back to their own true nature.

66

All streams flow to the sea   53
because it is lower than they are.
Humility gives it its power.

If you want to govern the people,   54
you must place yourself below them.
If you want to lead the people,
you must learn how to follow them.

The Master is above the people,   55
and no one feels oppressed.
She goes ahead of the people,
and no one feels manipulated.
The whole world is grateful to her.
Because she competes with no one,
no one can compete with her.

67

Some say that my teaching is nonsense.   56
Others call it lofty but impractical.
But to those who have looked inside themselves,
this nonsense makes perfect sense.
And to those who put it into practice,
this loftiness has roots that go deep.

I have just three things to teach: 57
simplicity, patience, compassion.
These three are your greatest treasures.
Simple in actions and in thoughts,
you return to the source of being.
Patient with both friends and enemies,
you accord with the way things are.
Compassionate toward yourself,
you reconcile all beings in the world.

75

When taxes are too high,   58
people go hungry.

When the government is too intrusive,
people lose their spirit.

Act for the people's benefit.   59
Trust them; leave them alone.

80

If a country is governed wisely,   60
its inhabitants will be content.
They enjoy the labor of their hands
and don't waste time inventing
labor-saving machines.
Since they dearly love their homes,
they aren't interested in travel.
There may be a few wagons and boats,
but these don't go anywhere.
There may be an arsenal of weapons,
but nobody ever uses them.
People enjoy their food,
take pleasure in being with their families,
spend weekends working in their gardens,
delight in the doings of the neighborhood.
And even though the next country is so close
that people can hear its roosters crowing and its dogs barking,
they are content to die of old age
without ever having gone to see it.

QUESTIONS FOR CRITICAL READING

1. According to Lao-tzu, what must the ruler provide the people with if
   they are to be happy? See especially Verse 66.
2. To what extent does Lao-tzu concern himself with individual happiness?
3. How would you describe Lao-tzu's attitude toward the people?
4. Why does Lao-tzu think the world cannot be improved? See Verse 29.
5. Which statements made in this selection do you feel support a materialist view of experience? Can they be resolved with Lao-tzu's overall
   thinking in the selection?
6. What are the limits and benefits of the expression: "Practice not-doing, /
   and everything will fall into place"? See Verse 3.
7. To what extent is Lao-tzu in favor of military action? What seem to be
   his views about the military? See Verse 31.

8. The term *Master* is used frequently in the selection. What can you tell about the character of the Master?

SUGGESTIONS FOR WRITING

1. The term *the Tao* is used often in this selection. Write a short essay that defines what Lao-tzu seems to mean by the term. If you were a politician and had the responsibility of governing a state, how would you follow the Tao as it is implied in Lao-tzu's statements? Is the Tao restrictive? Difficult? Open to interpretation? How well do you think it would work?

2. Write a brief essay that examines the following statements from the perspective of a young person today:

> The more prohibitions you have,
> the less virtuous people will be.
> The more weapons you have,
> the less secure people will be.
> The more subsidies you have,
> the less self-reliant people will be. (Verse 57)

To what extent do you agree with these statements, and to what extent do you feel they are statements that have a political importance? Do people in the United States seem to agree with these views, or do they disagree? What are the most visible political consequences of our nation's position regarding these ideas?

3. Some people have asserted that the American political system benefits the people most when the following views of Lao-tzu are carefully applied:

> Therefore the Master says:
> I let go of the law,
> and people become honest.
> I let go of economics,
> and people become prosperous.
> I let go of religion,
> and people become serene.
> I let go of all desire for the common good,
> and the good becomes common as grass. (Verse 57)

In a brief essay, decide to what extent American leaders follow these precepts. Whether you feel they do or not, do you think that they should follow these precepts? What are the likely results of their being put into practice?

4. Some of the statements Lao-tzu makes are so packed with meaning that it would take pages to explore them. One example is "When they think that they know the answers, / people are difficult to guide." Take this statement as the basis of a short essay and, in reference to a personal experience, explain the significance of this statement.

5. What does Lao-tzu imply about the obligation of the state to the individual it governs, and about the obligation of the individual to the state? Is one much more important than the other? Using the texts in this selection, establish what you feel is the optimum balance in the relationship between the two.

6. **CONNECTIONS** Compare Lao-tzu's view of government with that of Machiavelli in the next selection. Consider what seem to be the ultimate purposes of government, what seem to be the obligations of the leader to the people being led, and what seems to be the main work of the state. What comparisons can you make between Lao-tzu's Master and Machiavelli's prince?

NICCOLÒ MACHIAVELLI
The Qualities of the Prince

NICCOLÒ MACHIAVELLI (1469–1527) was an aristocrat whose fortunes wavered according to the shifts in power in Florence. Renaissance Italy was a collection of powerful city-states, which were sometimes volatile and unstable. When Florence's famed Medici princes were returned to power in 1512 after eighteen years of banishment, Machiavelli did not fare well. He was suspected of crimes against the state and imprisoned. Even though he was not guilty, he had to learn to support himself as a writer instead of continuing his career in civil service.

His works often contrast two forces: luck (one's fortune) and character (one's virtues). His own character outlasted his bad luck in regard to the Medicis, and he was returned to a position of responsibility. *The Prince* (1513), his most celebrated work, was a general treatise on the qualities the prince (that is, ruler) must have to maintain his power. In a more particular way, it was directed at the Medicis to encourage them to save Italy from the predatory incursions of France and Spain, whose troops were nibbling at the crumbling Italian principalities and who would, in time, control much of Italy.

The chapters presented here contain the core of the philosophy for which Machiavelli became famous. His instructions to the prince are curiously devoid of any high-sounding moralizing or any encouragement to be good as a matter of principle. Instead, Machiavelli recommends a very practical course of action for the prince: secure power by direct and effective means. It may be that Machiavelli fully expects that the prince will use his power for good ends—certainly he does not recommend tyranny. But he also supports using questionable means to achieve the final end of becoming

From *The Prince.* Translated by Peter Bondanella and Mark Musa.

and remaining the prince. Although Machiavelli recognizes that there is often a conflict between the ends and the means used to achieve them, he does not fret over the possible problems that may accompany the use of "unpleasant" means, such as punishment of upstarts, or the use of repression, imprisonment, and torture.

Through the years Machiavelli's view of human nature has come under criticism for its cynicism. For instance, he suggests that a morally good person would not remain long in any high office because that person would have to compete with the mass of people, who, he says, are basically bad. Machiavelli constantly tells us that he is describing the world as it really is, not as it should be. Perhaps Machiavelli is correct, but people have long condemned the way he approves of cunning, deceit, and outright lying as means of staying in power.

The contrast between Machiavelli's writings and Lao-tzu's opinions in the *Tao-te Ching* is instructive. Lao-tzu's advice issues from a detached view of a universal ruler; Machiavelli's advice is very personal, embodying a set of directives for a specific prince. Machiavelli expounds upon a litany of actions that must be taken; Lao-tzu, on the other hand, advises that judicious inaction will produce the best results.

Machiavelli's Rhetoric

Machiavelli's approach is less poetic and more pragmatic than Lao-tzu's. Whereas Lao-tzu's tone is almost biblical, Machiavelli's is that of a how-to book, relevant to a particular time and a particular place. Yet, like Lao-tzu, Machiavelli is brief and to the point. Each segment of the discussion is terse and economical.

Machiavelli announces his primary point clearly, refers to historical precedents to support his point, and then explains why his position is the best one by appealing to both common sense and historical experience. When he suspects the reader will not share his view wholeheartedly, he suggests an alternate argument and then explains why it is wrong. This is a very forceful way of presenting one's views. It gives the appearance of fairness and thoroughness—and, as we learn from reading Machiavelli, he is very much concerned with appearances. His method also gives his work fullness, a quality that makes us forget how brief it really is.

Another of his rhetorical methods is to discuss opposite pairings, including both sides of an issue. From the first he explores a number of oppositions—the art of war and the art of life, liberality and stinginess, cruelty and clemency, the fox and the lion. The method may seem simple, but it is important because it employs two of the basic techniques of rhetoric — comparison and contrast.

The aphorism is another of Machiavelli's rhetorical weapons. An aphorism is a saying — a concise statement of a principle — that has been accepted as true. Familiar examples are "A penny saved is a penny earned" and "There is no fool like an old fool." Machiavelli tells us: "A man who wishes to make a vocation of being good at all times will come to ruin among so many who are not good."

Such definite statements have several important qualities. One is that they are pithy: they seem to say a great deal in a few words. Another is that they appear to contain a great deal of wisdom, in part because they are delivered with such certainty, and in part because they have the ring of other aphorisms that we accept as true. Because they sound like aphorisms, they gain a claim to (unsubstantiated) truth, and we tend to accept them much more readily than perhaps we should. This may be why the speeches of contemporary politicians (modern versions of the prince) are often sprinkled with such expressions and illustrates why Machiavelli's rhetorical technique is still reliable, still effective, and still worth studying.

PREREADING QUESTIONS:
WHAT TO READ FOR

The following prereading questions may help you anticipate key issues in the discussion on Niccolò Machiavelli's "The Qualities of the Prince." Keeping them in mind during your first reading of the selection should help focus your reactions.

• Why does Machiavelli praise skill in warfare in his opening pages? How does that skill aid a prince?

• Is it better for a prince to be loved or to be feared?

The Qualities of the Prince

A Prince's Duty Concerning Military Matters

A prince, therefore, must not have any other object nor any   1
other thought, nor must he take anything as his profession but war, its institutions, and its discipline; because that is the only profession which befits one who commands; and it is of such importance that not only does it maintain those who were born princes, but many

times it enables men of private station to rise to that position; and, on the other hand, it is evident that when princes have given more thought to personal luxuries than to arms, they have lost their state. And the first way to lose it is to neglect this art; and the way to acquire it is to be well versed in this art.

Francesco Sforza[1] became Duke of Milan from being a private citizen because he was armed; his sons, since they avoided the inconveniences of arms, became private citizens after having been dukes. For, among the other bad effects it causes, being disarmed makes you despised; this is one of those infamies a prince should guard himself against, as will be treated below: for between an armed and an unarmed man there is no comparison whatsoever, and it is not reasonable for an armed man to obey an unarmed man willingly, nor that an unarmed man should be safe among armed servants; since, when the former is suspicious and the latter are contemptuous, it is impossible for them to work well together. And therefore, a prince who does not understand military matters, besides the other misfortunes already noted, cannot be esteemed by his own soldiers, nor can he trust them.

He must, therefore, never raise his thought from this exercise of war, and in peacetime he must train himself more than in time of war; this can be done in two ways: one by action, the other by the mind. And as far as actions are concerned, besides keeping his soldiers well disciplined and trained, he must always be out hunting, and must accustom his body to hardships in this manner; and he must also learn the nature of the terrain, and know how mountains slope, how valleys open, how plains lie, and understand the nature of rivers and swamps; and he should devote much attention to such activities. Such knowledge is useful in two ways: first, one learns to know one's own country and can better understand how to defend it; second, with the knowledge and experience of the terrain, one can easily comprehend the characteristics of any other terrain that it is necessary to explore for the first time; for the hills, valleys, plains, rivers, and swamps of Tuscany,[2] for instance, have certain similarities to those of other provinces; so that by knowing the lay of the land in one province one can easily understand it in others. And a prince who lacks this ability lacks the most important quality in a leader; because this skill teaches you to find the enemy, choose a

---

[1] **Francesco Sforza (1401–1466)** Became duke of Milan in 1450. He was, like most of Machiavelli's examples, a skilled diplomat and soldier. His court was a model of Renaissance scholarship and achievement.

[2] **Tuscany** Florence is in the region of Italy known as Tuscany.

campsite, lead troops, organize them for battle, and besiege towns to your own advantage.

Philopoemon, Prince of the Achaeans,[3] among the other praises 4 given to him by writers, is praised because in peacetime he thought of nothing except the means of waging war; and when he was out in the country with his friends, he often stopped and reasoned with them: "If the enemy were on that hilltop and we were here with our army, which of the two of us would have the advantage? How could we attack them without breaking formation? If we wanted to retreat, how could we do this? If they were to retreat, how could we pursue them?" And he proposed to them, as they rode along, all the contingencies that can occur in an army; he heard their opinions, expressed his own, and backed it up with arguments; so that, because of these continuous deliberations, when leading his troops no unforeseen incident could arise for which he did not have the remedy.

But as for the exercise of the mind, the prince must read histo- 5 ries and in them study the deeds of great men; he must see how they conducted themselves in wars; he must examine the reasons for their victories and for their defeats in order to avoid the latter and to imitate the former; and above all else he must do as some distinguished man before him has done, who elected to imitate someone who had been praised and honored before him, and always keep in mind his deeds and actions; just as it is reported that Alexander the Great imitated Achilles; Caesar, Alexander; Scipio, Cyrus.[4] And anyone who reads the life of Cyrus written by Xenophon then realizes how important in the life of Scipio that imitation was to his glory and how much, in purity, goodness, humanity, and generosity, Scipio conformed to those characteristics of Cyrus that Xenophon had written about.

Such methods as these a wise prince must follow, and never in 6 peaceful times must he be idle; but he must turn them diligently to his advantage in order to be able to profit from them in times of ad-

---

[3] **Philopoemon (252?–182 B.C.), Prince of the Achaeans** Philopoemon, from the city-state of Megalopolis, was a Greek general noted for skillful diplomacy. He led the Achaeans, a group of Greek states that formed the Achaean League, in several important expeditions, notably against Sparta. His cruelty in putting down a Spartan uprising caused him to be reprimanded by his superiors.

[4] **Cyrus (585?–529? B.C.)** Cyrus II (the Great), Persian emperor. Cyrus and the other figures featured in this sentence—Alexander the Great (356–323 B.C.); Achilles, hero of Homer's *Iliad;* Julius Caesar (100?–44 B.C.); and Scipio Africanus (236–184/3 B.C.), legendary Roman general—are all examples of politicians who were also great military geniuses. Xenophon (431–350? B.C.) was one of the earliest Greek historians; he chronicled the lives and military exploits of Cyrus and his son-in-law Darius.

versity, so that, when Fortune changes, she will find him prepared
to withstand such times.

On Those Things for Which Men, and Particularly Princes, Are Praised or Blamed

Now there remains to be examined what should be the methods   7
and procedures of a prince in dealing with his subjects and friends.
And because I know that many have written about this, I am afraid
that by writing about it again I shall be thought of as presumptuous,
since in discussing this material I depart radically from the procedures of others. But since my intention is to write something useful
for anyone who understands it, it seemed more suitable to me to
search after the effectual truth of the matter rather than its imagined
one. And many writers have imagined for themselves republics and
principalities that have never been seen nor known to exist in reality; for there is such a gap between how one lives and how one
ought to live that anyone who abandons what is done for what
ought to be done learns his ruin rather than his preservation: for a
man who wishes to make a vocation of being good at all times will
come to ruin among so many who are not good. Hence it is necessary for a prince who wishes to maintain his position to learn how
not to be good, and to use this knowledge or not to use it according
to necessity.

Leaving aside, therefore, the imagined things concerning a   8
prince, and taking into account those that are true, I say that all
men, when they are spoken of, and particularly princes, since they
are placed on a higher level, are judged by some of these qualities
which bring them either blame or praise. And this is why one is considered generous, another miserly (to use a Tuscan word, since
"avaricious" in our language is still used to mean one who wishes to
acquire by means of theft; we call "miserly" one who excessively
avoids using what he has); one is considered a giver, the other rapacious; one cruel, another merciful; one treacherous, another faithful;
one effeminate and cowardly, another bold and courageous; one humane, another haughty; one lascivious, another chaste; one trustworthy, another cunning; one harsh, another lenient; one serious,
another frivolous; one religious, another unbelieving; and the like.
And I know that everyone will admit that it would be a very praiseworthy thing to find in a prince, of the qualities mentioned above,
those that are held to be good, but since it is neither possible to have
them nor to observe them all completely, because human nature

does not permit it, a prince must be prudent enough to know how to escape the bad reputation of those vices that would lose the state for him, and must protect himself from those that will not lose it for him, if this is possible; but if he cannot, he need not concern himself unduly if he ignores these less serious vices. And, moreover, he need not worry about incurring the bad reputation of those vices without which it would be difficult to hold his state; since, carefully taking everything into account, one will discover that something which appears to be a virtue, if pursued, will end in his destruction; while some other thing which seems to be a vice, if pursued, will result in his safety and his well-being.

On Generosity and Miserliness

Beginning, therefore, with the first of the above-mentioned 9 qualities, I say that it would be good to be considered generous; nevertheless, generosity used in such a manner as to give you a reputation for it will harm you; because if it is employed virtuously and as one should employ it, it will not be recognized and you will not avoid the reproach of its opposite. And so, if a prince wants to maintain his reputation for generosity among men, it is necessary for him not to neglect any possible means of lavish display; in so doing such a prince will always use up all his resources and he will be obliged, eventually, if he wishes to maintain his reputation for generosity, to burden the people with excessive taxes and to do everything possible to raise funds. This will begin to make him hateful to his subjects, and, becoming impoverished, he will not be much esteemed by anyone; so that, as a consequence of his generosity, having offended many and rewarded few, he will feel the effects of any slight unrest and will be ruined at the first sign of danger; recognizing this and wishing to alter his policies, he immediately runs the risk of being reproached as a miser.

A prince, therefore, unable to use this virtue of generosity in a 10 manner which will not harm himself if he is known for it, should, if he is wise, not worry about being called a miser; for with time he will come to be considered more generous once it is evident that, as a result of his parsimony, his income is sufficient, he can defend himself from anyone who makes war against him, and he can undertake enterprises without overburdening his people, so that he comes to be generous with all those from whom he takes nothing, who are countless, and miserly with all those to whom he gives nothing, who are few. In our times we have not seen great deeds accomplished except by those who were considered miserly; all others were done away with. Pope Julius II,[5] although he made use of his reputation for generosity in order to gain the papacy, then decided not to maintain it in order to be able to wage war; the present King of France[6] has waged many wars without imposing extra taxes on his subjects, only because his habitual parsimony has provided for the additional expenditures; the present King of Spain,[7] if he had been considered generous, would not have engaged in nor won so many campaigns.

Therefore, in order not to have to rob his subjects, to be able to defend himself, not to become poor and contemptible, and not to be forced to become rapacious, a prince must consider it of little importance if he incurs the name of miser, for this is one of those vices that permits him to rule. And if someone were to say: Caesar with his generosity came to rule the empire, and many others, because they were generous and known to be so, achieved very high positions; I reply: you are either already a prince or you are on the way to becoming one; in the first instance such generosity is damaging; in the second it is very necessary to be thought generous. And Caesar was one of those who wanted to gain the principality of Rome; but if, after obtaining this, he had lived and had not moderated his expenditures, he would have destroyed that empire. And if someone were to reply: there have existed many princes who have accomplished great deeds with their armies who have been reputed to be generous; I answer you: a prince either spends his own money and that of his subjects or that of others; in the first case he must be economical; in the second he must not restrain any part of his generosity. And for that prince who goes out with his soldiers and lives by looting, sacking, and ransoms, who controls the property of others, such generosity is necessary; otherwise he would not be followed by his troops. And with what does not belong to you or to your subjects you can be a more liberal giver, as were Cyrus, Caesar, and Alexander; for spending the wealth of others does not lessen your reputation but adds to it; only the spending of your own is what harms you. And there is nothing that uses itself up faster than generosity, for as you employ it you lose the means of employing it, and

---

[5] **Pope Julius II (1443–1513)** Giuliano della Rovere, pope from 1503 to 1513. Like many of the popes of the day, Julius II was also a diplomat and a general.

[6] **present King of France** Louis XII (1462–1515). He entered Italy on a successful military campaign in 1494.

[7] **present King of Spain** Ferdinand V (1452–1516). A studied politician; he and Queen Isabella (1451–1504) financed Christopher Columbus's voyage to the New World in 1492.

you become either poor or despised or, in order to escape poverty, rapacious and hated. And above all other things a prince must guard himself against being despised and hated; and generosity leads you to both one and the other. So it is wiser to live with the reputation of a miser, which produces reproach without hatred, than to be forced to incur the reputation of rapacity, which produces reproach along with hatred, because you want to be considered as generous.

On Cruelty and Mercy and Whether It Is Better to Be Loved Than to Be Feared or the Contrary

Proceeding to the other qualities mentioned above, I say that 12 every prince must desire to be considered merciful and not cruel; nevertheless, he must take care not to misuse this mercy. Cesare Borgia[8] was considered cruel; nonetheless, his cruelty had brought order to Romagna,[9] united it, restored it to peace and obedience. If we examine this carefully, we shall see that he was more merciful than the Florentine people, who, in order to avoid being considered cruel, allowed the destruction of Pistoia.[10] Therefore, a prince must not worry about the reproach of cruelty when it is a matter of keeping his subjects united and loyal; for with a very few examples of cruelty he will be more compassionate than those who, out of excessive mercy, permit disorders to continue, from which arise murders and plundering; for these usually harm the community at large, while the executions that come from the prince harm one individual in particular. And the new prince, above all other princes, cannot escape the reputation of being called cruel, since new states are full of dangers. And Virgil, through Dido, states: "My difficult condition and the newness of my rule make me act in such a manner, and to set guards over my land on all sides."[11]

Nevertheless, a prince must be cautious in believing and in act- 13 ing, nor should he be afraid of his own shadow; and he should proceed in such a manner, tempered by prudence and humanity, so

---

[8] **Cesare Borgia (1476–1507)** He was known for his brutality and lack of scruples, not to mention his exceptionally good luck. He was a firm ruler, son of Pope Alexander VI.

[9] **Romagna** Region northeast of Tuscany; includes the towns of Bologna, Ferrara, Ravenna, and Rimini. Borgia united it as his base of power in 1501.

[10] **Pistoia** (also known as Pistoria) A town near Florence, disturbed in 1501 by a civil war that could have been averted by strong repressive measures.

[11] The quotation is from the *Aeneid* (II. 563–564), the greatest Latin epic poem, written by Virgil (70–19 B.C.). Dido, a woman general, ruled Carthage.

that too much trust may not render him imprudent nor too much distrust render him intolerable.

From this arises an argument: whether it is better to be loved   14
than to be feared, or the contrary. I reply that one should like to be
both one and the other; but since it is difficult to join them together,
it is much safer to be feared than to be loved when one of the two
must be lacking. For one can generally say this about men: that they
are ungrateful, fickle, simulators and deceivers, avoiders of danger,
greedy for gain; and while you work for their good they are completely yours, offering you their blood, their property, their lives,
and their sons, as I said earlier, when danger is far away; but when it
comes nearer to you they turn away. And that prince who bases his
power entirely on their words, finding himself stripped of other
preparations, comes to ruin; for friendships that are acquired by a
price and not by greatness and nobility of character are purchased
but are not owned, and at the proper moment they cannot be spent.
And men are less hesitant about harming someone who makes himself loved than one who makes himself feared because love is held
together by a chain of obligation which, since men are a sorry lot, is
broken on every occasion in which their own self-interest is concerned; but fear is held together by a dread of punishment which
will never abandon you.

A prince must nevertheless make himself feared in such a man-   15
ner that he will avoid hatred, even if he does not acquire love; since
to be feared and not to be hated can very well be combined; and this
will always be so when he keeps his hands off the property and the
women of his citizens and his subjects. And if he must take someone's life, he should do so when there is proper justification and
manifest cause; but, above all, he should avoid the property of others; for men forget more quickly the death of their father than the
loss of their patrimony. Moreover, the reasons for seizing their property are never lacking; and he who begins to live by stealing always
finds a reason for taking what belongs to others; on the contrary,
reasons for taking a life are rarer and disappear sooner.

But when the prince is with his armies and has under his com-   16
mand a multitude of troops, then it is absolutely necessary that he not
worry about being considered cruel; for without that reputation he
will never keep an army united or prepared for any combat. Among
the praiseworthy deeds of Hannibal[12] is counted this: that, having a

---

[12] **Hannibal (247–183 B.C.)** An amazingly inventive military tactician who
led the Carthaginian armies against Rome for more than fifteen years. He crossed the
Alps from Gaul (France) in order to surprise Rome. He was noted for use of the ambush and for "inhuman cruelty."

very large army, made up of all kinds of men, which he commanded in foreign lands, there never arose the slightest dissention, neither among themselves nor against their prince, both during his good and his bad fortune. This could not have arisen from anything other than his inhuman cruelty, which, along with his many other abilities, made him always respected and terrifying in the eyes of his soldiers; and without that, to attain the same effect, his other abilities would not have sufficed. And the writers of history, having considered this matter very little, on the one hand admire these deeds of his and on the other condemn the main cause of them.

And that it be true that his other abilities would not have been   17
sufficient can be seen from the example of Scipio, a most extraordinary man not only in his time but in all recorded history, whose armies in Spain rebelled against him; this came about from nothing other than his excessive compassion, which gave to his soldiers more liberty than military discipline allowed. For this he was censured in the senate by Fabius Maximus,[13] who called him the corruptor of the Roman militia. The Locrians,[14] having been ruined by one of Scipio's officers, were not avenged by him, nor was the arrogance of that officer corrected, all because of his tolerant nature; so that someone in the senate who tried to apologize for him said that there were many men who knew how not to err better than they knew how to correct errors. Such a nature would have, in time, damaged Scipio's fame and glory if he had maintained it during the empire; but, living under the control of the senate, this harmful characteristic of his not only concealed itself but brought him fame.

I conclude, therefore, returning to the problem of being feared   18
and loved, that since men love at their own pleasure and fear at the pleasure of the prince, a wise prince should build his foundation upon that which belongs to him, not upon that which belongs to others: he must strive only to avoid hatred, as has been said.

How a Prince Should Keep His Word

How praiseworthy it is for a prince to keep his word and to live   19
by integrity and not by deceit everyone knows; nevertheless, one sees from the experience of our times that the princes who have accomplished great deeds are those who have cared little for keeping

---

[13] **Fabius Maximus (?–203 B.C.)** Roman general who fought Hannibal. He was jealous of the younger Roman general Scipio.

[14] **Locrians** Inhabitants of Locri, an Italian town settled by the Greeks in c. 680 B.C.

their promises and who have known how to manipulate the minds
of men by shrewdness; and in the end they have surpassed those
who laid their foundations upon honesty.

You must, therefore, know that there are two means of fighting: 20
one according to the laws, the other with force; the first way is
proper to man, the second to beasts; but because the first, in many
cases, is not sufficient, it becomes necessary to have recourse to the
second. Therefore, a prince must know how to use wisely the natures of the beast and the man. This policy was taught to princes al-
legorically by the ancient writers, who described how Achilles and
many other ancient princes were given to Chiron[15] the Centaur to be
raised and taught under his discipline. This can only mean that,
having a half-beast and half-man as a teacher, a prince must know
how to employ the nature of the one and the other; and the one
without the other cannot endure.

Since, then, a prince must know how to make good use of the   21
nature of the beast, he should choose from among the beasts the fox
and the lion; for the lion cannot defend itself from traps and the
fox cannot protect itself from wolves. It is therefore necessary to be a
fox in order to recognize the traps and a lion in order to frighten the
wolves. Those who play only the part of the lion do not understand
matters. A wise ruler, therefore, cannot and should not keep his
word when such an observance of faith would be to his disadvantage and when the reasons which made him promise are removed.
And if men were all good, this rule would not be good; but since
men are a sorry lot and will not keep their promises to you, you
likewise need not keep yours to them. A prince never lacks legitimate reasons to break his promises. Of this one could cite an endless number of modern examples to show how many pacts, how
many promises have been made null and void because of the infi-
delity of princes; and he who has known best how to use the fox has
come to a better end. But it is necessary to know how to disguise
this nature well and to be a great hypocrite and a liar: and men are
so simpleminded and so controlled by their present necessities that
one who deceives will always find another who will allow himself to
be deceived.

I do not wish to remain silent about one of these recent in-   22
stances. Alexander VI[16] did nothing else, he thought about nothing
else, except to deceive men, and he always found the occasion to do

---

[15] **Chiron** A mythical figure, a centaur (half man, half horse). Unlike most cen-
taurs, he was wise and benevolent; he was also a legendary physician.

[16] **Alexander VI (1431–1503)** Roderigo Borgia, pope from 1492 to 1503. He
was Cesare Borgia's father and a corrupt but immensely powerful pope.

this. And there never was a man who had more forcefulness in his oaths, who affirmed a thing with more promises, and who honored his word less; nevertheless, his tricks always succeeded perfectly since he was well acquainted with this aspect of the world.

Therefore, it is not necessary for a prince to have all of the above-mentioned qualities, but it is very necessary for him to appear to have them. Furthermore, I shall be so bold as to assert this: that having them and practicing them at all times is harmful; and appearing to have them is useful; for instance, to seem merciful, faithful, humane, forthright, religious, and to be so; but his mind should be disposed in such a way that should it become necessary not to be so, he will be able and know how to change to the contrary. And it is essential to understand this: that a prince, and especially a new prince, cannot observe all those things by which men are considered good, for in order to maintain the state he is often obliged to act against his promise, against charity, against humanity, and against religion. And therefore, it is necessary that he have a mind ready to turn itself according to the way the winds of Fortune and the changeability of affairs require him; and, as I said above, as long as it is possible, he should not stray from the good, but he should know how to enter into evil when necessity commands. 23

A prince, therefore, must be very careful never to let anything slip from his lips which is not full of the five qualities mentioned above: he should appear, upon seeing and hearing him, to be all mercy, all faithfulness, all integrity, all kindness, all religion. And there is nothing more necessary than to seem to possess this last quality. And men in general judge more by their eyes than their hands; for everyone can see but few can feel. Everyone sees what you seem to be, few perceive what you are, and those few do not dare to contradict the opinion of the many who have the majesty of the state to defend them; and in the actions of all men, and especially of princes, where there is no impartial arbiter, one must consider the final result.[17] Let a prince therefore act to seize and to maintain the state; his methods will always be judged honorable and will be praised by all; for ordinary people are always deceived by appearances and by the outcome of a thing; and in the world there is nothing but ordinary people; and there is no room for the few, while the many have a place to lean on. A certain prince[18] of the present day, whom I shall refrain from naming, preaches nothing but peace 24

---

[17] The Italian original, *si guàrda al fine,* has often been mistranslated as "the ends justify the means," something Machiavelli never wrote. [Translators' note]

[18] **A certain prince** Probably King Ferdinand V of Spain (1452–1516).

and faith, and to both one and the other he is entirely opposed; and both, if he had put them into practice, would have cost him many times over either his reputation or his state.

On Avoiding Being Despised and Hated

But since, concerning the qualities mentioned above, I have spo- 25 ken about the most important, I should like to discuss the others briefly in this general manner: that the prince, as was noted above, should think about avoiding those things which make him hated and despised; and when he has avoided this, he will have carried out his duties and will find no danger whatsoever in other vices. As I have said, what makes him hated above all else is being rapacious and a usurper of the property and the women of his subjects; he must refrain from this; and in most cases, so long as you do not deprive them of either their property or their honor, the majority of men live happily; and you have only to deal with the ambition of a few, who can be restrained without difficulty and by many means. What makes him despised is being considered changeable, frivolous, effeminate, cowardly, irresolute; from these qualities a prince must guard himself as if from a reef, and he must strive to make everyone recognize in his actions greatness, spirit, dignity, and strength; and concerning the private affairs of his subjects, he must insist that his decision be irrevocable; and he should maintain himself in such a way that no man could imagine that he can deceive or cheat him.

That prince who projects such an opinion of himself is greatly 26 esteemed; and it is difficult to conspire against a man with such a reputation and difficult to attack him, provided that he is understood to be of great merit and revered by his subjects. For a prince must have two fears: one, internal, concerning his subjects; the other, external, concerning foreign powers. From the latter he can defend himself by his good troops and friends; and he will always have good friends if he has good troops; and internal affairs will always be stable when external affairs are stable, provided that they are not already disturbed by a conspiracy; and even if external conditions change, if he is properly organized and lives as I have said and does not lose control of himself, he will always be able to withstand every attack, just as I said that Nabis the Spartan[19] did. But concerning his subjects, when external affairs do not change, he has

---

[19] **Nabis the Spartan** Tyrant of Sparta from 207 to 192 B.C., routed by Philopoemon and the Achaean League.

to fear that they may conspire secretly: the prince secures himself from this by avoiding being hated or despised and by keeping the people satisfied with him; this is a necessary matter, as was treated above at length. And one of the most powerful remedies a prince has against conspiracies is not to be hated by the masses; for a man who plans a conspiracy always believes that he will satisfy the people by killing the prince; but when he thinks he might anger them, he cannot work up the courage to undertake such a deed; for the problems on the side of the conspirators are countless. And experience demonstrates that conspiracies have been many but few have been concluded successfully; for anyone who conspires cannot be alone, nor can he find companions except from amongst those whom he believes to be dissatisfied; and as soon as you have uncovered your intent to one dissatisfied man, you give him the means to make himself happy, since he can have everything he desires by uncovering the plot; so much is this so that, seeing a sure gain on the one hand and one doubtful and full of danger on the other, if he is to maintain faith with you he has to be either an unusually good friend or a completely determined enemy of the prince. And to treat the matter briefly, I say that on the part of the conspirator there is nothing but fear, jealousy, and the thought of punishment that terrifies him; but on the part of the prince there is the majesty of the principality, the laws, the defenses of friends and the state to protect him; so that, with the good will of the people added to all these things, it is impossible for anyone to be so rash as to plot against him. For, where usually a conspirator has to be afraid before he executes his evil deed, in this case he must be afraid, having the people as an enemy, even after the crime is performed, nor can he hope to find any refuge because of this.

One could cite countless examples on this subject; but I want to [27] satisfy myself with only one which occurred during the time of our fathers. Messer Annibale Bentivoglio, prince of Bologna and grandfather of the present Messer Annibale, was murdered by the Canneschi[20] family, who conspired against him; he left behind no heir except Messer Giovanni,[21] then only a baby. As soon as this murder occurred, the people rose up and killed all the Canneschi. This came about because of the good will that the house of the Bentivoglio enjoyed in those days; this good will was so great that with Annibale dead, and there being no one of that family left in the city who

---

[20] **Canneschi** Prominent family in Bologna.
[21] **Giovanni Bentivoglio (1443–1508)** Former tyrant of Bologna. In sequence he was a conspirator against, then a conspirator with, Cesare Borgia.

could rule Bologna, the Bolognese people, having heard that in Florence there was one of the Bentivoglio blood who was believed until that time to be the son of a blacksmith, went to Florence to find him, and they gave him the control of that city; it was ruled by him until Messer Giovanni became of age to rule.

I conclude, therefore, that a prince must be little concerned   28
with conspiracies when the people are well disposed toward him; but when the populace is hostile and regards him with hatred, he must fear everything and everyone. And well-organized states and wise princes have, with great diligence, taken care not to anger the nobles and to satisfy the common people and keep them contented; for this is one of the most important concerns that a prince has.

QUESTIONS FOR CRITICAL READING

1. The usual criticism of Machiavelli is that he advises his prince to be unscrupulous. Find examples for and against this claim.
2. Why do you agree or disagree with Machiavelli when he asserts that the great majority of people are not good? Does our government assume that to be true too?
3. Politicians—especially heads of state—are the contemporary counterparts of the prince. To what extent should successful heads of modern states show skill in war? Is modern war similar to wars in Machiavelli's era? If so, in what ways?
4. Clarify the advice Machiavelli gives concerning liberality and stinginess. Is this still good advice?
5. Are modern politicians likely to succeed by following all or most of Machiavelli's recommendations? Why or why not?

SUGGESTIONS FOR WRITING

1. In speaking of the prince's military duties, Machiavelli says that "being disarmed makes you despised." Choose an example or instance to strengthen your argument for or against this position. Is it possible that in modern society being defenseless is an advantage?
2. Find evidence within this excerpt to demonstrate that Machiavelli's attitude toward human nature is accurate. Remember that the usual criticism of Machiavelli is that he is cynical—that he thinks the worst of people rather than the best. Find quotations from the excerpt that support either or both of these views; then use them as the basis for an essay analyzing Machiavelli's views on human nature.
3. By referring to current events and leaders—either local, national, or international—decide whether Machiavelli's advice to the prince is

useful to the modern politician. Consider whether the advice is completely useless or completely reliable or whether its value depends on specific conditions. First state the advice, then show how it applies (or does not apply) to specific politicians, and finally critique its general effectiveness.

4. Probably the chief ethical issue raised by *The Prince* is the question of whether the desired ends justify the means used to achieve them. Write an essay in which you take a stand on this question. Begin by defining the issue: What does the concept "the ends justify the means" actually mean? What difficulties may arise when unworthy means are used to achieve worthy ends? Analyze Machiavelli's references to circumstances in which questionable means were (or should have been) used to achieve worthy ends. Use historical or personal examples to give your argument substance.

5. **CONNECTIONS**   One of Machiavelli's most controversial statements is: "A man who wishes to make a vocation of being good at all times will come to ruin among so many who are not good." How would Lao-tzu respond to this statement? How does the American political environment in the current decade support this statement? Under what conditions would such a statement become irrelevant?

6. **CONNECTIONS**   For some commentators, the prince that Machiavelli describes resembles the kind of ruler Hannah Arendt deplores in her essay "Ideology and Terror: A Novel Form of Government." Examine Machiavelli's views in terms of how his principles would result in a form of government similar to that which Arendt describes. Is terror a legitimate weapon for Machiavelli's prince? How would Machiavelli rationalize the prince's use of terror, should it become necessary?

JEAN-JACQUES ROUSSEAU
The Origin of Civil Society

JEAN-JACQUES ROUSSEAU (1712 – 1778) was the son of
Suzanne Bernard and Isaac Rousseau, a watchmaker in Geneva,
Switzerland. Shortly after his birth, Rousseau's mother died, and a
rash duel forced his father from Geneva. Rousseau was then ap-
prenticed at age thirteen to an engraver, a master who treated him
badly. He soon ran away from his master and found a home with a
Catholic noblewoman who at first raised him as her son and then,
when he was twenty, took him as her lover. In the process
Rousseau converted from Calvinist Protestantism to Roman
Catholicism. Eventually, he left Switzerland for Paris, where he
won an important essay contest and became celebrated in society.

Over the course of his lifetime, Rousseau produced a wide variety of literary and musical works, including a novel, *Emile* (1762),
an opera, *The Village Soothsayer* (1752), and an autobiography, *The
Confessions* (published posthumously in 1789). *The Social Contract*
(1762) was part of a never-completed longer work on political systems. In many ways Rousseau wrote in reaction to political
thinkers such as Hugo Grotius and Thomas Hobbes, to whom he
responds in the following selection. He contended that the Dutch
philosopher and legal expert Grotius unquestioningly accepted the
power of the aristocracy. He felt Grotius paid too much attention to
what was rather than what ought to be. On the other hand, Hobbes,
the English political philosopher, asserted that people had a choice
of being free or being ruled. In other words, those who were members of civil society chose to give up their freedom and submit to
the monarch's rule. Either they relinquished their freedom, or they
removed themselves from civil society to live a brutish existence.

From *Social Contract: Essays by Locke, Hume, and Rousseau.* Translated by Gerald
Hopkins.

Rousseau argued against Grotius by examining the way things ought to be. He argued against Hobbes by asserting that both the body politic and the monarch were sovereign and that when people created a civil society they surrendered their freedom to themselves as a group. If one person acted as sovereign or lawgiver, then that lawgiver had the responsibility of acting in accord with the will of the people. In a sense, this view parallels some of the views of Lao-tzu in the *Tao-te Ching*.

Popularly referred to as a defender of republicanism, Rousseau looked to the Republic of Geneva, his birthplace, as a model of government. He also idealized the generally democratic government of smaller Swiss cantons, such as Neuchatel, which used a form of town meeting where people gathered face to face to settle important issues. Ironically, Geneva put out a warrant for his arrest upon the publication of *The Social Contract* because although it praised Geneva's republicanism, it also condemned societies that depended on rule by a limited aristocracy. Unfortunately for Rousseau, at that time Geneva was governed by a small number of aristocratic families. Rousseau was deprived of his citizenship and could not return to his native home.

Similarly, Rousseau's controversial views were not easily received by those in power in France. After the publication of *Emile* offended the French Parliament, Rousseau was forced to abandon his comfortable rustic circumstances — living on country estates provided by patrons from the court — and spend the rest of his life in financial uncertainty. Ironically, in 1789, ten years after his death, Rousseau's philosophy was adopted by supporters of the French Revolution in their bloody revolt against the aristocracy.

Rousseau's Rhetoric

Rousseau's method is in many ways antagonistic: he establishes the views of other thinkers, counters them, and then offers his own ideas. An early example appears in the opening of paragraph 8: "Grotius denies that political power is ever exercised in the interests of the governed, and quotes the institution of slavery in support of his contention. His invariable method of arguing is to derive Right from Fact." Among other things, Rousseau expects his readers to know who Grotius was and what he said. He also expects his readers to agree that Grotius derives "Right from Fact" by understanding that the fact of monarchy justifies it as being right. As Rousseau tells us, that kind of circular reasoning is especially kind to tyrants, because it justifies them by their existence.

Rousseau uses analysis and examination of detail as his main rhetorical approaches. Whether he examines the ideas of others or presents ideas of his own, he is careful to examine the bases of the argument and to follow the arguments to their conclusions. He does this very thoroughly in his section "Of Slavery," in which he demonstrates that slavery is unacceptable no matter which of the current arguments are used to support it, including the widely held view that it was justifiable to enslave captured soldiers on the grounds that they owed their lives to their captors.

Rousseau also makes careful use of aphorism and analogy. His opening statement, "Man is born free, and everywhere he is in chains," is an aphorism that has been often quoted. It is a powerful and perplexing statement. How do people who are born free lose their freedom? Is it taken from them, or do they willingly surrender it? Rousseau spends considerable time examining this point.

The use of analogy is probably most striking in his comparison of government with the family. The force of the analogy reminds us that the members of a family are to be looked after by the family. As he tells us beginning in paragraph 5, the family is the only natural form of society. But instead of stopping there, he goes on to say that children are bound to the father only as long as they need him. Once they are able to be independent, they dissolve the natural bond and "return to a condition of equal independence." This analogy differs from the existing popular view that the monarch was like the father in a family and the people like his children; in fact, the analogy works against the legitimacy of the traditional monarchy as it was known in eighteenth-century France.

Rousseau also refers to other writers, using a rhetorical device known as *testimony:* he paraphrases the views of other authorities and moves on to promote his own. But in referring to other writers, Rousseau is unusually clever. For example, in paragraph 10 he begins with the analogy of the shepherd as the ruler in this fashion: "Just as the shepherd is superior in kind to his sheep, so, too, the shepherds of men, or, in other words, their rulers, are superior in kind to their peoples. This, according to Philo, was the argument advanced by Caligula, the Emperor, who drew from the analogy the perfectly true conclusion that either Kings are Gods or their subjects brute beasts." Caligula was a madman and an emperor guilty of enormous cruelty; from his point of view it may have seemed true that kings were gods. But Rousseau, in citing this questionable authority, disputes the validity of the analogy.

He argues as well against the view that might makes right in "Of the Right of the Strongest." The value of the social contract, he explains, is to produce a society that is not governed by the mightiest and most ruthless and that permits those who are not mighty to live peacefully and unmolested. Thus, those who participate in the social contract give up certain freedoms but gain many more—among them the freedom not to be dominated by physical brutality.

Rousseau concentrates on the question of man in nature, or natural society. His view is that natural society is dominated by the strongest individuals but that at some point natural society breaks down. Thus, in order to guarantee the rights of those who are not the strongest, the political order must change. "Some form of association" is developed "for the protection of the person and property of each constituent member." By surrendering some freedom to the group as a whole—to "the general will"—the individuals in the group can expect to prosper more widely and to live more happily. According to Rousseau, the establishment of a social contract ensures the stability of this form of civil society.

PREREADING QUESTIONS:
WHAT TO READ FOR

The following prereading questions may help you anticipate key issues in the discussion on Jean-Jacques Rousseau's "The Origin of Civil Society." Keeping them in mind as you read should help focus your reactions.

- When Rousseau says, "Man is born free, and everywhere he is in chains," does he seem to be referring literally to slaves in chains, or more figuratively to people in general?
- How convincing is Rousseau when he claims that the oldest form of government is the family?
- The "Social Contract" is one of Rousseau's chief ideas. What does it seem to mean?

The Origin of Civil Society

Note

It is my wish to inquire whether it be possible, within the civil 1 *order, to discover a legitimate and stable basis of Government. This I shall do by considering human beings as they are and laws as they might be. I shall attempt, throughout my investigations, to maintain a constant connection between what right permits and interest demands, in order that no separation may be made between justice and utility. I intend to begin without first proving the importance of my subject. Am I, it will be asked, either prince or legislator that I take it upon me to write of politics? My answer is—No; and it is for that very reason that I have chosen politics as the matter of my book. Were I either the one or the other I should not waste my time in laying down what has to be done. I should do it, or else hold my peace.*

I was born into a free state and am a member of its sovereign 2 *body. My influence on public affairs may be small, but because I have a right to exercise my vote, it is my duty to learn their nature, and it has been for me a matter of constant delight, while meditating on problems of Government in general, to find ever fresh reasons for regarding with true affection the way in which these things are ordered in my native land.*

The Subject of the First Book

Man is born free, and everywhere he is in chains. Many a man 3 believes himself to be the master of others who is, no less than they, a slave. How did this change take place? I do not know. What can make it legitimate? To this question I hope to be able to furnish an answer.

Were I considering only force and the effects of force, I should 4 say: "So long as a People is constrained to obey, and does, in fact, obey, it does well. So soon as it can shake off its yoke, and succeeds in doing so, it does better. The fact that it has recovered its liberty by virtue of that same right by which it was stolen, means either that it is entitled to resume it, or that its theft by others was, in the first place, without justification." But the social order is a sacred right which serves as a foundation for all other rights. This right, however, since it comes not by nature, must have been built upon conventions. To discover what these conventions are is the matter of our inquiry. But, before proceeding further, I must establish the truth of what I have so far advanced.

Of Primitive Societies

The oldest form of society—and the only natural one—is the 5 family. Children remain bound to their father for only just so long as they feel the need of him for their self-preservation. Once that need ceases the natural bond is dissolved. From then on, the children, freed from the obedience which they formerly owed, and the father, cleared of his debt of responsibility to them, return to a condition of equal independence. If the bond remain operative it is no longer something imposed by nature, but has become a matter of deliberate choice. The family is a family still, but by reason of convention only.

This shared liberty is a consequence of man's nature. Its first law is 6 that of self-preservation: its first concern is for what it owes itself. As soon as a man attains the age of reason he becomes his own master, because he alone can judge of what will best assure his continued existence.

We may, therefore, if we will, regard the family as the basic model 7 of all political associations. The ruler is the father writ large: the people are, by analogy, his children, and all, ruler and people alike, alienate their freedom only so far as it is to their advantage to do so. The only difference is that, whereas in the family the father's love for his children is sufficient reward to him for the care he has lavished on them, in the State, the pleasure of commanding others takes its place, since the ruler is not in a relation of love to his people.

Grotius[1] denies that political power is ever exercised in the in- 8 terests of the governed, and quotes the institution of slavery in support of his contention. His invariable method of arguing is to derive Right from Fact. It might be possible to adopt a more logical system of reasoning, but none which would be more favorable to tyrants.

According to Grotius, therefore, it is doubtful whether the term 9 "human race" belongs to only a few hundred men, or whether those few hundred men belong to the human race. From the evidence of his book it seems clear that he holds by the first of these alternatives, and on this point Hobbes[2] is in agreement with him. If this is so, then humanity is divided into herds of livestock, each with its "guardian" who watches over his charges only that he may ultimately devour them.

Just as the shepherd is superior in kind to his sheep, so, too, the 10 shepherds of men, or, in other words, their rulers, are superior in kind to their peoples. This, according to Philo,[3] was the argument

---

[1] **Hugo Grotius (1583–1645)** A Dutch lawyer who spent some time in exile in Paris. His fame as a child prodigy was considerable; his book on the laws of war (*De jure belli ac Pacis*) was widely known in Europe.

[2] **Thomas Hobbes (1588–1679)** Known as a materialist philosopher who did not credit divine influence in politics. An Englishman, he became famous for *Leviathan,* a study of politics that treated the state as if it were a monster (leviathan) with a life of its own.

[3] **Philo (13? B.C. – A.D. 47?)** A Jew who absorbed Greek culture and who wrote widely on many subjects. His studies on Mosaic law were considered important.

advanced by Caligula,[4] the Emperor, who drew from the analogy the perfectly true conclusion that either Kings are Gods or their subjects brute beasts.

The reasoning of Caligula, of Hobbes, and of Grotius is funda- 11 mentally the same. Far earlier, Aristotle, too, had maintained that men are not by nature equal, but that some are born to be slaves, others to be masters.

Aristotle[5] was right: but he mistook the effect for the cause. Noth- 12 ing is more certain than that a man born into a condition of slavery is a slave by nature. A slave in fetters loses everything—even the desire to be freed from them. He grows to love his slavery, as the companions of Ulysses grew to love their state of brutish transformation.[6]

If some men are by nature slaves, the reason is that they have 13 been made slaves *against* nature. Force made the first slaves: cowardice has perpetuated the species.

I have made no mention of King Adam or of the Emperor Noah, 14 the father of three great Monarchs[7] who divided up the universe between them, as did the children of Saturn,[8] whom some have been tempted to identify with them. I trust that I may be given credit for my moderation, since, being descended in a direct line from one of these Princes, and quite possibly belonging to the elder branch, I may, for all I know, were my claims supported in law, be even now the legitimate Sovereign of the Human Race.[9] However that may be, all will concur in the view that Adam was King of the World, as was

---

[4] **Caligula (A.D. 12–41)** Roman emperor of uncertain sanity. He loved his sister Drusilla so much that he had her deified when she died. A military commander, he was assassinated by an officer.

[5] **Aristotle (384–322 B.C.)** A student of Plato; his philosophical method became the dominant intellectual force in Western thought.

[6] **state of brutish transformation** This sentence refers to the Circe episode in Homer's *Odyssey* (X, XII). Circe was a sorceress who, by means of drugs, enchanted men and turned them into swine. Ulysses (Latin name of Odysseus), king of Ithaca, is the central figure of the *Odyssey*.

[7] **the father of three great Monarchs** Adam in the Bible (Genesis 4:1–25) fathered Cain, Abel, Enoch, and Seth. Noah's sons, Shem, Ham, and Japheth, repopulated the world after the Flood (Genesis 6:9–9:19).

[8] **children of Saturn** Saturn is a mythic god associated with the golden age of Rome and with the Greek god Cronus. It is probably the children of Cronus—Zeus, Poseidon, Hades, Demeter, and Hera—referred to here, because the Roman god Saturn had only one son, Picus.

[9] **Sovereign of the Human Race** Rousseau is being ironic; like the rest of us, he is descended from Adam (according to the Bible).

Robinson Crusoe of his island, only so long as he was its only inhabitant, and the great advantage of empire held on such terms was that the Monarch, firmly seated on his throne, had no need to fear rebellions, conspiracy, or war.

Of the Right of the Strongest

However strong a man, he is never strong enough to remain   15 master always, unless he transform his Might into Right, and Obedience into Duty. Hence we have come to speak of the Right of the Strongest, a right which, seemingly assumed in irony, has, in fact, become established in principle. But the meaning of the phrase has never been adequately explained. Strength is a physical attribute, and I fail to see how any moral sanction can attach to its effects. To yield to the strong is an act of necessity, not of will. At most it is the result of a dictate of prudence. How, then, can it become a duty?

Let us assume for a moment that some such Right does really   16 exist. The only deduction from this premise is inexplicable gibberish. For to admit that Might makes Right is to reverse the process of effect and cause. The mighty man who defeats his rival becomes heir to his Right. So soon as we can disobey with impunity, disobedience becomes legitimate. And, since the Mightiest is always right, it merely remains for us to become possessed of Might. But what validity can there be in a Right which ceases to exist when Might changes hands? If a man be constrained by Might to obey, what need has he to obey by Duty? And if he is not constrained to obey, there is no further obligation on him to do so. It follows, therefore, that the word Right adds nothing to the idea of Might. It becomes, in this connection, completely meaningless.

Obey the Powers that be. If that means Yield to Force, the pre-   17 cept is admirable but redundant. My reply to those who advance it is that no case will ever be found of its violation. All power comes from God. Certainly, but so do all ailments. Are we to conclude from such an argument that we are never to call in the doctor? If I am waylaid by a footpad at the corner of a wood, I am constrained by force to give him my purse. But if I can manage to keep it from him, is it my duty to hand it over? His pistol is also a symbol of Power. It must, then, be admitted that Might does not create Right, and that no man is under an obligation to obey any but the legitimate powers of the State. And so I continually come back to the question I first asked.

Of Slavery

Since no man has natural authority over his fellows, and since   18
Might can produce no Right, the only foundation left for legitimate
authority in human societies is Agreement.

If a private citizen, says Grotius, can alienate his liberty and   19
make himself another man's slave, why should not a whole people
do the same, and subject themselves to the will of a King? The argument contains a number of ambiguous words which stand in need
of explanation. But let us confine our attention to one only—*alienate*. To alienate means to give or to sell. Now a man who becomes
the slave of another does not give himself. He sells himself in return
for bare subsistence, if for nothing more. But why should a whole
people sell themselves? So far from furnishing subsistence to his
subjects, a King draws his own from them, and from them alone.
According to Rabelais,[10] it takes a lot to keep a King. Do we, then,
maintain that a subject surrenders his person on condition that his
property be taken too? It is difficult to see what he will have left.

It will be said that the despot guarantees civil peace to his sub-   20
jects. So be it. But how are they the gainers if the wars to which his
ambition may expose them, his insatiable greed, and the vexatious
demands of his Ministers cause them more loss than would any outbreak of internal dissension? How do they benefit if that very condition of civil peace be one of the causes of their wretchedness? One
can live peacefully enough in a dungeon, but such peace will hardly,
of itself, ensure one's happiness. The Greeks imprisoned in the cave
of Cyclops[11] lived peacefully while awaiting their turn to be devoured.

To say that a man gives himself for nothing is to commit oneself   21
to an absurd and inconceivable statement. Such an act of surrender
is illegitimate, null, and void by the mere fact that he who makes it
is not in his right mind. To say the same thing of a whole People is
tantamount to admitting that the People in question are a nation of
imbeciles. Imbecility does not produce Right.

Even if a man can alienate himself, he cannot alienate his chil-   22
dren. They are born free, their liberty belongs to them, and no one
but themselves has a right to dispose of it. Before they have attained
the age of reason their father may make, on their behalf, certain

---

[10] **François Rabelais (c. 1494–1553)** French writer, author of *Gargantua*
and *Pantagruel*, satires on politics and religion.

[11] **cave of Cyclops** The cyclops is a one-eyed giant cannibal whose cave is the
scene of one of Odysseus's triumphs in Homer's *Odyssey* (IX).

rules with a view to ensuring their preservation and well-being. But any such limitation of their freedom of choice must be regarded as neither irrevocable nor unconditional, for to alienate another's liberty is contrary to the natural order, and is an abuse of the father's rights. It follows that an arbitrary government can be legitimate only on condition that each successive generation of subjects is free either to accept or to reject it, and if this is so, then the government will no longer be arbitrary.

When a man renounces his liberty he renounces his essential manhood, his rights, and even his duty as a human being. There is no compensation possible for such complete renunciation. It is incompatible with man's nature, and to deprive him of his free will is to deprive his actions of all moral sanction. The convention, in short, which sets up on one side an absolute authority, and on the other an obligation to obey without question, is vain and meaningless. Is it not obvious that where we can demand everything we owe nothing? Where there is no mutual obligation, no interchange of duties, it must, surely, be clear that the actions of the commanded cease to have any moral value? For how can it be maintained that my slave has any "right" against me when everything that he has is my property? His right being *my* right, it is absurd to speak of it as ever operating to my disadvantage.   23

Grotius, and those who think like him, have found in the fact of war another justification for the so-called "right" of slavery. They argue that since the victor has a *right* to kill his defeated enemy, the latter may, if he so wish, ransom his life at the expense of his liberty, and that this compact is the more legitimate in that it benefits both parties.   24

But it is evident that this alleged *right* of a man to kill his enemies is not in any way a derivative of the state of war, if only because men, in their primitive condition of independence, are not bound to one another by any relationship sufficiently stable to produce a state either of war or of peace. They are not *naturally* enemies. It is the link between *things* rather than between *men* that constitutes war, and since a state of war cannot originate in simple personal relations, but only in relations between things, private hostility between man and man cannot obtain either in a state of nature where there is no generally accepted system of private property, or in a state of society where law is the supreme authority.   25

Single combats, duels, personal encounters are incidents which do not constitute a "state" of anything. As to those private wars which were authorized by the Ordinances of King Louis IX[12] and   26

---

[12] **King Louis IX (1214–1270)** King of France, also called St. Louis. He was looked upon as an ideal monarch.

suspended by the Peace of God, they were merely an abuse of Feudalism—that most absurd of all systems of government, so contrary was it to the principles of Natural Right and of all good polity.

War, therefore, is something that occurs not between man and 27 man, but between States. The individuals who become involved in it are enemies only by accident. They fight not as men or even as citizens, but as soldiers: not as members of this or that national group, but as its defenders. A State can have as its enemies only other States, not men at all, seeing that there can be no true relationship between things of a different nature.

This principle is in harmony with that of all periods, and with 28 the constant practice of every civilized society. A declaration of war is a warning, not so much to Governments as to their subjects. The foreigner—whether king, private person, or nation as a whole—who steals, murders, or holds in durance the subjects of another country without first declaring war on that country's Prince, acts not as an enemy but as a brigand. Even when war has been joined, the just Prince, though he may seize all public property in enemy territory, yet respects the property and possessions of individuals, and, in so doing, shows his concern for those rights on which his own laws are based. The object of war being the destruction of the enemy State, a commander has a perfect right to kill its defenders so long as their arms are in their hands: but once they have laid them down and have submitted, they cease to be enemies, or instruments employed by an enemy, and revert to the condition of men, pure and simple, over whose lives no one can any longer exercise a rightful claim. Sometimes it is possible to destroy a State without killing any of its subjects, and nothing in war can be claimed as a right save what may be necessary for the accomplishment of the victor's end. These principles are not those of Grotius, nor are they based on the authority of poets, but derive from the Nature of Things, and are founded upon Reason.

The Right of Conquest finds its sole sanction in the Law of the 29 Strongest. If war does not give to the victor the right to massacre his defeated enemies, he cannot base upon a nonexistent right any claim to the further one of enslaving them. We have the right to kill our enemies only when we cannot enslave them. It follows, therefore, that the right to enslave cannot be deduced from the right to kill, and that we are guilty of enforcing an iniquitous exchange if we make a vanquished foeman purchase with his liberty that life over which we have no right. Is it not obvious that once we begin basing the right of life and death on the right to enslave, and the right to enslave on the right of life and death, we are caught in a vicious circle? Even if we assume the existence of this terrible right to kill all

and sundry, I still maintain that a man enslaved, or a People conquered, in war is under no obligation to obey beyond the point at
which force ceases to be operative. If the victor spares the life of his
defeated opponent in return for an equivalent, he cannot be said to
have shown him mercy. In either case he destroys him, but in the
latter case he derives value from his act, while in the former he gains
nothing. His authority, however, rests on no basis but that of force.
There is still a state of war between the two men, and it conditions
the whole relationship in which they stand to one another. The enjoyment of the Rights of War presupposes that there has been no
treaty of Peace. Conqueror and conquered have, to be sure, entered
into a compact, but such a compact, far from liquidating the state of
war, assumes its continuance.

Thus, in whatever way we look at the matter, the "Right" to en-   30
slave has no existence, not only because it is without legal validity,
but because the very term is absurd and meaningless. The words
Slavery and *Right* are contradictory and mutually exclusive. Whether
we be considering the relation of one man to another man, or of an
individual to a whole People, it is equally idiotic to say—"You and I
have made a compact which represents nothing but loss to you and
gain to me. I shall observe it so long as it pleases me to do so—and
so shall you, until I cease to find it convenient."

That We Must Always Go Back
to an Original Compact

Even were I to grant all that I have so far refuted, the champions   31
of despotism would not be one whit the better off. There will always
be a vast difference between subduing a mob and governing a social
group. No matter how many isolated individuals may submit to the
enforced control of a single conqueror, the resulting relationship
will ever be that of Master and Slave, never of People and Ruler. The
body of men so controlled may be an agglomeration; it is not an association. It implies neither public welfare nor a body politic. An individual may conquer half the world, but he is still only an individual. His interests, wholly different from those of his subjects, are
private to himself. When he dies his empire is left scattered and dis-
integrated. He is like an oak which crumbles and collapses in ashes
so soon as the fire consumes it.

"A People," says Grotius, "may give themselves to a king." His   32
argument implies that the said People were already a People before
this act of surrender. The very act of gift was that of a political group
and presupposed deliberation. Before, therefore, we consider the act

by which a People chooses their king, it were well if we considered the act by which a People is constituted as such. For it necessarily precedes the other, and is the true foundation on which all Societies rest.

Had there been no original compact, why, unless the choice   33
were unanimous, should the minority ever have agreed to accept the decision of the majority? What right have the hundred who desire a master to vote for the ten who do not? The institution of the franchise is, in itself, a form of compact, and assumes that, at least once in its operation, complete unanimity existed.

Of the Social Pact

I assume, for the sake of argument, that a point was reached in   34
the history of mankind when the obstacles to continuing in a state of Nature were stronger than the forces which each individual could employ to the end of continuing in it. The original state of Nature, therefore, could no longer endure, and the human race would have perished had it not changed its manner of existence.

Now, since men can by no means engender new powers, but   35
can only unite and control those of which they are already possessed, there is no way in which they can maintain themselves save by coming together and pooling their strength in a way that will enable them to withstand any resistance exerted upon them from without. They must develop some sort of central direction and learn to act in concert.

Such a concentration of powers can be brought about only as   36
the consequence of an agreement reached between individuals. But the self-preservation of each single man derives primarily from his own strength and from his own freedom. How, then, can he limit these without, at the same time, doing himself an injury and neglecting that care which it is his duty to devote to his own concerns? This difficulty, in so far as it is relevant to my subject, can be expressed as follows:

"Some form of association must be found as a result of which   37
the whole strength of the community will be enlisted for the protection of the person and property of each constituent member, in such a way that each, when united to his fellows, renders obedience to his own will, and remains as free as he was before." That is the basic problem of which the Social Contract provides the solution.

The clauses of this Contract are determined by the Act of Association in such a way that the least modification must render them   38
null and void. Even though they may never have been formally

enunciated, they must be everywhere the same, and everywhere tacitly admitted and recognized. So completely must this be the case that, should the social compact be violated, each associated individual would at once resume all the rights which once were his, and regain his natural liberty, by the mere fact of losing the agreed liberty for which he renounced it.

It must be clearly understood that the clauses in question can be 39
reduced, in the last analysis, to one only, to wit, the complete alienation by each associate member to the community of *all his rights.* For, in the first place, since each has made surrender of himself without reservation, the resultant conditions are the same for all: and, because they are the same for all, it is in the interest of none to make them onerous to his fellows.

Furthermore, this alienation having been made unreservedly, 40
the union of individuals is as perfect as it well can be, none of the associated members having any claim against the community. For should there be any rights left to individuals, and no common authority be empowered to pronounce as between them and the public, then each, being in some things his own judge, would soon claim to be so in all. Were that so, a state of Nature would still remain in being, the conditions of association becoming either despotic or ineffective.

In short, whoso gives himself to all gives himself to none. And, 41
since there is no member of the social group over whom we do not acquire precisely the same rights as those over ourselves which we have surrendered to him, it follows that we gain the exact equivalent of what we lose, as well as an added power to conserve what we already have.

If, then, we take from the social pact everything which is not essential to it, we shall find it to be reduced to the following terms: 42
"each of us contributes to the group his person and the powers which he wields as a person under the supreme direction of the general will, and we receive into the body politic each individual as forming an indivisible part of the whole."

As soon as the act of association becomes a reality, it substitutes 43
for the person of each of the contracting parties a moral and collective body made up of as many members as the constituting assembly has votes, which body receives from this very act of constitution its unity, its dispersed *self,* and its will. The public person thus formed by the union of individuals was known in the old days as a *City,* but now as the *Republic* or *Body Politic.* This, when it fulfills a passive role, is known by its members as *The State,* when an active one, as *The Sovereign People,* and, in contrast to other similar bodies, as a *Power.* In respect of the constituent associates, it enjoys the collec-

tive name of *The People,* the individuals who compose it being known as *Citizens* in so far as they share in the sovereign authority, as *Subjects* in so far as they owe obedience to the laws of the State. But these different terms frequently overlap, and are used indiscriminately one for the other. It is enough that we should realize the difference between them when they are employed in a precise sense.

Of the Sovereign

It is clear from the above formula that the act of association im-   44
plies a mutual undertaking between the body politic and its constituent members. Each individual comprising the former contracts, so to speak, with himself and has a twofold function. As a member of the sovereign people he owes a duty to each of his neighbors, and, as a Citizen, to the sovereign people as a whole. But we cannot here apply that maxim of Civil Law according to which no man can be held to an undertaking entered into with himself, because there is a great difference between a man's duty to himself and to a whole of which he forms a part.

Here it should be pointed out that a public decision which can   45
enjoin obedience on all subjects to their Sovereign, by reason of the double aspect under which each is seen, cannot, on the contrary, bind the sovereign in his dealings with himself. Consequently, it is against the nature of the body politic that the sovereign should impose upon himself a law which he cannot infringe. For, since he can regard himself under one aspect only, he is in the position of an individual entering into a contract with himself. Whence it follows that there is not, nor can be, any fundamental law which is obligatory for the whole body of the People, not even the social contract itself. This does not mean that the body politic is unable to enter into engagements with some other Power, provided always that such engagements do not derogate from the nature of the Contract; for the relation of the body politic to a foreign Power is that of a simple individual.

But the body politic, or Sovereign, in that it derives its being   46
simply and solely from the sanctity of the said Contract, can never bind itself, even in its relations with a foreign Power, by any decision which might derogate from the validity of the original act. It may not, for instance, alienate any portion of itself, nor make submission to any other sovereign. To violate the act by reason of which it exists would be tantamount to destroying itself, and that which is nothing can produce nothing.

As soon as a mob has become united into a body politic, any at-   47
tack upon one of its members is an attack upon itself. Still more

important is the fact that, should any offense be committed against the body politic as a whole, the effect must be felt by each of its members. Both duty and interest, therefore, oblige the two contracting parties to render one another mutual assistance. The same individuals should seek to unite under this double aspect all the advantages which flow from it.

Now, the Sovereign People, having no existence, outside that of 48 the individuals who compose it, has, and can have, no interest at variance with theirs. Consequently, the sovereign power need give no guarantee to its subjects, since it is impossible that the body should wish to injure all its members, nor, as we shall see later, can it injure any single individual. The Sovereign, by merely existing, is always what it should be.

But the same does not hold true of the relation of subject to sov- 49 ereign. In spite of common interest, there can be no guarantee that the subject will observe his duty to the sovereign unless means are found to ensure his loyalty.

Each individual, indeed, may, as a man, exercise a will at vari- 50 ance with, or different from, that general will to which, as citizen, he contributes. His personal interest may dictate a line of action quite other than that demanded by the interest of all. The fact that his own existence as an individual has an absolute value, and that he is, by nature, an independent being, may lead him to conclude that what he owes to the common cause is something that he renders of his own free will; and he may decide that by leaving the debt unpaid he does less harm to his fellows than he would to himself should he make the necessary surrender. Regarding the moral entity constituting the State as a rational abstraction because it is not a man, he might enjoy his rights as a citizen without, at the same time, fulfilling his duties as a subject, and the resultant injustice might grow until it brought ruin upon the whole body politic.

In order, then, that the social compact may not be but a vain 51 formula, it must contain, though unexpressed, the single undertaking which can alone give force to the whole, namely, that whoever shall refuse to obey the general will must be constrained by the whole body of his fellow citizens to do so: which is no more than to say that it may be necessary to compel a man to be free—freedom being that condition which, by giving each citizen to his country, guarantees him from all personal dependence and is the foundation upon which the whole political machine rests, and supplies the power which works it. Only the recognition by the individual of the rights of the community can give legal force to undertakings entered into between citizens, which, otherwise, would become absurd, tyrannical, and exposed to vast abuses.

Of the Civil State

The passage from the state of nature to the civil state produces a 52
truly remarkable change in the individual. It substitutes justice for
instinct in his behavior, and gives to his actions a moral basis which
formerly was lacking. Only when the voice of duty replaces physical
impulse and when right replaces the cravings of appetite does the
man who, till then, was concerned solely with himself, realize that
he is under compulsion to obey quite different principles, and that
he must now consult his reason and not merely respond to the
promptings of desire. Although he may find himself deprived of
many advantages which were his in a state of nature, he will recognize that he has gained others which are of far greater value. By dint
of being exercised, his faculties will develop, his ideas take on a
wider scope, his sentiments become ennobled, and his whole soul
be so elevated, that, but for the fact that misuse of the new conditions still, at times, degrades him to a point below that from which
he has emerged, he would unceasingly bless the day which freed
him forever from his ancient state, and turned him from a limited
and stupid animal into an intelligent being and a Man.

Let us reduce all this to terms which can be easily compared. 53
What a man loses as a result of the Social Contract is his natural liberty and his unqualified right to lay hands on all that tempts him,
provided only that he can compass its possession. What he gains is
civil liberty and the ownership of what belongs to him. That we may
labor under no illusion concerning these compensations, it is well
that we distinguish between natural liberty which the individual enjoys so long as he is strong enough to maintain it, and civil liberty
which is curtailed by the general will. Between possessions which
derive from physical strength and the right of the first-comer, and
ownership which can be based only on a positive title.

To the benefits conferred by the status of citizenship might be 54
added that of Moral Freedom, which alone makes a man his own
master. For to be subject to appetite is to be a slave, while to obey
the laws laid down by society is to be free. But I have already said
enough on this point, and am not concerned here with the philosophical meaning of the word *liberty*.

Of Real Property

Each individual member of the Community gives himself to it at 55
the moment of its formation. What he gives is the whole man as he
then is, with all his qualities of strength and power, and everything

of which he stands possessed. Not that, as a result of this act of gift, such possessions, by changing hands and becoming the property of the Sovereign, change their nature. Just as the resources of strength upon which the City can draw are incomparably greater than those at the disposition of any single individual, so, too, is public possession when backed by a greater power. It is made more irrevocable, though not, so far, at least, as regards foreigners, more legitimate. For the State, by reason of the Social Contract which, within it, is the basis of all Rights, is the master of all its members' goods, though, in its dealings with other Powers, it is so only by virtue of its rights as first occupier, which come to it from the individuals who make it up.

The Right of "first occupancy," though more real than the "Right   56 of the strongest," becomes a genuine right only after the right of property has been established. All men have a natural right to what is necessary to them. But the positive act which establishes a man's claim to any particular item of property limits him to that and excludes him from all others. His share having been determined, he must confine himself to that, and no longer has any claim on the property of the community. That is why the right of "first occupancy," however weak it be in a state of nature, is guaranteed to every man enjoying the status of citizen. In so far as he benefits from this right, he withholds his claim, not so much from what is another's, as from what is not specifically his.

In order that the right of "first occupancy" may be legalized,   57 the following conditions must be present. (1) There must be no one already living on the land in question. (2) A man must occupy only so much of it as is necessary for his subsistence. (3) He must take possession of it, not by empty ceremony, but by virtue of his intention to work and to cultivate it, for that, in the absence of legal title, alone constitutes a claim which will be respected by others.

In effect, by according the right of "first occupancy" to a man's   58 needs and to his will to work, are we not stretching it as far as it will go? Should not some limits be set to this right? Has a man only to set foot on land belonging to the community to justify his claim to be its master? Just because he is strong enough, at one particular moment, to keep others off, can he demand that they shall never return? How can a man or a People take possession of vast territories, thereby excluding the rest of the world from their enjoyment, save by an act of criminal usurpation, since, as the result of such an act, the rest of humanity is deprived of the amenities of dwelling and subsistence which nature has provided for their common enjoyment? When Nuñez Balboa,[13] landing upon a strip of coast, claimed the Southern Sea and the whole of South America as the property of the crown of Castille, was he thereby justified in dispossessing its former inhabitants, and in excluding from it all the other princes of the earth? Grant that, and there will be no end to such vain ceremonies. It would be open to His Catholic Majesty[14] to claim from his Council Chamber possession of the whole Universe, only excepting those portions of it already in the ownership of other princes.

One can understand how the lands of individuals, separate but 59 contiguous, become public territory, and how the right of sovereignty, extending from men to the land they occupy, becomes at one real and personal—a fact which makes their owners more than ever dependent, and turns their very strength into a guarantee of their fidelity. This is an advantage which does not seem to have been considered by the monarchs of the ancient world, who, claiming to be no more than kings of the Persians, the Scythians, the Macedonians, seem to have regarded themselves rather as the rulers of men than as the masters of countries. Those of our day are cleverer, for they style themselves kings of France, of Spain, of England, and so forth. Thus, by controlling the land, they can be very sure of controlling its inhabitants.

The strange thing about this act of alienation is that, far from 60 depriving its members of their property by accepting its surrender, the Community actually establishes their claim to its legitimate ownership, and changes what was formerly mere usurpation into a right, by virtue of which they may enjoy possession. As owners they are Trustees for the Commonwealth. Their rights are respected by their fellow citizens and are maintained by the united strength of the community against any outside attack. From ceding their property to the State—and thus, to themselves—they derive nothing but advantage, since they have, so to speak, acquired all that they have surrendered. This paradox is easily explained once we realize the distinction between the rights exercised by the Sovereign and by the Owner over the same piece of property, as will be seen later.

It may so happen that a number of men begin to group them- 61 selves into a community before ever they own property at all, and that only later, when they have got possession of land sufficient to maintain them all, do they either enjoy it in common or parcel it be-

---

[13] **Nuñez Balboa (1475–1519)** Spanish explorer who discovered the Pacific Ocean.

[14] **His Catholic Majesty** A reference to the king of Spain, probably Ferdinand II of Aragon (1452–1516).

tween themselves in equal lots or in accordance with such scale of proportion as may be established by the sovereign. However this acquisition be made, the right exercised by each individual over his own particular share must always be subordinated to the overriding claim of the Community as such. Otherwise there would be no strength in the social bond, nor any real power in the exercise of sovereignty.

I will conclude this chapter, and the present Book, with a re- 62 mark which should serve as basis for every social system: that, so far from destroying natural equality, the primitive compact substitutes for it a moral and legal equality which compensates for all those physical inequalities from which men suffer. However unequal they may be in bodily strength or in intellectual gifts, they become equal in the eyes of the law, and as a result of the compact into which they have entered.

QUESTIONS FOR CRITICAL READING

1. Examine Rousseau's analogy of the family as the oldest and only natural form of government. Do you agree that the analogy is useful and that its contentions are true? Which aspects of this natural form of government do not work to help us understand the basis of government?
2. Rousseau seems to accept the family as a patriarchal structure. How would his views change if he accepted it as a matriarchal structure? How would they change if he regarded each member of the family as absolutely equal in authority from birth?
3. What does it mean to reason from what is fact instead of from what is morally right?
4. What features of Rousseau's social contract are like those of a legal contract? How does a person contract to be part of society?
5. What distinctions can be made between natural, moral, and legal equality? Which kind of equality is most important to a social system?

SUGGESTIONS FOR WRITING

1. When Rousseau wrote, "Man is born free, and everywhere he is in chains," the institution of slavery was widely practiced and justified by many authorities. Today slavery has been generally abolished. How is this statement relevant to people's condition in society now? What are some ways in which people relinquish their independence or freedom?
2. Clarify the difference between your duty to yourself and your duty to society (your social structure—personal, local, national). Establish

your duties in relation to each structure. How can these duties conflict with one another? How does the individual resolve the conflicts?

3. Do you agree with Rousseau when he says, "All men have a natural right to what is necessary to them"? What is necessary to all people, and in what sense do they have a right to what is necessary? Who should provide those necessities? Should necessities be provided for everyone or only for people who are unable to provide for themselves? If society will not provide these necessities, does the individual have the right to break the social contract by means of revolution?

4. What seems to be Rousseau's opinion regarding private property or the ownership of property? Beginning with paragraph 59, Rousseau distinguishes between monarchs with sovereignty over people and those with sovereignty over a region, such as France, Italy, or another country. What is Rousseau's view of the property that constitutes a state and who actually owns it? He mentions that the rights of individual owners must give way to the rights of the community in general. What is your response to this view?

5. Rousseau makes an important distinction between natural liberty and civil liberty. People in a state of nature enjoy natural liberty, and when they bind themselves together into a body politic, they enjoy civil liberty. What are the differences? Define each kind of liberty as carefully as you can, and take a stand on whether you feel civil liberty or natural liberty is superior. How is the conflict between the two forms of liberty felt today?

6. **CONNECTIONS** Rousseau's thinking emphasizes the role played by the common people in any civil society. How does that emphasis compare with Machiavelli's thinking? Consider the attitudes each writer has toward the essential goodness of people and the essential responsibilities of the monarch or government leader. In what ways is Lao-tzu closer in thinking to Rousseau or Machiavelli?

THOMAS JEFFERSON
The Declaration of Independence

THOMAS JEFFERSON (1743 – 1826) authored one of the most memorable statements in American history: the Declaration of Independence. He composed the work in 1776 under the watchful eyes of Benjamin Franklin, John Adams, and the rest of the Continental Congress, which spent two and a half days going over every word. Although the substance of the document was developed in committee, Jefferson, because of the grace of his writing style, was selected to craft the actual wording.

Jefferson rose to eminence in a time of great political upheaval. By the time he took a seat in the Virginia legislature in 1769, the colony was already on the course toward revolution. His pamphlet "A Summary View of the Rights of British America" (1774) brought him to the attention of those who were agitating for independence and established him as an ardent republican and revolutionary. In 1779 he was elected governor of Virginia. After the Revolutionary War he moved into the national political arena as the first secretary of state (1790 – 1793). He then served as John Adams's vice president (1797 – 1801) and was himself elected president in 1800. Perhaps one of his greatest achievements during his two terms (1801 – 1809) in office was his negotiation of the Louisiana Purchase, in which the United States acquired 828,000 square miles of land west of the Mississippi from France for about $15 million.

One of the fundamental paradoxes of Jefferson's personal and political life has been his attitude toward slavery. Like most wealthy Virginians, Jefferson owned slaves. However, in 1784 he tried to abolish slavery in the western territories that were being added to the United States. His "Report on Government for the Western Territory" failed by one vote. Historians have pointed out that Jefferson had an affair with Sally Hemmings, a mulatto slave who traveled with him abroad, and fathered several of her children.

However unclear his personal convictions, many of Jefferson's accomplishments, which extend from politics to agriculture and mechanical invention, still stand. One of the most versatile Americans of any generation, he wrote a book, *Notes on Virginia* (1782); designed and built Monticello, his famous homestead in Virginia; and in large part founded and designed the University of Virginia (1819).

Despite their revolutionary nature, the ideas Jefferson expressed in the Declaration of Independence were not entirely original. Rousseau's republican philosophies greatly influenced the work. When Jefferson states in the second paragraph that "all men are created equal, that they are endowed by their Creator with certain unalienable rights," he reflects Rousseau's emphasis on the political equality of men and on protecting certain fundamental rights (see Rousseau beginning with paragraph 39, p. 66). Jefferson also wrote that "Governments are instituted among Men, deriving their just powers from the consent of the governed." This is one of Rousseau's primary points, although it was Jefferson who immortalized it in these words.

Jefferson's Rhetoric

Jefferson's techniques include the use of the periodic sentence, which was especially typical of the age. The first sentence of the Declaration of Independence is periodic—that is, it is long and carefully balanced, and the main point comes at the end. Such sentences are not popular today, although an occasional periodic sentence can still be powerful in contemporary prose. Jefferson's first sentence says (in paraphrase): When one nation must sever its relations with a parent nation...and stand as an independent nation itself...the causes ought to be explained. Moreover, the main body of the Declaration of Independence lists the "causes" that lead to the final and most important element of the sentence. Causal analysis was a method associated with legal thought and reflects his training in eighteenth-century legal analysis. One understood things best when one understood their causes.

The periodic sentence demands certain qualities of balance and parallelism that all good writers should heed. The first sentence in paragraph 2 demonstrates both qualities. The balance is achieved by making each part of the sentence roughly the same length. The parallelism is achieved by linking words in deliberate repetition for effect (they are in italicized type in the following analysis). Note how the "truths" mentioned in the first clause are enumerated in the succession of noun clauses beginning with "that"; "Rights" are enumerated in the final clause:

We hold these truths to be self evident,
> *that* all men are created equal,
> *that* they are endowed by their Creator with certain unalienable Rights,
> *that* among these are Life, Liberty and the pursuit of Happiness.

Parallelism is one of the greatest stylistic techniques available to a writer sensitive to rhetoric. It is a natural technique: many untrained writers and speakers develop it on their own. The periodicity of the sentences and the balance of their parallelism suggest thoughtfulness, wisdom, and control.

Parallelism creates a natural link to the useful device of enumeration, or listing. Many writers using this technique establish their purpose from the outset — "I wish to address three important issues..." — and then number them: "First, I want to say...Second...," and so on. Jefferson devotes paragraphs 3 through 29 to enumerating the "causes" he mentions in paragraph 1. Each one constitutes a separate paragraph; thus, each has separate weight and importance. Each begins with "He" or "For" and is therefore in parallel structure. The technique of repetition of the same words at the beginning of successive lines is called *anaphora*. Jefferson's use of anaphora here is one of the best known and most effective in all literature. The "He" referred to is Britain's King George III (1738 – 1820), who is never mentioned by name. Congress is opposed not to a personality but to the sovereign of a nation that is oppressing the United States and a tyrant who is not dignified by being named. The "For" introduces grievous acts the king has given his assent to; these are offenses against the colonies.

However, Jefferson does not develop the causes in detail. We do not have specific information about what trade was cut off by the British, what taxes were imposed without consent, or how King George waged war or abdicated government in the colonies. Presumably, Jefferson's audience knew the details and was led by the twenty-seven paragraphs to observe how numerous the causes were. And all are serious; any one alone was enough cause for revolution. The effect of Jefferson's enumeration is to illustrate the patience of the colonies up to this point and to tell the world that the colonies have finally lost patience on account of the reasons listed. The Declaration of Independence projects the careful meditations and decisions of exceptionally calm, patient, and reasonable people.

The following prereading questions may help you anticipate key issues in the discussion on Thomas Jefferson's Declaration of Independence. Keeping them in mind during your first reading of the selection should help focus your reactions.

- Under what conditions may a people alter or abolish their government?

- Why does Jefferson consider King George a tyrant?

The Declaration of Independence

In Congress, July 4, 1776

The Unanimous Declaration of the Thirteen United States of America

When in the Course of human events, it becomes necessary for 1 one people to dissolve the political bands which have connected them with another, and to assume among the Powers of the earth, the separate and equal station to which the Laws of Nature and of Nature's God entitle them, a decent respect to the opinions of mankind requires that they should declare the causes which impel them to the separation.

We hold these truths to be self-evident, that all men are created 2 equal, that they are endowed by their Creator with certain inalienable Rights, that among these are Life, Liberty and the pursuit of Happiness. That to secure these rights, Governments are instituted among Men, deriving their just powers from the consent of the governed. That whenever any Form of Government becomes destructive of these ends, it is the Right of the People to alter or to abolish it, and to institute new Government, laying its foundation on such principles and organizing its powers in such form, as to them shall seem most likely to effect their Safety and Happiness. Prudence, indeed, will dictate that Governments long established should not be changed for light and transient causes; and accordingly all experience hath shown, that mankind are more disposed to suffer, while evils are sufferable, than to right themselves by abolishing the forms to which they are accustomed. But when a long train of abuses and usurpations, pursuing invariably the same Object evinces a design to reduce them under absolute Despotism, it is their right, it is their duty, to throw off such Government, and to provide new Guards for their future security. — Such has been the patient sufferance of these Colonies; and such is now the necessity which constrains them to alter their former Systems of Government. The history of the present King of Great Britain is a history of repeated injuries and usurpations, all having in direct object the establishment of an absolute Tyranny over these States. To prove this, let Facts be submitted to a candid world.

He has refused his Assent to Laws, the most wholesome and   3
necessary for the public good.

He has forbidden his Governors to pass Laws of immediate and   4
pressing importance, unless suspended in their operation till his Assent should be obtained; and when so suspended, he has utterly neglected to attend to them.

He has refused to pass other laws for the accommodation of   5
large districts of people, unless those people would relinquish the right of Representation in the Legislature, a right inestimable to them and formidable to tyrants only.

He has called together legislative bodies at places unusual, un-   6
comfortable, and distant from the depository of their Public Records, for the sole purpose of fatiguing them into compliance with his measures.

He has dissolved Representative Houses repeatedly, for oppos-   7
ing with manly firmness his invasions on the rights of the people.

He has refused for a long time, after such dissolutions, to cause   8
others to be elected; whereby the Legislative Powers, incapable of Annihilation, have returned to the People at large for their exercise; the State remaining in the mean time exposed to all the dangers of invasion from without, and convulsions within.

He has endeavoured to prevent the population of these States;[1]   9
for that purpose obstructing the Laws for Naturalization of Foreigners; refusing to pass others to encourage their migration hither, and raising the conditions of new Appropriations of Lands.

He has obstructed the Administration of Justice, by refusing his   10
Assent to Laws for establishing Judiciary Powers.

He has made Judges dependent on his Will alone, for the tenure   11
of their offices, and the amount and payment of their salaries.

He has erected a multitude of New Offices, and sent hither   12
swarms of Officers to harass our People, and eat out their substance.

---

[1] **prevent the population of these States** This meant limiting emigration to the Colonies, thus controlling their growth.

He has kept among us, in times of peace, Standing Armies with- 13
out the Consent of our legislature.

He has affected to render the Military independent of and supe- 14
rior to the Civil Power.

He has combined with others to subject us to a jurisdiction for- 15
eign to our constitution, and unacknowledged by our laws; giving
his Assent to their acts of pretended Legislation:

For quartering large bodies of armed troops among us: 16

For protecting them, by a mock Trial, from Punishment for any 17
Murders which they should commit on the Inhabitants of these
States:

For cutting off our Trade with all parts of the world: 18

For imposing taxes on us without our Consent: 19

For depriving us in many cases, of the benefits of Trial by Jury: 20

For transporting us beyond Seas to be tried for pretended of- 21
fences:

For abolishing the free System of English Laws in a neighbour- 22
ing Province, establishing therein an Arbitrary government, and enlarging its Boundaries so as to render it at once an example and fit
instrument for introducing the same absolute rule into these
Colonies:

For taking away our Charters, abolishing our most valuable 23
Laws, and altering fundamentally the Forms of our Governments:

For suspending our own Legislatures, and declaring themselves 24
invested with Power to legislate for us in all cases whatsoever.

He has abdicated Government here, by declaring us out of his 25
Protection and waging War against us.

He has plundered our seas, ravaged our Coasts, burnt our 26
towns, and destroyed the lives of our people.

He is at this time transporting large armies of foreign mercenar- 27
ies to compleat the works of death, desolation and tyranny, already
begun with circumstances of Cruelty & perfidy scarcely paralleled in
the most barbarous ages, and totally unworthy the Head of a civilized nation.

He has constrained our fellow Citizens taken Captive on the 28
high Seas to bear Arms against their Country, to become the executioners of their friends and Brethren, or to fall themselves by their
Hands.

He has excited domestic insurrections amongst us, and has en- 29
deavoured to bring on the inhabitants of our frontiers, the merciless
Indian Savages, whose known rule of warfare, is an undistinguished
destruction of all ages, sexes and conditions.

In every stage of these Oppressions We have Petitioned for Re- 30
dress in the most humble terms: Our repeated Petitions have been

answered only by repeated injury. A Prince, whose character is thus marked by every act which may define a Tyrant, is unfit to be the ruler of a free People.

Nor have We been wanting in attention to our British brethren.   31
We have warned them from time to time of attempts by their legislature to extend an unwarrantable jurisdiction over us. We have reminded them of the circumstances of our emigration and settlement here. We have appealed to their native justice and magnanimity, and we have conjured them by the ties of our common kindred to disavow these usurpations, which, would inevitably interrupt our connections and correspondence. They too have been deaf to the voice of justice and of consanguinity. We must, therefore, acquiesce in the necessity, which denounces our Separation, and hold them, as we hold the rest of mankind, Enemies in War, in Peace Friends.

We, therefore, the Representatives of the United States of Amer-   32
ica, in General Congress, Assembled, appealing to the Supreme Judge of the world for the rectitude of our intentions, do, in the Name, and by Authority of the good People of these Colonies, solemnly publish and declare, That these United Colonies are, and of Right ought to be Free and Independent States, that they are Absolved from all Allegiance to the British Crown, and that all political connection between them and the State of Great Britain, is and ought to be totally dissolved; and that as Free and Independent States, they have full Power to levy War, conclude Peace, contract Alliances, establish Commerce, and to do all other Acts and Things which Independent States may of right do. And for the support of this Declaration, with a firm reliance on the Protection of Divine Providence, we mutually pledge to each other our Lives, our Fortunes and our sacred Honor.

QUESTIONS FOR CRITICAL READING

1. What laws of nature does Jefferson refer to in paragraph 1?
2. What do you think Jefferson feels is the function of government (para. 2)?
3. What does Jefferson say about women? Is there any way you can determine his views from reading this document? Does he appear to favor a patriarchal system?
4. Find at least one use of parallel structure in the Declaration (see p. 76 in the section on Jefferson's Rhetoric for a description of parallelism). What key terms are repeated in identical or equivalent constructions, and to what effect?

5. Which causes listed in paragraphs 3 through 29 are the most serious? Are any trivial? Which ones are serious enough to cause a revolution?
6. What do you consider to be the most graceful sentence in the entire Declaration? Where is it placed in the Declaration? What purpose does it serve there?
7. In what ways does the king's desire for stable government interfere with Jefferson's sense of his own independence?

SUGGESTIONS FOR WRITING

1. Jefferson defines the inalienable rights of a citizen as "Life, Liberty and the pursuit of Happiness." Do you think these are indeed unalienable rights? Answer this question by including some sentences that use parallel structure and repeat key terms in similar constructions. Be certain that you define each of these rights both for yourself and for our time.
2. Write an essay discussing what you feel the function of government should be. Include at least three periodic sentences (underline them). You may first want to establish Jefferson's view of government and then compare or contrast it with your own.
3. Jefferson envisioned a government that allowed its citizens to exercise their rights to life, liberty, and the pursuit of happiness. Has Jefferson's revolutionary vision been achieved in America? Begin with a definition of these three key terms: "life," "liberty," and "the pursuit of happiness." Then, for each term use examples—drawn from current events, your own experience, American history—to take a clear and well-argued stand on whether the nation has achieved Jefferson's goal.
4. Slavery was legal in America in 1776, and Jefferson reluctantly owned slaves. He never presented his plan for gradual emancipation of the slaves to Congress because he realized that Congress would never approve it. But Jefferson and Franklin did finance a plan to buy slaves and return them to Africa, where in 1821 returning slaves founded the nation of Liberia. Agree or disagree with the following statement and defend your position: the ownership of slaves by the people who wrote the Declaration of Independence invalidates it. You may wish to read the relevant chapters on Jefferson and slavery in Merrill D. Peterson's *Thomas Jefferson and the New Nation* (1970).
5. What kind of government does Jefferson seem to prefer? In what ways would his government differ from that of the king he is reacting against? Is he talking about an entirely different system or about the same system but with a different kind of "prince" at the head? How would Jefferson protect the individual against the whim of the state, while also protecting the state against the whim of the individual?
6. **CONNECTIONS** Write an essay in which you examine the ways in which Jefferson agrees or disagrees with Lao-tzu's conception of human nature and of government. How does Jefferson share Lao-tzu's commitment to judicious inactivity? What evidence is there that the

king subscribes to it? Describe the similarities and differences between Jefferson's views and those of Lao-tzu.

7. **CONNECTIONS**   What principles does Jefferson share with Jean-Jacques Rousseau? Compare the fundamental demands of the Declaration of Independence with Rousseau's conceptions of liberty and independence. How would Rousseau have reacted to this Declaration?

HANNAH ARENDT
Ideology and Terror:
A Novel Form of Government

HANNAH ARENDT (1906 – 1975) was born and educated in Germany, earning her doctorate from the University of Heidelberg when she was twenty-two years old. She left Germany for Paris after Hitler came to power in 1933 and early in the development of Nazi ideology. In New York City she worked with Jewish relief groups and in 1940 married Heinrich Bluecher, a professor of philosophy. Arendt joined the faculty of the University of Chicago in 1963 and then taught as a visiting professor at a number of universities, eventually settling at the New School for Social Research in New York.

The Origins of Totalitarianism, from which this selection is excerpted, was first published in 1951 and solidified Arendt's reputation as an important political philosopher. She began work on the book in 1945, after Nazism was defeated in Europe, and finished most of it by 1949, during the period of growing tension between the United States and Russia that began the Cold War. Much of the book analyzes the politics of ideology in fascist and communist countries. Arendt went on to write a number of other influential works, such as *The Human Condition* (1958) and *Crises of the Republic* (1972), both of which address the problems she saw connected with a decline in moral values in modern society. One of her most controversial books, *Eichmann in Jerusalem* (1963), examined Adolf Eichmann, head of the Gestapo's Jewish section, who was tried and executed in Jerusalem. She observed that the nature of Eichmann's evil was essentially banal—that his crime involved going along with orders without taking the time to assess them critically. Her last work, *The Life of the Mind,* was not completed, although two of its planned three volumes were published posthumously in 1978.

"Ideology and Terror: A Novel Form of Government" is part of one of the last chapters in *The Origins of Totalitarianism.* The first part of the book sets forth a brief history of modern anti-Semitism because the rise of totalitarianism in Germany was based in large part on Hitler's belief that the Aryan race was biologically and morally more evolved than all other races. In this selection Hannah Arendt shows how the totalitarian state derives its power from propagating a set of ideas, or ideology, such as the view that one race is superior to all others. Once that premise is accepted, she demonstrates, then any and all atrocities against people of other races can be permitted and promoted.

In two instances, describing the ideology of fascist Germany and the ideology of communist Russia, Arendt demonstrates the ways in which the uncritical acceptance of an ideology provides the core of power for totalitarian states. In the case of Germany, racism led to the theory that if some races are inferior and debased then they must be destroyed for the good of humanity—a theory that was put into brutal practice by the Nazis. Arendt shows how this view derives from a misunderstanding of Darwin's theories of the survival of the fittest (see Darwin's "Natural Selection," p. 435). In the case of communist Russia, totalitarianism depended on the "scientific" theory of history put forth by Karl Marx (see Marx's "Communist Manifesto," p. 219) that insisted on class struggle and the need of the most "progressive class" to destroy the less progressive classes. Marx was referred to as the "Darwin of history" in part because his views reflected the same scientific logic as Darwin's theories of biology. According to Arendt, both the Nazi and communist totalitarian regimes claimed those laws of biology or history as the justification for their own brutal acts of terror.

Arendt's Rhetoric

Arendt's rhetorical approach is careful and thorough. However, she is not conclusively logical throughout. It is not that she is illogical but rather that she avoids the mistakes of the ideologies she critiques. For example, she does not establish one inviolable principle as her logical premise and then argue from it relentlessly.

Instead, she offers a descriptive analysis of the forms of totalitarianism that dominated the twentieth century. She tries to show that the absolute acceptance of racist and classist views results in terrorism. She examines the nature of government in terms of its normal expectations of lawfulness and claims that totalitarian governments make their ideology the law and thereby destroy lawfulness. As she says, in most forms of government the laws tell us what we must not do, whereas totalitarian governments tell us what we must do.

Arendt's paragraphs are long and carefully developed. In each she analyzes her terms and the circumstances she mentions. For example, she begins paragraph 10 with "In the interpretation of totalitarianism, all laws have become laws of movement." She then explains that Nazi ideology fastened onto a law of nature whereas communism fastened onto a law of history. In both cases these laws are "in motion" — meaning they describe a process of continuing development and change.

In several places Arendt develops the concept of terror, which goes beyond simple fear. According to Arendt, terror is the essence of the totalitarian state, and without it, the state collapses. Individual liberty and freedom are erased by the terror of the totalitarian state, and in this sense the values that Rousseau and Jefferson argue for are irrelevant. In some states, such as the state that Machiavelli imagined, terror might be useful for controlling the opposition. But in the totalitarian state it controls everyone. As Arendt says, "Terror becomes total when it becomes independent of all opposition; it rules supreme when nobody any longer stands in its way" (para. 13).

PREREADING QUESTIONS: WHAT TO READ FOR

The following prereading questions may help you anticipate key issues in the discussion on Hannah Arendt's "Ideology and Terror: A Novel Form of Government." Keeping them in mind during your first reading of the selection should help focus your reactions.

- What does *totalitarianism* mean?
- What is the relationship of terror to the law in a totalitarian state? What is the relationship of total terror to the essence of the totalitarian state?

Ideology and Terror:
A Novel Form of Government

In the preceding chapters we emphasized repeatedly that the   1
means of total domination are not only more drastic but that totalitarianism differs essentially from other forms of political oppression
known to us such as despotism, tyranny and dictatorship. Wherever
it rose to power, it developed entirely new political institutions and
destroyed all social, legal and political traditions of the country. No
matter what the specifically national tradition or the particular spiritual source of its ideology, totalitarian government always transformed classes into masses, supplanted the party system, not by
one-party dictatorships, but by a mass movement, shifted the center
of power from the army to the police, and established a foreign policy openly directed toward world domination. Present totalitarian
governments have developed from one-party systems; whenever
these became truly totalitarian, they started to operate according to a
system of values so radically different from all others, that none of
our traditional legal, moral, or common sense utilitarian categories
could any longer help us to come to terms with, or judge, or predict
their course of action.

If it is true that the elements of totalitarianism can be found by   2
retracing the history and analyzing the political implications of what
we usually call the crisis of our century, then the conclusion is unavoidable that this crisis is no mere threat from the outside, no mere
result of some aggressive foreign policy of either Germany or Russia,
and that it will no more disappear with the death of Stalin than it
disappeared with the fall of Nazi Germany. It may even be that the
true predicaments of our time will assume their authentic form—
though not necessarily the cruelest—only when totalitarianism has
become a thing of the past.

It is in the line of such reflections to raise the question whether   3
totalitarian government, born of this crisis and at the same time its
clearest and only unequivocal symptom, is merely a makeshift
arrangement, which borrows its methods of intimidation, its means
of organization and its instruments of violence from the well-known
political arsenal of tyranny, despotism and dictatorships, and owes
its existence only to the deplorable, but perhaps accidental failure of
the traditional political forces—liberal or conservative, national or
socialist, republican or monarchist, authoritarian or democratic. Or
whether, on the contrary, there is such a thing as the *nature* of totalitarian government, whether it has its own essence and can be com-

pared with and defined like other forms of government such as Western thought has known and recognized since the times of ancient philosophy. If this is true, then the entirely new and unprecedented forms of totalitarian organization and course of action must rest on one of the few basic experiences which men can have whenever they live together, and are concerned with public affairs. If there is a basic experience which finds its political expression in totalitarian domination, then, in view of the novelty of the totalitarian form of government, this must be an experience which, for whatever reason, has never before served as the foundation of a body politic and whose general mood — although it may be familiar in every other respect — never before has pervaded, and directed the handling of, public affairs.

If we consider this in terms of the history of ideas, it seems extremely unlikely. For the forms of government under which men live have been very few; they were discovered early, classified by the Greeks and have proved extraordinarily long-lived. If we apply these findings, whose fundamental idea, despite many variations, did not change in the two and a half thousand years that separate Plato from Kant,[1] we are tempted at once to interpret totalitarianism as some modern form of tyranny, that is a lawless government where power is wielded by one man. Arbitrary power, unrestricted by law, wielded in the interest of the ruler and hostile to the interests of the governed, on one hand, fear as the principle of action, namely fear of the people by the ruler and fear of the ruler by the people, on the other — these have been the hallmarks of tyranny throughout our tradition.

Instead of saying that totalitarian government is unprecedented, we could also say that it has exploded the very alternative on which all definitions of the essence of governments have been based in political philosophy, that is the alternative between lawful and lawless government, between arbitrary and legitimate power. That lawful government and legitimate power, on one side, lawlessness and arbitrary power on the other, belonged together and were inseparable has never been questioned. Yet, totalitarian rule confronts us with a totally different kind of government. It defies, it is true, all positive laws, even to the extreme of defying those which it has itself established (as in the case of the Soviet Constitution of 1936, to quote only the most outstanding example) or which it did not care to abol-

---

[1] **Immanuel Kant (1724–1804)** Modern philosopher who some rank with Plato (p. 313). Kant suggested that individuals should live as if a universal law could be derived from their behavior. Like Plato, Kant reflected on forms of government.

ish (as in the case of the Weimar Constitution which the Nazi government never revoked). But it operates neither without guidance of law nor is it arbitrary, for it claims to obey strictly and unequivocally those laws of Nature or of History from which all positive laws always have been supposed to spring.

It is the monstrous, yet seemingly unanswerable claim of totali- 6
tarian rule that, far from being "lawless," it goes to the sources of authority from which positive laws received their ultimate legitimation, that far from being arbitrary it is more obedient to these suprahuman forces than any government ever was before, and that far from wielding its power in the interest of one man, it is quite prepared to sacrifice everybody's vital immediate interests to the execution of what it assumes to be the law of History or the law of Nature. Its defiance of positive laws claims to be a higher form of legitimacy which, since it is inspired by the sources themselves, can do away with petty legality. Totalitarian lawfulness pretends to have found a way to establish the rule of justice on earth—something which the legality of positive law admittedly could never attain. The discrepancy between legality and justice could never be bridged because the standards of right and wrong into which positive law translates its own source of authority—"natural law" governing the whole universe, or divine law revealed in human history, or customs and traditions expressing the law common to the sentiments of all men—are necessarily general and must be valid for a countless and unpredictable number of cases, so that each concrete individual case with its unrepeatable set of circumstances somehow escapes it.

Totalitarian lawfulness, defying legality and pretending to estab- 7
lish the direct reign of justice on earth, executes the law of History or of Nature without translating it into standards of right and wrong for individual behavior. It applies the law directly to mankind without bothering with the behavior of men. The law of Nature or the law of History, if properly executed, is expected to produce mankind as its end product; and this expectation lies behind the claim to global rule of all totalitarian governments. Totalitarian policy claims to transform the human species into an active unfailing carrier of a law to which human beings otherwise would only passively and reluctantly be subjected. If it is true that the link between totalitarian countries and the civilized world was broken through the monstrous crimes of totalitarian regimes, it is also true that this criminality was not due to simple aggressiveness, ruthlessness, warfare and treachery, but to a conscious break of that *consensus iuris*[2]

---

[2] ***consensus iuris*** A general agreement about the laws that people must obey.

which, according to Cicero, constitutes a "people," and which, as international law, in modern times has constituted the civilized world insofar as it remains the foundation-stone of international relations even under the conditions of war. Both moral judgment and legal punishment presuppose this basic consent; the criminal can be judged justly only because he takes part in the *consensus iuris,* and even the revealed law of God can function among men only when they listen and consent to it.

At this point the fundamental difference between the totalitarian and all other concepts of law comes to light. Totalitarian policy does not replace one set of laws with another, does not establish its own *consensus iuris,* does not create, by one revolution, a new form of legality. Its defiance of all, even its own positive laws implies that it believes it can do without any *consensus iuris* whatever, and still not resign itself to the tyrannical state of lawlessness, arbitrariness and fear. It can do without the *consensus iuris* because it promises to release the fulfillment of law from all action and will of man; and it promises justice on earth because it claims to make mankind itself the embodiment of the law.   8

This identification of man and law, which seems to cancel the discrepancy between legality and justice that has plagued legal thought since ancient times, has nothing in common with the *lumen naturale*[3] or the voice of conscience, by which Nature or Divinity as the sources of authority for the *ius naturale*[4] or the historically revealed commands of God, are supposed to announce their authority in man himself. This never made man a walking embodiment of the law, but on the contrary remained distinct from him as the authority which demanded consent and obedience. Nature or Divinity as the source of authority for positive laws were thought of as permanent and eternal; positive laws were changing and changeable according to circumstances, but they possessed a relative permanence as compared with the much more rapidly changing actions of men; and they derived this permanence from the eternal presence of their source of authority. Positive laws, therefore, are primarily designed to function as stabilizing factors for the ever changing movements of men.   9

In the interpretation of totalitarianism, all laws have become laws of movement. When the Nazis talked about the law of nature or when the Bolsheviks talk about the law of history, neither nature   10

---

[3] **lumen naturale** Natural light—like common sense or individual conscience—that informs the individual about how to behave.

[4] **ius naturale** Natural law, thought to be common to all people, derived from nature rather than society.

nor history is any longer the stabilizing source of authority for the actions of mortal men; they are movements in themselves. Underlying the Nazis' belief in race laws as the expression of the law of nature in man, is Darwin's idea of man as the product of a natural development which does not necessarily stop with the present species of human beings, just as under the Bolsheviks' belief in class struggle as the expression of the law of history lies Marx's notion of society as the product of a gigantic historical movement which races according to its own law of motion to the end of historical times when it will abolish itself.

The difference between Marx's historical and Darwin's naturalistic approach has frequently been pointed out, usually and rightly in favor of Marx. This has led us to forget the great and positive interest Marx took in Darwin's theories; Engels[5] could not think of a greater compliment to Marx's scholarly achievements than to call him the "Darwin of history." If one considers, not the actual achievement, but the basic philosophies of both men, it turns out that ultimately the movement of history and the movement of nature are one and the same. Darwin's introduction of the concept of development into nature, his insistence that, at least in the field of biology, natural movement is not circular but unilinear, moving in an infinitely progressing direction, means in fact that nature is, as it were, being swept into history, that natural life is considered to be historical. The "natural" law of the survival of the fittest is just as much a historical law and could be used as such by racism as Marx's law of the survival of the most progressive class. Marx's class struggle, on the other hand, as the driving force of history is only the outward expression of the development of productive forces which in turn have their origin in the "labor-power" of men. Labor, according to Marx, is not a historical but a natural-biological force — released through man's "metabolism with nature" by which he conserves his individual life and reproduces the species. Engels saw the affinity between the basic convictions of the two men very clearly because he understood the decisive role which the concept of development played in both theories. The tremendous intellectual change which took place in the middle of the last [nineteenth] century consisted in the refusal to view or accept anything "as it is" and in the consistent interpretation of everything as being only a stage of some further develop-

11

---

[5] **Friedrich Engels (1820–1895)** Collaborator with Karl Marx on *The Communist Manifesto* (1848). He was the son of a textile mill owner and used some of his fortune to help Marx write *Das Kapital* (1867–1894). Engels lived most of his life in England.

ment. Whether the driving force of this development was called nature or history is relatively secondary. In these ideologies, the term "law" itself changed its meaning: from expressing the framework of stability within which human actions and motions can take place, it became the expression of the motion itself.

Totalitarian politics which proceeded to follow the recipes of ideologies has unmasked the true nature of these movements insofar as it clearly showed that there could be no end to this process. If it is the law of nature to eliminate everything that is harmful and unfit to live, it would mean the end of nature itself if new categories of the harmful and unfit-to-live could not be found; if it is the law of history that in a class struggle certain classes "wither away," it would mean the end of human history itself if rudimentary new classes did not form, so that they in turn could "wither away" under the hands of totalitarian rulers. In other words, the law of killing by which totalitarian movements seize and exercise power would remain a law of the movement even if they ever succeeded in making all of humanity subject to their rule. 12

By lawful government we understand a body politic in which positive laws are needed to translate and realize the immutable *ius naturale* or the eternal commandments of God into standards of right and wrong. Only in these standards, in the body of positive laws of each country, do the *ius naturale* or the Commandments of God achieve their political reality. In the body politic of totalitarian government, this place of positive laws is taken by total terror, which is designed to translate into reality the law of movement of history or nature. Just as positive laws, though they define transgressions, are independent of them—the absence of crimes in any society does not render laws superfluous but, on the contrary, signifies their most perfect rule—so terror in totalitarian government has ceased to be a mere means for the suppression of opposition, though it is also used for such purposes. Terror becomes total when it becomes independent of all opposition; it rules supreme when nobody any longer stands in its way. If lawfulness is the essence of non-tyrannical government and lawlessness is the essence of tyranny, then terror is the essence of totalitarian domination. 13

Terror is the realization of the law of movement; its chief aim is to make it possible for the force of nature or of history to race freely through mankind, unhindered by any spontaneous human action. As such, terror seeks to "stabilize" men in order to liberate the forces of nature or history. It is this movement which singles out the foes of mankind against whom terror is let loose, and no free action of either opposition or sympathy can be permitted to interfere with the elimination of the "objective enemy" of History or Nature, of the 14 class or the race. Guilt and innocence become senseless notions; "guilty" is he who stands in the way of the natural or historical process which has passed judgment over "inferior races," over individuals "unfit to live," over "dying classes and decadent peoples." Terror executes these judgments, and before its court, all concerned are subjectively innocent: the murdered because they did nothing against the system, and the murderers because they do not really murder but execute a death sentence pronounced by some higher tribunal. The rulers themselves do not claim to be just or wise, but only to execute historical or natural laws; they do not apply laws, but execute a movement in accordance with its inherent law. Terror is lawfulness, if law is the law of the movement of some suprahuman force, Nature or History.

Terror as the execution of a law of movement whose ultimate goal is not the welfare of men or the interest of one man but the fabrication of mankind, eliminates individuals for the sake of the species, sacrifices the "parts" for the sake of the "whole." The suprahuman force of Nature or History has its own beginning and its own end, so that it can be hindered only by the new beginning and the individual end which the life of each man actually is. 15

Positive laws in constitutional government are designed to erect boundaries and establish channels of communication between men whose community is continually endangered by the new men born into it. With each new birth, a new beginning is born into the world, a new world has potentially come into being. The stability of the laws corresponds to the constant motion of all human affairs, a motion which can never end as long as men are born and die. The laws hedge in each new beginning and at the same time assure its freedom of movement, the potentiality of something entirely new and unpredictable; the boundaries of positive laws are for the political existence of man what memory is for his historical existence: they guarantee the pre-existence of a common world, the reality of some continuity which transcends the individual life span of each generation, absorbs all new origins and is nourished by them. 16

Total terror is so easily mistaken for a symptom of tyrannical government because totalitarian government in its initial stages must behave like a tyranny and raze the boundaries of man-made law. But total terror leaves no arbitrary lawlessness behind it and does not rage for the sake of some arbitrary will or for the sake of despotic power of one man against all, least of all for the sake of a war of all against all. It substitutes for the boundaries and channels of communication between individual men a band of iron which holds them so tightly together that it is as though their plurality had disappeared into One Man of gigantic dimensions. To abolish the fences 17 of laws between men — as tyranny does — means to take away man's liberties and destroy freedom as a living political reality; for the space between men as it is hedged in by laws, is the living space of freedom. Total terror uses this old instrument of tyranny but destroys at the same time also the lawless, fenceless wilderness of fear and suspicion which tyranny leaves behind. This desert, to be sure, is no longer a living space of freedom, but it still provides some room for the fear-guided movements and suspicion-ridden actions of its inhabitants.

By pressing men against each other, total terror destroys the 18 space between them; compared to the condition within its iron band, even the desert of tyranny, insofar as it is still some kind of space, appears like a guarantee of freedom. Totalitarian government does not just curtail liberties or abolish essential freedoms; nor does it, at least to our limited knowledge, succeed in eradicating the love for freedom from the hearts of man. It destroys the one essential prerequisite of all freedom which is simply the capacity of motion which cannot exist without space.

Total terror, the essence of totalitarian government, exists nei- 19 ther for nor against men. It is supposed to provide the forces of nature or history with an incomparable instrument to accelerate their movement. This movement, proceeding according to its own law, cannot in the long run be hindered; eventually its force will always prove more powerful than the most powerful forces engendered by the actions and the will of men. But it can be slowed down and is slowed down almost inevitably by the freedom of man, which even totalitarian rulers cannot deny, for this freedom — irrelevant and arbitrary as they may deem it — is identical with the fact that men are being born and that therefore each of them is a new beginning, begins, in a sense, the world anew. From the totalitarian point of view, the fact that men are born and die can be only regarded as an annoying interference with higher forces. Terror, therefore, as the obedient servant of natural or historical movement has to eliminate from the process not only freedom in any specific sense, but the very source of freedom which is given with the fact of the birth of man and resides in his capacity to make a new beginning. In the iron band of terror, which destroys the plurality of men and makes out of many the One who unfailingly will act as though he himself were part of the course of history or nature, a device has been found not only to liberate the historical and natural forces, but to accelerate them to a speed they never would reach if left to themselves. Practically speaking, this means that terror executes on the spot the death sentences which Nature is supposed to have pronounced on races or individuals who are "unfit to live," or History on "dying classes," without waiting for the slower and less efficient processes of nature or history themselves.

In this concept, where the essence of government itself has be-   20
come motion, a very old problem of political thought seems to have found a solution similar to the one already noted for the discrepancy between legality and justice. If the essence of government is defined as lawfulness, and if it is understood that laws are the stabilizing forces in the public affairs of men (as indeed it always has been since Plato invoked Zeus, the god of the boundaries, in his *Laws*), then the problem of movement of the body politic and the actions of its citizens arises. Lawfulness sets limitations to actions, but does not inspire them; the greatness, but also the perplexity of laws in free societies is that they only tell what one should not, but never what one should do. The necessary movement of a body politic can never be found in its essence if only because this essence—again since Plato—has always been defined with a view to its permanence. Duration seemed one of the surest yardsticks for the goodness of a government. It is still for Montesquieu[6] the supreme proof for the badness of tyranny that only tyrannies are liable to be destroyed from within, to decline by themselves, whereas all other governments are destroyed through exterior circumstances. Therefore what the definition of governments always needed was what Montesquieu called a "principle of action" which, different in each form of government, would inspire government and citizens alike in their public activity and serve as a criterion, beyond the merely negative yardstick of lawfulness, for judging all action in public affairs. Such guiding principles and criteria of action are, according to Montesquieu, honor in a monarchy, virtue in a republic and fear in a tyranny.

In a perfect totalitarian government, where all men have become   21
One Man, where all action aims at the acceleration of the movement of nature or history, where every single act is the execution of a death sentence which Nature or History has already pronounced, that is, under conditions where terror can be completely relied upon to keep the movement in constant motion, no principle of action separate from its essence would be needed at all. Yet as long as totalitarian rule has not conquered the earth and with the iron band of terror made each single man a part of one mankind, terror in its double function as essence of government and principle, not of action, but of motion, cannot be fully realized. Just as lawfulness in

---

[6] **Baron de Montesquieu (1689–1755)** French legal authority. He developed the concept of the balance of powers in state government—balancing the monarch against the parliament. His most important book is *The Spirit of Laws* (1748).

constitutional government is insufficient to inspire and guide men's actions, so terror in totalitarian government is not sufficient to inspire and guide human behavior.

While under present conditions totalitarian domination still 22 shares with other forms of government the need for a guide for the behavior of its citizens in public affairs, it does not need and could not even use a principle of action strictly speaking, since it will eliminate precisely the capacity of man to act. Under conditions of total terror not even fear can any longer serve as an advisor of how to behave, because terror chooses its victims without reference to individual actions or thoughts, exclusively in accordance with the objective necessity of the natural or historical process. Under totalitarian conditions, fear probably is more widespread than ever before; but fear has lost its practical usefulness when actions guided by it can no longer help to avoid the dangers man fears. The same is true for sympathy or support of the regime; for total terror not only selects its victims according to objective standards; it chooses its executioners with as complete a disregard as possible for the candidate's conviction and sympathies. The consistent elimination of conviction as a motive for action has become a matter of record since the great purges in Soviet Russia and the satellite countries. The aim of totalitarian education has never been to instill convictions but to destroy the capacity to form any. The introduction of purely objective criteria into the selective system of the SS troops[7] was Himmler's[8] great organizational invention; he selected the candidates from photographs according to purely racial criteria. Nature itself decided, not only who was to be eliminated, but also who was to be trained as an executioner.

No guiding principle of behavior, taken itself from the realm of 23 human action, such as virtue, honor, fear, is necessary or can be useful to set into motion a body politic which no longer uses terror as a means of intimidation, but whose essence *is* terror. In its stead, it has introduced an entirely new principle into public affairs that dispenses with human will to action altogether and appeals to the craving need for some insight into the law of movement according to which the terror functions and upon which, therefore, all private destinies depend.

The inhabitants of a totalitarian country are thrown into and 24 caught in the process of nature or history for the sake of accelerating its movement; as such, they can only be executioners or victims of

---

[7] **SS troops** Elite Nazi storm troops.

[8] **Himmler** Heinrich Himmler (1900–1945) head of the Nazi gestapo, Hitler's secret police.

its inherent law. The process may decide that those who today eliminate races and individuals or the members of dying classes and
decadent peoples are tomorrow those who must be sacrificed. What
totalitarian rule needs to guide the behavior of its subjects is a
preparation to fit each of them equally well for the role of executioner and the role of victim. This two-sided preparation, the substitute for a principle of action, is the ideology.

Ideologies—isms which to the satisfaction of their adherents can   25
explain everything and every occurrence by deducing it from a single
premise—are a very recent phenomenon and, for many decades,
played a negligible role in political life. Only with the wisdom of hind-
sight can we discover in them certain elements which have made them
so disturbingly useful for totalitarian rule. Not before Hitler and Stalin
were the great political potentialities of the ideologies discovered.

Ideologies are known for their scientific character: they combine   26
the scientific approach with results of philosophical relevance and
pretend to be scientific philosophy. The word "ideology" seems to
imply that an idea can become the subject matter of a science just as
animals are the subject matter of zoology, and that the suffix -*logy* in
ideology, as in zoology, indicates nothing but the *logoi*, the scientific
statements made on it. If this were true, an ideology would indeed
be a pseudo-science and a pseudo-philosophy, transgressing at the
same time the limitations of science and the limitations of philosophy. Deism, for example, would then be the ideology which treats
the idea of God, with which philosophy is concerned, in the scientific manner of theology for which God is a revealed reality. (A theology which is not based on revelation as a given reality but treats
God as an idea would be as mad as a zoology which is no longer
sure of the physical, tangible existence of animals.) Yet we know
that this is only part of the truth. Deism, though it denies divine revelation, does not simply make "scientific" statements on a God
which is only an "idea," but uses the idea of God in order to explain
the course of the world. The "ideas" of isms—race in racism, God in
deism, etc.—never form the subject matter of the ideologies and the
suffix -*logy* never indicates simply a body of "scientific" statements.

An ideology is quite literally what its name indicates: it is the   27
logic of an idea. Its subject matter is history, to which the "idea" is
applied; the result of this application is not a body of statements
about something that *is*, but the unfolding of a process which is in
constant change. The ideology treats the course of events as though
it followed the same "law" as the logical exposition of its "idea." Ideologies pretend to know the mysteries of the whole historical
process—the secrets of the past, the intricacies of the present, the

uncertainties of the future—because of the logic inherent in their respective ideas.

Ideologies are never interested in the miracle of being. They are historical, concerned with becoming and perishing, with the rise and fall of cultures, even if they try to explain history by some "law of nature." The word "race" in racism does not signify any genuine curiosity about the human races as a field for scientific exploration, but is the "idea" by which the movement of history is explained as one consistent process. 28

The "idea" of an ideology is neither Plato's eternal essence grasped by the eyes of the mind nor Kant's regulative principle of reason but has become an instrument of explanation. To an ideology, history does not appear in the light of an idea (which would imply that history is seen *sub specie*[9] of some ideal eternity which itself is beyond historical motion) but as something which can be calculated by it. What fits the "idea" into this new role is its own "logic," that is a movement which is the consequence of the "idea" itself and needs no outside factor to set it into motion. Racism is the belief that there is a motion inherent in the very idea of race, just as deism is the belief that a motion is inherent in the very notion of God. 29

The movement of history and the logical process of this notion are supposed to correspond to each other, so that whatever happens, happens according to the logic of one "idea." However, the only possible movement in the realm of logic is the process of deduction from a premise. Dialectical logic, with its process from thesis through antithesis to synthesis which in turn becomes the thesis of the next dialectical movement, is not different in principle, once an ideology gets hold of it; the first thesis becomes the premise and its advantage for ideological explanation is that this dialectical device can explain away factual contradictions as stages of one identical, consistent movement. 30

As soon as logic as a movement of thought—and not as a necessary control of thinking—is applied to an idea, this idea is transformed into a premise. Ideological world explanations performed this operation long before it became so eminently fruitful for totalitarian reasoning. The purely negative coercion of logic, the prohibition of contradictions, became "productive" so that a whole line of thought could be initiated, and forced upon the mind, by drawing conclusions in the manner of mere argumentation. This argumentative process could be interrupted neither by a new idea (which would have been another premise with a different set of conse- 31

---

[9] **sub specie** As a kind of.

quences) nor by a new experience. Ideologies always assume that one idea is sufficient to explain everything in the development from the premise, and that no experience can teach anything because everything is comprehended in this consistent process of logical deduction. The danger in exchanging the necessary insecurity of philosophical thought for the total explanation of an ideology and its *Weltanschauung*,[10] is not even so much the risk of falling for some usually vulgar, always uncritical assumption as of exchanging the freedom inherent in man's capacity to think for the strait jacket of logic with which man can force himself almost as violently as he is forced by some outside power.

The *Weltanschauungen* and ideologies of the nineteenth century   32 are not in themselves totalitarian, and although racism and communism have become the decisive ideologies of the twentieth century they were not, in principle, any "more totalitarian" than the others; it happened because the elements of experience on which they were originally based—the struggle between the races for world domination, and the struggle between the classes for political power in the respective countries—turned out to be politically more important than those of other ideologies. In this sense the ideological victory of racism and communism over all other isms was decided before the totalitarian movements took hold of precisely these ideologies. On the other hand, all ideologies contain totalitarian elements, but these are fully developed only by totalitarian movements, and this creates the deceptive impression that only racism and communism are totalitarian in character. The truth is, rather, that the real nature of all ideologies was revealed only in the role that the ideology plays in the apparatus of totalitarian domination. Seen from this aspect, there appear three specifically totalitarian elements that are peculiar to all ideological thinking.

First, in their claim to total explanation, ideologies have the ten-   33 dency to explain not what is, but what becomes, what is born and passes away. They are in all cases concerned solely with the element of motion, that is, with history in the customary sense of the word. Ideologies are always oriented toward history, even when, as in the case of racism, they seemingly proceed from the premise of nature; here, nature serves merely to explain historical matters and reduce them to matters of nature. The claim to total explanation promises to explain all historical happenings, the total explanation of the past, the total knowledge of the present, and the reliable prediction of the future. Secondly, in this capacity ideological thinking becomes independent

---

[10] **Weltanschauung** World view.

of all experience from which it cannot learn anything new even if it is a question of something that has just come to pass. Hence ideological thinking becomes emancipated from the reality that we perceive with our five senses, and insists on a "truer" reality concealed behind all perceptible things, dominating them from this place of concealment and requiring a sixth sense that enables us to become aware of it. The sixth sense is provided by precisely the ideology, that particular ideological indoctrination which is taught by the educational institutions, established exclusively for this purpose, to train the "political soldiers" in the *Ordensburgen* of the Nazis or the schools of the Comintern and the Cominform.[11] The propaganda of the totalitarian movement also serves to emancipate thought from experience and reality; it always strives to inject a secret meaning into every public, tangible event and to suspect a secret intent behind every public political act. Once the movements have come to power, they proceed to change reality in accordance with their ideological claims. The concept of enmity is replaced by that of conspiracy, and this produces a mentality in which reality — real enmity or real friendship — is no longer experienced and understood in its own terms but is automatically assumed to signify something else.

Thirdly, since the ideologies have no power to transform reality, they achieve this emancipation of thought from experience through certain methods of demonstration. Ideological thinking orders facts into an absolutely logical procedure which starts from an axiomatically accepted premise, deducing everything else from it; that is, it proceeds with a consistency that exists nowhere in the realm of reality. The deducing may proceed logically or dialectically; in either case it involves a consistent process of argumentation which, because it thinks in terms of a process, is supposed to be able to comprehend the movement of the suprahuman, natural or historical processes. Comprehension is achieved by the mind's imitating, either logically or dialectically, the laws of "scientifically" established movements with which through the process of imitation it becomes integrated. Ideological argumentation, always a kind of logical deduction, corresponds to the two aforementioned elements of the ideologies — the element of movement and of emancipation from reality and experience — first, because its thought movement does not spring from experience but is self-generated, and, secondly, because it transforms the one and only point that is taken and accepted from experienced reality into an axiomatic premise, leaving from then on the subsequent argumentation process completely untouched from

34

---

[11] ***Ordensburgen*, Comintern, Cominform** Institutions of propaganda and political education in Germany and Russia.

any further experience. Once it has established its premise, its point of departure, experiences no longer interfere with ideological thinking, nor can it be taught by reality.

The device both totalitarian rulers used to transform their respec-   35
tive ideologies into weapons with which each of their subjects could force himself into step with the terror movement was deceptively simple and inconspicuous: they took them dead seriously, took pride the one in his supreme gift for "ice cold reasoning" (Hitler) and the other in the "mercilessness of his dialectics," and proceeded to drive ideological implications into extremes of logical consistency which, to the onlooker, looked preposterously "primitive" and absurd: a "dying class" consisted of people condemned to death; races that are "unfit to live" were to be exterminated. Whoever agreed that there are such things as "dying classes" and did not draw the consequence of killing their members, or that the right to live had something to do with race and did not draw the consequence of killing "unfit races," was plainly either stupid or a coward. This stringent logicality as a guide to action permeates the whole structure of totalitarian movements and governments. It is exclusively the work of Hitler and Stalin, who, although they did not add a single new thought to the ideas and propaganda slogans of their movements, for this reason alone must be considered ideologists of the greatest importance.

QUESTIONS FOR CRITICAL READING

1. Describe totalitarianism.
2. What role does science or pseudo-science play in the development of totalitarianism?
3. How can racism contribute to producing a totalitarian government?
4. What seem to be the primary goals of totalitarian governments? How do they differ from our own government?
5. How can the main ideas of an ideology proceed from a single premise? (See para. 25.)
6. Where do totalitarian governments operate today? What ideological organizations operate in the manner Arendt describes? What are their basic views?

SUGGESTIONS FOR WRITING

1. Arendt reflected the fears of her own time in this essay. For her the most terrifying and immediate totalitarian governments were Nazi Germany and communist Russia. What evidence do you see in our con-

temporary world that might suggest totalitarianism is not completely "dead"? What governments seem totalitarian in behavior today? How threatening are they? If you feel totalitarianism is not a threat today, what examples of ideology do you see at work in the modern world? Are there specific threatening ideologies that concern you? Write a brief essay on the existence of totalitarianism or on the threat of ideologies.

2. At the end of paragraph 32 Arendt tells us that "there appear three specifically totalitarian elements that are peculiar to all ideological thinking." She enumerates these in the next two paragraphs. Explain what they are and describe them in terms that you feel your peers would understand. Do you see examples of such elements in the ideological thinking that is represented in your immediate environment? Is it possible that some ideologies do not have these totalitarian elements? Be specific in your answer.

3. What is the role of law in the totalitarian state? Arendt points out that in Germany and Russia the laws were rewritten, not abolished, and that constitutions were preserved in unrevised form. What attitudes toward law enabled these governments to do things that other nations saw as breaking international law?

4. **CONNECTIONS**   What philosophical differences can you note between Lao-tzu and heads of totalitarian states? What do you think Lao-tzu would have to say about ideologies in general? Is he an ideologue? In what ways might Rousseau and Jefferson be considered ideologues? What is their first premise, and what logical progression must we take once we accept it?

5. **CONNECTIONS**   Although Machiavelli's prince could easily become a tyrant, is there anything in Machiavelli's advice that encourages the prince to accept a specific ideology? What are Machiavelli's attitudes toward the law and its relation to the prince? Would Machiavelli have accepted a totalitarian prince? How would Arendt evaluate Machiavelli's program? Would she consider him to be promoting an ideology?

PART TWO

JUSTICE

Aristotle
Frederick Douglass
Henry David Thoreau
Elizabeth Cady Stanton
Martin Luther King Jr.

INTRODUCTION

Ideas of justice have revolved historically around several closely related concepts: moral righteousness, equity of treatment, and reciprocity of action. Justice is an element of interpersonal relations, but philosophers usually link it to the individual's relationship to the state. In the Western tradition, the Greek philosopher Plato (428–347 B.C.) was the first to frame the concept of justice in terms of the health of the state. In his work *The Republic* he defined justice both as an overarching ideal and as a practical necessity for the functioning of a harmonious society. In his view, justice was served when each stratum of society (philosopher-rulers, soldiers, and artisans and workers) operated within its own sphere of action and did not interfere with others.

Like Plato, the Greek philosopher Aristotle (384–322 B.C.) viewed the general concept of justice as an important eternal quality that the individual should strive to uphold. He defined general justice as the overarching goal of moral righteousness that ensures a good society, legislative justice as the duty of the individual to comply with the laws of the society (civic virtue), and particular justice as the duty of the judge to redress inequalities in personal transactions. In turn each of these forms of justice works to maintain the overarching ideals of political and economic justice and thus protect the society from collapse. Ironically, although political justice centers on the concept of freedom and liberty, in Aristotle's time warring states enslaved defeated warriors and their families. Aristotle justified this practice by asserting that basic inequalities between people rendered some people natural slaves.

In later centuries, philosophers such as Thomas Hobbes (English, 1588–1679) drew on Aristotle's theories of natural justice — the justice found in a state of nature where the strong always impose their will on the weak. However, Hobbes found that because people actually live in communities with a political structure that leads them to suffer or commit injustices, the concept of justice becomes essentially moral. Hobbes wrestled with the moral parameters of justice and finally concluded that it is impossible to form a universal concept of justice and that justice is whatever laws are most useful and expedient for society.

This tension between justice as a moral ideal and its manifestation in society as practical law has been a hallmark of its evolution as an idea. Indeed, as the writers in this section so eloquently reveal, the laws that are meant to ensure justice within a society often enforce deep injustices. All five authors in this section investigate the relationship between the individual (or group of individuals) and society when the laws codified by that society are seen as unjust: either they enforce unequal treatment where no inherent inequality exists, or they require actions that conflict with individual conscience.

In the excerpt from his *Narrative of the Life of Frederick Douglass, an American Slave,* Douglass links the question of justice to the question of freedom. According to federal and state laws in the early nineteenth century that protected slavery in the South, Douglass was doomed to remain a slave until his dying day, unless his owner freed him or allowed him to purchase his freedom. In recording the circumstances of his life under a government that enforced slave laws—in both the North and the South—at the same time as it advocated independence, Douglass illustrates how deeply the injustice of slavery could damage the individual slave and slave holder.

The question of how the individual should react in the face of unjust laws is taken up by Henry David Thoreau. He refused to pay taxes that would be used in a war against Mexico that he felt was dishonorable, realized that he would have to pay a penalty for his views, and was willing to do so. Thoreau makes a special plea to conscience as a way of dealing with injustice by requiring the individual to place conscience first and law second. His "Civil Disobedience" reminds us that we are the citizens of the nation and that we ought to make our own will known. Thoreau stresses that there is a price for doing what is right, but that all honest citizens must pay it.

Elizabeth Cady Stanton relies on the rhetorical device of parody in her Declaration of Sentiments and Resolutions. Modeled directly on Thomas Jefferson's Declaration of Independence, Stanton's appeal serves as a reminder that Jefferson spoke only of men's independence, not that of women. Her demands are no less reasonable than Jefferson's, and it is a source of embarrassment to her that she has to redress such an omission after so much time has elapsed since Jefferson's Declaration was adopted.

Like Thoreau, Martin Luther King Jr. was also imprisoned for breaking a law his conscience deemed unjust. In his struggle against the Jim Crow laws enforcing segregation in the South, King acted on his belief that the individual can and should fight laws that treat members of society unjustly. King's *Letter from Birmingham Jail* provides a masterful and moving definition of what makes laws just or unjust. Furthermore, King develops the concept of nonviolent demonstration as a method by which the individual can protest unjust laws.

The writers in this section do not necessarily seek to define justice. Instead, each author illustrates injustice within society and extends the right of any individual—male or female, black or

white—to demand just laws and even to break the law when it contradicts the individual's moral conscience. The depth of commitment these writers have to the idea of justice, and the rhetorical
force of their arguments, compel us to respond by evaluating the
laws and attitudes that shape our lives.

ARISTOTLE
A Definition of Justice

ARISTOTLE (384–322 B.C.) is the great inheritor of Plato's influence in Greek philosophical thought. A student at the Academy
of Plato in Athens from age seventeen to thirty-seven, he was by all
accounts Plato's most brilliant pupil. He did not agree with Plato
on all issues, however, and seems to have broken with his master's
thinking around the time of Plato's death (347 B.C.). For example,
in Aristotle's comments on justice, drawn from his *Politics,* he
treats matters that Plato addressed as well. In the *Republic,* Plato
explored many issues of justice in the ideal state; Aristotle, however, is unconcerned with ideal states and examines justice only in
oligarchies and democracies, the states with which Athens was
familiar.

When Aristotle himself became a teacher in the Academy his
most distinguished student was Alexander the Great, the youthful
ruler who spread Greek values and laws to the rest of the known
world. There has been much speculation regarding what Aristotle
taught Alexander about justice; the thoroughness of the *Politics* implies that it may have been a great deal. A surviving fragment of a
letter from Aristotle to Alexander suggests that he advised Alexander to become the leader of the Greeks and the master of the so-
called barbarians of other cultures.

Aristotle discusses justice entirely in relation to the state. In
his time the state was a city-state, such as Athens with its surrounding areas. For him, the well-ordered state was the greatest of
human inventions, of such noble value that other ideals must take
second place to it. He did not put divinity or godliness first. A practical man, Aristotle was concerned with the life that human beings
know on earth.

In the passage that follows, which comes from Book III, Chapters 9–12 of the *Politics,* a few issues concerning Greek society
need to be clarified. The most startling information for the modern

111

reader may be the fact that Aristotle accepted the practice of slavery as the norm. During this era wars were frequent, and the losers were ordinarily killed or placed into slavery. Thus, for powerful and victorious states such as Athens, slaves were abundant. However, the classical Greek institution of slavery was unlike the modern institution in the West during the eighteenth and nineteenth centuries. For example, Greek slaves had some rights and privileges and were not debased as a matter of course.

In this passage Aristotle discusses the rights of the freeborn but not those of slaves, who have, he tells us, no choices in how they are to live. Indeed, Aristotle differed from many of his contemporaries in believing that slaves deserved to be slaves in the same way that prisoners deserved prison. (This view is not acceptable to us today, but it was a widely held belief for thousands of years, and not only in the West. Such a stance was not seriously challenged until the modern period beginning in the seventeenth century.) Justice, therefore, in Aristotle's view, was a question that centered on the relationship of the state to the noble and freeborn, and almost certainly only to the men among them.

At the beginning of the passage Aristotle also makes a distinction concerning how justice functions in two forms of government: oligarchy and democracy. An oligarchy is a government by the few, such as a clique of high-born military men or closely related men. In an oligarchy, justice is based on inequality: the small elite group is superior and all others are inferior. A democracy is a government by the many: the wealthy, the less wealthy, and the poor. For those who champion democracy, everyone is equal; the wealthy have the same vote as lesser property holders. During Aristotle's time, however, women and slaves had no voice in either form of government. Only free men were represented. In an oligarchy, Aristotle argues, justice implies inequality only between those people who are unequal. In other words, the oligarchs cannot declare themselves superior by arbitrary decree. If other people are superior to them, they must be recognized as such.

On the other hand, Aristotle tells us that democrats who say justice lies in equality must also recognize that some people are simply not equal to others. In examining the nature of equality, he points out that most people are "bad judges in their own affairs" (para. 1) because they are primarily concerned with themselves and cannot clearly see themselves in relation to others. Justice exists between equals, he says, but individuals talk holistically about justice when they are actually referring only to a part of it. Aristotle discusses matters of equality of wealth, equality of physiology and beauty, equality of virtue, and equality of talent, demonstrating that there are far too many kinds of equality for anyone to cite only one as the absolute. Consequently, politicians must concern themselves with the kinds of equality that relate to the responsibilities of being part of the state.

In discussing issues of justice, Aristotle also addresses the nature of the state. In an earlier portion of this discussion, Aristotle expresses a principle that would later be stated by Rousseau: the state begins with the family, proceeds to the village and then to the surrounding community, and ends with the city-state. This natural progression implies a very large size for a city-state in which intermarriage within the state is a defining feature. Trade and other interactions with neighboring states follow as a matter of course. Aristotle views these exchanges as based on friendship: "for the will to live together is friendship. The end of the state is the good life, and these are the means towards it" (para. 2).

Aristotle always sought the end consequence of every art he wrote about: "In all sciences and arts the end is a good, and the greatest good and in the highest degree a good in the most authoritative of all [arts]—this is the political science of which the good is justice, in other words, the common interest" (para. 10). This comment implies that the interest of the whole—the commonwealth that comprises the state—is superior to the interest of the individual. Thus, justice is key to the happiness of the community. He says at the end of the passage, "if wealth and freedom are necessary elements, justice and valour are equally so; for without the former qualities a state cannot exist at all, without the latter not well" (para. 10).

Aristotle's Rhetoric

Aristotle's *Rhetoric* is probably the most influential treatise on rhetoric worldwide. Yet this passage from *Politics*, like many of his scholarly discussions, does not use especially rousing or stirring rhetoric. The reason may lie in the fact that this work was meant as a teaching treatise, a document for students of political science. Indeed, the passage is structured as an argument that masquerades as an examination of the facts. Aristotle argues for a state that is democratic in nature, in which the wealthy do not necessarily have the largest say and in which the poor are not encouraged to pillage the rich in the name of equality. Moreover, in this state, the poor have a voice in government, although not at the highest levels. Women and slaves, being unequal, have no voice in government, yet their concerns are expected to be considered in a well-ordered state.

A number of interesting hypothetical questions arise in the course of the discussion. For example, Aristotle imagines a government in which those "who are not rich and have no personal merit" (para. 7) are permitted to share the greatest offices of the state. He sees them as eventually giving in to incompetence and crime. Yet he also believes it is essential to give them some role in government, and he uses the analogy of mixing "impure food" with "pure" to produce an "entire mass more wholesome than a small quantity of the pure would be" (para. 7). This argument is consistent with Aristotle's earlier discussion of who should rule. Should the best person rule? The wealthiest? The most valorous? He discards all these possibilities one by one in favor of democracy, that is, rule by the many. His argument centers on an astonishingly modern hypothesis: that the decisions of the many are less likely to be extreme and more likely to be right than the decisions of the few.

Aristotle is famously methodical in his approach to any question, breaking it down into parts, categorizing the parts, and addressing each in turn. He is careful not to lose the reader in the details, and he stops often to recapitulate the argument. He uses carefully chosen analogies to help his argument along. In the last paragraph, for example, he talks about flute players as analogies for citizens at large. If there are many good flute players and only a few excellent flutes, it is wise to give the best flutes to the best players, not to the wealthiest, the noblest, the most virtuous, or the most valorous. This analogy is an example of justice in relation to inequality. Nevertheless the point is that excellence (in this case, musical excellence) is recognized, and in being recognized justice is done. This forceful and sensible example works in the common interest. Therefore, in a community, proper recognition of equalities and inequalities among people will result in justice. And without justice no state can exist well.

PREREADING QUESTIONS:
WHAT TO READ FOR

The following prereading questions may help you anticipate key issues in the discussion on Aristotle's "A Definition of Justice." Keeping them in mind during your first reading of the selection should help focus your reactions.

- How does Aristotle define the state?
- Establish Aristotle's attitude toward the concept of equality and inequality.

A Definition of Justice

CHAPTER 9

Let us begin by considering the common definitions of oligarchy   1
and democracy,[1] and what is justice oligarchical and democratical. For
all men cling to justice of some kind, but their conceptions are imperfect and they do not express the whole idea. For example, justice is
thought by them to be, and is, equality, not, however, for all, but only
for equals. And inequality is thought to be, and is, justice; neither is
this for all, but only for unequals. When the persons are omitted, then
men judge erroneously. The reason is that they are passing judgement
on themselves, and most people are bad judges in their own case. And
whereas justice implies a relation to persons as well as to things, and a
just distribution, as I have already said in the *Ethics,* implies the same
ratio between the persons and between the things, they agree about
the equality of the things, but dispute about the equality of the persons, chiefly for the reason which I have just given — because they are
bad judges in their own affairs; and secondly, because both the parties
to the argument are speaking of a limited and partial justice, but imagine themselves to be speaking of absolute justice. For the one party, if
they are unequal in one respect, for example wealth, consider themselves to be unequal in all; and the other party, if they are equal in one
respect, for example free birth, consider themselves to be equal in all.
But they leave out the capital point. For if men met and associated out
of regard to wealth only, their share in the state would be proportioned to their property, and the oligarchical doctrine would then
seem to carry the day. It would not be just that he who paid one mina
should have the same share of a hundred minae, whether of the principal or of the profits, as he who paid the remaining ninety-nine. But a
state exists for the sake of a good life, and not for the sake of life only:
if life only were the object, slaves and brute animals might form a state,
but they cannot, for they have no share in happiness or in a life of free
choice. Nor does a state exist for the sake of alliance and security from

---

[1] **oligarchy and democracy** Government by the few and government by the
many, respectively.

injustice, nor yet for the sake of exchange and mutual intercourse; for then the Tyrrhenians and the Carthaginians, and all who have commercial treaties with one another, would be the citizens of one state. True, they have agreements about imports, and engagements that they will do no wrong to one another, and written articles of alliance. But there are no magistracies common to the contracting parties who will enforce their engagements; different states have each their own magistracies. Nor does one state take care that the citizens of the other are such as they ought to be, nor see that those who come under the terms of the treaty do no wrong or wickedness at all, but only that they do no injustice to one another. Whereas, those who care for good government take into consideration virtue and vice in states. Whence it may be further inferred that virtue must be the care of a state which is truly so called, and not merely enjoys the name: for without this end the community becomes a mere alliance which differs only in place from alliances of which the members live apart; and law is only a convention, "a surety to one another of justice," as the sophist[2] Lycophron says, and has no real power to make the citizens good and just.

This is obvious; for suppose distinct places, such as Corinth and 2 Megara, to be brought together so that their walls touched, still they would not be one city, not even if the citizens had the right to intermarry, which is one of the rights peculiarly characteristic of states. Again, if men dwelt at a distance from one another, but not so far off as to have no intercourse, and there were laws among them that they should not wrong each other in their exchanges, neither would this be a state. Let us suppose that one man is a carpenter, another a husbandman, another a shoemaker, and so on, and that their number is ten thousand: nevertheless, if they have nothing in common but exchange, alliance, and the like, that would not constitute a state. Why is this? Surely not because they are at a distance from one another: for even supposing that such a community were to meet in one place, but that each man had a house of his own, which was in a manner his state, and that they made alliance with one another, but only against evil-doers; still an accurate thinker would not deem this to be a state, if their intercourse with one another was of the same character after as before their union. It is clear then that a state is not a mere society, having a common place, established for the prevention of mutual crime and for the sake of exchange. These are conditions without which a state cannot exist; but all of them together do not constitute a state, which is a community of families and aggregations of families in well-being, for the sake of a perfect and self-

---

[2] **sophist:** Teacher of rhetoric.

sufficing life. Such a community can only be established among those who live in the same place and intermarry. Hence arise in cities family connexions, brotherhoods, common sacrifices, amusements which draw men together. But these are created by friendship, for the will to live together is friendship. The end of the state is the good life, and these are the means towards it. And the state is the union of families and villages in a perfect and self-sufficing life, by which we mean a happy and honourable life.

Our conclusion, then, is that political society exists for the sake 3
of noble actions, and not of mere companionship. Hence they who contribute most to such a society have a greater share in it than those who have the same or a greater freedom or nobility of birth but are inferior to them in political virtue; or than those who exceed them in wealth but are surpassed by them in virtue.

From what has been said it will be clearly seen that all the 4
partisans of different forms of government speak of a part of justice only.

Chapter 10

There is also a doubt as to what is to be the supreme power in 5
the state: —Is it the multitude? Or the wealthy? Or the good? Or the one best man? Or a tyrant? Any of these alternatives seems to involve disagreeable consequences. If the poor, for example, because they are more in number, divide among themselves the property of the rich—is not this unjust? No, by heaven (will be the reply), for the supreme authority justly willed it. But if this is not injustice, pray what is? Again, when in the first division all has been taken, and the majority divide anew the property of the minority, is it not evident, if this goes on, that they will ruin the state? Yet surely, virtue is not the ruin of those who possess her, nor is justice destructive of a state; and therefore this law of confiscation clearly cannot be just. If it were, all the acts of a tyrant must of necessity be just; for he only coerces other men by superior power, just as the multitude coerce the rich. But is it just then that the few and the wealthy should be the rulers? And what if they, in like manner, rob and plunder the people—is this just? If so, the other case will likewise be just. But there can be no doubt that all these things are wrong and unjust.

Then ought the good to rule and have supreme power? But in 6
that case everybody else, being excluded from power, will be dishonoured. For the offices of a state are posts of honour; and if one set of men always hold them, the rest must be deprived of them. Then will it be well that the one best man should rule? Nay, that is still more oligarchical, for the number of those who are dishonoured is thereby increased. Some one may say that it is bad in any case for

a man, subject as he is to all the accidents of human passion, to have the supreme power, rather than the law. But what if the law itself be democratical or oligarchical, how will that help us out of our difficulties? Not at all; the same consequences will follow.

CHAPTER 11

Most of these questions may be reserved for another occasion.   7
The principle that the multitude ought to be supreme rather than the few best is one that is maintained, and, though not free from difficulty, yet seems to contain an element of truth. For the many, of whom each individual is but an ordinary person, when they meet together may very likely be better than the few good, if regarded not individually but collectively, just as a feast to which many contribute is better than a dinner provided out of a single purse. For each individual among the many has a share of virtue and prudence, and when they meet together, they become in a manner one man, who has many feet, and hands, and senses; that is a figure of their mind and disposition. Hence the many are better judges than a single man of music and poetry; for some understand one part, and some another, and among them they understand the whole. There is a similar combination of qualities in good men, who differ from any individual of the many, as the beautiful are said to differ from those who are not beautiful, and works of art from realities, because in them the scattered elements are combined, although, if taken separately, the eye of one person or some other feature in another person would be fairer than in the picture. Whether this principle can apply to every democracy, and to all bodies of men, is not clear. Or rather, by heaven, in some cases it is impossible of application; for the argument would equally hold about brutes; and wherein, it will be asked, do some men differ from brutes? But there may be bodies of men about whom our statement is nevertheless true. And if so, the difficulty which has been already raised, and also another which is akin to it — viz. what power should be assigned to the mass of freemen and citizens, who are not rich and have no personal merit — are both solved. There is still a danger in allowing them to share the great offices of state, for their folly will lead them into error, and their dishonesty into crime. But there is a danger also in not letting them share, for a state in which many poor men are excluded from office will necessarily be full of enemies. The only way of escape is to assign to them some deliberative and judicial functions. For this reason Solon[3] and certain other legislators give them

---

[3] **Solon (c. 630–c. 560 B.C.)** Archon of Athens and one of its most famous lawgivers and reformers.

the power of electing to offices, and of calling the magistrates to account, but they do not allow them to hold office singly. When they meet together their perceptions are quite good enough, and combined with the better class they are useful to the state (just as impure food when mixed with what is pure sometimes makes the entire mass more wholesome than a small quantity of the pure would be), but each individual, left to himself, forms an imperfect judgement. On the other hand, the popular form of government involves certain difficulties. In the first place, it might be objected that he who can judge of the healing of a sick man would be one who could himself heal his disease, and make him whole—that is, in other words, the physician; and so in all professions and arts. As, then, the physician ought to be called to account by physicians, so ought men in general to be called to account by their peers. But physicians are of three kinds: —there is the ordinary practitioner, and there is the physician of the higher class, and thirdly the intelligent man who has studied the art: in all arts there is such a class; and we attribute the power of judging to them quite as much as to professors of the art. Secondly, does not the same principle apply to elections? For a right election can only be made by those who have knowledge; those who know geometry, for example, will choose a geometrician rightly, and those who know how to steer, a pilot; and, even if there be some occupations and arts in which private persons share in the ability to choose, they certainly cannot choose better than those who know. So that, according to this argument, neither the election of magistrates, nor the calling of them to account, should be entrusted to the many. Yet possibly these objections are to a great extent met by our old answer, that if the people are not utterly degraded, although individually they may be worse judges than those who have special knowledge—as a body they are as good or better. Moreover, there are some arts whose products are not judged of solely, or best, by the artists themselves, namely those arts whose products are recognized even by those who do not possess the art; for example, the knowledge of the house is not limited to the builder only; the user, or, in other words, the master, of the house will even be a better judge than the builder, just as the pilot will judge better of a rudder than the carpenter, and the guest will judge better of a feast than the cook.

This difficulty seems now to be sufficiently answered, but there is another akin to it. That inferior persons should have authority in greater matters than the good would appear to be a strange thing, yet the election and calling to account of the magistrates is the greatest of all. And these, as I was saying, are functions which in some states are assigned to the people, for the assembly is supreme in all 8

such matters. Yet persons of any age, and having but a small property qualification, sit in the assembly and deliberate and judge, although for the great officers of state, such as treasurers and generals,
a high qualification is required. This difficulty may be solved in the
same manner as the preceding, and the present practice of democracies may be really defensible. For the power does not reside in the
dicast,[4] or senator, or ecclesiast, but in the court, and the senate,
and the assembly, of which individual senators, or ecclesiasts, or di-
casts, are only parts or members. And for this reason the many may
claim to have a higher authority than the few; for the people, and
the senate, and the courts consist of many persons, and their property collectively is greater than the property of one or of a few individuals holding great offices. But enough of this.

   The discussion of the first question shows nothing so clearly as   9
that laws, when good, should be supreme; and that the magistrate or
magistrates should regulate those matters only on which the laws are
unable to speak with precision owing to the difficulty of any general
principle embracing all particulars. But what are good laws has not
yet been clearly explained; the old difficulty remains. The goodness
or badness, justice or injustice, of laws varies of necessity with the
constitutions of states. This, however, is clear, that the laws must be
adapted to the constitutions. But if so, true forms of government will
of necessity have just laws, and perverted forms of government will
have unjust laws.

CHAPTER 12

   In all sciences and arts the end is a good, and the greatest good   10
and in the highest degree a good in the most authoritative of all—
this is the political science of which the good is justice, in other
words, the common interest. All men think justice to be a sort of
equality; and to a certain extent they agree in the philosophical distinctions which have been laid down by us about Ethics. For they
admit that justice is a thing and has a relation to persons, and that
equals ought to have equality. But there still remains a question:
equality or inequality of what? Here is a difficulty which calls for political speculation. For very likely some persons will say that offices
of state ought to be unequally distributed according to superior excellence, in whatever respect, of the citizen, although there is no
other difference between him and the rest of the community; for
that those who differ in any one respect have different rights and

---

   [4] **dicast** Athens chose six thousand people each year to act as judge and jury
in civil cases. An ecclesiast is a member of the Athenian public assembly known as
the ecclesia.

claims. But, surely, if this is true, the complexion or height of a man, or any other advantage, will be a reason for his obtaining a greater share of political rights. The error here lies upon the surface, and may be illustrated from the other arts and sciences. When a number of flute-players are equal in their art, there is no reason why those of them who are better born should have better flutes given to them; for they will not play any better on the flute, and the superior instrument should be reserved for him who is the superior artist. If what I am saying is still obscure, it will be made clearer as we proceed. For if there were a superior flute-player who was far inferior in birth and beauty, although either of these may be a greater good than the art of flute-playing, and may excel flute-playing in a greater ratio than he excels the others in his art, still he ought to have the best flutes given to him, unless the advantages of wealth and birth contribute to excellence in flute-playing, which they do not. Moreover, upon this principle any good may be compared with any other. For if a given height may be measured against wealth and against freedom, height in general may be so measured. Thus if A excels in height more than B in virtue, even if virtue in general excels height still more, all goods will be commensurable; for if a certain amount is better than some other, it is clear that some other will be equal. But since no such comparison can be made, it is evident that there is good reason why in politics men do not ground their claim to office on every sort of inequality any more than in the arts. For if some be slow, and others swift, that is no reason why the one should have little and the others much; it is in gymnastic contests that such excellence is rewarded. Whereas the rival claims of candidates for office can only be based on the possession of elements which enter into the composition of a state. And therefore the noble, or freeborn, or rich, may with good reason claim office; for holders of offices must be freemen and tax-payers: a state can be no more composed entirely of poor men than entirely of slaves. But if wealth and freedom are necessary elements, justice and valour are equally so; for without the former qualities a state cannot exist at all, without the latter not well.

QUESTIONS FOR CRITICAL READING

1. In paragraph 1, justice is said to be "equality." What does that mean?
2. What is Aristotle's attitude toward "slaves and brute animals"?
3. Why do you think Aristotle believes the "right to intermarry" is "peculiarly characteristic of states" (para. 2)?

4. "The end of the state is the good life" (para. 2). What does Aristotle mean by this? How do you interpret the statement for yourself?
5. What role does friendship play in the creation of a state?
6. Why does Aristotle reject the notion that the most virtuous person should rule the state?
7. Aristotle holds firmly to the view that "the multitude ought to be supreme rather than the few best" (para. 7). Do you agree?
8. In paragraph 10 Aristotle says that the "good" of political science is justice, "in other words, the common interest." What does "the common interest" mean in this context?

SUGGESTIONS FOR WRITING

1. Aristotle says that when people argue about justice they usually are "speaking of a limited and partial justice." What does he mean? What examples do you see in his discussions of justice that back him up? Why is it so difficult to talk about justice in the larger sense of the word rather than to discuss a limited aspect of justice? For example, people talk about taxing the rich very heavily to help the poor as a form of justice. How would Aristotle regard that choice?
2. At the end of paragraph 1, Aristotle refers to a philosopher named Lycophron and reminds us that even though states can create just laws, the laws will not make the "citizens good and just." How true is that of our own time and place? What examples can you think of that illustrate how difficult it is for the nation to use laws to help make its citizens good and just? Is there any relationship between just laws and just citizens?
3. Aristotle tells us that "political society exists for the sake of noble actions, and not of mere companionship" (para. 3). In this sense, he reveals a need for high ideals in a state. How much does our own nation reveal a need for high ideals? Do citizens whom you know imagine the state as being capable of noble actions? How do politicians talk about their vision of the state? How would you talk about your vision and ideals if you were running for office?
4. Explain Aristotle's position on whether the "few and the wealthy" should be the rulers of the state (para. 5). What is your own view on this question? Do you feel that currently the nation is being run by the few and the wealthy, or does such a statement reflect a distortion of reality? What conditions in a modern state might lead to a situation in which the few and the wealthy are the rulers?
5. How do the laws of an oligarchy differ from those of a democracy? When the few and the powerful are the rulers, and the people have no vote and no power, what kinds of laws might be enacted to preserve that situation? Would they be just laws? On what basis would you establish your evaluation? How would you fare in an oligarchic society?

6. What are Aristotle's strongest arguments in favor of a government of the multitude as opposed to a government of the few? Which of these arguments do you feel affected the founders of our nation? Do you think Aristotle is correct in his judgment?

7. **CONNECTIONS**   Compare Aristotle's exploration of equality with the extensive discussion of equality in the essay "Created Equal" by Milton and Rose Friedman (in Part Three, p. 261). To what extent does your comparison reveal that the Friedmans are as interested in justice as Aristotle is? Which of the Friedmans' concerns for justice seem most similar to Aristotle's? Which are most different from Aristotle's?

8. **CONNECTIONS**   To what extent would Hannah Arendt and Henry David Thoreau agree with Aristotle when he says, "true forms of government will of necessity have just laws, and perverted forms of government will have unjust laws" (para. 9)? Examine the attitudes of Arendt and Thoreau toward various forms of government and, by extension, toward the ideals of justice under the law.

9. **CONNECTIONS**   Thomas Jefferson says in the Declaration of Independence that "all men are created equal." What could he mean? Do you think Jefferson read Aristotle? Does he seem to use the term *equal* in the same sense that Aristotle does?

FREDERICK DOUGLASS
From *Narrative of the Life of Frederick Douglass, an American Slave*

FREDERICK DOUGLASS (1817–1895) was born into slavery in Maryland; he died not only a free man but also a man who commanded the respect of his country, his government, and hosts of supporters. Ironically, it was his owner's wife, Mrs. Hugh Auld, a Northerner, who helped Douglass learn to read and write. Until her husband forcefully convinced her that teaching slaves was "unlawful, as well as unsafe," Mrs. Auld taught Douglass enough so that he could begin his own education—and escape to freedom. Mrs. Auld eventually surpassed her husband in her vehement opposition to having Douglass read, leading Douglass to conclude that slavery had a negative effect on slave and slave holder alike: both suffered the consequences of a political system that was inherently unjust.

The *Narrative* is filled with examples of the injustice of slavery. Douglass had little connection with his family. Separated from his mother, Harriet Bailey, Douglass never knew who his father was. In his *Narrative,* he records the beatings he witnessed as a slave, the conditions under which he lived, and the struggles he felt within himself to be a free man. Douglass himself survived brutal beatings and torture by a professional slave "breaker."

The laws of the time codified the injustices that Douglass and all American slaves suffered. The Fugitive Slave Act of 1793 tightened the hold on all slaves who had gone north in search of freedom. Federal marshals were enjoined to return slaves to their owners. The Underground Railroad helped so many runaway slaves find their way to Canada that a second Fugitive Slave Act was enacted in 1850 with stiff penalties for those who did not obey the law. In retaliation, many Northern states enacted personal freedom laws to counter the Fugitive Slave Act. Eventually, these laws became central to the South's decision to secede. However, Douglass's fate, when he eventually escaped in 1838 by impersonating an African American seaman (using his papers to board ship), was not secure. Abolitionists in New York helped him find work in shipyards in New Bedford. He changed his name from Auld to Douglass to protect himself, and he began his career as an orator in 1841 at an antislavery meeting in Nantucket.

To avoid capture after publication of an early version of his autobiography, Douglass spent two years on a speaking tour of Great Britain and Ireland (1845–1847). He then returned to the United States, bought his freedom, and rose to national fame as the founder and editor of the *North Star*, an abolitionist paper published in Rochester, New York. One of his chief concerns was for the welfare of the slaves who had managed to secure their freedom. When the Civil War began, there were no plans to free the slaves, but Douglass managed to convince Lincoln that it would further the war effort to free them; in 1863 the president delivered the Emancipation Proclamation.

However, the years after the war and Lincoln's death were not good for freed slaves. Terrorist groups in both the North and the South worked to keep them from enjoying freedom, and training programs for former slaves that might have been effective were never fully instituted. During this time Douglass worked in various capacities for the government—as assistant secretary of the Santo Domingo Commission, as an official in Washington, D.C., and as U.S. minister to Haiti (1889–1891). He was the first African American to become a national figure and to have influence with the government.

Douglass's Rhetoric

Douglass was basically self-taught, but he knew enough to read the powerful writers of his day. He was a commanding speaker in an age in which eloquence was valued and speakers were rewarded handsomely. This excerpt from the *Narrative*—Chapters 6, 7, and 8—is notable for its clear and direct style. The use of the first-person narrative is as simple as one could wish, yet the feelings projected are sincere and moving.

Douglass's structure is the chronological narrative, relating events in the order in which they occurred. He begins his story at the point of meeting a new mistress, a woman from whom he expected harsh treatment. Because she was new to the concept of slavery, however, she behaved in ways that were unusual, and Douglass remarks on her initially kind attitude. Douglass does not interrupt himself with flashbacks or leaps forward in time but tells the story as it happened. At critical moments, he slows the narrative to describe people or incidents in unusual detail and lets the reader infer from these details the extent of the injustice he suffered.

By today's standards, Douglass's style may seem formal. His sentences are often longer than those of modern writers, although they are always carefully balanced and punctuated by briefer sentences. Despite his long paragraphs, heavy with example and description, after a century and a half his work remains immediate and moving. No modern reader will have difficulty responding to what Frederick Douglass has to say. His views on justice are as accessible and as powerful now as when they were written.

PREREADING QUESTIONS: WHAT TO READ FOR

The following prereading questions may help you anticipate key issues in the discussion on the excerpt that follows from *Narrative of the Life of Frederick Douglass, an American Slave.* Keeping them in mind during your first reading of the selection should help focus your reactions.

• How did Douglass learn to read and write?

• Why was it thought dangerous for a slave to learn to read and write?

• What was the effect on Douglass of his learning to read?

From *Narrative of the Life of Frederick Douglass, an American Slave*

My new mistress proved to be all she appeared when I first met   1
her at the door,—a woman of the kindest heart and finest feelings. She had never had a slave under her control previously to myself, and prior to her marriage she had been dependent upon her own industry for a living. She was by trade a weaver; and by constant

application to her business, she had been in a good degree preserved from the blighting and dehumanizing effects of slavery. I was utterly astonished at her goodness. I scarcely knew how to behave towards her. She was entirely unlike any other white woman I had ever seen. I could not approach her as I was accustomed to approach other white ladies. My early instruction was all out of place. The crouching servility, usually so acceptable a quality in a slave, did not answer when manifested toward her. Her favor was not gained by it; she seemed to be disturbed by it. She did not deem it impudent or unmannerly for a slave to look her in the face. The meanest slave was put fully at ease in her presence, and none left without feeling better for having seen her. Her face was made of heavenly smiles, and her voice of tranquil music.

But, alas! this kind heart had but a short time to remain such. 2
The fatal poison of irresponsible power was already in her hands, and soon commenced its infernal work. That cheerful eye, under the influence of slavery, soon became red with rage; that voice, made all of sweet accord, changed to one of harsh and horrid discord; and that angelic face gave place to that of a demon.

Very soon after I went to live with Mr. and Mrs. Auld, she very 3
kindly commenced to teach me the A, B, C. After I had learned this, she assisted me in learning to spell words of three or four letters. Just at this point of my progress, Mr. Auld found out what was going on, and at once forbade Mrs. Auld to instruct me further, telling her, among other things, that it was unlawful, as well as unsafe, to teach a slave to read. To use his own words, further, he said, "If you give a nigger an inch, he will take an ell.[1] A nigger should know nothing but to obey his master—to do as he is told to do. Learning would *spoil* the best nigger in the world. Now," said he, "if you teach that nigger (speaking of myself) how to read, there would be no keeping him. It would forever unfit him to be a slave. He would at once become unmanageable, and of no value to his master. As to himself, it could do him no good, but a great deal of harm. It would make him discontented and unhappy." These words sank deep into my heart, stirred up sentiments within that lay slumbering, and called into existence an entirely new train of thought. It was a new and special revelation, explaining dark and mysterious things, with which my youthful understanding had struggled, but struggled in vain. I now understood what had been to me a most perplexing difficulty—to wit, the white man's power to enslave the black man. It was a grand achievement, and I prized it highly. From that mo-

---

[1]**ell** A measure about a yard in length.

ment, I understood the pathway from slavery to freedom. It was just what I wanted, and I got it at a time when I the least expected it. Whilst I was saddened by the thought of losing the aid of my kind mistress, I was gladdened by the invaluable instruction which, by the merest accident, I had gained from my master. Though conscious of the difficulty of learning without a teacher, I set out with high hope, and a fixed purpose, at whatever cost of trouble, to learn how to read. The very decided manner with which he spoke, and strove to impress his wife with the evil consequences of giving me instruction, served to convince me that he was deeply sensible of the truths he was uttering. It gave me the best assurance that I might rely with the utmost confidence on the results which, he said, would flow from teaching me to read. What he most dreaded, that I most desired. What he most loved, that I most hated. That which to him was a great evil, to be carefully shunned, was to me a great good, to be diligently sought; and the argument which he so warmly urged, against my learning to read, only served to inspire me with a desire and determination to learn. In learning to read, I owe almost as much to the bitter opposition of my master, as to the kindly aid of my mistress. I acknowledge the benefit of both.

I had resided but a short time in Baltimore before I observed a marked difference, in the treatment of slaves, from that which I had witnessed in the country. A city slave is almost a freeman, compared with a slave on the plantation. He is much better fed and clothed, and enjoys privileges altogether unknown to the slave on the plantation. There is a vestige of decency, a sense of shame, that does much to curb and check those outbreaks of atrocious cruelty so commonly enacted upon the plantation. He is a desperate slaveholder, who will shock the humanity of his nonslaveholding neighbors with the cries of his lacerated slave. Few are willing to incur the odium attaching to the reputation of being a cruel master; and above all things, they would not be known as not giving a slave enough to eat. Every city slaveholder is anxious to have it known of him, that he feeds his slaves well; and it is due to them to say, that most of them do give their slaves enough to eat. There are, however, some painful exceptions to this rule. Directly opposite to us, on Philpot Street, lived Mr. Thomas Hamilton. He owned two slaves. Their names were Henrietta and Mary. Henrietta was about twenty-two years of age, Mary was about fourteen; and of all the mangled and emaciated creatures I ever looked upon, these two were the most so. His heart must be harder than stone, that could look upon these unmoved. The head, neck, and shoulders of Mary were literally cut to pieces. I have frequently felt her head, and found it nearly covered with festering sores, caused by the lash of her cruel mistress. I do not know that her master ever whipped her, but I have been an eye-witness to the cruelty of Mrs. Hamilton. I used to be in Mr. Hamilton's house nearly every day. Mrs. Hamilton used to sit in a large chair in the middle of the room, with a heavy cowskin always by her side, and scarce an hour passed during the day but was marked by the blood of one of these slaves. The girls seldom passed her without her saying, "Move faster, you *black gip!*" at the same time giving them a blow with the cowskin over the head or shoulders, often drawing the blood. She would then say, "Take that, you *black gip!*"—continuing, "If you don't move faster, I'll move you!" Added to the cruel lashings to which these slaves were subjected, they were kept nearly half-starved. They seldom knew what it was to eat a full meal. I have seen Mary contending with the pigs for the offal thrown into the street. So much was Mary kicked and cut to pieces, that she was oftener called "*pecked*" than by her name.

I lived in Master Hugh's family about seven years. During this   5
time, I succeeded in learning to read and write. In accomplishing this, I was compelled to resort to various stratagems. I had no regular teacher. My mistress, who had kindly commenced to instruct me, had, in compliance with the advice and direction of her husband, not only ceased to instruct, but had set her face against my being instructed by any one else. It is due, however, to my mistress to say of her, that she did not adopt this course of treatment immediately. She at first lacked the depravity indispensable to shutting me up in mental darkness. It was at least necessary for her to have some training in the exercise of irresponsible power, to make her equal to the task of treating me as though I were a brute.

My mistress was, as I have said, a kind and tender-hearted   6
woman; and in the simplicity of her soul she commenced, when I first went to live with her, to treat me as she supposed one human being ought to treat another. In entering upon the duties of a slave-holder, she did not seem to perceive that I sustained to her the relation of a mere chattel, and that for her to treat me as a human being was not only wrong, but dangerously so. Slavery proved as injurious to her as it did to me. When I went there, she was a pious, warm, and tender-hearted woman. There was no sorrow or suffering for which she had not a tear. She had bread for the hungry, clothes for the naked, and comfort for every mourner that came within her reach. Slavery soon proved its ability to divest her of these heavenly qualities. Under its influence, the tender heart became stone, and the lamblike disposition gave way to one of tiger-like fierceness. The first step in her downward course was in her ceasing to instruct me. She now commenced to practise her husband's precepts. She finally

became even more violent in her opposition than her husband himself. She was not satisfied with simply doing as well as he had commanded; she seemed anxious to do better. Nothing seemed to make her more angry than to see me with a newspaper. She seemed to think that here lay the danger. I have had her rush at me with a face made all up of fury, and snatch from me a newspaper, in a manner that fully revealed her apprehension. She was an apt woman; and a little experience soon demonstrated, to her satisfaction, that education and slavery were incompatible with each other.

From this time I was most narrowly watched. If I was in a separate room any considerable length of time, I was sure to be suspected of having a book, and was at once called to give an account of myself. All this, however, was too late. The first step had been taken. Mistress, in teaching me the alphabet, had given me the *inch,* and no precaution could prevent me from taking the *ell.*

The plan which I adopted, and the one by which I was most successful, was that of making friends of all the little white boys whom I met in the street. As many of these as I could, I converted into teachers. With their kindly aid, obtained at different times and in different places, I finally succeeded in learning to read. When I was sent to errands, I always took my book with me, and by going one part of my errand quickly, I found time to get a lesson before my return. I used also to carry bread with me, enough of which was always in the house, and to which I was always welcome; for I was much better off in this regard than many of the poor white children in our neighborhood. This bread I used to bestow upon the hungry little urchins, who, in return, would give me that more valuable bread of knowledge. I am strongly tempted to give the names of two or three of those little boys, as a testimonial of the gratitude and affection I bear them; but prudence forbids;—not that it would injure me, but it might embarrass them; for it is almost an unpardonable offence to teach slaves to read in this Christian country. It is enough to say of the dear little fellows, that they lived on Philpot Street, very near Durgin and Bailey's ship-yard. I used to talk this matter of slavery over with them. I would sometimes say to them, I wished I could be as free as they would be when they got to be men. "You will be free as soon as you are twenty-one, *but I am a slave for life!* Have not I as good a right to be free as you have?" These words used to trouble them; they would express for me the liveliest sympathy, and console me with the hope that something would occur by which I might be free.

I was now about twelve years old, and the thought of being *a slave for life* began to bear heavily upon my heart. Just about this time, I got hold of a book entitled "The Columbian Orator." Every opportunity I got, I used to read this book. Among much of other interesting matter, I found in it a dialogue between a master and his slave. The slave was represented as having run away from his master three times. The dialogue represented the conversation which took place between them, when the slave was retaken the third time. In this dialogue, the whole argument in behalf of slavery was brought forward by the master, all of which was disposed of by the slave. The slave was made to say some very smart as well as impressive things in reply to his master—things which had the desired though unexpected effect; for the conversation resulted in the voluntary emancipation of the slave on the part of the master.

In the same book, I met with one of Sheridan's[2] mighty   10
speeches on and in behalf of Catholic emancipation. These were choice documents to me. I read them over and over again with unabated interest. They gave tongue to interesting thoughts of my own soul, which had frequently flashed through my mind, and died away for want of utterance. The moral which I gained from the dialogue was the power of truth over the conscience of even a slaveholder. What I got from Sheridan was a bold denunciation of slavery, and a powerful vindication of human rights. The reading of these documents enabled me to utter my thoughts, and to meet the arguments brought forward to sustain slavery; but while they relieved me of one difficulty, they brought on another even more painful than the one of which I was relieved. The more I read, the more I was led to abhor and detest my enslavers. I could regard them in no other light than a band of successful robbers, who had left their homes, and gone to Africa, and stolen us from our homes, and in a strange land reduced us to slavery. I loathed them as being the meanest as well as the most wicked of men. As I read and contemplated the subject, behold! that very discontentment which Master Hugh had predicted would follow my learning to read had already come, to torment and sting my soul to unutterable anguish. As I writhed under it, I would at times feel that learning to read had been a curse rather than a blessing. It had given me a view of my wretched condition, without the remedy. It opened my eyes to the horrible pit, but to no ladder upon which to get out. In moments of agony, I envied my fellow-slaves for their stupidity. I have often wished myself a beast. I preferred the condition of the meanest reptile to my own. Any thing, no matter what, to get rid of thinking! It was this everlasting thinking of

---

[2] **Richard Brinsley Sheridan (1751–1816)** Irish dramatist and orator. However, Douglass really refers to a speech by Daniel O'Connell (1775–1847) in favor of Irish Catholic emancipation.

my condition that tormented me. There was no getting rid of it. It was pressed upon me by every object within sight or hearing, animate or inanimate. The silver trump of freedom had roused my soul to eternal wakefulness. Freedom now appeared, to disappear no more forever. It was heard in every sound, and seen in every thing. It was ever present to torment me with a sense of my wretched condition. I saw nothing without seeing it, I heard nothing without hearing it, and felt nothing without feeling it. It looked from every star, it smiled in every calm, breathed in every wind, and moved in every storm.

I often found myself regretting my own existence, and wishing 11 myself dead; and but for the hope of being free, I have no doubt but that I should have killed myself, or done something for which I should have been killed. While in this state of mind, I was eager to hear any one speak of slavery. I was a ready listener. Every little while, I could hear something about the abolitionists.[3] It was some time before I found what the word meant. It was always used in such connections as to make it an interesting word to me. If a slave ran away and succeeded in getting clear, or if a slave killed his master, set fire to a barn, or did any thing very wrong in the mind of a slaveholder, it was spoken of as the fruit of *abolition.* Hearing the word in this connection very often, I set about learning what it meant. The dictionary afforded me little or no help. I found it was "the act of abolishing"; but then I did not know what was to be abolished. Here I was perplexed. I did not dare to ask any one about its meaning, for I was satisfied that it was something they wanted me to know very little about. After a patient waiting, I got one of our city papers, containing an account of the number of petitions from the north, praying for the abolition of slavery in the District of Columbia, and of the slave trade between the States. From this time I understood the words *abolition* and *abolitionist,* and always drew near when that word was spoken, expecting to hear something of importance to myself and fellow-slaves. The light broke in upon me by degrees. I went one day down on the wharf of Mr. Waters; and seeing two Irishmen unloading a scow of stone, I went, unasked, and helped them. When we had finished, one of them came to me and asked me if I were a slave. I told him I was. He asked, "Are ye a slave for life?" I told him that I was. The good Irishman seemed to be deeply affected by the statement. He said to the other that it was a pity so fine a little fellow as myself should be a slave for life. He said it was a shame to hold me. They both advised me to run away to the

---

[3] **abolitionists** Those who actively opposed slavery.

north; that I should find friends there, and that I should be free. I pretended not to be interested in what they said, and treated them as if I did not understand them; for I feared they might be treacherous. White men have been known to encourage slaves to escape, and then, to get the reward, catch them and return them to their masters. I was afraid that these seemingly good men might use me so; but I nevertheless remembered their advice, and from that time I resolved to run away. I looked forward to a time at which it would be safe for me to escape. I was too young to think of doing so immediately; besides, I wished to learn how to write, as I might have occasion to write my own pass. I consoled myself with the hope that I should one day find a good chance. Meanwhile, I would learn to write.

The idea as to how I might learn to write was suggested to me   12 by being in Durgin and Bailey's ship-yard, and frequently seeing the ship carpenters, after hewing, and getting a piece of timber ready for use, write on the timber the name of that part of the ship for which it was intended. When a piece of timber was intended for the larboard side, it would be marked thus—"L." When a piece was for the starboard side, it would be marked thus—"S." A piece for the larboard side forward, would be marked thus—"L.F." When a piece was for starboard side forward, it would be marked thus—"S.F." For larboard aft, it would be marked thus—"L.A." For starboard aft, it would be marked thus—"S.A." I soon learned the names of these letters, and for what they were intended when placed upon a piece of timber in the ship-yard. I immediately commenced copying them, and in a short time was able to make the four letters named. After that, when I met with any boy who I knew could write, I would tell him I could write as well as he. The next word would be, "I don't believe you. Let me see you try it." I would then make the letters which I had been so fortunate as to learn, and ask him to beat that. In this way I got a good many lessons in writing, which it is quite possible I should never have gotten in any other way. During this time, my copy-book was the board fence, brick wall, and pavement; my pen and ink was a lump of chalk. With these, I learned mainly how to write. I then commenced and continued copying the Italics in Webster's Spelling Book, until I could make them all without looking on the book. By this time, my little Master Thomas had gone to school, and learned how to write, and had written over a number of copy-books. These had been brought home, and shown to some of our near neighbors, and then laid aside. My mistress used to go to class meeting at the Wilk Street meeting-house every Monday afternoon, and leave me to take care of the house. When left thus, I used to spend the time in writing in the spaces left in Master Thomas's copy-book, copying what he had written. I continued to do this until I could write a hand very similar to that of Master Thomas. Thus, after a long, tedious effort for years, I finally succeeded in learning how to write.

In a very short time after I went to live at Baltimore, my old master's youngest son Richard died; and in about three years and six months after his death, my old master, Captain Anthony, died, leaving only his son, Andrew, and daughter, Lucretia, to share his estate. He died while on a visit to see his daughter at Hillsborough. Cut off thus unexpectedly, he left no will as to the disposal of his property. It was therefore necessary to have a valuation of the property, that it might be equally divided between Mrs. Lucretia and Master Andrew. I was immediately sent for, to be valued with the other property. Here again my feelings rose up in detestation of slavery. I had now a new conception of my degraded condition. Prior to this, I had become, if not insensible to my lot, at least partly so. I left Baltimore with a young heart overborne with sadness, and a soul full of apprehension. I took passage with Captain Rowe, in the schooner Wild Cat, and, after a sail of about twenty-four hours, I found myself near the place of my birth. I had now been absent from it almost, if not quite, five years. I, however, remembered the place very well. I was only about five years old when I left it, to go and live with my old master on Colonel Lloyd's plantation; so that I was now between ten and eleven years old. 13

We were all ranked together at the valuation. Men and women, old and young, married and single, were ranked with horses, sheep, and swine. There were horses and men, cattle and women, pigs and children, all holding the same rank in the scale of being, and were all subjected to the same narrow examination. Silvery-headed age and sprightly youth, maids and matrons, had to undergo the same indelicate inspection. At this moment, I saw more clearly than ever the brutalizing effects of slavery upon both slave and slaveholder. 14

After the valuation, then came the division. I have no language to express the high excitement and deep anxiety which were felt among us poor slaves during this time. Our fate for life was now to be decided. We had no more voice in that decision than the brutes among whom we were ranked. A single word from the white men was enough—against all our wishes, prayers, and entreaties—to sunder forever the dearest friends, dearest kindred, and strongest ties known to human beings. In addition to the pain of separation, there was the horrid dread of falling into the hands of Master Andrew. He was known to us all as being a most cruel wretch,—a 15 common drunkard, who had, by his reckless mismanagement and profligate dissipation, already wasted a large portion of his father's property. We all felt that we might as well be sold at once to the Georgia traders, as to pass into his hands; for we knew that that would be our inevitable condition,—a condition held by us all in the utmost horror and dread.

I suffered more anxiety than most of my fellow-slaves. I had known what it was to be kindly treated; they had known nothing of the kind. They had seen little or nothing of the world. They were in very deed men and women of sorrow, and acquainted with grief. Their backs had been made familiar with the bloody lash, so that they had become callous; mine was yet tender; for while at Baltimore I got few whippings, and few slaves could boast of a kinder master and mistress than myself; and the thought of passing out of their hands into those of Master Andrew—a man who, but a few days before, to give me a sample of his bloody disposition, took my little brother by the throat, threw him on the ground, and with the heel of his boot stamped upon his head till the blood gushed from his nose and ears—was well calculated to make me anxious as to my fate. After he had committed this savage outrage upon my brother, he turned to me, and said that was the way he meant to serve me one of these days,—meaning, I suppose, when I came into his possession. 16

Thanks to a kind Providence, I fell to the portion of Mrs. Lucretia, and was sent immediately back to Baltimore, to live again in the family of Master Hugh. Their joy at my return equalled their sorrow at my departure. It was a glad day to me. I had escaped a worse fate than lion's jaws. I was absent from Baltimore, for the purpose of valuation and division, just about one month, and it seemed to have been six. 17

Very soon after my return to Baltimore, my mistress, Lucretia, died, leaving her husband and child, Amanda; and in a very short time after her death, Master Andrew died. Now all the property of my old master, slaves included, was in the hands of strangers,—strangers who had had nothing to do with accumulating it. Not a slave was left free. All remained slaves, from the youngest to the oldest. If any one thing in my experience, more than another, served to deepen my conviction of the infernal character of slavery, and to fill me with unutterable loathing of slaveholders, it was their base ingratitude to my poor old grandmother. She had served my old master faithfully from youth to old age. She had been the source of all his wealth; she had peopled his plantation with slaves; she had become a great grandmother in his service. She had rocked him in infancy, attended him in childhood, served him through life, and at 18 his death wiped from his icy brow the cold death-sweat, and closed his eyes forever. She was nevertheless left a slave—a slave for life—a slave in the hands of strangers; and in their hands she saw her children, her grandchildren, and her great-grandchildren, divided, like so many sheep, without being gratified with the small privilege of a single word, as to their or her own destiny. And, to cap the climax of their base ingratitude and fiendish barbarity, my grandmother, who was now very old, having outlived my old master and all his children, having seen the beginning and end of all of them, and her present owners finding she was of but little value, her frame already racked with the pains of old age, and complete helplessness fast stealing over her once active limbs, they took her to the woods, built her a little hut, put up a little mud-chimney, and then made her welcome to the privilege of supporting herself there in perfect loneliness; thus virtually turning her out to die! If my poor old grandmother now lives, she lives to suffer in utter loneliness; she lives to remember and mourn over the loss of children, the loss of grandchildren, and the loss of great-grandchildren. They are, in the language of the slave's poet, Whittier,[4]—

> Gone, gone, sold and gone
> To the rice swamp dank and lone,
> Where the slave-whip ceaseless swings,
> Where the noisome insect stings,
> Where the fever-demon strews
> Poison with the falling dews,
> Where the sickly sunbeams glare
> Through the hot and misty air:—
>   Gone, gone, sold and gone
>   To the rice swamp dank and lone,
>   From Virginia hills and waters—
>   Woe is me, my stolen daughters!

The hearth is desolate. The children, the unconscious children, who once sang and danced in her presence, are gone. She gropes her way, in the darkness of age, for a drink of water. Instead of the voices of her children, she hears by day the moans of the dove, and by night the screams of the hideous owl. All is gloom. The grave is at the door. And now, when weighed down by the pains and aches of old age, when the head inclines to the feet, when the beginning and ending of human existence meet, and helpless infancy and painful old age combine together—at this time, this most needful time, the time for the exercise of that tenderness and affection which children

---

[4] **John Greenleaf Whittier (1807–1892)** New England abolitionist, journalist, and poet. The poem Douglass cites is "The Farewell" (1835).

only can exercise towards a declining parent—my poor old grandmother, the devoted mother of twelve children, is left all alone, in
yonder little hut, before a few dim embers. She stands—she sits—
she staggers—she falls—she groans—she dies—and there are
none of her children or grandchildren present, to wipe from her
wrinkled brow the cold sweat of death, or to place beneath the sod
her fallen remains. Will not a righteous God visit for these things?

In about two years after the death of Mrs. Lucretia, Master Thomas   20
married his second wife. Her name was Rowena Hamilton. She was
the eldest daughter of Mr. William Hamilton. Master now lived in St.
Michael's. Not long after his marriage, a misunderstanding took place
between himself and Master Hugh; and as a means of punishing his
brother, he took me from him to live with himself at St. Michael's.
Here I underwent another most painful separation. It, however, was
not so severe as the one I dreaded at the division of property; for, during this interval, a great change had taken place in Master Hugh and
his once kind and affectionate wife. The influence of brandy upon
him, and of slavery upon her, had effected a disastrous change in the
characters of both; so that, as far as they were concerned, I thought I
had little to lose by the change. But it was not to them that I was attached. It was to those little Baltimore boys that I felt the strongest attachment. I had received many good lessons from them, and was still
receiving them, and the thought of leaving them was painful indeed. I
was leaving, too, without the hope of ever being allowed to return.
Master Thomas had said he would never let me return again. The barrier betwixt himself and brother he considered impassable.

I then had to regret that I did not at least make the attempt to   21
carry out my resolution to run away; for the chances of success are
tenfold greater from the city than from the country.

I sailed from Baltimore for St. Michael's in the sloop Amanda,   22
Captain Edward Dodson. On my passage, I paid particular attention
to the direction which the steamboats took to go to Philadelphia. I
found, instead of going down, on reaching North Point they went
up the bay, in a north-easterly direction. I deemed this knowledge of
the utmost importance. My determination to run away was again revived. I resolved to wait only so long as the offering of a favorable
opportunity. When that came, I was determined to be off.

QUESTIONS FOR CRITICAL READING

1. Douglass describes Mrs. Auld as possessing "the fatal poison of irresponsible power" (para. 2). What precisely does he mean by this?

2. How does the absence of justice undermine the force of law?
3. Why did the slave holders believe learning to read would spoil a slave?
4. What were the results of Douglass's learning to read?
5. How did the slave holders regard their slaves? What differences does Douglass describe in their behavior?

SUGGESTIONS FOR WRITING

1. The society in which Douglass lived was governed by laws established by elected officials who had benefited from the writings of Rousseau and Jefferson, among others. How could they have conceived of their possession of slaves as an expression of justice?
2. What is the most important political issue raised in the essay? Douglass never talks about the law, but he implies a great deal about justice. What is the political truth regarding the law in Maryland at this time? What is the relationship between politics and justice in this essay?
3. One of the defenses of slavery was that it was for the good of the slaves. How might Frederick Douglass have argued against this defense?
4. Douglass assures us that Mrs. Auld was "a kind and tender-hearted woman" (para. 6) when he first went to live with her but that her behavior soon came to resemble that of other slave holders. How did her behavior alter, and what circumstances contributed to the change? Why does Douglass tell us about the change?
5. What, on the whole, is Douglass's attitude toward white people? Examine his statements about them, and establish as far as possible his feelings regarding their character. Is he bitter about his slavery experiences? Does he condemn the society that supported slavery?
6. How effective is the detailed description in the essay? Select the best descriptive passages and analyze them for their effectiveness in context. What does Douglass hope to accomplish by lavishing so much attention on such description?
7. **CONNECTIONS** Which writer on government would Douglass have found most important — Lao-tzu, Machiavelli, Rousseau, or Jefferson? Which would the slave holders agree with? What political ideals does Douglass hold? Trace their sources to one or more of these writers.
8. **CONNECTIONS** Apply the definitions of totalitarianism put forth by Hannah Arendt to the American institution of slavery. How does Douglass's essay describe or reveal the form of government that allowed him to live as a slave?

HENRY DAVID THOREAU
Civil Disobedience

HENRY DAVID THOREAU (1817–1862) began keeping a journal when he graduated from Harvard in 1837. The journal was preserved and published, and it shows us the seriousness, determination, and elevation of moral values characteristic of all his work. He is best known for *Walden* (1854), a record of his departure from the warm congeniality of Concord, Massachusetts, and the home of his close friend Ralph Waldo Emerson (1803–1882), for the comparative "wilds" of Walden Pond, where he built a cabin, planted a garden, and lived simply. In *Walden* Thoreau describes the deadening influence of ownership and extols the vitality and spiritual uplift that comes from living close to nature. He also argues that civilization's comforts sometimes rob a person of independence, integrity, and even conscience.

Thoreau and Emerson were prominent among the group of writers and thinkers who were referred to as the Transcendentalists. They believed in something that transcended the limits of sensory experience—in other words, something that transcended materialism. Their philosophy was based on the works of Immanuel Kant (1724–1804), the German idealist philosopher; Samuel Taylor Coleridge (1772–1834), the English poet; and Johann Wolfgang von Goethe (1749–1832), the German dramatist and thinker. These writers praised human intuition and the capacity to see beyond the limits of common experience.

Their philosophical idealism carried over into the social concerns of the day, expressing itself in works such as *Walden* and "Civil Disobedience," which was published with the title "Resistance to Civil Government" in 1849, a year after the publication of *The Communist Manifesto*. Although Thoreau all but denies his idealism in "Civil Disobedience," it is obvious that after spending a night in the Concord jail, he realizes he cannot quietly accept his government's behavior in regard to slavery. He begins to feel that it is not only appropriate but imperative to disobey unjust laws.

In Thoreau's time the most flagrantly unjust laws were those that supported slavery. The Transcendentalists strongly opposed slavery and spoke out against it. Abolitionists in Massachusetts harbored escaped slaves and helped them move to Canada and freedom. The Fugitive Slave Act, enacted in 1850, the year after "Civil Disobedience" was published, made Thoreau a criminal because he refused to comply with Massachusetts civil authorities when in 1851 they began returning escaped slaves to the South as the law required.

"Civil Disobedience" was much more influential in the twentieth century than it was in the nineteenth. Mohandas Gandhi (1869–1948) claimed that while he was editor of an Indian newspaper in South Africa, it helped to inspire his theories of nonviolent resistance. Gandhi eventually implemented these theories against the British empire and helped win independence for India. In the 1960s, Martin Luther King Jr. applied the same theories in the fight for racial equality in the United States. Thoreau's essay once again found widespread adherents among the many young men who resisted being drafted into the military to fight in Vietnam because they believed that the war was unjust.

"Civil Disobedience" was written after the Walden experience (which began on July 4, 1845, and ended on September 6, 1847). Thoreau quietly returned to Emerson's home and "civilization." His refusal to pay the Massachusetts poll tax—a "per head" tax imposed on all citizens to help support what he considered an unjust war against Mexico—landed him in the Concord jail. He spent just one day and one night there—his aunt paid the tax for him—but the experience was so extraordinary that he began examining it in his journal.

Thoreau's Rhetoric

Thoreau maintained his journal throughout his life and eventually became convinced that writing was one of the few professions by which he could earn a living. He made more money, however, from lecturing on the lyceum circuit. The lyceum, a New England institution, was a town adult education program, featuring important speakers such as the very successful Emerson and foreign lecturers. Admission fees were very reasonable, and in the absence of other popular entertainment, the lyceum was a popular proving ground for speakers interested in promoting their ideas.

"Civil Disobedience" was first outlined in rough-hewn form in the journal, where the main ideas appear and where experiments in phrasing began. (Thoreau was a constant reviser.) Then in February 1848, Thoreau delivered a lecture on "Civil Disobedience" at the Concord Lyceum urging people of conscience to actively resist a government that acted badly. Finally, the piece was prepared for publication in *Aesthetic Papers,* an intellectual journal edited by Elizabeth Peabody (1804–1894), the sister-in-law of another important New England writer, Nathaniel Hawthorne (1804–1864). There it was refined again, and certain important details were added.

"Civil Disobedience" bears many of the hallmarks of the spoken lecture. For one thing, it is written in the first person and addresses an audience that Thoreau expects will share many of his sentiments but certainly not all his conclusions. His message is to some extent anarchistic, virtually denying an unjust government any authority or respect.

Modern political conservatives generally take his opening quote—"That government is best which governs least"—as a rallying cry against governmental interference in everyday affairs. Such conservatives usually propose reducing government interference by reducing the government's capacity to tax wealth for unpopular causes. In fact, what Thoreau opposes is simply any government that is not totally just, totally moral, and totally respectful of the individual.

The easiness of the pace of the essay also derives from its original form as a speech. Even such locutions as "But to speak practically and as a citizen" (para. 3) connect the essay with its origins. Although Thoreau was not an overwhelming orator—he was short and somewhat homely, an unprepossessing figure—he ensured that his writing achieved what some speakers might have accomplished by means of gesture and theatrics.

Thoreau's language is marked by clarity. He speaks directly to every issue, stating his own position and recommending the position he feels his audience, as reasonable and moral people, should accept. One impressive achievement in this selection is Thoreau's capacity to shape memorable, virtually aphoristic statements that remain "quotable" generations later, beginning with his own quotation from the words of John L. O'Sullivan: "That government is best which governs least." Thoreau calls it a motto, as if it belonged on the great seal of a government or on a coin. It contains an interesting and impressive rhetorical flourish—the device of repeating "govern" and the near rhyme of "best" with "least."

His most memorable statements show considerable attention to the rhetorical qualities of balance, repetition, and pattern. "The only obligation which I have a right to assume is to do at any time what I think right" (para. 4) uses the word *right* in two senses: first, as a matter of personal volition; second, as a matter of moral rectitude. One's right, in other words, becomes the opportunity to do right. "For it matters not how small the beginning may seem to be: what is once well done is done forever" (para. 21) also relies on repetition for its effect and balances the concept of a beginning with its capacity to reach out into the future. The use of the rhetorical device of *chiasmus,* a criss-cross relationship between key words, marks "Under a government which imprisons any unjustly, the true place for a just man is also a prison" (para. 22). Here is the pattern:

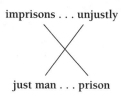

Such attention to phrasing is typical of speakers whose expressions must catch and retain the attention of listeners. Audiences do not have the advantage of referring to a text, so the words they hear must be forceful.

Thoreau relies also on analogy—comparing men with machines, people with plants, even the citizen with states considering secession from the Union. His analogies are effective and thus worth examining in some detail. He draws on the analysis of circumstance throughout the essay, carefully examining government actions to determine their qualities and their results. His questions include comments on politics (para. 1), on the Bible (para. 23), on Confucius (para. 24), and finally on his contemporary, Daniel Webster (1782–1852) (para. 42), demonstrating a wide range of influence but avoiding the pedantic tone that can come from using quotations too liberally or from citing obscure sources. This essay is simple, direct, and uncluttered. Its enduring influence is in part due to the clarity and grace that characterize Thoreau's writing at its best. Its power derives from Thoreau's demand that citizens act on the basis of conscience.

PREREADING QUESTIONS: WHAT TO READ FOR

The following prereading questions may help you anticipate key issues in the discussion on Henry David Thoreau's "Civil Disobedience." Keeping them in mind during your first reading of the selection should help focus your reactions.

- What kind of government does Thoreau feel would be most just?
- What is the individual's responsibility regarding supporting the government when it is wrong?
- How does Thoreau deal with unjust laws?

Civil Disobedience

I heartily accept the motto—"That government is best which 1 governs least,"[1] and I should like to see it acted up to more rapidly and systematically. Carried out, it finally amounts to this, which also I believe—"That government is best which governs not at all"; and when men are prepared for it, that will be the kind of government which they will have. Government is at best but an expedient; but most governments are usually, and all governments are sometimes, inexpedient. The objections which have been brought against a standing army, and they are many and weighty, and deserve to prevail, may also at last be brought against a standing government. The standing army is only an arm of the standing government. The government itself, which is only the mode which the people have chosen to execute their will, is equally liable to be abused and perverted before the people can act through it. Witness the present Mexican war,[2] the work of comparatively a few individuals using the standing government as their tool; for in the outset the people would not have consented to this measure.

This American government—what is it but a tradition, a recent 2 one, endeavoring to transmit itself unimpaired to posterity but each instant losing some of its integrity? It has not the vitality and force of a single living man; for a single man can bend it to his will. It is a

---

[1] **"...governs least"** John L. O'Sullivan (1813–1895) wrote in the *United States Magazine and Democratic Review* (1837) that "all government is evil, and the parents of evil.... The best government is that which governs least." Thomas Jefferson wrote, "That government is best which governs the least, because its people discipline themselves." Both comments echo the *Tao-te Ching*.

[2] **the present Mexican war (1846–1848)** The war was extremely unpopular in New England because it was an act of a bullying government anxious to grab land from a weaker nation. The United States had annexed Texas in 1845, precipitating a retaliation from Mexico.

sort of wooden gun to the people themselves. But it is not the less necessary for this; for the people must have some complicated machinery or other, and hear its din, to satisfy that idea of government which they have. Governments show thus how successfully men can be imposed on, even impose on themselves, for their own advantage. It is excellent, we must all allow. Yet this government never of itself furthered any enterprise but by the alacrity with which it got out of its way. *It* does not keep the country free. *It* does not settle the West. *It* does not educate. The character inherent in the American people has done all that has been accomplished; and it would have done somewhat more if the government had not sometimes got in its way. For government is an expedient by which men would fain succeed in letting one another alone; and, as has been said, when it is most expedient the governed are most let alone by it. Trade and commerce, if they were not made of India-rubber, would never manage to bounce over the obstacles which legislators are continually putting in their way; and, if one were to judge these men wholly by the effects of their actions and not partly by their intentions, they would deserve to be classed and punished with those mischievous persons who put obstructions on the railroads.

But to speak practically and as a citizen, unlike those who call 3 themselves no-government men, I ask for, not at once no government, but *at once* a better government. Let every man make known what kind of government would command his respect, and that will be one step toward obtaining it.

After all, the practical reason why, when the power is once in 4 the hands of the people, a majority are permitted, and for a long period continue, to rule is not because they are most likely to be in the right, nor because this seems fairest to the minority but because they are physically the strongest. But a government in which the majority rule in all cases cannot be based on justice, even as far as men understand it. Can there not be a government in which majorities do not virtually decide right and wrong but conscience?—in which majorities decide only those questions to which the rule of expediency is applicable? Must the citizen ever for a moment, or in the least degree, resign his conscience to the legislator? Why has every man a conscience then? I think that we should be men first and subjects afterward. It is not desirable to cultivate a respect for the law, so much as for the right. The only obligation which I have a right to assume is to do at any time what I think right. It is truly enough said that a corporation has no conscience; but a corporation of conscientious men is a corporation *with* a conscience. Law never made men a whit more just; and, by means of their respect for it, even the well-disposed are daily made the agents of injustice. A common and natural result of an undue respect for law is that you may see a file of soldiers, colonel, captain, corporal, privates, powder-monkeys,[3] and all, marching in admirable order over hill and dale to the wars, against their wills, ay, against their common sense and consciences, which makes it very steep marching indeed and produces a palpitation of the heart. They have no doubt that it is a damnable business in which they are concerned; they are all peaceably inclined. Now, what are they? Men at all? or small movable forts and magazines at the service of some unscrupulous man in power? Visit the Navy-Yard,[4] and behold a marine, such a man as an American government can make, or such as it can make a man with its black arts — a mere shadow and reminiscence of humanity, a man laid out alive and standing, and already, as one may say, buried under arms with funeral accompaniments, though it may be —

> Not a drum was heard, not a funeral note,
> As his corse to the rampart we hurried;
> Not a soldier discharged his farewell shot
> O'er the grave where our hero we buried.[5]

The mass of men serve the state thus, not as men mainly, but as machines, with their bodies. They are the standing army, and the militia, jailers, constables, posse comitatus,[6] &c. In most cases there is no free exercise whatever of the judgment or of the moral sense; but they put themselves on a level with wood and earth and stones; and wooden men can perhaps be manufactured that will serve the purpose as well. Such command no more respect than men of straw or a lump of dirt. They have the same sort of worth only as horses and dogs. Yet such as these even are commonly esteemed good citizens. Others — as most legislators, politicians, lawyers, ministers, and office-holders — serve the state chiefly with their heads; and, as they rarely make any moral distinctions, they are as likely to serve the Devil, without *intending* it, as God. A very few, as heroes, patriots, martyrs, reformers in the great sense, and *men,* serve the state with their consciences also and so necessarily resist it for the most part; and they are commonly treated as enemies by it. A wise man will only be useful as a man and will not submit to be "clay" and "stop a hole to keep the wind away," but leave that office to his dust at least:

---

³ **powder-monkeys** The boys who delivered gunpowder to cannons.

⁴ **Navy-Yard** This is apparently the U.S. naval yard at Boston.

⁵ These lines are from "Burial of Sir John Moore at Corunna" (1817) by the Irish poet Charles Wolfe (1791–1823).

⁶ **posse comitatus** Literally, the power of the county; the term means a law-enforcement group made up of ordinary citizens.

I am too high-born to be propertied,
To be a secondary at control,
Or useful serving-man and instrument
To any sovereign state throughout the world.[7]

He who gives himself entirely to his fellow-men appears to them   6
useless and selfish; but he who gives himself partially to them is pronounced a benefactor and philanthropist.

How does it become a man to behave toward this American   7
government today? I answer, that he cannot without disgrace be associated with it. I cannot for an instant recognize that political organization as *my* government which is the *slave's* government also.

All men recognize the right of revolution; that is, the right to   8
refuse allegiance to, and to resist the government when its tyranny
or its inefficiency are great and unendurable. But almost all say that
such is not the case now. But such was the case, they think, in the
Revolution of '75. If one were to tell me that this was a bad government because it taxed certain foreign commodities brought to its
ports, it is most probable that I should not make an ado about it, for
I can do without them. All machines have their friction; and possibly this does enough good to counterbalance the evil. At any rate, it
is a great evil to make a stir about it. But when the friction comes to
have its machine, and oppression and robbery are organized, I say
let us not have such a machine any longer. In other words, when a
sixth of the population of a nation which has undertaken to be the
refuge of liberty are slaves, and a whole country is unjustly overrun
and conquered by a foreign army and subjected to military law, I
think that it is not too soon for honest men to rebel and revolutionize. What makes this duty the more urgent is the fact that the country so overrun is not our own, but ours is the invading army.

Paley,[8] a common authority with many on moral questions, in   9
his chapter on the "Duty of Submission to Civil Government," resolves all civil obligation into expediency; and he proceeds to say,
"that so long as the interest of the whole society requires it, that is,
so long as the established government cannot be resisted or changed
without public inconveniency, it is the will of God that the established government be obeyed, and no longer. . . . This principle being

---

[7] **"clay," "stop a hole . . . wind away," I am too high-born . . .** These lines are
from Shakespeare; the first is from *Hamlet*, V.i.226–227. The verse is from *King
John*, V.ii.79–82.

[8] **William Paley (1743–1805)** An English theologian who lectured widely
on moral philosophy. Paley is famous for *A View of the Evidences of Christianity*
(1794). "Duty of Submission to Civil Government Explained" is Chapter 3 of Book 6
of *The Principles of Moral and Political Philosophy* (1785).

admitted, the justice of every particular case of resistance is reduced to a computation of the quantity of the danger and grievance on the one side, and of the probability and expense of redressing it on the other." Of this, he says, every man shall judge for himself. But Paley appears never to have contemplated those cases to which the rule of expediency does not apply, in which a people, as well as an individual, must do justice, cost what it may. If I have unjustly wrested a plank from a drowning man, I must restore it to him though I drown myself. This, according to Paley, would be inconvenient. But he that would save his life, in such a case, shall lose it. This people must cease to hold slaves and to make war on Mexico, though it cost them their existence as a people.

In their practice, nations agree with Paley; but does anyone   10
think that Massachusetts does exactly what is right at the present crisis?

> A drab of state, a cloth-o'-silver slut,
> To have her train borne up, and her soul trail in the dirt.[9]

Practically speaking, the opponents to a reform in Massachusetts are not a hundred thousand politicians at the South but a hundred thousand merchants and farmers here, who are more interested in commerce and agriculture than they are in humanity, and are not prepared to do justice to the slave and to Mexico, cost what it may. I quarrel not with far-off foes but with those who, near at home, co-operate with, and do the bidding of, those far away, and without whom the latter would be harmless. We are accustomed to say that the mass of men are unprepared; but improvement is slow because the few are not materially wiser or better than the many. It is not so important that many should be as good as you as that there be some absolute goodness somewhere; for that will leaven the whole lump. There are thousands who are in opinion opposed to slavery and to the war who yet in effect do nothing to put an end to them; who, es-teeming themselves children of Washington and Franklin, sit down with their hands in their pockets and say that they know not what to do, and do nothing; who even postpone the question of freedom to the question of free trade, and quietly read the prices-current along with the latest advices from Mexico after dinner and, it may be, fall asleep over them both. What is the price-current of an honest man and patriot today? They hesitate and they regret and sometimes they

---

[9] **A drab...** From Cyril Tourneur (1575?–1626), *Revenger's Tragedy* (1607), IV.iv.70–72. "Drab" is an obsolete term for a prostitute. Thoreau quotes the lines to imply that Massachusetts is a "painted lady" with a defiled soul.

petition; but they do nothing in earnest and with effect. They will wait, well disposed, for others to remedy the evil, that they may no longer have it to regret. At most, they give only a cheap vote, and a feeble countenance and God-speed, to the right, as it goes by them. There are nine hundred and ninety-nine patrons of virtue to one virtuous man. But it is easier to deal with the real possessor of a thing than with the temporary guardian of it.

All voting is a sort of gaming, like checkers or backgammon, with a slight moral tinge to it, a playing with right and wrong, with moral questions; and betting naturally accompanies it. The character of the voters is not staked. I cast my vote, perchance, as I think right; but I am not vitally concerned that that right should prevail. I am willing to leave it to the majority. Its obligation, therefore, never exceeds that of expediency. Even voting *for the right* is *doing* nothing for it. It is only expressing to men feebly your desire that it should prevail. A wise man will not leave the right to the mercy of chance, nor wish it to prevail through the power of the majority. There is but little virtue in the action of masses of men. When the majority shall at length vote for the abolition of slavery, it will be because they are indifferent to slavery, or because there is but little slavery left to be abolished by their vote. *They* will then be the only slaves. Only *his* vote can hasten the abolition of slavery who asserts his own freedom by his vote.

I hear of a convention to be held at Baltimore,[10] or elsewhere, for the selection of a candidate for the Presidency, made up chiefly of editors, and men who are politicians by profession; but I think, what is it to any independent, intelligent, and respectable man what decision they may come to? Shall we not have the advantage of his wisdom and honesty nevertheless? Can we not count upon some independent votes? Are there not many individuals in the country who do not attend conventions? But no: I find that the responsible man, so called, has immediately drifted from his position, and despairs of his country when his country has more reason to despair of him. He forthwith adopts one of the candidates thus selected as the only *available* one, thus proving that he is himself *available* for any purposes of the demagogue. His vote is of no more worth than that of any unprincipled foreigner or hireling native who may have been bought. O for a man who is a *man* and, as my neighbor says has a bone in his back which you cannot pass your hand through! Our

11

12

[10] **Baltimore** In 1848 the political environment was particularly intense; it was a seedbed for theoreticians of the Confederacy, which was only beginning to be contemplated seriously.

statistics are at fault: the population has been returned too large. How many *men* are there to a square thousand miles in this country? Hardly one. Does not America offer any inducement for men to settle here? The American has dwindled into an Odd Fellow[11] — one who may be known by the development of his organ of gregariousness and a manifest lack of intellect and cheerful self-reliance; whose first and chief concern, on coming into the world, is to see that the Almshouses are in good repair; and, before yet he has lawfully donned the virile garb, to collect a fund for the support of the widows and orphans that may be; who, in short, ventures to live only by the aid of the Mutual Insurance Company, which has promised to bury him decently.

It is not a man's duty, as a matter of course, to devote himself to   13 the eradication of any, even the most enormous wrong; he may still properly have other concerns to engage him; but it is his duty, at least, to wash his hands of it and, if he gives it no thought longer, not to give it practically his support. If I devote myself to other pursuits and contemplations, I must first see, at least, that I do not pursue them sitting upon another man's shoulders. I must get off him first, that he may pursue his contemplations too. See what gross inconsistency is tolerated. I have heard some of my townsmen say, "I should like to have them order me out to help put down an insurrection of the slaves, or to march to Mexico — see if I would go"; and yet these very men have each directly by their allegiance and so indirectly, at least, by their money, furnished a substitute. The soldier is applauded who refuses to serve in an unjust war by those who do not refuse to sustain the unjust government which makes the war; is applauded by those whose own act and authority he disregards and sets at naught; as if the State were penitent to that degree that it hired one to scourge it while it sinned, but not to that degree that it left off sinning for a moment. Thus, under the name of Order and Civil Government, we are all made at last to pay homage to and support our own meanness. After the first blush of sin comes its indifference; and from immoral it becomes, as it were, *unmoral*, and not quite unnecessary to that life which we have made.

The broadest and most prevalent error requires the most disin-   14 terested virtue to sustain it. The slight reproach to which the virtue of patriotism is commonly liable, the noble are most likely to incur. Those who, while they disapprove of the character and measures of

---

[11]**Odd Fellow** The Independent Order of Odd Fellows, a fraternal and benevolent secret society, founded in England in the eighteenth century and first established in the United States in 1819 in Baltimore.

a government, yield to it their allegiance and support, are undoubtedly its most conscientious supporters, and so frequently the most
serious obstacles to reform. Some are petitioning the State to dissolve the Union, to disregard the requisitions of the President. Why
do they not dissolve it themselves—the union between themselves
and the State—and refuse to pay their quota into its treasury? Do
not they stand in the same relation to the State that the State does to
the Union? And have not the same reasons prevented the State from
resisting the Union which have prevented them from resisting the
State?

How can a man be satisfied to entertain an opinion merely, and   15
enjoy *it*? Is there any enjoyment in it if his opinion is that he is aggrieved? If you are cheated out of a single dollar by your neighbor,
you do not rest satisfied with knowing that you are cheated, or with
saying that you are cheated, or even with petitioning him to pay you
your due; but you take effectual steps at once to obtain the full
amount and see that you are never cheated again. Action from principle, the perception and the performance of right, changes things
and relations; it is essentially revolutionary and does not consist
wholly with anything which was. It not only divides states and
churches, it divides families; ay, it divides the *individual,* separating
the diabolical in him from the divine.

Unjust laws exist: shall we be content to obey them, or shall we   16
endeavor to amend them and obey them until we have succeeded,
or shall we transgress them at once? Men generally, under such a
government as this, think that they ought to wait until they have
persuaded the majority to alter them. They think that if they should
resist the remedy would be worse than the evil. *It* makes it worse.
Why is it not more apt to anticipate and provide for reform? Why
does it not cherish its wise minority? Why does it cry and resist before it is hurt? Why does it not encourage its citizens to be on the
alert to point out its faults and *do* better than it would have them?
Why does it always crucify Christ and excommunicate Copernicus
and Luther[12] and pronounce Washington and Franklin rebels?

One would think that a deliberate and practical denial of its au-   17
thority was the only offence never contemplated by government;
else why has it not assigned its definite, its suitable and proportionate penalty? If a man who has no property refuses but once to earn
nine shillings for the State, he is put in prison for a period unlimited

---

[12]**Nicolaus Copernicus (1473–1543) and Martin Luther (1483–
1546)** Copernicus revolutionized astronomy and the way humankind perceives the
universe; Luther was a religious revolutionary who began the Reformation and created the first Protestant faith.

by any law that I know, and determined only by the discretion of those who placed him there; but if he should steal ninety times nine shillings from the State, he is soon permitted to go at large again.

If the injustice is part of the necessary friction of the machine of government, let it go, let it go: perchance it will wear smooth — certainly the machine will wear out. If the injustice has a spring or a pulley or a rope or a crank exclusively for itself, then perhaps you may consider whether the remedy will not be worse than the evil; but if it is of such a nature that it requires you to be the agent of injustice to another, then I say break the law. Let your life be a counter friction to stop the machine. What I have to do is to see, at any rate, that I do not lend myself to the wrong which I condemn.   18

As for adopting the ways which the State has provided for remedying the evil, I know not of such ways. They take too much time, and a man's life will be gone. I have other affairs to attend to. I came into this world, not chiefly to make this a good place to live in, but to live in it, be it good or bad. A man has not everything to do, but something; and because he cannot do *everything,* it is not necessary that he should do *something* wrong. It is not my business to be petitioning the Governor or the Legislature any more than it is theirs to petition me; and if they should not hear my petition what should I do then? But in this case the State has provided no way: its very Constitution is the evil. This may seem to be harsh and stubborn and unconciliatory; but it is to treat with the utmost kindness and consideration the only spirit that can appreciate or deserves it. So is all change for the better, like birth and death, which convulse the body.   19

I do not hesitate to say that those who call themselves Abolitionists should at once effectually withdraw their support, both in person and property, from the government of Massachusetts, and not wait till they constitute a majority of one before they suffer the right to prevail through them. I think that it is enough if they have God on their side, without waiting for that other one. Moreover, any man more right than his neighbors constitutes a majority of one already.   20

I meet this American government or its representative, the State government, directly and face to face once a year — no more — in the person of its tax-gatherer; this is the only mode in which a man situated as I am necessarily meets it; and it then says distinctly, Recognize me; and the simplest, the most effectual and, in the present posture of affairs, the indispensablest mode of treating with it on this head, of expressing your little satisfaction with and love for it, is to deny it then. My civil neighbor, the tax-gatherer, is the very man I have to deal with — for it is, after all, with men and not with parchment that I quarrel — and he has voluntarily chosen to be an agent   21 of the government. How shall he ever know well what he is and does as an officer of the government, or as a man, until he is obliged to consider whether he shall treat me, his neighbor, for whom he has respect, as a neighbor and well-disposed man, or as a maniac and disturber of the peace, and see if he can get over this obstruction to his neighborliness without a ruder and more impetuous thought or speech corresponding with his action. I know this well, that if one thousand, if one hundred, if ten men whom I could name—if ten *honest* men only—ay, if *one* HONEST man in this State of Massachusetts, *ceasing to hold slaves,* were actually to withdraw from this copartnership and be locked up in the county jail therefor, it would be the abolition of slavery in America. For it matters not how small the beginning may seem to be: what is once well done is done forever. But we love better to talk about it: that we say is our mission. Reform keeps many scores of newspapers in its service but not one man. If my esteemed neighbor,[13] the State's ambassador, who will devote his days to the settlement of the question of human rights in the Council Chamber, instead of being threatened with the prisons of Carolina, were to sit down the prisoner of Massachusetts, that State which is so anxious to foist the sin of slavery upon her sister—though at present she can discover only an act of inhospitality to be the ground of a quarrel with her—the Legislature would not wholly waive the subject the following winter.

Under a government which imprisons any unjustly, the true place for a just man is also a prison. The proper place today, the only place which Massachusetts has provided for her freer and less desponding spirits is in her prisons, to be put out and locked out of the State by her own act, as they have already put themselves out by their principles. It is there that the fugitive slave and the Mexican prisoner on parole and the Indian come to plead the wrongs of his race should find them; on that separate but more free and honorable ground where the State places those who are not *with* her but *against* her—the only house in a slave State in which a free man can abide with honor. If any think that their influence would be lost there, and their voices no longer afflict the ear of the State, that they would not be as an enemy within its walls, they do not know by how much truth is stronger than error, nor how much more eloquently and effectively he can combat injustice who has experienced a little in his

22

---

[13] **esteemed neighbor** Thoreau refers to Samuel Hoar (1778–1856), a Massachusetts congressman, who went to South Carolina to protest that state's practice of seizing black seamen from Massachusetts ships and enslaving them. South Carolina threatened Hoar and drove him out of the state. He did not secure the justice he demanded.

own person. Cast your whole vote, not a strip of paper merely, but your whole influence. A minority is powerless while it conforms to the majority; it is not even a minority then; but it is irresistible when it clogs by its whole weight. If the alternative is to keep all just men in prison or give up war and slavery, the State will not hesitate which to choose. If a thousand men were not to pay their tax-bills this year, that would not be a violent bloody measure, as it would be to pay them, and enable the State to commit violence and shed innocent blood. This is, in fact, the definition of a peaceable revolution, if any such is possible. If the tax-gatherer or any other public officer asks me, as one has done, "But what shall I do?" my answer is, "If you really wish to do anything, resign your office." When the subject has refused allegiance and the officer has resigned his office, then the revolution is accomplished. But even suppose blood should flow. Is there not a sort of blood shed when the conscience is wounded? Through this wound a man's real manhood and immortality flow out, and he bleeds to an everlasting death. I see this blood flowing now.

I have contemplated the imprisonment of the offender rather   23 than the seizure of his goods—though both will serve the same purpose—because they who assert the purest right, and consequently are most dangerous to a corrupt State, commonly have not spent much time in accumulating property. To such the State renders comparatively small service, and a slight tax is wont to appear exorbitant, particularly if they are obliged to earn it by special labor with their hands. If there were one who lived wholly without the use of money, the State itself would hesitate to demand it of him. But the rich man—not to make any invidious comparison—is always sold to the institution which makes him rich. Absolutely speaking, the more money, the less virtue; for money comes between a man and his objects and obtains them for him; and it was certainly no great virtue to obtain it. It puts to rest many questions which he would otherwise be taxed to answer; while the only new question which it puts is the hard but superfluous one, how to spend it. Thus his moral ground is taken from under his feet. The opportunities of living are diminished in proportion as what are called the "means" are increased. The best thing a man can do for his culture when he is rich is to endeavor to carry out those schemes which he entertained when he was poor. Christ answered the Herodians[14] according to their condition. "Show me the tribute-money," said he—and one

---

[14]**Herodians** Followers of King Herod who were opposed to Jesus Christ (see Matthew 22:16).

took a penny out of his pocket—if you use money which has the image of Caesar on it, and which he has made current and valuable, that is, if *you are men of the State* and gladly enjoy the advantages of Caesar's government, then pay him back some of his own when he demands it; "Render therefore to Caesar that which is Caesar's, and to God those things which are God's"—leaving them no wiser than before as to which was which; for they did not wish to know.

When I converse with the freest of my neighbors, I perceive that 24 whatever they may say about the magnitude and seriousness of the question, and their regard for the public tranquillity, the long and the short of the matter is that they cannot spare the protection of the existing government, and they dread the consequences to their property and families of disobedience to it. For my own part, I should not like to think that I ever rely on the protection of the State. But if I deny the authority of the State when it presents its tax-bill, it will soon take and waste all my property and so harass me and my children without end. This is hard. This makes it impossible for a man to live honestly, and at the same time comfortably, in outward respects. It will not be worth the while to accumulate property; that would be sure to go again. You must hire or squat somewhere and raise but a small crop and eat that soon. You must live within yourself and depend upon yourself always tucked up and ready for a start, and not have many affairs. A man may grow rich in Turkey even, if he will be in all respects a good subject of the Turkish government. Confucius[15] said: "If a state is governed by the principles of reason, poverty and misery are subjects of shame; if a state is not governed by the principles of reason, riches and honors are the subjects of shame." No; until I want the protection of Massachusetts to be extended to me in some distant Southern port, where my liberty is endangered, or until I am bent solely on building up an estate at home by peaceful enterprise, I can afford to refuse allegiance to Massachusetts and her right to my property and life. It costs me less in every sense to incur the penalty of disobedience to the State than it would to obey. I should feel as if I were worth less in that case.

Some years ago the State met me in behalf of the Church and 25 commanded me to pay a certain sum toward the support of a clergyman whose preaching my father attended, but never I myself. "Pay," it said, "or be locked up in the jail." I declined to pay. But, unfortu-

---

[15]**Confucius (551–479 B.C.)** The most important Chinese religious leader. His *Analects* (collection) treated not only religious but moral and political matters as well.

nately, another man saw fit to pay it. I did not see why the school-master should be taxed to support the priest, and not the priest the schoolmaster; for I was not the State's schoolmaster, but I supported myself by voluntary subscription. I did not see why the lyceum should not present its tax-bill and have the State to back its demand, as well as the Church. However, at the request of the selectmen, I condescended to make some such statement as this in writing: —
"Know all men by these presents, that I, Henry Thoreau, do not wish to be regarded as a member of any incorporated society which I have not joined." This I gave to the town clerk; and he has it. The State, having thus learned that I did not wish to be regarded as a member of that church, has never made a like demand on me since; though it said that it must adhere to its original presumption that time. If I had known how to name them, I should then have signed off in detail from all the societies which I never signed on to; but I did not know where to find a complete list.

I have paid no poll-tax[16] for six years. I was put into a jail once   26 on this account, for one night; and, as I stood considering the walls of solid stone, two or three feet thick, the door of wood and iron, a foot thick, and the iron grating which strained the light, I could not help being struck with the foolishness of that institution which treated me as if I were mere flesh and blood and bones, to be locked up. I wondered that it should have concluded at length that this was the best use it could put me to and had never thought to avail itself of my services in some way. I saw that if there was a wall of stone between me and my townsmen, there was a still more difficult one to climb or break through before they could get to be as free as I was. I did not for a moment feel confined, and the walls seemed a great waste of stone and mortar. I felt as if I alone of all my towns-men had paid my tax. They plainly did not know how to treat me but behaved like persons who are underbred. In every threat and in every compliment there was a blunder; for they thought that my chief desire was to stand the other side of that stone wall. I could not but smile to see how industriously they locked the door on my meditations, which followed them out again without let or hin-drance, and *they* were really all that was dangerous. As they could not reach me, they had resolved to punish my body; just as boys, if they cannot come at some person against whom they have a spite, will abuse his dog. I saw that the State was half-witted, that it was

---

[16]**poll-tax** A tax levied on every citizen living in a given area; *poll* means "head," so it is a tax per head. The tax Thoreau refers to, about $2, was used to support the Mexican War.

timid as a lone woman with her silver spoons, and that it did not know its friends from its foes, and I lost all my remaining respect for it and pitied it.

Thus the State never intentionally confronts a man's sense, intellectual or moral, but only his body, his senses. It is not armed with superior wit or honesty but with superior physical strength. I was not born to be forced. I will breathe after my own fashion. Let us see who is the strongest. What force has a multitude? They only can force me who obey a higher law than I. They force me to become like themselves. I do not hear of *men* being *forced* to live this way or that by masses of men. What sort of life were that to live? When I meet a government which says to me, "Your money or your life," why should I be in haste to give it my money? It may be in a great strait and not know what to do: I cannot help that. It must help itself; do as I do. It is not worth the while to snivel about it. I am not responsible for the successful working of the machinery of society. I am not the son of the engineer. I perceive that, when an acorn and a chestnut fall side by side, the one does not remain inert to make way for the other, but both obey their own laws and spring and grow and flourish as best they can till one, perchance, overshadows and destroys the other. If a plant cannot live according to its nature, it dies; and so a man. 27

The night in prison was novel and interesting enough. The prisoners in their shirt-sleeves were enjoying a chat and the evening air in the doorway when I entered. But the jailer said, "Come, boys, it is time to lock up"; and so they dispersed, and I heard the sound of their steps returning into the hollow apartments. My room-mate was introduced to me by the jailer as "a first-rate fellow and a clever man." When the door was locked, he showed me where to hang my hat and how he managed matters there. The rooms were whitewashed once a month; and this one, at least, was the whitest, most simply furnished, and probably the neatest apartment in the town. He naturally wanted to know where I came from and what brought me there; and when I had told him, I asked him in my turn how he came there, presuming him to be an honest man, of course; and, as the world goes, I believe he was. "Why," said he, "they accuse me of burning a barn; but I never did it." As near as I could discover, he had probably gone to bed in a barn when drunk and smoked his pipe there; and so a barn burnt. He had the reputation of being a clever man, had been there some three months waiting for his trial to come on, and would have to wait as much longer; but he was quite domesticated and contented, since he got his board for nothing and thought that he was well treated. 28

He occupied one window, and I the other; and I saw that if one   29
stayed there long, his principal business would be to look out the
window. I had soon read all the tracts that were left there and examined where former prisoners had broken out and where a grate had
been sawed off and heard the history of the various occupants of
that room; for I found that even here there was a history and a gossip which never circulated beyond the walls of the jail. Probably this
is the only house in the town where verses are composed, which afterward printed in a circular form but not published. I was shown
quite a long list of verses which were composed by some young men
who had been detected in an attempt to escape, who avenged themselves by signing them.

I pumped my fellow-prisoner as dry as I could, for fear I should   30
never see him again; but at length he showed me which was my bed
and left me to blow out the lamp.

It was like travelling into a far country, such as I had never ex-   31
pected to behold, to lie there for one night. It seemed to me that I
never had heard the town-clock strike before, nor the evening
sounds of the village; for we slept with the windows open, which
were inside the grating. It was to see my native village in the light of
the Middle Ages, and our Concord was turned into a Rhine stream,
and visions of knights and castles passed before me. They were the
voices of old burghers that I heard in the streets. I was an involuntary spectator and auditor of whatever was done and said in the
kitchen of the adjacent village-inn — a wholly new and rare experience to me. It was a closer view of my native town. I was fairly inside of it. I never had seen its institutions before. This is one of its
peculiar institutions; for it is a shire town.[17] I began to comprehend
what its inhabitants were about.

In the morning our breakfasts were put through the hole in the   32
door, in small oblong-square tin pans, made to fit, and holding a
pint of chocolate, with brown bread and an iron spoon. When they
called for the vessels again, I was green enough to return what bread
I had left; but my comrade seized it and said that I should lay that
up for lunch or dinner. Soon after he was let out to work at haying
in a neighboring field, whither he went every day, and would not be
back till noon; so he bade me good-day, saying that he doubted if he
should see me again.

When I came out of prison — for someone interfered and paid   33
that tax — I did not perceive that great changes had taken place on the

---

[17] **shire town** A county seat, which means the town had a court, county offices, and jails.

common, such as he observed who went in a youth and emerged a tottering and gray-headed man; and yet a change had to my eyes come over the scene — the town and State and country — greater than any that mere time could effect. I saw yet more distinctly the State in which I lived. I saw to what extent the people among whom I lived could be trusted as good neighbors and friends; that their friendship was for summer weather only; that they did not greatly propose to do right; that they were a distinct race from me by their prejudices and superstitions, as the Chinamen and Malays are; that, in their sacrifices to humanity, they ran no risks, not even to their property; that, after all, they were not so noble but they treated the thief as he had treated them and hoped, by a certain outward observance and a few prayers, and by walking in a particular straight though useless path from time to time, to save their souls. This may be to judge my neighbors harshly; for I believe that many of them are not aware that they have such an institution as the jail in their village.

34   It was formerly the custom in our village, when a poor debtor came out of jail, for his acquaintances to salute him, looking through their fingers, which were crossed to represent the grating of a jail window, "How do ye do?" My neighbors did not thus salute me but first looked at me and then at one another as if I had returned from a long journey. I was put into jail as I was going to the shoemaker's to get a shoe which was mended. When I was let out the next morning I proceeded to finish my errand, and having put on my mended shoe, joined a huckleberry party who were impatient to put themselves under my conduct; and in half an hour — for the horse was soon tackled — was in the midst of a huckleberry field on one of our highest hills two miles off, and then the State was nowhere to be seen.

35   This is the whole history of "My Prisons."

36   I have never declined paying the highway tax, because I am as desirous of being a good neighbor as I am of being a bad subject; and as for supporting schools I am doing my part to educate my fellow countrymen now. It is for no particular item in the tax-bill that I refuse to pay it. I simply wish to refuse allegiance to the State, to withdraw and stand aloof from it effectually. I do not care to trace the course of my dollar, if I could, till it buys a man or a musket to shoot one with — the dollar is innocent — but I am concerned to trace the effects of my allegiance. In fact, I quietly declare war with the State, after my fashion, though I will still make what use and get what advantage of her I can, as is usual in such cases.

37   If others pay the tax which is demanded of me from a sympathy with the State, they do but what they have already done in their own

case, or rather they abet injustice to a greater extent than the State requires. If they pay the tax from a mistaken interest in the individual taxed, to save his property, or prevent his going to jail, it is because they have not considered wisely how far they let their private feelings interfere with the public good.

This, then, is my position at present. But one cannot be too   38
much on his guard in such a case, lest his action be biassed by obstinacy or an undue regard for the opinions of men. Let him see that he does only what belongs to himself and to the hour.

I think sometimes, Why, this people mean well; they are   39
only ignorant; they would do better if they knew how: why give your neighbors this pain to treat you as they are not inclined to? But I think again, this is no reason why I should do as they do or permit others to suffer much greater pain of a different kind. Again, I sometimes say to myself, When many millions of men, without heat, without ill will, without personal feeling of any kind, demand of you a few shillings only, without the possibility, such is their constitution, of retracting or altering their present demand, and without the possibility, on your side, of appeal to any other millions, why expose yourself to this overwhelming brute force? You do not resist cold and hunger, the winds and the waves, thus obstinately; you quietly submit to a thousand similar necessities. You do not put your head into the fire. But just in proportion as I regard this as not wholly a brute force but partly a human force, and consider that I have relations to those millions as to so many millions of men, and not of mere brute or inanimate things, I see that appeal is possible, first and instantaneously, from them to the Maker of them, and secondly, from them to themselves. But if I put my head deliberately into the fire, there is no appeal to fire or to the Maker of fire, and I have only myself to blame. If I could convince myself that I have any right to be satisfied with men as they are, and to treat them accordingly, and not according, in some respects, to my requisitions and expectations of what they and I ought to be, then, like a good Mussulman[18] and fatalist, I should endeavor to be satisfied with things as they are and say it is the will of God. And, above all, there is this difference between resisting this and a purely brute or natural force, that I can resist this with some effect; but I cannot expect, like Orpheus,[19] to change the nature of the rocks and trees and beasts.

---

[18] **Mussulman** Muslim; a follower of the religion of Islam.
[19] **Orpheus** In Greek mythology Orpheus was a poet whose songs were so plaintive that they affected animals, trees, and even stones.

I do not wish to quarrel with any man or nation. I do not wish   40
to split hairs, to make fine distinctions, or set myself up as better
than my neighbors. I seek rather, I may say, even an excuse for con-
forming to the laws of the land. I am but too ready to conform to
them. Indeed, I have reason to suspect myself on this head; and each
year, as the tax-gatherer comes round, I find myself disposed to review the acts and position of the general and State governments, and
the spirit of the people, to discover a pretext for conformity.

> We must affect our country as our parents;
> And if at any time we alienate
> Our love or industry from doing it honor,
> We must respect effects and teach the soul
> Matter of conscience and religion,
> And not desire of rule or benefit.[20]

I believe that the State will soon be able to take all my work of this
sort out of my hands, and then I shall be no better a patriot than my
fellow-countrymen. Seen from a lower point of view, the Constitution, with all its faults, is very good; the law and the courts are very
respectable; even this State and this American government are, in
many respects, very admirable and rare things, to be thankful for,
such as a great many have described them; but seen from a point of
view a little higher, they are what I have described them; seen from a
higher still, and the highest, who shall say what they are, or that
they are worth looking at or thinking of at all?

However, the government does not concern me much, and I   41
shall bestow the fewest possible thoughts on it. It is not many moments that I live under a government, even in this world. If a man is
thought-free, fancy-free, imagination-free, that which *is not* never for
a long time appearing *to be* to him, unwise rulers or reformers cannot fatally interrupt him.

I know that most men think differently from myself; but those   42
whose lives are by profession devoted to the study of these or kindred subjects content me as little as any. Statesmen and legislators,
standing so completely within the institution, never distinctly and
nakedly behold it. They speak of moving society but have no
resting-place without it. They may be men of a certain experience
and discrimination and have no doubt invented ingenious and even

----

[20] **We must affect...** From George Peele (1556–1596), *The Battle of Alcazar*
(acted 1588–1589, printed 1594), II.ii. Thoreau added these lines in a later printing
of the essay. They emphasize the fact that one is disobedient to the state as one is to
a parent—with love and affection and from a cause of conscience. Disobedience is
not taken lightly.

useful systems, for which we sincerely thank them; but all their wit and usefulness lie within certain not very wide limits. They are wont to forget that the world is not governed by policy and expediency. Webster[21] never goes behind government and so cannot speak with authority about it. His words are wisdom to those legislators who contemplate no essential reform in the existing government; but for thinkers, and those who legislate for all time, he never once glances at the subject. I know of those whose serene and wise speculations on this theme would soon reveal the limits of his mind's range and hospitality. Yet, compared with the cheap professions of most reformers, and the still cheaper wisdom and eloquence of politicians in general, his are almost the only sensible and valuable words, and we thank Heaven for him. Comparatively, he is always strong, original, and, above all, practical. Still his quality is not wisdom but prudence. The lawyer's truth is not Truth but consistency, or a consistent expediency. Truth is always in harmony with herself and is not concerned chiefly to reveal the justice that may consist with wrongdoing. He well deserves to be called, as he has been called, the Defender of the Constitution. There are really no blows to be given by him but defensive ones. He is not a leader but a follower. His leaders are the men of '87.[22] "I have never made an effort," he says, "and never propose to make an effort; I have never countenanced an effort, and never mean to countenance an effort, to disturb the arrangement as originally made, by which the various States came into the Union." Still thinking of the sanction which the Constitution gives to slavery, he says, "Because it was a part of the original compact—let it stand." Notwithstanding his special acuteness and ability, he is unable to take a fact out of its merely political relations and behold it as it lies absolutely to be disposed of by the intellect—what, for instance, it behooves a man to do here in America today with regard to slavery but ventures, or is driven, to make some such desperate answer as the following, while professing to speak absolutely, and as a private man—from which what new and singular code of social duties might be inferred? "The manner," says he, "in which the governments of those States where slavery exists are to regulate it, is for their own consideration, under their responsibility to their constituents, to the general laws of propriety, humanity, and

---

[21] **Daniel Webster (1782–1852)** One of the most brilliant orators of his time. He was secretary of state from 1841 to 1843, which is why Thoreau thinks he cannot be a satisfactory critic of government.

[22] **men of '87** The men who framed the Constitution in 1787.

justice, and to God. Associations formed elsewhere, springing from a feeling of humanity, or any other cause, have nothing whatever to do with it. They have never received any encouragement from me, and they never will."[23]

They who know of no purer sources of truth, who have traced   43
up its stream no higher, stand, and wisely stand, by the Bible and the Constitution, and drink at it there with reverence and humility; but they who behold where it comes trickling into this lake or that pool gird up their loins once more and continue their pilgrimage toward its fountain-head.

No man with a genius for legislation has appeared in America.   44
They are rare in the history of the world. There are orators, politicians, and eloquent men by the thousand; but the speaker has not yet opened his mouth to speak who is capable of settling the much-vexed questions of the day. We love eloquence for its own sake and not for any truth which it may utter or any heroism it may inspire. Our legislators have not yet learned the comparative value of free-trade and of freedom, of union, and of rectitude, to a nation. They have no genius or talent for comparatively humble questions of taxation and finance, commerce and manufacturers and agriculture. If we were left solely to the wordy wit of legislators in Congress for our guidance, uncorrected by the seasonable experience and the effectual complaints of the people, America would not long retain her rank among the nations. For eighteen hundred years, though perchance I have no right to say it, the New Testament has been written; yet where is the legislator who has wisdom and practical talent enough to avail himself of the light which it sheds on the science of legislation?

The authority of government, even such as I am willing to sub-   45
mit to — for I will cheerfully obey those who know and can do better than I, and in many things even those who neither know nor can do so well — is still an impure one: to be strictly just, it must have the sanction and consent of the governed. It can have no pure right over my person and property but what I concede to it. The progress from an absolute to a limited monarchy, from a limited monarchy to a democracy, is a progress toward a true respect for the individual. Even the Chinese philosopher[24] was wise enough to regard the individual as the basis of the empire. Is a democracy such as we know it the last improvement possible in government? Is it not possible to

---

[23] These extracts have been inserted since the Lecture was read. [Thoreau's note]

[24] **Chinese philosopher** Thoreau probably means Confucius.

take a step further towards recognizing and organizing the rights of man? There will never be a really free and enlightened State until the State comes to recognize the individual as a higher and independent power, from which all its own power and authority are derived, and treats him accordingly. I please myself with imagining a State at last which can afford to be just to all men and to treat the individual with respect as a neighbor; which even would not think it inconsistent with its own repose if a few were to live aloof from it, not meddling with it, nor embraced by it, who fulfilled all the duties of neighbors and fellow-men. A State which bore this kind of fruit and suffered it to drop off as fast as it ripened would prepare the way for a still more perfect and glorious State, which also I have imagined but not yet anywhere seen.

QUESTIONS FOR CRITICAL READING

1. How would you characterize the tone of Thoreau's address? Is he chastising his audience? Is he praising it? What opinion do you think he has of his audience?
2. Explain what Thoreau means when he says, "But a government in which the majority rule in all cases cannot be based on justice, even as far as men understand it" (para. 4).
3. How is injustice "part of the necessary friction of the machine of government" (para. 18)?
4. Why does Thoreau provide us with "the whole history of 'My Prisons'" (paras. 28–35)? Describe what being in jail taught Thoreau. Why do you think Thoreau reacted so strongly to being in a local jail for a single day?
5. Choose an example of Thoreau's use of irony, and comment on its effectiveness. (One example appears in para. 25.)
6. How might Thoreau view the responsibility of the majority to a minority within the sphere of government?
7. How clear are Thoreau's concepts of justice? On what are they based?
8. Is it possible that when Thoreau mentions "the Chinese philosopher" (para. 45) he means Lao-tzu? Would Lao-tzu agree that the individual is "the basis of the empire"?

SUGGESTIONS FOR WRITING

1. Thoreau insists, "Law never made men a whit more just" (para. 4). He introduces the concept of conscience as a monitor of law and government. Explain his views on conscience and the conscientious person.

How can conscience help create justice? Why is it sometimes difficult for law to create justice?

2. Do you agree with Thoreau when he says, "All voting is a sort of gaming" (para. 11)? Examine his attitude toward elections and the relationship of elections to the kind of justice one can expect from a government.

3. Answer Thoreau's question: "Unjust laws exist: shall we be content to obey them, or shall we endeavor to amend them and obey them until we have succeeded, or shall we transgress them at once?" (para. 16). Thoreau reminds us that the law has been created by the majority and to disobey would put him in a minority—a "wise minority." Why should the wise minority have the right to disobey laws created by the majority?

4. In what ways was the United States government of Thoreau's time built on the individual or on the individual's best interests? In what way is our current government based on the individual's best interests? How can satisfying the individual's best interests be reconciled with satisfying the community's interest? Which would produce more justice?

5. Examine quotations from Thoreau that focus on justice for the individual, and write an essay that establishes the values of the government Thoreau describes. How might that government see its obligations to the governed? How would it treat matters of justice and moral issues? Describe Thoreau's view of the American government of his time in enough detail to give a clear sense of the essay to someone who has not read it.

6. Reread Thoreau's question in item 3 above. Answer it in an essay that focuses on issues that are significant to you. Be as practical and cautious as you feel you should be, and provide your own answer—not the one you feel Thoreau might have given. Then describe the forms that Thoreau's disobedience would be likely to take. What probably would be the limits of his actions?

7. **CONNECTIONS** Analyze passages from Hannah Arendt's "Ideology and Terror" in relation to what Thoreau says in "Civil Disobedience." Would Arendt have disobeyed a law that was perceived as immoral? Would she have gone to jail to protest unjust laws? During the late 1930s German law would have required Arendt to turn herself in as a Jew, although to do so would have been to face almost certain death. Should she have broken the law?

8. **CONNECTIONS** Thoreau admits (para. 41) that he is not very concerned with government because he does not have to pay much attention to it. His life goes on regardless of government. He also says that "[t]he authority of government . . . is still an impure one: to be strictly just, it must have the sanction and consent of the governed" (para. 45). How would Jefferson have reacted to Thoreau's attitudes toward government? Would he have agreed with Thoreau's view that it is essentially unimportant to the individual? Does Thoreau derive from Jefferson his view that the success of a government depends on the sanction

of the governed? Or did Jefferson have a different idea about the relationship between the government and the governed?

9. **CONNECTIONS**   Thoreau was especially sympathetic to the plight of African American slaves and would likely have shared the views of Frederick Douglass and Martin Luther King Jr. What advice might he have given them? Write an essay that applies the basic ideas of "Civil Disobedience" to the circumstances in which Douglass and King found themselves.

ELIZABETH CADY STANTON
Declaration of Sentiments and Resolutions

ELIZABETH CADY STANTON (1815–1902) was exceptionally intelligent, and because her lawyer father was willing to indulge her gifts, she was provided the best education a woman in her time in America could expect. Born and raised in Johnstown, New York, she was one of six children, five girls and one boy, Eleazar, in whom all the hopes of the family rested. When Eleazar died after graduating from college, Elizabeth strove to replace him in the admiration of her father. She studied Greek so successfully that she was admitted as the only young woman in the local secondary school, where she demonstrated her abilities—which on the whole were superior to those of the boys with whom she studied.

Nonetheless, she did not win the esteem she hoped for. Her father, although he loved and cared for her, continually told her he wished she had been born a boy. In Johnstown, as elsewhere, women had few rights and rather low expectations. The question of education was a case in point: it was a profound exception for Elizabeth Cady to go to school with boys or even to study what they studied. She had no hopes of following in their paths because all the professions they aimed for were closed to women. This fact was painfully brought home to her when she finished secondary school. All the boys she studied with went on to Union College in Schenectady, but she was barred from attending the all-male institution. Instead, she attended a much inferior Troy Female Seminary, run by a pioneer of American education, Emma Willard (1787–1870).

From the *History of Woman Suffrage.*

169

Troy was as good a school as any woman in America could attend; yet it emphasized a great many traditional womanly pursuits as well as the principles of Calvinism, which Elizabeth Cady came to believe were at the root of the problem women had in American society. In the 1830s women did not have the vote; if they were married, they could not own property; and they could not sue for divorce no matter how ugly their marital situation. A husband expected a dowry from his wife, and he could spend it exactly as he wished: on gambling, carousing, or speculating. Not until 1848, the year of the Seneca Falls Convention, did New York pass laws to change this situation.

Elizabeth Cady married when she was twenty-four years old. Her husband, Henry Stanton, was a prominent abolitionist and journalist. He had little money, and the match was not entirely blessed by Elizabeth's father. In characteristic fashion she had the word *obey* struck from the marriage vows; thus she had trouble finding a preacher who would adhere to her wishes. And, preferring never to be known as Mrs. Stanton, she was always addressed as Elizabeth Cady Stanton.

Early on, their life was settled in Boston, where Elizabeth found considerable intellectual companionship and stimulation. Good servants made her household tasks minimal. But soon Henry Stanton's health demanded that they move to Seneca Falls, New York, where there were few servants of any caliber, and where there were few people of intellectual independence to stimulate her. Her lot in life became much like that of any housewife, and she could not abide it.

After a discussion at tea with a number of like-minded women, she proposed a woman's convention to discuss their situation. On July 14, 1848 (a year celebrated for revolutions in every major capital of Europe), the following notice appeared in the *Seneca County Courier,* a semiweekly journal:

SENECA FALLS CONVENTION

WOMAN'S RIGHTS CONVENTION.—A Convention to discuss the social, civil, and religious condition and rights of woman, will be held in the Wesleyan Chapel, at Seneca Falls, N.Y., on Wednesday and Thursday, the 19th and 20th of July, current; commencing at 10 o'clock A.M. During the first day the meeting will be exclusively for women, who are earnestly invited to attend. The public generally are invited to be present on the second day, when Lucretia Mott, of Philadelphia, and other ladies and gentlemen, will address the convention.

On the appointed day, less than a week after the notice, carriages and other vehicles tied up the streets around the Wesleyan Chapel with a large number of interested people. The first shock was that the chapel was locked, and the first order of business was for a man to climb through an open window to unlock the doors. The chapel was filled immediately, but not only with women. Many men were present, including Frederick Douglass, and the women decided that because they were already there, the men could stay.

The convention was a significant success, establishing a pattern that has been repeated frequently since. Elizabeth Cady Stanton, in her Declaration, figured as a radical in the assembly, proposing unheard-of reforms such as granting women the vote, which most of the moderates in the assembly could not agree on. For a while the assembly wished to omit the question of the vote, but Elizabeth, by presenting it as her first statement in the Declaration, made it clear that without the right to vote on legislation and legislators, women would never be able to change the status quo. Eventually, with the help of Douglass and others, the convention accepted her position, and the women's movement in America was under way.

Stanton's Rhetoric

Because the Seneca Falls Declaration is modeled directly on Jefferson's Declaration of Independence, we cannot get a good idea of Stanton's rhetorical gifts. However, by relying on Jefferson, she exercised a powerful wit (for which her other writing is well known) by reminding her audience that when the Declaration of Independence was uttered, no thought was given to half its potential audience — women. Thus, the Seneca Falls Declaration is a parody, and it is especially effective in the way it parodies its model so closely.

The same periodic sentences, parallelism, and balance are used and largely to the same effect. She employed the same profusion of one-paragraph utterances and exactly the same opening for each of them. Stanton played a marvelous trick, however. In place of the tyrannical foreign King George — Jefferson's "He" — she has put the tyrant man. Because of the power of her model, her Declaration gathers strength and ironically undercuts the model.

The most interesting aspect of Stanton's rhetorical structure has to do with the order in which she includes the abuses and wrongs that she asks to be made right. She begins with the vote, just as Jefferson began with the law. Both are essential to the entire argument, and both are the key to change. Whereas Jefferson demands an entirely new government, Elizabeth Cady Stanton ends by demanding the "equal participation" of women with men in the government they have already won.

PREREADING QUESTIONS: WHAT TO READ FOR

The following prereading questions may help you anticipate key issues in the discussion on Elizabeth Cady Stanton's Declaration of Sentiments and Resolutions. Keeping them in mind during your first reading of the selection should help focus your reactions.

• What power has man had over women, according to Stanton?

• What is Stanton's attitude toward just and unjust laws?

Declaration of Sentiments and Resolutions

Adopted by the Seneca Falls Convention, July 19–20, 1848

When, in the course of human events, it becomes necessary for   1
one portion of the family of man to assume among the people of the earth a position different from that which they have hitherto occupied, but one to which the laws of nature and of nature's God entitle them, a decent respect to the opinions of mankind requires that they should declare the causes that impel them to such a course.

We hold these truths to be self-evident: that all men and women   2
are created equal; that they are endowed by their Creator with certain inalienable rights; that among these are life, liberty, and the pursuit of happiness; that to secure these rights governments are instituted, deriving their just powers from the consent of the governed. Whenever any form of government becomes destructive of these ends, it is the right of those who suffer from it to refuse allegiance to it, and to insist upon the institution of a new government, laying its foundation on such principles, and organizing its powers in such form, as to them shall seem most likely to effect their safety and happiness. Prudence,

indeed, will dictate that governments long established should not be changed for light and transient causes; and accordingly all experience hath shown that mankind are more disposed to suffer, while evils are sufferable, than to right themselves by abolishing the forms to which they were accustomed. But when a long train of abuses and unsurpations, pursuing invariably the same object, evinces a design to reduce them under absolute despotism, it is their duty to throw off such government, and to provide new guards for their future security. Such has been the patient sufferance of the women under this government, and such is now the necessity which constrains them to demand the equal station to which they are entitled.

The history of mankind is a history of repeated injuries and   3
usurpations on the part of man toward woman, having in direct object the establishment of an absolute tyranny over her. To prove this, let facts be submitted to a candid world.

He has never permitted her to exercise her inalienable right to   4
the elective franchise.

He has compelled her to submit to laws, in the formation of   5
which she had no voice.

He has withheld from her rights which are given to the most ig-   6
norant and degraded men — both natives and foreigners.

Having deprived her of this first right of a citizen, the elective   7
franchise, thereby leaving her without representation in the halls of legislation, he has oppressed her on all sides.

He has made her, if married, in the eye of the law, civilly dead.   8

He has taken from her all right in property, even to the wages   9
she earns.

He has made her, morally, an irresponsible being, as she can   10
commit many crimes with impunity, provided they be done in the presence of her husband. In the covenant of marriage, she is compelled to promise obedience to her husband, he becoming to all intents and purposes, her master — the law giving him power to deprive her of her liberty, and to administer chastisement.

He has so framed the laws of divorce, as to what shall be the   11
proper causes, and in case of separation, to whom the guardianship of the children shall be given, as to be wholly regardless of the happiness of women — the law, in all cases, going upon a false supposition of the supremacy of man, and giving all power into his hands.

After depriving her of all rights as a married woman, if single,   12
and the owner of property, he has taxed her to support a government which recognizes her only when her property can be made profitable to it.

He has monopolized nearly all the profitable employments, and   13
from those she is permitted to follow, she receives but a scanty

remuneration. He closes against her all the avenues to wealth and distinction which he considers most honorable to himself. As a teacher of theology, medicine, or law, she is not known.

He has denied her the facilities for obtaining a thorough educa-   14 tion, at colleges being closed against her.

He allows her in Church, as well as State, but a subordinate po-   15 sition, claiming Apostolic authority for her exclusion from the ministry, and, with some exceptions, from any public participation in the affairs of the Church.

He has created a false public sentiment by giving to the world a   16 different code of morals for men and women, by which moral delinquencies which exclude women from society, are not only tolerated, but deemed of little account in man.

He has usurped the prerogative of Jehovah himself, claiming it   17 as his right to assign for her a sphere of action, when that belongs to her conscience and to her God.

He has endeavored, in every way that he could, to destroy her   18 confidence in her own powers, to lessen her self-respect, and to make her willing to lead a dependent and abject life.

Now, in view of this entire disfranchisement of one-half the   19 people of this country, their social and religious degradation—in view of the unjust laws above mentioned, and because women do feel themselves aggrieved, oppressed, and fraudulently deprived of their most sacred rights, we insist that they have immediate admission to all the rights and privileges which belong to them as citizens of the United States.

In entering upon the great work before us, we anticipate no   20 small amount of misconception, misrepresentation, and ridicule; but we shall use every instrumentality within our power to effect our object. We shall employ agents, circulate tracts, petition the State and National legislatures, and endeavor to enlist the pulpit and the press in our behalf. We hope this Convention will be followed by a series of Conventions embracing every part of the country.

[The following resolutions were discussed by Lucretia Mott,   21 Thomas and Mary Ann McClintock, Amy Post, Catharine A. F. Stebbins, and others, and were adopted:]

WHEREAS, The great precept of nature is conceded to be, that "man shall   22 pursue his own true and substantial happiness." Blackstone[1] in his

---

[1] **Sir William Blackstone (1723–1780)** The most influential of English scholars of the law. His *Commentaries of the Laws of England* (4 vols., 1765–1769) form the basis of the study of law in England.

Commentaries remarks, that this law of Nature being coeval[2] with mankind, and dictated by God himself, is of course superior in obligation to any other. It is binding over all the globe, in all countries and at all times; no human laws are of any validity if contrary to this, and such of them as are valid, derive all their force, and all their validity, and all their authority, mediately and immediately, from this original; therefore,

Resolved, That such laws as conflict, in any way, with the true 23 and substantial happiness of woman, are contrary to the great precept of nature and of no validity, for this is "superior in obligation to any other."

Resolved, That all laws which prevent woman from occupying 24 such a station in society as her conscience shall dictate, or which place her in a position inferior to that of man, are contrary to the great precept of nature, and therefore of no force or authority.

Resolved, That woman is man's equal—was intended to be so by 25 the Creator, and the highest good of the race demands that she should be recognized as such.

Resolved, That the women of this country ought to be enlight- 26 ened in regard to the laws under which they live, that they may no longer publish their degradation by declaring themselves satisfied with their present position, nor their ignorance, by asserting that they have all the rights they want.

Resolved, That inasmuch as man, while claiming for himself in- 27 tellectual superiority, does accord to woman moral superiority, it is pre-eminently his duty to encourage her to speak and teach, as she has an opportunity, in all religious assemblies.

Resolved, That the same amount of virtue, delicacy, and refine- 28 ment of behavior that is required of woman in the social state, should also be required of man, and the same transgressions should be visited with equal severity on both man and woman.

Resolved, That the objection of indelicacy and impropriety, 29 which is so often brought against woman when she addresses a public audience, comes with a very ill-grace from those who encourage, by their attendance, her appearance on the stage, in the concert, or in feats of the circus.

Resolved, That woman has too long rested satisfied in the 30 circumscribed limits which corrupt customs and a perverted application of the Scriptures have marked out for her, and that it is time she should move in the enlarged sphere which her great Creator has assigned her.

Resolved, That it is the duty of the women of this country to se- 31 cure to themselves their sacred right to the elective franchise.

—————

[2] **being coeval** Existing simultaneously.

Resolved, That the equality of human rights results necessarily 32 from the fact of the identity of the race in capabilities and responsibilities.

Resolved, therefore, That, being invested by the Creator with the 33 same capabilities, and the same consciousness of responsibility for their exercise, it is demonstrably the right and duty of woman, equally with man, to promote every righteous cause by every righteous means; and especially in regard to the great subjects of morals and religion, it is self-evidently her right to participate with her brother in teaching them, both in private and in public, by writing and by speaking, by any instrumentalities proper to be used, and in any assemblies proper to be held; and this being a self-evident truth growing out of the divinely implanted principles of human nature, any custom or authority adverse to it, whether modern or wearing the hoary sanction of antiquity, is to be regarded as a self-evident falsehood, and at war with mankind.

[At the last session Lucretia Mott[3] offered and spoke to the fol- 34 lowing resolution:]

Resolved, That the speedy success of our cause depends upon 35 the zealous and untiring efforts of both men and women, for the overthrow of the monopoly of the pulpit, and for the securing to woman an equal participation with men in the various trades, professions, and commerce.

QUESTIONS FOR CRITICAL READING

1. Stanton begins her Declaration with a diatribe against the government. To what extent is the government responsible for the wrongs she complains about?
2. Exactly what is Stanton complaining about? What are the wrongs that have been done? Do they seem important to you?
3. How much of the effect of the selection depends upon the parody of the Declaration of Independence?
4. Which of the individual declarations is the most important? Which is the least important?
5. Is any of the declarations serious enough to warrant starting a revolution?

---

[3] **Lucretia Mott (1793–1880)** One of the founders of the 1848 convention at which these resolutions were presented. She was one of the earliest and most important of the feminists who struggled to proclaim their rights. She was also a prominent abolitionist.

6. Why do you think the suggestion that women deserve the vote was so hard to put across at the convention?

SUGGESTIONS FOR WRITING

1. Make a careful comparison between the Declaration and Jefferson's Declaration of Independence. What are the similarities? What are the differences? Why would Stanton's Declaration be particularly more distinguished because it is a parody of such a document? What weaknesses might be implied because of the close resemblance?

2. Write an essay that is essentially a declaration in the same style Stanton uses. Choose a cause carefully and follow the same pattern that Stanton does in the selection. Establish the appropriate relationship between government and the cause you are interested in defending or promoting.

3. To what extent is it useful to petition a government to redress the centuries of wrongs done to women? Is it the government's fault that women were treated so badly? Is the government able to have a significant effect on helping to change the unpleasant circumstances of women? Is it appropriate or inappropriate for Stanton to attack government in her search for equality?

4. The Declaration of Independence was aimed at justifying a war. Is the question of war anywhere implied in Stanton's address? If war is not the question, what is? Is there any substitute for war in Stanton's essay?

5. Read down the list of declarations and resolutions that Stanton enumerates. Have all of these issues been dealt with in our times? Would such a declaration as this still be appropriate, or has the women's movement accomplished all its goals?

6. Examine the issues treated in paragraph 16, concerning "a different code of morals" for men and women. Explain exactly what Stanton meant by that expression, and consider how different things are today from what they were in Stanton's day.

7. **CONNECTIONS** To what extent do you think Henry David Thoreau would have agreed with Elizabeth Cady Stanton? What aspects of her Declaration would he have found most useful for his own position? Would he have urged women to practice civil disobedience on behalf of women's rights, or would he have accepted the general point of view of his time and concerned himself only with the independence of men?

8. **CONNECTIONS** What is Frederick Douglass's attitude toward women? How would his views have supported Elizabeth Cady Stanton's position in her Declaration? Do you think Stanton should have parodied Frederick Douglass rather than Thomas Jefferson? How is her sense of injustice similar to that of Douglass?

MARTIN LUTHER KING JR.
Letter from Birmingham Jail

MARTIN LUTHER KING JR. (1929–1968) was the most influential civil rights leader in America for a period of more than fifteen years. He was an ordained minister with a doctorate in theology from Boston University. He worked primarily in the South, where he labored steadily to overthrow laws that promoted segregation and to increase the number of black voters registered in southern communities.

From 1958 to 1968 demonstrations and actions opened up opportunities for African Americans who in the South hitherto had been prohibited from sitting in certain sections of buses, using facilities such as water fountains in bus stations, and sitting at luncheon counters with whites. Such laws—unjust and insulting, not to mention unconstitutional—were not challenged by local authorities. Martin Luther King Jr., who became famous for supporting a program to integrate buses in Montgomery, Alabama, was asked by the Southern Christian Leadership Conference (SCLC) to assist in the fight for civil rights in Birmingham, Alabama, where an SCLC meeting was to be held.

King was arrested as the result of a program of sit-ins at luncheon counters and wrote the letter printed here to a group of clergymen who had criticized his position. King had been arrested before and would be arrested again—resembling Thoreau somewhat in his attitude toward laws that did not conform to moral justice.

King, like Thoreau, was willing to suffer for his views, especially when he found himself faced with punitive laws denying civil rights to all citizens. His is a classic case in which the officers of the government pled that they were dedicated to maintaining a stable civil society, even as they restricted King's individual rights. In 1963, many of the good people to whom King addressed this letter firmly believed that peace and order might be threatened by granting African Americans the true independence and freedom that King insisted were their rights and indeed were guaranteed under the constitution. This is why King's letter objects to an injustice that was rampant in Frederick Douglass's time but inexcusable in the time of John F. Kennedy.

Eventually the causes King promoted were victorious. His efforts helped change attitudes in the South and spur legislation that has benefited all Americans. His views concerning nonviolence spread throughout the world, and by the early 1960s he had become famous as a man who stood for human rights and human dignity virtually everywhere. He won the Nobel Peace Prize in 1964.

Although King himself was nonviolent, his program left both him and his followers open to the threat of violence. The sit-ins and voter registration programs spurred countless bombings, threats, and murders by members of the white community. King's life was often threatened, his home bombed, his followers harassed. He was assassinated at the Lorraine Motel in Memphis, Tennessee, on April 4, 1968. But before he died he saw — largely through his own efforts, influence, and example — the face of America change.

King's Rhetoric

The most obvious rhetorical tradition King assumes in this important work is that of the books of the Bible that were originally letters, such as Paul's Epistle to the Ephesians and his several letters to the Corinthians. Many of Paul's letters were written while he was in prison in Rome, and he established a moral position that could inspire the citizens who received the letters. At the same time Paul carried out the most important work of the early Christian church — spreading the word of Jesus to those who wished to be Christians but who needed clarification and encouragement.

It is not clear that the clergymen who received King's letter fully appreciated the rhetorical tradition he drew upon — but they were men who preached from the Bible and certainly should have understood it. The text itself alludes to the mission of Paul and to his communications to his people. King works with this rhetorical tradition not only because it is effective but because it resonates with the deepest aspect of his calling — spreading the gospel of Christ. Brotherhood and justice were his message.

King's tone is one of utmost patience with his critics. He seems bent on winning them over to his point of view, just as he seems confident that — because they are, like him, clergymen — their goodwill should help them see the justice of his views.

His method is that of careful reasoning, focusing on the substance of their criticism, particularly on their complaints that his actions were "unwise and untimely" (para. 1). King takes each of those charges in turn, carefully analyzes it against his position, and then follows with the clearest possible statement of his own views and why he feels they are worth adhering to. The "Letter from Birmingham Jail" is a model of close and reasonable analysis of a very complex situation. It succeeds largely because it remains concrete, treating one issue after another carefully, refusing to be caught up in passion or posturing. Above all, King remains grounded in logic, convinced that his arguments will in turn convince his audience.

PREREADING QUESTIONS: WHAT TO READ FOR

The following prereading questions may help you anticipate key issues in the discussion on Martin Luther King's "Letter from Birmingham Jail." Keeping them in mind during your first reading of the selection should help focus your reactions.

- What kind of injustice did Martin Luther King find in Birmingham?

- Why was Martin Luther King disappointed in the white churches?

Letter from Birmingham Jail

April 16, 1963

MY DEAR FELLOW CLERGYMEN:[1]

While confined here in the Birmingham city jail, I came across   1
your recent statement calling my present activities "unwise and untimely." Seldom do I pause to answer criticism of my work and

---

[1] This response to a published statement by eight fellow clergymen from Alabama (Bishop C. C. J. Carpenter, Bishop Joseph A. Durick, Rabbi Milton L. Grafman, Bishop Paul Hardin, Bishop Nolan B. Harmon, the Reverend George M. Murray, the Reverend Edward V. Ramage, and the Reverend Earl Stallings) was composed under somewhat constricting circumstances. Begun on the margins of the newspaper in which the statement appeared while I was in jail, the letter was continued on scraps of writing paper supplied by a friendly Negro trusty, and concluded on a pad my attorneys were eventually permitted to leave me. Although the text remains in substance unaltered, I have indulged in the author's prerogative of polishing it for publication. [King's note]

ideas. If I sought to answer all the criticisms that cross my desk, my
secretaries would have little time for anything other than such correspondence in the course of the day, and I would have no time for
constructive work. But since I feel that you are men of genuine good
will and that your criticisms are sincerely set forth, I want to try to
answer your statement in what I hope will be patient and reasonable
terms.

I think I should indicate why I am here in Birmingham, since   2
you have been influenced by the view which argues against "out-
siders coming in." I have the honor of serving as president of the
Southern Christian Leadership Conference, an organization operating in every southern state, with headquarters in Atlanta, Georgia.
We have some eighty-five affiliated organizations across the South,
and one of them is the Alabama Christian Movement for Human
Rights. Frequently we share staff, educational, and financial resources with our affiliates. Several months ago the affiliate here in
Birmingham asked us to be on call to engage in a nonviolent direct-
action program if such were deemed necessary. We readily consented, and when the hour came we lived up to our promise. So I,
along with several members of my staff, am here because I was invited here. I am here because I have organizational ties here.

But more basically, I am in Birmingham because injustice is   3
here. Just as the prophets of the eighth century B.C. left their villages
and carried their "thus saith the Lord" far beyond the boundaries of
their home towns, and just as the Apostle Paul left his village of Tarsus[2] and carried the gospel of Jesus Christ to the far corners of the
Greco-Roman world, so am I compelled to carry the gospel of freedom beyond my own home town. Like Paul, I must constantly respond to the Macedonian call for aid.[3]

Moreover, I am cognizant of the interrelatedness of all commu-   4
nities and states. I cannot sit idly by in Atlanta and not be concerned
about what happens in Birmingham. Injustice anywhere is a threat
to justice everywhere. We are caught in an inescapable network of
mutuality, tied in a single garment of destiny. Whatever affects one
directly, affects all indirectly. Never again can we afford to live with
the narrow, provincial, "outside agitator" idea. Anyone who lives

---

[2] **village of Tarsus** Birthplace of St. Paul (? – A.D. 67), in Asia Minor, present-
day Turkey, close to Syria.
[3] **the Macedonian call for aid** The citizens of Philippi, in Macedonia (northern Greece), were among the staunchest Christians. Paul went to their aid frequently; he also had to resolve occasional bitter disputes within the Christian community there (see Philippians 2:2 – 14).

inside the United States can never be considered an outsider anywhere within its bounds.

You deplore the demonstrations taking place in Birmingham. 5
But your statement, I am sorry to say, fails to express a similar concern for the conditions that brought about the demonstrations. I am
sure that none of you would want to rest content with the superficial
kind of social analysis that deals merely with effects and does not
grapple with underlying causes. It is unfortunate that demonstrations are taking place in Birmingham, but it is even more unfortunate that the city's white power structure left the Negro community
with no alternative.

In any nonviolent campaign there are four basic steps: collec- 6
tion of the facts to determine whether injustices exist; negotiation;
self-purification; and direct action. We have gone through all these
steps in Birmingham. There can be no gainsaying the fact that racial
injustice engulfs this community. Birmingham is probably the most
thoroughly segregated city in the United States. Its ugly record of
brutality is widely known. Negroes have experienced grossly unjust
treatment in the courts. There have been more unsolved bombings
of Negro homes and churches in Birmingham than in any other city
in the nation. These are the hard brutal facts of the case. On the
basis of these conditions, Negro leaders sought to negotiate with the
city fathers. But the latter consistently refused to engage in good-
faith negotiation.

Then, last September, came the opportunity to talk with leaders 7
of Birmingham's economic community. In the course of the negotiations, certain promises were made by the merchants—for example,
to remove the stores' humiliating racial signs. On the basis of these
promises, the Reverend Fred Shuttlesworth and the leaders of the
Alabama Christian Movement for Human Rights agreed to a morato-
rium on all demonstrations. As the weeks and months went by, we
realized that we were the victims of a broken promise. A few signs,
briefly removed, returned; the others remained.

As in so many past experiences, our hopes had been blasted, 8
and the shadow of deep disappointment settled upon us. We had no
alternative except to prepare for direct action, whereby we would
present our very bodies as a means of laying our case before the conscience of the local and the national community. Mindful of the
difficulties involved, we decided to undertake a process of self-
purification. We began a series of workshops on nonviolence, and
we repeatedly asked ourselves: "Are you able to accept blows without retaliating?" "Are you able to endure the ordeal of jail?" We decided to schedule our direct-action program for the Easter season,
realizing that except for Christmas, this is the main shopping period

of the year. Knowing that a strong economic-withdrawal program would be the by-product of direct action, we felt that this would be the best time to bring pressure to bear on the merchants for the needed change.

Then it occurred to us that Birmingham's mayoral election was   9
coming up in March, and we speedily decided to postpone action until after election day. When we discovered that the Commissioner of Public Safety, Eugene "Bull" Connor, had piled up enough votes to be in the run-off, we decided again to postpone action until the day after the run-off so that the demonstrations could not be used to cloud the issues. Like many others, we waited to see Mr. Connor defeated, and to this end we endured postponement after postponement. Having aided in this community need, we felt that our direct-action program could be delayed no longer.

You may well ask, "Why direct action? Why sit-ins, marches,   10
and so forth? Isn't negotiation a better path?" You are quite right in calling for negotiation. Indeed, this is the very purpose of direct action. Nonviolent direct action seeks to create such a crisis and foster such a tension that a community which has constantly refused to negotiate is forced to confront the issue. It seeks so to dramatize the issue that it can no longer be ignored. My citing the creation of tension as part of the work of the nonviolent resister may sound rather shocking. But I must confess that I am not afraid of the word "tension." I have earnestly opposed violent tension, but there is a type of constructive, nonviolent tension which is necessary for growth. Just as Socrates[4] felt that it was necessary to create a tension in the mind so that individuals could rise from the bondage of myths and half truths to the unfettered realm of creative analysis and objective appraisal, so must we see the need for nonviolent gadflies to create the kind of tension in society that will help men rise from the dark depths of prejudice and racism to the majestic heights of understanding and brotherhood.

The purpose of our direct-action program is to create a situation   11
so crisis-packed that it will inevitably open the door to negotiation. I therefore concur with you in your call for negotiation. Too long has our beloved Southland been bogged down in a tragic effort to live in monologue rather than dialogue.

---

[4] **Socrates (470?–399 B.C.)** The "tension in the mind" King refers to is created by the question-answer technique known as the Socratic method. By posing questions in the beginning of the paragraph, King shows his willingness to share Socrates' rhetorical techniques. Socrates was imprisoned and killed for his civil disobedience (see para. 21). He was the greatest of the Greek philosophers.

One of the basic points in your statement is that the action that I   12
and my associates have taken in Birmingham is untimely. Some have
asked: "Why didn't you give the new city administration time to
act?" The only answer that I can give to this query is that the new
Birmingham administration must be prodded about as much as the
outgoing one, before it will act. We are sadly mistaken if we feel that
the election of Albert Boutwell as mayor will bring the millennium[5]
to Birmingham. While Mr. Boutwell is a much more gentle person
than Mr. Connor, they are both segregationists, dedicated to maintenance of the status quo. I have hoped that Mr. Boutwell will be reasonable enough to see the futility of massive resistance to desegregation. But he will not see this without pressure from devotees of civil
rights. My friends, I must say to you that we have not made a single
gain in civil rights without determined legal and nonviolent pressure. Lamentably, it is an historical fact that privileged groups seldom give up their privileges voluntarily. Individuals may see the
moral light and voluntarily give up their unjust posture; but, as
Reinhold Niebuhr[6] has reminded us, groups tend to be more immoral than individuals.

We know through painful experience that freedom is never vol-   13
untarily given by the oppressor; it must be demanded by the oppressed. Frankly, I have yet to engage in a direct-action campaign
that was "well timed" in the view of those who have not suffered unduly from the disease of segregation. For years now I have heard the
word "Wait!" It rings in the ear of every Negro with piercing familiarity. This "Wait" has almost always meant "Never." We must come
to see, with one of our distinguished jurists, that "justice too long
delayed is justice denied."[7]

We have waited for more than 340 years for our constitutional and   14
God-given rights. The nations of Asia and Africa are moving with jet-
like speed toward gaining political independence, but we still creep at
horse-and-buggy pace toward gaining a cup of coffee at a lunch

---

[5] **the millennium** A reference to Revelation 20, according to which the second
coming of Christ will be followed by one thousand years of peace, when the devil
will be incapacitated. After this will come a final battle between good and evil, followed by the Last Judgment.

[6] **Reinhold Niebuhr (1892–1971)** Protestant American philosopher who
urged church members to put their beliefs into action against social injustice. He
urged Protestantism to develop and practice a code of social ethics and wrote in
Moral Man and Immoral Society (1932) of the point King mentions here.

[7] **"justice too long delayed is justice denied"** Chief Justice Earl Warren's
expression in 1954 was adapted from English writer Walter Savage Landor's phrase
"Justice delayed is justice denied."

counter. Perhaps it is easy for those who have never felt the stinging darts of segregation to say, "Wait." But when you have seen vicious mobs lynch your mothers and fathers at will and drown your sisters and brothers at whim; when you have seen hate-filled policemen curse, kick, and even kill your black brothers and sisters; when you see the vast majority of your twenty million Negro brothers smothering in an airtight cage of poverty in the midst of an affluent society; when you suddenly find your tongue twisted and your speech stammering as you seek to explain to your six-year-old daughter why she can't go to the public amusement park that has just been advertised on television, and see tears welling up in her eyes when she is told that Funtown is closed to colored children, and see ominous clouds of inferiority beginning to form in her little mental sky, and see her beginning to distort her personality by developing an unconscious bitterness toward white people; when you have to concoct an answer for a five-year-old son who is asking, "Daddy, why do white people treat colored people so mean?"; when you take a cross-country drive and find it necessary to sleep night after night in the uncomfortable corners of your automobile because no motel will accept you; when you are humiliated day in and day out by nagging signs reading "white" and "colored"; when your first name becomes "nigger," your middle name becomes "boy" (however old you are) and your last name becomes "John," and your wife and mother are never given the respected title "Mrs."; when you are harried by day and haunted by night by the fact that you are a Negro, living constantly at tiptoe stance, never quite knowing what to expect next, and are plagued with inner fears and outer resentments; when you are forever fighting a degenerating sense of "nobodiness"—then you will understand why we find it difficult to wait. There comes a time when the cup of endurance runs over, and men are no longer willing to be plunged into the abyss of despair. I hope, sirs, you can understand our legitimate and unavoidable impatience.

You express a great deal of anxiety over our willingness to break   15
laws. This is certainly a legitimate concern. Since we so diligently urge people to obey the Supreme Court's decision of 1954 outlawing segregation in the public schools, at first glance it may seem rather paradoxical for us consciously to break laws. One may well ask: "How can you advocate breaking some laws and obeying others?" The answer lies in the fact that there are two types of laws: just and unjust. I would be the first to advocate obeying just laws. One has not only a legal but a moral responsibility to obey just laws. Conversely, one has a moral responsibility to disobey unjust laws. I would agree with St. Augustine[8] that "an unjust law is no law at all."

[8] **St. Augustine (354–430)** Early bishop of the Christian Church who deeply influenced the spirit of Christianity for many centuries.

Now, what is the difference between the two? How does one de-   16
termine whether a law is just or unjust? A just law is a manmade
code that squares with the moral law or the law of God. An unjust
law is a code that is out of harmony with the moral law. To put it in
the terms of St. Thomas Aquinas:[9] An unjust law is a human law
that is not rooted in eternal law and natural law. Any law that uplifts
human personality is just. Any law that degrades human personality
is unjust. All segregation statutes are unjust because segregation distorts the soul and damages the personality. It gives the segregator a
false sense of superiority and the segregated a false sense of inferiority. Segregation, to use the terminology of the Jewish philosopher
Martin Buber,[10] substitutes an "I-it" relationship for an "I-thou" relationship and ends up relegating persons to the status of things.
Hence segregation is not only politically, economically, and socio-
logically unsound, it is morally wrong and sinful. Paul Tillich[11] has
said that sin is separation. Is not segregation an existential expression of man's tragic separation, his awful estrangement, his terrible
sinfulness? Thus it is that I can urge men to obey the 1954 decision
of the Supreme Court, for it is morally right; and I can urge them to
disobey segregation ordinances, for they are morally wrong.

Let us consider a more concrete example of just and unjust   17
laws. An unjust law is a code that a numerical or power majority
group compels a minority group to obey but does not make binding
on itself. This is *difference* made legal. By the same token, a just law
is a code that a majority compels a minority to follow and that it is
willing to follow itself. This is *sameness* made legal.

Let me give another explanation. A law is unjust if it is inflicted   18
on a minority that, as a result of being denied the right to vote, had
no part in enacting or devising the law. Who can say that the legislature of Alabama which set up that state's segregation laws was democratically elected? Throughout Alabama all sorts of devious methods are used to prevent Negroes from becoming registered voters,
and there are some counties in which, even though Negroes constitute a majority of the population, not a single Negro is registered.

---

[9] **St. Thomas Aquinas (1225–1274)** The greatest of the medieval Christian
philosophers and one of the greatest church authorities.

[10] **Martin Buber (1878–1965)** Jewish theologian. *I and Thou* (1923) is his
most famous book.

[11] **Paul Tillich (1886–1965)** An important twentieth-century Protestant theologian who held that Christianity was reasonable and effective in modern life.
Tillich saw sin as an expression of man's separation from God, from himself, and
from his fellow man. King sees the separation of the races as a further manifestation
of man's sinfulness. Tillich, who was driven out of Germany by the Nazis, stresses
the need for activism and the importance of action in determining moral vitality, just
as King does.

Can any law enacted under such circumstances be considered democratically structured?

Sometimes a law is just on its face and unjust in its application. 19
For instance, I have been arrested on a charge of parading without a permit. Now, there is nothing wrong in having an ordinance which requires a permit for a parade. But such an ordinance becomes unjust when it is used to maintain segregation and to deny citizens the First Amendment privilege of peaceful assembly and protest.

I hope you are able to see the distinction I am trying to point 20
out. In no sense do I advocate evading or defying the law, as would the rabid segregationist. That would lead to anarchy. One who breaks an unjust law must do so openly, lovingly, and with a willingness to accept the penalty. I submit that an individual who breaks a law that conscience tells him is unjust, and who willingly accepts the penalty of imprisonment in order to arouse the conscience of the community over its injustice, is in reality expressing the highest respect for law.

Of course, there is nothing new about this kind of civil disobe- 21
dience. It was evidenced subliminally in the refusal of Shadrach, Meshach, and Abednego to obey the laws of Nebuchadnezzar,[12] on the ground that a higher moral law was at stake. It was practiced superbly by the early Christians, who were willing to face hungry lions and the excruciating pain of chopping blocks rather than submit to certain unjust laws of the Roman Empire. To a degree, academic freedom is a reality today because Socrates practiced civil disobedience. In our own nation, the Boston Tea Party represented a massive act of civil disobedience.

We should never forget that everything Adolf Hitler did in Ger- 22
many was "legal" and everything the Hungarian freedom fighters[13] did in Hungary was "illegal." It was "illegal" to aid and comfort a Jew in Hitler's Germany. Even so, I am sure that, had I lived in Germany at the time, I would have aided and comforted my Jewish brothers. If today I lived in a Communist country where certain principles dear to the Christian faith are suppressed, I would openly advocate disobeying that country's antireligious laws.

---

[12] **Nebuchadnezzar (c. 630–562 B.C.)** Chaldean king who twice attacked Jerusalem. He ordered Shadrach, Meshach, and Abednego to worship a golden image. They refused, were cast into a roaring furnace, and were saved by God (see Daniel 1:7–3:30).

[13] **Hungarian freedom fighters** The Hungarians rose in revolt against Soviet rule in 1956. Russian tanks put down the uprising with great force that shocked the world. Many freedom fighters died, and many others escaped to the West.

I must make two honest confessions to you, my Christian and   23
Jewish brothers. First, I must confess that over the past few years I
have been gravely disappointed with the white moderate. I have almost reached the regrettable conclusion that the Negro's great stum-
bling block in his stride toward freedom is not the White Citizen's
Counciler[14] or the Ku Klux Klanner, but the white moderate, who is
more devoted to "order" than to justice; who prefers a negative
peace which is the absence of tension to a positive peace which is
the presence of justice; who constantly says, "I agree with you in the
goal you seek, but I cannot agree with your methods of direct action"; who paternalistically believes he can set the timetable for another man's freedom; who lives by a mythical concept of time and
who constantly advises the Negro to wait for a "more convenient
season." Shallow understanding from people of good will is more
frustrating than absolute misunderstanding from people of ill will.
Lukewarm acceptance is much more bewildering than outright
rejection.

I had hoped that the white moderate would understand that law   24
and order exist for the purpose of establishing justice and that when
they fail in this purpose they become the dangerously structured
dams that block the flow of social progress. I had hoped that the
white moderate would understand that the present tension in the
South is a necessary phase of the transition from an obnoxious negative peace, in which the Negro passively accepted his unjust plight,
to a substantive and positive peace, in which all men will respect the
dignity and worth of human personality. Actually, we who engage in
nonviolent direct action are not the creators of tension. We merely
bring to the surface the hidden tension that is already alive. We
bring it out in the open, where it can be seen and dealt with. Like a
boil that can never be cured so long as it is covered up but must be
opened with all its ugliness to the natural medicines of air and light,
injustice must be exposed, with all the tension its exposure creates,
to the light of human conscience and the air of national opinion, before it can be cured.

In your statement you assert that our actions, even though   25
peaceful, must be condemned because they precipitate violence. But
is this a logical assertion? Isn't this like condemning a robbed man
because his possession of money precipitated the evil act of robbery?

---

[14] **White Citizen's Counciler** White Citizen's Councils organized in southern
states in 1954 to fight school desegregation as ordered by the Supreme Court in May
1954. The councils were not as secret or violent as the Klan; they were also ineffective.

Isn't this like condemning Socrates because his unswerving commitment to truth and his philosophical inquiries precipitated the act by the misguided populace in which they made him drink hemlock? Isn't this like condemning Jesus because his unique God-consciousness and never-ceasing devotion to God's will precipitated the evil act of crucifixion? We must come to see that, as the federal courts have consistently affirmed, it is wrong to urge an individual to cease his efforts to gain his basic constitutional rights because the quest may precipitate violence. Society must protect the robbed and punish the robber.

I had also hoped that the white moderate would reject the myth   26
concerning time in relation to the struggle for freedom. I have just received a letter from a white brother in Texas. He writes: "All Christians know that the colored people will receive equal rights eventually, but it is possible that you are in too great a religious hurry. It has taken Christianity almost two thousand years to accomplish what it has. The teachings of Christ take time to come to earth." Such an attitude stems from a tragic misconception of time, from the strangely irrational notion that there is something in the very flow of time that will inevitably cure all ills. Actually, time itself is neutral; it can be used either destructively or constructively. More and more I feel that the people of ill will have used time much more effectively than have the people of good will. We will have to repent in this generation not merely for the hateful words and actions of the bad people, but for the appalling silence of the good people. Human progress never rolls in on wheels of inevitability; it comes through the tireless efforts of men willing to be co-workers with God, and without this hard work, time itself becomes an ally of the forces of social stagnation. We must use time creatively, in the knowledge that the time is always ripe to do right. Now is the time to make real the promise of democracy and transform our pending national elegy into a creative psalm of brotherhood. Now is the time to lift our national policy from the quicksand of racial injustice to the solid rock of human dignity.

You speak of our activity in Birmingham as extreme. At first I   27
was rather disappointed that fellow clergymen would see my nonviolent efforts as those of an extremist. I began thinking about the fact that I stand in the middle of two opposing forces in the Negro community. One is a force of complacency, made up in part of Negroes who, as a result of long years of oppression, are so drained of self-respect and a sense of "somebodiness" that they have adjusted to segregation; and in part of a few middle-class Negroes who, because of a degree of academic and economic security and because in some ways they profit by segregation, have become insensitive to the

problems of the masses. The other force is one of bitterness and hatred, and it comes perilously close to advocating violence. It is expressed in the various black nationalist groups that are springing up across the nation, the largest and best known being Elijah Muhammad's Muslim movement.[15] Nourished by the Negro's frustration over the continued existence of racial discrimination, this movement is made up of people who have lost faith in America, who have absolutely repudiated Christianity, and who have concluded that the white man is an incorrigible "devil."

28   I have tried to stand between these two forces, saying that we need emulate neither the "do-nothingism" of the complacent nor the hatred and despair of the black nationalist. For there is the more excellent way of love and nonviolent protest. I am grateful to God that, through the influence of the Negro church, the way of nonviolence became an integral part of our struggle.

29   If this philosophy had not emerged, by now many streets of the South would, I am convinced, be flowing with blood. And I am further convinced that if our white brothers dismiss as "rabble-rousers" and "outside agitators" those of us who employ nonviolent direct action, and if they refuse to support our nonviolent efforts, millions of Negroes will, out of frustration and despair, seek solace and security in black nationalist ideologies—a development that would inevitably lead to a frightening racial nightmare.[16]

30   Oppressed people cannot remain oppressed forever. The yearning for freedom eventually manifests itself, and that is what has happened to the American Negro. Something within has reminded him of his birthright of freedom, and something without has reminded him that it can be gained. Consciously or unconsciously, he has been caught up by the *Zeitgeist*,[17] and with his black brothers of Africa and his brown and yellow brothers of Asia, South America, and the Caribbean, the United States Negro is moving with a sense of great urgency toward the promised land of racial justice. If one

---

[15] **Elijah Muhammad's Muslim movement** The Black Muslim movement, which began in the 1920s but flourished in the 1960s under its leader, Elijah Muhammad (1897–1975). Among notable figures who became Black Muslims were the poet Imamu Amiri Baraka (b. 1934), the world championship prizefighter Muhammad Ali (b. 1942), and the controversial reformer and religious leader Malcolm X (1925–1965). King saw their rejection of white society (and consequently brotherhood) as a threat.

[16] **a frightening racial nightmare** The black uprisings of the 1960s in all major American cities, and the conditions that led to them, were indeed a racial nightmare. King's prophecy was quick to come true.

[17] *Zeitgeist* German word for the intellectual, moral, and cultural spirit of the times.

recognizes this vital urge that has engulfed the Negro community, one should readily understand why public demonstrations are taking place. The Negro has many pent-up resentments and latent frustrations, and he must release them. So let him march; let him make prayer pilgrimages to the city hall; let him go on freedom rides[18]— and try to understand why he must do so. If his repressed emotions are not released in nonviolent ways, they will seek expression through violence; this is not a threat but a fact of history. So I have not said to my people, "Get rid of your discontent." Rather, I have tried to say that this normal and healthy discontent can be channeled into the creative outlet of nonviolent direct action. And now this approach is being termed extremist.

But though I was initially disappointed at being categorized as   31 an extremist, as I continued to think about the matter I gradually gained a measure of satisfaction from the label. Was not Jesus an extremist for love: "Love your enemies, bless them that curse you, do good to them that hate you, and pray for them which despitefully use you, and persecute you." Was not Amos an extremist for justice: "Let justice roll down like waters and righteousness like an everflowing stream." Was not Paul an extremist for the Christian gospel: "I bear in my body the marks of the Lord Jesus." Was not Martin Luther an extremist: "Here I stand; I cannot do otherwise, so help me God." And John Bunyan: "I will stay in jail to the end of my days before I make a butchery of my conscience." And Abraham Lincoln: "This nation cannot survive half slave and half free." And Thomas Jefferson: "We hold these truths to be self-evident, that all men are created equal..."[19] So the question is not whether we will be extremists, but what kind of extremists we will be. Will we be extremists for hate or for love? Will we be extremists for the preservation of injustice or for the extension of justice? In that dramatic scene on Calvary's hill three men were crucified. We must never forget that all three were crucified for the same crime—the crime of extrem-

---

[18] **freedom rides** In 1961 the Congress of Racial Equality (CORE) organized rides of whites and blacks to test segregation in southern buses and bus terminals with interstate passengers. More than 600 federal marshals were needed to protect the riders, most of whom were arrested.

[19] **Amos, Old Testament prophet (eighth century B.C.); Paul (?–A.D. 67); Martin Luther (1483–1546); John Bunyan (1628–1688); Abraham Lincoln (1809–1865); and Thomas Jefferson (1743–1826)** These figures are all noted for religious, moral, or political innovations that changed the world. Amos was a prophet who favored social justice; Paul argued against Roman law; Luther began the Reformation of the Christian Church; Bunyan was imprisoned for preaching the gospel according to his own understanding; Lincoln freed America's slaves; Jefferson drafted the Declaration of Independence.

ism. Two were extremists for immorality, and thus fell below their environment. The other, Jesus Christ, was an extremist for love, truth, and goodness, and thereby rose above his environment. Perhaps the South, the nation, and the world are in dire need of creative extremists.

I had hoped that the white moderate would see this need. Perhaps 32 I was too optimistic; perhaps I expected too much. I suppose I should have realized that few members of the oppressor race can understand the deep groans and passionate yearnings of the oppressed race, and still fewer have the vision to see that injustice must be rooted out by strong, persistent, and determined action. I am thankful, however, that some of our white brothers in the South have grasped the meaning of this social revolution and committed themselves to it. They are still all too few in quantity, but they are big in quality. Some — such as Ralph McGill, Lillian Smith, Harry Golden, James McBride Dabbs, Ann Braden, and Sarah Patton Boyle — have written about our struggle[20] in eloquent and prophetic terms. Others have marched with us down nameless streets of the South. They have languished in filthy, roach-infested jails, suffering the abuse and brutality of policemen who view them as "dirty nigger-lovers." Unlike so many of their moderate brothers and sisters, they have recognized the urgency of the moment and sensed the need for powerful "action" antidotes to combat the disease of segregation.

Let me take note of my other major disappointment. I have been 33 so greatly disappointed with the white church and its leadership. Of course, there are some notable exceptions. I am not unmindful of the fact that each of you has taken some significant stands on this issue. I commend you, Reverend Stallings, for your Christian stand on this past Sunday, in welcoming Negroes to your worship service on a nonsegregated basis. I commend the Catholic leaders of this state for integrating Spring Hill College several years ago.

But despite these notable exceptions, I must honestly reiterate 34 that I have been disappointed with the church. I do not say this as one of those negative critics who can always find something wrong with the church. I say this as a minister of the gospel, who loves the church; who was nurtured in its bosom; who has been sustained by its spiritual blessings and who will remain true to it as long as the cord of life shall lengthen.

---

[20]**written about our struggle** These are all prominent southern writers who expressed their feelings regarding segregation in the South. Some of them, like Smith and Golden, wrote very popular books with a wide influence. Some, like McGill and Smith, were severely rebuked by white southerners.

When I was suddenly catapulted into the leadership of the bus   35
protest in Montgomery, Alabama, a few years ago, I felt we would be
supported by the white church. I felt that the white ministers,
priests, and rabbis of the South would be among our strongest allies.
Instead, some have been outright opponents, refusing to understand
the freedom movement and misrepresenting its leaders; all too many
others have been more cautious than courageous and have remained
silent behind the anesthetizing security of stained-glass windows.

   In spite of my shattered dreams, I came to Birmingham with the   36
hope that the white religious leadership of this community would
see the justice of our cause and, with deep moral concern, would
serve as the channel through which our just grievances could reach
the power structure. I had hoped that each of you would understand. But again I have been disappointed. . . .

   There was a time when the church was very powerful—in the   37
time when the early Christians rejoiced at being deemed worthy to
suffer for what they believed. In those days the church was not
merely a thermometer that recorded the ideas and principles of popular opinion; it was a thermostat that transformed the mores of society. Whenever the early Christians entered a town, the people in
power became disturbed and immediately sought to convict the
Christians for being "disturbers of the peace" and "outside agitators."
But the Christians pressed on, in the conviction that they were
"a colony of heaven," called to obey God rather than man. Small
in number, they were big in commitment. They were too God-
intoxicated to be "astronomically intimidated." By their effort and
example they brought an end to such ancient evils as infanticide and
gladiatorial contests.

   Things are different now. So often the contemporary church is a   38
weak, ineffectual voice with an uncertain sound. So often it is an
archdefender of the status quo. Far from being disturbed by the
presence of the church, the powerful structure of the average community is consoled by the church's silent—and often even vocal—
sanction of things as they are.

   But the judgment of God is upon the church as never before. If   39
today's church does not recapture the sacrificial spirit of the early
church, it will lose its authenticity, forfeit the loyalty of millions, and
be dismissed as an irrelevant social club with no meaning for the
twentieth century. Every day I meet young people whose disappointment with the church has turned into outright disgust.

   Perhaps I have once again been too optimistic. Is organized reli-   40
gion too inextricably bound to the status quo to save our nation and
the world? Perhaps I must turn my faith to the inner spiritual

church, the church within the church, as the true *ekklesia*[21] and the hope of the world. But again I am thankful to God that some noble souls from the ranks of organized religion have broken loose from the paralyzing chains of conformity and joined us as active partners in the struggle for freedom. They have left their secure congregations and walked the streets of Albany, Georgia, with us. They have gone down the highways of the South on torturous rides for freedom. Yes, they have gone to jail with us. Some have been dismissed from their churches, have lost the support of their bishops and fellow ministers. But they have acted in the faith that right defeated is stronger than evil triumphant. Their witness has been the spiritual salt that has preserved the true meaning of the gospel in these troubled times. They have carved a tunnel of hope through the dark mountain of disappointment.

I hope the church as a whole will meet the challenge of this decisive hour. But even if the church does not come to the aid of justice, I have no despair about the future. I have no fear about the outcome of our struggle in Birmingham, even if our motives are at present misunderstood. We will reach the goal of freedom in Birmingham and all over the nation, because the goal of America is freedom. Abused and scorned though we may be, our destiny is tied up with America's destiny. Before the pilgrims landed at Plymouth, we were here. Before the pen of Jefferson etched the majestic words of the Declaration of Independence across the pages of history, we were here. For more than two centuries our forebears labored in this country without wages; they made cotton king; they built the homes of their masters while suffering gross injustice and shameful humiliation—and yet out of a bottomless vitality they continued to thrive and develop. If the inexpressible cruelties of slavery could not stop us, the opposition we now face will surely fail. We will win our freedom because the sacred heritage of our nation and the eternal will of God are embodied in our echoing demands.   41

Before closing I feel impelled to mention one other point in your statement that has troubled me profoundly. You warmly commended the Birmingham police force for keeping "order" and "preventing violence." I doubt that you would have so warmly commended the police force if you had seen its dogs sinking their teeth into unarmed, nonviolent Negroes. I doubt that you would so quickly commend the policemen if you were to observe their ugly   42

---

[21] **ekklesia** Greek word for "church" meaning not just the institution but the spirit of the church.

and inhumane treatment of Negroes here in the city jail; if you were to watch them push and curse old Negro women and young Negro girls; if you were to see them slap and kick old Negro men and young boys; if you were to observe them, as they did on two occasions, refuse to give us food because we wanted to sing our grace together. I cannot join you in your praise of the Birmingham police department.

It is true that the police have exercised a degree of discipline in handling the demonstrators. In this sense they have conducted themselves rather "nonviolently" in public. But for what purpose? To preserve the evil system of segregation. Over the past few years I have consistently preached that nonviolence demands that the means we use must be as pure as the ends we seek. I have tried to make clear that it is wrong to use immoral means to attain moral ends. But now I must affirm that it is just as wrong, or perhaps even more so, to use moral means to preserve immoral ends. Perhaps Mr. Connor and his policemen have been rather nonviolent in public, as was Chief Pritchett in Albany, Georgia, but they have used the moral means of nonviolence to maintain the immoral end of racial injustice. As T. S. Eliot[22] has said, "The last temptation is the greatest treason: To do the right deed for the wrong reason."

I wish you had commended the Negro sit-inners and demonstrators of Birmingham for their sublime courage, their willingness to suffer, and their amazing discipline in the midst of great provocation. One day the South will recognize its real heroes. They will be the James Merediths,[23] with the noble sense of purpose that enables them to face jeering and hostile mobs, and with the agonizing loneliness that characterizes the life of the pioneer. They will be old, oppressed, battered Negro women, symbolized in a seventy-two-year-old woman in Montgomery, Alabama, who rose up with a sense of dignity and with her people decided not to ride segregated buses, and who responded with ungrammatical profundity to one who inquired about her weariness: "My feets is tired, but my soul is at rest."

43

44

---

[22]**Thomas Stearns Eliot (1888–1965)** Renowned as one of the twentieth century's major poets, Eliot was born in the United States but in 1927 became a British subject and a member of the Church of England. Many of his poems focused on religious and moral themes. These lines are from Eliot's play *Murder in the Cathedral,* about Saint Thomas à Becket (1118–1170), the archbishop of Canterbury, who was martyred for his opposition to King Henry II.

[23]**the James Merediths** James Meredith (b. 1933) was the first black to become a student at the University of Mississippi. His attempt to register for classes in 1962 created the first important confrontation between federal and state authorities, when Governor Ross Barnett personally blocked Meredith's entry to the university. Meredith graduated in 1963 and went on to study law at Columbia University.

They will be the young high school and college students, the young ministers of the gospel and a host of their elders, courageously and nonviolently sitting in at lunch counters and willingly going to jail for conscience' sake. One day the South will know that when these disinherited children of God sat down at lunch counters, they were in reality standing up for what is best in the American dream and for the most sacred values in our Judaeo-Christian heritage, thereby bringing our nation back to those great wells of democracy which were dug deep by the founding fathers in their formulation of the Constitution and the Declaration of Independence.

Never before have I written so long a letter. I'm afraid it is much too long to take your precious time. I can assure you that it would have been much shorter if I had been writing from a comfortable desk, but what else can one do when he is alone in a narrow jail cell, other than write long letters, think long thoughts, and pray long prayers?   45

If I have said anything in this letter that overstates the truth and indicates an unreasonable impatience, I beg you to forgive me. If I have said anything that understates the truth and indicates my having a patience that allows me to settle for anything less than brotherhood, I beg God to forgive me.   46

I hope this letter finds you strong in the faith. I also hope that circumstances will soon make it possible for me to meet each of you, not as an integrationist or a civil rights leader but as a fellow clergyman and a Christian brother. Let us all hope that the dark clouds of racial prejudice will soon pass away and the deep fog of misunderstanding will be lifted from our fear-drenched communities, and in some not too distant tomorrow the radiant stars of love and brotherhood will shine over our great nation with all their scintillating beauty.   47

> Yours in the cause of
> Peace and Brotherhood,
> MARTIN LUTHER KING, JR.

QUESTIONS FOR CRITICAL READING

1. Define "nonviolent direct action" (para. 2). In what areas of human experience is it best implemented? Is politics its best area of application? What are the four steps in a nonviolent campaign?
2. Do you agree that "law and order exist for the purpose of establishing justice" (para. 24)? Why? Describe how law and order either do or do not establish justice in your community. Compare notes with your peers.

3. King describes an unjust law as "a code that a numerical or power majority group compels a minority group to obey but does not make binding on itself" (para. 17). Devise one or two other definitions of an unjust law. What unjust laws currently on the books do you disagree with?

4. What do you think is the best-written paragraph in the essay? Why?

5. King cites "tension" in paragraph 10 and elsewhere as a beneficial force. Do you agree? What kind of tension does he mean?

6. In what ways was King an extremist (paras. 30–31)?

7. In his letter, to what extent does King consider the needs of women? Would he feel that issues of women's rights are unrelated to issues of racial equality?

8. According to King, how should a government function in relation to the needs of the individual? Does he feel, like Thoreau's "Chinese philosopher," that the empire is built on the individual?

SUGGESTIONS FOR WRITING

1. Write a brief letter protesting an injustice that you feel may not be entirely understood by people you respect. Clarify the nature of the injustice, the reasons that people hold an unjust view, and the reasons your views should be accepted. Consult King's letter, and use his techniques.

2. In paragraph 43, King says, "I have consistently preached that nonviolence demands that the means we use must be as pure as the ends we seek." What does he mean by this? Define the ends he seeks and the means he approves. Do you agree with him on this point? If you have read the selection from Machiavelli, contrast their respective views. Which view seems more reasonable to you?

3. The first part of the letter defends King's journey to Birmingham as a Christian to help his fellows gain justice. He challenges the view that he is an outsider, using such expressions as "network of mutuality" and "garment of destiny" (para. 4). How effective is his argument? Examine the letter for other expressions that justify King's intervention on behalf of his brothers and sisters. Using his logic, describe other social areas where you might be justified in acting on your own views on behalf of humanity. Do you expect your endeavors would be welcomed? Are there any areas where you think it would be wrong to intervene?

4. In paragraphs 15–22, King discusses two kinds of laws—those that are morally right and those that are morally wrong. Which laws did King regard as morally right? Which laws did he consider morally wrong? Analyze one or two current laws that you feel are morally wrong. Be sure to be fair in describing the laws and establishing their nature. Then explain why you feel they are morally wrong. Would you

feel justified in breaking these laws? Would you feel prepared, as King was, to pay the penalties demanded of one who breaks the law?

5. Compare King's letter with sections of Paul's letters to the faithful in the New Testament. Either choose a single letter, such as the Epistle to the Romans, or select passages from Romans, the two letters to the Corinthians, the Galatians, the Ephesians, the Thessalonians, or the Philippians. How did Paul and King agree and disagree about brotherly love, the mission of Christ, the mission of the church, concern for the law, and the duties of the faithful? Inventory the New Testament letters and King's letter carefully for concrete evidence of similar or contrary positions.

6. **CONNECTIONS**   To what extent do Martin Luther King Jr.'s views about government coincide with those of Lao-tzu? Is there a legitimate comparison to be made between King's policy of nonviolent resistance and Lao-tzu's judicious inactivity? To what extent would King have agreed with Lao-tzu's views? Would Lao-tzu have supported King's position in his letter, or would he have interpreted events differently?

7. **CONNECTIONS**   King cites conscience as a guide to obeying just laws and defying unjust laws. How close is his position to that of Thoreau? Do you think that he had read Thoreau's "Civil Disobedience" as an important document regarding justice and injustice? Compare and contrast the positions of these two writers.

PART THREE

WEALTH AND POVERTY

Adam Smith
Karl Marx
John Kenneth Galbraith
Milton and Rose Friedman
Robert B. Reich

INTRODUCTION

Ancient writers talk about wealth in terms of a surplus of necessary or desirable goods and products. After the invention of coins—which historians attribute to the Lydians, whose civilization flourished in the eastern Mediterranean region from 800 to 200 B.C.—wealth also became associated with money. However, the relationship of wealth to money has long been debated. According to Aristotle, people misunderstand wealth when they think of it as "only a quantity of coin." For him, money was useful primarily as a means of representing and purchasing goods but was not sustaining in and of itself.

Writers like Aristotle have argued that wealth benefits the state by ensuring stability, growth, security, and cultural innovations and that it benefits the individual by providing leisure time, mobility, and luxury. Most societies, however, have struggled with the problems caused by unequal distribution of wealth, either among individuals or between citizens and the state. The Spartan leader Lycurgus is said to have tackled the problem in the ninth century B.C. by convincing the inhabitants of the Greek city-state of Sparta that they needed to redistribute their wealth. Land and household goods were redistributed among the citizens, and Lycurgus was hailed as a hero. However, Lycurgus's model has not been the norm in subsequent civilizations, and questions about the nature of wealth and its role and distribution in society have persisted.

The selections in this section present ideas on wealth and poverty from a variety of perspectives. Adam Smith begins by tracing the natural evolution of wealth from farming to trade. Karl Marx expounds on what he feels are the corrosive effects of excessive wealth on the individual and on the problems caused by unequal distribution of wealth between laborers and business owners. Milton and Rose Friedman discuss the relationships they see between equality of opportunity and freedom. For them, any restriction on opportunity and individualism represents a move toward the kinds of limitation on freedom that were typical in Communist countries before the collapse of the Soviet Union. John Kenneth Galbraith and Robert B. Reich further investigate the problems that an unequal distribution of wealth poses for society as a whole.

Adam Smith was known originally as a moral philosopher with a professorship at Glasgow, but he wrote at a time of extraordinary expansion in Great Britain. As industrial power grew in the late eighteenth century, England became more wealthy and began to dominate trade in important areas of commerce. In his own mind, Smith's interest in wealth may have been connected with his studies in morality, or it may have grown from his considerable curiosity about a broad range of subjects. Regardless, he produced one of the century's most important and extensive books on economics, *The Wealth of Nations*. It is still consulted by economists today.

Smith's "Of the Natural Progress of Opulence" is an attempt to understand the "natural" steps to wealth. Smith posits an interesting relationship between the country, where food and plants, such as cotton and flax, supply the necessities of life, and the city, which produces no food but takes the surplus from the country and turns it into manufactured goods. Smith's ideas concerning this process center on surplus. The farmers produce more than they can consume, and therefore they can market their goods to the city. The city takes some of the goods from the farmers and turns them into manufactured products, which can be sold back to the people in the country. When there is a surplus of manufactured goods, they can be sold abroad. That process can produce wealth—on a grand scale.

Karl Marx's *Communist Manifesto* clarifies the relationship between a people's condition and the economic system in which they live. Marx saw that capitalism provided opportunities for the wealthy and powerful to take advantage of labor. He argued that because labor cannot efficiently sell its product, management can keep labor in perpetual economic bondage.

Marx knew poverty firsthand, but one of his close associates, Friedrich Engels, who collaborated on portions of the *Manifesto,* was the son of a factory owner and so was able to observe closely how the rich can oppress the poor. For both of them, the economic system of capitalism produced a class struggle between the rich (bourgeoisie) and the laboring classes (proletariat).

John Kenneth Galbraith's selection, "The Position of Poverty," dates from the middle of the twentieth century and addresses an issue that earlier thinkers avoided: the question of poverty. It is not that earlier writers were unaware that poverty existed—most mention it in passing—but their main concern was the accumulation and preservation of wealth. Galbraith, in his study of the economics of contemporary America, also focuses on wealth; the title of his most famous book is *The Affluent Society* (1958; rev. 1998). He, however, points toward something greater than the issue of attaining affluence. His concern is with the allocation of the wealth that American society has produced. His fears that selfishness and waste will dominate the affluent society have led him to write about what he considers the most important social issue related to economics: poverty and its effects. If Smith was correct in seeing wealth as appropriate subject matter for economic study, then Galbraith has pointed to the opposite of wealth as being equally worthy of close examination.

Milton and Rose Friedman are unconcerned with the distinctions of wealth or poverty—at least in the sense that neither economic state commands their attention. Instead, they focus on the efforts of the state that aim to produce what they call equality of outcome. They are fierce believers in equality of opportunity, but they assert that any effort to guarantee an equality of outcome will restrict the freedom of high achievers in a society. For them, equality of outcome means guaranteeing the economic well-being of people who may not have earned it, while restricting the economic well-being of those who have. Indirectly, the Friedmans offer an argument whose outcome would help preserve the wealth of those with unusual talents for business. They see their position as close to Jefferson's and completely opposed to Marx's.

Robert B. Reich, formerly a lecturer at Harvard University until he was appointed secretary of labor in the first Clinton administration, has taught courses in economics and published widely. His 1991 book, *The Work of Nations,* echoes the title of Adam Smith's eighteenth-century masterpiece of capitalist theory, *The Wealth of Nations.* Although Reich's views on labor are distinct from Smith's, his essay focuses on labor with the same intensity Smith brings to money. His views consider how worldwide economic developments will affect labor in the next decades. According to Reich, labor falls into three groups—routine workers, in-person servers, and symbolic analysts—each of which will fare differently in the coming years.

Most of these theorists agree that a healthy economy can relieve the misery and suffering of a population. Most agree that wealth and plenty are preferable to impoverishment and want. But some are also concerned with the effects of materialism and greed on the spiritual life of a nation. Galbraith sees a society with enormous power to bring about positive social change, the capacity to make positive moral decisions. But, for all his optimism, Galbraith reminds us that we have made very little progress in an area of social concern that has been a focus of thought and action for a generation.

ADAM SMITH
Of the Natural Progress of Opulence

ADAM SMITH (1723–1790) was born in Kirkcaldy on the eastern coast of Scotland. He attended Glasgow University and received a degree from Oxford, after which he gave a successful series of lectures on rhetoric in his hometown. This resulted in his appointment as professor of logic at Glasgow in 1751. A year later he moved to a professorship in moral philosophy that had been vacated by Thomas Craggie, one of his former teachers. He held this position for twelve years. Smith's early reputation was built entirely on his work in moral philosophy, which included theology, ethics, justice, and political economy.

In many ways Adam Smith's views are striking in their modernity; in fact, his work continues to inform our understanding of current economic trends. His classic and best-known book, *An Inquiry into the Nature and Causes of the Wealth of Nations* (1776), examines the economic system of the modern nation that has reached, as England had, the commercial level of progress. According to Smith, a nation has to pass through a number of levels of culture — from hunter-gatherer to modern commercial — on its way to becoming modern. In this sense, he was something of an evolutionist in economics.

Wealth of Nations is quite different in both tone and concept from Smith's earlier success, *Theory of Moral Sentiments* (1759). The earlier work postulates a social order based, in part, on altruism — an order in which individuals aid one another — whereas *Wealth of Nations* asserts that the best economic results are obtained when individuals work for their own interests and their own gain. This kind of effort, Smith assures us, results in the general improvement of a society because the industry of the individual

From *An Inquiry into the Nature and Causes of the Wealth of Nations*.

benefits everyone in the nation by producing more wealth; the greater the wealth of the nation, the better the lot of every individual in the nation.

There is no question that Smith was an ardent capitalist who felt an almost messianic need to spread the doctrine of capitalism. He maintained throughout his life that *Wealth of Nations* was one with his writings on moral and social issues and that when his work was complete it would encompass the basic elements of any society.

In "Of the Natural Progress of Opulence," Smith outlines a microcosm of the progress of capitalism as he understood it. His purpose is to establish the steps by which a nation creates its wealth and the steps by which a region becomes wealthy. For the most part, he is interested in the development of capitalism in Great Britain, including his native Scotland. His perspective includes the natural developments that he observed in his own time in the late eighteenth century as well as developments that he could imagine from earlier times. Because he wrote and published his book just before the American Revolution and the subsequent industrial revolution, his primary concerns are farming and agriculture. In earlier sections of *Wealth of Nations,* Smith focused on metal—silver and gold—as a measure of wealth, then later on corn (by which he usually meant wheat or barley) as a measure of wealth. In this selection, he is more emphatic about land as a convenient instrument of wealth.

His primary point is related to what he sees as a natural progression. People in the country have land on which they plant crops, which they sell, in part, to people in the town. The people in the town, lacking land but possessing skills such as weaving, building, and the like, create a market for the goods from the country. They take the product of the land and, with the surplus beyond their daily needs for food and sustenance, manufacture useful goods. In turn, they sell the desirable goods to people in the country, and both manage to accumulate wealth in the process. In this view the manufactures of the town are important but by no means as essential as the food that sustains the nation. Indeed, Smith regards surplus production as the key to the move toward wealth, which accumulates into opulence.

It is interesting that Smith does not emphasize the trade of goods among nations. He does emphasize the fact that the interchange between the country and the town in England also has a counterpart in international trade. However, Smith seems a bit uneasy in contemplating the usefulness of international trade as a means to accumulate wealth. Land, he reminds the reader, is secure, controllable, and not likely to yield to the whimsy of foul winds, leaky ships, or dishonest foreign merchants. One realizes that regardless of what he might say in praise of other possibilities, Smith himself would likely prefer a life in the country on a spread of his own land, collecting rent from tenants who produce food and flax and other goods that help him accumulate wealth.

Smith's Rhetoric

Adam Smith is widely regarded as one of the most influential economic thinkers of the eighteenth century. His *Wealth of Nations* is a gigantic book with many complex arguments regarding the nature of money and the role of capital in trade. This selection is a relatively straightforward statement regarding what he feels is the usual progress that all nations experience in the creation and accumulation of wealth. However, the normal eighteenth-century paragraph is much longer than those of today. By the same token, the normal eighteenth-century sentence is more complex in structure than we are used to today. For that reason, many readers will pause for reflection as they read Smith's work.

Still, his sentences are ultimately clear and direct. His opening sentence, for example, is a mighty declaration: "The great commerce of every civilized society, is that carried on between the inhabitants of the town and those of the country." In this sentence Smith makes a clear pronouncement, a statement about *every* society. Such a sweeping generalization is likely to invite attack and skepticism, but he feels totally secure in his assertion and proceeds to argue his position point by point.

On a more modest note, when Smith says, "Upon equal, or nearly equal profits, most men will chuse to employ their capitals rather in the improvement and cultivation of land, than either in manufactures or in foreign trade" (para. 3), he expects the reader to see the simple wisdom of trusting the land and distrusting instruments of trade. However, many readers—even in his own time—would see this sentence as revealing a personal preference rather than a general rule. Even in the seventeenth century, many merchants were growing rich by ignoring land and trusting trade on the high seas.

Smith's view on this issue reflects an aspect of his conservatism, a stance that remains recognizably conservative even by today's standards. Nevertheless, his principles have guided traders as well as farmers for more than two hundred years. In his time, the workers in agriculture outnumbered workers in manufactures by a factor of eighty or ninety. But today, workers in agriculture have decreased progressively since the industrial revolution. Now, as a result of more efficient farming manufactures, only two or three people out of a hundred work on farms producing food and other goods. It would be interesting to know how Smith might react to this dramatic shift in occupations.

In helping the reader to work through his argument, Smith includes inset "summaries" of the content of each paragraph. For paragraph 2, he includes two insets. The first — *"The cultivation of the country must be prior to the increase of the town,"* — alerts the reader to look for his explanation of why this claim is true. The second inset — *"though the town may sometimes be distant from the country from which it derives its subsistence"* — helps readers focus on the implications of distances from agriculture and manufacture for the local population. Those who grow corn nearest the city will make more money than those who live at a distance and must pay for its transportation to market. It is interesting to note that later ages developed relatively inexpensive means of transport — such as canals and railroads — to even out the cost of carriage in relation to fixed prices.

Smith depends on the clear, step-by-step argument to hold the attention of his reader. He establishes and examines each major point, clarifies his own position, then moves on to the next related point. For example, he talks about nations with uncultivated land, or large areas of land, and how the procedure he outlines works. Then he introduces the situation of a nation that has no uncultivated land available, or land available only at very high cost. Under such circumstances, people will turn to manufacture but not rely on selling their products locally. In those conditions, they will risk foreign sales.

It is also worth noting that when Smith talks about the American colonies, he reminds the reader that there is plenty of land for people to work. As a result, little or no manufacture is produced for sale abroad. He sees this as an indication that the Americans are fiercely independent, demanding land of their own so as to guarantee that they will have adequate sustenance in the future. Throughout the selection Smith establishes a clear sense of the progress of nations toward the accumulation of wealth, and he provides the reader with a blueprint for financial success.

PREREADING QUESTIONS:
WHAT TO READ FOR

The following prereading questions may help you anticipate key issues in the discussion on Adam Smith's "Of the Natural Progress of Opulence." Keeping them in mind during your first reading of the selection should help focus your reactions.

- What is the nature of the commerce between the country and the town?

- What does Smith think is the natural order of things in the development of commerce?

Of the Natural Progress of Opulence

The great commerce is that between town and country, which is obviously advantageous to both.

The great commerce of every civilized society, 1 is that carried on between the inhabitants of the town and those of the country. It consists in the exchange of rude for manufactured produce, either immediately, or by the intervention of money, or of some sort of paper which represents money. The country supplies the town with the means of subsistence, and the materials of manufacture. The town repays this supply by sending back a part of the manufactured produce to the inhabitants of the country. The town, in which there neither is nor can be any reproduction of substances, may very properly be said to gain its whole wealth and subsistence from the country. We must not, however, upon this account, imagine that the gain of the town is the loss of the country. The gains of both are mutual and reciprocal, and the division of labour is in this, as in all other cases, advantageous to all the different persons employed in the various occupations into which it is subdivided. The inhabitants of the country purchase of the town a greater quantity of manufactured goods, with the produce of a much smaller quantity of their own labour, than they must have employed had they attempted to prepare them themselves. The town affords a market for the surplus produce of the country, or what is over and above the maintenance of the cultivators, and it is there that the inhabitants of the country exchange it for something else which is in demand among them. The greater the number and revenue of the inhabitants of the town, the more extensive is the market which it affords to those of the country; and the more extensive that market, it is always the more advantageous to a great number. The corn which grows within a mile of the town, sells there for the same price with that which comes from twenty miles distance. But the price of the latter must generally, not only pay the expence of raising and bringing it to market, but afford too the ordinary profits of agriculture to the farmer. The proprietors and cultivators of the country, therefore, which lies in the neighbourhood of the town, over and above the ordinary profits of agriculture, gain, in the price of what they sell, the whole value of the carriage of the like produce that is brought from more distant parts, and they save, besides, the whole value of this carriage in the price of what they buy. Compare the cultivation of the lands in the neighbourhood of any considerable town, with that of those which lie at some distance from it, and you will easily satisfy yourself how much the country is benefited by the commerce of the town. Among all the absurd speculations that have been propagated concerning the balance of trade, it has never been pretended that either the country loses by its commerce with the town, or the town by that with the country which maintains it.

The cultivation of the country must be prior to the increase of the town,

As subsistence is, in the nature of things, prior 2 to conveniency and luxury, so the industry which procures the former, must necessarily be prior to that which ministers to the latter. The cultivation and improvement of the country, therefore, which affords subsistence, must, necessarily, be prior to the increase of the town, which furnishes only the means of conveniency and luxury. It is the surplus produce of the country only, or what is over and above the maintenance of the cultivators, that constitutes the subsistence of the town, which can therefore increase only with the increase of this surplus produce. The town, indeed, may not always derive its whole subsistence from the country in its neighbourhood, or even from the territory to which it belongs, but from very distant countries; and this, though it forms no exception from the general rule, has occasioned considerable variations in the progress of opulence in different ages and nations.

though the town may sometimes be distant from the country from which it derives its subsistence.

That order of things which necessity imposes 3 in general, though not in every particular country,

This order of things is favoured by the natural preference of man for agriculture.

is, in every particular country, promoted by the natural inclinations of man. If human institutions had never thwarted those natural inclinations, the towns could no-where have increased beyond what the improvement and cultivation of the territory in which they were situated could support; till such time, at least, as the whole of that territory was completely cultivated and improved. Upon equal, or nearly equal profits, most men will chuse to employ their capitals rather in the improvement and cultivation of land, than either in manufactures or in foreign trade. The man who employs his capital in land, has it more under his view and command, and his fortune is much less liable to accidents, than that of the trader, who is obliged frequently to commit it, not only to the winds and the waves, but to the more uncertain elements of human folly and injustice, by giving great credits in distant countries to men, with whose character and situation he can seldom be thoroughly acquainted. The capital of the landlord, on the contrary, which is fixed in the improvement of his land, seems to be as well secured as the nature of human affairs can admit of. The beauty of the country besides, the pleasures of a country life, the tranquillity of mind which it promises, and wherever the injustice of human laws does not disturb it, the independency which it really affords, have charms that more or less attract every body; and as to cultivate the ground was the original destination of man, so in every stage of his existence he seems to retain a predilection for this primitive employment.

Cultivators require the assistance of artificers, who settle together and form a village, and their employment augments with the improvement of the country.

Without the assistance of some artificers, indeed, the cultivation of land cannot be carried on, but with great inconveniency and continual interruption. Smiths, carpenters, wheel-wrights, and plough-wrights, masons, and bricklayers, tanners, shoemakers, and taylors, are people, whose service the farmer has frequent occasion for. Such artificers too stand, occasionally, in need of the assistance of one another; and as their residence is not, like that of the farmer, necessarily tied down to a precise spot, they naturally settle in the neighbourhood of one another, and thus form a small town or village. The butcher, the brewer, and the baker, soon join them, together with many other artificers and retailers, necessary or useful for supplying their occasional wants, and who contribute still further to augment the town. The inhabitants of the town and those of the country are mutually the servants of one another. The town is a continual fair or market, to which the inhabitants of the country resort in order to exchange their rude for manufactured produce. It is this commerce which supplies the inhabitants of the town both with the materials of their work, and the means of their subsistence. The quantity of the finished work which they sell to the inhabitants of the country, necessarily regulates the quantity of the materials and provisions which they buy. Neither their employment nor subsistence, therefore, can augment, but in proportion to the augmentation of the demand from the country for finished work; and this demand can augment only in proportion to the extension of improvement and cultivation. Had human institutions, therefore, never disturbed the natural course of things, the progressive wealth and increase of the towns would, in every political society, be consequential, and in proportion to the improvement and cultivation of the territory or country.

In the American colonies an artificer who has acquired sufficient stock becomes a planter instead of manufacturing for distant sale,

In our North American colonies, where uncultivated land is still to be had upon easy terms, no manufactures for distant sale have ever yet been established in any of their towns. When an artificer has acquired a little more stock than is necessary for carrying on his own business in supplying the neighbouring country, he does not, in North America, attempt to establish with it a manufacture for more distant sale, but employs it in the purchase and improvement of uncultivated land. From artificer he becomes planter, and neither the large wages nor the easy subsistence which that country affords to artificers, can bribe him rather to work for other people than for himself. He feels that an artificer is the servant of his customers, from whom he derives his subsistence; but that a planter who cultivates his own land, and derives his necessary subsistence from the labour of his own family, is really a master, and independent of all the world.

as in countries where no uncultivated land can be procured.

In countries, on the contrary, where there is 6 either no uncultivated land, or none that can be had upon easy terms, every artificer who has acquired more stock than he can employ in the occasional jobs of the neighbourhood, endeavours to prepare work for more distant sale. The smith erects some sort of iron, the weaver some sort of linen or woollen manufactory. Those different manufactures come, in process of time, to be gradually subdivided, and thereby improved and refined in a great variety of ways, which may easily be conceived, and which it is therefore unnecessary to explain any further.

Manufactures are naturally preferred to foreign commerce.

In seeking for employment to a capital, manu- 7 factures are, upon equal or nearly equal profits, naturally preferred to foreign commerce, for the same reason that agriculture is naturally preferred to manufactures. As the capital of the landlord or farmer is more secure than that of the manufacturer, so the capital of the manufacturer, being at all times more within his view and command, is more secure than that of the foreign merchant. In every period, indeed, of every society, the surplus part both of the rude and manufactured produce, or that for which there is no demand at home, must be sent abroad in order to be exchanged for something for which there is some demand at home. But whether the capital, which carries this surplus produce abroad, be a foreign or a domestic one, is of very little importance. If the society has not acquired sufficient capital both to cultivate all its lands, and to manufacture in the completest manner the whole of its rude produce, there is even a considerable advantage that that rude produce should be exported by a foreign capital, in order that the whole stock of the society may be employed in more useful purposes. The wealth of ancient Egypt, that of China and Indostan, sufficiently demonstrate that a nation may attain a very high degree of opulence, though the greater part of its exportation trade be carried on by foreigners. The progress of our North American and West Indian colonies would have been much less rapid, had no capital but what belonged to themselves been employed in exporting their surplus produce.

So the natural course of things is first agriculture, then manufactures, and finally foreign commerce.

According to the natural course of things, therefore, the greater part of the capital of every growing society is, first, directed to agriculture, afterwards to manufactures, and last of all to foreign commerce. This order of things is so very natural, that in every society that had any territory, it has always, I believe, been in some degree observed. Some of their lands must have been cultivated before any considerable towns could be established, and some sort of coarse industry of the manufacturing kind must have been carried on in those towns, before they could well think of employing themselves in foreign commerce. 8

But this order has been in many respects inverted.

But though this natural order of things must have taken place in some degree in every such society, it has, in all the modern states of Europe, been, in many respects, entirely inverted. The foreign commerce of some of their cities has introduced all their finer manufactures, or such as were fit for distant sale; and manufactures and foreign commerce together, have given birth to the principal improvements of agriculture. The manners and customs which the nature of their original government introduced, and which remained after that government was greatly altered, necessarily forced them into this unnatural and retrograde order. 9

QUESTIONS FOR CRITICAL READING

1. How does manufacture eventually help agriculture?
2. Why is it more important to cultivate land than foreign trade?
3. What is special about the civilizations of Egypt, China, and Indostan?
4. Why did the American and West Indian colonies grow so rapidly?
5. In unpopulated countries, what is the natural way people treat the land?
6. How do the town manufactures profit from the country's surplus goods?
7. What is an artificer?

SUGGESTIONS FOR WRITING

1. Explain how you know that Adam Smith favors country living over town life. What seems to be his opinion of each way of living?

2. Explain what Smith means by "subsistence is, in the nature of things, prior to conveniency and luxury, so the industry which procures the former, must necessarily be prior to that which ministers to the latter" (para. 2). Smith makes this claim several times. Is he correct even today?

3. Examine Smith's discussion and write an essay that takes issue with his conclusions. Base your argument on the changes that have occurred in world economy since Smith's time. How have things changed economically to render his arguments less valid or less applicable?

4. In paragraph 3, Smith talks about the "natural inclinations of man." What are they? What relevance do they have to Smith's argument? Have man's "natural inclinations" changed substantially since Smith wrote *Wealth of Nations*?

5. Smith says, "The town affords a market for the surplus produce of the country" (para 1). What does he mean by this statement? Is it still true today? What are the implications of this statement for the theories that Smith attempts to establish? Why is a surplus essential for his theory on the natural progress of opulence to be persuasive?

6. **CONNECTIONS** Examine Thomas Jefferson's Declaration of Independence for issues that relate well to the questions that Adam Smith raises. What are the economic and capitalist underpinnings of Jefferson's statements? In what ways does Jefferson agree or disagree with Smith's concepts of the development of opulence?

7. **CONNECTIONS** Smith is the most important theorist of capitalism prior to the twentieth century. How do his ideas contrast with Karl Marx's views about capitalism and how capitalists work? What would Marx take issue with in Smith's argument? What can you tell about the nature of capitalism in the worlds of Adam Smith in 1776 and of Karl Marx in 1850?

8. **CONNECTIONS** How does Robert B. Reich's analysis of the "new economy" alter the basic wisdom of Adam Smith's views on the natural progress of an economy's development from agriculture to manufactures to foreign trade? What novelties in the "new economy" alter your view of Smith's theory?

KARL MARX
The Communist Manifesto

KARL MARX (1818–1883) was born in Germany to Jewish parents who converted to Lutheranism. A scholarly man, Marx studied literature and philosophy, ultimately earning a doctorate in philosophy at the University of Jena. After being denied a university position, however, he turned to make a living from journalism.

Soon after beginning his journalistic career, Marx came into conflict with Prussian authorities because of his radical social views, and after a period of exile in Paris he moved to Brussels. After several more moves, Marx found his way to London, where he finally settled in absolute poverty; his friend Friedrich Engels (1820–1895) contributed money to prevent Marx and his family from starving. During this time in London, Marx wrote the books for which he is famous while also writing for and editing newspapers. His contributions to the *New York Daily Tribune* number over 300 items between the years 1851 and 1862.

Marx is best known for his theories of socialism, as expressed in *The Communist Manifesto* (1848)—which, like much of his important work, was written with Engels's help—and in the three-volume *Das Kapital* (*Capital*), the first volume of which was published in 1867. In his own lifetime he was not well known, nor were his ideas widely debated. Yet he was part of an ongoing movement composed mainly of intellectuals. Vladimir Lenin (1870–1924) was a disciple whose triumph in the Russian Revolution of 1917 catapulted Marx to the forefront of world thought. Since 1917 Marx's thinking has been scrupulously analyzed, debated, and argued. Capitalist thinkers have found him unconvincing, whereas Communist thinkers have found him a prophet and keen analyst of social structures.

Translated by Samuel Moore. Part III of *The Communist Manifesto,* "Socialist and Communist Literature," is omitted here.

In England, Marx's studies centered on the concept of an ongoing class struggle between those who owned property—the bourgeoisie—and those who owned nothing but whose work produced wealth—the proletariat. Marx was concerned with the forces of history, and his view of history was that it is progressive and, to an extent, inevitable. This view is prominent in *The Communist Manifesto,* particularly in Marx's review of the overthrow of feudal forms of government by the bourgeoisie. He thought it inevitable that the bourgeoisie and the proletariat would engage in a class struggle, from which the proletariat would emerge victorious. In essence, Marx took a materialist position. He denied the providence of God in the affairs of humans and defended the view that economic institutions evolve naturally and that, in their evolution, they control the social order. Thus, communism was an inevitable part of the process, and in the *Manifesto* he worked to clarify the reasons for its inevitability.

One of Marx's primary contentions was that capital is "not a personal, it is a social power" (para. 78). Thus, according to Marx, the "past dominates the present" (para. 83), because the accumulation of past capital determines how people will live in the present society. Capitalist economists, however, see capital as a personal power, but a power that, as John Kenneth Galbraith might say, should be used in a socially responsible way.

Marx's Rhetoric

The selection included here omits one section, the least important for the modern reader. The first section has a relatively simple rhetorical structure that depends on comparison. The title, "Bourgeois and Proletarians," tells us that the section will clarify the nature of each class and then go on to make some comparisons and contrasts. These concepts were by no means as widely discussed or thought about in 1848 as they are today, so Marx is careful to define his terms. At the same time, he establishes his theories regarding history by making further comparisons with class struggles in earlier ages.

Marx's style is simple and direct. He moves steadily from point to point, establishing his views on the nature of classes, on the nature of bourgeois society, and on the questions of industrialism and its effects on modern society. He considers wealth, worth, nationality, production, agriculture, and machinery. Each point is addressed in turn, usually in its own paragraph.

The organization of the next section, "Proletarians and Communists" (paras. 60–133), is not, despite its title, comparative in nature. Rather, with the proletariat defined as the class of the future, Marx tries to show that the Communist cause is the proletarian cause. In the process, Marx uses a clever rhetorical strategy. He assumes that he is addressed by an antagonist—presumably a bourgeois or a proletarian who is in sympathy with the bourgeoisie. He then proceeds to answer each popular complaint against communism. He shows that it is not a party separate from other workers' parties (para. 61). He clarifies the question of abolishing existing property relations (paras. 68–93). He emphasizes the antagonism between capital and wage labor (para. 76); he discusses the disappearance of culture (para. 94); he clarifies the questions of the family (paras. 98–100) and of the exploitation of children (para. 101). He brings up the new system of public education (paras. 102–4). He raises the touchy issue of the "community of women" (paras. 105–10), as well as the charge that Communists want to abolish nations (paras. 111–15). He brushes aside religion (para. 116). When he is done with the complaints, he gives us a rhetorical signal: "But let us have done with the bourgeois objections to Communism" (para. 126).

The rest of the second section contains a brief summary, and then Marx presents his ten-point program (para. 131). The structure is simple, direct, and effective. In the process of answering the charges against communism, Marx is able to clarify exactly what it is and what it promises. In contrast to his earlier arguments, the ten points of his Communist program seem clear, easy, and (again by contrast) almost acceptable. Although the style is not dashing (despite a few memorable lines), the rhetorical structure is extraordinarily effective for the purposes at hand.

In the last section (paras. 135 – 45), in which Marx compares the Communists with other reform groups such as those agitating for redistribution of land and other agrarian reforms, he indicates that the Communists are everywhere fighting alongside existing groups for the rights of people who are oppressed by their societies. As Marx says, "In short, the Communists everywhere support every revolutionary movement against the existing social and political order of things" (para. 141). Nothing could be a more plain and direct declaration of sympathies.

PREREADING QUESTIONS: WHAT TO READ FOR

The following prereading questions may help you anticipate key issues in the discussion on Karl Marx's *Communist Manifesto*. Keeping them in mind during your first reading of the selection should help focus your reactions.

- What is the economic condition of the bourgeoisie? What is the economic condition of the proletariat?
- How does the expanding world market for goods affect national identity?
- What benefits does Marx expect communism to provide the proletariat?

The Communist Manifesto

A specter is haunting Europe—the specter of Communism. All the Powers of old Europe have entered into a holy alliance to exorcise this specter; Pope and Czar, Metternich[1] and Guizot,[2] French Radicals[3] and German police-spies.   1

Where is the party in opposition that has not been decried as communistic by its opponents in power? Where the Opposition that has not hurled back the branding reproach of Communism against the more advanced opposition parties, as well as against its reactionary adversaries?   2

Two things result from this fact.   3

I. Communism is already acknowledged by all European Powers to be itself a Power.   4

II. It is high time that Communists should openly, in the face of the whole world, publish their views, their aims, their tendencies, and meet this nursery tale of the specter of Communism with a Manifesto of the party itself.   5

To this end, Communists of various nationalities have assembled in London and sketched the following Manifesto, to be published in the English, French, German, Italian, Flemish and Danish languages.   6

---

[1] **Prince Klemens von Metternich (1773–1859)** Foreign minister of Austria (1809–1848) who had a hand in establishing the peace after the final defeat in 1815 of Napoleon (1769–1821); Metternich was highly influential in the crucial Congress of Vienna (1814–1815).

[2] **François Pierre Guizot (1787–1874)** Conservative French statesman, author, and philosopher. Like Metternich, he was opposed to communism.

[3] **French Radicals** Actually middle-class liberals who wanted a return to a republic in 1848 after the eighteen-year reign of Louis-Philippe (1773–1850), the "citizen king."

Bourgeois and Proletarians[4]

The history of all hitherto existing society is the history of class   7
struggles.

Freeman and slave, patrician and plebeian, lord and serf, guild-   8
master and journeyman, in a word, oppressor and oppressed, stood
in constant opposition to one another, carried on uninterrupted,
now hidden, now open fight, a fight that each time ended, either in
a revolutionary re-constitution of society at large, or in the common
ruin of the contending classes.

In the earlier epochs of history we find almost everywhere a   9
complicated arrangement of society into various orders, a manifold
gradation of social rank. In ancient Rome we have patricians,
knights, plebeians, slaves; in the Middle Ages, feudal lords, vassals,
guild-masters, journeymen, apprentices, serfs; in almost all of these
classes, again, subordinate gradations.

The modern bourgeois society that has sprouted from the ruins   10
of feudal society, has not done away with class antagonisms. It has
but established new classes, new conditions of oppression, new
forms of struggle in place of the old ones.

Our epoch, the epoch of the bourgeoisie, possesses, however,   11
this distinctive feature; it has simplified the class antagonisms. Society as a whole is more and more splitting up into two great hostile
camps, into two great classes directly facing each other: Bourgeoisie
and Proletariat.

From the serfs of the Middle Ages sprang the chartered burghers   12
of the earliest towns. From these burgesses the first elements of the
bourgeoisie were developed.

The discovery of America, the rounding of the Cape,[5] opened   13
up fresh ground for the rising bourgeoisie. The East Indian and Chinese markets, the colonization of America, trade with the colonies,
the increase in the means of exchange and in commodities generally,
gave to commerce, to navigation, to industry, an impulse never before known, and thereby, to the revolutionary element in the tottering feudal society, a rapid development.

---

[4] By bourgeois is meant the class of modern Capitalists, owners of the means of
social production and employers of wage labor. By proletarians, the class of modern
wage laborers who, having no means of production of their own, are reduced to selling their labor-power in order to live. [Engels's note]

[5] **the Cape** The Cape of Good Hope, at the southern tip of Africa. This was a
main sea route for trade with India and the Orient. Europe profited immensely from
the opening up of these new markets in the sixteenth century.

The feudal system of industry, under which industrial produc-   14
tion was monopolized by closed guilds, now no longer sufficed for
the growing wants of the new market. The manufacturing system
took its place. The guild-masters were pushed on one side by the
manufacturing middle-class: division of labor between the different
corporate guilds vanished in the face of division of labor in each
single workshop.

Meantime the markets kept ever growing, the demand ever ris-   15
ing. Even manufacture no longer sufficed. Thereupon, steam and
machinery revolutionized industrial production. The place of manufacture was taken by the giant, Modern Industry, the place of the industrial middle-class, by industrial millionaires, the leaders of whole
industrial armies, the modern bourgeois.

Modern industry has established the world-market, for which   16
the discovery of America paved the way. This market has given an
immense development to commerce, to navigation, to communication by land. This development has, in its turn, reacted on the extension of industry; and in proportion as industry, commerce, navigation, railways extended, in the same proportion the bourgeoisie
developed, increased its capital, and pushed into the background
every class handed down from the Middle Ages.

We see, therefore, how the modern bourgeoisie is itself the   17
product of a long course of development, of a series of revolutions in
the modes of production and of exchange.

Each step in the development of the bourgeoisie was accompa-   18
nied by a corresponding political advance of that class. An oppressed class under the sway of the feudal nobility, an armed and
self-governing association in the medieval commune,[6] here independent urban republic (as in Italy and Germany), there taxable "third
estate"[7] of the monarchy (as in France), afterwards, in the period of
manufacture proper, serving either the semi-feudal or the absolute
monarchy as a counterpoise against nobility, and, in fact, corner
stone of the great monarchies in general, the bourgeoisie has at last,
since the establishment of Modern Industry and of the world-
market, conquered for itself, in the modern representative State, exclusive political sway. The executive of the modern State is but a committee for managing the common affairs of the whole bourgeoisie.

The bourgeoisie, historically, has played a most revolutionary   19
part.

----

[6] **the medieval commune** Refers to the growth in the eleventh century of
towns whose economy was highly regulated by mutual interest and agreement.

[7] **"third estate"** The clergy was the first estate, the aristocracy the second estate, and the bourgeoisie the third estate.

The bourgeoisie, wherever it has got the upper hand, has put an 20
end to all feudal, patriarchal, idyllic relations. It has pitilessly torn
asunder the motley feudal ties that bound man to his "natural superiors," and has left no other nexus between man and man than
naked self-interest, than callous "cash payment." It has drowned the
most heavenly ecstasies of religious fervor,[8] of chivalrous enthusiasm, of Philistine sentimentalism, in the icy water of egotistical calculation. It has resolved personal worth into exchange value, and in
place of the numberless indefeasible chartered freedoms, has set up
that single, unconscionable freedom—Free Trade. In one word, for
exploitation, veiled by religious and political illusions, it has substi-
tuted naked, shameless, direct, brutal exploitation.

The bourgeoisie has stripped of its halo every occupation hith- 21
erto honored and looked up to with reverent awe. It has converted
the physician, the lawyer, the priest, the poet, the man of science,
into its paid wage laborers.

The bourgeoisie has torn away from the family its sentimental 22
veil, and has reduced the family relation to a mere money relation.

The bourgeoisie has disclosed how it came to pass that the bru- 23
tal display of vigor in the Middle Ages, which reactionists so much
admire, found its fitting complement in the most slothful indolence.
It has been the first to show what man's activity can bring about. It
has accomplished wonders far surpassing Egyptian pyramids,
Roman aqueducts and Gothic cathedrals; it has conducted expeditions that put in the shade all former Exoduses of nations and
crusades.

The bourgeoisie cannot exist without constantly revolutionizing 24
the instruments of production, and thereby the relations of production, and with them the whole relations of society. Conservation of
the old modes of production in unaltered form was, on the contrary,
the first condition of existence for all earlier industrial classes. Constant revolutionizing of production, uninterrupted disturbance of all
social conditions, everlasting uncertainty and agitation distinguish
the bourgeois epoch from all earlier ones. All fixed, fast frozen relations, with their train of ancient and venerable prejudices and

---

[8] **religious fervor** This and other terms in this sentence contain a compressed
historical observation. "Religious fervor" refers to the Middle Ages; "chivalrous enthusiasm" refers to the rise of the secular state and to the military power of knights;
"Philistine sentimentalism" refers to the development of popular arts and literature
in the sixteenth, seventeenth, and eighteenth centuries. "Philistine" refers to those
who were generally uncultured, that is, the general public. "Sentimentalism" is a
code word for the encouragement of emotional response rather than rational
thought.

opinions, are swept away, all new formed ones become antiquated before they can ossify. All that is solid melts into the air, all that is holy is profaned, and man is at last compelled to face with sober senses, his real conditions of life, and his relations with his kind.

The need of a constantly expanding market for its prod-   25
ucts chases the bourgeoisie over the whole surface of the globe. It must nestle everywhere, settle everywhere, establish connections everywhere.

The bourgeoisie has through its exploitation of the world-   26
market given a cosmopolitan character to production and consumption in every country. To the great chagrin of reactionists, it has drawn from under the feet of industry the national ground on which it stood. All old-established national industries have been destroyed or are daily being destroyed. They are dislodged by new industries, whose introduction becomes a life and death question for all civilized nations, by industries that no longer work up indigenous raw material, but raw material drawn from the remotest zones; industries whose products are consumed, not only at home, but in every quarter of the globe. In place of the old wants, satisfied by the productions of the country, we find new wants, requiring for their satisfaction the products of distant lands and climes. In place of the old local and national seclusion and self-sufficiency, we have intercourse in every direction, universal interdependence of nations. And as in material, so also in intellectual production. The intellectual creations of individual nations become common property. National onesidedness and narrowmindedness become more and more impossible, and from the numerous national and local literatures there arises a world-literature.

The bourgeoisie, by the rapid improvement of all instruments of   27
production, by the immensely facilitated means of communication, draws all, even the most barbarian nations into civilization. The cheap prices of its commodities are the heavy artillery with which it batters down all Chinese walls, with which it forces the barbarians' intensely obstinate hatred of foreigners to capitulate. It compels all nations, on pain of extinction, to adopt the bourgeois mode of production; it compels them to introduce what it calls civilization into their midst, i.e., to become bourgeois themselves. In a word, it creates a world after its own image.

The bourgeoisie has subjected the country to the rule of the   28
towns. It has created enormous cities, has greatly increased the urban population as compared with the rural and has thus rescued a considerable part of the population from the idiocy of rural life. Just as it has made the country dependent on the towns, so it has made barbarian and semi-barbarian countries dependent on civilized

ones, nations of peasants on nations of bourgeois, the East on the West.

The bourgeoisie keeps more and more doing away with the 29 scattered state of the population, of the means of production, and of property. It has agglomerated population, centralized means of production, and has concentrated property in a few hands. The necessary consequence of this was political centralization. Independent, or but loosely connected provinces, with separate interests, laws, governments and systems of taxation, became lumped together in one nation, with one government, one code of laws, one national class interest, one frontier and one customs tariff.

The bourgeoisie, during its rule of scarce one hundred years, 30 has created more massive and more colossal productive forces than have all preceding generations together. Subjection of Nature's forces to man, machinery, application of chemistry to industry and agriculture, steam-navigation, railways, electric telegraphs, clearing of whole continents for cultivation, canalization of rivers, whole populations conjured out of the ground—what earlier century had even a presentiment that such productive forces slumbered in the lap of social labor?

We see then: the means of production and of exchange on 31 whose foundation the bourgeoisie built itself up, were generated in feudal society. At a certain stage in the development of these means of production and of exchange, the conditions under which feudal society produced and exchanged, the feudal organization of agriculture and manufacturing industry, in one word, the feudal relations of property became no longer compatible with the already developed productive forces; they became so many fetters. They had to burst asunder; they were burst asunder.

Into their place stepped free competition, accompanied by a so- 32 cial and political constitution adapted to it, and by the economical and political sway of the bourgeois class.

A similar movement is going on before our own eyes. Modern 33 bourgeois society with its relations of production, of exchange and of property, a society that has conjured up such gigantic means of production and of exchange, is like the sorcerer, who is no longer able to control the powers of the nether world whom he has called up by his spells. For many a decade past, the history of industry and commerce is but the history of the revolt of modern productive forces against modern conditions of production, against the property relations that are the conditions for the existence of the bourgeoisie and of its rule. It is enough to mention the commercial crises that by their periodical return put on its trial, each time more threateningly, the existence of the entire bourgeois society. In these crises a great part not only of the existing products, but also of the previously created productive forces, are periodically destroyed. In these crises there breaks out an epidemic that, in all earlier epochs, would have seemed an absurdity—the epidemic of overproduction. Society suddenly finds itself put back into a state of momentary barbarism; it appears as if a famine, a universal war of devastation, had cut off the supply of every means of subsistence; industry and commerce seem to be destroyed; and why? Because there is too much civilization, too much means of subsistence, too much industry, too much commerce. The productive forces at the disposal of society no longer tend to further the development of the conditions of the bourgeois property; on the contrary, they have become too powerful for these conditions by which they are fettered, and as soon as they overcome these fetters they bring disorder into the whole of bourgeois society, endanger the existence of bourgeois property. The conditions of bourgeois society are too narrow to comprise the wealth created by them. And how does the bourgeoisie get over these crises? On the one hand by enforced destruction of a mass of productive forces; on the other, by the conquest of new markets, and by the more thorough exploitation of the old ones. That is to say, by paving the way for more extensive and more destructive crises, and by diminishing the means whereby crises are prevented.

The weapons with which the bourgeoisie felled feudalism to the 34 ground are now turned against the bourgeoisie itself.

But not only has the bourgeoisie forged the weapons that bring 35 death to itself; it has also called into existence the men who are to wield those weapons—the modern working class—the proletarians.

In proportion as the bourgeoisie, i.e., capital, is developed, in 36 the same proportion is the proletariat, the modern working class, developed, a class of laborers who live only so long as they find work, and who find work only so long as their labor increases capital. These laborers, who must sell themselves piecemeal, are a commodity, like every other article of commerce, and are consequently exposed to all the vicissitudes of competition, to all the fluctuations of the market.

Owing to the extensive use of machinery and to division of 37 labor, the work of the proletarians has lost all individual character, and, consequently, all charm for the workman. He becomes an appendage of the machine, and it is only the most simple, most monotonous and most easily acquired knack that is required of him. Hence, the cost of production of a workman is restricted almost entirely to the means of subsistence that he requires for his maintenance, and for the propagation of his race. But the price of a commodity, and also of labor, is equal to its cost of production. In proportion, therefore, as the repulsiveness of the work increases the wage decreases. Nay more, in proportion as the use of machinery and division of labor increases, in the same proportion the burden of toil increases, whether by prolongation of the working hours, by increase of the work enacted in a given time, or by increased speed of the machinery, etc.

Modern industry has converted the little workshop of the patri- 38 archal master into the great factory of the industrial capitalist. Masses of laborers, crowded into factories, are organized like soldiers. As privates of the industrial army they are placed under the command of a perfect hierarchy of officers and sergeants. Not only are they the slaves of the bourgeois class and of the bourgeois state, they are daily and hourly enslaved by the machine, by the overlooker, and, above all, by the individual bourgeois manufacturer himself. The more openly this despotism proclaims gain to be its end and aim, the more petty, the more hateful and the more embittering it is.

The less the skill and exertion or strength implied in manual 39 labor, in other words, the more modern industry becomes developed, the more is the labor of men superseded by that of women. Differences of age and sex have no longer any distinctive social validity for the working class. All are instruments of labor, more or less expensive to use, according to their age and sex.

No sooner is the exploitation of the laborer by the manufac- 40 turer, so far at an end, that he receives his wages in cash, than he is set upon by the other portions of the bourgeoisie, the landlord, the shopkeeper, the pawnbroker, etc.

The lower strata of the middle class—the small trades-people, 41 shopkeepers and retired tradesmen generally, the handicraftsmen and peasants—all these sink gradually into the proletariat, partly because their diminutive capital does not suffice for the scale on which Modern Industry is carried on, and is swamped in the competition with the large capitalists, partly because their specialized skill is rendered worthless by new methods of production. Thus the proletariat is recruited from all classes of the population.

The proletariat goes through various stages of development. 42 With its birth begins its struggle with the bourgeoisie. At first the contest is carried on by individual laborers, then by the workpeople of a factory, then by the operatives of one trade, in one locality, against the individual bourgeois who directly exploits them. They direct their attacks not against the bourgeois conditions of production, but against the instruments of production themselves; they destroy imported wares that compete with their labor, they smash to pieces machinery, they set factories ablaze, they seek to restore by force the vanished status of the workman of the Middle Ages.

At this stage the laborers still form an incoherent mass scattered   43 over the whole country, and broken up by their mutual competition. If anywhere they unite to form more compact bodies, this is not yet the consequence of their own active union, but of the union of the bourgeoisie, which class, in order to attain its own political ends, is compelled to set the whole proletariat in motion, and is moreover yet, for a time, able to do so. At this stage, therefore, the proletarians do not fight their enemies, but the enemies of their enemies, the remnants of absolute monarchy, the landowners, the nonindustrial bourgeois, the petty bourgeoisie. Thus the whole historical movement is concentrated in the hands of the bourgeoisie, every victory so obtained is a victory for the bourgeoisie.

But with the development of industry the proletariat not only   44 increases in number; it becomes concentrated in greater masses, its strength grows and it feels that strength more. The various interests and conditions of life within the ranks of the proletariat are more and more equalized, in proportion as machinery obliterates all distinctions of labor, and nearly everywhere reduces wages to the same low level. The growing competition among the bourgeois, and the resulting commercial crisis, make the wages of the workers even more fluctuating. The unceasing improvement of machinery, ever more rapidly developing, makes their livelihood more and more precarious; the collisions between individual workmen and individual bourgeois take more and more the character of collisions between two classes. Thereupon the workers begin to form combinations (Trades' Unions)[9] against the bourgeois; they club together in order to keep up the rate of wages; they found permanent associations in order to make provision beforehand for these occasional revolts. Here and there the contest breaks out into riots.

Now and then the workers are victorious, but only for a time.   45 The real fruit of their battle lies not in the immediate result but in the ever-expanding union of workers. This union is helped on by the improved means of communication that are created by modern industry, and that places the workers of different localities in contact with one another. It was just this contact that was needed to centralize the numerous local struggles, all of the same character, into one

---

[9] **combinations (Trades' Unions)** The labor movement was only beginning in 1848. It consisted of trades' unions that started as social clubs but soon began agitating for labor reform. They represented an important step in the growth of socialism in Europe.

national struggle between classes. But every class struggle is a political struggle. And that union, to attain which the burghers of the Middle Ages with their miserable highways, required centuries, the modern proletarians, thanks to railways, achieve in a few years.

This organization of the proletarians into a class, and conse- 46 quently into a political party, is continually being upset again by the competition between the workers themselves. But it ever rises up again, stronger, firmer, mightier. It compels legislative recognition of particular interests of the workers by taking advantage of the divisions among the bourgeoisie itself. Thus the ten hours' bill in England[10] was carried.

Altogether collisions between the classes of the old society fur- 47 ther, in many ways, the course of development of the proletariat. The bourgeoisie finds itself involved in a constant battle. At first with the aristocracy; later on, with those portions of the bourgeoisie itself whose interests have become antagonistic to the progress of industry; at all times, with the bourgeoisie of foreign countries. In all these battles it sees itself compelled to appeal to the proletariat, to ask for its help, and thus, to drag it into the political arena. The bourgeoisie itself, therefore, supplies the proletariat with its own elements of political and general education; in other words, it furnishes the proletariat with weapons for fighting the bourgeoisie.

Further, as we have already seen, entire sections of the ruling 48 classes are, by the advance of industry, precipitated into the proletariat, or are at least threatened in their conditions of existence. These also supply the proletariat with fresh elements of enlightenment and progress.

Finally, in times when the class struggle nears the decisive hour, 49 the process of dissolution going on within the ruling class—in fact, within the whole range of an old society—assumes such a violent, glaring character that a small section of the ruling class cuts itself adrift and joins the revolutionary class, the class that holds the future in its hands. Just as, therefore, at an earlier period, a section of the nobility went over to the bourgeoisie, so now a portion of the bourgeoisie goes over to the proletariat, and in particular, a portion of the bourgeois ideologists, who have raised themselves to the level of comprehending theoretically the historical movements as a whole.

----

[10] **the ten hours' bill in England** This bill (1847) was an important labor reform. It limited the working day for women and children in factories to only ten hours, at a time when it was common for some people to work sixteen hours a day. The bill's passage was a result of political division, not of benevolence on the managers' part.

Of all the classes that stand face to face with the bourgeoisie   50
today the proletariat alone is a really revolutionary class. The other
classes decay and finally disappear in the face of Modern Industry;
the proletariat is its special and essential product.

The lower middle class, the small manufacturer, the shop-   51
keeper, the artisan, the peasant, all these fight against the bourgeoisie, to save from extinction their existence as fractions of the
middle class. They are therefore not revolutionary, but conservative.
Nay, more; they are reactionary, for they try to roll back the wheel
of history. If by chance they are revolutionary, they are so only in
view of their impending transfer into the proletariat; they thus defend not their present, but their future interests; they desert their
own standpoint to place themselves at that of the proletariat.

The "dangerous class," the social scum, that passively rotting   52
mass thrown off by the lowest layers of old society, may, here and
there, be swept into the movement by a proletarian revolution; its
conditions of life, however, prepare it far more for the part of a
bribed tool of reactionary intrigue.

In the conditions of the proletariat, those of the old society at large   53
are already virtually swamped. The proletarian is without property; his
relation to his wife and children has no longer anything in common
with the bourgeois family relations; modern industrial labor, modern
subjection to capital, the same in England as in France, in America as in
Germany, has stripped him of every trace of national character. Law,
morality, religion, are to him so many bourgeois prejudices, behind
which lurk in ambush just as many bourgeois interests.

All the preceding classes that got the upper hand sought to for-   54
tify their already acquired status by subjecting society at large to
their conditions of appropriation. The proletarians cannot become
masters of the productive forces of society, except by abolishing
their own previous mode of appropriation, and thereby also every
other previous mode of appropriation. They have nothing of their
own to secure and to fortify; their mission is to destroy all previous
securities for and insurances of individual property.

All previous historical movements were movements of minori-   55
ties, or in the interest of minorities. The proletarian movement is the
self-conscious, independent movement of the immense majority.
The proletariat, the lowest stratum of our present society, cannot
stir, cannot raise itself up without the whole superincumbent strata
of official society being sprung into the air.

Though not in substance, yet in form, the struggle of the pro-   56
letariat with the bourgeoisie is at first a national struggle. The
proletariat of each country must, of course, first of all settle matters
with its own bourgeoisie.

In depicting the most general phases of the development of the 57
proletariat, we traced the more or less veiled civil war, raging within
existing society, up to the point where that war breaks out into open
revolution, and where the violent overthrow of the bourgeoisie, lays
the foundations for the sway of the proletariat.

Hitherto every form of society has been based, as we have al- 58
ready seen, on the antagonism of oppressing and oppressed classes.
But in order to oppress a class, certain conditions must be assured to
it under which it can, at least, continue its slavish existence. The
serf, in the period of serfdom, raised himself to membership in the
commune, just as the petty bourgeois, under the yoke of feudal ab-
solutism, managed to develop into a bourgeois. The modern laborer,
on the contrary, instead of rising with the progress of industry, sinks
deeper and deeper below the conditions of existence of his own
class. He becomes a pauper, and pauperism develops more rapidly
than population and wealth. And here it becomes evident that the
bourgeoisie is unfit any longer to be the ruling class in society, and
to impose its conditions of existence upon society as an over-riding
law. It is unfit to rule, because it is incompetent to assure an existence to its slave within his slavery, because it cannot help letting
him sink into such a state that it has to feed him, instead of being
fed by him. Society can no longer live under this bourgeoisie; in
other words, its existence is no longer compatible with society.

The essential condition for the existence, and for the sway of the 59
bourgeois class, is the formation and augmentation of capital; the
condition for capital is wage labor. Wage labor rests exclusively on
competition between the laborers. The advance of industry, whose
involuntary promoter is the bourgeoisie, replaces the isolation of the
laborers, due to competition, by their involuntary combination, due
to association. The development of Modern Industry, therefore, cuts
from under its feet the very foundation on which the bourgeoisie
produces and appropriates products. What the bourgeoisie therefore
produces, above all, are its own grave diggers. Its fall and the victory
of the proletariat are equally inevitable.

Proletarians and Communists

In what relation do the Communists stand to the proletarians as 60
a whole?

The Communists do not form a separate party opposed to other 61
working class parties.

They have no interests separate and apart from those of the pro- 62
letariat as a whole.

They do not set up any sectarian principles of their own, by 63
which to shape and mold the proletarian movement.

The Communists are distinguished from the other working class 64
parties by this only: 1. In the national struggles of the proletarians of
the different countries, they point out and bring to the front the
common interests of the entire proletariat, independently of all nationality. 2. In the various stages of development which the struggle
of the working class against the bourgeoisie has to pass through,
they always and everywhere represent the interests of the movement
as a whole.

The Communists, therefore, are on the one hand practically the 65
most advanced and resolute section of the working class parties of
every country, that section which pushes forward all others; on the
other hand, theoretically, they have over the great mass of the proletariat the advantage of clearly understanding the line of march, the
conditions, and the ultimate general results of the proletarian
movement.

The immediate aim of the Communists is the same as that of all 66
the other proletarian parties: formation of the proletariat into a class,
overthrow of the bourgeois of supremacy, conquest of political
power by the proletariat.

The theoretical conclusions of the Communists are in no way 67
based on ideas or principles that have been invented or discovered
by this or that would-be universal reformer.

They merely express, in general terms, actual relations springing 68
from an existing class struggle, from a historical movement going on
under our very eyes. The abolition of existing property relations is
not at all a distinctive feature of Communism.

All property relations in the past have continually been sub- 69
ject to historical change consequent upon the change in historical
conditions.

The French Revolution, for example, abolished feudal property 70
in favor of bourgeois property.

The distinguishing feature of Communism is not the abolition 71
of property generally, but the abolition of bourgeois property. But
modern bourgeois private property is the final and most complete
expression of the system of producing and appropriating products,
that is based on class antagonism, on the exploitation of the many
by the few.

In this sense, the theory of the Communists may be summed up 72
in the single sentence: Abolition of private property.

We Communists have been reproached with the desire of abol- 73
ishing the right of personally acquiring property as the fruit of a
man's own labor, which property is alleged to be the groundwork of
all personal freedom, activity and independence.

Hard won, self-acquired, self-earned property! Do you mean the 74
property of the petty artisan and of the small peasant, a form of
property that preceded the bourgeois form? There is no need to
abolish that; the development of industry has to a great extent already destroyed it, and is still destroying it daily.

Or do you mean modern bourgeois private property? 75

But does wage labor create any property for the laborer? Not a 76
bit. It creates capital, i.e., that kind of property which exploits wage
labor, and which cannot increase except upon condition of getting a
new supply of wage labor for fresh exploitation. Property, in its
present form, is based on the antagonism of capital and wage labor.
Let us examine both sides of this antagonism.

To be a capitalist is to have not only a purely personal, but a so- 77
cial status in production. Capital is a collective product, and only by
the united action of many members, nay, in the last resort, only by
the united action of all members of society, can it be set in motion.

Capital is therefore not a personal, it is a social power. 78

When, therefore, capital is converted into common property, 79
into the property of all members of society, personal property is not
thereby transformed into social property. It is only the social character of the property that is changed. It loses its class character.

Let us now take wage labor. 80

The average price of wage labor is the minimum wage, i.e., that 81
quantum of the means of subsistence which is absolutely requisite to
keep the laborer in bare existence as a laborer. What, therefore, the
wage laborer appropriates by means of his labor, merely suffices to
prolong and reproduce a bare existence. We by no means intend to
abolish this personal appropriation of the products of labor, an appropriation that is made for the maintenance and reproduction of
human life, and that leaves no surplus wherewith to command the
labor of others. All that we want to do away with is the miserable
character of this appropriation, under which the laborer lives merely
to increase capital and is allowed to live only in so far as the interests
of the ruling class require it.

In bourgeois society, living labor is but a means to increase ac- 82
cumulated labor. In Communist society accumulated labor is but a
means to widen, to enrich, to promote the existence of the laborer.

In bourgeois society, therefore, the past dominates the present; 83
in Communist society the present dominates the past. In bourgeois
society, capital is independent and has individuality, while the living
person is dependent and has no individuality.

And the abolition of this state of things is called by the bour- 84
geois abolition of individuality and freedom! And rightly so. The
abolition of bourgeois individuality, bourgeois independence and
bourgeois freedom is undoubtedly aimed at.

By freedom is meant, under the present bourgeois conditions of 85 production, free trade, free selling and buying.

But if selling and buying disappears, free selling and buying disappears also. This talk about free selling and buying, and all the other "brave words" of our bourgeoisie about freedom in general have a meaning, if any, only in contrast with restricted selling and buying, with the fettered traders of the Middle Ages, but have no meaning when opposed to the Communistic abolition of buying and selling, of the bourgeois conditions of production, and of the bourgeoisie itself.

You are horrified at our intending to do away with private prop- 87 erty. But in your existing society private property is already done away with for nine-tenths of the population; its existence for the few is solely due to its non-existence in the hands of those nine-tenths. You reproach us, therefore, with intending to do away with a form of property, the necessary condition for whose existence is the nonexistence of any property for the immense majority of society.

In one word, you reproach us with intending to do away with 88 your property. Precisely so: that is just what we intend.

From the moment when labor can no longer be converted into 89 capital, money, or rent, into a social power capable of being monopolized, i.e., from the moment when individual property can no longer be transformed into bourgeois property, into capital, from that moment, you say, individuality vanishes.

You must, therefore, confess that by "individual" you mean no 90 other person than the bourgeois, than the middle-class owner of property. This person must, indeed, be swept out of the way and made impossible.

Communism deprives no man of the power to appropriate the 91 products of society: all that it does is to deprive him of the power to subjugate the labor of others by means of such appropriation.

It has been objected that upon the abolition of private property 92 all work will cease and universal laziness will overtake us.

According to this, bourgeois society ought long ago to have 93 gone to the dogs through sheer idleness; for those of its members who work acquire nothing, and those who acquire anything do not work. The whole of this objection is but another expression of the tautology:[11] that there can no longer be any wage labor when there is no longer any capital.

All objections urged against the Communistic mode of produc- 94 ing and appropriating material products have, in the same way, been

---

[11] **tautology** A statement whose two parts say essentially the same thing. The second half of the previous sentence is a tautology.

urged against the Communistic modes of producing and appropriating intellectual products. Just as, to the bourgeois, the disappearance of class property is the disappearance of production itself, so the disappearance of class culture is to him identical with the disappearance of all culture.

That culture, the loss of which he laments, is, for the enormous 95 majority, a mere training to act as a machine.

But don't wrangle with us so long as you apply, to our intended 96 abolition of bourgeois property, the standard of your bourgeois notions of freedom, culture, law, etc. Your very ideas are but the outgrowth of the conditions of your bourgeois production and bourgeois property, just as your jurisprudence is but the will of your class made into a law for all, a will whose essential character and direction are determined by the economical conditions of existence of your class.

The selfish misconception that induces you to transform into 97 eternal laws of nature and of reason the social forms springing from your present mode of production and form of property—historical relations that rise and disappear in the progress of production—this misconception you share with every ruling class that has preceded you. What you see clearly in the case of ancient property, what you admit in the case of feudal property, you are of course forbidden to admit in the case of your own bourgeois form of property.

Abolition of the family! Even the most radical flare up at this in- 98 famous proposal of the Communists.

On what foundation is the present family, the bourgeois family, 99 based? On capital, on private gain. In its completely developed form this family exists only among the bourgeoisie. But this state of things finds its complement in the practical absence of the family among the proletarians, and in public prostitution.

The bourgeois family will vanish as a matter of course when its 100 complement vanishes, and both will vanish with the vanishing of capital.

Do you charge us with wanting to stop the exploitation of chil- 101 dren by their parents? To this crime we plead guilty.

But, you will say, we destroy the most hallowed of relations 102 when we replace home education by social.

And your education! Is not that also social, and determined by 103 the social conditions under which you educate; by the intervention, direct or indirect, of society by means of schools, etc.? The Communists have not invented the intervention of society in education; they do but seek to alter the character of that intervention, and to rescue education from the influence of the ruling class.

The bourgeois clap-trap about the family and education, about 104 the hallowed correlation of parent and child, become all the more disgusting, the more, by the action of Modern Industry, all family ties among the proletarians are torn asunder and their children transformed into simple articles of commerce and instruments of labor.

But you Communists would introduce community of women, 105 screams the whole bourgeoisie chorus.

The bourgeois sees in his wife a mere instrument of production. 106 He hears that the instruments of production are to be exploited in common, and, naturally, can come to no other conclusion, than that the lot of being common to all will likewise fall to the women.

He has not even a suspicion that the real point aimed at is to do 107 away with the status of women as mere instruments of production.

For the rest, nothing is more ridiculous than the virtuous indig- 108 nation of our bourgeois at the community of women which, they pretend, is to be openly and officially established by the Communists. The Communists have no need to introduce community of women, it has existed almost from time immemorial.

Our bourgeois, not content with having the wives and daugh- 109 ters of their proletarians at their disposal, not to speak of common prostitutes, take the greatest pleasure in seducing each others' wives.

Bourgeois marriage is in reality a system of wives in common, 110 and thus, at the most, what the Communists might possibly be reproached with, is that they desire to introduce, in substitution for a hypocritically concealed, an openly legalized community of women. For the rest, it is self-evident that the abolition of the present system of production must bring with it the abolition of the community of women springing from that system, i.e., of prostitution both public and private.

The Communists are further reproached with desiring to abol- 111 ish countries and nationalities.

The working men have no country. We cannot take from them 112 what they don't possess. Since the proletariat must first of all acquire political supremacy, must rise to be the leading class of the nation, must constitute itself the nation, it is, so far, itself national, though not in the bourgeois sense of the word.

National differences and antagonisms between peoples are daily 113 more and more vanishing, owing to the development of the bourgeoisie, to freedom of commerce, to the world-market, to uniformity in the mode of production and in the conditions of life corresponding thereto.

The supremacy of the proletariat will cause them to vanish still 114 faster. United action, of the leading civilized countries at least, is one of the first conditions for the emancipation of the proletariat.

In proportion as the exploitation of one individual by another is 115 put an end to, the exploitation of one nation by another will also be put an end to. In proportion as the antagonism between classes within the nation vanishes, the hostility of one nation to another will come to an end.

The charges against Communism made from a religious, a 116 philosophical, and generally, from an ideological standpoint, are not deserving of serious examination.

Does it require deep intuition to comprehend that man's ideas, 117 views and conceptions, in one word, man's consciousness, changes with every change in the conditions of his material existence, in his social relations and in his social life?

What else does the history of ideas prove than that intellectual 118 production changes in character in proportion as material production is changed? The ruling ideas of each age have ever been the ideas of its ruling class.

When people speak of ideas that revolutionize society they do 119 but express the fact that within the old society the elements of a new one have been created, and that the dissolution of the old ideas keeps even pace with the dissolution of the old conditions of existence.

When the ancient world was in its last throes the ancient reli- 120 gions were overcome by Christianity. When Christian ideas succumbed in the 18th century to rationalist ideas, feudal society fought its death battle with the then revolutionary bourgeoisie. The ideas of religious liberty and freedom of conscience merely gave expression to the sway of free competition within the domain of knowledge.

"Undoubtedly," it will be said, "religious, moral, philosophical 121 and judicial ideas have been modified in the course of historical development. But religion, morality, philosophy, political science, and law, constantly survived this change.

"There are, besides, eternal truths such as Freedom, Justice, etc., 122 that are common to all states of society. But Communism abolishes eternal truths, it abolishes all religion and all morality, instead of constituting them on a new basis; it therefore acts in contradiction to all past historical experience."

What does this accusation reduce itself to? The history of all 123 past society has consisted in the development of class antagonisms, antagonisms that assumed different forms at different epochs.

But whatever form they may have taken, one fact is common to 124 all past ages, viz., the exploitation of one part of society by the other. No wonder, then, that the social consciousness of past ages, despite all the multiplicity and variety it displays, moves within certain common forms, or general ideas, which cannot completely vanish except with the total disappearance of class antagonisms.

The Communist revolution is the most radical rupture with tra- 125 ditional property relations; no wonder that its development involves the most radical rupture with traditional ideas.

But let us have done with the bourgeois objections to Com- 126 munism.

We have seen above that the first step in the revolution by the 127 working class is to raise the proletariat to the position of ruling class, to win the battle of democracy.

The proletariat will use its political supremacy to wrest, by de- 128 grees, all capital from the bourgeoisie, to centralize all instruments of production in the hands of the State, i.e., of the proletariat organized as a ruling class; and to increase the total productive forces as rapidly as possible.

Of course, in the beginning, this cannot be effected except by 129 means of despotic inroads on the rights of property, and on the conditions of bourgeois production; by means of measures, therefore, which appear economically insufficient and untenable, but which in the course of the movement outstrip themselves, necessitate further inroads upon the old social order, and are unavoidable as a means of entirely revolutionizing the mode of production.

These measures will of course be different in different countries. 130

Nevertheless in the most advanced countries the following will 131 be pretty generally applicable:

1. Abolition of property in land and application of all rents of land to public purposes.
2. A heavy progressive or graduated income tax.
3. Abolition of all right of inheritance.
4. Confiscation of the property of all emigrants and rebels.
5. Centralization of credit in the hands of the State, by means of a national bank with State capital and an exclusive monopoly.
6. Centralization of the means of communication and transport in the hands of the State.
7. Extension of factories and instruments of production owned by the State; the bringing into cultivation of waste lands, and the improvement of the soil generally in accordance with a common plan.
8. Equal liability of all to labor. Establishment of industrial armies, especially for agriculture.
9. Combination of agriculture with manufacturing industries; gradual abolition of the distinction between town and country by a more equable distribution of the population over the country.
10. Free education for all children in public schools. Abolition of children's factory labor in its present form. Combination of education with industrial production, etc., etc.

When, in the course of development, class distinctions have dis- 132
appeared, and all production has been concentrated in the hands of
a vast association of the whole nation, the public power will lose its
political character. Political power, properly so called, is merely the
organized power of one class for oppressing another. If the proletariat during its contest with the bourgeoisie is compelled, by the
force of circumstances, to organize itself as a class, if, by means of a
revolution, it makes itself the ruling class, and, as such, sweeps away
by force the old conditions of production, then it will, along with
these conditions, have swept away the conditions for the existence
of class antagonism, and of classes generally, and will thereby have
abolished its own supremacy as a class.

In place of the old bourgeois society, with its classes and class 133
antagonisms, we shall have an association in which the free development of each is the condition for the free development of all....

Position of the Communists in Relation to
the Various Existing Opposition Parties

[The preceding section] has made clear the relations of the 134
Communists to the existing working class parties, such as the
Chartists in England and the Agrarian Reforms[12] in America.

The Communists fight for the attainment of the immediate 135
aims, for the enforcement of the momentary interests of the working
class; but in the movement of the present they also represent and
take care of the future of that movement. In France the Communists
ally themselves with the Social-Democrats[13] against the conservative
and radical bourgeoisie, reserving, however, the right to take up a
critical position in regard to phrases and illusions traditionally
handed down from the great Revolution.

In Switzerland they support the Radicals,[14] without losing sight 136
of the fact that this party consists of antagonistic elements, partly

---

[12] **Agrarian Reforms** Agrarian reform was a very important issue in America
after the Revolution. The Chartists were a radical English group established in 1838;
they demanded political and social reforms. They were among the more violent revolutionaries of the day. Agrarian reform, or redistribution of the land, was slow to
come, and the issue often sparked violence between social classes.

[13] **Social-Democrats** In France in the 1840s, a group that proposed the ideal
of labor reform through the establishment of workshops supplied with government
capital.

[14] **Radicals** By 1848, European Radicals, taking their name from the violent
revolutionaries of the French Revolution (1789–1799), were a nonviolent group
content to wait for change.

of Democratic Socialists, in the French sense, partly of radical bourgeois.

In Poland they support the party that insists on an agrarian rev- 137 olution, as the prime condition for national emancipation, that party which fomented the insurrection of Cracow in 1846.[15]

In Germany they fight with the bourgeoisie whenever it acts in a 138 revolutionary way, against the absolute monarchy, the feudal squirearchy, and the petty bourgeoisie.

But they never cease for a single instant to instill into the work- 139 ing class the clearest possible recognition of the hostile antagonism between bourgeoisie and proletariat, in order that the German workers may straightway use, as so many weapons against the bourgeoisie, the social and political conditions that the bourgeoisie must necessarily introduce along with its supremacy, and in order that, after the fall of the reactionary classes in Germany, the fight against the bourgeoisie itself may immediately begin.

The Communists turn their attention chiefly to Germany, be- 140 cause that country is on the eve of a bourgeois revolution,[16] that is bound to be carried out under more advanced conditions of European civilization, and with a more developed proletariat, than that of England was in the seventeenth and of France in the eighteenth century, and because the bourgeois revolution in Germany will be but the prelude to an immediately following proletarian revolution.

In short, the Communists everywhere support every revolution- 141 ary movement against the existing social and political order of things.

In all these movements they bring to the front, as the leading 142 question in each, the property question, no matter what its degree of development at the time.

Finally, they labor everywhere for the union and agreement of 143 the democratic parties of all countries.

The Communists disdain to conceal their views and aims. They 144 openly declare that their ends can be attained only by the forcible overthrow of all existing social conditions. Let the ruling classes tremble at a Communistic revolution. The proletarians have nothing to lose but their chains. They have a world to win.

Working men of all countries, unite!   145

---

[15] **the insurrection of Cracow in 1846** Cracow was an independent city in 1846. The insurrection was designed to join Cracow with Poland and to further large-scale social reforms.

[16] **on the eve of a bourgeois revolution** Ferdinand Lassalle (1825–1864) developed the German labor movement and was in basic agreement with Marx, who was nevertheless convinced that Lassalle's approach was wrong. The environment in Germany seemed appropriate for revolution, in part because of its fragmented political structure and in part because no major revolution had yet occurred there.

QUESTIONS FOR CRITICAL READING

1. Begin by establishing your understanding of the terms *bourgeois* and *proletarian*. Does Marx make a clear distinction between the terms? Are such terms applicable to American society today? Which of these groups, if any, do you feel that you belong to?
2. Marx makes the concept of social class fundamental to his theories. Can "social class" be easily defined? Are social classes evident in our society? Are they engaged in a struggle of the sort Marx assumes to be inevitable?
3. What are Marx's views about the value of work in the society he describes? What is his attitude toward wealth?
4. Marx says that every class struggle is a political struggle. Do you agree?
5. Examine the first part. Which class gets more paragraphs—the bourgeoisie or the proletariat? Why?
6. Is the modern proletariat a revolutionary class?
7. Is Marx's analysis of history clear? Try to summarize his views on the progress of history.
8. Is capital a social force, or is it a personal force? Do you think of your savings (either now or in the future) as belonging to you alone or as in some way belonging to your society?
9. What, in Marx's view, is the responsibility of wealthy citizens?

SUGGESTIONS FOR WRITING

1. Defend or attack Marx's statement: "The executive of the modern State is but a committee for managing the common affairs of the whole bourgeoisie" (para. 18). Is this generally true? Take three "affairs of the whole bourgeoisie" and test each one in turn.
2. Examine Marx's statements regarding women. Refer especially to paragraphs 39, 98, 105, and 110. Does he imply that his views are in conflict with those of his general society? After you have a list of his statements, see if you can establish exactly what he is recommending. Do you approve of his recommendations?
3. Marx's program of ten points is listed in paragraph 131. Using the technique that Marx himself uses—taking each point in its turn, clarifying the problems with the point, and finally deciding for or against the point—evaluate his program. Which points do you feel are most beneficial to society? Which are detrimental to society? What is your overall view of the general worth of the program? Do you think it would be possible to put such a program into effect?
4. All Marx's views are predicated on the present nature of property ownership and the changes that communism will institute. He claims, for example, that a rupture with property relations "involves the most radical rupture with traditional ideas" (para. 125). And he discusses in depth his proposal for the rupture of property relations (paras. 68–93). Clarify traditional property relations—what can be owned and by

whom—and then contrast with these the proposals Marx makes. Establish your own views as you go along. Include your reasons for taking issue or expressing agreement with Marx. What kinds of property relations do you see around you? What kinds are most desirable for a healthy society?

5. What is the responsibility of the state toward the individual in the kind of economic circumstances that Marx describes? How can the independence of individuals who have amassed great wealth and wish to operate freely be balanced against the independence of those who are poor and have no wealth to manipulate? What kinds of abuse are possible in such circumstances, and what remedies can a state achieve through altering the economic system? What specific remedies does Marx suggest? Are they workable?

6. Do you feel that Marx's suggestions are desirable? Or that they are likely to produce the effects he desires? Critics sometimes complain about Marx's misunderstanding of human nature. Do you feel he has an adequate understanding of human nature? What do you see as impediments to the full success of his program?

7. How accurate is Marx's view of the bourgeoisie? He identifies the bourgeoisie with capital and capitalists. He also complains that the bourgeoisie has established a world market for goods and by doing so has destroyed national and regional identities. Examine his analysis in paragraphs 22–36 in terms of what you see happening in the economic world today and decide whether or not his ideas about how the bourgeoisie functions still apply and ring true. Has Marx foreseen the problems of globalization that incited protests and riots such as those aimed at the World Bank, the World Trade Organization, and the International Monetary Fund during the last years of the twentieth century into the early part of the twenty-first century?

8. **CONNECTIONS**   Hannah Arendt suggests that Marx invokes a law of history in insisting that there will be a clash between people from different economic classes. Examine this document to see how much of Arendt's position can be defended by reference to Marx. How were Marx's views used to produce a totalitarian state in the Soviet Union? In other words, is Arendt's analysis of Marx accurate?

9. **CONNECTIONS**   Marx's philosophy differs from that of Robert B. Reich. How would Marx respond to Reich's analysis of the future of labor in the next few decades? Would Marx see signs of a coming class struggle in the distinctions Reich draws between the routine workers, the in-person servers, and the symbolic analysts? Does Reich's essay take any of Marx's theories into account?

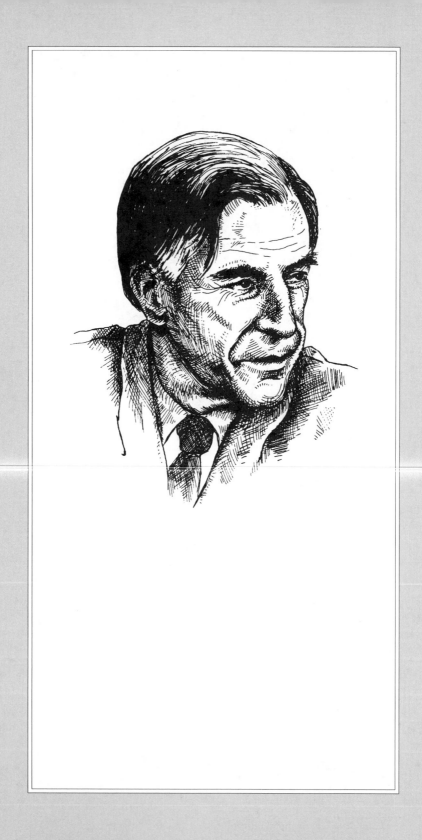

JOHN KENNETH GALBRAITH
The Position of Poverty

JOHN KENNETH GALBRAITH (b. 1908) was born in Canada but has been an American citizen since 1937. He grew up on a farm in Ontario and took his first university degree in agricultural science. This background may have contributed to the success of his many books on subjects such as economics, the State Department, Indian art, and government, which have always explained complex concepts with a clarity easily grasped by laypeople. Sometimes he has been criticized for oversimplifying issues, but on the whole, he has made a brilliant success of writing with wit and humor about perplexing and sometimes troubling issues.

Galbraith was professor of economics at Harvard University for many years. During the presidential campaigns of Adlai Stevenson in 1952 and 1956, he assisted the Democrats as a speechwriter and economics adviser. He performed the same tasks for John F. Kennedy in 1960. Kennedy appointed Galbraith ambassador to India, a post that he maintained for a little over two years, including the period during which India and China fought a border war. His experiences in India resulted in *Ambassador's Journal: A Personal Account of the Kennedy Years* (1969). Kennedy called Galbraith his finest ambassadorial appointment.

Galbraith's involvement with politics was somewhat unusual for an academic economist at that time. It seems to have stemmed from strongly held personal views on the social issues of his time. One of the most important contributions of his best-known and probably most significant book, *The Affluent Society* (1958; rev. eds. 1969, 1976, 1998), was its analysis of America's economic ambitions. He pointed out that at that time the economy was entirely

From *The Affluent Society.*

tied up in the measurement and growth of the gross national product. Economists and government officials concentrated on boosting output, a goal that he felt was misdirected because it would result in products that people really did not need and that would not benefit them. Creating artificial needs for things that had no ultimate value and building in a "planned obsolescence" seemed to him to be wasteful and ultimately destructive.

Galbraith suggested that America concentrate on genuine needs and satisfy them immediately. He was deeply concerned about the environment and suggested that clean air was a priority that should take precedence over industry. He supported development of the arts and stressed the importance of improving housing across the nation. His effort was directed at trying to help Americans change certain basic values by giving up the pursuit of useless consumer novelties and substituting a program of genuine social development. The commitment to consumer products as the basis of the economy naturally argued against a redirection of effort toward the solution of social problems.

Galbraith is so exceptionally clear in his essay that little commentary is needed to establish its importance. He is insightful in clarifying two kinds of poverty: case poverty and insular poverty. Case poverty is restricted to an individual and his or her family and often seems to be caused by alcoholism, ignorance, mental deficiency, discrimination, or specific handicaps. It is an individual, not a group, disorder. Insular poverty affects a group in a given area—an "island" within the larger society. He points to poverty in Appalachia and in the slums of major cities, where most of the people in those "islands" are at or below the poverty level. Insular poverty is linked to the environment, and its causes are somehow derived from that environment.

Galbraith's analysis is perceptive and influential, and although little or no progress has been made in solving the problem of poverty since 1959, he assures us that there are steps that can be taken to help eradicate it. Such steps demand the nation's will, however, and he warns that the nation may lack the will. He also reasons that because the poor are a minority, few politicians make their plight a campaign issue. Actually, in this belief he is wrong. Kennedy in 1960, Lyndon Johnson in 1964, and Jimmy Carter in 1976 made programs for the poor central among their governmental concerns. Because of the war in Vietnam and other governmental policies, however, the 1960s and early 1970s were a time of staggering inflation, wiping out any of the advances the poor had made.

Galbraith's Rhetoric

The most important rhetorical achievement of the piece is its style. This is an example of the elevated plain style: a clear, direct, and basically simple approach to language that only occasionally admits a somewhat learned vocabulary—as in the use of a very few words such as *opulent, unremunerative,* and *ineluctable.* Most of the words he uses are ordinary ones.

He breaks the essay into five carefully numbered sections. In this way he highlights its basic structure and informs us that he has clearly separated its elements into related groups so that he can speak directly to aspects of his subject rather than to the entire topic. This rhetorical technique of division contributes to clarity and confers a sense of authority on the writer.

Galbraith relies on statistical information that the reader can examine if necessary. This information is treated in the early stages of the piece as a prologue. Once such information has been given, Galbraith proceeds in the manner of a logician establishing premises and deriving the necessary conclusions. The subject is sober and sobering, involving issues that are complex, uncertain, and difficult, but the style is direct, confident, and essentially simple. This is the secret of the success of the book from which this selection comes. *The Affluent Society* has been translated into well over a dozen languages and has been a best-seller around the globe, and almost fifty years after its first publication it remains an influential book. Its fundamental insights are such that it is likely to be relevant to the economy of the United States for generations to come.

PREREADING QUESTIONS: WHAT TO READ FOR

The following prereading questions may help you anticipate key issues in the discussion on John Kenneth Galbraith's "The Position of Poverty." Keeping them in mind during your first reading of the selection should help focus your reactions.

• Why is modern poverty different from that of a century ago?

• What is case poverty?

• What is insular poverty?

The Position of Poverty

"The study of the causes of poverty," Alfred Marshall observed   1
at the turn of the century, "is the study of the causes of the degradation of a large part of mankind." He spoke of contemporary England
as well as of the world beyond. A vast number of people both in
town and country, he noted, had insufficient food, clothing and
house-room; they were: "Overworked and undertaught, weary and
careworn, without quiet and without leisure." The chance of their
succor, he concluded, gave to economic studies "their chief and
their highest interest."[1]

No contemporary economist would be likely to make such an   2
observation about the United States. Conventional economic discourse makes obeisance to the continued existence of some poverty.
"We must remember that we still have a great many poor people." In
the nineteen-sixties, poverty promised, for a time, to become a subject of serious political concern. Then the Vietnam war came and the
concern evaporated or was displaced. For economists of conventional mood, the reminders that the poor still exist are a useful way
of allaying uneasiness about the relevance of conventional economic
goals. For some people, wants must be synthesized. Hence, the
importance of the goods to them is not *per se* very high. So much
may be conceded. But others are far closer to physical need. And
hence we must not be cavalier about the urgency of providing them
with the most for the least. The sales tax may have merit for the opulent, but it still bears heavily on the poor. The poor get jobs more
easily when the economy is expanding. Thus poverty survives in
economic discourse partly as a buttress to the conventional economic wisdom.

The privation of which Marshall spoke was, going on to a cen-   3
tury ago, the common lot at least of all who worked without special
skill. As a general affliction, it was ended by increased output which,
however imperfectly it may have been distributed, nevertheless ac-
crued in substantial amount to those who worked for a living. The
result was to reduce poverty from the problem of a majority to that
of a minority. It ceased to be a general case and became a special
case. It is this which has put the problem of poverty into its peculiar
modern form.

---

[1] *Principles of Economics*, 8th ed. (London: Macmillan, 1927), pp. 2–4. [Gal-
braith's note] Alfred Marshall (1842–1924) was an English economist whose *Principles of Economics* (1890) was long a standard text and is still relied on by some
economists for its theories of costs, values, and distribution.

II

For poverty does survive. In part, it is a physical matter; those 4
afflicted have such limited and insufficient food, such poor clothing,
such crowded, cold and dirty shelter that life is painful as well as
comparatively brief. But just as it is far too tempting to say that, in
matters of living standards, everything is relative, so it is wrong to
rest everything on absolutes. People are poverty-stricken when their
income, even if adequate for survival, falls radically behind that of
the community. Then they cannot have what the larger community
regards as the minimum necessary for decency; and they cannot
wholly escape, therefore, the judgment of the larger community that
they are indecent. They are degraded for, in the literal sense, they
live outside the grades or categories which the community regards
as acceptable.

Since the first edition of this book appeared, and one hopes 5
however slightly as a consequence, the character and dimension of
this degradation have become better understood. There have also
been fulsome promises that poverty would be eliminated. The performance on these promises has been less eloquent.

The degree of privation depends on the size of the family, the 6
place of residence—it will be less with given income in rural areas
than in the cities—and will, of course, be affected by changes in living costs. One can usefully think of deprivation as falling into two
broad categories. First, there is what may be called *case* poverty.
This one encounters in every community, rural or urban, however
prosperous that community or the times. Case poverty is the poor
farm family with the junk-filled yard and the dirty children playing
in the bare dirt. Or it is the gray-black hovel beside the railroad
tracks. Or it is the basement dwelling in the alley.

Case poverty is commonly and properly related to some charac- 7
teristic of the individuals so afflicted. Nearly everyone else has mas-
tered his or her environment; this proves that it is not intractable.
But some quality peculiar to the individual or family involved—
mental deficiency, bad health, inability to adapt to the discipline of
industrial life, uncontrollable procreation, alcohol, discrimination
involving a very limited minority, some educational handicap unrelated to community shortcoming, or perhaps a combination of several of theses handicaps—has kept these individuals from participating in the general well-being.

Second, there is what may be called *insular* poverty—that 8
which manifests itself as an "island" of poverty. In the island, everyone or nearly everyone is poor. Here, evidently, it is not easy to explain matters by individual inadequacy. We may mark individuals

down as intrinsically deficient in social performance; it is not proper or even wise so to characterize an entire community. The people of the island have been frustrated by some factor common to their environment.

Case poverty exists. It has also been useful to those who have ⁹ needed a formula for keeping the suffering of others from causing suffering to themselves. Since this poverty is the result of the deficiencies, including the moral shortcomings, of the persons concerned, it is possible to shift the responsibility to them. They are worthless and, as a simple manifestation of social justice, they suffer for it. Or, at a somewhat higher level of social perception and compassion, it means that the problem of poverty is sufficiently solved by private and public charity. This rescues those afflicted from the worst consequences of their inadequacy or misfortune; no larger social change or reorganization is suggested. Except as it may be insufficient in its generosity, the society is not at fault.

Insular poverty yields to no such formulas. In earlier times, ¹⁰ when agriculture and extractive industries were the dominant sources of livelihood, something could be accomplished by shifting the responsibility for low income to a poor natural endowment and thus, in effect, to God. The soil was thin and stony, other natural resources absent and hence the people were poor. And, since it is the undoubted preference of many to remain in the vicinity of the place of their birth, a homing instinct that operates for people as well as pigeons, the people remained in the poverty which heaven had decreed for them. It is an explanation that is nearly devoid of empirical application. Connecticut is very barren and stony and incomes are very high. Similarly Wyoming. West Virginia is well watered with rich mines and forests and the people are very poor. The South is much favored in soil and climate and similarly poor and the very richest parts of the South, such as the Mississippi-Yazoo Delta, have long had a well-earned reputation for the greatest deprivation. Yet so strong is the tendency to associate poverty with natural causes that even individuals of some modest intelligence will still be heard, in explanation of insular poverty, to say, "It's basically a poor country." "It's a pretty barren region."

Most modern poverty is insular in character and the islands are ¹¹ the rural and urban slums. From the former, mainly in the South, the southern Appalachians and Puerto Rico, there has been until recent times a steady flow of migrants, some white but more black, to the latter. Grim as life is in the urban ghetto, it still offers more hope, income and interest than in the rural slum.

The most important characteristic of insular poverty is forces, ¹² common to all members of the community, that restrain or prevent participation in economic life at going rates of return. These restraints are several. Race, which acts to locate people by their color rather than by the proximity to employment, is obviously one. So are poor educational facilities. (And this effect is further exaggerated when the poorly educated, endemically a drug on the labor market, are brought together in dense clusters by the common inadequacy of the schools available to blacks and the poor.) So is the disintegration of family life in the slum which leaves households in the hands of women. Family life itself is in some measure a manifestation of affluence. And so, without doubt, is the shared sense of helplessness and rejection and the resulting demoralization which is the product of the common misfortune.

The most certain thing about this poverty is that it is not reme- 13
died by a general advance in income. Case poverty is not remedied because the specific individual inadequacy precludes employment and participation in the general advance. Insular poverty is not directly alleviated because the advance does not remove the specific frustrations of environment to which the people of these areas are subject. This is not to say that it is without effect. If there are jobs outside the ghetto or away from the rural slum, those who are qualified, and not otherwise constrained, can take them and escape. If there are no such jobs, none can escape. But it remains that advance cannot improve the position of those who, by virtue of self or environment, cannot participate.

III

With the transition of the very poor from a majority to a com- 14
parative minority position, there has been a change in their political position. Any tendency of a politician to identify himself with those of the lowest estate usually brought the reproaches of the well-to-do. Political pandering and demagoguery were naturally suspected. But, for the man so reproached, there was the compensating advantage of alignment with a large majority. Now any politician who speaks for the very poor is speaking for a small and generally inarticulate minority. As a result, the modern liberal politician regularly aligns himself not with the poverty-ridden members of the community but with the far more numerous people who enjoy the far more affluent income of (say) the modern trade union member or the intellectual. Ambrose Bierce, in *The Devil's Dictionary*, called poverty "a file provided for the teeth of the rats of reform."[2] It is so no longer. Reform

---

[2] **Ambrose Bierce (1842–1914?)** A southern American writer noted for satirical writings such as the one quoted.

now concerns itself with the needs of people who are relatively well-to-do—whether the comparison be with their own past or with those who are really at the bottom of the income ladder.

In consequence, a notable feature of efforts to help the very poor is their absence of any very great political appeal.[3] Politicians have found it possible to be indifferent where they could not be derisory. And very few have been under a strong compulsion to support these efforts.

The concern for inequality and deprivation had vitality only so long as the many suffered while a few had much. It did not survive as a decisive political issue in a time when the many had much even though others had much more. It is our misfortune that when inequality declined as an issue, the slate was not left clean. A residual and in some ways rather more hopeless problem remained.

IV

An affluent society that is also both compassionate and rational would, no doubt, secure to all who needed it the minimum income essential for decency and comfort. The corrupting effect on the human spirit of unearned revenue has unquestionably been exaggerated as, indeed, have the character-building values of hunger and privation. To secure to each family a minimum income, as a normal function of the society, would help ensure that the misfortunes of parents, deserved or otherwise, were not visited on their children. It would help ensure that poverty was not self-perpetuating. Most of the reaction, which no doubt would be adverse, is based on obsolete attitudes. When poverty was a majority phenomenon, such action could not be afforded. A poor society, as this essay has previously shown, had to enforce the rule that the person who did not work could not eat. And possibly it was justified in the added cruelty of applying the rule to those who could not work or whose efficiency was far below par. An affluent society has no similar excuse for such rigor. It can use the forthright remedy of providing income for those without. Nothing requires such a society to be compassionate. But it no longer has a high philosophical justification for callousness.

The notion that income is a remedy for indigency has a certain forthright appeal.[4] It would also ease the problems of economic management by reducing the reliance on production as a source of

---

[3]This was true of the Office of Economic Opportunity—the so-called poverty program—and was ultimately the reason for its effective demise. [Galbraith's note]

[4]As earlier noted, in the first edition the provision of a guaranteed income was discussed but dismissed as "beyond reasonable hope." [Galbraith's note]

income. The provision of such a basic source of income must henceforth be the first and the strategic step in the attack on poverty.

But it is only one step. In the past, we have suffered from the supposition that the only remedy for poverty lies in remedies that allow people to look after themselves—to participate in the economy. Nothing has better served the conscience of people who wished to avoid inconvenient or expensive action than an appeal, on this issue, to Calvinist precept—"The only sound way to solve the problem of poverty is to help people help themselves." But this does not mean that steps to allow participation and to keep poverty from being self-perpetuating are unimportant. On the contrary. It requires that the investment in children from families presently afflicted be as little below normal as possible. If the children of poor families have first-rate schools and school attendance is properly enforced; if the children, though badly fed at home, are well nourished at school; if the community has sound health services, and the physical well-being of the children is vigilantly watched; if there is opportunity for advanced education for those who qualify regardless of means; and if, especially in the case of urban communities, housing is ample and housing standards are enforced, the streets are clean, the laws are kept, and recreation is adequate—then there is a chance that the children of the very poor will come to maturity without inhibiting disadvantage. In the case of insular poverty, this remedy requires that the services of the community be assisted from outside. Poverty is self-perpetuating partly because the poorest communities are poorest in the services which would eliminate it. To eliminate poverty efficiently, we must, indeed, invest more than proportionately in the children of the poor community. It is there that high-quality schools, strong health services, special provision for nutrition and recreation are most needed to compensate for the very low investment which families are able to make in their own offspring. 19

The effect of education and related investment in individuals is to help them overcome the restraints that are imposed by their environment. These need also to be attacked even more directly—by giving the mobility that is associated with plentiful, good and readily available housing, by provision of comfortable, efficient and economical mass transport, by making the environment pleasant and safe, and by eliminating the special health handicaps that afflict the poor. 20

Nor is case poverty entirely resistant to such remedies. Much can be done to treat those characteristics which cause people to reject or be rejected by the modern industrial society. Educational deficiencies can be overcome. Mental deficiencies can be treated. 21

Physical handicaps can be remedied. The limiting factor is not a lack of knowledge of what can be done. Overwhelmingly, it is a shortage of money.

V

It will be clear that, to a remarkable extent, the remedy for 22 poverty leads to the same requirements as those for social balance. The restraints that confine people to the ghetto are those that result from insufficient investment in the public sector. And the means to escape from these constraints and to break their hold on subsequent generations just mentioned—better nutrition and health, better education, more and better housing, better mass transport, an environment more conducive to effective social participation—all, with rare exceptions, call for massively greater investment in the public sector. In recent years, the problems of the urban ghetto have been greatly discussed but with little resultant effect. To a certain extent, the search for deeper social explanations of its troubles has been motivated by the hope that these (together with more police) might lead to solutions that would somehow elide the problem of cost. It is an idle hope. The modern urban household is an extremely expensive thing. We have not yet taken the measure of the resources that must be allocated to its public tasks if it is to be agreeable or even tolerable. And first among the symptoms of an insufficient allocation is the teeming discontent of the modern ghetto.

A further feature of these remedies is to be observed. Their con- 23 sequence is to allow of participation in the economic life of the larger community—to make people and the children of people who are now idle productive. This means that they will add to the total output of goods and services. We see once again that even by its own terms the present preoccupation with the private sector of the economy as compared with the whole spectrum of human needs is inefficient. The parallel with investment in the supply of trained and educated manpower discussed above will be apparent.

But increased output of goods is not the main point. Even to the 24 most intellectually reluctant reader, it will now be evident that enhanced productive efficiency is not the motif of this volume. The very fact that increased output offers itself as a by-product of the effort to eliminate poverty is one of the reasons. No one would be called upon to write at such length on a problem so easily solved as that of increasing production. The main point lies elsewhere. Poverty—grim, degrading and ineluctable—is not remarkable in India. For relatively few, the fate is otherwise. But in the United States, the survival of poverty is remarkable. We ignore it because we share with all societies at all times the capacity for not seeing what we do not wish to see. Anciently this has enabled the nobleman to enjoy his dinner while remaining oblivious to the beggars around his door. In our own day, it enables us to travel in comfort through the South Bronx and into the lush precincts of midtown Manhattan. But while our failure to notice can be explained, it cannot be excused. "Poverty," Pitt[5] exclaimed, "is no disgrace but it is damned annoying." In the contemporary United States, it is not annoying but it is a disgrace.

QUESTIONS FOR CRITICAL READING

1. What is the fundamental difference between the attitude Alfred Marshall held toward the poor (para. 1) and the attitude contemporary economists hold?
2. Galbraith avoids a specific definition of poverty because he says it changes from society to society. How would you define poverty as it exists in our society? What are its major indicators?
3. According to Galbraith, what is the relationship of politics to poverty?
4. What, according to this essay, seem to be the causes of poverty?
5. Clarify the distinctions Galbraith makes between case poverty and insular poverty. Are they reasonable distinctions?
6. Does Galbraith oversimplify the issues of poverty in America?
7. Galbraith first published this piece in 1958. How much have attitudes toward poverty changed since then? What kinds of progress seem to have been made toward eradicating poverty?

SUGGESTIONS FOR WRITING

1. In paragraph 4, Galbraith says, "People are poverty-stricken when their income, even if adequate for survival, falls radically behind that of the community. Then they cannot have what the larger community regards as the minimum necessary for decency; and they cannot wholly escape, therefore, the judgment of the larger community that they are indecent. They are degraded for, in the literal sense, they live outside the grades or categories which the community regards as acceptable." Examine what he says here, and explain what he means. Is this an accurate description of poverty? How would you amend it? If you accept his description of poverty, what public policy would you recommend

---

[5] **William Pitt, the Younger (1759–1806)** British prime minister from 1783 to 1801 and, briefly, again in 1804 and 1805.

to deal with it? What would be the consequences of accepting Galbraith's description?

2. Galbraith points out some anomalies of poverty and place. For example, he notes that West Virginia is rich in resources but that its people have been notable for their poverty. Connecticut, on the other hand, is poor in resources, with stony, untillable land, and its people have been notable for their wealth. Some economists have also pointed out that when the Americas were settled, South America had gold, was home to lush tropics that yielded food and fruit for the asking, and held the promise of immense wealth. North America had a harsh climate, stubborn soil conditions, and dense forests that needed clearing. Yet North America has less poverty now than does South America. Write a brief essay in which you consider whether what is said above is too simplified to be useful. If it is not, what do you think is the reason for the economic distinctions that Galbraith and others point out?

3. What personal experiences have you had with poverty? Are you familiar with examples of case poverty? If so, describe them in such a way as to help others understand them. What causes produced the poverty? What is the social situation of the people in your examples? How might they increase their wealth?

4. Examine the newspapers for the last several days, and look through back issues of magazines such as *Time, Newsweek,* the *New Republic,* the *New Leader,* or *U.S. News & World Report.* How many stories does each devote to the question of poverty? Present a survey of the views you find, and compare them with Galbraith's. How much agreement or disagreement is there? Would the level of the nation's concern with poverty please Galbraith?

5. Write a brief essay about current political attitudes toward poverty. If possible, gather some recent statements made by politicians. Analyze them to see how closely they tally with Galbraith's concerns and views. Do any specific politicians act as spokespeople for the poor?

6. Galbraith says that poverty has undergone a dramatic change in our society: once most people were poor and only a few were affluent, and now most people are affluent and only a few are poor. Is Galbraith correct in this assessment? Interview your parents and grandparents and their friends to establish or disprove the validity of Galbraith's claim, and then explain what you feel are the problems the poor face as a result of their minority status. If possible, during your interviews ask what feelings your parents and their friends have about the poor. What feelings do you have? Are they shared by your friends?

7. **CONNECTIONS**   What might Karl Marx say in reaction to Galbraith's definition of poverty and his terms for case poverty and insular poverty? Should Galbraith have examined the role of the bourgeoisie in creating, maintaining, or ignoring poverty? Galbraith wrote the original version of this piece during the 1950s, while world communism was at its height. How might he have accommodated the issues that Marx felt were most important for the working person?

8. **CONNECTIONS**   To what extent would Milton and Rose Friedman be sympathetic to Galbraith's attitude toward the poor? What would the Friedmans react to most negatively in Galbraith's discussion? What would they take issue with concerning the role of politicians in solving the problems of poverty? What would Galbraith expect of politicians that the Friedmans would not?

MILTON AND ROSE FRIEDMAN
Created Equal

MILTON FRIEDMAN (b. 1912) is a senior research fellow at the Hoover Institution and Paul Snowden Russell Distinguished Service Professor Emeritus of Economics at the University of Chicago. He taught at the University of Chicago from 1946 to 1976. Friedman won the Nobel Prize for Economics in 1976 and is widely regarded as the leading expert in monetarist economics. (A monetarist is an economist who studies the relation of the supply of money to the growth of the economy.) Friedman's theories regarding money supply have been influential on most U.S. government policy since the 1960s.

ROSE DIRECTOR FRIEDMAN studied at Reed College and then at the University of Chicago, where she received a Bachelor of Philosophy degree and went on to study for the Ph.D. in economics. She did all the work for the degree except for the thesis. She married Milton Friedman in 1937 and worked with the Federal Deposit Insurance Corporation and the National Bureau of Economic Research. She has collaborated with her husband on three books, and together they created the Milton and Rose D. Friedman Foundation, whose focus is on helping parents have a say in the schools their children attend.

Milton Friedman is a prominent laissez-faire economist. The term *laissez-faire* translates loosely as "let them do as they will," and its use in economics implies a policy in which the government avoids interfering with business. Friedman sees the government's primary role as limited to regulating the supply of money in order to balance prices, output, and employment. He has been a champion of free market economy, in which tariffs and trade barriers are removed, and has advised a number of conservative politicians, from Barry Goldwater to Richard Nixon to Ronald Reagan. His policies are largely those that Margaret Thatcher put into action in her government in England in the 1980s.

Friedman's most important books are *Taxing to Prevent Infla-tion* (1943); *Essays in Positive Economics* (1953); *A Theory of the Consumption Function* (1957); the book many say is his most influential, *A Monetary History of the United States 1867–1960* (1963), with Anna Schwartz; *The Optimum Quantity of Money* (1969); and *Free to Choose: A Personal Statement* (1980). Rose D. Friedman co-authored the last book as well as *Capitalism and Freedom* (1962) and *Tyranny of the Status Quo* (1984). Milton and Rose Friedman have also published a memoir, *Two Lucky People* (1998), recounting their struggles and achievements. The Friedmans' work centers on monetary policy but also encompasses larger issues, such as the relationship of government to business and the relationship of the individual to capital and capitalism. Much of Milton Friedman's early work was written in the shadow of fascism and world communism, and his views strongly support more rather than less freedom. For him, freedom works in helping to produce wealth and to avoid poverty.

The essay that follows, "Created Equal," was published originally in *Free to Choose: A Personal Statement* (1980). The concept of equality interested the French statesman and author Alexis de Tocqueville, whose own essay on equality appears in this volume in the section on American Culture. Tocqueville wrote in the nineteenth century and responded to the development of the United States as a new nation in which nobility and aristocratic classes had no place and in which people regarded each other as being on an essentially equal footing. For Tocqueville, that situation was a novelty. Thomas Jefferson, too, emphasized issues of equality in the eighteenth century, and it is there that the Friedmans center their opening remarks.

The Friedmans explore exactly what the founding fathers meant by equality when they declared that "all men are created equal." The problems associated with the existence of slavery and its essential contradiction of equality persisted for one hundred fifty years until the Civil War and emancipation in 1862. The emphasis on equality before God reminds us that the concept of equality is qualified by a number of distinctions, both politically and economically. The Friedmans review some of those distinctions and attempt to clarify points that are central to their own understanding of equality.

For example, they state that when Jefferson declared that all men are created equal, he also knew that all men were very different from one another and that because they were not the same, they remained distinct in sometimes problematic ways. Jefferson himself was a man of enormous talent. He was an architect, a successful farmer, a scientist and inventor, and a founder of a great university. He also grew wealthy enough to own a large number of slaves. The Friedmans point out that he was successful to such a degree that he might be thought superior in achievement to most contemporary Americans. In other words, he was a member of the wealthy elite.

Rather than seeing this as a problem, the Friedmans insist that this is the nature of the world: "Life is not fair" (para. 35). Some people have more talent, luck, and success than others. Yet all are equal before God and equal before the law. According to the Friedmans, the freedom to succeed — to acquire more wealth than some others, to achieve more good works than some others, to flourish more than some others — is central to the American experiment.

Government policies that restrict the freedom to succeed, whether they be excessive taxation, restrictive laws, or specific prohibitions, are forms of oppression. The Friedmans' greatest fear concerns the distinction of *equality of outcome*. The term simply means that rather than promoting equality of opportunity, the government wishes at times to guarantee that a number of people will achieve the same outcome. This desire necessitates some form of restriction that permits all people to share the wealth relatively equally — something like a handicap in horse racing. For the Friedmans, such constraints are the worst form of economic tyranny and a denial of personal freedom.

The Friedmans' Rhetoric

The primary strategy of the first parts of the passage centers on definition of terms. The Friedmans present an argument in favor of freedom and free markets, but they realize that their argument will succeed or fail in terms of the clarity of their premises and the intelligibility of their definitions. The terms *equality* and *freedom* mean different things to different people, and if the Friedmans do not clarify their terms right away, they could end up arguing at cross purposes with their readers. The Friedmans also help their argument by structuring it carefully, using six subheads to clarify its organization: "Equality before God," "Equality of Opportunity," "Equality of Outcome," "Who Favors Equality of Outcome?," "Consequences of Egalitarian Policies," and "Capitalism and Equality."

The authors' first efforts are to establish the importance of liberty for the individual and then to show how various government policies can actually impinge on individual liberty in the name of

doing something many feel is desirable: guaranteeing a good outcome for all people equally. Their views generally support the free
market, which implies that individuals should be free to build a
business as they see fit. They should not be hindered by heavy taxation designed to redistribute wealth from people who earn a great
deal to those who earn very little. The Friedmans' argument relies
on careful comparisons with Communist countries and undeveloped countries to demonstrate the calamities that can result from
such programs.

One of the interesting strategies of the argument is the use of
historical comparisons, both with recent nations and with classical
civilizations. Milton Friedman is widely known in Japan (which
has benefited from his economic theories) and introduces examples
and comparisons from Asia as well as from Europe and the United
States. However, he also understands the civilizations of early
Greece and Rome and comments on the effects that modern
"mechanical improvement" might have had on individuals in those
cultures. He points out that even in Communist Russia—which
still existed when he wrote this essay—the concept of equality was
contradicted by the fact that the party members and the Politburo
represented an upper class with wealth and privileges, whereas the
ordinary workers made do with shabby goods and limited choice in
the marketplace.

Ultimately this argument favors freedom of choice, freedom of
opportunity, and the free capitalist market. Anything else, the
Friedmans imply, suggests a restriction of freedom and ultimate
unhappiness. Moreover, and most important, such restrictions contradict the principles of freedom on which the concept of equality
is based.

PREREADING QUESTIONS:
WHAT TO READ FOR

The following prereading questions may help you anticipate key issues
in the discussion on Milton and Rose Friedman's "Created Equal." Keeping
them in mind during your first reading of the selection should help focus
your reactions.

- In the Friedmans' view, what is the relationship between equality and
liberty?

- Why do the Friedmans disapprove of the concept of "equality of outcome"?

Created Equal

"Equality," "liberty"—what precisely do these words from the 1
Declaration of Independence mean? Can the ideals they express be
realized in practice? Are equality and liberty consistent one with the
other, or are they in conflict?

Since well before the Declaration of Independence, these ques- 2
tions have played a central role in the history of the United States.
The attempt to answer them has shaped the intellectual climate of
opinion, led to bloody war, and produced major changes in economic and political institutions. This attempt continues to dominate
our political debate. It will shape our future as it has our past.

In the early decades of the Republic, equality meant equality be- 3
fore God; liberty meant the liberty to shape one's own life. The obvious conflict between the Declaration of Independence and the institution of slavery occupied the center of the stage. That conflict was
finally resolved by the Civil War. The debate then moved to a different level. Equality came more and more to be interpreted as "equality of opportunity" in the sense that no one should be prevented by
arbitrary obstacles from using his capacities to pursue his own objectives. That is still its dominant meaning to most citizens of the
United States.

Neither equality before God nor equality of opportunity pre- 4
sented any conflict with liberty to shape one's own life. Quite the
opposite. Equality and liberty were two faces of the same basic
value—that every individual should be regarded as an end in
himself.

A very different meaning of equality has emerged in the United 5
States in recent decades—equality of outcome. Everyone should
have the same level of living or of income, should finish the race at
the same time. Equality of outcome is in clear conflict with liberty.
The attempt to promote it has been a major source of bigger and
bigger government, and of government-imposed restrictions on our
liberty.

Equality before God

When Thomas Jefferson, at the age of thirty-three, wrote "all 6
men are created equal," he and his contemporaries did not take
these words literally. They did not regard "men"—or as we would
say today, "persons"—as equal in physical characteristics, emotional reactions, mechanical and intellectual abilities. Thomas

Jefferson himself was a most remarkable person. At the age of twenty-six he designed his beautiful house at Monticello (Italian for "little mountain"), supervised its construction, and, indeed, is said to have done some of the work himself. In the course of his life, he was an inventor, a scholar, an author, a statesman, governor of the State of Virginia, President of the United States, Minister to France, founder of the University of Virginia—hardly an average man.

The clue to what Thomas Jefferson and his contemporaries   7
meant by equal is in the next phrase of the Declaration—"endowed by their Creator with certain unalienable rights; that among these are Life, Liberty, and the pursuit of Happiness." Men were equal before God. Each person is precious in and of himself. He has unalienable rights, rights that no one else is entitled to invade. He is entitled to serve his own purposes and not to be treated simply as an instrument to promote someone else's purposes. "Liberty" is part of the definition of equality, not in conflict with it.

Equality before God—personal equality[1]—is important pre-   8
cisely because people are not identical. Their different values, their different tastes, their different capacities will lead them to want to lead very different lives. Personal equality requires respect for their right to do so, not the imposition on them of someone else's values or judgment. Jefferson had no doubt that some men were superior to others, that there was an elite. But that did not give them the right to rule others.

If an elite did not have the right to impose its will on others,   9
neither did any other group, even a majority. Every person was to be his own ruler—provided that he did not interfere with the similar right of others. Government was established to protect that right—from fellow citizens and from external threat—not to give a majority unbridled rule. Jefferson had three achievements he wanted to be remembered for inscribed on his tombstone: the Virginia statute for religious freedom (a precursor of the U.S. Bill of Rights designed to protect minorities against domination by majorities), authorship of the Declaration of Independence, and the founding of the University of Virginia. The goal of the framers of the Constitution of the United States, drafted by Jefferson's contemporaries, was a national government strong enough to defend the country and promote the general welfare but at the same time sufficiently limited in power to protect the individual citizen, and the separate state governments, from domination by the national government. Democratic, in the sense of

---

[1] See J. R. Pole, *The Pursuit of Equality in American History* (Berkeley and Los Angeles: University of California Press, 1978), pp. 51–58. [Friedmans' note]

widespread participation in government, yes; in the political sense of majority rule, clearly no.

Similarly, Alexis de Tocqueville, the famous French political philosopher and sociologist, in his classic *Democracy in America*, written after a lengthy visit in the 1830s, saw equality, not majority rule, as the outstanding characteristic of America. "In America," he wrote, 10

> the aristocratic element has always been feeble from its birth; and if at the present day it is not actually destroyed, it is at any rate so completely disabled, that we can scarcely assign to it any degree of influence on the course of affairs. The democratic principle, on the contrary, has gained so much strength by time, by events, and by legislation, as to have become not only predominant but all-powerful. There is no family or corporate authority. . . .
>
> America, then, exhibits in her social state a most extraordinary phenomenon. Men are there seen on a greater equality in point of fortune and intellect, or, in other words, more equal in their strength, than in any other country of the world, or in any age of which history has preserved the remembrance.[2]

Tocqueville admired much of what he observed, but he was by no means an uncritical admirer, fearing that democracy carried too far might undermine civic virtue. As he put it, "There is . . . a manly and lawful passion for equality which incites men to wish all to be powerful and honored. This passion tends to elevate the humble to the rank of the great; but there exists also in the human heart a depraved taste for equality, which impels the weak to attempt to lower the powerful to their own level, and reduces men to prefer equality in slavery to inequality with freedom."[3] 11

It is striking testimony to the changing meaning of words that in recent decades the Democratic party of the United States has been the chief instrument for strengthening that government power which Jefferson and many of his contemporaries viewed as the greatest threat to democracy. And it has striven to increase government power in the name of a concept of "equality" that is almost the opposite of the concept of equality Jefferson identified with liberty and Tocqueville with democracy. 12

Of course the practice of the founding fathers did not always correspond to their preaching. The most obvious conflict was 13

---

[2] Alexis de Tocqueville, *Democracy in America,* 2 vols., 2d ed., trans. Henry Reeve, ed. Francis Bowen (Boston: John Allyn, Publisher, 1863), vol. I, pp. 66–67. (First French edition published in 1835.) [Friedmans' note]

[3] Ibid., pp. 67–68. [Friedmans' note]

slavery. Thomas Jefferson himself owned slaves until the day he died—July 4, 1826. He agonized repeatedly about slavery, suggested in his notes and correspondence plans for eliminating slavery, but never publicly proposed any such plans or campaigned against the institution.

Yet the Declaration he drafted had either to be blatantly violated   14 by the nation he did so much to create and form, or slavery had to be abolished. Little wonder that the early decades of the Republic saw a rising tide of controversy about the institution of slavery. That controversy ended in a civil war that, in the words of Abraham Lincoln's Gettysburg Address, tested whether a "nation, conceived in liberty and dedicated to the proposition that all men are created equal...can long endure." The nation endured, but only at a tremendous cost in lives, property, and social cohesion.

Equality of Opportunity

Once the Civil War abolished slavery and the concept of per-   15 sonal equality—equality before God and the law—came closer to realization, emphasis shifted, in intellectual discussion and in government and private policy, to a different concept—equality of opportunity.

Literal equality of opportunity—in the sense of "identity"—is   16 impossible. One child is born blind, another with sight. One child has parents deeply concerned about his welfare who provide a background of culture and understanding; another has dissolute, improvident parents. One child is born in the United States, another in India, or China, or Russia. They clearly do not have identical opportunities open to them at birth, and there is no way that their opportunities can be made identical.

Like personal equality, equality of opportunity is not to be inter-   17 preted literally. Its real meaning is perhaps best expressed by the French expression dating from the French Revolution: *Une carrière ouverte aux talents*—a career open to the talents. No arbitrary obstacles should prevent people from achieving those positions for which their talents fit them and which their values lead them to seek. Not birth, nationality, color, religion, sex, nor any other irrelevant characteristic should determine the opportunities that are open to a person—only his abilities.

On this interpretation, equality of opportunity simply spells out   18 in more detail the meaning of personal equality, of equality before the law. And like personal equality, it has meaning and importance precisely because people are different in their genetic and cultural characteristics, and hence both want to and can pursue different careers.

Equality of opportunity, like personal equality, is not inconsistent with liberty; on the contrary, it is an essential component of liberty. If some people are denied access to particular positions in life for which they are qualified simply because of their ethnic background, color, or religion, that is an interference with their right to "Life, Liberty, and the pursuit of Happiness." It denies equality of opportunity and, by the same token, sacrifices the freedom of some for the advantage of others. 19

Like every ideal, equality of opportunity is incapable of being fully realized. The most serious departure was undoubtedly with respect to the blacks, particularly in the South but in the North as well. Yet there was also tremendous progress for blacks and for other groups. The very concept of a "melting pot" reflected the goal of equality of opportunity. So also did the expansion of "free" education at elementary, secondary, and higher levels—though...this development has not been an unmixed blessing. 20

The priority given to equality of opportunity in the hierarchy of values generally accepted by the public after the Civil War is manifested particularly in economic policy. The catchwords were free enterprise, competition, laissez-faire. Everyone was to be free to go into any business, follow any occupation, but any property, subject only to the agreement of the other parties to the transaction. Each was to have the opportunity to reap the benefits if he succeeded, to suffer the costs if he failed. There were to be no arbitrary obstacles. Performance, not birth, religion, or nationality, was the touchstone. 21

One corollary was the development of what many who regarded themselves as the cultural elite sneered at as vulgar materialism—an emphasis on the almighty dollar, on wealth as both the symbol and the seal of success. As Tocqueville pointed out, this emphasis reflected the unwillingness of the community to accept the traditional criteria in feudal and aristocratic societies, namely birth and parentage. Performance was the obvious alternative, and the accumulation of wealth was the most readily available measure of performance. 22

Another corollary, of course, was an enormous release of human energy that made America an increasingly productive and dynamic society in which social mobility was an everyday reality. Still another, perhaps surprisingly, was an explosion in charitable activity. This explosion was made possible by the rapid growth in wealth. It took the form it did—of nonprofit hospitals, privately endowed colleges and universities, a plethora of charitable organizations directed to helping the poor—because of the dominant values of the society, including, especially, promotion of equality of opportunity. 23

Of course, in the economic sphere as elsewhere, practice did 24
not always conform to the ideal. Government *was* kept to a minor
role; no major obstacles to enterprise were erected, and by the
end of the nineteenth century, positive government measures, especially the Sherman Anti-Trust Law, were adopted to eliminate private barriers to competition. But extralegal arrangements continued
to interfere with the freedom of individuals to enter various businesses or professions, and social practices unquestionably gave
special advantages to persons born in the "right" families, of the
"right" color, and practicing the "right" religion. However, the rapid
rise in the economic and social position of various less privileged groups demonstrates that these obstacles were by no means
insurmountable.

In respect of government measures, one major deviation from 25
free markets was in foreign trade, where Alexander Hamilton's *Report on Manufactures* had enshrined tariff protection for domestic industries as part of the American way. Tariff protection was inconsistent with thoroughgoing equality of opportunity... and, indeed,
with the free immigration of persons, which was the rule until
World War I, except only for Orientals. Yet it could be rationalized
both by the needs of national defense and on the very different
ground that equality stops at the water's edge—an illogical rational-
ization that is adopted also by most of today's proponents of a very
different concept of equality.

Equality of Outcome

That different concept, equality of outcome, has been gaining 26
ground in this century. It first affected government policy in Great
Britain and on the European continent. Over the past half-century it
has increasingly affected government policy in the United States as
well. In some intellectual circles the desirability of equality of outcome has become an article of religious faith: everyone should finish
the race at the same time. As the Dodo said in *Alice in Wonderland,*
"*Everybody* has won, and *all* must have prizes."

For this concept, as for the other two, "equal" is not to be inter- 27
preted literally as "identical." No one really maintains that everyone,
regardless of age or sex or other physical qualities, should have
identical rations of each separate item of food, clothing, and so on.
The goal is rather "fairness," a much vaguer notion—indeed, one
that it is difficult, if not impossible, to define precisely. "Fair shares
for all" is the modern slogan that has replaced Karl Marx's "To each
according to his needs, from each according to his ability."

This concept of equality differs radically from the other two. 28
Government measures that promote personal equality or equality of
opportunity enhance liberty; government measures to achieve "fair
shares for all" reduce liberty. If what people get is to be determined
by "fairness," who is to decide what is "fair"? As a chorus of voices
asked the Dodo, "But who is to give the prizes?" "Fairness" is not an
objectively determined concept once it departs from identity. "Fairness," like "needs," is in the eye of the beholder. If all are to have
"fair shares," someone or some group of people must decide what
shares are fair—and they must be able to impose their decisions on
others, taking from those who have more than their "fair" share and
giving to those who have less. Are those who make and impose such
decisions equal to those for whom they decide? Are we not in
George Orwell's *Animal Farm,* where "all animals are equal, but
some animals are more equal than others"?

In addition, if what people get is determined by "fairness" and 29
not by what they produce, where are the "prizes" to come from?
What incentive is there to work and produce? How is it to be decided who is to be the doctor, who the lawyer, who the garbage collector, who the street sweeper? What assures that people will accept
the roles assigned to them and perform those roles in accordance
with their abilities? Clearly, only force or the threat of force will do.

The key point is not merely that practice will depart from the 30
ideal. Of course it will, as it does with respect to the other two concepts of equality as well. The point is rather that there is a fundamental conflict between the *ideal* of "fair shares" or of its precursor,
"to each according to his needs," and the *ideal* of personal liberty.
This conflict has plagued every attempt to make equality of outcome
the overriding principle of social organization. The end result has
invariably been a state of terror: Russia, China, and, more recently,
Cambodia offer clear and convincing evidence. And even terror has
not equalized outcomes. In every case, wide inequality persists by
any criterion; inequality between the rulers and the ruled, not only
in power, but also in material standards of life.[4]

The far less extreme measures taken in Western countries in the 31
name of equality of outcome have shared the same fate to a lesser
extent. They, too, have restricted individual liberty. They, too, have
failed to achieve their objective. It has proved impossible to define
"fair shares" in a way that is generally acceptable, or to satisfy the

---

[4] See Smith, *The Russians,* and Kaiser, *Russia: The People and the Power.* Nick
Eberstadt, "Has China Failed?" *The New York Review of Books,* April 5, 1979, p. 37,
notes, "In China,...income distribution seems *very roughly* to have been the same
since 1953." [Friedmans' note]

members of the community that they are being treated "fairly." On the contrary, dissatisfaction has mounted with every additional attempt to implement equality of outcome.

Much of the moral fervor behind the drive for equality of outcome comes from the widespread belief that it is not fair that some children should have a great advantage over others simply because they happen to have wealthy parents. Of course it is not fair. However, unfairness can take many forms. It can take the form of the inheritance of property—bonds and stocks, houses, factories; it can also take the form of the inheritance of talent—musical ability, strength, mathematical genius. The inheritance of property can be interfered with more readily than the inheritance of talent. But from an ethical point of view, is there any difference between the two? Yet many people resent the inheritance of property but not the inheritance of talent.

Look at the same issue from the point of view of the parent. If you want to assure your child a higher income in life, you can do so in various ways. You can buy him (or her) an education that will equip him to pursue an occupation yielding a high income; or you can set him up in a business that will yield a higher income than he could earn as a salaried employee; or you can leave him property, the income from which will enable him to live better. Is there any ethical difference among these three ways of using your property? Or again, if the state leaves you any money to spend over and above taxes, should the state permit you to spend it on riotous living but not to leave it to your children?

The ethical issues involved are subtle and complex. They are not to be resolved by such simplistic formulas as "fair shares for all." Indeed, if we took that seriously, youngsters with less musical skill should be given the greatest amount of musical training in order to compensate for their inherited disadvantage, and those with greater musical aptitude should be prevented from having access to good musical training; and similarly with all other categories of inherited personal qualities. That might be "fair" to the youngsters lacking in talent, but would it be "fair" to the talented, let alone to those who had to work to pay for training the youngsters lacking talent, or to the persons deprived of the benefits that might have come from the cultivation of the talents of the gifted?

Life is not fair. It is tempting to believe that government can rectify what nature has spawned. But it is also important to recognize how much we benefit from the very unfairness we deplore.

There's nothing fair about Marlene Dietrich's having been born with beautiful legs that we all want to look at; or about Muhammad Ali's having been born with the skill that made him a great fighter. But on the other side, millions of people who have enjoyed looking at Marlene Dietrich's legs or watching one of Muhammad Ali's fights have benefited from nature's unfairness in producing a Marlene Dietrich and a Muhammad Ali. What kind of a world would it be if everyone were a duplicate of everyone else?

It is certainly not fair that Muhammad Ali should be able to earn 37 millions of dollars in one night. But wouldn't it have been even more unfair to the people who enjoyed watching him if, in the pursuit of some abstract ideal of equality, Muhammad Ali had not been permitted to earn more for one night's fight — or for each day spent in preparing for a fight — than the lowest man on the totem pole could get for a day's unskilled work on the docks? It might have been possible to do that, but the result would have been to deny people the opportunity to watch Muhammad Ali. We doubt very much that he would have been willing to undergo the arduous regimen of training that preceded his fights, or to subject himself to the kind of fights he has had, if he were limited to the pay of an unskilled dockworker.

Still another facet of this complex issue of fairness can be illus- 38 trated by considering a game of chance, for example, an evening at baccarat. The people who choose to play may start the evening with equal piles of chips, but as the play progresses, those piles will become unequal. By the end of the evening, some will be big winners, others big losers. In the name of the ideal of equality, should the winners be required to repay the losers? That would take all the fun out of the game. Not even the losers would like that. They might like it for the one evening, but would they come back again to play if they knew that whatever happened, they'd end up exactly where they started?

This example has a great deal more to do with the real world 39 than one might at first suppose. Every day each of us makes decisions that involve taking a chance. Occasionally it's a big chance — as when we decide what occupation to pursue, whom to marry, whether to buy a house or make a major investment. More often it's a small chance, as when we decide what movie to go to, whether to cross the street against the traffic, whether to buy one security rather than another. Each time the question is, who is to decide what chances we take? That in turn depends on who bears the consequences of the decision. If we bear the consequences, we can make the decision. But if someone else bears the consequences, should we or will we be permitted to make the decision? If you play baccarat as an agent for someone else with his money, will he, or should he, permit you unlimited scope for decision making? Is he not almost certain to set some limit to your discretion? Will he not lay down some rules for you to observe? To take a very different example, if the government (i.e., your fellow taxpayers) assumes the costs of flood damage to your house, can you be permitted to decide freely whether to build your house on a floodplain? It is no accident that increasing government intervention into personal decisions has gone hand in hand with the drive for "fair shares for all."

The system under which people make their own choices—and bear most of the consequences of their decisions—is the system that has prevailed for most of our history. It is the system that gave the Henry Fords, the Thomas Alva Edisons, the George Eastmans, the John D. Rockefellers, the James Cash Penneys the incentive to transform our society over the past two centuries. It is the system that gave other people an incentive to furnish venture capital to finance the risky enterprises that these ambitious inventors and captains of industry undertook. Of course, there were many losers along the way—probably more losers than winners. We don't remember their names. But for the most part they went in with their eyes open. They knew they were taking chances. And win or lose, society as a whole benefited from their willingness to take a chance.   40

The fortunes that this system produced came overwhelmingly from developing new products or services, or new ways of producing products or services, or of distributing them widely. The resulting addition to the wealth of the community as a whole, to the well-being of the masses of the people, amounted to many times the wealth accumulated by the innovators. Henry Ford acquired a great fortune. The country acquired a cheap and reliable means of transportation and the techniques of mass production. Moreover, in many cases the private fortunes were largely devoted in the end to the benefit of society. The Rockefeller, Ford, and Carnegie foundations are only the most prominent of the numerous private benefactions which are so outstanding a consequence of the operation of a system that corresponded to "equality of opportunity" and "liberty" as these terms were understood until recently.   41

One limited sample may give the flavor of the outpouring of philanthropic activity in the nineteenth and early twentieth century. In a book devoted to "cultural philanthropy in Chicago from the 1880's to 1917," Helen Horowitz writes: 42

> At the turn of the century, Chicago was a city of contradictory impulses: it was both a commercial center dealing in the basic commodities of an industrial society and a community caught in the winds of cultural uplift. As one commentator put it, the city was "a strange combination of pork and Plato."
>
> A major manifestation of Chicago's drive toward culture was the establishment of the city's great cultural institutions in the 1880's and early 1890's (the Art Institute, the Newberry Library,

the Chicago Symphony Orchestra, the University of Chicago, the Field Museum, the Crerar Library)....

These institutions were a new phenomenon in the city. Whatever the initial impetus behind their founding, they were largely organized, sustained, and controlled by a group of businessmen.... Yet while privately supported and managed, the institutions were designed for the whole city. Their trustees had turned to cultural philanthropy not so much to satisfy personal aesthetic or scholarly yearnings as to accomplish social goals. Disturbed by social forces they could not control and filled with idealistic notions of culture, these businessmen saw in the museum, the library, the symphony orchestra, and the university a way to purify their city and to generate a civic renaissance.[5]

43   Philanthropy was by no means restricted to cultural institutions. There was, as Horowitz writes in another connection, "a kind of explosion of activity on many different levels." And Chicago was not an isolated case. Rather, as Horowitz puts it, "Chicago seemed to epitomize America."[6] The same period saw the establishment of Hull House in Chicago under Jane Addams, the first of many settlement houses established throughout the nation to spread culture and education among the poor and to assist them in their daily problems. Many hospitals, orphanages, and other charitable agencies were set up in the same period.

44   There is no inconsistency between a free market system and the pursuit of broad social and cultural goals, or between a free market system and compassion for the less fortunate, whether that compassion takes the form, as it did in the nineteenth century, of private charitable activity, or, as it has done increasingly in the twentieth, of assistance through government—provided that in both cases it is an expression of a desire to help others. There is all the difference in the world, however, between two kinds of assistance through government that seem superficially similar: first, 90 percent of us agreeing to impose taxes on ourselves in order to help the bottom 10 percent, and second, 80 percent voting to impose taxes on the top 10 percent to help the bottom 10 percent—William Graham Sumner's famous example of B and C deciding what D shall do for A.[7] The first may be wise or unwise, an effective or an ineffective way to help

---

[5] Helen Lefkowitz Horowitz, *Culture and the City* (Lexington: University Press of Kentucky, 1976), pp. ix–x. [Friedmans' note]

[6] Ibid., pp. 212 and 31. [Friedmans' note]

[7] "The Forgotten Man," in Albert G. Keller and Maurice R. Davis, eds., *Essays of William G. Sumner* (New Haven: Yale University Press, 1934), vol. I, pp. 466–96. [Friedmans' note]

the disadvantaged—but it is consistent with belief in both equality of opportunity and liberty. The second seeks equality of outcome and is entirely antithetical to liberty.

Who Favors Equality of Outcome?

There is little support for the goal of equality of outcome despite   45
the extent to which it has become almost an article of religious faith among intellectuals and despite its prominence in the speeches of politicians and the preambles of legislation. The talk is belied alike by the behavior of government, of the intellectuals who most ardently espouse egalitarian sentiments, and of the public at large.

For government, one obvious example is the policy toward lot-   46
teries and gambling. New York State—and particularly New York City—is widely and correctly regarded as a stronghold of egalitarian sentiment. Yet the New York State government conducts lotteries and provides facilities for off-track betting on races. It advertises extensively to induce its citizens to buy lottery tickets and bet on the races—at terms that yield a very large profit to the government. At the same time it tries to suppress the "numbers" game, which, as it happens, offers better odds than the government lottery (especially when account is taken of the greater ease of avoiding tax on winnings). Great Britain, a stronghold, if not the birthplace, of egalitarian sentiment, permits private gambling clubs and betting on races and other sporting events. Indeed, wagering is a national pastime and a major source of government income.

For intellectuals, the clearest evidence is their failure to practice   47
what so many of them preach. Equality of outcome can be promoted on a do-it-yourself basis. First, decide exactly what you mean by equality. Do you want to achieve equality within the United States? In a selected group of countries as a whole? In the world as a whole? Is equality to be judged in terms of income per person? Per family? Per year? Per decade? Per lifetime? Income in the form of money alone? Or including such nonmonetary items as the rental value of an owned home; food grown for one's own use; services rendered by members of the family not employed for money, notably the housewife? How are physical and mental handicaps or advantages to be allowed for?

However you decide these issues, you can, if you are an egalitar-   48
ian, estimate what money income would correspond to your concept of equality. If your actual income is higher than that, you can keep that amount and distribute the rest to people who are below that level. If your criterion were to encompass the world—as most

egalitarian rhetoric suggests it should—something less than, say, $200 a year (in 1979 dollars) per person would be an amount that would correspond to the conception of equality that seems implicit in most egalitarian rhetoric. That is about the average income per person worldwide.

What Irving Kristol has called the "new class"—government 49 bureaucrats, academics whose research is supported by government funds or who are employed in government financed "think-tanks," staffs of the many so-called "general interest" or "public policy" groups, journalists and others in the communications industry—are among the most ardent preachers of the doctrine of equality. Yet they remind us very much of the old, if unfair, saw about the Quakers: "They came to the New World to do good, and ended up doing well." The members of the new class are in general among the highest paid persons in the community. And for many among them, preaching equality and promoting or administering the resulting legislation has proved an effective means of achieving such high incomes. All of us find it easy to identify our own welfare with the welfare of the community.

Of course, an egalitarian may protest that he is but a drop in the 50 ocean, that he would be willing to redistribute the excess of his income over his concept of an equal income if everyone else were compelled to do the same. On one level this contention that compulsion would change matters is wrong—even if everyone else did the same, his specific contribution to the income of others would still be a drop in the ocean. His individual contribution would be just as large if he were the only contributor as if he were one of many. Indeed, it would be more valuable because he could target his contribution to go to the very worst off among those he regards as appropriate recipients. On another level compulsion would change matters drastically: the kind of society that would emerge if such acts of redistribution were voluntary is altogether different—and, by our standards, infinitely preferable—to the kind that would emerge if redistribution were compulsory.

Persons who believe that a society of enforced equality is prefer- 51 able can also practice what they preach. They can join one of the many communes in this country and elsewhere, or establish new ones. And, of course, it is entirely consistent with a belief in personal equality or equality of opportunity and liberty that any group of individuals who wish to live in that way should be free to do so. Our thesis that support for equality of outcome is word-deep receives strong support from the small number of persons who have wished to join such communes and from the fragility of the communes that have been established.

Egalitarians in the United States may object that the fewness of   52
communes and their fragility reflect the opprobrium that a predominantly "capitalist" society visits on such communes and the resulting
discrimination to which they are subjected. That may be true for the
United States but as Robert Nozick[8] has pointed out, there is one
country where that is not true, where, on the contrary, egalitarian
communes are highly regarded and prized. That country is Israel. The
kibbutz played a major role in early Jewish settlement in Palestine and
continues to play an important role in the state of Israel. A dispropor-
tionate fraction of the leaders of the Israeli state were drawn from the
kibbutzim. Far from being a source of disapproval, membership in a
kibbutz confers social status and commands approbation. Everyone is
free to join or leave a kibbutz, and kibbutzim have been viable social
organizations. Yet at no time, and certainly not today, have more than
about 5 percent of the Jewish population of Israel chosen to be members of a kibbutz. That percentage can be regarded as an upper estimate of the fraction of people who would voluntarily choose a system
enforcing equality of outcome in preference to a system characterized
by inequality, diversity, and opportunity.

Public attitudes about graduated income taxes are more mixed.   53
Recent referenda on the introduction of graduated state income
taxes in some states that do not have them, and on an increase in the
extent of graduation in other states, have generally been defeated.
On the other hand, the federal income tax is highly graduated, at
least on paper, though it also contains a large number of provisions
("loopholes") that greatly reduce the extent of graduation in practice. On this showing, there is at least public tolerance of a moderate
amount of redistributive taxation.

However, we venture to suggest that the popularity of Reno, Las   54
Vegas, and now Atlantic City is no less faithful an indication of the
preferences of the public than the federal income tax, the editorials
in the *New York Times* and the *Washington Post,* and the pages of the
New York Review of Books.

Consequences of Egalitarian Policies

In shaping our own policy, we can learn from the experience of   55
Western countries with which we share a common intellectual and
cultural background, and from which we derive many of our values.

---

[8] Robert Nozick, "Who Would Choose Socialism?" *Reason,* May 1978, pp. 22–
23. [Friedmans' note]

Perhaps the most instructive example is Great Britain, which led the way in the nineteenth century toward implementing equality of opportunity and in the twentieth toward implementing equality of outcome.

Since the end of World War II, British domestic policy has been 56 dominated by the search for greater equality of outcome. Measure after measure has been adopted designed to take from the rich and give to the poor. Taxes were raised on income until they reached a top rate of 98 percent on property income and 83 percent on "earned" income, and were supplemented by ever heavier taxes on inheritances. State-provided medical, housing, and other welfare services were greatly expanded, along with payments to the unemployed and the aged. Unfortunately, the results have been very different from those that were intended by the people who were quite properly offended by the class structure that dominated Britain for centuries. There has been a vast redistribution of wealth, but the end result is not an equitable distribution.

Instead, new classes of privileged have been created to replace 57 or supplement the old: the bureaucrats, secure in their jobs, protected against inflation both when they work and when they retire; the trade unions that profess to represent the most downtrodden workers but in fact consist of the highest paid laborers in the land— the aristocrats of the labor movement; and the new millionaires— people who have been cleverest at finding ways around the laws, the rules, the regulations that have poured from Parliament and the bureaucracy, who have found ways to avoid paying taxes on their income and to get their wealth overseas beyond the grasp of the tax collectors. A vast reshuffling of income and wealth, yes; greater equity, hardly.

The drive for equality in Britain failed, not because the wrong 58 measures were adopted—though some no doubt were; not because they were badly administered—though some no doubt were; not because the wrong people administered them—though no doubt some did. The drive for equality failed for a much more fundamental reason. It went against one of the most basic instincts of all human beings. In the words of Adam Smith, "The uniform, constant, and uninterrupted effort of every man to better his condition"[9]—and, one may add, the condition of his children and his children's children. Smith, of course, meant by "condition" not merely material well-being, though certainly that was one component. He had a much broader concept in mind, one that included all

---

[9] *Wealth of Nations*, vol. I, p. 325 (Book II, Chap. III). [Friedmans' note]

of the values by which men judge their success — in particular the kind of social values that gave rise to the outpouring of philanthropic activities in the nineteenth century.

When the law interferes with people's pursuit of their own values, they will try to find a way around. They will evade the law, they will break the law, or they will leave the country. Few of us believe in a moral code that justifies forcing people to give up much of what they produce to finance payments to persons they do not know for purposes they may not approve of. When the law contradicts what most people regard as moral and proper, they will break the law — whether the law is enacted in the name of a noble ideal such as equality or in the naked interest of one group at the expense of another. Only fear of punishment, not a sense of justice and morality, will lead people to obey the law. 59

When people start to break one set of laws, the lack of respect for the law inevitably spreads to all laws, even those that everyone regards as moral and proper — laws against violence, theft, and vandalism. Hard as it may be to believe, the growth of crude criminality in Britain in recent decades may well be one consequence of the drive for equality. 60

In addition, that drive for equality has driven out of Britain some of its ablest, best-trained, most vigorous citizens, much to the benefit of the United States and other countries that have given them a greater opportunity to use their talents for their own benefit. Finally, who can doubt the effect that the drive for equality has had on efficiency and productivity? Surely, that is one of the main reasons why economic growth in Britain has fallen so far behind its continental neighbors, the United States, Japan, and other nations over the past few decades. 61

We in the United States have not gone as far as Britain in promoting the goal of equality of outcome. Yet many of the same consequences are already evident — from a failure of egalitarian measures to achieve their objectives, to a reshuffling of wealth that by no standards can be regarded as equitable, to a rise in criminality, to a depressing effect on productivity and efficiency. 62

Capitalism and Equality

Everywhere in the world there are gross inequities of income and wealth. They offend most of us. Few can fail to be moved by the contrast between the luxury enjoyed by some and the grinding poverty suffered by others. 63

In the past century a myth has grown up that free market capi-   64
talism — equality of opportunity as we have interpreted that term —
increases such inequalities, that it is a system under which the rich
exploit the poor.

Nothing could be further from the truth. Wherever the free   65
market has been permitted to operate, wherever anything approaching equality of opportunity has existed, the ordinary man has been
able to attain levels of living never dreamed of before. Nowhere is
the gap between rich and poor wider, nowhere are the rich richer
and the poor poorer, than in those societies that do not permit the
free market to operate. That is true of feudal societies like medieval
Europe, India before independence, and much of modern South
America, where inherited status determines position. It is equally
true of centrally planned societies, like Russia or China or India
since independence, where access to government determines position. It is true even where central planning was introduced, as in all
three of these countries, in the name of equality.

Russia is a country of two nations: a small privileged upper class   66
of bureaucrats, Communist party officials, technicians; and a great
mass of people living little better than their great-grandparents did.
The upper class has access to special shops, schools, and luxuries of
all kind; the masses are condemned to enjoy little more than the basic
necessities. We remember asking a tourist guide in Moscow the cost
of a large automobile that we saw and being told, "Oh, those aren't for
sale; they're only for the Politburo." Several recent books by American
journalists document in great detail the contrast between the privileged life of the upper classes and the poverty of the masses.[10] Even on
a simpler level, it is noteworthy that the average wage of a foreman is
a larger multiple of the average wage of an ordinary worker in a Russian factory than in a factory in the United States — and no doubt he
deserves it. After all, an American foreman only has to worry about
being fired; a Russian foreman also has to worry about being shot.

China, too, is a nation with wide differences in income — be-   67
tween the politically powerful and the rest; between city and countryside; between some workers in the cities and other workers. A perceptive student of China writes that "the inequality between rich and
poor regions in China was more acute in 1957 than in any of the larger
nations of the world except perhaps Brazil." He quotes another
scholar as saying, "These examples suggest that the Chinese industrial

---

[10] See Smith, *The Russians,* and Kaiser, *Russia: The People and the Power.* [Fried-
mans' note]

wage structure is not significantly more egalitarian than that of other countries." And he concludes his examination of equality in China, "How evenly distributed would China's income be today? Certainly, it would not be as even as Taiwan's or South Korea's.... On the other hand, income distribution in China is obviously more even than in Brazil or South America.... We must conclude that China is far from being a society of complete equality. In fact, income differences in China may be quite a bit greater than in a number of countries commonly associated with 'fascist' elites and exploited masses."[11]

Industrial progress, mechanical improvement, all of the great   68
wonders of the modern era have meant relatively little to the wealthy. The rich in Ancient Greece would have benefited hardly at all from modern plumbing: running servants replaced running water. Television and radio—the patricians of Rome could enjoy the leading musicians and actors in their home, could have the leading artists as domestic retainers. Ready-to-wear clothing, supermarkets—all these and many other modern developments would have added little to their life. They would have welcomed the improvements in transportation and in medicine, but for the rest, the great achievements of Western capitalism have redounded primarily to the benefit of the ordinary person. These achievements have made available to the masses conveniences and amenities that were previously the exclusive prerogative of the rich and powerful.

In 1848 John Stuart Mill wrote: 69

> Hitherto it is questionable if all the mechanical inventions yet made have lightened the day's toil of any human being. They have enabled a greater population to live the same life of drudgery and imprisonment, and an increased number of manufacturers and others to make fortunes. They have increased the comforts of the middle classes. But they have not yet begun to effect those great changes in human destiny, which it is in their nature and in their futurity to accomplish.[12]

No one could say that today. You can travel from one end of the   70
industrialized world to the other and almost the only people you will find engaging in backbreaking toil are people who are doing it for sport. To find people whose day's toil has not been lightened by mechanical invention, you must go to the noncapitalist world: to Russia, China, India or Bangladesh, parts of Yugoslavia; or to the more

---

[11] Nick Eberstadt, "China: How Much Success," *New York Review of Books*, May 3, 1979, pp. 40–41. [Friedmans' note]

[12] John Stuart Mill, *The Principles of Political Economy* (1848), 9th ed. (London: Longmans, Green & Co., 1886), vol. II, p. 332 (Book IV, Chap. VI). [Friedmans' note]

backward capitalist countries—in Africa, the Mideast, South America; and until recently, Spain or Italy.

Conclusion

A society that puts equality—in the sense of equality of out- 71
come—ahead of freedom will end up with neither equality nor freedom. The use of force to achieve equality will destroy freedom, and the force, introduced for good purposes, will end up in the hands of people who use it to promote their own interests.

On the other hand, a society that puts freedom first will, as a 72
happy by-product, end up with both greater freedom and greater equality. Though a by-product of freedom, greater equality is not an accident. A free society releases the energies and abilities of people to pursue their own objectives. It prevents some people from arbitrarily suppressing others. It does not prevent some people from achieving positions of privilege, but so long as freedom is maintained, it prevents those positions of privilege from becoming institutionalized; they are subject to continued attack by other able, ambitious people. Freedom means diversity but also mobility. It preserves the opportunity for today's disadvantaged to become tomorrow's privileged and, in the process, enables almost everyone, from top to bottom, to enjoy a fuller and richer life.

QUESTIONS FOR CRITICAL READING

1. What is the difference between equality of opportunity and equality of outcome?
2. What effect does a policy that guarantees equality of outcome have on freedom?
3. Explain the Friedmans' attitude toward the concept of "Equality before God" (paras. 6–14).
4. What is the meaning of "laissez-faire"?
5. What role should government play in regulating the nation's economic system?
6. What is "personal equality"?
7. What advantages does a free market give the "right people"?

SUGGESTIONS FOR WRITING

1. The Friedmans make a strong case for equality of opportunity. However, some critics might say that they actually make a case for permitting the highly advantaged to exploit the less advantaged. This would

give those with exceptional economic talent and skills a free reign to make millions while those who are ordinary would spend a life in relative poverty. The Friedmans explain that life is not fair, so such distinctions will naturally occur. How can you defend their views? How can you attack their views?

2. The Friedmans discuss the inheritance of property and the inheritance of talent in paragraphs 32 to 34. If government stands aside on the question of inheritance of talent —which could contribute considerably to the economic success of an individual —why should it not stand aside on the question of inheritance of property? Compare the two and take your own stand on what role government should have in relation to the inheritance of qualities or property that might give an individual a considerable advantage in life.

3. Examine the question of fairness in this essay. The complex idea of "fair share," which is discussed in detail in paragraphs 34 to 41, is dealt with in a manner that is intended to convince you that the Friedmans' position is accurate and desirable. Analyze their position and decide whether or not they are right.

4. In paragraphs 17 to 25, the Friedmans closely examine whether or not we can expect equality of opportunity "to be interpreted literally." Establish their position on this question and then argue the question for yourself. How do you interpret this idea, and what do you personally believe in? Attempt to convince someone who does not agree with you.

5. The Friedmans argue that "[e]quality of opportunity, like personal equality, is not inconsistent with liberty; on the contrary, it is an essential component of liberty" (para. 19). Why would they feel it necessary to make this statement? Is there any sense in which equality of opportunity might actually be inconsistent with liberty? Examine the entire essay in an effort to make an argument that contradicts the Friedmans' assumption. If possible, draw on your own research.

6. **CONNECTIONS** The Friedmans have something to say about the effect of machines and mechanical inventions on working people in underdeveloped countries. Karl Marx also comments on the use of machines and its effect on worker morale. How, ultimately, do machines affect the working class in terms of either limiting or expanding personal opportunity?

7. **CONNECTIONS** This essay assumes that Jefferson's ideas in the Declaration of Independence generally agree with the positions espoused by the Friedmans. Re-read Jefferson and evaluate this assumption for yourself: Does Jefferson seem to be in absolute agreement with the Friedmans, or have the Friedmans reinterpreted Jefferson for their own purposes? Use quotations from Jefferson's Declaration to support your answer.

ROBERT B. REICH
Why the Rich Are Getting Richer and the Poor, Poorer

ROBERT B. REICH (b. 1946), University Professor in the Heller Graduate School at Brandeis University, who served as secretary of labor in the first Clinton administration, holds a graduate degree from Yale Law School, and unlike his former colleagues in the John F. Kennedy School of Government at Harvard, he does not hold a Ph.D. in economics. Nonetheless, he has written numerous books on economics and has been a prominent lecturer for a dozen years. One of his most recent books, *Locked in the Cabinet* (1997), is a memoir of his four years as secretary of labor. *The Work of Nations* (1991), from which this essay comes, is the distillation of many years' analysis of modern economic trends.

As a college student, Reich was an activist but not a radical. In 1968 he was a Rhodes scholar, studying at Oxford University with Bill Clinton and a number of others who became influential American policymakers. Reich is a specialist in policy studies — that is, the relationship of governmental policy to the economic health of the nation. Unlike those who champion free trade and unlimited expansion, Reich questions the existence of free trade by pointing to the effect of government taxation on business enterprise. Taxation — like many governmental policies regarding immigration, tariffs, and money supply — directly shapes the behavior of most companies. Reich feels that government must establish and execute an industrial policy that will benefit the nation.

Even though organized labor groups, such as industrial unions, have rejected much of his theorizing about labor, Reich has developed a reputation as a conciliator who can see opposite sides of a question and resolve them. He is known for his denunciation of mergers, lawsuits, takeovers, and other deals that he believes simply churn money around rather than produce wealth. He feels that such maneuvers enrich a few predatory people but do not benefit labor in general—and, indeed, that the debt created by such deals harms labor in the long run.

In *The Next American Frontier* (1983), Reich insists that government, unions, and businesses must cooperate to create a workable program designed to improve the economy. Trusting to chance and free trade, he argues, will not work in the current economy. He also has said that the old assembly-line methods must give way to what he calls "flexible production," involving smaller, customized runs of products for specific markets.

Reich's *The Work of Nations* (1991), whose title draws on Adam Smith's classic *The Wealth of Nations* (1776), examines the borderless nature of contemporary corporations. Multinational corporations are a reality, and as he points out in the following essay, their flexibility makes it possible for them to thrive by moving manufacturing plants from nation to nation. The reasons for moving are sometimes connected to lower wages but more often are connected to the infrastructure of a given nation. Reliable roads, plentiful electricity, well-educated workers, low crime rates, and political stability are all elements that make a location attractive to a multinational corporation.

Reich's Rhetoric

The structure of "Why the Rich Are Getting Richer and the Poor, Poorer" is built on a metaphor: that of boats rising or falling with the tide. As Reich notes, "All Americans used to be in roughly the same economic boat" (para. 2), and when the economic tide rose, most people rose along with it. However, today "national borders no longer define our economic fates"; Reich therefore views Americans today as being in different boats, depending on their role in the economy, and his essay follows the fates of three distinct kinds of workers.

Examining the routine worker, he observes, "The boat containing routine producers is sinking rapidly" (para. 3). As he demonstrates, the need for routine production has declined in part because of improvements in production facilities. Much labor-intensive work has been replaced by machines. Modern factories often scramble to locate in places where production costs are lowest. People in other nations work at a fraction of the hourly rate of American workers, and because factories are relatively cheap to establish, they can be easily moved.

Reich continues the boat metaphor with "in-person servers." The boat that carries these workers, he says, "is sinking as well, but somewhat more slowly and unevenly" (para. 20). Workers in restaurants, retail outlets, car washes, and other personal service industries often work part-time and have few health or other benefits. Their jobs are imperiled by machines as well, although not as much as manufacturing jobs are. Although the outlook for such workers is buoyed by a declining population, which will reduce competition for their jobs, increased immigration may cancel this benefit.

Finally, Reich argues that the "vessel containing America's symbolic analysts is rising" (para. 28). This third group contains the population that identifies and solves problems and brokers ideas. "Almost everyone around the world is buying the skills and insights of Americans who manipulate oral and visual symbols" (para. 33). Engineers, consultants, marketing experts, publicists, and those in entertainment fields all manage to cross national boundaries and prosper at a rate that is perhaps startling. As a result of an expanding world market, symbolic analysts do not depend only on the purchasing power of routine and in-service workers. Instead, they rely on the same global web that dominates the pattern of corporate structure.

Reich's essay follows the fate of these three groups in turn to establish the pattern of change and expectation that will shape America's economic future. His metaphor is deftly handled, and he includes details, examples, facts, and careful references to support his position.

PREREADING QUESTIONS:
WHAT TO READ FOR

The following prereading questions may help you anticipate key issues in the discussion on Robert B. Reich's "Why the Rich Are Getting Richer and the Poor, Poorer." Keeping them in mind during your first reading of the selection should help focus your reactions.

- Why and how does an individual's position in the world economy depend on the function he/she performs in it?
- What are "routine producers"? What will be their fate in the future?
- Who are the "symbolic analysts" in our economy? How does one become a symbolic analyst?

Why the Rich Are Getting Richer
and the Poor, Poorer

The division of labour is limited by the extent of the market.
—ADAM SMITH,
*An Inquiry into the Nature
and Causes of the Wealth of Nations* (1776)

Regardless of how your job is officially classified (manufactur- 1
ing, service, managerial, technical, secretarial, and so on), or the industry in which you work (automotive, steel, computer, advertising,
finance, food processing), your real competitive position in the
world economy is coming to depend on the function you perform in
it. Herein lies the basic reason why incomes are diverging. The fortunes of routine producers are declining. In-person servers are also
becoming poorer, although their fates are less clear-cut. But symbolic analysts—who solve, identify, and broker new problems—
are, by and large, succeeding in the world economy.

All Americans used to be in roughly the same economic boat. 2
Most rose or fell together as the corporations in which they were
employed, the industries comprising such corporations, and the national economy as a whole became more productive—or languished. But national borders no longer define our economic fates.
We are now in different boats, one sinking rapidly, one sinking
more slowly, and the third rising steadily.

The boat containing routine producers is sinking rapidly. Recall 3
that by midcentury routine production workers in the United States
were paid relatively well. The giant pyramidlike organizations at the
core of each major industry coordinated their prices and investments—avoiding the harsh winds of competition and thus maintaining healthy earnings. Some of these earnings, in turn, were rein-
vested in new plant and equipment (yielding ever-larger-scale
economies); another portion went to top managers and investors.
But a large and increasing portion went to middle managers and
production workers. Work stoppages posed such a threat to high-
volume production that organized labor was able to exact an ever-
larger premium for its cooperation. And the pattern of wages established within the core corporations influenced the pattern
throughout the national economy. Thus the growth of a relatively affluent middle class, able to purchase all the wondrous things produced in high volume by the core corporations.

But, as has been observed, the core is rapidly breaking down 4
into global webs which earn their largest profits from clever
problem-solving, -identifying, and brokering. As the costs of transporting standard things and of communicating information about
them continue to drop, profit margins on high-volume, standardized
production are thinning, because there are few barriers to entry.
Modern factories and state-of-the-art machinery can be installed almost anywhere on the globe. Routine producers in the United States,
then, are in direct competition with millions of routine producers in
other nations. Twelve thousand people are added to the world's population every hour, most of whom, eventually, will happily work for
a small fraction of the wages of routine producers in America.[1]

The consequence is clearest in older, heavy industries, where 5
high-volume, standardized production continues its ineluctable
move to where labor is cheapest and most accessible around the
world. Thus, for example, the Maquiladora factories cluttered along
the Mexican side of the U.S. border in the sprawling shanty towns of
Tijuana, Mexicali, Nogales, Agua Prieta, and Ciudad Juárez — factories owned mostly by Americans, but increasingly by Japanese — in
which more than a half million routine producers assemble parts
into finished goods to be shipped into the United States.

The same story is unfolding worldwide. Until the late 1970s, 6
AT&T had depended on routine producers in Shreveport,
Louisiana, to assemble standard telephones. It then discovered
that routine producers in Singapore would perform the same
tasks at a far lower cost. Facing intense competition from other
global webs, AT&T's strategic brokers felt compelled to switch. So
in the early 1980s they stopped hiring routine producers in Shreveport and began hiring cheaper routine producers in Singapore. But
under this kind of pressure for ever-lower high-volume production
costs, today's Singaporean can easily end up as yesterday's
Louisianan. By the late 1980s, AT&T's strategic brokers found that
routine producers in Thailand were eager to assemble telephones for
a small fraction of the wages of routine producers in Singapore.
Thus, in 1989, AT&T stopped hiring Singaporeans to make
telephones and began hiring even cheaper routine producers in
Thailand.

----

[1] The reader should note, of course, that lower wages in other areas of the
world are of no particular attraction to global capital unless workers there are sufficiently productive to make the labor cost of producing *each unit* lower there than in
higher-wage regions. Productivity in many low-wage areas of the world has improved due to the ease with which state-of-the-art factories and equipment can be
installed there. [Reich's note]

The search for ever-lower wages has not been confined to heavy 7
industry. Routine data processing is equally footloose. Keypunch
operators located anywhere around the world can enter data into
computers, linked by satellite or transoceanic fiber-optic cable, and
take it out again. As the rates charged by satellite networks continue
to drop, and as more satellites and fiber-optic cables become available (reducing communication costs still further), routine data
processors in the United States find themselves in ever more direct
competition with their counterparts abroad, who are often eager to
work for far less.

By 1990, keypunch operators in the United States were earning, 8
at most, $6.50 per hour. But keypunch operators throughout the
rest of the world were willing to work for a fraction of this. Thus,
many potential American data-processing jobs were disappearing,
and the wages and benefits of the remaining ones were in decline. Typical was Saztec International, a $20-million-a-year data-
processing firm headquartered in Kansas City, whose American
strategic brokers contracted with routine data processors in Manila
and with American-owned firms that needed such data-processing
services. Compared with the average Philippine income of $1,700
per year, data-entry operators working for Saztec earn the princely
sum of $2,650. The remainder of Saztec's employees were American
problem-solvers and -identifiers, searching for ways to improve the
worldwide system and find new uses to which it could be put.[2]

By 1990, American Airlines was employing over 1,000 data 9
processors in Barbados and the Dominican Republic to enter names
and flight numbers from used airline tickets (flown daily to Barbados from airports around the United States) into a giant computer
bank located in Dallas. Chicago publisher R. R. Donnelley was sending entire manuscripts to Barbados for entry into computers in
preparation for printing. The New York Life Insurance Company
was dispatching insurance claims to Castleisland, Ireland, where
routine producers, guided by simple directions, entered the claims
and determined the amounts due, then instantly transmitted the
computations back to the United States. (When the firm advertised
in Ireland for twenty-five data-processing jobs, it received six hundred applications.) And McGraw-Hill was processing subscription
renewal and marketing information for its magazines in nearby Gal-
way. Indeed, literally millions of routine workers around the world
were receiving information, converting it into computer-readable

---

[2] John Maxwell Hamilton, "A Bit Player Buys into the Computer Age," *New York
Times Business World,* December 3, 1989, p. 14. [Reich's note]

form, and then sending it back—at the speed of electronic impulses—whence it came.

The simple coding of computer software has also entered into 10 world commerce. India, with a large English-speaking population of technicians happy to do routine programming cheaply, is proving to be particularly attractive to global webs in need of this service. By 1990, Texas Instruments maintained a software development facility in Bangalore, linking fifty Indian programmers by satellite to TI's Dallas headquarters. Spurred by this and similar ventures, the Indian government was building a teleport in Poona, intended to make it easier and less expensive for many other firms to send their routine software design specifications for coding.[3]

This shift of routine production jobs from advanced to develop- 11 ing nations is a great boon to many workers in such nations who otherwise would be jobless or working for much lower wages. These workers, in turn, now have more money with which to purchase symbolic-analytic services from advanced nations (often embedded within all sorts of complex products). The trend is also beneficial to everyone around the world who can now obtain high-volume, standardized products (including information and software) more cheaply than before.

But these benefits do not come without certain costs. In particu- 12 lar the burden is borne by those who no longer have good-paying routine production jobs within advanced economies like the United States. Many of these people used to belong to unions or at least benefited from prevailing wage rates established in collective bargaining agreements. But as the old corporate bureaucracies have flattened into global webs, bargaining leverage has been lost. Indeed, the tacit national bargain is no more.

Despite the growth in the number of new jobs in the United 13 States, union membership has withered. In 1960, 35 percent of all nonagricultural workers in America belonged to a union. But by 1980 that portion had fallen to just under a quarter, and by 1989 to about 17 percent. Excluding government employees, union membership was down to 13.4 percent.[4] This was a smaller proportion even than in the early 1930s, before the National Labor Relations Act created a legally protected right to labor representation. The drop in membership has been accompanied by a growing number of

---

[3] Udayan Gupta, "U.S.-Indian Satellite Link Stands to Cut Software Costs," *Wall Street Journal,* March 6, 1989, p. B2. [Reich's note]

[4] *Statistical Abstract of the United States* (Washington, D.C.: U.S. Government Printing Office, 1989), p. 416, table 684. [Reich's note]

collective bargaining agreements to freeze wages at current levels, reduce wage levels of entering workers, or reduce wages overall. This is an important reason why the long economic recovery that began in 1982 produced a smaller rise in unit labor costs than any of the eight recoveries since World War II—the low rate of unemployment during its course notwithstanding.

Routine production jobs have vanished fastest in traditional unionized industries (autos, steel, and rubber, for example), where average wages have kept up with inflation. This is because the jobs of older workers in such industries are protected by seniority; the youngest workers are the first to be laid off. Faced with a choice of cutting wages or cutting the number of jobs, a majority of union members (secure in the knowledge that there are many who are junior to them who will be laid off first) often have voted for the latter.

Thus the decline in union membership has been most striking among young men entering the work force without a college education. In the early 1950s, more than 40 percent of this group joined unions; by the late 1980s, less than 20 percent (if public employees are excluded, less than 10 percent).[5] In steelmaking, for example, although many older workers remained employed, almost half of all routine steelmaking jobs in America vanished between 1974 and 1988 (from 480,000 to 260,000). Similarly with automobiles: During the 1980s, the United Auto Workers lost 500,000 members—one-third of their total at the start of the decade. General Motors alone cut 150,000 American production jobs during the 1980s (even as it added employment abroad). Another consequence of the same phenomenon: the gap between the average wages of unionized and nonunionized workers widened dramatically—from 14.6 percent in 1973 to 20.4 percent by end of the 1980s.[6] The lesson is clear. If you drop out of high school or have no more than a high school diploma, do not expect a good routine production job to be awaiting you.

Also vanishing are lower- and middle-level management jobs involving routine production. Between 1981 and 1986, more than 780,000 foremen, supervisors, and section chiefs lost their jobs through plant closings and layoffs.[7] Large numbers of assistant divi-

---

[5] Calculations from Current Population Surveys by L. Katz and A. Revenga, "Changes in the Structure of Wages: U.S. and Japan," National Bureau of Economic Research, September 1989. [Reich's note]

[6] U.S. Department of Commerce, Bureau of Labor Statistics, "Wages of Unionized and Non-Unionized Workers," various issues. [Reich's note]

[7] U.S. Department of Labor, Bureau of Labor Statistics, "Reemployment Increases Among Displaced Workers," BLS News, USDL 86-414, October 14, 1986, table 6. [Reich's note]

sion heads, assistant directors, assistant managers, and vice presidents also found themselves jobless. GM shed more than 40,000 white-collar employees and planned to eliminate another 25,000 by the mid-1990s.[8] As America's core pyramids metamorphosed into global webs, many middle-level routine producers were as obsolete as routine workers on the line.

As has been noted, foreign-owned webs are hiring some Americans to do routine production in the United States. Philips, Sony, and Toyota factories are popping up all over—to the self-congratulatory applause of the nation's governors and mayors, who have lured them with promises of tax abatements and new sewers, among other amenities. But as these ebullient politicians will soon discover, the foreign-owned factories are highly automated and will become far more so in years to come. Routine production jobs account for a small fraction of the cost of producing most items in the United States and other advanced nations, and this fraction will continue to decline sharply as computer-integrated robots take over. In 1977 it took routine producers thirty-five hours to assemble an automobile in the United States; it is estimated that by the mid-1990s, Japanese-owned factories in America will be producing finished automobiles using only eight hours of a routine producer's time.[9]

The productivity and resulting wages of American workers who run such robotic machinery may be relatively high, but there may not be many such jobs to go around. A case in point: in the late 1980s, Nippon Steel joined with America's ailing Inland Steel to build a new $400 million cold-rolling mill fifty miles west of Gary, Indiana. The mill was celebrated for its state-of-the-art technology, which cut the time to produce a coil of steel from twelve days to about one hour. In fact, the entire plant could be run by a small team of technicians, which became clear when Inland subsequently closed two of its old cold-rolling mills, laying off hundreds of routine workers. Governors and mayors take note: your much-ballyhooed foreign factories may end up employing distressingly few of your constituents.

Overall, the decline in routine jobs has hurt men more than women. This is because the routine production jobs held by men in high-volume metal-bending manufacturing industries had paid higher wages than the routine production jobs held by women in textiles and data processing. As both sets of jobs have been lost,

17

18

19

---

[8] *Wall Street Journal*, February 16, 1990, p. A5. [Reich's note]
[9] Figures from the International Motor Vehicles Program, Massachusetts Institute of Technology, 1989. [Reich's note]

American women in routine production have gained more equal footing with American men—equally poor footing, that is. This is a major reason why the gender gap between male and female wages began to close during the 1980s.

The second of the three boats, carrying in-person servers, is   20
sinking as well, but somewhat more slowly and unevenly. Most in-person servers are paid at or just slightly above the minimum wage and many work only part-time, with the result that their take-home pay is modest, to say the least. Nor do they typically receive all the benefits (health care, life insurance, disability, and so forth) gar-nered by routine producers in large manufacturing corporations or by symbolic analysts affiliated with the more affluent threads of global webs.[10] In-person servers are sheltered from the direct effects of global competition and, like everyone else, benefit from access to lower-cost products from around the world. But they are not im-mune to its indirect effects.

For one thing, in-person servers increasingly compete with for-   21
mer routine production workers, who, no longer able to find well-paying routine production jobs, have few alternatives but to seek in-person service jobs. The Bureau of Labor Statistics estimates that of the 2.8 million manufacturing workers who lost their jobs during the early 1980s, fully one-third were rehired in service jobs paying at least 20 percent less.[11] In-person servers must also compete with high school graduates and dropouts who years before had moved easily into routine production jobs but no longer can. And if demo-graphic predictions about the American work force in the first decades of the twenty-first century are correct (and they are likely to be, since most of the people who will comprise the work force are already identifiable), most new entrants into the job market will be black or Hispanic men, or women—groups that in years past have possessed relatively weak technical skills. This will result in an even larger number of people crowding into in-person services. Finally, in-person servers will be competing with growing numbers of immi-grants, both legal and illegal, for whom in-person services will comprise the most accessible jobs. (It is estimated that between the

---

[10] The growing portion of the American labor force engaged in in-person ser-vices, relative to routine production, thus helps explain why the number of Ameri-cans lacking health insurance increased by at least 6 million during the 1980s. [Reich's note]

[11] U.S. Department of Labor, Bureau of Labor Statistics, "Reemployment In-creases Among Disabled Workers," October 14, 1986. [Reich's note]

mid-1980s and the end of the century, about a quarter of all workers entering the American labor force will be immigrants.[12])

Perhaps the fiercest competition that in-person servers face 22 comes from labor-saving machinery (much of it invented, designed, fabricated, or assembled in other nations, of course). Automated tellers, computerized cashiers, automatic car washes, robotized vending machines, self-service gasoline pumps, and all similar gadgets substitute for the human beings that customers once encountered. Even telephone operators are fast disappearing, as electronic sensors and voice simulators become capable of carrying on conversations that are reasonably intelligent and always polite. Retail sales workers—among the largest groups of in-person servers—are similarly imperiled. Through personal computers linked to television screens, tomorrow's consumers will be able to buy furniture, appliances, and all sorts of electronic toys from their living rooms—examining the merchandise from all angles, selecting whatever color, size, special features, and price seem most appealing, and then transmitting the order instantly to warehouses from which the selections will be shipped directly to their homes. So, too, with financial transactions, airline and hotel reservations, rental car agreements, and similar contracts, which will be executed between consumers in their homes and computer banks somewhere else on the globe.[13]

Advanced economies like the United States will continue to 23 generate sizable numbers of new in-person service jobs, of course, the automation of older ones notwithstanding. For every bank teller who loses her job to an automated teller, three new jobs open for aerobics instructors. Human beings, it seems, have an almost insatiable desire for personal attention. But the intense competition nevertheless ensures that the wages of in-person servers will remain relatively low. In-person servers—working on their own, or else dispersed widely amid many small establishments, filling all sorts of personal-care niches—cannot readily organize themselves into labor unions or create powerful lobbies to limit the impact of such competition.

In two respects, demographics will work in favor of in-person 24 servers, buoying their collective boat slightly. First, as has been noted, the rate of growth of the American work force is slowing. In

---

[12] Federal Immigration and Naturalization Service, *Statistical Yearbook* (Washington, D.C.: U.S. Government Printing Office, 1986, 1987). [Reich's note]

[13] See Claudia H. Deutsch, "The Powerful Push for Self-Service," *New York Times,* April 9, 1989, section 3, p. 1. [Reich's note]

particular, the number of young workers is shrinking. Between 1985
and 1995, the number of the eighteen- to twenty-four-year-olds will
have declined by 17.5 percent. Thus, employers will have more incentive to hire and train in-person servers whom they might previously have avoided. But this demographic relief from the competitive pressures will be only temporary. The cumulative procreative
energies of the postwar baby-boomers (born between 1946 and
1964) will result in a new surge of workers by 2010 or there-
abouts.[14] And immigration—both legal and illegal—shows every
sign of increasing in years to come.

Next, by the second decade of the twenty-first century, the   25
number of Americans aged sixty-five and over will be rising precipi-
tously, as the baby-boomers reach retirement age and live longer.
Their life expectancies will lengthen not just because fewer of them
will have smoked their way to their graves and more will have eaten
better than their parents, but also because they will receive all sorts
of expensive drugs and therapies designed to keep them alive—
barely. By 2035, twice as many Americans will be elderly as in 1988,
and the number of octogenarians is expected to triple. As these decaying baby-boomers ingest all the chemicals and receive all the
treatments, they will need a great deal of personal attention. Millions
of deteriorating bodies will require nurses, nursing-home operators,
hospital administrators, orderlies, home-care providers, hospice
aides, and technicians to operate and maintain all the expensive machinery that will monitor and temporarily stave off final disintegration. There might even be a booming market for euthanasia specialists. In-person servers catering to the old and ailing will be in strong
demand.[15]

One small problem: the decaying baby-boomers will not have   26
enough money to pay for these services. They will have used up
their personal savings years before. Their Social Security payments
will, of course, have been used by the government to pay for the
previous generation's retirement and to finance much of the budget
deficits of the 1980s. Moreover, with relatively fewer young Americans in the population, the supply of housing will likely exceed the
demand, with the result that the boomers' major investments—
their homes—will be worth less (in inflation-adjusted dollars) when

---

[14] U.S. Bureau of the Census, Current Population Reports, Series P-23, no. 138,
tables 2-1, 4-6. See W. Johnson, A. Packer, et al., Workforce 2000: Work and Workers
for the 21st Century (Indianapolis: Hudson Institute, 1987). [Reich's note]

[15] The Census Bureau estimates that by the year 2000, at least 12 million Americans will work in health services—well over 6 percent of the total work force.
[Reich's note]

they retire than they planned for. In consequence, the huge cost of caring for the graying boomers will fall on many of the same people who will be paid to care for them. It will be like a great sump pump: in-person servers of the twenty-first century will have an abundance of health-care jobs, but a large portion of their earnings will be devoted to Social Security payments and income taxes, which will in turn be used to pay their salaries. The net result: no real improvement in their standard of living.

The standard of living of in-person servers also depends, indirectly, on the standard of living of the Americans they serve who are engaged in world commerce. To the extent that *these* Americans are richly rewarded by the rest of the world for what they contribute, they will have more money to lavish upon in-person services. Here we find the only form of "trickle-down" economics that has a basis in reality. A waitress in a town whose major factory has just been closed is unlikely to earn a high wage or enjoy much job security; in a swank resort populated by film producers and banking moguls, she is apt to do reasonably well. So, too, with nations. In-person servers in Bangladesh may spend their days performing roughly the same tasks as in-person servers in the United States, but have a far lower standard of living for their efforts. The difference comes in the value that their customers add to the world economy. 27

Unlike the boats of routine producers and in-person servers, however, the vessel containing America's symbolic analysts is rising. Worldwide demand for their insights is growing as the ease and speed of communicating them steadily increases. Not every symbolic analyst is rising as quickly or as dramatically as every other, of course; symbolic analysts at the low end are barely holding their own in the world economy. But symbolic analysts at the top are in such great demand worldwide that they have difficulty keeping track of all their earnings. Never before in history has opulence on such a scale been gained by people who have earned it, and done so legally. 28

Among symbolic analysts in the middle range are American scientists and researchers who are busily selling their discoveries to global enterprise webs. They are not limited to American customers. If the strategic brokers in General Motors' headquarters refuse to pay a high price for a new means of making high-strength ceramic engines dreamed up by a team of engineers affiliated with Carnegie Mellon University in Pittsburgh, the strategic brokers of Honda or Mercedes-Benz are likely to be more than willing. 29

So, too, with the insights of America's ubiquitous management consultants, which are being sold for large sums to eager entrepreneurs in Europe and Latin America. Also, the insights of America's 30 energy consultants, sold for even larger sums to Arab sheikhs. American design engineers are providing insights to Olivetti, Mazda, Siemens, and other global webs; American marketers, techniques for learning what worldwide consumers will buy; American advertisers, ploys for ensuring that they actually do. American architects are issuing designs and blueprints for opera houses, art galleries, museums, luxury hotels, and residential complexes in the world's major cities; American commercial property developers, marketing these properties to worldwide investors and purchasers.

Americans who specialize in the gentle art of public relations are 31 in demand by corporations, governments, and politicians in virtually every nation. So, too, are American political consultants, some of whom, at this writing, are advising the Hungarian Socialist Party, the remnant of Hungary's ruling Communists, on how to salvage a few parliamentary seats in the nation's first free election in more than forty years. Also at this writing, a team of American agricultural consultants is advising the managers of a Soviet farm collective employing 1,700 Russians eighty miles outside Moscow. As noted, American investment bankers and lawyers specializing in financial circumnavigations are selling their insights to Asians and Europeans who are eager to discover how to make large amounts of money by moving large amounts of money.

Developing nations, meanwhile, are hiring American civil engi- 32 neers to advise on building roads and dams. The present thaw in the Cold War will no doubt expand these opportunities. American engineers from Bechtel (a global firm notable for having employed both Caspar Weinberger and George Shultz for much larger sums than either earned in the Reagan administration) have begun helping the Soviets design and install a new generation of nuclear reactors. Nations also are hiring American bankers and lawyers to help them renegotiate the terms of their loans with global banks, and Washington lobbyists to help them with Congress, the Treasury, the World Bank, the IMF, and other politically sensitive institutions. In fits of obvious desperation, several nations emerging from communism have even hired American economists to teach them about capitalism.

Almost everyone around the world is buying the skills and in- 33 sights of Americans who manipulate oral and visual symbols—musicians, sound engineers, film producers, makeup artists, directors, cinematographers, actors and actresses, boxers, scriptwriters, songwriters, and set designers. Among the wealthiest of symbolic analysts are Steven Spielberg, Bill Cosby, Charles Schulz, Eddie Murphy, Sylvester Stallone, Madonna, and other star directors and performers—who are almost as well known on the streets of Dresden and Tokyo as in the Back Bay of Boston. Less well rewarded but no less renowned are the unctuous anchors on Turner Broadcasting's Cable News, who appear daily, via satellite, in places ranging from Vietnam to Nigeria. Vanna White is the world's most-watched game-show hostess. Behind each of these familiar faces is a collection of American problem-solvers, -identifiers, and brokers who train, coach, advise, promote, amplify, direct, groom, represent, and otherwise add value to their talents.[16]

There are also the insights of senior American executives who   34
occupy the world headquarters of global "American" corporations and the national or regional headquarters of global "foreign" corporations. Their insights are duly exported to the rest of the world through the webs of global enterprise. IBM does not export many machines from the United States, for example. Big Blue makes machines all over the globe and services them on the spot. Its prime American exports are symbolic and analytic. From IBM's world headquarters in Armonk, New York, emanate strategic brokerage and related management services bound for the rest of the world. In return, IBM's top executives are generously rewarded.

The most important reason for this expanding world market   35
and increasing global demand for the symbolic and analytic insights of Americans has been the dramatic improvement in worldwide communication and transportation technologies. Designs, instructions, advice, and visual and audio symbols can be communicated more and more rapidly around the globe, with ever-greater precision and at ever-lower cost. Madonna's voice can be transported to billions of listeners, with perfect clarity, on digital compact discs. A new invention emanating from engineers in Battelle's laboratory in Columbus, Ohio, can be sent almost anywhere via modem, in a form that will allow others to examine it in three dimensions through enhanced computer graphics. When face-to-face meetings are still required—and videoconferencing will not suffice—it is relatively easy for designers, consultants, advisers, artists, and executives to board supersonic jets and, in a matter of hours, meet directly with their worldwide clients, customers, audiences, and employees.

With rising demand comes rising compensation. Whether in the   36
form of licensing fees, fees for service, salaries, or shares in final profits, the economic result is much the same. There are also nonpecuniary rewards. One of the best-kept secrets among symbolic

---

[16] In 1989, the entertainment business summoned to the United States $5.5 billion in foreign earnings—making it among the nation's largest export industries, just behind aerospace. U.S. Department of Commerce, International Trade Commission, "Composition of U.S. Exports," various issues. [Reich's note]

analysts is that so many of them enjoy their work. In fact, much of it does not count as work at all, in the traditional sense. The work of routine producers and in-person servers is typically monotonous; it causes muscles to tire or weaken and involves little independence or discretion. The "work" of symbolic analysts, by contrast, often involves puzzles, experiments, games, a significant amount of chatter, and substantial discretion over what to do next. Few routine producers or in-person servers would "work" if they did not need to earn the money. Many symbolic analysts would "work" even if money were no object.

At midcentury, when America was a national market dominated 37 by core pyramid-shaped corporations, there were constraints on the earnings of people at the highest rungs. First and most obviously, the market for their services was largely limited to the borders of the nation. In addition, whatever conceptual value they might contribute was small relative to the value gleaned from large scale — and it was dependent on large scale for whatever income it was to summon. Most of the problems to be identified and solved had to do with enhancing the efficiency of production and improving the flow of materials, parts, assembly, and distribution. Inventors searched for the rare breakthrough revealing an entirely new product to be made in high volume; management consultants, executives, and engineers thereafter tried to speed and synchronize its manufacture, to better achieve scale efficiencies; advertisers and marketers sought then to whet the public's appetite for the standard item that emerged. Since white-collar earnings increased with larger scale, there was considerable incentive to expand the firm; indeed, many of America's core corporations grew far larger than scale economies would appear to have justified.

By the 1990s, in contrast, the earnings of symbolic analysts 38 were limited neither by the size of the national market nor by the volume of production of the firms with which they were affiliated. The marketplace was worldwide, and conceptual value was high relative to value added from scale efficiencies.

There had been another constraint on high earnings, which also 39 gave way by the 1990s. At midcentury, the compensation awarded to top executives and advisers of the largest of America's core corporations could not be grossly out of proportion to that of low-level production workers. It would be unseemly for executives who engaged in highly visible rounds of bargaining with labor unions, and who routinely responded to government requests to moderate prices, to take home wages and benefits wildly in excess of what other Americans earned. Unless white-collar executives restrained themselves, moreover, blue-collar production workers could not be expected to restrain their own demands for higher wages. Unless both groups exercised restraint, the government could not be expected to forbear from imposing direct controls and regulations.

At the same time, the wages of production workers could not be   40 allowed to sink too low, lest there be insufficient purchasing power in the economy. After all, who would buy all the goods flowing out of American factories if not American workers? This, too, was part of the tacit bargain struck between American managers and their workers.

Recall the oft-repeated corporate platitude of the era about the   41 chief executive's responsibility to carefully weigh and balance the interests of the corporation's disparate stakeholders. Under the stewardship of the corporate statesman, no set of stakeholders—least of all white-collar executives—was to gain a disproportionately large share of the benefits of corporate activity; nor was any stakeholder—especially the average worker—to be left with a share that was disproportionately small. Banal though it was, this idea helped to maintain the legitimacy of the core American corporation in the eyes of most Americans, and to ensure continued economic growth.

But by the 1990s, these informal norms were evaporating, just   42 as (and largely because) the core American corporation was vanishing. The links between top executives and the American production worker were fading: an ever-increasing number of subordinates and contractees were foreign, and a steadily growing number of American routine producers were working for foreign-owned firms. An entire cohort of middle-level managers, who had once been deemed "white collar," had disappeared; and, increasingly, American executives were exporting their insights to global enterprise webs.

As the American corporation itself became a global web almost   43 indistinguishable from any other, its stakeholders were turning into a large and diffuse group, spread over the world. Such global stakeholders were less visible, and far less noisy, than national stakeholders. And as the American corporation sold its goods and services all over the world, the purchasing power of American workers became far less relevant to its economic survival.

Thus have the inhibitions been removed. The salaries and bene-   44 fits of America's top executives, and many of their advisers and consultants, have soared to what years before would have been unimaginable heights, even as those of other Americans have declined.

QUESTIONS FOR CRITICAL READING

1. What are symbolic analysts? Give some examples from your own experience.

2. What is the apparent relationship between higher education and an educated worker's prospects for wealth?
3. To what extent do you agree or disagree with Reich's description and analysis of routine workers and in-service workers?
4. If Reich's analysis is correct, which gender or social groups are likely to be most harmed by modern economic circumstances in America? Which are most likely to become wealthy? Why?
5. Are symbolic analysts inherently more valuable to our society than routine or in-service workers? Why do symbolic analysts command so much more wealth?
6. Which of the three groups Reich mentions do you see as having the greatest potential for growth in the next thirty years?

SUGGESTIONS FOR WRITING

1. Judging from the views that Reich holds about decreasing job opportunities for all three groups of workers, how will increased immigration affect the American economy? Is immigration a hopeful sign? Is it a danger to the economy? How do most people seem to perceive the effect of increased immigration?
2. To what extent do you think Reich is correct about the growing wealth of symbolic analysts? He says, "Never before in history has opulence on such a scale been gained by people who have earned it, and done so legally" (para. 28). Do you see yourself as a symbolic analyst? How do you see your future in relation to the three economic groups Reich describes?
3. Reich says, "Few routine producers or in-person servers would 'work' if they did not need to earn the money. Many symbolic analysts would 'work' even if money were no object" (para. 36). Is this true? Examine your own experience—along with the experience of others you know—and defend or attack this view. How accurate do you consider Reich to be in his analysis of the way various workers view their work?
4. Describe the changes that have taken place in the American economy since 1960, according to this essay. How have they affected the way Americans work and the work that Americans can expect to find? How have your personal opportunities been broadened or narrowed by the changes? Do you feel the changes have been good for the country or not? Why?
5. Reich's view of the great success of Japanese corporations and of their presence as manufacturing giants in the United States and elsewhere is largely positive. He has pointed out elsewhere that Honda and other manufacturers in the United States provide jobs and municipal income that would otherwise go to other nations. What is your view of the presence of large Japanese corporations in the United States? What is your view of other nations' manufacturing facilities in the United States?

6. Why are the rich getting richer and the poor, poorer? Examine the kinds of differences between the rich and the poor that Reich describes. Is the process of increasing riches for the rich and increasing poverty for the poor inevitable, or will it begin to change in the near future?

7. **CONNECTIONS**   To what extent do you think Reich agrees with the position of Milton and Rose Friedman regarding the global free market economy as an economic blessing? Does Reich assume that equality of opportunity is essential in a global context? Does he feel that the economic system he describes is fair to those who have talent and ability? What reservations, if any, does Reich make for protecting the rights of the poor? Is poverty an important issue for either Reich or the Friedmans?

PART FOUR

MIND

Plato
Sigmund Freud
Carl Jung
Karen Horney
Howard Gardner
Francis Crick

INTRODUCTION

Ideas about the nature of the human mind have abounded throughout history. Philosophers and scientists have sought to discern the mind's components and functions and have distinguished humans from other animals according to the qualities associated with the mind, such as reason and self-awareness. The ancient Greeks formulated the concept of the psyche (from which we derive the term *psychology*) as the center of consciousness and reason as well as emotions. During the Renaissance, René Descartes (1596–1650) concluded *Cogito ergo sum* ("I think, therefore I am") and proposed that the mind was the source of human identity and that reason was the key to comprehending the material world. Influenced by Descartes, John Locke (1632–1704) developed a theory of the mind as a *tabula rasa,* or blank slate, that was shaped entirely by external experiences. The selections in this section further explore these questions about the nature of the mind and its relationship to consciousness, knowledge, intellect, and the other means by which we work to understand ourselves and our world.

The first selection, by Plato, contains one of the most formative ideas about the nature of mind. Plato posited that the world of sensory experience is not the real world and that our senses are in fact incapable of experiencing reality. In Plato's view, reality is an ideal that exists only in an environment something akin to the concept of heaven. He suggested that people are born with knowledge of that reality. The infant, in other words, possesses the ideas of reality to start with, having gained them from heaven and retaining them in memory. For Plato, education was the process by which students regained such "lost" memories and made them part of their conscious understanding. Although he never uses the terms *conscious* and *unconscious* in describing the mind, Plato's views foreshadow the later theories of psychologists such as William James (1842–1910), Sigmund Freud, and Carl Jung.

Sigmund Freud, one of the founders of psychoanalysis, is perhaps most famous for his studies of the unconscious. His theories regarding the relationship of the conscious mind to the unconscious mind have become central to the thinking of many modern psychiatrists. His essay from *The Interpretation of Dreams* presents the main outlines of his theory that dreams are products of the psychical activity of the individual and that they offer insight into the content of the unconscious. Until Freud's time, the primary thinking about dreams ignored a connection with the conscious mind of the wakeful individual. Books on the subject had long treated all dreams as categorical and assumed that a meaning could be assigned to a dream on the basis of its structure rather than on the basis of the life of the individual. Freud's careful analysis of dreams demonstrates that the dream is connected to the conscious mind of the dreamer and therefore must be interpreted in terms of the individual's life.

Carl Jung began his studies with Freud's views of the content of the unconscious, but one of his analyses led him in a novel direction. He concluded that some of the content of the unconscious mind could not have begun in the conscious mind because it was not the product of the individual's conscious experience. Jung reasoned that certain images present in the unconscious were common to all members of a culture. He called these images *archetypal* because they seemed fundamental and universal, such as the archetype of the father and the archetype of the mother. He then hypothesized that part of the mind's content is derived from cultural history. Unlike Freud, Jung saw the unconscious as containing images that represent deep instinctual longings belonging to an entire culture, not just to the individual.

A contemporary of both Freud and Jung, Karen Horney incorporates ideas from both these thinkers while advancing her own theories on the relations between men and women. "The Distrust Between the Sexes" describes certain habits of mind that may be thought of as culturally induced but that may also reflect genuine differences in individual minds. Like Jung, Horney argues that if the culture has produced an archetypal male and an archetypal female, no matter what the experiences of the individual, the unconscious registers those archetypes. Horney also talks about culturally induced behavior that begins in "formative years," but because she is a follower of Freud, she does not propose that the distinctions are as clearly gender-linked as Jung insists that archetypes are culturally linked. However, some of her theories about how one sex views the other imply that gender plays a significant role in forming attitudes. In this sense, certain of Horney's views are interpretable in Jungian terms.

Howard Gardner's interest is intelligence, which he approaches from a pluralist point of view. His idea of seven distinct intelligences, as opposed to the conventional views represented by standardized IQ tests, is at once traditional and revolutionary. In drawing on the model of ancient Greek education, he urges us to examine the virtues of all seven forms of intelligence and not rely on the logical-mathematical model that dominates contemporary education. Gardner notes that certain forms of intelligence are culturally linked, but he leaves open the question of whether they are gender-linked.

. Francis Crick, famous for describing the double-helix of DNA, introduces the quest for the secret of consciousness in this chapter from his book *The Astonishing Hypothesis*. In his book's subtitle, he calls this pursuit "The Scientific Search for the Soul." His essay is simply a beginning, an examination of the landscape of consciousness and what has been said about it. What interests us most in his essay is the method by which he establishes his search. He wishes to be scientific while at the same time taking into account the complexity of our feelings about the nature of the soul. (The Greek term for "mind" was *psyche,* which also translates as "soul," as does the later Roman term, *anima.*) The result is an attempt to give us a roadmap that will begin to lead to an understanding of the phenomenon of mind we call consciousness.

These essays approach the problem of mind from different positions and are concerned with different questions of consciousness, thought, limitation, and intelligence. They raise some of the most basic questions concerning the mind, such as, What are its components? What can it know? What should we most value in its function? In answering these questions, each essay provides us with ideas that provoke more thought and still more questions.

PLATO
The Allegory of the Cave

PLATO (428–347 B.C.) was born into an aristocratic, probably Athenian, family and educated according to the best precepts available. He eventually became a student of Socrates and later involved himself closely with Socrates' work and teaching. Plato was not only Socrates' finest student but also the one who immortalized Socrates in his works. Most of Plato's works are philosophical essays in which Socrates speaks as a character in a dialogue with one or more students or listeners.

Both Socrates and Plato lived in turbulent times. In 404 B.C. Athens was defeated by Sparta and its government was taken over by tyrants. Political life in Athens became dangerous. Plato felt, however, that he could effect positive change in Athenian politics until Socrates was tried unjustly for corrupting the youth of Athens and sentenced to death in 399 B.C. After that, Plato withdrew from public life and devoted himself to writing and to the Academy he founded in an olive grove in Athens. The Academy endured for almost a thousand years, which tells us how greatly Plato's thought was valued.

Although it is not easy to condense Plato's views, he may be said to have held the world of sense perception to be inferior to the world of ideal entities that exist only in a pure spiritual realm. These ideals, or forms, Plato argued, are perceived directly by everyone before birth and then dimly remembered here on earth. But the memory, dim as it is, enables people to understand what the senses perceive, despite the fact that the senses are unreliable and their perceptions imperfect.

This view of reality has long been important to philosophers because it gives a philosophical basis to antimaterialistic thought.

From *The Republic.* Translated and glossed by Benjamin Jowett.

It values the spirit first and frees people from the tyranny of sensory perception and sensory reward. In the case of love, Plato held that Eros leads individuals to revere the body and its pleasures; but the thrust of his teaching is that the body is a metaphor for spiritual delights. Plato maintains that the body is only a starting point, which eventually can lead to both spiritual fulfillment and the appreciation of true beauty.

On the one hand, "The Allegory of the Cave" is a discussion of politics: *The Republic,* from which it is taken, is a treatise on justice and the ideal government. On the other hand, it has long stood as an example of the notion that if we rely on our perceptions to know the truth about the world, then we will know very little about it. In order to live ethically, it is essential to know what is true and, therefore, what is important beyond the world of sensory perception.

Plato's allegory has been persuasive for centuries and remains at the center of thought that attempts to counter the pleasures of the sensual life. Most religions aim for spiritual enlightenment and praise the qualities of the soul, which lies beyond perception. Thus, it comes as no surprise that Christianity and other religions have developed systems of thought that bear a close resemblance to Plato's. Later refinements of his thought, usually called Neo-Platonism, have been influential even into modern times.

Plato's Rhetoric

Two important rhetorical techniques are at work in the following selection. The first and more obvious—at least on one level— is the device of the allegory, a story in which the characters and situations actually represent people and situations in another context. It is a difficult technique to sustain, although Aesop's fables were certainly successful in using animals to represent people and their foibles. The advantage of the technique is that a complex and sometimes unpopular argument can be fought and won before the audience realizes that an argument is under way. The disadvantage of the technique is that the terms of the allegory may only approximate the situation it represents; thus, the argument may fail to be convincing.

The second rhetorical technique Plato uses is the dialogue. In fact, this device is a hallmark of Plato's work; indeed, most of his writings are called dialogues. The *Symposium, Apology, Phaedo, Crito, Meno,* and most of his famous works are written in dialogue form. Usually in these works Socrates is speaking to a student or a friend about highly abstract issues, asking questions that require simple answers. Slowly, the questioning proceeds to elucidate the answers to complex issues.

This question-and-answer technique basically constitutes the Socratic method. Socrates analyzes the answer to each question, examines its implications, and then asserts the truth. The method works partly because Plato believes that people do not learn things but remember them. That is, people originate from heaven, where they knew the truth; they already possess knowledge and must recover it by means of the dialogue. Socrates' method is ideally suited to that purpose.

Beyond these techniques, however, we must look at Plato's style. It is true that he is working with difficult ideas, but his style is so clear, simple, and direct that few people would have trouble understanding what he is saying at any given moment. Considering the influence this work has had on world thought and the reputation Plato had earned by the time he wrote *The Republic,* its style is remarkably plain and accessible. Plato's respect for rhetoric and its proper uses is part of the reason he can express himself with such impressive clarity.

PREREADING QUESTIONS: WHAT TO READ FOR

The following prereading questions may help you anticipate key issues in the discussion on Plato's "The Allegory of the Cave." Keeping them in mind during your first reading of the selection should help focus your reactions.

- In what ways are we like the people in the cave looking at shadows?

- Why is the world of sensory perception somewhat illusory?

- For Plato, what is the difference between the upper world and the lower world?

The Allegory of the Cave

SOCRATES, GLAUCON. *The den, the prisoners: the light at a distance;*

And now, I said, let me show in a figure how 1 far our nature is enlightened or unenlightened:— Behold! human beings living in an underground den, which has a mouth open towards the light and reaching all along the den; here they have been from their childhood, and have their legs and necks chained so that they cannot move, and can only see before them, being prevented by the chains from turning round their heads. Above and behind them a fire is blazing at a distance, and between the fire and the prisoners there is a raised way; and you will see, if you look, a low wall built along the way, like the screen which marionette players have in front of them, over which they show the puppets.

I see. 2

the low wall, and the moving figures of which the shadows are seen on the opposite wall of the den.

And do you see, I said, men passing along the 3 wall carrying all sorts of vessels, and statues and figures of animals made of wood and stone and various materials, which appear over the wall? Some of them are talking, others silent.

You have shown me a strange image, and they 4 are strange prisoners.

Like ourselves, I replied; and they see only 5 their own shadows, or the shadows of one another, which the fire throws on the opposite wall of the cave?

True, he said; how could they see anything but 6 the shadows if they were never allowed to move their heads?

And of the objects which are being carried in 7 like manner they would only see the shadows?

Yes, he said. 8

And if they were able to converse with one an- 9 other, would they not suppose that they were naming what was actually before them?

Very true. 10

The prisoners would mistake the shadows for realities.

And suppose further that the prison had an 11 echo which came from the other side, would they not be sure to fancy when one of the passers-by spoke that the voice which they heard came from the passing shadow?

No question, he replied. 12

To them, I said, the truth would be literally 13 nothing but the shadows of the images.

That is certain. 14

And now look again, and see what will natu- 15 rally follow if the prisoners are released and disabused of their error. At first, when any of them is liberated and compelled suddenly to stand up and turn his neck round and walk and look towards the light, he will suffer sharp pains; the glare will distress him, and he will be unable to see the realities of which in his former state he had seen the shadows; and then conceive someone saying to him, that what he saw before was an illusion, but that now, when he is approaching nearer to being and his eye is turned towards more real existence, he has a clearer vision—what will be his reply? And you may further imagine that his instructor is pointing to the objects as they pass and requiring him to name them,—will he not be perplexed? Will he not fancy that the shadows which he formerly saw are truer than the objects which are now shown to him?

And when released, they would still persist in maintaining the superior truth of the shadows.

Far truer. 16

And if he is compelled to look straight at the 17 light, will he not have a pain in his eyes which will make him turn away to take refuge in the objects of vision which he can see, and which he will conceive to be in reality clearer than the things which are now being shown to him?

True, he said. 18

And suppose once more, that he is reluctantly 19 dragged up a steep and rugged ascent, and held fast until he is forced into the presence of the sun himself, is he not likely to be pained and irritated? When he approaches the light his eyes will be dazzled, and he will not be able to see anything at all of what are now called realities.

When dragged upwards, they would be dazzled by excess of light.

Not all in a moment, he said. 20

He will require to grow accustomed to the 21 sight of the upper world. And first he will see the shadows best, next the reflections of men and other objects in the water, and then the objects themselves; then he will gaze upon the light of the moon and the stars and the spangled heaven; and he will see the sky and the stars by night better than the sun or the light of the sun by day?

Certainly. 22

Last of all he will be able to see the sun, and 23 not mere reflections of him in the water, but he

At length they will see the sun and understand his nature.

will see him in his own proper place, and not in another; and he will contemplate him as he is.

Certainly.   24

He will then proceed to argue that this is he 25 who gives the season and the years, and is the guardian of all that is in the visible world, and in a certain way the cause of all things which he and his fellows have been accustomed to behold?

Clearly, he said, he would first see the sun and 26 then reason about him.

And when he remembered his old habitation, 27 and the wisdom of the den and his fellow prison-

They would then pity their old companions of the den.

ers, do you not suppose that he would felicitate himself on the change, and pity them?

Certainly, he would.   28

And if they were in the habit of conferring 29 honors among themselves on those who were quickest to observe the passing shadows and to re-mark which of them went before, and which fol-lowed after, and which were together; and who were therefore best able to draw conclusions as to the future, do you think that he would care for such honors and glories, or envy the possessors of them? Would he not say with Homer,

Better to be the poor servant of a poor master,

and to endure anything, rather than think as they do and live after their manner?

Yes, he said, I think that he would rather suffer 30 anything than entertain these false notions and live in this miserable manner.

Imagine once more, I said, such an one coming 31 suddenly out of the sun to be replaced in his old situation; would he not be certain to have his eyes full of darkness?

To be sure, he said.   32

But when they returned to the den, they would see much worse than those who had never left it.

And if there were a contest, and he had to 33 compete in measuring the shadows with the pris-oners who had never moved out of the den, while his sight was still weak, and before his eyes had be-come steady (and the time which would be needed to acquire this new habit of sight might be very considerable), would he not be ridiculous? Men would say of him that up he went and down he came without his eyes; and that it was better not even to think of ascending; and if any one tried to loose another and lead him up to the light, let them only catch the offender, and they would put him to death.

No question, he said. 34

The prison is the world of sight, the light of the fire is the sun.

This entire allegory, I said, you may now append, dear Glaucon, to the previous argument; the prison house is the world of sight, the light of the fire is the sun, and you will not misapprehend me if you interpret the journey upwards to be the ascent of the soul into the intellectual world according to my poor belief, which, at your desire, I have expressed—whether rightly or wrongly God knows. But, whether true or false, my opinion is that in the world of knowledge the idea of good appears last of all, and is seen only with an effort; and, when seen, is also inferred to be the universal author of all things beautiful and right, parent of light and of the lord of light in this visible world, and the immediate source of reason and truth in the intellectual; and that this is the power upon which he who would act rationally either in public or private life must have his eye fixed. 35

I agree, he said, as far as I am able to understand you. 36

Moreover, I said, you must not wonder that those who attain to this beatific vision are unwilling to descend to human affairs; for their souls are ever hastening into the upper world where they desire to dwell; which desire of theirs is very natural, if our allegory may be trusted. 37

Yes, very natural. 38

Nothing extraordinary in the philosopher being unable to see in the dark.

And is there anything surprising in one who passes from divine contemplations to the evil state of man, misbehaving himself in a ridiculous manner; if, while his eyes are blinking and before he has become accustomed to the surrounding darkness, he is compelled to fight in courts of law, or in other places, about the images or the shadows of images of justice, and is endeavoring to meet the conceptions of those who have never yet seen absolute justice? 39

Anything but surprising, he replied. 40

The eyes may be blinded in two ways, by excess or by defect of light.

Anyone who has common sense will remember that the bewilderments of the eyes are of two kinds, and arise from two causes, either from coming out of the light or from going into the light, which is true of the mind's eye, quite as much as of the bodily eye; and he who remembers this when he sees anyone whose vision is perplexed and weak, will not be too ready to laugh; he will first ask whether that soul of man has come out of the brighter life, and is unable to see because unaccustomed to the dark, or having turned from darkness to the day is dazzled by excess of light. And he will count the one happy in his condition and state of being, and he will pity the other; or, if he have a mind to laugh at the soul which comes from below into the light, there will be more reason in this than in the laugh which greets him who returns from above out of the light into the den. 41

That, he said, is a very just distinction. 42

The conversion of the soul is the turning round the eye from darkness to light.

But then, if I am right, certain professors of education must be wrong when they say that they can put a knowledge into the soul which was not there before, like sight into blind eyes. 43

They undoubtedly say this, he replied. 44

Whereas, our argument shows that the power and capacity of learning exists in the soul already; and that just as the eye was unable to turn from darkness to light without the whole body, so too the instrument of knowledge can only by the movement of the whole soul be turned from the world of becoming into that of being, and learn by degrees to endure the sight of being, and of the brightest and best of being, or in other words, of the good. 45

Very true. 46

And must there not be some art which will effect conversion in the easiest and quickest manner; not implanting the faculty of sight, for that exists already, but has been turned in the wrong direction, and is looking away from the truth? 47

Yes, he said, such an art may be presumed. 48

And whereas the other so-called virtues of the soul seem to be akin to bodily qualities, for even when they are not originally innate they can be im- 49

The virtue of wisdom has a divine power which may be turned either towards good or towards evil.

planted later by habit and exercise, the virtue of wisdom more than anything else contains a divine element which always remains, and by this conversion is rendered useful and profitable; or, on the other hand, hurtful and useless. Did you never observe the narrow intelligence flashing from the keen eye of a clever rogue—how eager he is, how clearly his paltry soul sees the way to his end; he is the reverse of blind, but his keen eyesight is forced into the service of evil, and he is mischievous in proportion to his cleverness?

Very true, he said. 50

But what if there had been a circumcision of 51 such natures in the days of their youth; and they had been severed from those sensual pleasures, such as eating and drinking, which, like leaden weights, were attached to them at their birth, and which drag them down and turn the vision of their souls upon the things that are below—if, I say, they had been released from these impediments and turned in the opposite direction, the very same faculty in them would have seen the truth as keenly as they see what their eyes are turned to now.

Very likely. 52

Neither the uneducated nor the over-educated will be good servants of the State.

Yes, I said; and there is another thing which is 53 likely, or rather a necessary inference from what has preceded, that neither the uneducated and uninformed of the truth, nor yet those who never make an end of their education, will be able ministers of State; not the former, because they have no single aim of duty which is the rule of all their actions, private as well as public; nor the latter, because they will not act at all except upon compulsion, fancying that they are already dwelling apart in the islands of the blessed.

Very true, he replied. 54

Then, I said, the business of us who are the 55 founders of the State will be to compel the best minds to attain that knowledge which we have already shown to be the greatest of all—they must continue to ascend until they arrive at the good; but when they have ascended and seen enough we must not allow them to do as they do now.

Men should ascend to the upper world, but they should also return to the lower.

What do you mean? 56

I mean that they remain in the upper world: 57 but this must not be allowed; they must be made to descend again among the prisoners in the den, and partake of their labors and honors, whether they are worth having or not.

But is not this unjust? he said; ought we to give 58 them a worse life, when they might have a better?

You have again forgotten, my friend, I said, the 59 intention of the legislator, who did not aim at making any one class in the State happy above the rest; the happiness was to be in the whole State, and he held the citizens together by persuasion and necessity, making them benefactors of the State, and therefore benefactors of one another; to this end he created them, not to please themselves, but to be his instruments in binding up the State.

True, he said, I had forgotten. 60

The duties of philosophers.

Observe, Glaucon, that there will be no injus- 61 tice in compelling our philosophers to have a care and providence of others; we shall explain to them that in other States, men of their class are not obliged to share in the toils of politics: and this is reasonable, for they grow up at their own sweet will, and the government would rather not have them. Being self-taught, they cannot be expected to show any gratitude for a culture which they have never received. But we have brought you into the world to be rulers of the hive, kings of yourselves and of the other citizens, and have educated you far better and more perfectly than they have been educated, and you are better able to share in the double duty. Wherefore each of you, when his turn comes, must go down to the general underground abode, and get the habit of seeing in the dark.

Their obligations to their country will induce them to take part in her government.

When you have acquired the habit, you will see ten thousand times better than the inhabitants of the den, and you will know what the several images are, and what they represent, because you have seen the beautiful and just and good in their truth. And thus our State, which is also yours, will be a reality, and not a dream only, and will be administered in a spirit unlike that of other States, in which men fight with one another about shadows only and are distracted in the struggle for power, which in their eyes is a great good. Whereas the truth is that the State in which the rulers are most reluctant to govern is always the best and most quietly governed, and the State in which they are most eager, the worst.

Quite true, he replied.   62

And will our pupils, when they hear this,   63 refuse to take their turn at the toils of State, when they are allowed to spend the greater part of their time with one another in the heavenly light?

They will be willing but not anxious to rule.

Impossible, he answered; for they are just   64 men, and the commands which we impose upon them are just; there can be no doubt that every one of them will take office as a stern necessity, and not after the fashion of our present rulers of State.

The statesman must be provided with a better life than that of a ruler; and then he will not covet office.

Yes, my friend, I said; and there lies the point.   65 You must contrive for your future rulers another and a better life than that of a ruler, and then you may have a well-ordered State; for only in the State which offers this, will they rule who are truly rich, not in silver and gold, but in virtue and wisdom, which are the true blessings of life. Whereas if they go to the administration of public affairs, poor and hungering after their own private advantage, thinking that hence they are to snatch the chief good, order there can never be; for they will be fighting about office, and the civil and domestic broils which thus arise will be the ruin of the rulers themselves and of the whole State.

Most true, he replied.   66

And the only life which looks down upon the   67 life of political ambition is that of true philosophy. Do you know of any other?

Indeed, I do not, he said.   68

QUESTIONS FOR CRITICAL READING

1. What is the relationship between Socrates and Glaucon? Are they equal in intellectual authority? Are they concerned with the same issues?

2. How does the allegory of the prisoners in the cave watching shadows on a wall relate to us today? What shadows do we see, and how do they distort our sense of what is real?
3. Are we prisoners in the same sense that Plato's characters are?
4. If Plato is right that the material world is an illusion, how would too great a reliance on materialism affect ethical decisions?
5. What ethical issues, if any, are raised by Plato's allegory?
6. In paragraph 49, Plato states that the virtue of wisdom "contains a divine element." What is "a divine element"? What does this statement seem to mean? Do you agree with Plato?
7. What distinctions does Plato make between the public and the private? Would you make the same distinctions (see paras. 53–55)?

SUGGESTIONS FOR WRITING

1. Analyze the allegory of the cave for its strengths and weaknesses. Consider what the allegory implies for people living in a world of the senses and for what might lie behind that world. To what extent are people like (or unlike) the figures in the cave? To what extent is the world we know like the cave?
2. Socrates ends the dialogue by saying that rulers of the state must be able to look forward to a better life than that of being rulers. He and Glaucon agree that only one life "looks down upon the life of political ambition"—"that of true philosophy" (para. 67). What is the life of true philosophy? Is it superior to that of governing (or anything else)? How would you define its superiority? What would its qualities be? What would its concerns be? Would you be happy leading such a life?
3. In what ways would depending on the material world for one's highest moral values affect ethical behavior? What is the connection between ethics and materialism? Write a brief essay that defends or attacks materialism as a basis for ethical action. How can people aspire to the good if they root their greatest pleasures in the senses? What alternatives do modern people have if they choose to base their actions on nonmaterialistic, or spiritual, values? What are those values? How can they guide our ethical behavior? Do you think they should?
4. In paragraph 61, Socrates outlines a program that would assure Athens of having good rulers and good government. Clarify exactly what the program is, what its problems and benefits are, and how it could be put into action. Then decide whether the program would work. You may consider whether it would work for our time, for Socrates' time, or both. If possible, use examples (hypothetical or real) to bolster your argument.
5. Socrates states unequivocally that Athens should compel the best and the most intelligent young men to be rulers of the state. Review his reasons for saying so, consider what his concept of the state is, and then take a stand on the issue. Is it right to compel the best and most

intelligent young people to become rulers? If so, would it be equally proper to compel those well suited for the professions of law, medicine, teaching, or religion to follow those respective callings? Would an ideal society result if all people were forced to practice the calling for which they had the best aptitude?

6. **CONNECTIONS** Plato has a great deal to say about goodness as it relates to government. Compare his views with those of Lao-tzu and Machiavelli. Which of those thinkers would Plato have agreed with most? In comparing these three writers and their political views, consider the nature of goodness they required in a ruler. Do you think that we hold similar attitudes today in our expectations for the goodness of our government?

SIGMUND FREUD
From *The Interpretation of Dreams*

SIGMUND FREUD (1856–1939) is, in the minds of many, the founder of modern psychiatry. He developed the psychoanalytic method: the examination of the mind using dream analysis, the analysis of the unconscious through free association, and the correlation of findings with attitudes toward sexuality and sexual development. His theories changed the way people treated neurosis and most other mental disorders. Today we use terms he either invented or championed, such as *psychoanalysis, penis envy, Oedipus complex,* and *wish-fulfillment.*

Freud was born in Freiberg, Moravia (now Pribor in the Czech Republic), and moved to Vienna, Austria, when he was four. He pursued a medical career and soon began exploring neurology, which stimulated him to begin his psychoanalytic methods. *The Interpretation of Dreams* (1899) is one of his first important books. It was followed in rapid succession by a number of ground-breaking studies: *The Psychopathology of Everyday Life* (1904), *Three Essays on the Theory of Sexuality* (1905), *Totem and Taboo* (1913), *Beyond the Pleasure Principle* (1920), and *Civilization and Its Discontents* (1930). Freud's personal life was essentially uneventful in Vienna until he was put under house arrest by the Nazis in 1938 because he was Jewish. He was released and moved to London, where he died the following year.

As a movement, psychoanalysis shocked most of the world by postulating a superego, which establishes high standards of personal behavior; an ego, which corresponds to the apparent

From *The Interpretation of Dreams.* Translated by James Strachey.

personality; an id, which includes the deepest primitive forces of life; and an unconscious, into which thoughts and memories we cannot face are repressed or sublimated. The origin of much mental illness, the theory presumes, lies in the inability of the mind to find a way to sublimate—express in harmless and often creative ways—the painful thoughts that have been repressed. Dreams and unconscious actions sometimes act as releases or harmless expressions of these thoughts and memories.

Before Freud's work, books that interpreted classic dreams existed, but they assumed dreams were universal in importance rather than personal. In *The Interpretation of Dreams,* Freud reviews these historical approaches to dreams and draws the revolutionary conclusion that dreams can be interpreted as important personal psychological events. The second part of Freud's book offers a sample interpretation of one of his own dreams concerning injections given to a patient named Irma (he refers to the analysis in this selection). In that analysis he shows how his dream reveals his own uncertainties about his patient.

Freud's theory of the dream as wish-fulfillment is first introduced in this chapter and is developed further in the last section of his book. In this chapter he explores evidence indicating that dreams express the unfulfilled wishes of the individual. He offers a number of examples from his own dreams as well as from dreams of family members. He also makes some interesting observations about the dreams of children, with examples from his own children's dreams. His examples are familiar and pertinent to his family circumstances, but they are universal enough to help readers interpret their own dreams.

Freud's Rhetoric

Freud's style is simple and direct in this chapter. His language is relaxed, clear, and familiar, as is the material he introduces, because most of it comes from his own family's experiences. He tells us about his trips, his mountain walks, his family around him, and their desires and hopes. He states that when they are disappointed, their dreams supply the pleasures that they were denied.

Freud's basic effort is that of argumentation—although his style is so unthreatening that for many readers the argument will be invisible. Freud expects to convince his readers by the method of supplying a number of examples and offering analyses of the examples. Once the reader has read through these analyzed examples, he or she is expected to be convinced that dreams are, indeed, wish-fulfillments. Freud was unable to offer examples of dream analyses from other analysts because, as he tells us in the early part of his book, no other analyst approaches dreams as he does. He does offer us a dream or two from nonfamily members, but the analyses are his own.

One interesting rhetorical device that seems to underlie the entire selection is a simple metaphor expressed in the opening paragraph, where he likens the reader's present position to someone who has ascended a mountaintop and paused to enjoy the view. The heights, attainable only through effort, are a metaphor for the exertions of the psychoanalyst that raise the sights of the patient or the reader. Only from the promontory can one see the true topography of the locale, and Freud's work takes us to that promontory. Moreover, several of the examples Freud later uses are also drawn from mountain climbing—walks by himself and others through the foothills leading to the mountain. He tells of his child growing impatient with the foothills because he wishes to gain the mountaintop immediately. All this is a convenient metaphor for the preparations that the analyst must make to understand the truth about the meaning of dreams.

In a letter Freud wrote to an associate while he was working on the book, he describes his rhetorical approach in the following manner: "The whole thing is planned on the model of an imaginary walk. First comes the dark wood of the authorities (who cannot see the trees), where there is no clear view and it is easy to go astray. Then there is a cavernous defile through which I lead my readers— my specimen dream with its peculiarities, its details, its indiscretions and its bad jokes—and then, all at once, the high ground and the open prospect" (August 6, 1899).

Not all of Freud's writing is as approachable as this example. But when Freud writes about universal experiences, his style is often clear and direct. In large part because of Freud's rhetorical skill, the concept of the dream as wish-fulfillment has become part of our language.

PREREADING QUESTIONS: WHAT TO READ FOR

The following prereading questions may help you anticipate key issues in the discussion on the excerpt that follows from Sigmund Freud's *The Interpretation of Dreams*. Keeping them in mind during your first reading of the selection should help focus your reactions.

• How does a dream express wish-fulfillment?

• What is the source of the material that forms a dream?

From *The Interpretation of Dreams*

When, after passing through a narrow defile, we suddenly   1
emerge upon a piece of high ground, where the path divides and the
finest prospects open up on every side, we may pause for a moment
and consider in which direction we shall first turn our steps. Such is
the case with us, now that we have surmounted the first interpretation of a dream. We find ourselves in the full daylight of a sudden
discovery. Dreams are not to be likened to the unregulated sounds
that rise from a musical instrument struck by the blow of some external force instead of by a player's hand; they are not meaningless,
they are not absurd; they do not imply that one portion of our store
of ideas is asleep while another portion is beginning to wake. On the
contrary, they are psychical phenomena of complete validity—fulfillments of wishes; they can be inserted into the chain of intelligible
waking mental acts; they are constructed by a highly complicated
activity of the mind.

But no sooner have we begun to rejoice at this discovery than   2
we are assailed by a flood of questions. If, as we are told by dream-
interpretation, a dream represents a fulfilled wish, what is the origin
of the remarkable and puzzling form in which the wish-fulfillment is
expressed? What alteration have the dream-thoughts undergone before being changed into the manifest dream which we remember
when we wake up? How does that alteration take place? What is the
source of the material that has been modified into the dream? What
is the source of the many peculiarities that are to be observed in the
dream-thoughts—such, for instance, as the fact that they may be
mutually contradictory? Can a dream tell us anything new about our
internal psychical processes? Can its content correct opinions we
have held during the day?

I propose that for the moment we should leave all these ques-   3
tions on one side and pursue our way further along one particular
path. We have learnt that a dream can represent a wish as fulfilled.
Our first concern must be to enquire whether this is a universal
characteristic of dreams or whether it merely happened to be the
content of the particular dream (the dream of Irma's injection)
which was the first that we analyzed. For even if we are prepared to
find that every dream has a meaning and a psychical value, the possibility must remain open of this meaning not being the same in
every dream. Our first dream was the fulfillment of a wish; a second
one might turn out to be a fulfilled fear; the content of a third might
be a reflection; while a fourth might merely reproduce a memory.

Shall we find other wishful dreams besides this one? Or are there perhaps no dreams but wishful ones?

It is easy to prove that dreams often reveal themselves without   4
any disguise as fulfillments of wishes; so that it may seem surprising that the language of dreams was not understood long ago. For instance, there is a dream that I can produce in myself as often as I like—experimentally, as it were. If I eat anchovies or olives or any other highly salted food in the evening, I develop thirst during the night which wakes me up. But my waking is preceded by a dream; and this always has the same content, namely, that I am drinking. I dream I am swallowing down water in great gulps, and it has the delicious taste that nothing can equal but a cool drink when one is parched with thirst. Then I wake up and have to have a real drink. This simple dream is occasioned by the thirst which I become aware of when I wake. The thirst gives rise to a wish to drink, and the dream shows me that wish fulfilled. In doing so it is performing a function—which it was easy to divine. I am a good sleeper and not accustomed to be woken by any physical need. If I can succeed in appeasing my thirst by *dreaming* that I am drinking, then I need not wake up in order to quench it. This, then, is a dream of convenience. Dreaming has taken the place of action, as it often does elsewhere in life. Unluckily my need for water to quench my thirst cannot be satisfied by a dream in the same way as my thirst for revenge against my friend Otto and Dr. M.; but the good intention is there in both cases. Not long ago this same dream of mine showed some modification. I had felt thirsty even before I fell asleep, and I had emptied a glass of water that stood on the table beside my bed. A few hours later during the night I had a fresh attack of thirst, and this had inconvenient results. In order to provide myself with some water I should have had to get up and fetch the glass standing on the table by my wife's bed. I therefore had an appropriate dream that my wife was giving me a drink out of a vase; this vase was an Etruscan cinerary urn which I had brought back from a journey to Italy and had since given away. But the water in it tasted so salty (evidently because of the ashes in the urn) that I woke up. It will be noticed how conveniently everything was arranged in this dream. Since its only purpose was to fulfil [sic] a wish, it could be completely egoistical. A love of comfort and convenience is not really compatible with consideration for other people. The introduction of the cinerary urn was probably yet another wish-fulfillment. I was sorry that the vase was no longer in my possession—just as the glass of water on my wife's table was out of my reach. The urn with its ashes fitted in, too, with the salty taste in my mouth which had now grown stronger and which I knew was bound to wake me.

Dreams of convenience like these were very frequent in my 5 youth. Having made it a practice as far back as I can remember to work late into the night, I always found it difficult to wake early. I used then to have a dream of being out of bed and standing by the washing stand; after a while I was no longer able to disguise from myself the fact that I was really still in bed, but in the meantime I had had a little more sleep. A slothful dream of this kind, which was expressed in a particularly amusing and elegant form, has been reported to me by a young medical colleague who seems to share my liking for sleep. The landlady of his lodgings in the neighborhood of the hospital had strict instructions to wake him in time every morning but found it no easy job to carry them out. One morning sleep seemed peculiarly sweet. The landlady called through the door: "Wake up, Herr Pepi! It's time to go to the hospital!" In response to this he had a dream that he was lying in bed in a room in the hospital, and that there was a card over the bed on which was written: "Pepi H., medical student, age 22." While he was dreaming, he said to himself "As I'm already *in* the hospital, there's no need for me to go there"—and turned over and went on sleeping. In this way he openly confessed the motive for his dream.

Here is another dream in which once again the stimulus pro- 6 duced its effect during actual sleep. One of my women patients, who had been obliged to undergo an operation on her jaw which had taken an unfavorable course, was ordered by her doctors to wear a cooling apparatus on the side of her face day and night. But as soon as she fell asleep she used to throw it off. One day, after she had once more thrown the apparatus on the floor, I was asked to speak to her seriously about it. "This time I really couldn't help it," she answered. "It was because of a dream I had in the night. I dreamed I was in a box at the opera and very much enjoying the performance. But Herr Karl Meyer was in the nursing home and complaining bitterly of pains in his jaw. So I told myself that as I hadn't any pain I didn't need the apparatus; and I threw it away." The dream of this poor sufferer seems almost like a concrete representation of a phrase that sometimes forces its way on to people's lips in unpleasant situations: "I must say I could think of something more agreeable than this." The dream gives a picture of this more agreeable thing. The Herr Karl Meyer on to whom the dreamer transplanted her pains was the most indifferent young man of her acquaintance that she could call to mind.

The wish-fulfillment can be detected equally easily in some 7 other dreams which I have collected from normal people. A friend of mine, who knows my theory of dreams and has told his wife of it, said to me one day: "My wife has asked me to tell you that she had a dream yesterday that she was having her period. You can guess what that means." I could indeed guess it. The fact that this young married woman dreamed that she was having her period meant that she had missed her period. I could well believe that she would have been glad to go on enjoying her freedom a little longer before shouldering the burden of motherhood. It was a neat way of announcing her first pregnancy. Another friend of mine wrote and told me that, not long before, his wife had dreamed that she had noticed some milk stains on the front of her vest. This too was an announcement of pregnancy, but not of a first one. The young mother was wishing that she might have more nourishment to give her second child than she had had for her first.

A young woman had been cut off from society for weeks on end 8 while she nursed her child through an infectious illness. After the child's recovery, she had a dream of being at a party at which, among others, she met Alphonse Daudet, Paul Bourget, and Marcel Prévost;[1] they were all most affable to her and highly amusing. All of the authors resembled their portraits, except Marcel Prévost, of whom she had never seen a picture; and he looked like . . . the disinfection officer who had fumigated the sick room the day before and who had been her first visitor for so long. Thus it seems possible to give a complete translation of the dream: "It's about time for something more amusing than this perpetual sick-nursing."

These examples will perhaps be enough to show that dreams 9 which can only be understood as fulfillments of wishes and which bear their meaning upon their faces without disguise are to be found under the most frequent and various conditions. They are mostly short and simple dreams, which afford a pleasant contrast to the confused and exuberant compositions that have in the main attracted the attention of the authorities. Nevertheless, it will repay us to pause for a moment over these simple dreams. We may expect to find the very simplest forms of dreams in *children,* since there can be no doubt that their psychical productions are less complicated than those of adults. Child psychology, in my opinion, is destined to perform the same useful services for adult psychology that the investigation of the structure or development of the lower animals has performed for research into the structure of the higher classes of animals. Few deliberate efforts have hitherto been made to make use of child psychology for this purpose.

The dreams of young children are frequently pure wish- 10 fulfillments and are in that case quite uninteresting compared with

---

[1] **Alphonse Daudet (1840–1897), Paul Bourget (1852–1935), and Marcel Prévost (1862–1941)** All French novelists.

the dreams of adults. They raise no problems for solution; but on the other hand they are of inestimable importance in proving that, in their essential nature, dreams represent fulfillments of wishes. I have been able to collect a few instances of such dreams from material provided by my own children.

I have to thank an excursion which we made from Aussee to the lovely village of Hallstatt in the summer of 1896 for two dreams: One of these was dreamed by my daughter, who was then eight and a half, and the other by her brother of five and a quarter. I must explain by way of preamble that we had been spending the summer on a hillside near Aussee, from which, in fine weather, we enjoyed a splendid view of the Dachstein. The Simony Hütte could be clearly distinguished through a telescope. The children made repeated attempts at seeing it through the telescope—I cannot say with what success. Before our excursion, I had told the children that Hallstatt lay at the foot of the Dachstein. They very much looked forward to the day. From Hallstatt we walked up the Echerntal, which delighted the children with its succession of changing landscapes. One of them, however, the five-year-old boy, gradually became fretful. Each time a new mountain came into view he asked if that was the Dachstein and I had to say, "No, only one of the foothills." After he had asked the question several times, he fell completely silent; and he refused point blank to come with us up the steep path to the waterfall. I thought he was tired. But next morning he came to me with a radiant face and said: "Last night I dreamed we were at the Simony Hütte." I understood him then. When I had spoken about the Dachstein, he had expected to climb the mountain in the course of our excursion to Hallstatt and to find himself at close quarters with the hut which there had been so much talk about in connection with the telescope. But when he found that he was being fobbed off[2] with foothills and a waterfall, he felt disappointed and out of spirits. The dream was a compensation. I tried to discover its details, but they were scanty: "You have to climb up steps for six hours"— which was what he had been told.

The same excursion stirred up wishes in the eight-and-a-half-year-old girl as well—wishes which had to be satisfied in a dream. We had taken our neighbor's twelve-year-old son with us to Hallstatt. He was already a full-blown gallant, and there were signs that he had engaged the young lady's affections. Next morning she told me the following dream: "Just fancy! I had a dream that Emil was one of the family and called you 'Father' and 'Mother' and slept with

11

12

---

[2] **fobbed off** Deceived.

us in the big room like the boys. Then Mother came in and threw a handful of big bars of chocolate, wrapped up in blue and green paper, under our beds." Her brothers, who have evidently not inherited a faculty for understanding dreams, followed the lead of the authorities and declared that the dream was nonsense. The girl herself defended one part of the dream at least; and it throws light on the theory of neuroses to learn *which* part. "Of course it's nonsense Emil being one of the family; but the part about the bars of chocolate isn't." It had been precisely on that point that I had been in the dark, but the girl's mother now gave me the explanation. On their way home from the station the children had stopped in front of a slot machine from which they were accustomed to obtain bars of chocolate of that very kind, wrapped in shiny metallic paper. They had wanted to get some; but their mother rightly decided that the day had already fulfilled enough wishes and left this one over to be fulfilled by the dream. I myself had not observed the incident. But the part of the dream which had been proscribed by my daughter was immediately clear to me. I myself had heard our well-behaved guest telling the children on the walk to wait till Father and Mother caught up with them. The little girl's dream turned this temporary kinship into permanent adoption. Her affection was not yet able to picture any other forms of companionship than those which were represented in the dream and which were based on her relation to her brothers. It was of course impossible to discover without questioning her why the bars of chocolate were thrown under the beds.

A friend of mine has reported a dream to me which was very 13 much like my son's. The dreamer was an eight-year-old girl. Her father had started off with several children on a walk to Dornbach, with the idea of visiting the Rohrer Hütte. As it was getting late, however, he had turned back, promising the children to make up for the disappointment another time. On their way home they had passed the sign post that marks the path up to the Hameau. The children had then asked to be taken up to the Hameau; but once again for the same reason they had to be consoled with the promise of another day. Next morning the eight-year-old girl came to her father and said in satisfied tones: "Daddy, I dreamed last night that you went with us to the Rohrer Hütte and the Hameau." In her impatience she had anticipated the fulfillment of her father's promises.

Here is an equally straightforward dream, provoked by the 14 beauty of the scenery at Aussee in another of my daughters, who was at that time three and a quarter. She had crossed the lake for the first time, and the crossing had been too short for her: When we reached the landing-stage she had not wanted to leave the boat and had wept bitterly. Next morning she said: "Last night I went on the lake." Let us hope that her dream-crossing had been of a more satis-fying length.

My eldest boy, then eight years old, already had dreams of his 15 fantasies coming true: He dreamed that he was driving in a chariot with Achilles and that Diomede was the charioteer. As may be guessed, he had been excited the day before by a book on the leg-ends of Greece which had been given to his elder sister.

If I may include words spoken by children in their sleep under 16 the heading of dreams, I can at this point quote one of the most youthful dreams in my whole collection. My youngest daughter, then nineteen months old, had had an attack of vomiting one morn-ing and had consequently been kept without food all day. During the night after this day of starvation she was heard calling out excit-edly in her sleep: "Anna Fweud, stwawbewwies, wild stwawbew-wies, omblet, pudden!" At that time she was in the habit of using her own name to express the idea of taking possession of something. The menu included pretty well everything that must have seemed to her to make up a desirable meal. The fact that strawberries appeared in it in two varieties was a demonstration against the domestic health regulations. It was based upon the circumstance, which she had no doubt observed, that her nurse had attributed her indisposi-tion to a surfeit of strawberries. She was thus retaliating in her dream against this unwelcome verdict.

Though we think highly of the happiness of childhood because 17 it is still innocent of sexual desires, we should not forget what a fruitful source of disappointment and renunciation, and conse-quently what a stimulus to dreaming, may be provided by the other of the two great vital instincts. Here is another instance of this. My nephew, aged 22 months, had been entrusted with the duty of con-gratulating me on my birthday and of presenting me with a basket of cherries, which are still scarcely in season at that time of year. He seems to have found the task a hard one, for he kept on repeating "Chewwies in it" but could not be induced to hand the present over. However, he found a means of compensation. He had been in the habit every morning of telling his mother that he had a dream of the "white soldier"—a Guards officer in his white cloak whom he had once gazed at admiringly in the street. On the day after his birthday sacrifice he awoke with a cheerful piece of news, which could only have originated from a dream: "Hermann eaten all the chewwies!"

I do not myself know what animals dream of. But a proverb, to 18 which my attention was drawn by one of my students, does claim to know. "What," asks the proverb, "do geese dream of?" And it replies: "Of maize." The whole theory that dreams are wish-fulfillments is contained in these two phrases.

It will be seen that we might have arrived at our theory of the 19
hidden meaning of dreams most rapidly merely by following linguistic usage. It is true that common language sometimes speaks of
dreams with contempt. (The phrase "*Träume sind Schäume* [Dreams
are froth]" seems intended to support the scientific estimate of
dreams.) But, on the whole, ordinary usage treats dreams above all
as the blessed fulfillers of wishes. If ever we find our expectation
surpassed by the event, we exclaim in our delight: "I should never
have imagined such a thing even in my wildest dreams."

QUESTIONS FOR CRITICAL READING

1. Why is it important to consider dreams as related to waking mental
   events?
2. What do you think dreams reveal about the way your mind works?
   How does your view compare to Freud's?
3. How do the dreams Freud mentions seem to fulfill wishes?
4. Do your own dreams seem to be wish-fulfillment dreams? Give some
   examples, and see how the dreams are analyzed by others.
5. How useful is it to rely on the dreams of oneself and one's family to develop a theory of dreams? Does Freud convince you that his theory is
   viable?
6. Freud says, "We may expect to find the very simplest forms of dreams
   in *children*" (para. 9). Do you agree or disagree with him on this point?
   Why?
7. In paragraph 4 Freud mentions "dream[s] of convenience." What are
   they? Have you had such dreams?

SUGGESTIONS FOR WRITING

1. What does Freud's theory of dreams tell us about the nature of the
   human mind? Freud insists that dreams are important psychic events
   that are a product of the individual's mind and are not something impressed on the mind by outside sources. If they are mental events that
   need to be analyzed to be understood, what can be inferred about the
   mind that created them?
2. In paragraph 3 Freud mentions a dream he calls "a fulfilled fear." Examine your own dreams for a few evenings, write down a dream that
   fits this description, and offer your own interpretation of the dream.
3. Freud says that compared with the dreams of adults, the dreams of
   children seem to be "pure" wish-fulfillments. Collect some dreams
   from children, and analyze them. Decide whether they are as obviously
   wish-fulfillments as Freud's examples are.

4. Do animals dream? Freud raises this interesting question late in the discussion. Have you any evidence to suggest that animals dream? If so, write a brief essay that examines the possible content of an animal's dream. What might be the likely function of the dream in the animal's psychic life?

5. Which of your dreams do you believe is definitely not a wish-fulfillment dream? Describe it carefully, and analyze it in relation to your life. If you prove it is not a wish-fulfillment dream, what does that imply about Freud's views?

6. **CONNECTIONS** Plato's concerns in his "Allegory of the Cave" point to a level of reality that humans cannot reach because of the limitations of sensory apprehension. Is it also true that the dream world represents a level of reality that is impossible to reach because of the limitations of the conscious, waking mind? Which part of the mind—the conscious or the unconscious—does Freud seem to regard as primary in his discussion? Is there the sense that he regards one or the other as possessing a greater "reality"? How do his views fit with those of Plato?

7. **CONNECTIONS** Freud's approach to the study of dreams depends largely on the detailed report of the dreams of patients, members of his family, and himself. In essence, Freud is studying the unconscious—because dreamers are asleep and not conscious. Does Freud's method correspond in any significant way with the scientific method Francis Crick uses to study consciousness? How would Freud and Crick react to each other's methods? Is Freud satisfactorily scientific?

CARL JUNG
The Personal and the Collective Unconscious

CARL GUSTAV JUNG (1875–1961), Freud's most famous disciple, was a Swiss physician who collaborated with Freud from 1907 to 1912, when the two argued about the nature of the unconscious. Jung's *Psychology of the Unconscious* (1912) posits an unconscious that is composed of more than the ego, superego, and id. According to Jung, an additional aspect of the unconscious is a collection of archetypal images that can be inherited by members of the same group. Experience clarifies these images, but the images in turn direct experience.

In one of his essays on the collective unconscious, Jung asserts that the great myths express the archetypes of actions and heroes stored in the unconscious by elucidating them for the individual and society. These archetypes represent themselves in mythic literature in images, such as the great father or the great mother, or in patterns of action, such as disobedience and self-sacrifice. They transcend social barriers and exemplify themselves similarly in most people in any given cultural group. For Jung, the individual must adapt to the archetypes that reveal themselves in the myths in order to be psychically healthy.

Like Freud, Jung postulates a specific model of the way the mind works: he claims the existence not only of a conscious mind — which all of us can attest to from experience and common sense — but also of an unconscious component to the mind. He argues that we are unaware of the content of our unconscious mind except, perhaps, in dreams (which occur when we are unconscious), which Freud and

---

Translated by Cary F. Baynes (London and New York, 1931), republished in *Psyche and Symbol* (New York, 1958).

others insist speak to us in symbols rather than in direct language. Jung also acknowledges the symbolic nature of the unconscious but disagrees with the source of the content of the unconscious mind.

In "The Personal and the Collective Unconscious" (1916), Jung describes the pattern of psychological transference that most psychoanalysts experience with their patients. In the case presented here, the patient's problems were associated with her father, and the transference was the normal one of conceiving of the doctor — in this case, Jung — in terms of the father. When this transference occurs, the patient often is cured of the problems that brought her to the psychoanalyst, but in this case the transference was incomplete. Jung offers a detailed analysis of the dreams that revealed the problems with the transference and describes the intellectual state of the woman whose dreams form the basis of the discussion. She is intelligent, conscious of the mechanism of transference, and careful about her own inner life. Yet the dream that Jung analyzes had a content that he could not relate to her personal life.

In an attempt to explain his inability to analyze the woman's dream strictly in terms of her personal life, Jung reexamines Freud's definition of the unconscious. As Jung explains Freud's view, the unconscious is a repository for material that is produced by the conscious mind and later repressed so as not to interfere with the function of the conscious mind. Thus, painful memories and unpleasant fears are often repressed and rarely become problems because they are sublimated — transformed into harmless activity, often dreams — and released. According to Freud, the material in the unconscious mind develops solely from personal experience.

Jung, however, argues that personal experiences form only part of the individual's unconscious, what he calls the "personal unconscious" (para. 17). For the patient in this essay, the images in the dream that he and the patient at first classified as a transference dream (in which the doctor became the father/lover figure) had qualities that could not be explained fully by transference. Instead, the dream seemed to represent a primordial figure, a god. From this, Jung develops the view that such a figure is cultural in nature and not personal. Nothing in the patient's life pointed to her concern for a god of the kind that developed in her dream. Jung proposes that the images that constituted the content of her dream were not a result of personal experience or education but, instead, were inherited. Jung defines this portion of the unconscious as the "collective unconscious" (para. 19).

Jung's theories proved unacceptable to Freud. After their collaboration ended, Jung studied the world's myths and mythic systems, including alchemy and occult literature. In them he saw many of the archetypal symbols that he felt were revealed in dreams—including symbolic quests, sudden transformations, dramatic or threatening landscapes, and images of God. His conclusions were that this literature, most or all of which was suppressed or rejected by modern religions such as Christianity, was a repository for the symbols of the collective unconscious—at least of Western civilization and perhaps of other civilizations.

Jung's Rhetoric

Like Freud, Jung tells a story. His selection is a narrative beginning with a recapitulation of Freud's view of the unconscious. Jung tells us that according to the conventional view the contents of the unconscious have passed "the threshold of consciousness" (para. 2): in other words they were once in the conscious mind of the individual. However, Jung also asserts that "the unconscious also contains components that have *not yet* reached the threshold of consciousness" (para. 3). At least two questions arise from this assertion: What is that content, and where did it come from?

Jung then provides the "example" (para. 5) of the woman whose therapy he was conducting. He tells us, as one would tell a story, about the woman's treatment and how such treatment works in a general sense. He explains the phenomenon of transference, claiming that "a successful transference can . . . cause the whole neurosis to disappear" (para. 5). Near the end of this patient's treatment he analyzed her dreams and found something he did not expect. He relates the narrative of the dream (para. 10), which includes the image of a superhuman father figure in a field of wheat swaying in the wind. From this he concludes that the image of the dream is not the doctor/father/lover figure that is common to transference—and that the patient was thoroughly aware of—but something of an entirely different order. He connects it to an archetype of God and proceeds to an analysis that explains the dream in terms of a collective unconscious whose content is shared by groups of people rather than created by the individual alone.

Jung's rhetorical strategy here is an argument proceeding from both example and analysis. The example is given in detail, along with enough background to make it useful to the reader. Then the example is narrated carefully, and its content is examined through a process of analysis familiar to those in psychiatry.

Some of the material in this selection is relatively challenging because Jung uses technical language and occasionally obscure references. However, the simplicity of the technique of narrative, telling a story of what happened, makes the selection intelligible, even though it deals with highly complex and controversial ideas.

PREREADING QUESTIONS: WHAT TO READ FOR

The following prereading questions may help you anticipate key issues in the discussion on Carl Jung's "The Personal and the Collective Unconscious." Keeping them in mind during your first reading of the selection should help focus your reactions.

• What are some of the contents of the unconscious?

• What is the difference between the personal and the collective unconscious?

The Personal and the Collective Unconscious

In Freud's view, as most people know, the contents of the unconscious are limited to infantile tendencies which are repressed because of their incompatible character. Repression is a process that begins in early childhood under the moral influence of the environment and lasts throughout life. Through analysis the repressions are removed and the repressed wishes made conscious. 1

According to this theory, the unconscious contains only those parts of the personality which could just as well be conscious and are in fact suppressed only through upbringing. Although from one point of view the infantile tendencies of the unconscious are the most conspicuous, it would nonetheless be incorrect to define or evaluate the unconscious entirely in these terms. The unconscious has still another side to it: it includes not only repressed contents, but also all psychic material that lies below the threshold of consciousness. It is impossible to explain the subliminal nature of all this material on the principle of repression; otherwise, through the removal of repressions, a man would acquire a phenomenal memory which would thenceforth forget nothing. 2

We therefore emphatically say that in addition to the repressed material the unconscious contains all those psychic components that 3

have fallen below the threshold, including subliminal sense perceptions. Moreover we know, from abundant experience as well as for
theoretical reasons, that the unconscious also contains components
that have *not yet* reached the threshold of consciousness. These are
the seeds of future conscious contents. Equally we have reason to
suppose that the unconscious is never at rest in the sense of being
inactive, but is continually engaged in grouping and regrouping its
contents. Only in pathological cases can this activity be regarded as
completely autonomous; normally it is co-ordinated with the conscious mind in a compensatory relationship.

It is to be assumed that all these contents are personal in so far   4
as they are acquired during the individual's life. Since this life is limited, the number of acquired contents in the unconscious must also
be limited. This being so, it might be thought possible to empty the
unconscious either by analysis or by making a complete inventory of
unconscious contents, on the ground that the unconscious cannot
produce anything more than is already known and accepted in the
conscious mind. We should also have to infer, as already indicated,
that if one could stop the descent of conscious contents into the unconscious by doing away with repression, unconscious productivity
would be paralyzed. This is possible only to a very limited extent, as
we know from experience. We urge our patients to hold fast to repressed contents that have been re-associated with consciousness,
and to assimilate them into their plan of life. But this procedure, as
we may daily convince ourselves, makes no impression on the unconscious, since it calmly continues to produce dreams and fantasies
which, according to Freud's original theory, must arise from personal repressions. If in such cases we pursue our observations systematically and without prejudice, we shall find material which, although similar in form to the previous personal contents, yet seems
to contain allusions that go far beyond the personal sphere.

Casting about in my mind for an example to illustrate what I   5
have just said, I have a particularly vivid memory of a woman patient with a mild hysterical neurosis which, as we expressed it in
those days, had its principal cause in a "father complex." By this we
wanted to denote the fact that the patient's peculiar relationship to
her father stood in her way. She had been on very good terms with
her father, who had since died. It was a relationship chiefly of feeling. In such cases it is usually the intellectual function that is developed, and this later becomes the bridge to the world. Accordingly
our patient became a student of philosophy. Her energetic pursuit of
knowledge was motivated by her need to extricate herself from the
emotional entanglement with her father. This operation may succeed if her feelings can find an outlet on the new intellectual level,

perhaps in the formation of an emotional tie with a suitable man, equivalent to the former tie. In this particular case, however, the transition refused to take place, because the patient's feelings remained suspended, oscillating between her father and a man who was not altogether suitable. The progress of her life was thus held up, and that inner disunity so characteristic of a neurosis promptly made its appearance. The so-called normal person would probably be able to break the emotional bond in one or the other direction by a powerful act of will, or else—and this is perhaps the more usual thing—he would come through the difficulty unconsciously, on the smooth path of instinct, without ever being aware of the sort of conflict that lay behind his headaches or other physical discomforts. But any weakness of instinct (which may have many causes) is enough to hinder a smooth unconscious transition. Then all progress is delayed by conflict, and the resulting stasis of life is equivalent to a neurosis. In consequence of the standstill, psychic energy flows off in every conceivable direction, apparently quite uselessly. For instance, there are excessive innervations of the sympathetic system, which lead to nervous disorders of the stomach and intestines; or the vagus (and consequently the heart) is stimulated; or fantasies and memories, uninteresting enough in themselves, become overvalued and prey on the conscious mind (mountains out of molehills). In this state a new motive is needed to put an end to the morbid suspension. Nature herself paves the way for this, unconsciously and indirectly, through the phenomenon of the transference (Freud). In the course of treatment the patient transfers the father imago[1] to the doctor, thus making him, in a sense, the father, and in the sense that he is *not* the father, also making him a substitute for the man she cannot reach. The doctor therefore becomes both a father and a kind of lover—in other words, the object of conflict. In him the opposites are united, and for this reason he stands for a quasi-ideal solution of the conflict. Without in the least wishing it, he draws upon himself an overvaluation that is almost incredible to the outsider, for to the patient he seems like a savior or a god. This way of speaking is not altogether so laughable as it sounds. It is indeed a bit much to be a father and lover at once. Nobody could possibly stand up to it in the long run, precisely because it is too much of a good thing. One would have to be a demigod at least to sustain such a role without a break, for all the time one would have to be the giver. To the patient in the state of transference, this provisional solution naturally seems ideal, but only at first; in the end she comes

---

[1] **imago** Idealized image of a person.

to a standstill that is just as bad as the neurotic conflict was. Fundamentally, nothing has yet happened that might lead to a real solution. The conflict has merely been transferred. Nevertheless a successful transference can—at least temporarily—cause the whole neurosis to disappear, and for this reason it has been very rightly recognized by Freud as a healing factor of first-rate importance, but, at the same time, as a provisional state only, for although it holds out the possibility of a cure, it is far from being the cure itself.

This somewhat lengthy discussion seemed to me essential if my 6
example was to be understood, for my patient had arrived at the state of transference and had already reached the upper limit where the standstill begins to make itself disagreeable. The question now arose: what next? I had of course become the complete savior, and the thought of having to give me up was not only exceedingly distasteful to the patient, but positively terrifying. In such a situation "sound common sense" generally comes out with a whole repertory of admonitions: "you simply must," "you really ought," "you just cannot," etc. So far as sound common sense is, happily, not too rare and not entirely without effect (pessimists, I know, exist), a rational motive can, in the exuberant feeling of health you get from transference, release so much enthusiasm that a painful sacrifice can be risked with a mighty effort of will. If successful—and these things sometimes are—the sacrifice bears blessed fruit, and the erstwhile patient leaps at one bound into the state of being practically cured. The doctor is generally so delighted that he fails to tackle the theoretical difficulties connected with this little miracle.

If the leap does not succeed—and it did not succeed with my 7
patient—one is then faced with the problem of severing the transference. Here "psychoanalytic" theory shrouds itself in a thick darkness. Apparently we are to fall back on some nebulous trust in fate: somehow or other the matter will settle itself. "The transference stops automatically when the patient runs out of money," as a slightly cynical colleague once remarked to me. Or the ineluctable demands of life make it impossible for the patient to linger on in the transference—demands which compel the involuntary sacrifice, sometimes with a more or less complete relapse as a result. (One may look in vain for accounts of such cases in the books that sing the praises of psychoanalysis!)

To be sure, there are hopeless cases where nothing helps; but 8
there are also cases that do not get stuck and do not inevitably leave the transference situation with bitter hearts and sore heads. I told myself, at this juncture with my patient, that there must be a clear and respectable way out of the impasse. My patient had long since run out of money—if indeed she ever possessed any—but I was

curious to know what means nature would devise for a satisfactory way out of the transference deadlock. Since I never imagined that I was blessed with that "sound common sense" which always knows exactly what to do in every tangled situation, and since my patient knew as little as I, I suggested to her that we could at least keep an eye open for any movements coming from a sphere of the psyche uncontaminated by our superior wisdom and our conscious plannings. That meant first and foremost her dreams.

Dreams contain images and thought associations which we do 9 not create with conscious intent. They arise spontaneously without our assistance and are representatives of a psychic activity withdrawn from our arbitrary will. Therefore the dream is, properly speaking, a highly objective, natural product of the psyche, from which we might expect indications, or at least hints, about certain basic trends in the psychic process. Now, since the psychic process, like any other life process, is not just a causal sequence, but is also a process with a teleological orientation,[2] we might expect dreams to give us certain indicia about the objective causality as well as about the objective tendencies, because they are nothing less than self-portraits of the psychic life process.

On the basis of these reflections, then, we subjected the dreams 10 to a careful examination. It would lead too far to quote word for word all the dreams that now followed. Let it suffice to sketch their main character: the majority referred to the person of the doctor, that is to say, the actors were unmistakably the dreamer herself and her doctor. The latter, however, seldom appeared in this natural shape, but was generally distorted in a remarkable way. Sometimes his figure was of supernatural size, sometimes he seemed to be extremely aged, then again he resembled her father, but was at the same time curiously woven into nature, as in the following dream: *Her father (who in reality was of small stature) was standing with her on a hill that was covered with wheat fields. She was quite tiny beside him, and he seemed to her like a giant. He lifted her up from the ground and held her in his arms like a little child. The wind swept over the wheat fields, and as the wheat swayed in the wind, he rocked her in his arms.*

From this dream and from others like it I could discern various 11 things. Above all I got the impression that her unconscious was holding unshakably to the idea of my being the father-lover, so that the fatal tie we were trying to undo appeared to be doubly strengthened. Moreover one could hardly avoid seeing that the unconscious

---

[2] **teleological orientation** Possessing a sense of design; directed toward an end or purpose.

placed a special emphasis on the supernatural, almost "divine" nature of the father-lover, thus accentuating still further the overvaluation occasioned by the transference. I therefore asked myself whether the patient had still not understood the wholly fantastic character of her transference, or whether perhaps the unconscious could never be reached by understanding at all, but must blindly and idiotically pursue some nonsensical chimera. Freud's idea that the unconscious can "do nothing but wish," Schopenhauer's[3] blind and aimless Will, the gnostic demi-urge who in his vanity deems himself perfect and then in the blindness of his limitation creates something lamentably imperfect — all these pessimistic suspicions of an essentially negative background to the world and the soul came threateningly near. And indeed there would be nothing to set against this except a well-meaning "you ought," reinforced by a stroke of the ax that would cut down the whole phantasmagoria for good and all.

But as I turned the dreams over and over in my mind, there   12
dawned on me another possibility. I said to myself: it cannot be denied that the dreams continue to speak in the same old metaphors with which our conversations have made both doctor and patient sickeningly familiar. But the patient has an undoubted understanding of her transference fantasy. She knows that I appear to her as a semidivine father-lover, and she can, at least intellectually, distinguish this from my factual reality. Therefore the dreams are obviously reiterating the conscious standpoint minus the conscious criticism, which they completely ignore. They reiterate the conscious contents, not *in toto,* but insist on the fantastic standpoint as opposed to "sound common sense."

I naturally asked myself what was the source of this obstinacy and   13
what was its purpose? That it must have some purposive meaning I was convinced, for there is no truly living thing that does not have a final meaning, that can in other words be explained as a mere leftover from antecedent facts. But the energy of the transference is so strong that it gives one the impression of a vital instinct. That being so, what is the purpose of such fantasies? A careful examination and analysis of the dreams, especially of the one just quoted, revealed a very marked tendency — in contrast to conscious criticism, which always seeks to reduce things to human proportions — to endow the person of the doctor with superhuman attributes. He had to be gigantic, primordial, huger than the father, like the wind that sweeps over the earth — was he then to be made into a god? Or, I said to myself, was it rather

---

[3] **Arthur Schopenhauer (1788–1860)** German pessimistic philosopher.

the case that the unconscious was trying to *create* a god out of the person of the doctor, as it were to free a vision of God from the veils of the personal, so that the transference to the person of the doctor was no more than a misunderstanding on the part of the conscious mind, a stupid trick played by "sound common sense"? Was the urge of the unconscious perhaps only apparently reaching out towards the person, but in a deeper sense towards a god? Could the longing for a god be a *passion* welling up from our darkest, instinctual nature, a passion unswayed by any outside influences, deeper and stronger perhaps than the love for a human person? Or was it perhaps the highest and truest meaning of that inappropriate love we call transference, a little bit of real *Gottesminne*,[4] that has been lost to consciousness ever since the fifteenth century?

No one will doubt the reality of a passionate longing for a   14
human person; but that a fragment of religious psychology, an historical anachronism, indeed something of a medieval curiosity—we are reminded of Mechtild of Magdeburg[5]—should come to light as an immediate living reality in the middle of the consulting room, and be expressed in the prosaic figure of the doctor, seems almost too fantastic to be taken seriously.

A genuinely scientific attitude must be unprejudiced. The sole   15
criterion for the validity of an hypothesis is whether or not it possesses an heuristic—i.e., explanatory—value. The question now is, can we regard the possibilities set forth above as a valid hypothesis? There is no a priori[6] reason why it should not be just as possible that the unconscious tendencies have a goal beyond the human person, as that the unconscious can "do nothing but wish." Experience alone can decide which is the more suitable hypothesis.

This new hypothesis was not entirely plausible to my very criti-   16
cal patient. The earlier view that I was the father-lover, and as such presented an ideal solution of the conflict, was incomparably more attractive to her way of feeling. Nevertheless her intellect was sufficiently clear to appreciate the theoretical possibility of the new hypothesis. Meanwhile the dreams continued to disintegrate the person of the doctor and swell them to ever vaster proportions. Concurrently with this there now occurred something which at first I alone perceived, and with the utmost astonishment, namely a kind of subterranean undermining of the transference. Her relations with

---

[4] **Gottesminne** Love of God.
[5] **Mechtild of Magdeburg** Thirteenth-century German mystic, writer, and saint.
[6] **a priori** Based on theory rather than on experiment or evidence.

a certain friend deepened perceptibly, notwithstanding the fact that consciously she still clung to the transference. So that when the time came for leaving me, it was no catastrophe, but a perfectly reasonable parting. I had the privilege of being the only witness during the process of severance. I saw how the transpersonal control point developed—I cannot call it anything else—a *guiding function* and step by step gathered to itself all the former personal overvaluations; how, with this afflux of energy, it gained influence over the resisting conscious mind without the patient's consciously noticing what was happening. From this I realized that the dreams were not just fantasies, but self-representations of unconscious developments which allowed the psyche of the patient gradually to grow out of the pointless personal tie.

This change took place, as I showed, through the unconscious development of a transpersonal control point; a virtual goal, as it were, that expressed itself symbolically in a form which can only be described as a vision of God. The dreams swelled the human person of the doctor to superhuman proportions, making him a gigantic primordial father who is at the same time the wind, and in whose protecting arms the dreamer rests like an infant. If we try to make the patient's conscious, and traditionally Christian, idea of God responsible for the divine image in the dreams, we would still have to lay stress on the distortion. In religious matters the patient had a critical and agnostic attitude, and her idea of a possible deity had long since passed into the realm of the inconceivable, i.e., had dwindled into a complete abstraction. In contrast to this, the god-image of the dreams corresponded to the archaic conception of a nature demon, something like Wotan.[7] *Theos to pneûma,* "God is spirit," is here translated back into its original form where *pneûma* means "wind": God is the wind, stronger and mightier than man, an invisible breath-spirit. As in the Hebrew *ruach,* so in Arabic *ruh* means breath and spirit. Out of the purely personal form the dreams developed an archaic god-image that is infinitely far from the conscious idea of God. It might be objected that this is simply an infantile image, a childhood memory. I would have no quarrel with this assumption if we were dealing with an old man sitting on a golden throne in heaven. But there is no trace of any sentimentality of that kind; instead, we have a primitive conception that can correspond only to an archaic mentality. These primitive conceptions, of which I have given a large number of examples in my *Symbols of Transformation,* tempt one to make, in regard to unconscious material, a

17

---

[7] **Wotan** Supreme God; character in Richard Wagner's *Ring* cycle of operas.

distinction very different from that between "preconscious" and "unconscious" or "subconscious" and "unconscious." The justification for these distinctions need not be discussed here. They have a definite value and are worth refining further as points of view. The fundamental distinction which experience has forced upon me merely claims the value of a further point of view. From what has been said it is clear that we have to distinguish in the unconscious a layer which we may call the *personal unconscious*. The materials contained in this layer are of a personal nature in so far as they have the character partly of acquisitions derived from the individual's life and partly of psychological factors which could just as well be conscious. It is readily understandable that incompatible psychological elements are liable to repression and therefore become unconscious; but on the other hand we also have the possibility of making and keeping the repressed contents conscious, once they have been recognized. We recognize them as personal contents because we can discover their effects, or their partial manifestation, or their specific origin in our personal past. They are the integral components of the personality, they belong to its inventory, and their loss to consciousness produces an inferiority in one or the other respect—an inferiority, moreover, that has the psychological character not so much of an organic mutilation or an inborn defect as of a want which gives rise to a feeling of moral resentment. The sense of moral inferiority always indicates that the missing element is something which, one feels, should not be missing, or which could be made conscious if only one took enough trouble. The feeling of moral inferiority does not come from a collision with the generally accepted and, in a sense, arbitrary moral law, but from the conflict with one's own self which, for reasons of psychic equilibrium, demands that the deficit be redressed. Whenever a sense of moral inferiority appears, it shows that there is not only the demand to assimilate an unconscious component, but also the possibility of assimilating it. In the last resort it is a man's moral qualities which force him, either through direct recognition of the necessity to do so, or indirectly through a painful neurosis, to assimilate his unconscious self and to keep himself fully conscious. Whoever progresses along this road of realizing the unconscious self must inevitably bring into consciousness the contents of the personal unconscious, thus widening the scope of his personality. I should add at once that this "widening" primarily concerns the moral consciousness, one's self-knowledge, for the unconscious contents that are released and brought into consciousness by analysis are usually unpleasant—which is precisely why these wishes, memories, tendencies, plans, etc. were repressed. These are the contents that are brought to light in much the same way by a thorough confession, though to a much more limited extent. The rest comes out as a rule in dream analysis. It is often very interesting to watch how the dreams fetch up the essential points, bit by bit and with the nicest choice. The total material that is added to consciousness causes a considerable widening of the horizon, a deepened self-knowledge which, more than anything else, is calculated to humanize a man and make him modest. But even self-knowledge, assumed by all wise men to be the best and most efficacious, has different effects on different characters. We make very remarkable discoveries in this respect in practical analysis, but I shall deal with this question in the next chapter.

As my example of the archaic idea of God shows, the unconscious   18
seems to contain other things besides personal acquisitions and belongings. My patient was quite unconscious of the derivation of "spirit" from "wind," or of the parallelism between the two. This content was not the product of her thinking, nor had she ever been taught it. The critical passage in the New Testament was inaccessible to her—*to pneûma pneî hopou thelei*—since she knew no Greek. If we must take it as a wholly personal acquisition, it might be a case of so-called cryptomnesia,[8] the unconscious recollection of a thought which the dreamer had once read somewhere. I have nothing against such a possibility in this particular case; but I have seen a sufficient number of other cases—many of them are to be found in the book mentioned above—where cryptomnesia can be excluded with certainty. Even if it were a case of cryptomnesia, which seems to me very improbable, we should still have to explain what the predisposition was that caused just this image to be retained and later, as Semon puts it, "ecphorated" (*ekphoreîn*, Latin *efferre*, "to produce"). In any case, cryptomnesia or no cryptomnesia, we are dealing with a genuine and thoroughly primitive god image that grew up in the unconscious of a civilized person and produced a living effect—an effect which might well give the psychologist of religion food for reflection. There is nothing about this image that could be called personal: it is a wholly collective image, the ethnic origin of which has long been known to us. Here is an historical image of world-wide distribution that has come into existence again through a natural psychic function. This is not so very surprising, since my patient was born into the world with a human brain which presumably still functions today much as it did of

---

[8] Cf. Théodore Flournoy, *Des Indes à la planète Mars: Étude sur un cas de somnambulisme avec glossolalie* (Paris and Geneva, 1900; trans. by D. B. Vermilye as *From India to the Planet Mars,* New York, 1900), and Jung, "Psychology and Pathology of So-called Occult Phenomena," *Coll. Works,* Vol. 1, pp. 81ff. [Jung's note]

old. We are dealing with a reactivated archetype, as I have elsewhere called these primordial images. These ancient images are restored to life by the primitive, analogical mode of thinking peculiar to dreams. It is not a question of inherited ideas, but of inherited thought patterns.

In view of these facts we must assume that the unconscious con-   19
tains not only personal, but also impersonal, collective components in the form of inherited categories or archetypes. I have therefore advanced the hypothesis that at its deeper levels the unconscious possesses collective contents in a relatively active state. That is why I speak of the collective unconscious.

QUESTIONS FOR CRITICAL READING

1. What is Jung's view of the relationship of the unconscious mind to the conscious mind? How does it compare to Freud's?
2. What is repression? Why does repression work as it does?
3. How does transference work in psychoanalytic treatment? Is it a good thing or not?
4. What is unusual about Jung's patient's dream? What about it can he not fit into a normal pattern of transference?
5. What is the distinction between the personal unconscious and the collective unconscious?
6. Do you agree that "Dreams contain images and thought associations which we do not create with conscious intent" (para. 9)? Why or why not?

SUGGESTIONS FOR WRITING

1. Jung talks about common sense and its limitations. For some people, common sense denies the existence of an unconscious mind. Relying on Jung, your own personal experiences, and any other sources you choose, defend the existence of an unconscious mind. At the same time, do your best to explain the content of the unconscious and why it is important to the individual.
2. With reference to your own dreams, argue for or against the belief that dreams are products of the conscious mind. Have you had dreams whose content did not pass the "threshold" of your conscious mind?
3. Although the adult Jung was not religious, as the son of a Swiss pastor he was well acquainted with religion. In paragraph 13, Jung asserts that his patient's dream reveals a fundamental human longing for God. As he puts it, "Could the longing for a god be a *passion* welling up from our darkest, instinctual nature?" Examine the possibility that such a

psychological phenomenon has affected your attitude toward religion and religious belief.

4. Jung suggests that mythic literature maintains some of the images that make up the collective unconscious of a group of people. Select a myth (consult Ovid's *Metamorphosis,* Grimm's fairy tales, or the Greek myths, or choose a pattern of mythic behavior repeated in popular films) and analyze the instinctual longing it represents for us. What does the myth reveal about our culture?

5. **CONNECTIONS** Jung was a follower of Freud until he eventually broke from him. The break was not altogether friendly, and the feelings between the two—on professional matters—were often strained. Compare Jung's approach to the subject of the unconscious with Freud's. In what respects do they differ? In what ways are their methods either compatible or incompatible with each other? Do you find Jung's methods more or less useful than Freud's? Explain why.

KAREN HORNEY
The Distrust between the Sexes

KAREN HORNEY (1885–1952) was a distinguished psychia-
trist who developed her career somewhat independently of the influence of Sigmund Freud. In her native Germany, she taught in the
Berlin Psychoanalytic Institute from the end of World War I until
1932, a year before Hitler came to power. She was influenced by
Freud's work—as was every other psychoanalyst—but she found
that although brilliant, it did not satisfactorily explain important
issues in female sexuality.

In Germany, Horney's early research was centered on questions about female psychology. This selection, first published in
German in 1931, is part of these early studies. Horney's conclusion
was that penis envy, like many other psychological issues in
women, was determined by cultural factors and that these issues
were not purely psychological or libidinal in origin. She thought
Freud oversimplified female sexuality and that the truth, demonstrated through her own analysis, was vastly different. She began a
significant theoretical shift that saw neurosis as a product of both
psychological and cultural conflicts rather than of psychological
stress alone.

In 1932, Horney emigrated to America, where she began writing a distinguished series of publications on neurosis. Her career in
Chicago was remarkable. Not only did she found the American Institute for Psychoanalysis (1941) and the *American Journal of Psychoanalysis,* she also wrote such important books as *The Neurotic
Personality of Our Time* (1937), *New Ways in Psychoanalysis* (1939),
and *Self-Analysis* (1942). Her work was rooted in cultural studies,
and one of her principal arguments was that neuroses, including

From *Feminine Psychology* (1967). Translated by Harold Kelman.

sexual problems, are caused by cultural influences and pressures that the individual simply cannot deal with. Freud thought the reverse, placing the causal force of neuroses in sexuality.

Her studies constantly brought her back to the question of interpersonal relations, and she saw neurotic patterns developed in childhood as the main cause of many failed relationships. The selection focuses particularly on the relationship that individuals establish with their mother or their father. Her insistence that childhood patterns affect adult behavior is consonant with Freudianism; however, her interpretations of those patterns are somewhat different. Like Jung, she looks toward anthropological studies of tribal behavior for help in interpreting the behavior of modern people.

Horney claims that the distrust between the sexes cannot be explained away as existing only in individuals but is a widespread phenomenon that arises out of psychological forces present in men and women. She discusses a number of cultural practices in primitive peoples in an effort to suggest that even without modern cultural trappings, the two sexes suffer anxieties in their relationships. She also looks at the individual in a family setting, showing that normal expectations of child-parent relations can sometimes be frustrated, with seriously harmful results.

In addition, she examines the nature of culture, reminding us that early societies were often matriarchal—that is, centered not on men and their activities but on women. Her views about matriarchy, that the mystery of a woman is connected to her biologically creative nature, are quite suggestive in psychological terms. The envy as she sees it is on the part of men, who compensate for their inability to create life by spending their energies creating "state, religion, art, and science" (para. 14).

Horney speaks directly about sexual matters and about what she sees as male anxieties. She holds that there are distinct areas of conflict between men and women and that they are psychological in origin.

Horney's Rhetoric

This is an expository essay, establishing the truth of hypothesis by pointing to a range of evidence from a variety of sources. Horney's view is that the distrust between the sexes is the result of cultural forces of which the individual is only dimly aware. In this sense she aligns herself with the Freudians, who constantly point to influences on the individual that are subconscious in nature and, therefore, not part of the individual's self-awareness.

To some degree her essay is itself an analysis of the relationship between men and women, with a look back at the history of culture. Her technique—a review of older societies—establishes that the current nature of the relationship between men and women is colored by the fact that most modern societies are dominated by patriarchal institutions. In ancient times, however, societies may well have been matriarchal.

This selection was originally delivered as a lecture to the German Women's Medical Association in November 1930, and most of the audience members were women. Consequently, the nature of the imagery, the frankness of the discourse, and the cultural focus concern issues that would have a distinct impact on women. On reading this essay, it becomes clear that Karen Horney is speaking with a particular directness that she might have modified for a mixed audience.

Her method of writing is analytical, as she says several times. She is searching for causes within the culture as well as within the individual. Her range of causal analysis includes the comparative study of cultures (ethnology) as well as personal psychology. Her capacity to call on earlier writers and cultures reveals her enormous scope of knowledge and also helps convince the reader of the seriousness of her inquiry.

PREREADING QUESTIONS: WHAT TO READ FOR

The following prereading questions may help you anticipate key issues in the discussion on Karen Horney's "The Distrust between the Sexes." Keeping them in mind during your first reading of the selection should help focus your reactions.

- How can a woman's attitude toward men be influenced by childhood conflicts?
- How do patriarchal traditions affect men's attitudes toward women?

The Distrust between the Sexes

As I begin to talk to you today about some problems in the rela- 1
tionship between the sexes, I must ask you not to be disappointed. I
will not concern myself primarily with the aspect of the problem

that is most important to the physician. Only at the end will I briefly deal with the question of therapy. I am far more concerned with pointing out to you several psychological reasons for the distrust between the sexes.

The relationship between men and women is quite similar to that between children and parents, in that we prefer to focus on the positive aspects of these relationships. We prefer to assume that love is the fundamentally given factor and that hostility is an accidental and avoidable occurrence. Although we are familiar with slogans such as "the battle of the sexes" and "hostility between the sexes," we must admit that they do not mean a great deal. They make us over-focus on sexual relations between men and women, which can very easily lead us to a too one-sided view. Actually, from our recollection of numerous case histories, we may conclude that love relationships are quite easily destroyed by overt or covert hostility. On the other hand we are only too ready to blame such difficulties on individual misfortune, on incompatibility of the partners, and on social or economic causes.

The individual factors, which we find causing poor relations between men and women, may be the pertinent ones. However, because of the great frequency, or better, the regular occurrence of disturbances in love relations, we have to ask ourselves whether the disturbances in the individual cases might not arise from a common background; whether there are common denominators for this easily and frequently arising suspiciousness between the sexes?

It is almost impossible to attempt within the framework of a brief lecture to give you a complete survey of so large a field. I therefore will not even mention such factors as the origin and effects of such social institutions as marriage. I merely intend to select at random some of the factors that are psychologically understandable and pertain to the causes and effects of the hostility and tension between the sexes.

I would like to start with something very commonplace — namely, that a good deal of this atmosphere of suspiciousness is understandable and even justifiable. It apparently has nothing to do with the individual partner, but rather with the intensity of the affects[1] and with the difficulty of taming them.

We know or may dimly sense, that these affects can lead to ecstasy, to being beside oneself, to surrendering oneself, which means a leap into the unlimited and the boundless. This is perhaps why real passion is so rare. For like a good businessman, we are loath to

---

[1] **affects** Feelings, emotions, or passions.

put all our eggs in one basket. We are inclined to be reserved and ever ready to retreat. Be that as it may, because of our instinct for self preservation, we all have a natural fear of losing ourselves in another person. That is why what happens to love, happens to education and psychoanalysis; everybody thinks he knows all about them, but few do. One is inclined to overlook how little one gives of oneself, but one feels all the more this same deficiency in the partner, the feeling of "You never really loved me." A wife who harbors suicidal thoughts because her husband does not give her all his love, time, and interest, will not notice how much of her own hostility, hidden vindictiveness, and aggression are expressed through her attitude. She will feel only despair because of her abundant "love," while at the same time she will feel most intensely and see most clearly the lack of love in her partner. Even Strindberg[2] [who was a misogynist] defensively managed to say on occasion that he was no woman hater, but that women hated and tortured him.

Here we are not dealing with pathological phenomena at all. In 7 pathological cases we merely see a distortion and exaggeration of a general and normal occurrence. Anybody, to a certain extent, will be inclined to overlook his own hostile impulses, but under pressure of his own guilty conscience, may project them onto the partner. This process must, of necessity, cause some overt or covert distrust of the partner's love, fidelity, sincerity, or kindness. This is the reason why I prefer to speak of distrust between the sexes and not of hatred; for in keeping with our own experience we are more familiar with the feeling of distrust.

A further, almost unavoidable, source of disappointment and dis- 8 trust in our normal love life derives from the fact that the very intensity of our feelings of love stirs up all of our secret expectations and longings for happiness, which slumber deep inside us. All our unconscious wishes, contradictory in their nature and expanding boundlessly on all sides, are waiting here for their fulfillment. The partner is supposed to be strong, and at the same time helpless, to dominate us and be dominated by us, to be ascetic and to be sensuous. He should rape us and be tender, have time for us exclusively and also be intensely involved in creative work. As long as we assume that he could actually fulfill all these expectations, we invest him with the glitter of sexual overestimation. We take the magnitude of such overvaluation for the measure of our love, while in reality it merely expresses the magnitude of our expectations. The very nature of our claims makes

---

[2]**August Strindberg (1849–1912)** A Swedish playwright and novelist whose dark portraits of women were influenced by his misogyny (hatred of women).

their fulfillment impossible. Herein lies the origin of the disappointments with which we may cope in a more or less effective way. Under
favorable circumstances we do not even have to become aware of the
great number of our disappointments, just as we have not been aware
of the extent of our secret expectations. Yet there remain traces of distrust in us, as in a child who discovers that his father cannot get him
the stars from the sky after all.

   Thus far, our reflections certainly have been neither new nor   9
specifically analytical and have often been better formulated in the
past. The analytical approach begins with the question: What special
factors in human development lead to the discrepancy between expectations and fulfillment and what causes them to be of special
significance in particular cases? Let us start with a general consideration. There is a basic difference between human and animal development—namely, the long period of the infant's helplessness and
dependency. The paradise of childhood is most often an illusion
with which adults like to deceive themselves. For the child, however, this paradise is inhabited by too many dangerous monsters.
Unpleasant experiences with the opposite sex seem to be unavoidable. We need only recall the capacity that children possess, even in
their very early years, for passionate and instinctive sexual desires
similar to those of adults and yet different from them. Children are
different in the aims of their drives, but above all, in the pristine integrity of their demands. They find it hard to express their desires
directly, and where they do, they are not taken seriously. Their seriousness sometimes is looked upon as being cute, or it may be overlooked or rejected. In short, children will undergo painful and humiliating experiences of being rebuffed, being betrayed, and being
told lies. They also may have to take second place to a parent or a
sibling, and they are threatened and intimidated when they seek, in
playing with their own bodies, those pleasures that are denied them
by adults. The child is relatively powerless in the face of all this. He
is not able to ventilate his fury at all, or only to a minor degree, nor
can he come to grips with the experience by means of intellectual
comprehension. Thus, anger and aggression are pent up within him
in the form of extravagant fantasies, which hardly reach the daylight
of awareness, fantasies that are criminal when viewed from the
standpoint of the adult, fantasies that range from taking by force and
stealing, to those about killing, burning, cutting to pieces, and chok-
ing. Since the child is vaguely aware of these destructive forces
within him, he feels, according to the talion law,[3] equally threatened

---

[3] **talion law** Law that demands that the criminal be given the same punishment as was suffered by the victim—an eye for an eye.

by the adults. Here is the origin of those infantile anxieties of which no child remains entirely free. This already enables us to understand better the fear of love of which I have spoke before. Just here, in this most irrational of all areas, the old childhood fears of a threatening father or mother are reawakened, putting us instinctively on the defensive. In other words, the fear of love will always be mixed with the fear of what we might do to the other person, or what the other person might do to us. A lover in the Aru Islands,[4] for example, will never make a gift of a lock of hair to his beloved, because should an argument arise, the beloved might burn it, thus causing the partner to get sick.

I would like to sketch briefly how childhood conflicts may affect   10
the relationship to the opposite sex in later life. Let us take as an example a typical situation: The little girl who was badly hurt through some great disappointment by her father, will transform her innate instinctual wish to receive from the man, into a vindictive one of taking from him by force. Thus the foundation is laid for a direct line of development to a later attitude, according to which she will not only deny her maternal instincts, but will have only one drive, i.e., to harm the male, to exploit him, and to suck him dry. She has become a vampire. Let us assume that there is a similar transformation from the wish to receive to the wish to take away. Let us further assume that the latter wish was repressed due to anxiety from a guilty conscience; then we have here the fundamental constellation for the formation of a certain type of woman who is unable to relate to the male because she fears that every male will suspect her of wanting something from him. This really means that she is afraid that he might guess her repressed desires. Or by completely projecting onto him her repressed wishes, she will imagine that every male merely intends to exploit her, that he wants from her only sexual satisfaction, after which he will discard her. Or let us assume that a reaction formation of excessive modesty will mask the repressed drive for power. We then have the type of woman who shies away from demanding or accepting anything from her husband. Such a woman, however, due to the return of the repressed, will react with depression to the nonfulfillment of her unexpressed, and often unformulated, wishes. She thus unwittingly jumps from the frying pan into the fire, as does her partner, because a depression will hit him much harder than direct aggression. Quite often the repression of aggression against the male drains all her vital energy. The woman then feels helpless to meet life. She will shift the entire responsibility

---

[4] **Aru Islands** Islands in Indonesia whose inhabitants were especially interesting for modern anthropologists.

for her helplessness onto the man, robbing him of the very breath of life. Here you have the type of woman who, under the guise of being helpless and childlike, dominates her man.

These are examples that demonstrate how the fundamental attitude of women toward men can be disturbed by childhood conflicts. In an attempt to simplify matters, I have stressed only one point, which, however, seems crucial to me — the disturbance in the development of motherhood. 11

I shall now proceed to trace certain traits of male psychology. I do not wish to follow individual lines of development, though it might be very instructive to observe analytically how, for instance, even men who consciously have a very positive relationship with women and hold them in high esteem as human beings, harbor deep within themselves a secret distrust of them; and how this distrust relates back to feelings toward their mothers, which they experienced in their formative years. I shall focus rather on certain typical attitudes of men toward women and how they have appeared during various eras of history and in different cultures, not only as regards sexual relationships with women, but also, and often more so, in nonsexual situations, such as in their general evaluation of women. 12

I shall select some random examples, starting with Adam and Eve. Jewish culture, as recorded in the Old Testament, is outspokenly patriarchal. This fact reflects itself in their religion, which has no maternal goddesses; in their morals and customs, which allow the husband the right to dissolve the marital bond simply by dismissing his wife. Only by being aware of this background can we recognize the male bias in two incidents of Adam's and Eve's history. First of all, woman's capacity to give birth is partly denied and partly devaluated: Eve was made of Adam's rib and a curse was put on her to bear children in sorrow. In the second place, by interpreting her tempting Adam to eat of the tree of knowledge as a sexual temptation, woman appears as the sexual temptress, who plunges man into misery. I believe that these two elements, one born out of resentment, the other out of anxiety, have damaged the relationship between the sexes from the earliest times to the present. Let us follow this up briefly. Man's fear of woman is deeply rooted in sex, as is shown by the simple fact that it is only the sexually attractive woman of whom he is afraid and who, although he strongly desires her, has to be kept in bondage. Old women, on the other hand, are held in high esteem, even by cultures in which the young woman is dreaded and therefore suppressed. In some primitive cultures the old woman may have the decisive voice in the affairs of the tribe; among Asian nations also she enjoys great power and prestige. On the other hand, in primitive tribes woman is surrounded by taboos during the entire period of her sexual maturity. Women of the 13

Arunta tribe are able to magically influence the male genitals. If they sing to a blade of grass and then point it at a man or throw it at him, he becomes ill or loses his genitals altogether. Women lure him to his doom. In a certain East African tribe, husband and wife do not sleep together, because her breath might weaken him. If a woman of a South African tribe climbs over the leg of a sleeping man, he will be unable to run; hence the general rule of sexual abstinence two to five days prior to hunting, warfare, or fishing. Even greater is the fear of menstruation, pregnancy, and childbirth. Menstruating women are surrounded by extensive taboos—a man who touches a menstruating woman will die. There is one basic thought at the bottom of all this: Woman is a mysterious being who communicates with spirits and thus has magic powers that she can use to hurt the male. He must therefore protect himself against her powers by keeping her subjugated. Thus the Miri in Bengal do not permit their women to eat the flesh of the tiger, lest they become too strong. The Watawela of East Africa keep the art of making fire a secret from their women, lest women become their rulers. The Indians of California have ceremonies to keep their women in submission; a man is disguised as a devil to intimidate the women. The Arabs of mecca exclude women from religious festivities to prevent familiarity between women and their overlords. We find similar customs during the Middle Ages—the Cult of the Virgin[5] side by side with the burning of witches; the adoration of "pure" motherliness, completely divested of sexuality, next to the cruel destruction of the sexually seductive woman. Here again is the implication of underlying anxiety, for the witch is in communication with the devil. Nowadays, with our more humane forms of aggression, we burn women only figuratively, sometimes with undisguised hatred, sometimes with apparent friendliness. In any case "The Jew must burn."[6] In friendly and secret autos-da-fé,[7] many nice things are said about women, but it is just unfortunate that in her God-given natural state, she is not the

---

[5] **Cult of the Virgin** During the Medieval period (c. 700–1300), the Roman Catholic Church promoted a strong emotional attachment to the Virgin Mary, which resulted in the production of innumerable paintings and sculptures. Horney points out the irony of venerating the mother of God while tormenting human women by burning them at the stake.

[6] **"The Jew must burn."** This is a quote from *Nathan the Wise* by the eighteenth-century German author Gotthold Ephraim Lessing, a humanist and a spokesman for enlightenment and rationality. The expression became a colloquialism. It meant no matter how worthy and well-intentioned his acts, by virtue of being a Jew, a man was guilty. [Translator's note]

[7] **autos-da-fé** Literally, acts of faith. It was a term used to refer to the hearing at which the Holy Inquisition gave its judgment on a case of heresy, and its most common use is to refer to the burning of heretics at the stake.

equal of the male. Möbius[8] pointed out that the female brain weighs less than the male one, but the point need not be made in so crude a way. On the contrary, it can be stressed that woman is not at all inferior, only different, but that unfortunately she has fewer or none of those human or cultural qualities that man holds in such high esteem. She is said to be deeply rooted in the personal and emotional spheres, which is wonderful; but unfortunately, this makes her incapable of exercising justice and objectivity, therefore disqualifying her for positions in law and government and in the spiritual community. She is said to be at home only in the realm of eros. Spiritual matters are alien to her innermost being, and she is at odds with cultural trends. She therefore is, as Asians frankly state, a second-rate being. Woman may be industrious and useful but is, alas, incapable of productive and independent work. She is, indeed, prevented from real accomplishment by the deplorable, bloody tragedies of menstruation and childbirth. And so every man silently thanks his God, just as the pious Jew does in his prayers, that he was not created a woman.

Man's attitude toward motherhood is a large and complicated chapter. One is generally inclined to see no problem in this area. Even the misogynist is obviously willing to respect woman as a mother and to venerate her motherliness under certain conditions, as mentioned above regarding the Cult of the Virgin. In order to obtain a clearer picture, we have to distinguish between two attitudes: men's attitudes toward motherliness, as represented in its purest form in the Cult of the Virgin, and their attitude toward motherhood as such, as we encounter it in the symbolism of the ancient mother goddesses. Males will always be in favor of motherliness, as expressed in certain spiritual qualities of women, i.e., the nurturing, selfless, self-sacrificing mother; for she is the ideal embodiment of the woman who could fulfill all his expectations and longings. In the ancient mother goddesses, man did not venerate motherliness in the spiritual sense, but rather motherhood in its most elemental meaning. Mother goddesses are earthy goddesses, fertile like the soil. They bring forth new life and they nurture it. It was this life-creating power of woman, an elemental force, that filled man with admiration. And this is exactly the point where problems arise. For it is contrary to human nature to sustain appreciation without resentment toward capabilities that one does not possess. Thus, a man's

14

---

[8] **Paul Julius Möbius (1853–1907)** German neurologist and student of the pathological traits of geniuses such as Rousseau, Goethe, Schopenhauer, and Nietzsche.

minute share in creating new life became, for him, an immense incitement to create something new on his part. He has created values of which he might well be proud. State, religion, art, and science are essentially his creations, and our entire culture bears the masculine imprint.

However, as happens elsewhere, so it does here; even the greatest satisfactions or achievements, if born out of sublimation, cannot fully make up for something for which we are not endowed by nature. Thus there has remained an obvious residue of general resentment of men against women. This resentment expresses itself, also in our times, in men's distrustful defensive maneuvers against the threat of women's invasion of their domains; hence their tendency to devalue pregnancy and childbirth and to overemphasize male genitality. This attitude does not express itself in scientific theories alone, but is also of far-reaching consequence for the entire relationship between the sexes, and for sexual morality in general. Motherhood, especially illegitimate motherhood, is very insufficiently protected by laws—with the one exception of a recent attempt at improvement in Russia. Conversely, there is ample opportunity for the fulfillment of the male's sexual needs. Emphasis on irresponsible sexual indulgence, and devaluation of women to an object of purely physical needs, are further consequences of this masculine attitude.

From Bachofen's[9] investigations we know that this state of the cultural supremacy of the male has not existed since the beginning of time, but that women once occupied a central position. This was the era of the so-called matriarchy, when law and custom were centered around the mother. Matricide was then, as Sophocles[10] showed in the *Eumenides,* the unforgivable crime, while patricide, by comparison, was a minor offense. Only in recorded historical times have men begun, with minor variations, to play the leading role in the political, economical, and judicial fields, as well as in the area of sexual morality. At present we seem to be going through a period of struggle in which women once more dare to fight for their equality. This is a phase, the duration of which we are not yet able to survey.

I do not want to be misunderstood as having implied that all disaster results from male supremacy and that relations between the sexes would improve if women were given the ascendancy.

---

[9] **J. J. Bachofen (1815–1887)** One of the earliest German ethnologists who proposed, in 1861, that a pattern of matriarchy—in which the female was the dominant figure in society—had existed in the earliest societies.

[10] **Sophocles (496?–406 B.C.)** A great Greek tragedian. However, Horney is probably referring to Aeschylus (525–456 B.C.), who wrote the *Eumenides,* the play she mentions.

However, we must ask ourselves why there should have to be any power struggle at all between the sexes. At any given time, the more powerful side will create an ideology suitable to help maintain its position and to make this position acceptable to the weaker one. In this ideology the differentness of the weaker one will be interpreted as inferiority, and it will be proven that these differences are unchangeable, basic, or God's will. It is the function of such an ideology to deny or conceal the existence of a struggle. Here is one of the answers to the question raised initially as to why we have so little awareness of the fact that there is a struggle between the sexes. It is in the interest of men to obscure this fact; and the emphasis they place on their ideologies has caused women, also, to adopt these theories. Our attempt at resolving these rationalizations and at examining these ideologies as to their fundamental driving forces, is merely a step on the road taken by Freud.[11]

I believe that my exposition shows more clearly the origin of resentment than the origin of dread, and I therefore want to discuss briefly the latter problem. We have seen that the male's dread of the female is directed against her as a sexual being. How is this to be understood? The clearest aspect of this dread is revealed by the Arunta tribe. They believe that the woman has the power to magically influence the male genital. This is what we mean by castration anxiety in analysis. It is an anxiety of psychogenic origin that goes back to feelings of guilt and old childhood fears. Its anatomical-psychological nucleus lies in the fact that during intercourse the male has to entrust his genitals to the female body, that he presents her with his semen and interprets this as a surrender of vital strength to the woman, similar to his experiencing the subsiding of erection after intercourse as evidence of having been weakened by the woman. Although the following idea has not been thoroughly worked through yet, it is highly probable, according to analytical and ethnological data, that the relationship to the mother is more strongly and directly associated with the fear of death than the relationship to the father. We have learned to understand the longing for death as the longing for reunion with the mother. In African fairy tales it is a woman who brings death into the world. The great mother goddesses also brought death and destruction. It is as though we were possessed by the idea that the one who gives life is also capable of taking it away. There is a third aspect of the male's dread of the female that is more difficult to understand and to prove, but that can

18

---

[11] **Sigmund Freud (1856–1939)** See the introduction to his selection in this part.

be demonstrated by observing certain recurrent phenomena in the animal world. We can see that the male is quite frequently equipped with certain specific stimulants for attracting the female, or with specific devices for seizing her during sexual union. Such arrangements would be incomprehensible if the female animal possessed equally urgent or abundant sexual needs as does the male. As a matter of fact, we see that the female rejects the male unconditionally, after fertilization has occurred. Although examples taken from the animal world may be applied to human beings only with the greatest of caution, it is permissible, in this context, to raise the following question: Is it possible that the male is sexually dependent on the female to a higher degree than the woman is on him, because in women part of the sexual energy is linked to generative processes? Could it be that men, therefore, have a vital interest in keeping women dependent on them? So much for the factors that seem to be at the root of the great power struggle between men and women, insofar as they are of a psychogenic nature and related to the male.

That many-faceted thing called love succeeds in building 19 bridges from the loneliness on this shore to the loneliness on the other one. These bridges can be of great beauty, but they are rarely built for eternity and frequently they cannot tolerate too heavy a burden without collapsing. Here is the other answer to the question posed initially of why we see love between the sexes more distinctly than we see hate—because the union of the sexes offers us the greatest possibilities for happiness. We therefore are naturally inclined to overlook how powerful are the destructive forces that continually work to destroy our chances for happiness.

We might ask in conclusion, how can analytical insights con- 20 tribute to diminish the distrust between the sexes? There is no uniform answer to this problem. The fear of the power of the affects and the difficulty in controlling them in a love relationship, the resulting conflict between surrender and self-preservation, between the I and the Thou[12] is an entirely comprehensible, unmitigatable, and as it were, normal phenomenon. The same thing applies in essence to our readiness for distrust, which stems from unresolved childhood conflicts. These childhood conflicts, however, can vary greatly in intensity, and will leave behind traces of variable depth. Analysis not only can help in individual cases to improve the relationship with the opposite sex, but it can also attempt to improve

---

[12] **the I and the Thou** A reference to Martin Buber's book *I and Thou*. Buber (1878–1965), a Jewish theologian and philosopher, is associated with modern existentialism.

the psychological conditions of childhood and forestall excessive conflicts. This, of course, is our hope for the future. In the momentous struggle for power, analysis can fulfill an important function by uncovering the real motives of this struggle. This uncovering will not eliminate the motives, but it may help to create a better chance for fighting the struggle on its own ground instead of relegating it to peripheral issues.

QUESTIONS FOR CRITICAL READING

1. Do you agree that there is hostility between the sexes? What evidence can you cite?
2. What are some of the most important childhood experiences that can affect adult behavior toward the opposite sex?
3. This selection was originally a lecture delivered in Germany in 1930. To what extent are its concerns no longer relevant? To what extent are they still relevant?
4. Do you think this essay could promote better relations between men and women?
5. What kinds of expectations do women seem to have of men, and vice versa? Do these expectations tend to contribute to hostility in specific ways? Consider Horney's description of expectations in paragraph 8.
6. How do the examples of behavior in primitive cultures contribute to an understanding of the relationship between the sexes in our culture?
7. Is Horney pessimistic or optimistic about relationships between the sexes?

SUGGESTIONS FOR WRITING

1. In paragraph 9, Horney says that "unpleasant experiences with the opposite sex seem to be unavoidable." In your experience, is this true? What unpleasant experiences have you had with the opposite sex? What unpleasant experiences have you observed?
2. Horney mentions that the intensity of our feelings can stir up secret longings for, and expectations of, the opposite sex (para. 8). What kinds of secret expectations do you feel each sex might have about the other in a relationship? Why would such expectations remain secret? Does such secrecy contribute to problems? Does it contribute to hostility?
3. Deep in the essay, in paragraph 14, Horney mentions envy as contributing to the hostility between the sexes. She says, "For it is contrary to human nature to sustain appreciation without resentment toward capabilities that one does not possess." Do you agree with her? Do you

think envy may have something to do with the hostility between the sexes? Examine your own experience to see whether you recall instances of envy on your part toward a member of the opposite sex (or vice versa).

4. At one point, Horney says, "Man's fear of woman is deeply rooted in sex" (para. 13). Do you think this is true? Is woman's fear of man similarly rooted? Examine this question by comparing two men's magazines and two women's magazines to determine what they reveal about the psychology of men and women. Compare their visual material, particularly photographs of members of the opposite sex. Also compare the fiction, and look for signs of a specifically male or female form of fantasy. Compare the advertising to identify the interests of men and women — and try to relate these to psychological concerns.

5. Horney is very direct in her discussion of male dominance in society, not only saying that it exists but asking, "Could it be that men, therefore, have a vital interest in keeping women dependent on them?" (para. 18). Conduct an interview with one man and one woman. Find out whether they have the same or different feelings about this question. Ask them if they see an effort on the part of men to keep women dependent, and then ask them what form any such dependency takes. Do they agree? Where do you stand on this issue?

6. At one point, Horney discusses how different men are from women. Write an essay in which you show the extent to which women are different from men. If possible, sample others' opinions and see if they note important differences. To what extent would differences between men and women contribute to hostility?

7. What are the most important psychic phenomena in Horney's discussion? Her concerns are primarily cultural, but she also describes a psychological situation that has its root in mental experience. What are the most important mental experiences, and how do they manifest themselves in the mental life of individuals?

8. **CONNECTIONS**   Jung discusses the personal and collective unconscious. Horney's argument is that there are personal and cultural aspects to the development of the minds of men and women. How close is Horney to Jung's position regarding what is personal and what is cultural in gender distinction? Does Jung's or Freud's work with dreams clarify the distinctions?

HOWARD GARDNER
A Rounded Version: The Theory of Multiple Intelligences

HOWARD GARDNER (b. 1943), professor of education and adjunct professor of psychology at Harvard University, is codirector of Harvard's Project Zero, a program dedicated to improving education in schools by emphasizing creativity in thinking and problem solving. By emphasizing the arts and the newer electronic technologies associated with learning, the program cultivates a "culture of thinking" in the classroom as opposed to a culture of rote learning. Gardner has received a MacArthur Foundation award (1981), which supported his research for five years, and has won a number of important awards in the field of education, including the Grawemeyer Award in Education (1990), given for the first time to an American. Among his many books are *Leading Minds: An Anatomy of Leadership* (1995) and *Extraordinary Minds: Portraits of Exceptional Individuals and an Examination of Our Extraordinariness* (1997).

Perhaps the most important and best-known product of Project Zero is the theory of multiple intelligences, which Gardner first published in *Frames of Mind* (1983). (His more recent book, *Intelligence Reframed: Multiple Intelligence for the 21st Century* [1999], offers a revisitation and more detailed elaboration on multiple intelligence theory and its application.) In *Frames of Mind*, he noted that the general attitude toward intelligence centers on the IQ (intelligence quotient) test that Alfred Binet (1857–1911) devised. Binet believed that intelligence is measurable and that IQ tests result in numerical scores that are reliable indicators of a more or less permanent basic intelligence. Gardner offered several objections to that view. One

From *Multiple Intelligences: The Theory in Practice.*

373

was that IQ predictors might point to achievement in schools and colleges but not necessarily to achievement in life. For example, students with middling scores performed at extraordinary levels in business, politics, and other walks of life, whereas high-achieving students often settled for middling careers. The reports on high-performing executives indicated a considerable intelligence at work, but it was not necessarily the kind of intelligence that could be measured by the Binet tests.

Gardner also was intrigued by findings that local regions of the brain controlled specific functions of the mind. For example, studies had established that certain regions of the brain were specialized for language functions, whereas others were specialized for physical movement, music, mathematics, and other skills. When those portions of the brain suffered damage, as with stroke or accident, the functions for which they were specialized were adversely affected. These observations, which were plentiful in the work of neurologists during and after World War II, led Gardner to propose the existence of a variety of intelligences rather than only one.

As he explains in the following essay from his book *Multiple Intelligences: The Theory in Practice* (1993), his studies led him to propose seven distinct intelligences. The first is linguistic, which naturally includes language. This intelligence applies not only to learning languages but also to using language well—as, for example, in the case of poets and writers. The second is logical-mathematical, which refers to the applications of mathematics and of logical reasoning. Our society uses these verbal-mathematical forms of intelligence as the practical measure of intelligence: the SATs, for instance, depend almost entirely on measuring these forms.

Gardner adds five more forms of intelligence. Spatial intelligence concerns the ways in which we perceive and imagine spatial relations. Some people, such as architects and sculptors, are clearly more gifted than others at imagining space. Musical intelligence is seen as distinct from other forms of intelligence if only because some people, such as child prodigies, are apparently born with superior musical abilities. Bodily-kinesthetic intelligence shows up in dancers and athletes, like Mikhail Barishnikov and the late Jackie Joyner-Kersee, who perform extraordinarily with their bodies. But bodily-kinesthetic intelligence also applies to detailed physical work, such as the manipulations necessary for the work of surgeons, dentists, and craftspeople, such as weavers, potters, metal-workers, and jewelers.

Finally, Gardner also defines two kinds of personal intelligence that are difficult to isolate and study but that he feels must be regarded as forms of intelligence. Interpersonal intelligence concerns the way we get along with other people. People with a high interpersonal intelligence might be salespeople, teachers, politicians, or evangelists. They respond to others and are sensitive to their needs and their concerns. They understand cooperation, compromise, and respect for other people's views. The second kind of personal intelligence—intrapersonal—refers to how one understands oneself. The self-knowledge to recognize one's strengths and weaknesses and to avoid an inflated sense of self-importance constitutes a high degree of intrapersonal intelligence.

Gardner sees all these intelligences working together in the individual. As he says, when one of them dominates, the individual can appear freakish, as the person with autism who easily multiplies huge numbers in his head but cannot relate to other human beings. Because the individual must nurture all these intelligences to develop into a complete person, Gardner is working to revise educational practices to reflect all varieties of intelligence.

Greeks in the time of Plato and Aristotle seem to have understood much of what Gardner says. They included music and dance, for example, in the curriculum of their schools. They developed linguistic and interpersonal skills in the teaching of rhetoric and made logic and mathematics central to their teaching. One of Socrates' most famous statements, in fact—"Know thyself"—admonishes us to develop intrapersonal intelligence.

Gardner's Rhetoric

Rather than open the essay by describing the multiple intelligences, Gardner starts with a dramatic scene and a hypothetical story. He describes two eleven-year-old children who take an IQ test and then are regarded in special ways by their teachers: one is expected to do well in school, the other is expected to do less well. The expectations are met. But years later the student with the lower IQ is vastly more successful in business than the student who scored higher. Why is this so? The rest of the essay answers that implied rhetorical question.

One of the most important devices Gardner relies on is enumeration. He has seven different kinds of intelligence to discuss and takes each one in turn. The reader is not aware of a special range of importance to the seven forms of intelligence: the first, musical intelligence, is not necessarily the most important or the first to be recognized in an individual. Bodily-kinesthetic is not necessarily less important because it comes after musical intelligence. By placing logical-mathematical intelligence in the middle of the sequence, Gardner suggests that this form of intelligence, which our society traditionally treats as first in importance, should take its place beside a range of intelligences that are all more or less equal in value.

Just as important as the use of enumeration is Gardner's use of parallelism in the structure of each of the intelligences he enumerates. For each he offers a subhead that identifies the specific intelligence and then a "sketch with a thumbnail biography" that helps establish the nature of the intelligence. Then Gardner discusses the details of each intelligence and suggests ways in which it may relate to other forms of intelligence. This method has the advantage of extreme clarity. Likewise, paralleling examples and quotations in describing each intelligence makes the point over and over and ultimately produces a convincing argument without the appearance of argument.

Gardner makes another important rhetorical decision regarding the size and nature of the paragraphs. Modern readers, conditioned by newspapers and magazines, expect paragraphs to be short and direct. Gardner's paragraphs reflect a decision to communicate with a general reading audience rather than an audience of specialists or specially educated readers. For that reason, a single subject may sometimes be discussed in two or more adjacent paragraphs, with the paragraph break acting as a "breather" (see paras. 19–20 and 22–23).

All these rhetorical devices aid the reader in absorbing complex material. Gardner's primary efforts in this essay are to facilitate communication. He keeps his language simple, his sentences direct, and his paragraphs brief. For the modern reader, this is a recipe for understanding.

PREREADING QUESTIONS: WHAT TO READ FOR

The following prereading questions may help you anticipate key issues in the discussion on Howard Gardner's "A Rounded Version: The Theory of Multiple Intelligences." Keeping them in mind during your first reading of the selection should help focus your reactions.

• What constitutes an intelligence, according to Gardner?

• What is the most compelling evidence for the theory of multiple intelligences?

A Rounded Version: The Theory of Multiple Intelligences

Coauthored by Joseph Walters

Two eleven-year-old children are taking a test of "intelligence." 1
They sit at their desks laboring over the meanings of different
words, the interpretation of graphs, and the solutions to arithmetic
problems. They record their answers by filling in small circles on a
single piece of paper. Later these completed answer sheets are
scored objectively: the number of right answers is converted into a
standardized score that compares the individual child with a population of children of similar age.

The teachers of these children review the different scores. They 2
notice that one of the children has performed at a superior level; on
all sections of the test, she answered more questions correctly than
did her peers. In fact, her score is similar to that of children three to
four years older. The other child's performance is average—his
scores reflect those of other children his age.

A subtle change in expectations surrounds the review of these 3
test scores. Teachers begin to expect the first child to do quite well
during her formal schooling, whereas the second should have only
moderate success. Indeed these predictions come true. In other
words, the test taken by the eleven-year-olds serves as a reliable predictor of their later performance in school.

How does this happen? One explanation involves our free use of 4
the word "intelligence": the child with the greater "intelligence" has
the ability to solve problems, to find the answers to specific questions, and to learn new material quickly and efficiently. These skills
in turn play a central role in school success. In this view, "intelligence" is a singular faculty that is brought to bear in any problem-
solving situation. Since schooling deals largely with solving problems of various sorts, predicting this capacity in young children
predicts their future success in school.

"Intelligence," from this point of view, is a general ability that is 5
found in varying degrees in all individuals. It is the key to success in
solving problems. This ability can be measured reliably with standardized pencil-and-paper tests that, in turn, predict future success
in school.

What happens after school is completed? Consider the two indi- 6
viduals in the example. Looking further down the road, we find that
the "average" student has become a highly successful mechanical

engineer who has risen to a position of prominence in both the professional community of engineers as well as in civic groups in his community. His success is no fluke—he is considered by all to be a talented individual. The "superior" student, on the other hand, has had little success in her chosen career as a writer; after repeated rejections by publishers, she has taken up a middle management position in a bank. While certainly not a "failure," she is considered by her peers to be quite "ordinary" in her adult accomplishments. So what happened?

This fabricated example is based on the facts of intelligence testing. IQ tests predict school performance with considerable accuracy, but they are only an indifferent predictor of performance in a profession after formal schooling.[1] Furthermore, even as IQ tests measure only logical or logical-linguistic capacities, in this society we are nearly "brain-washed" to restrict the notion of intelligence to the capacities used in solving logical and linguistic problems.   7

To introduce an alternative point of view, undertake the following "thought experiment." Suspend the usual judgment of what constitutes intelligence and let your thoughts run freely over the capabilities of humans—perhaps those that would be picked out by the proverbial Martian visitor. In this exercise, you are drawn to the brilliant chess player, the world-class violinist, and the champion athlete; such outstanding performers deserve special consideration. Under this experiment, a quite different view of *intelligence* emerges. Are the chess player, violinist, and athlete "intelligent" in these pursuits? If they are, then why do our tests of "intelligence" fail to identify them? If they are not "intelligent," what allows them to achieve such astounding feats? In general, why does the contemporary construct "intelligence" fail to explain large areas of human endeavor?   8

In this chapter we approach these problems through the theory of multiple intelligences (MI). As the name indicates, we believe that human cognitive competence is better described in terms of a set of abilities, talents, or mental skills, which we call "intelligences." All normal individuals possess each of these skills to some extent; individuals differ in the degree of skill and in the nature of their combination. We believe this theory of intelligence may be more humane and more veridical than alternative views of intelligence and that it more adequately reflects the data of human "intelligent" behavior. Such a theory has important educational implications, including ones for curriculum development.   9

---

[1] Jencks, C. (1972). *Inequality*. New York: Basic Books. [Gardner's note]

What Constitutes an Intelligence?

The question of the optimal definition of intelligence looms large in our inquiry. Indeed, it is at the level of this definition that the theory of multiple intelligences diverges from traditional points of view. In a traditional view, intelligence is defined operationally as the ability to answer items on tests of intelligence. The inference from the test scores to some underlying ability is supported by statistical techniques that compare responses of subjects at different ages; the apparent correlation of these test scores across ages and across different tests corroborates the notion that the general faculty of intelligence, g, does not change much with age or with training or experience. It is an inborn attribute or faculty of the individual.

Multiple intelligences theory, on the other hand, pluralizes the traditional concept. An intelligence entails the ability to solve problems or fashion products that are of consequence in a particular cultural setting or community. The problem-solving skill allows one to approach a situation in which a goal is to be obtained and to locate the appropriate route to that goal. The creation of a *cultural* product is crucial to such functions as capturing and transmitting knowledge or expressing one's views or feelings. The problems to be solved range from creating an end for a story to anticipating a mating move in chess to repairing a quilt. Products range from scientific theories to musical compositions to successful political campaigns.

MI theory is framed in light of the biological origins of each problem-solving skill. Only those skills that are universal to the human species are treated. Even so, the biological proclivity to participate in a particular form of problem solving must also be coupled with the cultural nurturing of that domain. For example, language, a universal skill, may manifest itself particularly as writing in one culture, as oratory in another culture, and as the secret language of anagrams in a third.

Given the desire of selecting intelligences that are rooted in biology, and that are valued in one or more cultural settings, how does one actually identify an "intelligence"? In coming up with our list, we consulted evidence from several different sources: knowledge about normal development and development in gifted individuals; information about the breakdown of cognitive skills under conditions of brain damage; studies of exceptional populations, including prodigies, idiots savants, and autistic children; data about the evolution of cognition over the millennia; cross-cultural accounts of cognition; psychometric studies, including examinations of correlations among tests; and psychological training studies, particularly measures of transfer and generalization across tasks. Only those candidate intelligences that satisfied all or a majority of the criteria were selected as bona fide intelligences. A more complete discussion of each of these criteria for an "intelligence" and the seven intelligences that have been proposed so far, is found in *Frames of Mind.*[2] This book also considers how the theory might be disproven and compares it to competing theories of intelligence.

In addition to satisfying the aforementioned criteria, each intel-   14
ligence must have an identifiable core operation or set of operations. As a neutrally based computational system, each intelligence is activated or "triggered" by certain kinds of internally or externally presented information. For example, one core of musical intelligence is the sensitivity to pitch relations, whereas one core of linguistic intelligence is the sensitivity to phonological features.

An intelligence must also be susceptible to encoding in a symbol   15
system — a culturally contrived system of meaning, which captures and conveys important forms of information. Language, picturing, and mathematics are but three nearly worldwide symbol systems that are necessary for human survival and productivity. The relationship of a candidate intelligence to a human symbol system is no accident. In fact, the existence of a core computational capacity anticipates the existence of a symbol system that exploits that capacity. While it may be possible for an intelligence to proceed without an accompanying symbol system, a primary characteristic of human intelligence may well be its gravitation toward such an embodiment.

The Seven Intelligences

Having sketched the characteristics and criteria of an intelli-   16
gence, we turn now to a brief consideration of each of the seven intelligences. We begin each sketch with a thumbnail biography of a person who demonstrates an unusual facility with that intelligence. These biographies illustrate some of the abilities that are central to the fluent operation of a given intelligence. Although each biography illustrates a particular intelligence, we do not wish to imply that in adulthood intelligences operate in isolation. Indeed, except for abnormal individuals, intelligences always work in concert, and any sophisticated adult role will involve a melding of several of them. Following each biography we survey the various sources of data that support each candidate as an "intelligence."

---

[2] Gardner, H. (1983). *Frames of Mind: The Theory of Multiple Intelligences.* New York: Basic Books. [Gardner's note]

Musical Intelligence

When he was three years old, Yehudi Menuhin was smuggled into the San Francisco Orchestra concerts by his parents. The sound of Louis Persinger's violin so entranced the youngster that he insisted on a violin for his birthday and Louis Persinger as his teacher. He got both. By the time he was ten years old, Menuhin was an international performer.[3]

Violinist Yehudi Menuhin's musical intelligence manifested itself even before he had touched a violin or received any musical training. His powerful reaction to that particular sound and his rapid progress on the instrument suggest that he was biologically prepared in some way for that endeavor. In this way evidence from child prodigies supports our claim that there is a biological link to a particular intelligence. Other special populations, such as autistic children who can play a musical instrument beautifully but who cannot speak, underscore the independence of musical intelligence.   17

A brief consideration of the evidence suggests that musical skill passes the other tests for an intelligence. For example, certain parts of the brain play important roles in perception and production of music. These areas are characteristically located in the right hemisphere, although musical skill is not as clearly "localized," or located in a specifiable area, as language. Although the particular susceptibility of musical ability to brain damage depends on the degree of training and other individual differences, there is clear evidence for "amusia" or loss of musical ability.   18

Music apparently played an important unifying role in Stone Age (Paleolithic) societies. Birdsong provides a link to other species. Evidence from various cultures supports the notion that music is a universal faculty. Studies of infant development suggest that there is a "raw" computational ability in early childhood. Finally, musical notation provides an accessible and lucid symbol system.   19

In short, evidence to support the interpretation of musical ability as an "intelligence" comes from many different sources. Even though musical skill is not typically considered an intellectual skill like mathematics, it qualifies under our criteria. By definition it deserves consideration; and in view of the data, its inclusion is empirically justified.   20

Bodily-Kinesthetic Intelligence

Fifteen-year-old Babe Ruth played third base. During one game his team's pitcher was doing very poorly and Babe loudly criticized him from third base. Brother Mathias, the coach, called out,

---

[3] Menuhin, Y. (1977). *Unfinished Journey.* New York: Knopf. [Gardner's note]

"Ruth, if you know so much about it, YOU pitch!" Babe was surprised and embarrassed because he had never pitched before, but Brother Mathias insisted. Ruth said later that at the very moment he took the pitcher's mound, he KNEW he was supposed to be a pitcher and that it was "natural" for him to strike people out. Indeed, he went on to become a great major league pitcher (and, of course, attained legendary status as a hitter).[4]

Like Menuhin, Babe Ruth was a child prodigy who recognized   21
his "instrument" immediately upon his first exposure to it. This recognition occurred in advance of formal training.

Control of bodily movement is, of course, localized in the motor   22
cortex, with each hemisphere dominant or controlling bodily movements on the contra-lateral side. In right-handers, the dominance for such movement is ordinarily found in the left hemisphere. The ability to perform movements when directed to do so can be impaired even in individuals who can perform the same movements reflexively or on a nonvoluntary basis. The existence of specific *apraxia* constitutes one line of evidence for a bodily-kinesthetic intelligence.

The evolution of specialized body movements is of obvious advantage to the species, and in humans this adaptation is extended   23
through the use of tools. Body movement undergoes a clearly defined developmental schedule in children. And there is little question of its universality across cultures. Thus it appears that bodily-kinesthetic "knowledge" satisfies many of the criteria for an intelligence.

The consideration of bodily-kinesthetic knowledge as "problem   24
solving" may be less intuitive. Certainly carrying out a mime sequence or hitting a tennis ball is not solving a mathematical equation. And yet, the ability to use one's body to express an emotion (as in a dance), to play a game (as in a sport), or to create a new product (as in devising an invention) is evidence of the cognitive features of body usage. The specific computations required to solve a particular bodily-kinesthetic *problem*, hitting a tennis ball, are summarized by Tim Gallwey:

> At the moment the ball leaves the server's racket, the brain calculates approximately where it will land and where the racket will intercept it. This calculation includes the initial velocity of the ball, combined with an input for the progressive decrease in

[4] Connor, A. (1982). *Voices from Cooperstown.* New York: Collier. (Based on a quotation taken from *The Babe Ruth Story,* Babe Ruth & Bob Considine. New York: Dutton, 1948.) [Gardner's note]

velocity and the effect of wind and after the bounce of the ball. Simultaneously, muscle orders are given: not just once, but constantly with refined and updated information. The muscles must cooperate. A movement of the feet occurs, the racket is taken back, the face of the racket kept at a constant angle. Contact is made at a precise point that depends on whether the order was given to hit down the line or cross-court, an order not given until after a split-second analysis of the movement and balance of the opponent.

To return an average serve, you have about one second to do this. To hit the ball at all is remarkable and yet not uncommon. The truth is that everyone who inhabits a human body possesses a remarkable creation.[5]

Logical-Mathematical Intelligence.   In 1983 Barbara McClin- 25 tock won the Nobel Prize in medicine or physiology for her work in microbiology. Her intellectual powers of deduction and observation illustrate one form of logical-mathematical intelligence that is often labeled "scientific thinking." One incident is particularly illuminating. While a researcher at Cornell in the 1920s McClintock was faced one day with a problem: while *theory* predicted 50-percent pollen sterility in corn, her research assistant (in the "field") was finding plants that were only 25- to 30-percent sterile. Disturbed by this discrepancy, McClintock left the cornfield and returned to her office, where she sat for half an hour, thinking:

> Suddenly I jumped up and ran back to the (corn) field. At the top of the field (the others were still at the bottom) I shouted "Eureka, I have it! I know what the 30% sterility is!" . . . They asked me to prove it. I sat down with a paper bag and a pencil and I started from scratch, which I had not done at all in my laboratory. It had all been done so fast; the answer came and I ran. Now I worked it out step by step—it was an intricate series of steps—and I came out with [the same result]. [They] looked at the material and it was exactly as I'd said it was; it worked out exactly as I had diagrammed it. Now, why did I know, without having done it on paper? Why was I so sure?[6]

This anecdote illustrates two essential facts of the logical- 26 mathematical intelligence. First, in the gifted individual, the process of problem solving is often remarkably rapid—the successful scientist copes with many variables at once and creates numerous

---

[5] Gallwey, T. (1976). *Inner Tennis.* New York: Random House. [Gardner's note]
[6] Keller, E. (1983). *A Feeling for the Organism* (p. 104). Salt Lake City: W. H. Freeman. [Gardner's note]

hypotheses that are each evaluated and then accepted or rejected in turn.

The anecdote also underscores the *nonverbal* nature of the intelligence. A solution to a problem can be constructed *before* it is articulated. In fact, the solution process may be totally invisible, even to the problem solver. This need not imply, however, that discoveries of this sort—the familiar "Aha!" phenomenon—are mysterious, intuitive, or unpredictable. The fact that it happens more frequently to some people (perhaps Nobel Prize winners) suggests the opposite. We interpret this as the work of theological-mathematical intelligence. 27

Along with the companion skill of language, logical-mathematical reasoning provides the principal basis for IQ tests. This form of intelligence has been heavily investigated by traditional psychologists, and it is the archetype of "raw intelligence" or the problem-solving faculty that purportedly cuts across domains. It is perhaps ironic, then, that the actual mechanism by which one arrives at a solution to a logical-mathematical problem is not as yet properly understood. 28

This intelligence is supported by our empirical criteria as well. Certain areas of the brain are more prominent in mathematical calculation than others. There are idiots savants who perform great feats of calculation even though they remain tragically deficient in most other areas. Child prodigies in mathematics abound. The development of this intelligence in children has been carefully documented by Jean Piaget and other psychologists. 29

Linguistic Intelligence

At the age of ten, T. S. Eliot created a magazine called "Fireside" to which he was the sole contributor. In a three-day period during his winter vacation, he created eight complete issues. Each one included poems, adventure stories, a gossip column, and humor. Some of this material survives and it displays the talent of the poet.[7]

As with the logical intelligence, calling linguistic skill an "intelligence" is consistent with the stance of traditional psychology. Linguistic intelligence also passes our empirical tests. For instance, a specific area of the brain, called "Broca's Area," is responsible for the production of grammatical sentences. A person with damage to this 30

---

[7] Soldo, J. (1982). Jovial juvenilia: T. S. Eliot's first magazine. *Biography, 5,* 25–37. [Gardner's note]

area can understand words and sentences quite well but has difficulty putting words together in anything other than the simplest of sentences. At the same time, other thought processes may be entirely unaffected.

The gift of language is universal, and its development in children is strikingly constant across cultures. Even in deaf populations where a manual sign language is not explicitly taught, children will often "invent" their own manual language and use it surreptitiously! We thus see how an intelligence may operate independently of a specific input modality or output channel.   31

Spatial Intelligence

Navigation around the Caroline Islands in the South Seas is accomplished without instruments. The position of the stars, as viewed from various islands, the weather patterns, and water color are the only sign posts. Each journey is broken into a series of segments; and the navigator learns the position of the stars within each of these segments. During the actual trip the navigator must envision mentally a reference island as it passes under a particular star and from that he computes the number of segments completed, the proportion of the trip remaining, and any corrections in heading that are required. The navigator cannot *see* the islands as he sails along; instead he maps their locations in his mental "picture" of the journey.[8]

Spatial problem solving is required for navigation and in the use   32
of the notational system of maps. Other kinds of spatial problem solving are brought to bear in visualizing an object seen from a different angle and in playing chess. The visual arts also employ this intelligence in the use of space.

Evidence from brain research is clear and persuasive. Just as the   33
left hemisphere has, over the course of evolution, been selected as the site of linguistic processing in right-handed persons, the right hemisphere proves to be the site most crucial for spatial processing. Damage to the right posterior regions causes impairment of the ability to find one's way around a site, to recognize faces or scenes, or to notice fine details.

Patients with damage specific to regions of the right hemisphere   34
will attempt to compensate for their spacial deficits with linguistic strategies. They will try to reason aloud, to challenge the task, or

---

[8] Gardner, H. (1983). *Frames of Mind: The Theory of Multiple Intelligences.* New York: Basic Books. [Gardner's note]

even make up answers. But such nonspatial strategies are rarely successful.

Blind populations provide an illustration of the distinction between the spatial intelligence and visual perception. A blind person can recognize shapes by an indirect method: running a hand along the object translates into length of time of movement, which in turn is translated into the size of the object. For the blind person, the perceptual system of the tactile modality parallels the visual modality in the seeing person. The analogy between the spatial reasoning of the blind and the linguistic reasoning of the deaf is notable.   35

There are few child prodigies among visual artists, but there are idiots savants such as Nadia.[9] Despite a condition of severe autism, this preschool child made drawings of the most remarkable representational accuracy and finesse.   36

Interpersonal Intelligence.   With little formal training in special education and nearly blind herself, Anne Sullivan began the intimidating task of instructing a blind and deaf seven-year-old Helen Keller. Sullivan's efforts at communication were complicated by the child's emotional struggle with the world around her. At their first meal together, this scene occurred: 37

> Annie did not allow Helen to put her hand into Annie's plate and take what she wanted, as she had been accustomed to do with her family. It became a test of wills—hand thrust into plate, hand firmly put aside. The family, much upset, left the dining room. Annie locked the door and proceeded to eat her breakfast while Helen lay on the floor kicking and screaming, pushing and pulling at Annie's chair. [After half an hour] Helen went around the table looking for her family. She discovered no one else was there and that bewildered her. Finally, she sat down and began to eat her breakfast, but with her hands. Annie gave her a spoon. Down on the floor it clattered, and the contest of wills began anew.[10]

Anne Sullivan sensitively responded to the child's behavior. She wrote home: "The greatest problem I shall have to solve is how to discipline and control her without breaking her spirit. I shall go rather slowly at first and try to win her love."   38

---

[9] Selfe, L. (1977). *Nadia: A Case of Extraordinary Drawing in an Autistic Child.* New York: Academic Press. [Gardner's note]

[10] Lash, J. (1980). *Helen and Teacher: The Story of Helen Keller and Anne Sullivan Macy* (p. 52). New York: Delacorte. [Gardner's note]

In fact, the first "miracle" occurred two weeks later, well before 39
the famous incident at the pumphouse. Annie had taken Helen to a
small cottage near the family's house, where they could live alone.
After seven days together, Helen's personality suddenly underwent a
profound change — the therapy had worked:

> My heart is singing with joy this morning. A miracle has hap-
> pened! The wild little creature of two weeks ago has been trans-
> formed into a gentle child.[11]

It was just two weeks after this that the first breakthrough in 40
Helen's grasp of language occurred; and from that point on, she pro-
gressed with incredible speed. The key to the miracle of language
was Anne Sullivan's insight into the *person* of Helen Keller.

Interpersonal intelligence builds on a core capacity to notice 41
distinctions among others; in particular, contrasts in their moods,
temperaments, motivations, and intentions. In more advanced
forms, this intelligence permits a skilled adult to read the intentions
and desires of others, even when these have been hidden. This skill
appears in a highly sophisticated form in religious or political leaders, teachers, therapists, and parents. The Helen Keller–Anne Sullivan story suggests that this interpersonal intelligence does not depend on language.

All indices in brain research suggest that the frontal lobes play a 42
prominent role in interpersonal knowledge. Damage in this area can
cause profound personality changes while leaving other forms of
problem solving unharmed — a person is often "not the same person" after such an injury.

Alzheimer's disease, a form of presenile dementia, appears to 43
attack posterior brain zones with a special ferocity, leaving spatial, logical, and linguistic computations severely impaired. Yet,
Alzheimer's patients will often remain well groomed, socially
proper, and continually apologetic for their errors.. In contrast,
Pick's disease, another variety of presenile dementia that is more
frontally oriented, entails a rapid loss of social graces.

Biological evidence for interpersonal intelligence encompasses 44
two additional factors often cited as unique to humans. One factor is
the prolonged childhood of primates, including the close attachment to the mother. In those cases where the mother is removed
from early development, normal interpersonal development is in serious jeopardy. The second factor is the relative importance in humans of social interaction. Skills such as hunting, tracking, and

---

[11] Lash (p. 54). [Gardner's note]

killing in prehistoric societies required participation and cooperation of large numbers of people. The need for group cohesion, leadership, organization, and solidarity follows naturally from this.

Intrapersonal Intelligence.   In an essay called "A Sketch of the   45
Past," written almost as a diary entry, Virginia Woolf discusses the
"cotton wool of existence"—the various mundane events of life. She
contrasts this "cotton wool" with three specific and poignant memories from her childhood: a fight with her brother, seeing a particular
flower in the garden, and hearing of the suicide of a past visitor:

> These are three instances of exceptional moments. I often tell
> them over, or rather they come to the surface unexpectedly. But
> now for the first time I have written them down, and I realize
> something that I have never realized before. Two of these mo-
> ments ended in a state of despair. The other ended, on the con-
> trary, in a state of satisfaction.
> The sense of horror (in hearing of the suicide) held me
> powerless. But in the case of the flower, I found a reason; and was
> thus able to deal with the sensation. I was not powerless.
> Though I still have the peculiarity that I receive these sudden
> shocks, they are now always welcome; after the first surprise, I al-
> ways feel instantly that they are particularly valuable. And so I go
> on to suppose that the shock-receiving capacity is what makes me
> a writer. I hazard the explanation that a shock is at once in my
> case followed by the desire to explain it. I feel that I have had a
> blow; but it is not, as I thought as a child, simply a blow from an
> enemy hidden behind the cotton wool of daily life; it is or will be-
> come a revelation of some order; it is a token of some real thing
> behind appearances; and I make it real by putting it into words.[12]

This quotation vividly illustrates the intrapersonal intelligence—   46
knowledge of the internal aspects of a person: access to one's own
feeling life, one's range of emotions, the capacity to effect discrimina-
tions among these emotions and eventually to label them and to
draw upon them as a means of understanding and guiding one's own
behavior. A person with good intrapersonal intelligence has a viable
and effective model of himself or herself. Since this intelligence is the
most private, it requires evidence from language, music, or some
other more expressive form of intelligence if the observer is to detect
it at work. In the above quotation, for example, linguistic intelligence
is drawn upon to convey intrapersonal knowledge; it embodies the

---

[12] Woolf, V. (1976). *Moments of Being* (pp. 69–70). Sussex: The University
Press. [Gardner's note]

interaction of intelligences, a common phenomenon to which we will return later.

We see the familiar criteria at work in the intrapersonal intelli-   47
gence. As with the interpersonal intelligence, the frontal lobes play a central role in personality change. Injury to the lower area of the frontal lobes is likely to produce irritability or euphoria; while injury to the higher regions is more likely to produce indifference, listlessness, slowness, and apathy—a kind of depressive personality. In such "frontal-lobe" individuals, the other cognitive functions often remain preserved. In contrast, among aphasics who have recovered sufficiently to describe their experiences, we find consistent testimony: while there may have been a diminution of general alertness and considerable depression about the condition, the individual in no way felt himself to be a different person. He recognized his own needs, wants, and desires and tried as best he could to achieve them.

The autistic child is a prototypical example of an individual   48
with impaired intrapersonal intelligence; indeed, the child may not even be able to refer to himself. At the same time, such children often exhibit remarkable abilities in the musical, computational, spatial, or mechanical realms.

Evolutionary evidence for an intrapersonal faculty is more diffi-   49
cult to come by, but we might speculate that the capacity to transcend the satisfaction of instinctual drives is relevant. This becomes increasingly important in a species not perennially involved in the struggle for survival.

In sum, then, both interpersonal and intrapersonal faculties pass   50
the tests of an intelligence. They both feature problem-solving endeavors with significance for the individual and the species. Interpersonal intelligence allows one to understand and work with others; intrapersonal intelligence allows one to understand and work with oneself. In the individual's sense of self, one encounters a melding of inter- and intrapersonal components. Indeed, the sense of self emerges as one of the most marvelous of human inventions—a symbol that represents all kinds of information about a person and that is at the same time an invention that all individuals construct for themselves.

Summary: The Unique Contributions
of the Theory

As human beings, we all have a repertoire of skills for solving   51
different kinds of problems. Our investigation has begun, therefore, with a consideration of these problems, the contexts they are found

in, and the culturally significant products that are the outcome. We have not approached "intelligence" as a reified[13] human faculty that is brought to bear in literally any problem setting; rather, we have begun with the problems that humans *solve* and worked back to the "intelligences" that must be responsible.

Evidence from brain research, human development, evolution, and cross-cultural comparisons was brought to bear in our search for the relevant human intelligences: a candidate was included only if reasonable evidence to support its membership was found across these diverse fields. Again, this tack differs from the traditional one: since no candidate faculty is *necessarily* an intelligence, we could choose on a motivated basis. In the traditional approach to "intelligence," there is no opportunity for this type of empirical decision.   52

We have also determined that these multiple human faculties, the intelligences, are to a significant extent *independent.* For example, research with brain-damaged adults repeatedly demonstrates that particular faculties can be lost while others are spared. This independence of intelligences implies that a particularly high level of ability in one intelligence, say mathematics, does not require a similarly high level in another intelligence, like language or music. This independence of intelligences contrasts sharply with traditional measures of IQ that find high correlations among test scores. We speculate that the usual correlations among subtests of IQ tests come about because all of these tasks in fact measure the ability to respond rapidly to items of a logical-mathematical or linguistic sort; we believe that these correlations would be substantially reduced if one were to survey in a contextually appropriate way the full range of human problem-solving skills.   53

Until now, we have supported the fiction that adult roles depend largely on the flowering of a single intelligence. In fact, however, nearly every cultural role of any degree of sophistication requires a combination of intelligences. Thus, even an apparently straightforward role, like playing the violin, transcends a reliance on simple musical intelligence. To become a successful violinist requires bodily-kinesthetic dexterity and the interpersonal skills of relating to an audience and, in a different way, choosing a manager; quite possibly it involves an intrapersonal intelligence as well. Dance requires skills in bodily-kinesthetic, musical, interpersonal, and spatial intelligences in varying degrees. Politics requires an interpersonal skill, a linguistic facility, and perhaps some logical aptitude.   54

---

[13] **reified** Regarding an abstraction (e.g., intelligence) as if it were a concrete thing.

Inasmuch as nearly every cultural role requires several intelligences, it becomes important to consider individuals as a collection of aptitudes rather than as having a singular problem-solving faculty that can be measured directly through pencil-and-paper tests. Even given a relatively small number of such intelligences, the diversity of human ability is created through the differences in these profiles. In fact, it may well be that the "total is greater than the sum of the parts." An individual may not be particularly gifted in any intelligence; and yet, because of a particular combination or blend of skills, he or she may be able to fill some niche uniquely well. Thus it is of paramount importance to assess the particular combination of skills that may earmark an individual for a certain vocational or avocational niche.

QUESTIONS FOR CRITICAL READING

1. In the heading preceding paragraph 10, Gardner asks, "What Constitutes an Intelligence?" After reading this essay, how would you answer that question? How effectively does Gardner answer it?
2. What is the relation of culture to intelligence? See paragraph 11.
3. Why does society value logical-mathematical intelligence so highly? Do you feel it is reasonable to do so? Why?
4. What relationship do you see between intelligence and problem solving? What relationship do you see between education and problem solving?
5. Do you think that education can enhance these seven forms of intelligence? What evidence can you cite that intelligence is not fixed but can be altered by experience?
6. Why is it important "to assess the particular combination of skills that may earmark an individual" (para. 54)?

SUGGESTIONS FOR WRITING

1. Gardner says that his theory of MI (multiple intelligences) was shaped by his observations of "the biological origins of each problem-solving skill" (para. 12). Why is this important to his theory? How has he connected each of the intelligences to a biological origin? What biological issues are not fully accounted for in the theory of multiple intelligences?
2. In which of these seven forms of intelligence do you excel? Describe your achievements in these forms by giving specific examples that help your reader relate your abilities to the intelligences you have cited.

Now that you have identified your primary intelligences, what implications do they suggest for your later life?

3. Gardner is keenly interested in reforming education in light of his theory of multiple intelligences. How could education be altered to best accommodate seven forms of intelligence? What would be done differently in schools? Who would benefit from the differences you propose? How would society in general benefit from those differences?

4. Describe a problem-solving situation that requires two or more of the intelligences that Gardner describes. If possible, draw your example from your own experience or the experience of someone you know. Describe how the several intelligences work together to help solve the problem.

5. In some discussions of the forms of intelligence, commentators add an eighth—the naturalist's ability to recognize fine distinctions and patterns in the natural world. What might be the biological origin for that intelligence? In what cultural context might that intelligence be crucial? Do you feel that there is such an intelligence as represented by the naturalist or that it is included in other forms of intelligence?

6. **CONNECTIONS**   What relationship do you see between Plato's discussion of the soul and Gardner's discussion of intelligence? See paragraphs 41–55 in Plato. Which of Gardner's intelligences does Socrates seem to favor in Plato's dialogue?

7. **CONNECTIONS**   Which writers in this section of the book could best adapt Gardner's theories to their own? Consider Plato's discussion of the cave and the implied limits of knowledge. What are the limits of the seven intelligences? How might Karen Horney have used Gardner's theories to explain the different ways in which the sexes regard each other? Do the different sexes excel in different forms of intelligence? How might Gardner or Horney defend or argue against such a view? Might Francis Crick use Gardner's theories to suggest different forms of consciousness?

FRANCIS CRICK
The General Nature of Consciousness

FRANCIS CRICK (b. 1916) moved with his family from Northampton, England, to London after World War I. He received his early schooling in London and studied physics at University College London. He began a Ph.D. degree in physics but discontinued his studies during World War II, when he joined the British Admiralty to work on underwater mines. When the war ended, he began to study in Cambridge at the Strangeways Research Laboratory. In 1947, he decided to work on crystallography and X-ray diffraction and found it necessary to study molecular biology from the bottom up. He said that after the war he rethought his intellectual interests and realized that the molecular nature of life was his primary interest.

The research Crick did in the 1950s led to one of the most important discoveries of the twentieth century: the double-helix structure of DNA (deoxyribonucleic acid). DNA is the structure that is largely responsible for passing on hereditary characteristics. In 1962, Crick shared the Nobel Prize in Physiology or Medicine with his collaborator, James Dewey Watson, for their work on DNA structure. (In 1968, Watson published a "personal account" of his and Crick's efforts in a now famous book, *The Double Helix*.) Crick's work has led to successive significant discoveries in genetic science, including the move to map the human genome.

Crick's books include *Of Molecules and Men* (1966), which explains the implications of the radical changes that were taking place in the study of biology during the twentieth century, and *Life Itself: Its Origins in Nature* (1981), in which he suggested that life may have originated on earth as a result of a "seed" from another planet or asteroid.

From *The Astonishing Hypothesis: The Scientific Search for the Soul.*

Crick's interests, right after World War II, were two. One was the nature of life itself, an interest that prompted him to study biology. The second was the nature of consciousness. He regarded it as a concept that remained baffling to scientists and psychologists alike. He felt that psychologists had largely ignored the concept in their emphasis on behaviorism as a primary area of research. Crick, who has continued his studies at the Salk Institute for Biological Studies in California, and an associate, Christof Koch, of the California Institute of Technology, have pursued research into the nature of consciousness despite the fact that in this area the challenges to scientific method are considerable.

As Crick explains here, most previous research on the nature of consciousness has been very unscientific. He blames this partly on the way in which scientists, philosophers, and psychologists have addressed the question: they focus on the results of consciousness rather than on its causes. Crick assures us that the problem is most interesting on the neuronal level, that is, the level at which individual neurons work. Conceding that there may be as many neurons in a human brain as there are stars in our solar system, he admits that his job is extremely difficult. Moreover, experiments on human brains are limited. Many important discoveries have come from examining people with minor brain damage, usually as a result of accidents. Other researches have focused on primates such as the macaque monkey, whose brain closely resembles that of humans.

Although he does not go into detail in this introductory essay, Crick and Koch have focused on a single aspect of consciousness: visual perception. One of Crick's contentions is that visual perception is a major component of consciousness that is vastly more complex than we realize. He asserts that two important features of consciousness are at work in the act of visual perception: memory and attention. The eye is drawn to a movement or a distinct visual characteristic, and the memory records the event. However, because the visual world is complex and our experience governs the ways in which we see, Crick also contends that we actually invent for ourselves much of what we see. In the act of ignoring unimportant visual elements in our field of vision, we impose a structure that matches our attentive concerns. Thus, consciousness is, in part, always an imaginative construct.

However, in this essay Crick merely touches on that point. More important, he reviews the work of other thinkers in regard to consciousness. He also touches on the question of where consciousness resides in the brain. Although he does not reveal his views explicitly in this essay (a chapter from *The Astonishing*

Hypothesis: The Scientific Search for the Soul [1994]), he makes it clear in the rest of the book that he believes consciousness resides in a locale or connected locales in the brain. He even suggests that the concept of the soul, which usually implies an aspect of the conscious self, can be related to a specific place in the brain. In the book's Afterword, he also identifies a location in the brain for free will. He bases his judgment on the experiences of people with brain damage in a specific area that produced an absence of will as well as a conflict of will. (He mentions a patient whose left hand actually grabbed things involuntarily; the hand had to be yelled at before it would let go of the object in question!)

For us, this essay begins to bring the highly complex concept of consciousness to the center of our attention. Most people regard consciousness as a given, something we constantly have in our possession. However, when one examines the behavior of schizophrenics, manic depressives, or those with brain damage, understanding the concept becomes very difficult. This is also true in trying to determine the kind of consciousness that other animals may possess.

Crick's Rhetoric

Crick seems to use a method very similar to that of Aristotle. He begins with a simple declaration that it is important to "know what we have to explain." He breaks down the problems associated with consciousness and shows us that we have to find original ways to approach them. Like Aristotle, he also starts by establishing categories that can be addressed individually so as to gain a more powerful grip on the issue. However, unlike Aristotle, who rarely refers to earlier work by other scientists, Crick begins his essay in a traditional way for modern scientific and humanistic writing: he surveys what has been done and said about his subject by other authorities, especially psychologists, philosophers, and neuroscientists. He reviews the work of numerous thinkers, including William James, Sigmund Freud, and Carl Jung. Ultimately, he reduces their basic conclusions to a short list:

1. Not all the operations of the brain correspond to consciousness.

2. Consciousness involves some form of memory, probably a very short term one.

3. Consciousness is closely associated with attention. (para. 8)

This simple enumeration at the end of a survey of prior thought is designed not only to help clarify the work done earlier but also to establish the principles upon which Crick will build his own theory. Interestingly, he goes on to suggest that thus far, none of these thinkers has addressed the question of consciousness in a specific and scientific fashion. This rhetorical technique is inherently convincing and establishes a level of clarity to which the rest of the essay will aspire.

Crick uses the same method of enumeration later, in paragraphs 31 to 37, when he lists the questions that he feels are not important to answer at this time. (Even though he is very clear about why he will not address them, in reading through these questions you may find that some of them are exactly the ones you want to have addressed. For example, Crick does not consider the question of self-consciousness in either this essay or the rest of the book.)

The nature of consciousness remains elusive throughout the essay, but by establishing these basic principles Crick hopes to shed some light on an otherwise obscure issue. In reviewing the work of contemporary thinkers regarding consciousness, Crick explains their position and notes possible difficulties with their thinking. In discussing psychologists beginning in paragraph 12, he describes the work of researchers such as Philip Johnson-Laird, a cognitive scientist with an interest in language, an element that is thought to be unique to humans and an essential part of human consciousness. Crick goes on to consider the work of Ray Jackendoff, a professor of linguistics and cognitive science. By focusing on these two thinkers, Crick can explain some of the most promising work while at the same time suggesting areas for further research to help identify the nature of consciousness.

Crick admits that understanding the nature of consciousness is difficult. As he explains, understanding the structure of DNA, by contrast, is relatively easy because as a basic building block of life, it developed very early in evolution. On the other hand, consciousness is a late evolutionary development. Indeed, Crick asserts that human consciousness does not go back much further than one hundred thousand years. Having taken so much longer to develop, it is likely a much more complex process and will resist understanding longer than did the nature of genetic replication.

PREREADING QUESTIONS: WHAT TO READ FOR

The following prereading questions may help you anticipate key issues in the discussion on Francis Crick's "The General Nature of Consciousness." Keeping them in mind during your first reading of the selection should help focus your reactions.

- How does Crick propose studying consciousness "in a scientific manner"?
- Why does Crick settle on a problem in perception as a means of studying consciousness?
- What is the role of memory and attention in our understanding of consciousness?

The General Nature of Consciousness

In any field find the strangest thing and then explore it.
— JOHN ARCHIBALD WHEELER

To come to grips with the problem of consciousness, we first need to know what we have to explain. Of course, in a general way we all know what consciousness is like. Unfortunately that is not enough. Psychologists have frequently shown that our common-sense ideas about the workings of the mind can be misleading. The obvious first step, then, is to find out what psychologists over the years have considered to be the essential features of consciousness. They may not have got it quite right, but at least their ideas on the subject will provide us with a starting point.

Since the problem of consciousness is such a central one, and since consciousness appears so mysterious, one might have expected that psychologists and neuroscientists would now direct major efforts toward understanding it. This, however, is far from being the case. The majority of modern psychologists omit any mention of the problem, although much of what they study enters into consciousness. Most modern neuroscientists ignore it.

This was not always so. When psychology began as an experimental science, largely in the latter part of the nineteenth century, there was much interest in consciousness, even though it was admitted that the exact meaning of the word was unclear. The major method of studying it, especially in Germany, was by detailed and systematic introspection. It was hoped that psychology might become more scientific by refining introspection until it became a reliable technique.

The American psychologist William James (the brother of novelist Henry James) discussed consciousness at some length. In his monumental work *The Principles of Psychology,* first published in 1890, he described five properties of what he called "thought." Every thought, he wrote, tends to be part of personal consciousness. Thought is always changing, is sensibly continuous, and appears to deal with ob-

1

2

3

4

jects independent of itself. In addition, thought focuses on some objects to the exclusion of others. In other words, it involves attention. Of attention he wrote, in an oft-quoted passage: "Everyone knows what attention is. It is the taking possession by the mind, in clear and vivid form, of one out of what seem several simultaneously possible objects or trains of thought. . . . It implies withdrawal from some things in order to deal effectively with others."

In the nineteenth century we can also find the idea that consciousness is closely associated with memory. James quotes the Frenchman Charles Richet, who wrote in 1884 that "to suffer for only a hundredth of a second is not to suffer at all; and for my part I would readily agree to undergo a pain, however acute and intense it might be, provided it should last only a hundredth of a second, and leave after it neither reverberation nor recall." 5

Not all operations of the brain were thought to be conscious. Many psychologists believed that some processes are subliminal or subconscious. For example, Hermann von Helmholtz, the nineteenth-century German physicist and physiologist, often spoke of perception in terms of "unconscious inference." By this he meant that perception was similar in its logical structure to what we normally mean by inference, but that it was largely unconscious. 6

In the early twentieth century the concepts of the preconscious and the unconscious were made widely popular, especially in literary circles, by Freud, Jung, and their associates, mainly because of the sexual flavor they gave to them. By modern standards, Freud can hardly be regarded as a scientist but rather as a physician who had many novel ideas and who wrote persuasively and unusually well. He became the main founder of the new cult of psychoanalysis. 7

Thus, as long as one hundred years ago we see that three basic ideas were already current: 8

1. Not all the operations of the brain correspond to consciousness.
2. Consciousness involves some form of memory, probably a very short term one.
3. Consciousness is closely associated with attention.

Unfortunately, a movement arose in academic psychology that denied the usefulness of consciousness as a psychological concept. This was partly because experiments involving introspection did not appear to be leading anywhere and partly because it was hoped that psychology could become more scientific by studying behavior (in particular, animal behavior) that could be observed unambiguously by the experimenter. This was the Behaviorist movement. It became taboo to talk about mental events. All behavior had to be explained in terms of the stimulus and the response.

Behaviorism was especially strong in the United States, where it   9
was started by John B. Watson and others before World War I. It
flourished in the 1930s and 1940s when B. F. Skinner was its most
celebrated exponent. Other schools of psychology existed in Europe,
such as the Gestalt school, but it was not until the rise of cognitive
psychology in the late 1950s and 1960s that it became intellectually
respectable, at least in the United States, for a psychologist to talk
about mental events. It then became possible to study visual imagery,[1] for example, and to postulate psychological models for various mental processes, usually based on concepts used to describe
the behavior of digital computers. Even so, consciousness was seldom mentioned and there was little attempt to distinguish between
conscious and unconscious activity in the brain.

Much the same was true of neuroscientists studying the brains   10
of experimental animals. Neuroanatomists worked almost entirely
on dead animals (including human beings) while neurophysiologists
largely studied anesthetized animals who are not conscious. For example, they do not feel any pain during such experiments. This was
especially true after the epoch-making discovery by the neurobiolo-
gists David Hubel and Torsten Wiesel in the late fifties. They found
that nerve cells in the visual cortex of the brain of an anesthetized
cat showed a whole series of interesting responses when light was
shone on the cat's opened eyes, even though its brain waves showed
it to be more asleep than awake. For this and subsequent work they
were awarded a Nobel Prize in 1981.

It is far more difficult to study the response of these brain cells   11
in an alert animal (not only must its head be restrained but eye
movements must either be prevented or carefully observed). For this
reason very few experiments have been done to compare the responses of the same brain cell to the same visual signals under two
conditions: when the animal is asleep and again when it is awake.
Not only have neuroscientists traditionally avoided the problem of
consciousness because of these experimental difficulties but also because they considered the problem both too subjective and too
"philosophical," and thus not easily amenable to experimental study.
It would not have been easy for a neuroscientist to get a grant for the
purpose of studying consciousness.

Physiologists are still reluctant to worry about consciousness,   12
but in the last few years a number of psychologists have begun to

---

[1] Kosslyn, S. M. (1983). *Ghosts in the Mind's Machine*. New York: W. W. Norton
& Co. [Crick's note]

address the matter. I will sketch briefly the ideas of three of them. What they have in common is a neglect or, at best, a distant interest in nerve cells. Instead, they hope to contribute to an understanding of consciousness mainly by using the standard methods of psychology. They treat the brain as an impenetrable "black box" of which we know only the outputs—the behaviors it produces—caused by various inputs, such as those signalled by the senses. And they construct models that use general ideas based on our commonsense understanding of the mind, which they express in engineering or computing terms. All three authors would probably describe themselves as cognitive scientists.

Philip Johnson-Laird, now a professor of psychology at Princeton University, is a distinguished British cognitive scientist with a major interest in language, especially in the meaning of words, sentences, and narratives. These are issues unique to humans. It is not surprising that Johnson-Laird pays little attention to the brain, since much of our detailed information about the primate brain is derived from monkeys and they have no true language. His two books, *Mental Models* and *The Computer and the Mind,* are concerned with the problem of how to describe the mind—the activities of the brain— and the relevance of modern computers to that description.[2,3] He stresses that the brain is, as we shall see, a highly parallel mechanism (meaning that millions of processes are going on at the same time) and that we are unconscious of much of what it does.[4]   13

Johnson-Laird believes that any computer, and especially a highly parallel computer, must have an operating system that controls the rest of its functions, even though it may not have complete control over them. He proposes that it is the workings of this operating system that correspond most closely to consciousness and that it is located at a high level in the hierarchies of the brain.   14

Ray Jackendoff, professor of linguistics and cognitive science at Brandeis University, is a well-known American cognitive scientist with a special interest in language and music. Like most cognitive scientists, he believes that the mind is best thought of as a biological information-processing system. However, he differs from many of them in that he regards, as one of the most fundamental issues of psychology, the question "What makes our conscious experience the way it is?"   15

---

[2] Johnson-Laird, P. N. (1983). *Mental Models.* Cambridge, MA: Harvard University Press. [Crick's note]

[3] Johnson-Laird, P. N. (1988). *The Computer and the Mind: An Introduction to Cognitive Science.* Cambridge, MA: Harvard University Press. [Crick's note]

[4] Johnson-Laird is especially interested in self-reflection and self-awareness, topics that, for tactical reasons, I shall leave to one side. [Crick's note]

His Intermediate-Level Theory of Consciousness states that   16
awareness is derived neither from the raw elements of perception
nor from high-level thought but from a level of representation intermediate between the most peripheral (sensationlike) and the most
central (thoughtlike). He rightly emphasizes that this is a quite novel
point of view.[5]

Like Johnson-Laird, Jackendoff has been strongly influenced by   17
the analogy of the brain to a modern computer. He points out that
this analogy provides some immediate dividends. For example, in a
computer, a great deal of the information is stored but only a small
part is active at any one time. The same is true of the brain.

However, not all of the activity in the brain is conscious. He thus   18
makes a distinction not merely between the brain and the mind but
between the brain, the computational mind, and what he calls the
"phenomenological mind," meaning (roughly) what we are conscious
of. He agrees with Johnson-Laird that what we are conscious of is the
result of computations rather than the computations themselves.[6]

He also believes there is an intimate connection between aware-   19
ness and short-term memory. He expresses this by saying that
"awareness is supported by the contents of short-term memory,"
going on to add that short-term memory involves "fast" processes
and that slow processes have no direct phenomenological effect.

As to attention, he suggests that the computational effect of at-   20
tention is that the material being attended to is undergoing especially intensive and detailed processing. He believes that this is what
accounts for attention's limited capacity.

Jackendoff and Johnson-Laird are both functionalists. Just as it   21
is not necessary to know about the actual wiring of a computer
when writing programs for it, so a functionalist investigates the information processed by the brain, and the computational processes
the brain performs on this information, without considering the
neurological implementation of these processes. He usually regards
such considerations as totally irrelevant or, at best, premature.[7]

This attitude does not help when one wants to *discover* the   22
workings of an immensely complicated apparatus like the brain.

---

[5] Jackendoff, R. (1987). *Consciousness and the Computational Mind.* Cambridge, MA: Bradford Books, MIT Press. [Crick's note]

[6] Jackendoff expresses this in jargon of his own. What I have called "the results" he calls "information structures." [Crick's note]

[7] Genetics is also concerned with information transfer, both between genera-tions and within an individual, but the real breakthrough came when the structure of DNA showed very clearly the idiom in which this information was expressed. [Crick's note]

Why not look inside the black box and observe how its components behave? It is not sensible to tackle a very difficult problem with one hand tied behind one's back. When, eventually, we know in some detail how the brain works, then a high-level description (which is what functionalism is) may be a useful way to think about its overall behavior. Such ideas can always be checked for accuracy by using detailed information from lower levels, such as the cellular or molecular levels. Our provisional high-level descriptions should be thought of as rough guides to help us unravel the intricate operations of the brain.

Bernard J. Baars, an institute faculty professor at the Wright Institute in Berkeley, California, has written a book entitled *A Cognitive Theory of Consciousness*.[8] Although Baars is a cognitive scientist, he is rather more interested in the human brain than either Jackendoff or Johnson-Laird.   23

He calls his basic idea the Global Workspace. He identifies the information that exists at any one time in this workspace as the content of consciousness. The workspace, which acts as a central informational exchange, is connected to many unconscious receiving processors. These specialists are highly efficient in their own domains but not outside them. In addition, they can cooperate and compete for access to the workspace. Baars elaborates this basic model in several ways. For example, the receiving processors can reduce uncertainty by interacting until they reach agreement on only one active interpretation.[9]   24

In broader terms, he considers consciousness to be profoundly active and that there are attentional control mechanisms for access to consciousness. He believes we are conscious of some items in short-term memory but not all.   25

These three cognitive theoreticians share a loose consensus on three points about the nature of consciousness. They all agree that not all the activities of the brain correspond directly with consciousness, and that consciousness is an active process. They all believe that attention and some form of short-term memory is involved in consciousness. And they would probably agree that the information in consciousness can be fed into both long-term episodic memory as well as into the higher, planning levels of the motor system that controls voluntary movements. Beyond that their ideas diverge somewhat.   26

---

[8] Baars, B. (1988). *A Cognitive Theory of Consciousness*. Cambridge, England: Cambridge University Press. [Crick's note]

[9] I have not attempted to describe all the complications of Baars's model. Many of these have been added because he wishes to explain many aspects of consciousness, such as consciousness of self, self-monitoring, and also other psychological activities such as unconscious contexts, volition, hypnosis, and so on. [Crick's note]

Let us keep all three sets of ideas in mind while exploring an ap-   27
proach that tries to see what we can learn by combining them with
our growing knowledge of the structure and activity of the nerve
cells in the brain.

Most of my own ideas on consciousness have been developed in   28
collaboration with a younger colleague, Christof Koch, now a professor of computation and neural systems at the California Institute
of Technology (Caltech). Christof and I have known each other from
the time in the early eighties when he was a graduate student of
Tomaso Poggio in Tübingen. Our approach is essentially a scientific
one.[10] We believe that it is hopeless to try to solve the problems of
consciousness by general philosophical arguments; what is needed
are suggestions for new experiments that might throw light on these
problems. To do this we need a tentative set of theoretical ideas that
may have to be modified or discarded as we proceed. It is characteristic of a scientific approach that one does not try to construct some
all-embracing theory that purports to explain *all* aspects of consciousness. Nor does such an approach concentrate on studying language simply because it is uniquely human. Rather, one tries to select the most favorable system for the study of consciousness, as it
appears at this time, and study it from as many aspects as possible.
In a battle, you do not usually attack on all fronts. You probe for the
weakest place and then concentrate your efforts there.

We made two basic assumptions. The first is that there is some-   29
thing that requires a scientific explanation. There is general agreement that people are not conscious of all the processes going on in
their heads, although exactly which might be a matter of dispute.
While you are aware of many of the results of perceptual and memory processes, you have only limited access to the processes that
produce this awareness (e.g., "How did I come up with the first
name of my grandfather?"). In fact, some psychologists have suggested that you have only very limited introspective access to the
origins of even higher order cognitive processes. It seems probable,
however, that at any one moment some active neuronal processes in
your head correlate with consciousness, while others do not. *What
are the differences between them?*

Our second assumption was tentative: that all the different   30
aspects of consciousness, for example pain and visual awareness,

---

[10] In what follows, I quote extensively from ideas that Koch and I published on
this subject in 1990 in the journal called *Seminars in the Neurosciences (SIN).*[11]
[Crick's note]

[11] Crick, F., and Koch, C. (1990). Towards a neurobiological theory of consciousness. *Seminars Neurosc* 2:263–275. [Crick's note]

employ a basic common mechanism or perhaps a few such mechanisms. If we could understand the mechanisms for one aspect, then
we hope we will have gone most of the way to understanding them
all. Paradoxically, consciousness appears to be so odd and, at first
sight, so difficult to understand that only a rather special explanation is likely to work. The general nature of consciousness may be
easier to discover than more mundane operations, such as how the
brain processes information so that you see in three dimensions,
which can, in principle, be explained in many different ways.
Whether this is really true remains to be seen.

Christof and I suggested that several topics should be set aside   31
or merely stated outright without further discussion, for experience
has shown that otherwise much valuable time can be wasted arguing
about them.

1. Everyone has a rough idea of what is meant by conscious-   32
ness. It is better to avoid a *precise* definition of consciousness because of the dangers of premature definition. Until the problem is
understood much better, any attempt at a formal definition is likely
to be either misleading or overly restrictive, or both.[12]

2. Detailed arguments about what consciousness is for are   33
probably premature, although such an approach may give useful
hints about its nature. It is, after all, a bit surprising that one should
worry too much about the function of something when we are
rather vague about what it is. It is known that without consciousness you can deal only with familiar, rather routine, situations or respond to very limited information in new situations.

3. It is plausible that some species of animals—and in particu-   34
lar the higher mammals—possess some of the essential features of
consciousness, but not necessarily all. For this reason, appropriate
experiments on such animals may be relevant to finding the mechanisms underlying consciousness. It follows that a language system
(of the type found in humans) is not essential for consciousness—
that is, one can have the key features of consciousness without language. This is not to say that language may not considerably enrich
consciousness.

4. It is not profitable at this stage to argue about whether   35
"lower" animals, such as octopus, fruit flies, or nematodes, are conscious. It is probable, however, that consciousness correlates to
some extent with the degree of complexity of any nervous system.

---

[12] If this seems like cheating, try defining for me the word *gene*. So much is now
known about genes that any simple definition is likely to be inadequate. How much
more difficult, then, to define a biological term when rather little is known about it.
[Crick's note]

When we clearly understand, both in detail and in principle, what consciousness involves in humans, then will be the time to consider the problem of consciousness in much lower animals.

For the same reason I won't ask whether some parts of our own 36 nervous system have a special, isolated, consciousness of their own. If you say, "Of course my spinal cord is conscious but it's not telling me," I am not, at this stage, going to spend time arguing with you about it.

5. There are many forms of consciousness, such as those 37 associated with seeing, thinking, emotion, pain, and so on. Self-consciousness—that is, the self-referential aspect of consciousness—is probably a special case of consciousness. In our view, it is better left to one side for the moment. Various rather unusual states, such as the hypnotic state, lucid dreaming, and sleep walking, will not be considered here since they do not seem to have special features that would make them experimentally advantageous.

How can we approach consciousness in a scientific manner? 38 Consciousness takes many forms, but as I have already explained, for an initial scientific attack it usually pays to concentrate on the form that appears easiest to study. Christof Koch and I chose visual awareness rather than other forms of consciousness, such as pain or self-awareness, because humans are very visual animals and our visual awareness is especially vivid and rich in information. In addition, its input is often highly structured yet easy to control. For these reasons much experimental work has already been done on it.

The visual system has another advantage. There are many ex- 39 periments that, for ethical reasons, cannot be done on humans but can be done on animals. Fortunately, the visual system of higher primates appears somewhat similar to our own, and many experiments on vision have already been done on animals such as the macaque monkey. If we had chosen to study the language system there would have been no suitable experimental animal to work on.

Because of our detailed knowledge of the visual system in the 40 primate brain, we can see how the visual parts of the brain take the picture (the visual field) apart, but we do not yet know how the brain puts it all together to provide our highly organized view of the world—that is, what we see. It seems as if the brain needs to impose some global unity on certain activities in its different parts so that the attributes of a single object—its shape, color, movement, location, and so on—are in some way brought together without at the same time confusing them with the attributes of other objects in the visual field.

This global process requires mechanisms that could well be de- 41
scribed as "attention" and involves some form of very short term
memory. It has been suggested that this global unity might be expressed by the *correlated* firing of the neurons involved. Loosely
speaking, this means that the neurons that respond to the properties
of that particular object tend to fire at the same moment, whereas
other active neurons, corresponding to other objects, do not fire in
synchrony with the correlated set. To approach the problem we
must first understand something of the psychology of vision.

QUESTIONS FOR CRITICAL READING

1. Crick says we have a general sense of what consciousness is like. How
   would you describe it?
2. What does it mean to say that "consciousness is an active process"
   (para. 26)?
3. Do you agree with Crick that consciousness is "something that requires
   a scientific explanation" (para. 29)?
4. Crick says, "Consciousness takes many forms" (para. 38). What are
   some?
5. Why does Crick choose the visual system for his exclusive study of
   consciousness?
6. What are some of the ways in which early psychologists regarded consciousness (paras. 4–8)?
7. What are some of the principles of behavioral psychology? Why do
   they interfere with the study of consciousness?
8. What does Crick mean when he says that physiologists treat the brain
   as a "black box" (para. 12)?

SUGGESTIONS FOR WRITING

1. Using the two principles that Crick isolates as essential for consciousness—memory and attention—explain how you perceive consciousness to work. Try to accommodate as many aspects of consciousness as
   possible: perception, pain, self-awareness, complex thought, imagination. Essentially, your job is to describe the workings of consciousness
   to someone who has not thought about it as extensively as you.
2. If memory is an aspect of consciousness, and if consciousness is active,
   as Crick suggests, then the processes of consciousness may have reor-
   ganized or restructured memories in order to satisfy psychological
   needs. Using an example from your memory or the memory of someone you know well, describe a situation in which the reality of experience "changed" in some way when it became a memory. Try to de-

scribe how the consciousness altered the reality to which the memory refers. Then try to establish how such a change "improved" the reality. Does the "improvement" benefit the individual in some way?

3. Crick does not personally enjoy using a computer. He owns one or more, but he uses computers for household tasks and prefers pencil and paper for his work. This detail may explain why he does not encourage us to compare the human mind to a computer. However, the nature of memory, memory storage, and the capacity to learn (e.g., playing chess) implies there is a comparison to be made. In addition, Crick constantly talks about neurons and mechanisms that produce responses in the brain. Given those details, what do you think the chances are that a computer will ultimately develop a consciousness?

4. One interesting question that Crick has decided to omit from his discussion relates to the "use of consciousness." What do you feel is the ultimate use of consciousness in the natural world? Of what advantage is consciousness for the individual? If we assume that many living things—such as all plants, presumably all or most insects, and all or most invertebrates—have little or no consciousness, of what advantage could it be for higher animals such as ourselves and other mammals and primates?

5. Crick insists that his "approach is essentially a scientific one" (para. 28). This statement implies experiments that can be replicated by others. How would you address the question of consciousness from a nonscientific approach? Such an approach might be, in Crick's terms, philosophical or even religious. How would you describe consciousness and at the same time raise some of the important questions that must be addressed when contemplating the nature of consciousness?

6. **CONNECTIONS**   Both Freud and Jung address the unconscious. How would Crick address the unconscious from a scientific standpoint? Would he be satisfied with the approaches that Freud and Jung take to discussing the unconscious? Are their approaches scientific enough for Crick? Are they scientific enough for you?

PART FIVE

NATURE

Francis Bacon
Charles Darwin
Rachel Carson
Stephen Jay Gould
Michio Kaku
Richard P. Feynman

INTRODUCTION

Ideas of nature—of the world that exists outside human invention—have formed the core of human inquiry since the beginning of society. Early civilizations viewed nature as a willfully creative and destructive force and structured their religions around gods and goddesses who personified components of the natural world. For example, many early Egyptian and Greek religions worshiped a sun god, such as Ra or Apollo, and performed rituals meant to gain the favor of these gods.

This affiliation of nature with divine forces was gradually joined by a new approach: scientific inquiry. The basic premise of scientific inquiry was that the physical world could be understood through careful observation and described through consistent and logical rules. Lucretius, a prominent Roman thinker who lived during the first century B.C., wrote one of the first treatises on natural science. In his work *On the Nature of Things,* he argued that nature should be viewed in purely materialistic terms and that the universe was composed of minute pieces of matter, or "atoms." During the Renaissance the pursuit of a scientific understanding of the world culminated with Nicolaus Copernicus's (1473–1543) heliocentric (sun-centered) model of the universe. In the seventeenth century Sir Isaac Newton (1642–1727) further developed these methods of objective observation while formulating his laws of physics. Although nature was still believed to be the creation of a divine force, its workings were gradually becoming more and more accessible to human understanding. In the process, humans began to reevaluate their own place in nature.

The six writers in this section offer various ideas on nature, from the origin of life to the structure of the universe. Many of their theories were contended in their time and continue to be debated and rethought, but they share the underlying mission of deciphering the forces that shape our world and our lives.

At the time Francis Bacon wrote, before the advent of sophisticated scientific instruments, most scientists relied on their five senses and their theoretical preconceptions to investigate the workings of the world around them. In "The Four Idols," Bacon raises questions about these modes of scientific inquiry by asking, What casts of mind are essential to gaining knowledge? What prevents us from understanding nature clearly? By thus critiquing traditional presumptions and methods of investigation, Bacon challenges his readers to examine nature with new mental tools.

In "Natural Selection," Charles Darwin proposes a theory that is still controversial today. While on a voyage around South America in the HMS *Beagle,* Darwin observed remarkable similarities in the structures of various animals. He approached these discoveries with the advantages of a good education, a deep knowledge of the Bible and theology (he was trained as a minister), and a systematic and inquiring mind. Ultimately, he developed his theories of evolution to explain the significance of resemblances he detected among his scientific samples of insects and flowers and other forms of life. Explaining the nature of nature forms the underpinnings of Darwin's work.

Rachel Carson's "Nature Fights Back" is a classic essay describing the ways in which ignorance of the environmental effects of insecticides has come back to haunt us. When this essay was published in *Silent Spring* in 1962, people began to realize the damage that had been done in the name of preserving agriculture by spraying DDT and other toxic chemicals as a means of controlling crop pests. By disturbing the balance of nature with these sprays, chemical corporations inadvertently permitted the unlimited growth of other undesirable insects by killing off a large number of their predators. In some cases the results included far more damage and far more widespread invasion of pests than had ever been seen before. Carson shows how nature alters itself, even at the genetic level, to fight back against the devastation of pesticides.

Stephen Jay Gould, in "Nonmoral Nature," examines the results of the kind of thinking that Bacon deplored in the seventeenth century but that nevertheless flourished in the nineteenth century. Interpreting the world of nature as if it were fashioned by someone with the same prejudices as the Victorian scientist—usually also a minister—led people to see good and evil in animal and insect behavior. Even today most of us see the world in such terms. To Gould, however, moral issues relate to people—not to, say, dolphins or sharks. For him, thinking like a naturalist means achieving detachment: how we approach the evidence before us, in other words, is as important as what we actually observe. Gould wants us to give up anthropomorphic ways of interpreting evidence in favor of a more rational approach. As he demonstrates, this is not easy to achieve.

Puzzling out the most current thinking in theoretical physics requires speculation that borders on what Michio Kaku calls craziness. One of the craziest theories concerns dark matter, a form of matter in the universe that cannot be seen or touched. Yet according to the calculations of physicists and astronomers, the universe may be made up of more than 90 percent dark matter. In "The Mystery of Dark Matter," Kaku explains that were it not for the existence of dark matter, our galaxy would spin apart and the universe itself would not hold together. In passing, Kaku also alludes to another theory that contradicts common sense: the superstring theory. Instead of postulating hard particles at the heart of the atom, Kaku suggests that the smallest entities in the atom are vibrating strings of energy. This theory not only explains why there are so many particles but also resolves the inherent contradictions between the two great theories in modern physics, quantum theory and the theory of relativity.

Richard P. Feynman, one of the nation's most respected physicists, is best known for his work on quantum mechanics and for having discovered the cause of the crash of the *Challenger* space shuttle in 1986. A Nobel Prize winner (1965) and one of the most important physicists of his generation, he worked on the atomic bomb during World War II, then turned his attention to advanced problems in particle physics, hoping to understand the nature of the atom.

The essay that appears here, "The Relation of Science and Religion," is something of a departure for Feynman, but it reflects one of his personal interests: defining the relationship between the scientific viewpoint and the religious viewpoint. Both are distinct perspectives, and the problem is to see how or whether they will interrelate. Feynman wrote the essay for readers of a technical journal, but he relied on simple and direct language that can be understood by humanists as well as scientists. The question of whether the scientific cast of mind permits the scientist to be religious is at the heart of the discussion.

Although Francis Bacon probably would not understand the astonishing theories that the other writers in this section discuss, he would appreciate the methods they used to reason about their hypotheses and to establish their conclusions. All these writers are joined in their desire to understand the workings of nature and in their profound respect for the questions that remain.

FRANCIS BACON
The Four Idols

FRANCIS BACON, Lord Verulam (1561–1626), lived during
one of the most exciting times in history. Among his contemporaries were the essayist Michel de Montaigne; the playwrights
Christopher Marlowe and William Shakespeare; the adventurer Sir
Francis Drake; and Queen Elizabeth I, in whose reign Bacon held
several high offices. He became lord high chancellor of England in
1618 but fell from power in 1621 through a complicated series of
events, among which was his complicity in a bribery scheme. His
so-called crimes were minor, but he paid dearly for them. His book
Essayes (1597) was exceptionally popular during his lifetime, and
when he found himself without a proper job, he devoted himself to
what he declared to be his own true work: writing about philosophy and science.

His purpose in *Novum Organum* (The new organon), published
in 1620, was to replace the old organon, or instrument of thought,
Aristotle's treatises on logic and thought. Despite Aristotle's perva-
sive influence on sixteenth- and seventeenth-century thought — his
texts were used in virtually all schools and colleges — Bacon thought
that Aristotelian deductive logic produced error. In *Novum Organum*
he tried to set the stage for a new attitude toward logic and scientific
inquiry. He proposed a system of reasoning usually referred to as induction. This quasi-scientific method involves collecting and listing
observations from nature. Once a mass of observations is gathered
and organized, Bacon believed, the truth about what is observed will
become apparent.

Bacon is often mistakenly credited with having invented the
scientific method of inquiring into nature; but although he was
right about the need for collecting and observing, he was wrong

---

From *Novum Organum*. Translated by Francis Headlam and R. L. Ellis.

about the outcome of such endeavors. After all, one could watch an infinite number of apples (and oranges, too) fall to the ground without ever having the slightest sense of why they do so. What Bacon failed to realize—and he died before he could become scientific enough to realize it—is the creative function of the scientist as expressed in the hypothesis. The hypothesis—an educated guess about why something happens—must be tested by the kinds of observations Bacon recommended.

Nonetheless, "The Four Idols" is a brilliant work. It does establish the requirements for the kind of observation that produces true scientific knowledge. Bacon despaired of any thoroughly objective inquiry in his own day, in part because no one paid attention to the ways in which the idols, limiting preconceptions, strangled thought, observation, and imagination. He realized that the would-be natural philosopher was foiled even before he began. Bacon was a farsighted man. He was correct about the failures of science in his time; and he was correct, moreover, in his assessment that advancement would depend on sensory perception and on aids to perception, such as microscopes and telescopes. The real brilliance of "The Four Idols" lies in Bacon's focus not on what is observed but on the instrument of observation—the human mind. Only when the instrument is freed of error can we rely on its observations to reveal the truth.

Bacon's Rhetoric

Bacon was trained during the great age of rhetoric, and his prose (even though in this case it is translated from Latin) shows the clarity, balance, and organization that characterize the prose writing of seventeenth-century England. The most basic device Bacon uses is enumeration: stating clearly that there are four idols and implying that he will treat each one in turn.

Enumeration is one of the most common and most reliable rhetorical devices. The listener hears a speaker say "I have only three things I want to say today" and is alerted to listen for all three, while feeling secretly grateful that there are only three. When encountering complex material, the reader is always happy to have such "road signs" as "The second aspect of this question is . . ."

"The Four Idols," after a three-paragraph introduction, proceeds with a single paragraph devoted to each idol, so that we have an early definition of each and a sense of what to look for. Paragraphs 8 to 16 cover only the issues related to the Idols of the

Tribe: the problems all people have simply because they are people. Paragraphs 17 to 22 consider the Idols of the Cave: those particular fixations individuals have because of their special backgrounds or limitations. Paragraphs 23 to 26 address the questions related to Idols of the Marketplace, particularly those that deal with the way people misuse words and abuse definitions. The remainder of the selection treats the Idols of the Theater, which relate entirely to philosophic systems and preconceptions—all of which tend to narrow the scope of research and understanding.

Enumeration is used within each of these groups of paragraphs as well. Bacon often begins a paragraph with such statements as "There is one principal . . . distinction between different minds" (para. 19). Or he says, "The idols imposed by words on the understanding are of two kinds" (para. 24). The effect is to ensure clarity where confusion could easily reign.

As an added means of achieving clarity, Bacon sets aside a single paragraph—the last—to summarize the main points that he has made, in the order in which they were made.

Within any section of this selection, Bacon depends on observation, example, and reason to make his points. When he speaks of a given idol, he defines it, gives several examples to make it clearer, discusses its effects on thought, and then dismisses it as dangerous. He then goes on to the next idol. Where appropriate, in some cases he names those who are victims of a specific idol. In each case he tries to be thorough, explanatory, and convincing.

Not only is this work a landmark in thought; it is also, because of its absolute clarity, a beacon. We can still profit from its light.

PREREADING QUESTIONS: WHAT TO READ FOR

The following prereading questions may help you anticipate key issues in the discussion on Francis Bacon's "The Four Idols." Keeping them in mind during your first reading of the selection should help focus your reactions.

- What are the four idols?
- Why do the four idols make it difficult for us to see the truth?
- What are some chief characteristics of human understanding?

The Four Idols

The idols[1] and false notions which are now in possession of the   1
human understanding, and have taken deep root therein, not only
so beset men's minds that truth can hardly find entrance, but even
after entrance obtained, they will again in the very instauration[2] of
the sciences meet and trouble us, unless men being forewarned of
the danger fortify themselves as far as may be against their assaults.

There are four classes of idols which beset men's minds. To   2
these for distinction's sake I have assigned names—calling the first
class *Idols of the Tribe*; the second, *Idols of the Cave*; the third, *Idols of
the Marketplace*; the fourth, *Idols of the Theater*.

The formation of ideas and axioms by true induction[3] is no   3
doubt the proper remedy to be applied for the keeping off and clearing away of idols. To point them out, however, is of great use; for
the doctrine of idols is to the interpretation of nature what the doctrine of the refutation of sophisms[4] is to common logic.

The *Idols of the Tribe* have their foundation in human nature it-   4
self, and in the tribe or race of men. For it is a false assertion that the
sense of man is the measure of things. On the contrary, all perceptions as well of the sense as of the mind are according to the measure of the individual and not according to the measure of the universe. And the human understanding is like a false mirror, which,
receiving rays irregularly, distorts and discolors the nature of things
by mingling its own nature with it.

The *Idols of the Cave* are the idols of the individual man. For   5
everyone (besides the errors common to human nature in general)
has a cave or den of his own, which refracts[5] and discolors the light
of nature; owing either to his own proper and peculiar nature; or to
his education and conversation with others; or to the reading of
books, and the authority of those whom he esteems and admires; or

---

[1] **idols** By this term Bacon means phantoms or illusions. The Greek philosopher Democritus spoke of *eidola,* tiny representations of things that impressed themselves on the mind (see note 21).

[2] **instauration** Institution.

[3] **induction** Bacon championed induction as the method by which new knowledge is developed. As he saw it, induction involved a patient gathering and categorizing of facts in the hope that a large number of them would point to the truth. As a
process of gathering evidence from which inferences are drawn, induction is contrasted with Aristotle's method, *deduction,* according to which a theory is established
and the truth deduced. Deduction places the stress on the authority of the expert;
induction places the stress on the facts themselves.

[4] **sophisms** Apparently intelligent statements that are wrong; false wisdom.

[5] **refracts** Deflects, bends back, alters.

to the differences of impressions, accordingly as they take place in a mind preoccupied and predisposed or in a mind indifferent and settled; or the like. So that the spirit of man (according as it is meted out to different individuals) is in fact a thing variable and full of perturbation,[6] and governed as it were by chance. Whence it was well observed by Heraclitus[7] that men look for sciences in their own lesser worlds, and not in the greater or common world.

There are also idols formed by the intercourse and association of   6 men with each other, which I call *Idols of the Marketplace,* on account of the commerce and consort of men there. For it is by discourse that men associate; and words are imposed according to the apprehension of the vulgar.[8] And therefore the ill and unfit choice of words wonderfully obstructs the understanding. Nor do the definitions or explanations wherewith in some things learned men are wont[9] to guard and defend themselves, by any means set the matter right. But words plainly force and overrule the understanding, and throw all into confusion and lead men away into numberless empty controversies and idle fancies.

Lastly, there are idols which have immigrated into men's minds   7 from the various dogmas of philosophies, and also from wrong laws of demonstration.[10] These I call *Idols of the Theater;* because in my judgment all the received systems[11] are but so many stage-plays, representing worlds of their own creation after an unreal and scenic fashion. Nor is it only of the systems now in vogue, or only of the ancient sects and philosophies, that I speak; for many more plays of the same kind may yet be composed and in like artificial manner set forth; seeing that errors the most widely different have nevertheless causes for the most part alike. Neither again do I mean this only of entire systems, but also of many principles and axioms in science, which by tradition, credulity, and negligence, have come to be received.

But of these several kinds of idols I must speak more largely and   8 exactly, that the understanding may be duly cautioned.

---

[6] **perturbation** Uncertainty, disturbance. In astronomy, the motion caused by the gravity of nearby planets.

[7] **Heraclitus (535?–475? B.C.)** Greek philosopher who believed that there was no reality except in change; all else was illusion. He also believed that fire was the basis of all the world and that everything we see is a transformation of it.

[8] **vulgar** Common people.

[9] **wont** Accustomed.

[10] **laws of demonstration** Bacon may be referring to Aristotle's logical system of syllogism and deduction.

[11] **received systems** Official or authorized views of scientific truth.

The human understanding is of its own nature prone to suppose   9
the existence of more order and regularity in the world than it finds.
And though there be many things in nature which are singular and
unmatched, yet it devises for them parallels and conjugates and relatives[12] which do not exist. Hence the fiction that all celestial bodies
move in perfect circles; spirals and dragons being (except in name)
utterly rejected. Hence too the element of fire with its orb is brought
in, to make up the square with the other three which the sense perceives. Hence also the ratio of density[13] of the so-called elements is
arbitrarily fixed at ten to one. And so on of other dreams. And these
fancies affect not dogmas only, but simple notions also.

The human understanding when it has once adopted an opin-   10
ion (either as being the received opinion or as being agreeable to itself) draws all things else to support and agree with it. And though
there be a greater number and weight of instances to be found on
the other side, yet these it either neglects and despises, or else by
some distinction sets aside and rejects; in order that by this great
and pernicious predetermination the authority of its former conclusions may remain inviolate. And therefore it was a good answer that
was made by one who when they showed him hanging in a temple a
picture of those who had paid their vows as having escaped ship-
wreck, and would have him say whether he did not now acknowledge the power of the gods—"Ay," asked he again, "but where are
they painted that were drowned after their vows?" And such is the
way of all superstition, whether in astrology, dreams, omens, divine
judgments, or the like; wherein men having a delight in such vani-
ties, mark the events where they are fulfilled, but where they fail,
though this happen much oftener, neglect and pass them by. But
with far more subtlety does this mischief insinuate itself into philosophy and the sciences; in which the first conclusion colors and
brings into conformity with itself all that come after, though far
sounder and better. Besides, independently of that delight and vanity which I have described, it is the peculiar and perpetual error of
the human intellect to be more moved and excited by affirmatives
than by negatives; whereas it ought properly to hold itself indifferently disposed towards both alike. Indeed, in the establishment of
any true axiom, the negative instance is the more forcible of the two.

---

[12] **parallels and conjugates and relatives** A reference to the habit of assuming that phenomena are regular and ordered, consisting of squares, triangles, circles,
and other regular shapes.

[13] **ratio of density** The false assumption that the relationship of mass or weight
to volume was ten to one. This is another example of Bacon's complaint, establishing
a convenient regular "relative," or relationship.

The human understanding is moved by those things most 11
which strike and enter the mind simultaneously and suddenly, and
so fill the imagination; and then it feigns and supposes all other
things to be somehow, though it cannot see how, similar to those
few things by which it is surrounded. But for that going to and fro to
remote and heterogeneous instances, by which axioms are tried as in
the fire,[14] the intellect is altogether slow and unfit, unless it be
forced thereto by severe laws and overruling authority.

The human understanding is unquiet; it cannot stop or rest, and 12
still presses onward, but in vain. Therefore it is that we cannot conceive of any end or limit to the world, but always as of necessity it
occurs to us that there is something beyond. Neither again can it be
conceived how eternity has flowed down to the present day; for that
distinction which is commonly received of infinity in time past and
in time to come can by no means hold; for it would thence follow
that one infinity is greater than another, and that infinity is wasting
away and tending to become finite. The like subtlety arises touching
the infinite divisibility of lines,[15] from the same inability of thought
to stop. But this inability interferes more mischievously in the discovery of causes:[16] for although the most general principles in nature ought to be held merely positive, as they are discovered, and
cannot with truth be referred to a cause; nevertheless, the human
understanding being unable to rest still seeks something prior in the
order of nature. And then it is that in struggling towards that which
is further off, it falls back upon that which is more nigh at hand;
namely, on final causes: which have relation clearly to the nature of
man rather than to the nature of the universe, and from this source

---

[14] **tried as in the fire** Trial by fire is a figure of speech representing thorough,
rigorous testing even to the point of risking what is tested. An axiom is a statement
of apparent truth that has not yet been put to the test of examination and investigation.

[15] **infinite divisibility of lines** This gave rise to the paradox of Zeno, the Greek
philosopher of the fifth century B.C. who showed that it was impossible to get from
one point to another because one had to pass the midpoint of the line determined by
the two original points, and then the midpoint of the remaining distance, and then
of that remaining distance, down to an infinite number of points. By using accepted
truths to "prove" an absurdity about motion, Zeno actually hoped to prove that motion itself did not exist. This is the "subtlety," or confusion, Bacon says is produced
by the "inability of thought to stop."

[16] **discovery of causes** Knowledge of the world was based on four causes: efficient (who made it?), material (what is it made of?), formal (what is its shape?),
and final (what is its purpose?). The scholastics concentrated their thinking on the
first and last, whereas the "middle causes," related to matter and shape, were the
proper subject matter of science because they alone yielded to observation. (See
para. 34.)

have strangely defiled philosophy. But he is no less an unskilled and shallow philosopher who seeks causes of that which is most general, than he who in things subordinate and subaltern[17] omits to do so.

The human understanding is no dry light, but receives an 13 infusion from the will and affections;[18] whence proceed sciences which may be called "sciences as one would." For what a man had rather were true he more readily believes. Therefore he rejects difficult things from impatience of research; sober things, because they narrow hope; the deeper things of nature, from superstition; the light of experience, from arrogance and price, lest his mind should seem to be occupied with things mean and transitory; things not commonly believed, out of deference to the opinion of the vulgar. Numberless in short are the ways, and sometimes imperceptible, in which the affections color and infect the understanding.

But by far the greatest hindrance and aberration of the human 14 understanding proceeds from the dullness, incompetency, and deceptions of the senses; in that things which strike the sense outweigh things which do not immediately strike it, though they be more important. Hence it is that speculation commonly ceases where sight ceases; insomuch that of things invisible there is little or no observation. Hence all the working of the spirits[19] enclosed in tangible bodies lies hid and unobserved of men. So also all the more subtle changes of form in the parts of coarser substances (which they commonly call alteration, though it is in truth local motion through exceedingly small spaces) is in like manner unobserved. And yet unless these two things just mentioned be searched out and brought to light, nothing great can be achieved in nature, as far as the production of works is concerned. So again the essential nature of our common air, and of all bodies less dense than air (which are very many) is almost unknown. For the sense by itself is a thing infirm and erring; neither can instruments for enlarging or sharpening the senses do much; but all the truer kind of interpretation of nature is effected by instances and experiments fit and apposite;[20] wherein the sense decides touching the experiment only, and the experiment touching the point in nature and the thing itself.

---

[17] **subaltern** Lower in status.
[18] **will and affections** Human free will and emotional needs and responses.
[19] **spirits** The soul or animating force.
[20] **apposite** Appropriate; well related.

The human understanding is of its own nature prone to abstrac-   15
tions and gives a substance and reality to things which are fleeting.
But to resolve nature into abstractions is less to our purpose than to
dissect her into parts; as did the school of Democritus,[21] which went
further into nature than the rest. Matter rather than forms should be
the object of our attention, its configurations and changes of configuration, and simple action, and law of action or motion; for forms
are figments of the human mind, unless you will call those laws of
action forms.

Such then are the idols which I call *Idols of the Tribe;* and which   16
take their rise either from the homogeneity of the substance of the
human spirit,[22] or from its preoccupation, or from its narrowness,
or from its restless motion, or from an infusion of the affections,
or from the incompetency of the senses, or from the mode of
impression.

The *Idols of the Cave* take their rise in the peculiar constitution,   17
mental or bodily, of each individual; and also in education, habit,
and accident. Of this kind there is a great number and variety; but I
will instance those the pointing out of which contains the most important caution, and which have most effect in disturbing the clear-
ness of the understanding.

Men become attached to certain particular sciences and specula-   18
tions, either because they fancy themselves the authors and inventors thereof, or because they have bestowed the greatest pains upon
them and become most habituated to them. But men of this kind, if
they betake themselves to philosophy and contemplations of a general character, distort and color them in obedience to their former
fancies; a thing especially to be noticed in Aristotle,[23] who made his
natural philosophy[24] a mere bondservant to his logic, thereby ren-
dering it contentious and well nigh useless. The race of chemists[25]

---

[21] **Democritus (460?–370? B.C.)** Greek philosopher who thought the world
was composed of atoms. Bacon felt such "dissection" to be useless because it was impractical. Yet Democritus's concept of the *eidola,* the mind's impressions of things,
may have contributed to Bacon's idea of "the idol."

[22] **human spirit** Human nature.

[23] **Aristotle (384–322 B.C.)** Greek philosopher whose *Organon* (system of
logic) dominated the thought of Bacon's time. Bacon sought to overthrow Aristotle's
hold on science and thought.

[24] **natural philosophy** The scientific study of nature in general—biology, zoology, geology, etc.

[25] **chemists** Alchemists had developed a "fantastic philosophy" from their experimental attempts to transmute lead into gold.

again out of a few experiments of the furnace have built up a fantastic philosophy, framed with reference to a few things; and Gilbert[26] also, after he had employed himself most laboriously in the study and observation of the loadstone, proceeded at once to construct an entire system in accordance with his favorite subject.

There is one principal and, as it were, radical distinction be- 19
tween different minds, in respect of philosophy and the sciences, which is this: that some minds are stronger and apter to mark the differences of things, others to mark their resemblances. The steady and acute mind can fix its contemplations and dwell and fasten on the subtlest distinctions: the lofty and discursive mind recognizes and puts together the finest and most general resemblances. Both kinds however easily err in excess, by catching the one at gradations, the other at shadows.

There are found some minds given to an extreme admiration of 20
antiquity, others to an extreme love and appetite for novelty; but few so duly tempered that they can hold the mean, neither carping at what has been well laid down by the ancients, nor despising what is well introduced by the moderns. This however turns to the great injury of the sciences and philosophy; since these affectations of antiquity and novelty are the humors[27] of partisans rather than judgments; and truth is to be sought for not in the felicity of any age, which is an unstable thing, but in the light of nature and experience, which is eternal. These factions therefore must be abjured,[28] and care must be taken that the intellect be not hurried by them into assent.

Contemplations of nature and of bodies in their simple form 21
break up and distract the understanding, while contemplations of nature and bodies in their composition and configuration overpower and dissolve the understanding: a distinction well seen in the school of Leucippus[29] and Democritus as compared with the other philosophies. For that school is so busied with the particles that it hardly attends to the structure; while the others are so lost in admiration of the structure that they do not penetrate to the simplicity of nature. These kinds of contemplation should therefore be alternated and taken by turns; that so the understanding may be rendered at once

---

[26] **William Gilbert (1544–1603)** An English scientist who studied magnetism and codified many laws related to magnetic fields. He was particularly ridiculed by Bacon for being too narrow in his researches.

[27] **humors** Used in a medical sense to mean a distortion caused by imbalance.

[28] **abjured** Renounced, sworn off, repudiated.

[29] **Leucippus (fifth century B.C.)** Greek philosopher; teacher of Democritus and inventor of the atomistic theory. His works survive only in fragments.

penetrating and comprehensive, and the inconveniences above mentioned, with the idols which proceed from them, may be avoided.

Let such then be our provision and contemplative prudence for 22 keeping off and dislodging the *Idols of the Cave,* which grow for the most part either out of the predominance of a favorite subject, or out of an excessive tendency to compare or to distinguish, or out of partiality for particular ages, or out of the largeness or minuteness of the objects contemplated. And generally let every student of nature take this as a rule — that whatever his mind seizes and dwells upon with peculiar satisfaction is to be held in suspicion, and that so much the more care is to be taken in dealing with such questions to keep the understanding even and clear.

But the *Idols of the Marketplace* are the most troublesome of all: 23 idols which have crept into the understanding through the alliances of words and names. For men believe that their reason governs words; but it is also true that words react on the understanding; and this it is that has rendered philosophy and the sciences sophistical and inactive. Now words, being commonly framed and applied according to the capacity of the vulgar, follow those lines of division which are most obvious to the vulgar understanding. And whenever an understanding of greater acuteness or a more diligent observation would alter those lines to suit the true divisions of nature, words stand in the way and resist the change. Whence it comes to pass that the high and formal discussions of learned men end oftentimes in disputes about words and names; with which (according to the use and wisdom of the mathematicians) it would be more prudent to begin, and so by means of definitions reduce them to order. Yet even definitions cannot cure this evil in dealing with natural and material things; since the definitions themselves consist of words, and those words beget others: so that it is necessary to recur to individual instances, and those in due series and order; as I shall say presently when I come to the method and scheme for the formation of notions and axioms.[30]

The idols imposed by words on the understanding are of two 24 kinds. They are either names of things which do not exist (for as there are things left unnamed through lack of observation, so likewise are there names which result from fantastic suppositions and to which nothing in reality responds), or they are names of things which exist, but yet confused and ill-defined, and hastily and irregularly derived from realities. Of the former kind are Fortune, the Prime Mover, Planetary Orbits, Element of Fire, and like fictions

---

[30] **notions and axioms** Conceptions and definitive statements of truth.

which owe their origin to false and idle theories.[31] And this class of idols is more easily expelled, because to get rid of them it is only necessary that all theories should be steadily rejected and dismissed as obsolete.

But the other class, which springs out of a faulty and unskillful 25 abstraction, is intricate and deeply rooted. Let us take for example such a word as *humid;* and see how far the several things which the word is used to signify agree with each other; and we shall find the word *humid* to be nothing else than a mark loosely and confusedly applied to denote a variety of actions which will not bear to be reduced to any constant meaning. For it both signifies that which easily spreads itself round any other body; and that which in itself is indeterminate and cannot solidize; and that which readily yields in every direction; and that which easily divides and scatters itself; and that which easily unites and collects itself; and that which readily flows and is put in motion; and that which readily clings to another body and wets it; and that which is easily reduced to a liquid, or being solid easily melts. Accordingly when you come to apply the word—if you take it in one sense, flame is humid; if in another, air is not humid; if in another, fine dust is humid; if in another, glass is humid. So that it is easy to see that the notion is taken by abstraction only from water and common and ordinary liquids, without any due verification.

There are however in words certain degrees of distortion and 26 error. One of the least faulty kinds is that of names of substances, especially of lowest species and well-deduced (for the notion of *chalk* and of *mud* is good, of *earth* bad);[32] a more faulty kind is that of actions, as *to generate, to corrupt, to alter;* the most faulty is of qualities (except such as are the immediate objects of the sense), as *heavy, light, rare, dense,* and the like. Yet in all these cases some notions are of necessity a little better than others, in proportion to the greater variety of subjects that fall within the range of the human sense.

But the *Idols of the Theater* are not innate, nor do they steal into 27 the understanding secretly, but are plainly impressed and received into the mind from the play-books of philosophical systems and the

---

[31] **idle theories** These are things that cannot be observed and thus do not exist. Fortune is fate; the Prime Mover is God or some "first" force; the notion that planets orbited the sun was considered as "fantastic" as these others or as the idea that everything was made up of fire and its many permutations.

[32] **earth bad** Chalk and mud were useful in manufacture; hence they were terms of approval. *Earth* is used here in the sense we use *dirt,* as in "digging in the dirt."

perverted rules of demonstration.[33] To attempt refutations in this case would be merely inconsistent with what I have already said: for since we agree neither upon principles nor upon demonstrations, there is no place for argument. And this is so far well, inasmuch as it leaves the honor of the ancients untouched. For they are no wise disparaged—the question between them and me being only as to the way. For as the saying is, the lame man who keeps the right road outstrips the runner who takes a wrong one. Nay, it is obvious that when a man runs the wrong way, the more active and swift he is the further he will go astray.

But the course I propose for the discovery of sciences is such as   28
leaves but little to the acuteness and strength of wits, but places all wits[34] and understandings nearly on a level. For as in the drawing of a straight line or perfect circle, much depends on the steadiness and practice of the hand, if it be done by aim of hand only, but if with the aid of rule or compass, little or nothing; so is it exactly with my plan. But though particular confutations[35] would be of no avail, yet touching the sects and general divisions of such systems I must say something; something also touching the external signs which show that they are unsound; and finally something touching the causes of such great infelicity and of such lasting and general agreement in error; that so the access to truth may be made less difficult, and the human understanding may the more willingly submit to its purgation and dismiss its idols.

Idols of the Theater, or of systems, are many, and there can be   29
and perhaps will be yet many more. For were it not that now for many ages men's minds have been busied with religion and theology; and were it not that civil governments, especially monarchies, have been averse to such novelties, even in matters speculative; so that men labor therein to the peril and harming of their fortunes— not only unrewarded, but exposed also to contempt and envy; doubtless there would have arisen many other philosophical sects like to those which in great variety flourished once among the Greeks. For as on the phenomena of the heavens many hypotheses may be constructed, so likewise (and more also) many various dogmas may be set up and established on the phenomena of philosophy. And in the plays of this philosophical theater you may

---

[33] **perverted rules of demonstration** Another complaint against Aristotle's logic as misapplied in Bacon's day.

[34] **wits** Intelligence, powers of reasoning.

[35] **confutations** Specific counterarguments. Bacon means that he cannot offer particular arguments against each scientific sect; thus he offers a general warning.

observe the same thing which is found in the theater of the poets, that stories invented for the stage are more compact and elegant, and more as one would wish them to be, than true stories out of history.

In general, however, there is taken for the material of philoso- 30 phy either a great deal out of a few things, or a very little out of many things; so that on both sides philosophy is based on too narrow a foundation of experiment and natural history, and decides on the authority of too few cases. For the rational school of philosophers[36] snatches from experience a variety of common instances, neither duly ascertained nor diligently examined and weighed, and leaves all the rest to meditation and agitation of wit.

There is also another class of philosophers,[37] who having be- 31 stowed much diligent and careful labor on a few experiments, have thence made bold to educe and construct systems; wresting all other facts in a strange fashion to conformity therewith.

And there is yet a third class,[38] consisting of those who out of 32 faith and veneration mix their philosophy with theology and traditions; among whom the vanity of some has gone so far aside as to seek the origin of sciences among spirits and genii.[39] So that this parent stock of errors—this false philosophy—is of three kinds; the sophistical, the empirical, and the superstitious. . . .

But the corruption of philosophy by superstition and an admix- 33 ture of theology is far more widely spread, and does the greatest harm, whether to entire systems or to their parts. For the human understanding is obnoxious to the influence of the imagination no less than to the influence of common notions. For the contentious and sophistical kind of philosophy ensnares the understanding; but this kind, being fanciful and tumid[40] and half poetical, misleads it more

---

[36] **rational school of philosophers** Platonists who felt that human reason alone could discover the truth and that experiment was unnecessary. Their observation of experience produced only a "variety of common instances" from which they reasoned.

[37] **another class of philosophers** William Gilbert (1544–1603) experimented tirelessly with magnetism, from which he derived numerous odd theories. Though Gilbert was a true scientist, Bacon thought of him as limited and on the wrong track.

[38] **a third class** Pythagoras (580?–500? B.C.) was a Greek philosopher who experimented rigorously with mathematics and a tuned string. He is said to have developed the musical scale. His theory of reincarnation, or the transmigration of souls, was somehow based on his travels in India and his work with scales. The superstitious belief in the movement of souls is what Bacon complains of.

[39] **genii** Oriental demons or spirits; a slap at Pythagoras, who traveled in the Orient.

[40] **tumid** Overblown, swollen.

by flattery. For there is in man an ambition of the understanding, no less than of the will, especially in high and lofty spirits.

Of this kind we have among the Greeks a striking example in 34 Pythagoras, though he united with it a coarser and more cumbrous superstition; another in Plato and his school,[41] more dangerous and subtle. It shows itself likewise in parts of other philosophies, in the introduction of abstract forms and final causes and first causes, with the omission in most cases of causes intermediate, and the like. Upon this point the greatest caution should be used. For nothing is so mischievous as the apotheosis of error; and it is a very plague of the understanding for vanity to become the object of veneration. Yet in this vanity some of the moderns have with extreme levity indulged so far as to attempt to found a system of natural philosophy on the first chapter of Genesis, on the book of Job, and other parts of the sacred writings; seeking for the dead among the living: which also makes the inhibition and repression of it the more important, because from this unwholesome mixture of things human and divine there arises not only a fantastic philosophy but also an heretical religion. Very meet it is therefore that we be sober-minded, and give to faith that only which is faith's. . . .

So much concerning the several classes of Idols, and their 35 equipage: all of which must be renounced and put away with a fixed and solemn determination, and the understanding thoroughly freed and cleansed; the entrance into the kingdom of man, founded on the sciences, being not much other than the entrance into the kingdom of heaven, whereunto none may enter except as a little child.

QUESTIONS FOR CRITICAL READING

1. Which of Bacon's idols is the most difficult to understand? Do your best to define it.
2. Which of these idols do we still need to worry about? Why? What dangers does it present?
3. What does Bacon mean by implying that our senses are weak (para. 14)? In what ways do you agree or disagree with that opinion?
4. Occasionally Bacon says something that seems a bit like an aphorism (see the introduction to Machiavelli, p. 37). Find at least one such expression in this selection. On examination, does the expression have as much meaning as it seems to have?

---

[41] **Plato and his school** Plato's religious bent was further developed by Plotinus (A.D. 205–270) in his *Enneads*. Although Plotinus was not a Christian, his Neoplatonism was welcomed as a philosophy compatible with Christianity.

5. What kind of readers did Bacon expect for this piece? What clues does his way of communicating provide regarding the nature of his anticipated readers?

SUGGESTIONS FOR WRITING

1. Which of Bacon's idols most seriously affects the way you as a person observe nature? Using enumeration, arrange the idols in order of their effect on your own judgment. If you prefer, you may write about the idol you believe is most effective in slowing investigation into nature.

2. Is it true, as Bacon says in paragraph 10, that people are in general "more moved and excited by affirmatives than by negatives"? Do we really stress the positive and deemphasize the negative in the conduct of our general affairs? Find at least three instances in which people seem to gravitate toward the positive or the negative in everyday situations. Try to establish whether Bacon has, in fact, described what is a habit of mind.

3. In paragraph 13, Bacon states that the "will and affections" enter into matters of thought. By this he means that our understanding of what we observe is conditioned by what we want and what we feel. Thus, when he says, "For what a man had rather were true he more readily believes," he tells us that people tend to believe what they want to believe. Test this statement by means of observation. Find out, for example, how many older people are convinced that the world is deteriorating, how many younger people feel that there is a plot on the part of older people to hold them back, how many women feel that men consciously oppress women, and how many men feel that feminists are not as feminine as they should be. What other beliefs can you discover that seem to have their origin in what people want to believe rather than in what is true?

4. Bacon's views on religion have always been difficult to define. He grew up in a very religious time, but his writings rarely discuss religion positively. In this work he talks about giving "to faith that only which is faith's" (para. 34). He seems to feel that scientific investigation is something quite separate from religion. Examine the selection carefully to determine what you think Bacon's view on this question is. Then take a stand on the issue of the relationship between religion and science. Should science be totally independent of religious concerns? Should religious issues control scientific experimentation? What does Bacon mean when he complains about the vanity of founding "a system of natural philosophy on the first chapter of Genesis, on the book of Job, and other parts of the sacred writings" (para. 34)? "Natural philosophy" means biology, chemistry, physics, and science in general. Are Bacon's complaints justified? Would his complaints be relevant today?

5. **CONNECTIONS**   How has the reception of Darwin's work been affected by a general inability of the public to see beyond Bacon's four
idols? Read both Darwin's essay and that of Stephen Jay Gould. Which
of those two writers is more concerned with the lingering effects of the
four idols? Do you feel that the effects have seriously affected people's
beliefs regarding Darwinian theory?

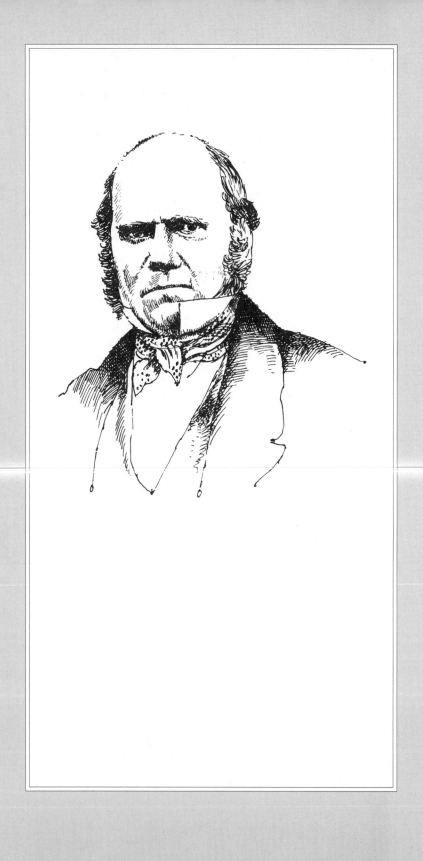

CHARLES DARWIN
Natural Selection

CHARLES DARWIN (1809–1882) was trained as a minister in the Church of England, but he was also the grandson of one of England's greatest horticulturists, Erasmus Darwin. Partly as a way of putting off ordination in the church and partly because of his natural curiosity, Darwin found himself performing the functions of a naturalist on HMS *Beagle,* which was engaged in scientific explorations around South America during the years 1831 to 1836. Darwin's book *Journal of Researches into the Geology and Natural History of the Various Countries Visited by H. M. S. Beagle, 1832–36* (1839) details the experiences he had and offers some views of his self-education as a naturalist.

His journeys on the *Beagle* led him to note variations in species of animals he found in various separate locales, particularly between remote islands and the mainland. Varieties—his term for any visible (or invisible) differences in markings, coloration, size or shape of appendages, organs, or bodies—were of some peculiar use, he believed, for animals in the environment in which he found them. He was not certain about the use of these varieties, and he did not know whether the changes that created the varieties resulted from the environment or from some chance operation of nature. Ultimately, he concluded that varieties in nature were caused by three forces: (1) natural selection, in which varieties occur spontaneously by chance but are then "selected for" because they are aids to survival; (2) direct action of the environment, in which

From *On the Origin of Species by Means of Natural Selection.* This text is from the first edition, published in 1859. In the five subsequent editions, Darwin hedged more and more on his theory, often introducing material in defense against objections. The first edition is vigorous and direct; this edition jolted the worlds of science and religion out of their complaisance. In later editions, this chapter was titled "Natural Selection; or, Survival of the Fittest."

nonadaptive varieties do not survive because of climate, food conditions, or the like; and (3) the effects of use or disuse of a variation (for example, the short beak of a bird mentioned in para. 9). Darwin later regarded sexual selection, which figures prominently in this work, as less significant.

The idea of evolution—the gradual change of species through some kind of modification of varieties—had been in the air for many years when Darwin began his work. The English scientists W. C. Wells in 1813 and Patrick Matthew in 1831 had both proposed theories of natural selection, although Darwin was unaware of their work. Alfred Russel Wallace (1823–1913), a younger English scientist, revealed in 1858 that he was about to propose the same theory of evolution as was Darwin. They jointly published brief versions of their theories in 1858, and the next year Darwin rushed the final version of his book *On the Origin of Species by Means of Natural Selection* to press.

Darwin did not mention human beings as part of the evolutionary process in *On the Origin of Species;* because he was particularly concerned about the probable adverse reactions of theologians, he merely promised later discussion of that subject. It came in *The Descent of Man and Selection in Relation to Sex* (1871), the companion to *On the Origin of Species.*

When Darwin returned to England after completing his research on the *Beagle,* he supplemented his knowledge with information gathered from breeders of pigeons, livestock, dogs, and horses. This research, it must be noted, involved relatively few samples and was conducted according to comparatively unscientific practices. Yet although limited, it corresponded with his observations of nature. Humans could and did cause changes in species; Darwin's task was to show that nature—through the process of natural selection—could do the same thing.

The Descent of Man stirred up a great deal of controversy between the church and Darwin's supporters. Not since the Roman Catholic Church denied the fact that the earth went around the sun, which Galileo proved scientifically by 1632 (and was placed under house arrest for his pains), had there been a more serious confrontation between science and religion. Darwin was ridiculed by ministers and doubted by older scientists; but his views were stoutly defended by younger scientists, many of whom had arrived at similar conclusions. In the end, Darwin's views were accepted by the Church of England, and when he died in 1882 he was lionized and buried at Westminster Abbey in London. Only recently has controversy concerning his work arisen again.

Darwin's Rhetoric

Despite the complexity of the material it deals with, Darwin's writing is fluent, smooth, and stylistically sophisticated and keeps the reader engaged. Darwin's rhetorical method depends entirely on the yoking of thesis and demonstration. He uses definition frequently, but most often he uses testimony, gathering information and instances, both real and imaginary, from many different sources.

Interestingly enough, Darwin claimed that he used Francis Bacon's method of induction in his research, gathering evidence of many instances of a given phenomenon, from which the truth—or a natural law—emerges. In fact, Darwin did not quite follow this path. Like most modern scientists, he established a hypothesis after a period of observation, and then he looked for evidence that confirmed or refuted the hypothesis. He was careful to include examples that argued against his view, but like most scientists, he emphasized the importance of the supportive samples.

Induction plays a part in the rhetoric of this selection in that it is dominated by examples from bird breeding, birds in nature, domestic farm animals and their breeding, and botany, including the breeding of plants and the interdependence of certain insects and certain plants. Erasmus Darwin was famous for his work with plants, and it is natural that such observations would play an important part in his grandson's thinking.

The process of natural selection is carefully discussed, particularly in paragraph 8 and thereafter. Darwin emphasizes its positive nature and its differences from selection by human breeders. The use of comparison, which appears frequently in the selection, is most conspicuous in these paragraphs. He postulates a nature in which the fittest survive because they are best adapted for survival, but he does not dwell on the fate of those who are unfit individuals. It was left to later writers, often misapplying his theories, to do that.

PREREADING QUESTIONS: WHAT TO READ FOR

The following prereading questions may help you anticipate key issues in the discussion on Charles Darwin's "Natural Selection." Keeping them in mind during your first reading of the selection should help focus your reactions.

• What is the basic principle of natural selection?

• How does "human" selection differ from nature's selection?

Natural Selection

How will the struggle for existence . . . act in regard to varia- 1
tion? Can the principle of selection, which we have seen is so potent
in the hands of man, apply in nature? I think we shall see that it can
act most effectually. Let it be borne in mind in what an endless
number of strange peculiarities our domestic productions, and, in a
lesser degree, those under nature, vary; and how strong the hereditary tendency is. Under domestication, it may be truly said that the
whole organization becomes in some degree plastic.[1] Let it be borne
in mind how infinitely complex and close-fitting are the mutual relations of all organic beings to each other and to their physical conditions of life. Can it, then, be thought improbable, seeing that
variations useful to man have undoubtedly occurred, that other variations useful in some way to each being in the great and complex
battle of life, should sometimes occur in the course of thousands of
generations? If such do occur, can we doubt (remembering that
many more individuals are born than can possibly survive) that individuals having any advantage, however slight, over others, would
have the best chance of surviving and or procreating their kind? On
the other hand, we may feel sure that any variation in the least degree injurious would be rigidly destroyed. This preservation of favorable variations and the rejection of injurious variations, I call
Natural Selection. Variations neither useful nor injurious would not
be affected by natural selection, and would be left a fluctuating element, as perhaps we see in the species called polymorphic.[2]

We shall best understand the probable course of natural selec- 2
tion by taking the case of a country undergoing some physical
change, for instance, of climate. The proportional numbers of its inhabitants would almost immediately undergo a change, and some
species might become extinct. We may conclude, from what we
have seen of the intimate and complex manner in which the inhabitants of each country are bound together, that any change in the numerical proportions of some of the inhabitants, independently of the
change of climate itself, would most seriously affect many of the others. If the country were open on its borders, new forms would certainly immigrate, and this also would seriously disturb the relations
of some of the former inhabitants. Let it be remembered how powerful the influence of a single introduced tree or mammal has been

---

[1] **plastic** Capable of being shaped and changed.
[2] **species called polymorphic** Species that have more than one form over the
course of their lives, such as butterflies.

shown to be. But in the case of an island, or of a country partly surrounded by barriers, into which new and better adapted forms
could not freely enter, we should then have places in the economy
of nature which would assuredly be better filled up, if some of the
original inhabitants were in some manner modified; for, had the
area been open to immigration, these same places would have been
seized on by intruders. In such case, every slight modification,
which in the course of ages chanced to arise, and which in any way
favored the individuals of any of the species, by better adapting
them to their altered conditions, would tend to be preserved; and
natural selection would thus have free scope for the work of improvement.

We have reason to believe . . . that a change in the conditions of   3
life, by specially acting on the reproductive system, causes or increases variability; and in the foregoing case the conditions of life are
supposed to have undergone a change, and this would manifestly be
favorable to natural selection, by giving a better chance of profitable
variations occurring; and unless profitable variations do occur, natural selection can do nothing. Not that, as I believe, any extreme
amount of variability is necessary; as man can certainly produce
great results by adding up in any given direction mere individual
differences, so could Nature, but far more easily, from having incomparably longer time at her disposal. Nor do I believe that any
great physical change, as of climate, or any unusual degree of isolation to check immigration, is actually necessary to produce new and
unoccupied places for natural selection to fill up by modifying and
improving some of the varying inhabitants. For as all the inhabitants
of each country are struggling together with nicely balanced forces,
extremely slight modifications in the structure or habits of one inhabitant would often give it an advantage over others; and still
further modifications of the same kind would often still further increase the advantage. No country can be named in which all the native inhabitants are now so perfectly adapted to each other and to
the physical conditions under which they live, that none of them
could anyhow be improved; for in all countries, the natives have
been so far conquered by naturalized productions, that they have allowed foreigners to take firm possession of the land. And as foreigners have thus everywhere beaten some of the natives, we may safely
conclude that the natives might have been modified with advantage,
so as to have better resisted such intruders.

As man can produce and certainly has produced a great result   4
by his methodical and unconscious means of selection, what may
not nature effect? Man can act only on external and visible characters; nature cares nothing for appearances, except in so far as they

may be useful to any being. She can act on every internal organ, on every shade of constitutional difference, on the whole machinery of life. Man selects only for his own good; Nature only for that of the being which she tends. Every selected character is fully exercised by her; and the being is placed under well-suited conditions of life. Man keeps the natives of many climates in the same country; he seldom exercises each selected character in some peculiar and fitting manner; he feeds a long and a short beaked pigeon on the same food; he does not exercise a long-backed or long-legged quadruped in any peculiar manner; he exposes sheep with long and short wool to the same climate. He does not allow the most vigorous males to struggle for the females. He does not rigidly destroy all inferior animals, but protects during each varying season, as far as lies in his power, all his productions. He often begins his selection by some half-monstrous form; or at least by some modification prominent enough to catch the eye, or to be plainly useful to him. Under nature, the slightest difference of structure or constitution may well turn the nicely balanced scale in the struggle for life, and so be preserved. How fleeting are the wishes and efforts of man! how short his time! and consequently how poor will his products be, compared with those accumulated by nature during whole geological periods. Can we wonder, then, that nature's productions should be far "truer" in character than man's productions; that they should be infinitely better adapted to the most complex conditions of life, and should plainly bear the stamp of far higher workmanship?

It may be said that natural selection is daily and hourly scruti- 5
nizing, throughout the world, every variation, even the slightest; rejecting that which is bad, preserving and adding up all that is good; silently and insensibly working, whenever and wherever opportunity offers, at the improvement of each organic being in relation to its organic and inorganic conditions of life. We see nothing of these slow changes in progress, until the hand of time has marked the long lapse of ages, and then so imperfect is our view into long past geological ages, that we only see that the forms of life are now different from what they formerly were.

Although natural selection can act only through and for the 6
good of each being, yet characters and structures, which we are apt to consider as of very trifling importance, may thus be acted on. When we see leaf-eating insects green, and bark-feeders mottled-grey; the alpine ptarmigan white in winter, the red-grouse the color of heather, and the black-grouse that of peaty earth, we must believe that these tints are of service to these birds and insects in preserving them from danger. Grouse, if not destroyed at some period of their lives, would increase in countless numbers; they are known to suffer

largely from birds of prey; and hawks are guided by eyesight to their prey—so much so that on parts of the Continent[3] persons are warned not to keep white pigeons, as being the most liable to destruction. Hence I can see no reason to doubt that natural selection might be most effective in giving the proper color to each kind of grouse, and in keeping that color, when once acquired, true and constant. Nor ought we to think that the occasional destruction of an animal of any particular color would produce little effect; we should remember how essential it is in a flock of white sheep to destroy every lamb with the faintest trace of black. In plants, the down on the fruit and the color of the flesh are considered by botanists as characters of the most trifling importance; yet we hear from an excellent horticulturist, Downing,[4] that in the United States, smooth-skinned fruits suffer far more from a beetle, a curculio,[5] than those with down; that purple plums suffer far more from a certain disease than yellow plums; whereas another disease attacks yellow-fleshed peaches far more than those with other colored flesh. If, with all the aids of art, these slight differences make a great difference in cultivating the several varieties, assuredly, in a state of nature, where the trees would have to struggle with other trees and with a host of enemies, such differences would effectually settle which variety, whether a smooth or downy, a yellow or purple fleshed fruit, should succeed.

In looking at many small points of difference between species, 7 which, as far as our ignorance permits us to judge, seem to be quite unimportant, we must not forget that climate, food, etc., probably produce some slight and direct effect. It is, however, far more necessary to bear in mind that there are many unknown laws of correlation[6] of growth, which, when one part of the organization is modified through variation and the modifications are accumulated by natural selection for the good of the being, will cause other modifications, often of the most unexpected nature.

As we see that those variations which under domestication ap- 8 pear at any particular period of life, tend to reappear in the offspring at the same period—for instance, in the seeds of the many varieties

---

[3] **Continent** European continent; the contiguous land mass of Europe, which excludes the British Isles.

[4] **Andrew Jackson Downing (1815–1852)** American horticulturist and specialist in fruit and fruit trees.

[5] **curculio** A weevil.

[6] **laws of correlation** In certain plants and animals, one condition relates to another, as in the case of blue-eyed white cats, which are often deaf; the reasons are not clear but have to do with genes and their locations.

of our culinary and agricultural plants; in the caterpillar and cocoon stages of the varieties of the silkworm; in the eggs of poultry, and in the color of the down of their chickens; in the horns of our sheep and cattle when nearly adult—so in a state of nature, natural selection will be enabled to act on and modify organic beings at any age, by the accumulation of profitable variations at that age, and by their inheritance at a corresponding age. If it profit a plant to have its seeds more and more widely disseminated by the wind, I can see no greater difficulty in this being effected through natural selection than in the cotton-planter increasing and improving by selection the down in the pods on his cotton-trees. Natural selection may modify and adapt the larva of an insect to a score of contingencies, wholly different from those which concern the mature insect. These modifications will no doubt effect, through the laws of correlation, the structure of the adult; and probably in the case of those insects which live only for a few hours, and which never feed, a large part of their structure is merely the correlated result of successive changes in the structure of their larvae. So, conversely, modifications in the adult will probably often affect the structure of the larva; but in all cases natural selection will ensure that modifications consequent on other modifications at a different period of life, shall not be in the least degree injurious: for if they became so, they would cause the extinction of the species.

Natural selection will modify the structure of the young in rela- 9 tion to the parent, and of the parent in relation to the young. In social animals it will adapt the structure of each individual for the benefit of the community, if each in consequence profits by the selected change. What natural selection cannot do is to modify the structure of one species, without giving it any advantage, for the good of another species; and though statements to this effect may be found in works of natural history, I cannot find one case which will bear investigation. A structure used only once in an animal's whole life, if of high importance to it, might be modified to any extent by natural selection; for instance, the great jaws possessed by certain insects, and used exclusively for opening the cocoon—or the hard tip to the beak of nestling birds, used for breaking the egg. It has been asserted that of the best short-beaked tumbler-pigeons, more perish in the egg than are able to get out of it; so that fanciers[7] assist in the act of hatching. Now, if nature had to make the beak of a full-grown pigeon very short for the bird's own advantage, the process of modification would be very slow, and there would be simultaneously the

---

[7] **fanciers** Amateurs who raise and race pigeons.

most rigorous selection of the young birds within the egg, which had the most powerful and hardest beaks, for all with weak beaks would inevitably perish; or, more delicate and more easily broken shells might be selected, the thickness of the shell being known to vary like every other structure.

Sexual Selection

Inasmuch as peculiarities often appear under domestication in one sex and become hereditarily attached to that sex, the same fact probably occurs under nature, and if so, natural selection will be able to modify one sex in its functional relations to the other sex, or in relation to wholly different habits of life in the two sexes, as is sometimes the case with insects. And this leads me to say a few words on what I call Sexual Selection. This depends, not on a struggle for existence, but on a struggle between the males for possession of the females; the result is not death to the unsuccessful competitor, but few or no offspring. Sexual selection is, therefore, less rigorous than natural selection. Generally, the most vigorous males, those which are best fitted for their places in nature, will leave most progeny. But in many cases, victory will depend not on general vigor, but on having special weapons, confined to the male sex. A hornless stag or spurless cock would have a poor chance of leaving offspring. Sexual selection by always allowing the victor to breed might surely give indomitable courage, length to the spur, and strength to the wing to strike in the spurred leg, as well as the brutal cock fighter,[8] who knows well that he can improve his breed by careful selection of the best cocks. How low in the scale of nature this law of battle descends, I know not; male alligators have been described as fighting, bellowing, and whirling round, like Indians in a wardance, for the possession of the females; male salmons have been seen fighting all day long; male stag-beetles often bear wounds from the huge mandibles[9] of other males. The war is, perhaps, severest between the males of polygamous animals,[10] and these seem oftenest provided with special weapons. The males of carnivorous animals are already well armed; though to them and to others, special means of defense may be given through means of sexual selection, as the

10

---

[8] **brutal cock fighter** Cockfights were a popular spectator sport in England, especially for gamblers, but many people considered them a horrible brutality.

[9] **mandibles** Jaws.

[10] **polygamous animals** Animals that typically have more than one mate.

mane to the lion, the shoulder-pad to the boar, and the hooked jaw to the male salmon; for the shield may be as important for victory as the sword or spear.

Among birds, the contest is often of a more peaceful character. All those who have attended to the subject believe that there is the severest rivalry between the males of many species to attract, by singing, the females. The rock-thrush of Guiana,[11] birds of paradise, and some others, congregate; and successive males display their gorgeous plumage and perform strange antics before the females, which standing by as spectators, at last choose the most attractive partner. Those who have closely attended to birds in confinement well know that they often take individual preferences and dislikes: thus Sir R. Heron[12] has described how one pied peacock was eminently attractive to all his hen birds. It may appear childish to attribute any effect to such apparently weak means: I cannot here enter on the details necessary to support this view; but if man can in a short time give elegant carriage and beauty to his bantams,[13] according to his standard of beauty, I can see no good reason to doubt that female birds, by selecting, during thousands of generations, the most melodious or beautiful males, according to their standard of beauty, might produce a marked effect. I strongly suspect that some well-known laws with respect to the plumage of male and female birds, in comparison with the plumage of the young, can be explained on the view of plumage having been chiefly modified by sexual selection, acting when the birds have come to the breeding age or during the breeding season; the modifications thus produced being inherited at corresponding ages or seasons, either by the males alone, or by the males and females; but I have not space here to enter on this subject.

Thus it is, as I believe, that when the males and females of any animal have the same general habits of life, but differ in structure, color, or ornament, such differences have been mainly caused by sexual selection; that is, individual males have had, in successive generations, some slight advantage over other males, in their weapons, means of defense, or charms; and have transmitted these advantages to their male offspring. Yet, I would not wish to attribute all such sexual differences to this agency: for we see peculiarities arising and becoming attached to the male sex in our domestic

11

12

---

[11] **Guiana** Formerly British Guiana, now Guyana, on the northeast coast of South America.

[12] **Sir Robert Heron (1765–1854)** English politician who maintained a menagerie of animals.

[13] **bantams** Cocks bred for fighting.

animals (as the wattle in male carriers, horn-like protuberances in the cocks of certain fowls, etc.), which we cannot believe to be either useful to the males in battle, or attractive to the females. We see analogous cases under nature, for instance, the tuft of hair on the breast of the turkey-cock, which can hardly be either useful or ornamental to this bird; indeed, had the tuft appeared under domestication, it would have been called a monstrosity.

Illustrations of the Action of Natural Selection

In order to make it clear how, as I believe, natural selection acts,   13
I must beg permission to give one or two imaginary illustrations. Let us take the case of a wolf, which preys on various animals, securing some by craft, some by strength, and some by fleetness; and let us suppose that the fleetest prey, a deer for instance, had from any change in the country increased in numbers, or that other prey had decreased in numbers, during that season of the year when the wolf is hardest pressed for food. I can under such circumstances see no reason to doubt that the swiftest and slimmest wolves would have the best chance of surviving, and so be preserved or selected, provided always that they retained strength to master their prey at this or at some other period of the year, when they might be compelled to prey on other animals. I can see no more reason to doubt this, than that man can improve the fleetness of his greyhounds by careful and methodical selection, or by that unconscious selection which results from each man trying to keep the best dogs without any thought of modifying the breed.

Even without any change in the proportional numbers of the   14
animals on which our wolf preyed, a cub might be born with an innate tendency to pursue certain kinds of prey. Nor can this be thought very improbable; for we often observe great differences in the natural tendencies of our domestic animals; one cat, for instance, taking to catch rats, another mice; one cat, according to Mr. St. John,[14] bringing home winged game, another hares or rabbits, and another hunting on marshy ground and almost nightly catching woodcocks or snipes. The tendency to catch rats rather than mice is known to be inherited. Now, if any slight innate change of habit or of structure benefited an individual wolf, it would have the best chance of surviving and of leaving offspring. Some of its young

---

[14] **Charles George William St. John (1809–1856)** An English naturalist whose book *Wild Sports and Natural History of the Highlands* was published in 1846.

would probably inherit the same habits or structure, and by the repetition of this process, a new variety might be formed which would either supplant or coexist with the parent-form of wolf. Or, again, the wolves inhabiting a mountainous district, and those frequenting the lowlands, would naturally be forced to hunt different prey; and from the continued preservation of the individuals best fitted for the two sites, two varieties might slowly be formed. These varieties would cross and blend where they met; but to this subject of intercrossing we shall soon have to return. I may add, that, according to Mr. Pierce,[15] there are two varieties of the wolf inhabiting the Catskill Mountains in the United States, one with a light greyhound-like form, which pursues deer, and the other more bulky, with shorter legs, which more frequently attacks the shepherd's flocks.

Let us now take a more complex case. Certain plants excrete a sweet juice, apparently for the sake of eliminating something injurious from their sap; this is effected by glands at the base of the stipules[16] in some Leguminosæ, and at the back of the leaf of the common laurel. This juice, though small in quantity, is greedily sought by insects. Let us now suppose a little sweet juice or nectar to be excreted by the inner bases of the petals of a flower. In this case insects in seeking the nectar would get dusted with pollen, and would certainly often transport the pollen from one flower to the stigma of another flower. The flowers of two distinct individuals of the same species would thus get crossed; and the act of crossing, we have good reason to believe (as will hereafter be more fully alluded to), would produce very vigorous seedlings, which consequently would have the best chance of flourishing and surviving. Some of these seedlings would probably inherit the nectar-excreting power. Those individual flowers which had the largest glands or nectaries, and which excreted most nectar, would be oftenest visited by insects, and would be oftenest crossed; and so in the long-run would gain the upper hand. Those flowers, also, which had their stamens and pistils[17] placed, in relation to the size and habits of the particular insects which visited them, so as to favor in any degree the transportal of their pollen from flower to flower, would likewise be favored or selected. We might have taken the case of insects visiting flowers for the sake of collecting pollen instead of nectar; and as pollen is formed for the sole object of fertilization, its destruction appears a simple loss to the plant; yet if a little pollen were carried, at first oc-

---

[15] **Pierce** Unidentified.

[16] **stipules** Spines at the base of a leaf.

[17] **stamens and pistils** Sexual organs of plants. The male and female organs appear together in the same flower.

casionally and then habitually, by the pollen-devouring insects from flower to flower, and a cross thus effected, although nine-tenths of the pollen were destroyed, it might still be a great gain to the plant; and those individuals which produced more and more pollen, and had larger and larger anthers,[18] would be selected.

When our plant, by this process of the continued preservation or natural selection of more and more attractive flowers, had been rendered highly attractive to insects, they would, unintentionally on their part, regularly carry pollen from flower to flower; and that they can most effectually do this, I could easily show by many striking instances. I will give only one—not as a very striking case, but as likewise illustrating one step in the separation of the sexes of plants, presently to be alluded to. Some holly-trees bear only male flowers, which have four stamens producing rather a small quantity of pollen, and a rudimentary pistil; other holly-trees bear only female flowers; these have a full-sized pistil, and four stamens with shrivelled anthers, in which not a grain of pollen can be detected. Having found a female tree exactly sixty yards from a male tree, I put the stigmas[19] of twenty flowers, taken from different branches, under the microscope, and on all, without exception, there were pollen-grains, and on some a profusion of pollen. As the wind had set for several days from the female to the male tree, the pollen could not thus have been carried. The weather had been cold and boisterous, and therefore not favorable to bees; nevertheless every female flower which I examined had been effectually fertilized by the bees, accidentally dusted with pollen, having flown from tree to tree in search of nectar. But to return to our imaginary case: as soon as the plant had been rendered so highly attractive to insects that pollen was regularly carried from flower to flower, another process might commence. No naturalist doubts the advantage of what has been called the "physiological division of labor"; hence we may believe that it would be advantageous to a plant to produce stamens alone in one flower or on one whole plant, and pistils alone in another flower or on another plant. In plants under culture and placed under new conditions of life, sometimes the male organs and sometimes the female organs become more or less impotent; now if we suppose this to occur in ever so slight a degree under nature, then as pollen is already carried regularly from flower to flower, and as a more complete separation of the sexes of our plant would be advantageous on the principle of the division of labor, individuals with this tendency

[16]

---

[18] **anthers** An anther is that part of the stamen that contains pollen.
[19] **stigmas** Where the plant's pollen develops.

more and more increased, would be continually favored or selected, until at last a complete separation of the sexes would be effected.

Let us now turn to the nectar-feeding insects in our imaginary   17
case: we may suppose the plant of which we have been slowly increasing the nectar by continued selection, to be a common plant; and that certain insects depended in main part on its nectar for food. I could give many facts, showing how anxious bees are to save time; for instance, their habit of cutting holes and sucking the nectar at the bases of certain flowers, which they can, with a very little more trouble, enter by the mouth. Bearing such facts in mind, I can see no reason to doubt that an accidental deviation in the size and form of the body, or in the curvature and length of the proboscis,[20] etc., far too slight to be appreciated by us, might profit a bee or other insect, so that an individual so characterized would be able to obtain its food more quickly, and so have a better chance of living and leaving descendants. Its descendants would probably inherit a tendency to a similar slight deviation of structure. The tubes of the corollas[21] of the common red and incarnate clovers (Trifolium pratense and incarnatum) do not on a hasty glance appear to differ in length; yet the hive-bee can easily suck the nectar out of the incarnate clover, but not out of the common red clover, which is visited by humble-bees[22] alone; so that whole fields of the red clover offer in vain an abundant supply of precious nectar to the hive-bee. Thus it might be a great advantage to the hive-bee to have a slightly longer or differently constructed proboscis. On the other hand, I have found by experiment that the fertility of clover greatly depends on bees visiting and moving parts of the corolla, so as to push the pollen on to the stigmatic surface. Hence, again, if humble-bees were to become rare in any country, it might be a great advantage to the red clover to have a shorter or more deeply divided tube to its corolla, so that the hive-bee could visit its flowers. Thus I can understand how a flower and a bee might slowly become, either simultaneously or one after the other, modified and adapted in the most perfect manner to each other, by the continued preservation of individuals presenting mutual and slightly favorable deviations of structure.

I am well aware that this doctrine of natural selection, exempli-   18
fied in the above imaginary instances, is open to the same objections which were at first urged against Sir Charles Lyell's noble views[23] on

---

[20] **proboscis** Snout.

[21] **corollas** Inner set of floral petals.

[22] **humble-bees** Bumblebees.

[23] **Sir Charles Lyell's noble views** Lyell (1797–1875) was an English geologist whose landmark work, *Principles of Geology* (1830–1833), Darwin read while on the *Beagle*. The book inspired Darwin, and the two scientists became friends. Lyell was shown portions of *On the Origin of Species* while Darwin was writing it.

"the modern changes of the earth, as illustrative of geology"; but we now very seldom hear the action, for instance, of the coast-waves, called a trifling and insignificant cause, when applied to the excavation of gigantic valleys or to the formation of the longest lines of inland cliffs. Natural selection can act only by the preservation and accumulation of infinitesimally small inherited modifications, each profitable to the preserved being; and as modern geology has almost banished such views as the excavation of a great valley by a single diluvial[24] wave, so will natural selection, if it be a true principle, banish the belief of the continued creation of new organic beings, or of any great and sudden modification in their structure.

QUESTIONS FOR CRITICAL READING

1. Darwin's metaphor "battle of life" (para. 1) introduces issues that might be thought extraneous to a scientific inquiry. What is the danger of using such a metaphor? What is the advantage of doing so?
2. Many religious groups reject Darwin's concept of natural selection, but they heartily accept human selection in the form of controlled breeding. Why would there be such a difference between the two?
3. Do you feel that the theory of natural selection is a positive force? Could it be directed by divine power?
4. In this work, there is no reference to human beings in terms of the process of selection. How might the principles at work on animals also work on people? Do you think that Darwin assumes this?
5. When this chapter was published in a later edition, Darwin added to its title "Survival of the Fittest." What issues or emotions does that new title raise that "Natural Selection" does not?

SUGGESTIONS FOR WRITING

1. In paragraph 13, Darwin uses imaginary examples. Compare the value of his genuine examples and these imaginary ones. How effective is the use of imaginary examples in an argument? What requirements should an imaginary example meet to be forceful in an argument? Do you find Darwin's imaginary examples to be strong or weak?

---

[24] **diluvial** Pertaining to a flood. Darwin means that geological changes, such as those that caused the Grand Canyon, were no longer thought of as occurring instantly by flood (or other catastrophes) but were considered to have developed over a long period of time, as he imagines happened in the evolution of the species.

2. From paragraph 14 on, Darwin discusses the process of modification of a species through its beginning in the modification of an individual. Explain, insofar as you understand the concept, how a species could be modified by a variation occurring in just one individual. In your explanation, use Darwin's rhetorical technique of the imaginary example.

3. Write an essay that takes as its thesis statement the following sentence from paragraph 18: "Natural selection can act only by the preservation and accumulation of infinitesimally small inherited modifications, each profitable to the preserved being." Be sure to examine the work carefully for other statements by Darwin that add strength, clarity, and meaning to this one. You may also employ the Darwinian device of presenting imaginary instances in your essay.

4. A controversy exists concerning the Darwinian theory of evolution. Explore the *Readers' Guide to Periodical Literature* (a reference book you can find at your local or college library), and the Internet for up-to-date information on the creationist-evolutionist conflict in schools. Look up either or both terms to see what articles you can find. Define the controversy and take a stand on it. Use your knowledge of natural selection gained from this piece. Remember, too, that Darwin was trained as a minister of the church and was concerned about religious opinion.

5. When Darwin wrote this piece, he believed that sexual selection was of great importance in evolutionary changes in species. Assuming that this belief is true, establish the similarities between sexual selection in plants and animals and sexual selection, as you have observed it, in people. Paragraphs 10 to 12 discuss this issue. Darwin does not discuss selection in human beings, but it is clear that physical and stylistic distinctions between the sexes have some bearing on selection. Assuming that to be true, what qualities in people (physical and mental) are likely to survive? Why?

6. **CONNECTIONS** Which of Francis Bacon's four idols would have made it most difficult for Darwin's contemporaries to accept the theory of evolution, despite the mass of evidence he presented? Do the idols interfere with people's ability to evaluate evidence?

7. **CONNECTIONS** In "Ideology and Terror: A Novel Form of Government," Hannah Arendt claims that the social applications of Darwinian views are central to the efficient operation of a terrorist government. Now that you have read Darwin's ideas on natural selection and his comments on the survival of species, can you verify that Arendt's views are reasonable and probable? Describe how one could construct a political ideology using the ideas in Darwin's selection.

RACHEL CARSON
Nature Fights Back

RACHEL CARSON (1907–1964) was educated at the Pennsylvania College for Women (now Chatham College) and Johns Hopkins University, where she received a master's degree in zoology in 1932. She continued her studies at the Marine Biological Laboratory of the Woods Hole Oceanographic Institute in Massachusetts. After teaching biology at the University of Maryland, Carson joined the Bureau of Fisheries (now the United States Fish and Wildlife Service) in 1936. She became editor-in-chief of its publications in 1949. Her first best-selling book on science, *The Sea around Us* (1951), earned her a National Book Award, among many other prizes. In 1952 she left government service to devote herself to research and writing.

Although Rachel Carson was not a distinguished scientist, she was frequently praised for her science writing, which distinguished her from others in her field. She was a painstaking writer who, by her own admission, wrote late into the night and subjected her work to many revisions. In addition to magazine articles she wrote a number of books, including *Under the Sea-Wind: A Naturalist's Picture of Ocean Life* (1941), *The Edge of the Sea* (1955), and *Silent Spring* (1962). She was eventually elected to the British Royal Society of Literature and the American Institute of Arts and Letters.

In the late 1950s, people were noticing that many common birds and insects no longer appeared on the landscape. The effect of powerful insecticides such as DDT had killed off not just the pests that hampered crop growth but also many desirable and beautiful animals that were part of the food chain depending on those insects. *Silent Spring,* in which "Nature Fights Back" appears, is an attack on the wholesale use of pesticides in agriculture.

From *Silent Spring.*

"Nature Fights Back" describes the efforts made in the early part of the twentieth century to control agricultural pests through extensive spraying of powerful insecticides such as DDT and Malathion. Carson's detailed descriptions of the insect populations affected by sprays reveal that there is no clear way to use chemical insecticides without upsetting the balance of nature. When the pests are killed, so are the predatory insects that usually control those populations. When that happens, different undesirable insect populations balloon and cause more havoc. Carson's thorough knowledge of insecticidal spray programs that have been instituted in the past allows her to give a focused picture of the ways in which human efforts at pest control have been frustrated. She presents a portrait of nature that was in harmony in the past, and then she shows how that harmony has been disturbed.

One important point she makes is that many entomologists (insect specialists), despite having the knowledge to understand the situation continue to develop powerful insecticides. The reason is clear: the giant chemical corporations that profit from insecticide spraying support entomologists in graduate school with generous research grants. In other words, the corporations "buy off" the very scientists who might make a difference in informing the public about the dangers of spraying.

Carson is not absolute in her views on the issue of spraying, however. She realizes that some insecticides have to be used under certain circumstances, as she demonstrates at the end of the essay. However, she emphasizes that restrictions need to be placed on the use of insecticides, especially in terms of their strength and the area of their use. Natural means of pest control, she insists, are always preferable to widespread spraying, if only because such spraying produces unwanted results.

Carson herself was unprepared for the overwhelming reception of *Silent Spring:* it not only sold over 500,000 copies but also shocked the public into awareness of the dangers of wholesale damage to the environment. Another result of Carson's book was a government investigation during the Kennedy administration; it eventually led to the banning of DDT in 1972 and resulted in legislation attempting to reverse the effect of indiscriminate spraying and pesticide use. The ecological movement in full swing today was triggered in large part by the frightening picture of pesticide use that Rachel Carson painted in *Silent Spring.*

Carson's Rhetoric

Rachel Carson was praised for her ability to communicate scientific truths to a wide audience. In college, she was an English major before she switched to biology; her rhetorical style, although not specifically literary in this essay, is characterized by careful writing, vivid description, and metaphors designed to move her audience. In other words, she aims to affect her readers as well as to inform them.

This essay represents a carefully calculated argument in favor of restricting insecticide use not only in the United States but throughout the world. When Carson wrote *Silent Spring*, most people were unaware of the astonishing damage that DDT had done to worldwide bird populations. The insecticide had gotten into the food chain, and one result was that the shells of birds' eggs were so weak they could not survive to full term. Carson helped bring that fact to the attention of Americans; one result is that the bald eagle, which was once on the edge of extinction, has now been restored to much of its original wild population.

Carson gives so many details in this essay, and offers so many careful descriptions of the relationship between predators and host insects, because she knows her audience is unaware of the facts that have been piling up in scientific journals that only specialists read. The examples she brings forth are so numerous that few readers can scoff at her and insist that she is referring to isolated examples. However, this rhetorical technique risks a great deal because Carson cannot be sure that the reader will stay with her and permit her to get all the evidence out.

Because she understands the limitations of even a willing reader, Carson takes great care in making her writing both exceptionally clear and very engaging, using metaphors and comparisons that are intelligible and relevant. She also engages the reader by creating brief stories—or what seem like stories—explaining the behavior of the praying mantis, the *Polistes* wasp, the many kinds of borers, and the tiny lady bug. Each insect has its own drama, and by emphasizing that drama Carson holds the reader's attention.

For readers who may fear her position is extreme, she introduces testimony from a number of experts who have long worked in this field. She begins by quoting a Dutch biologist, C. J. Briejèr. She ends the essay by quoting a Canadian entomologist, G. C. Ullyett. In between, as an aid to her argument, she cites the experiences and researches of several other specialists.

In fact, Carson's argument was very successful. She remains a pioneer and a hero in the field of environmental studies. Her greatest concern was the damage done to the environment by well-intentioned people who were unaware of the devastation they caused. As a result of her work, the world has awakened from a dangerously ignorant sleep. As she tells us, however, it is not too late to begin to undo the damage.

**PREREADING QUESTIONS:
WHAT TO READ FOR**

The following prereading questions may help you anticipate key issues in the discussion on Rachel Carson's "Nature Fights Back." Keeping them in mind during your first reading of the selection should help focus your reactions.

• How are insect populations naturally controlled?

• What effect do insecticide sprays have on insect populations?

Nature Fights Back

To have risked so much in our efforts to mold nature to our sat-   1
isfaction and yet to have failed in achieving our goal would indeed
be the final irony. Yet this, it seems, is our situation. The truth, seldom mentioned but there for anyone to see, is that nature is not so
easily molded and that the insects are finding ways to circumvent
our chemical attacks on them.

"The insect world is nature's most astonishing phenomenon,"   2
said the Dutch biologist C. J. Briejèr. "Nothing is impossible to it;
the most improbable things commonly occur there. One who penetrates deeply into its mysteries is continually breathless with wonder. He knows that anything can happen, and that the completely
impossible often does."

The "impossible" is now happening on two broad fronts. By a   3
process of genetic selection, the insects are developing strains resistant to chemicals. . . . But the broader problem, which we shall look
at now, is the fact that our chemical attack is weakening the defenses
inherent in the environment itself, defenses designed to keep the
various species in check. Each time we breach these defenses a
horde of insects pours through.

From all over the world come reports that make it clear we are   4
in a serious predicament. At the end of a decade or more of intensive
chemical control, entomologists were finding that problems they
had considered solved a few years earlier had returned to plague
them. And new problems had arisen as insects once present only in
insignificant numbers had increased to the status of serious pests. By
their very nature chemical controls are self-defeating, for they have
been devised and applied without taking into account the complex
biological systems against which they have been blindly hurled. The

chemicals may have been pretested against a few individual species, but not against living communities.

In some quarters nowadays it is fashionable to dismiss the balance of nature as a state of affairs that prevailed in an earlier, simpler world—a state that has now been so thoroughly upset that we might as well forget it. Some find this a convenient assumption, but as a chart for a course of action it is highly dangerous. The balance of nature is not the same today as in Pleistocene times,[1] but it is still there: a complex, precise, and highly integrated system of relationships between living things which cannot safely be ignored any more than the law of gravity can be defied with impunity by a man perched on the edge of a cliff. The balance of nature is not a *status quo;*[2] it is fluid, ever shifting, in a constant state of adjustment. Man, too, is part of this balance. Sometimes the balance is in his favor; sometimes—and all too often through his own activities—it is shifted to his disadvantage.

Two critically important facts have been overlooked in designing the modern insect control programs. The first is that the really effective control of insects is that applied by nature, not by man. Populations are kept in check by something the ecologists call the resistance of the environment, and this has been so since the first life was created. The amount of food available, conditions of weather and climate, the presence of competing or predatory species, all are critically important. "The greatest single factor in preventing insects from overwhelming the rest of the world is the internecine warfare which they carry out among themselves," said the entomologist Robert Metcalf. Yet most of the chemicals now used kill all insects, our friends and enemies alike.

The second neglected fact is the truly explosive power of a species to reproduce once the resistance of the environment has been weakened. The fecundity of many forms of life is almost beyond our power to imagine, though now and then we have suggestive glimpses. I remember from student days the miracle that could be wrought in a jar containing a simple mixture of hay and water merely by adding to it a few drops of material from a mature culture of protozoa. Within a few days the jar would contain a whole galaxy of whirling, darting life—uncountable trillions of the slipper animalcule, *Paramecium,* each small as a dust grain, all multiplying without restraint in their temporary Eden of favorable temperatures, abundant food, absence of enemies. Or I think of shore rocks white

5

6

7

---

[1] **Pleistocene times** Epoch of ice ages occurring 1,600,000 to 10,000 years ago.
[2] *status quo* The existing state of things.

with barnacles as far as the eye can see, or of the spectacle of passing through an immense school of jellyfish, mile after mile, with seemingly no end to the pulsing, ghostly forms scarcely more substantial than the water itself.

We see the miracle of nature's control at work when the cod 8 move through winter seas to their spawning grounds, where each female deposits several millions of eggs. The sea does not become a solid mass of cod as it would surely do if all the progeny of all the cod were to survive. The checks that exist in nature are such that out of the millions of young produced by each pair only enough, on the average, survive to adulthood to replace the parent fish.

Biologists used to entertain themselves by speculating as to what 9 would happen if, through some unthinkable catastrophe, the natural restraints were thrown off and all the progeny of a single individual survived. Thus Thomas Huxley[3] a century ago calculated that a single female aphis (which has the curious power of reproducing without mating) could produce progeny in a single year's time whose total weight would equal that of the inhabitants of the Chinese empire of his day.

Fortunately for us such an extreme situation is only theoretical, 10 but the dire results of upsetting nature's own arrangements are well known to students of animal populations. The stockman's zeal for eliminating the coyote has resulted in plagues of field mice, which the coyote formerly controlled. The oft repeated story of the Kaibab deer in Arizona is another case in point. At one time the deer population was in equilibrium with its environment. A number of predators—wolves, pumas, and coyotes—prevented the deer from outrunning their food supply. Then a campaign was begun to "conserve" the deer by killing off their enemies. Once the predators were gone, the deer increased prodigiously and soon there was not enough food for them. The browse line on the trees went higher and higher as they sought food, and in time many more deer were dying of starvation than had formerly been killed by predators. The whole environment, moreover, was damaged by their desperate efforts to find food.

The predatory insects of field and forests play the same role as 11 the wolves and coyotes of the Kaibab. Kill them off and the population of the prey insect surges upward.

No one knows how many species of insects inhabit the earth be- 12 cause so many are yet to be identified. But more than 700,000 have al-

---

[3] **Thomas Henry Huxley (1825–1895)** British naturalist who was a strong champion of Darwin and his theory of evolution.

ready been described. This means that in terms of the number of species, 70 to 80 per cent of the earth's creatures are insects. The vast majority of these insects are held in check by natural forces, without any intervention by man. If this were not so, it is doubtful that any conceivable volume of chemicals—or any other methods—could possibly keep down their populations.

The trouble is that we are seldom aware of the protection af- 13 forded by natural enemies until it fails. Most of us walk unseeing through the world, unaware alike of its beauties, its wonders, and the strange and sometimes terrible intensity of the lives that are being lived about us. So it is that the activities of the insect predators and parasites are known to few. Perhaps we may have noticed an oddly shaped insect of ferocious mien on a bush in the garden and been dimly aware that the praying mantis lives at the expense of other insects. But we see with understanding eye only if we have walked in the garden at night and here and there with a flashlight have glimpsed the mantis stealthily creeping upon her prey. Then we sense something of the drama of the hunter and the hunted. Then we begin to feel something of that relentlessly pressing force by which nature controls her own.

The predators—insects that kill and consume other insects— 14 are of many kinds. Some are quick and with the speed of swallows snatch their prey from the air. Others plod methodically along a stem, plucking off and devouring sedentary insects like the aphids. The yellowjackets capture soft-bodied insects and feed the juices to their young. Muddauber wasps build columned nests of mud under the eaves of houses and stock them with insects on which their young will feed. The horseguard wasp hovers above herds of grazing cattle, destroying the blood-sucking flies that torment them. The loudly buzzing syrphid fly, often mistaken for a bee, lays its eggs on leaves of aphis-infested plants; the hatching larvae then consume immense numbers of aphids. Ladybugs or lady beetles are among the most effective destroyers of aphids, scale insects, and other plant-eating insects. Literally hundreds of aphids are consumed by a single ladybug to stoke the little fires of energy which she requires to produce even a single batch of eggs.

Even more extraordinary in their habits are the parasitic insects. 15 These do not kill their hosts outright. Instead, by a variety of adaptations they utilize their victims for the nurture of their own young. They may deposit their eggs within the larvae or eggs of their prey, so that their own developing young may find food by consuming the host. Some attach their eggs to a caterpillar by means of a sticky solution; on hatching, the larval parasite bores through the skin of the host. Others, led by an instinct that simulates foresight, merely lay their eggs on a leaf so that a browsing caterpillar will eat them inadvertently.

Everywhere, in field and hedgerow and garden and forest, the   16
insect predators and parasites are at work. Here, above a pond, the
dragonflies dart and the sun strikes fire from their wings. So their
ancestors sped through swamps where huge reptiles lived. Now, as
in those ancient times, the sharp-eyed dragonflies capture mosquitoes in the air, scooping them in with basket-shaped legs. In the waters below, their young, the dragonfly nymphs, or naiads, prey on
the aquatic stages of mosquitoes and other insects.

Or there, almost invisible against a leaf, is the lacewing, with   17
green gauze wings and golden eyes, shy and secretive, descendant of
an ancient race that lived in Permian times.[4] The adult lacewing
feeds mostly on plant nectars and the honeydew of aphids, and in
time she lays her eggs, each on the end of a long stalk which she fastens to a leaf. From these emerge her children—strange, bristled
larvae called aphis lions, which live by preying on aphids, scales, or
mites, which they capture and suck dry of fluid. Each may consume
several hundred aphids before the ceaseless turning of the cycle of
its life brings the time when it will spin a white silken cocoon in
which to pass the pupal stage.

And there are many wasps, and flies as well, whose very exis-   18
tence depends on the destruction of the eggs or larvae of other insects through parasitism. Some of the egg parasites are exceedingly
minute wasps, yet by their numbers and their great activity they
hold down the abundance of many crop-destroying species.

All these small creatures are working—working in sun and   19
rain, during the hours of darkness, even when winter's grip has
damped down the fires of life to mere embers. Then this vital force
is merely smoldering, awaiting the time to flare again into activity
when spring awakens the insect world. Meanwhile, under the white
blanket of snow, below the frost-hardened soil, in crevices in the
bark of trees, and in sheltered caves, the parasites and the predators
have found ways to tide themselves over the season of cold.

The eggs of the mantis are secure in little cases of thin parch-   20
ment attached to the branch of a shrub by the mother who lived her
life span with the summer that is gone.

The female *Polistes* wasp, taking shelter in a forgotten corner of   21
some attic, carries in her body the fertilized eggs, the heritage on
which the whole future of her colony depends. She, the lone survivor, will start a small paper nest in the spring, lay a few eggs in its

---

[4] **Permian times** Geologic period, 286 to 245 million years ago.

cells, and carefully rear a small force of workers. With their help she will then enlarge the nest and develop the colony. Then the workers, foraging ceaselessly through the hot days of summer, will destroy countless caterpillars.

Thus, through the circumstances of their lives, and the nature of   22 our own wants, all these have been our allies in keeping the balance of nature tilted in our favor. Yet we have turned our artillery against our friends. The terrible danger is that we have grossly underestimated their value in keeping at bay a dark tide of enemies that, without their help, can overrun us.

The prospect of a general and permanent lowering of environ-   23 mental resistance becomes grimly and increasingly real with each passing year as the number, variety, and destructiveness of insecticides grows. With the passage of time we may expect progressively more serious outbreaks of insects, both disease-carrying and crop-destroying species, in excess of anything we have ever known.

"Yes, but isn't this all theoretical?" you may ask. "Surely it won't   24 really happen—not in my lifetime, anyway."

But it is happening, here and now. Scientific journals had al-   25 ready recorded some 50 species involved in violent dislocations of nature's balance by 1958. More examples are being found every year. A recent review of the subject contained references to 215 papers reporting or discussing unfavorable upsets in the balance of insect populations caused by pesticides.

Sometimes the result of chemical spraying has been a tremen-   26 dous upsurge of the very insect the spraying was intended to control, as when blackflies in Ontario became 17 times more abundant after spraying than they had been before. Or when in England an enormous outbreak of the cabbage aphid—an outbreak that had no parallel on record—followed spraying with one of the organic phosphorus chemicals.

At other times spraying, while reasonably effective against the   27 target insect, has let loose a whole Pandora's box[5] of destructive pests that had never previously been abundant enough to cause trouble. The spider mite, for example, has become practically a worldwide pest as DDT and other insecticides have killed off its enemies. The spider mite is not an insect. It is a barely visible eight-legged creature belonging to the group that includes spiders, scorpions, and ticks. It has mouth parts adapted for piercing and

----

[5] **Pandora's box** In Greek myth Pandora received a box from the gods, which she was forbidden to open. When she opened it anyway, the evils and miseries contained within it poured out upon the world.

sucking, and a prodigious appetite for the chlorophyll that makes the world green. It inserts these minute and stiletto-sharp mouth parts into the outer cells of leaves and evergreen needles and extracts the chlorophyll. A mild infestation gives trees and shrubbery a mottled or salt-and-pepper appearance; with a heavy mite population, foliage turns yellow and falls.

This is what happened in some of the western national forests a   28 few years ago, when in 1956 the United States Forest Service sprayed some 885,000 acres of forested lands with DDT. The intention was to control the spruce budworm, but the following summer it was discovered that a problem worse than the budworm damage had been created. In surveying the forests from the air, vast blighted areas could be seen where the magnificent Douglas firs were turning brown and dropping their needles. In the Helena National Forest and on the western slopes of the Big Belt Mountains, then in other areas of Montana and down into Idaho the forests looked as though they had been scorched. It was evident that this summer of 1957 had brought the most extensive and spectacular infestation of spider mites in history. Almost all of the sprayed area was affected. Nowhere else was the damage evident. Searching for precedents, the foresters could remember other scourges of spider mites, though less dramatic than this one. There had been similar trouble along the Madison River in Yellowstone Park in 1929, in Colorado 20 years later, and then in New Mexico in 1956. *Each of these outbreaks had followed forest spraying with insecticides.* (The 1929 spraying, occurring before the DDT era, employed lead arsenate.)

Why does the spider mite appear to thrive on insecticides? Be-   29 sides the obvious fact that it is relatively insensitive to them, there seem to be two other reasons. In nature it is kept in check by various predators such as ladybugs, a gall midge, predaceous mites and several pirate bugs, all of them extremely sensitive to insecticides. The third reason has to do with population pressure within the spider mite colonies. An undisturbed colony of mites is a densely settled community, huddled under a protective webbing for concealment from its enemies. When sprayed, the colonies disperse as the mites, irritated though not killed by the chemicals, scatter out in search of places where they will not be disturbed. In so doing they find a far greater abundance of space and food than was available in the former colonies. Their enemies are now dead so there is no need for the mites to spend their energy in secreting protective webbing. Instead, they pour all their energies into producing more mites. It is not uncommon for their egg production to be increased threefold — all through the beneficent effect of insecticides.

In the Shenandoah Valley of Virginia, a famous apple-growing region, hordes of a small insect called the red-banded leaf roller arose to plague the growers as soon as DDT began to replace arsenate of lead. Its depredations had never before been important; soon its toll rose to 50 per cent of the crop and it achieved the status of the most destructive pest of apples, not only in this region but throughout much of the East and Midwest, as the use of DDT increased.

The situation abounds in ironies. In the apple orchards of Nova Scotia in the late 1940's the worst infestations of the codling moth (cause of "wormy apples") were in the orchards regularly sprayed. In unsprayed orchards the moths were not abundant enough to cause real trouble.

Diligence in spraying had a similarly unsatisfactory reward in the eastern Sudan, where cotton growers had a bitter experience with DDT. Some 60,000 acres of cotton were being grown under irrigation in the Gash Delta. Early trials of DDT having given apparently good results, spraying was intensified. It was then that trouble began. One of the most destructive enemies of cotton is the bollworm. But the more cotton was sprayed, the more bollworms appeared. The unsprayed cotton suffered less damage to fruits and later to mature bolls than the sprayed, and in twice-sprayed fields the yield of seed cotton dropped significantly. Although some of the leaf-feeding insects were eliminated, any benefit that might thus have been gained was more than offset by bollworm damage. In the end the growers were faced with the unpleasant truth that their cotton yield would have been greater had they saved themselves the trouble and expense of spraying.

In the Belgian Congo and Uganda the results of heavy applications of DDT against an insect pest of the coffee bush were almost "catastrophic." The pest itself was found to be almost completely unaffected by the DDT, while its predator was extremely sensitive.

In America, farmers have repeatedly traded one insect enemy for a worse one as spraying upsets the population dynamics of the insect world. Two of the mass-spraying programs recently carried out have had precisely this effect. One was the fire ant eradication program in the South; the other was the spraying for the Japanese beetle in the Midwest.

When a wholesale application of heptachlor was made to the farmlands in Louisiana in 1957, the result was the unleashing of one of the worst enemies of the sugarcane crop—the sugarcane borer. Soon after the heptachlor treatment, damage by borers increased sharply. The chemical aimed at the fire ant had killed off the enemies of the borer. The crop was so severely damaged that farmers sought to bring suit against the state for negligence in not warning them that this might happen.

The same bitter lesson was learned by Illinois farmers. After the   36
devastating bath of dieldrin recently administered to the farmlands in eastern Illinois for the control of the Japanese beetle, farmers discovered that corn borers had increased enormously in the treated area. In fact, corn grown in fields within this area contained almost twice as many of the destructive larvae of this insect as did the corn grown outside. The farmers may not yet be aware of the biological basis of what has happened, but they need no scientists to tell them they have made a poor bargain. In trying to get rid of one insect, they have brought on a scourge of a much more destructive one. According to Department of Agriculture estimates, total damage by the Japanese beetle in the United States adds up to about 10 million dollars a year, while damage by the corn borer runs to about 85 million.

It is worth noting that natural forces had been heavily relied on   37
for control of the corn borer. Within two years after this insect was accidentally introduced from Europe in 1917, the United States Government had mounted one of its most intensive programs for locating and importing parasites of an insect pest. Since that time 24 species of parasites of the corn borer have been brought in from Europe and the Orient at considerable expense. Of these, 5 are recognized as being of distinct value in control. Needless to say, the results of all this work are now jeopardized as the enemies of the corn borer are killed off by the sprays.

If this seems absurd, consider the situation in the citrus groves   38
of California, where the world's most famous and successful experiment in biological control was carried out in the 1880's. In 1872 a scale insect that feeds on the sap of citrus trees appeared in California and within the next 15 years developed into a pest so destructive that the fruit crop in many orchards was a complete loss. The young citrus industry was threatened with destruction. Many farmers gave up and pulled out their trees. Then a parasite of the scale insect was imported from Australia, a small lady beetle called the vedalia. Within only two years after the first shipment of the beetles, the scale was under complete control throughout the citrus-growing sections of California. From that time on one could search for days among the orange groves without finding a single scale insect.

Then in the 1940's the citrus growers began to experiment with   39
glamorous new chemicals against other insects. With the advent of DDT and the even more toxic chemicals to follow, the populations of the vedalia in many sections of California were wiped out. Its im-

portation had cost the government a mere $5000. Its activities had saved the fruit growers several millions of dollars a year, but in a moment of heedlessness the benefit was canceled out. Infestations of the scale insect quickly reappeared and damage exceeded anything that had been seen for fifty years.

"This possibly marked the end of an era," said Dr. Paul DeBach 40 of the Citrus Experiment Station in Riverside. Now control of the scale has become enormously complicated. The vedalia can be maintained only by repeated releases and by the most careful attention to spray schedules, to minimize their contact with insecticides. And regardless of what the citrus growers do, they are more or less at the mercy of the owners of adjacent acreages, for severe damage has been done by insecticidal drift.

All these examples concern insects that attack agricultural 41 crops. What of those that carry disease? There have already been warnings. On Nissan Island in the South Pacific, for example, spraying had been carried on intensively during the Second World War, but was stopped when hostilities came to an end. Soon swarms of a malaria-carrying mosquito reinvaded the island. All of its predators had been killed off and there had not been time for new populations to become established. The way was therefore clear for a tremendous population explosion. Marshall Laird, who has described this incident, compares chemical control to a treadmill; once we have set foot on it we are unable to stop for fear of the consequences.

In some parts of the world disease can be linked with spraying 42 in quite a different way. For some reason, snail-like mollusks seem to be almost immune to the effects of insecticides. This has been observed many times. In the general holocaust that followed the spraying of salt marshes in eastern Florida, aquatic snails alone survived. The scene as described was a macabre picture—something that might have been created by a surrealist brush. The snails moved among the bodies of the dead fishes and the moribund crabs, devouring the victims of the death rain of poison.

But why is this important? It is important because many aquatic 43 snails serve as hosts of dangerous parasitic worms that spend part of their life cycle in a mollusk, part in a human being. Examples are the blood flukes, or schistosoma, that cause serious disease in man when they enter the body by way of drinking water or through the skin when people are bathing in infested waters. The flukes are released into the water by the host snails. Such diseases are especially prevalent in parts of Asia and Africa. Where they occur, insect control measures that favor a vast increase of snails are likely to be followed by grave consequences.

And of course man is not alone in being subject to snail-borne 44
disease. Liver disease in cattle, sheep, goats, deer, elk, rabbits, and
various other warm-blooded animals may be caused by liver flukes
that spend part of their life cycles in fresh-water snails. Livers infested with these worms are unfit for use as human food and are
routinely condemned. Such rejections cost American cattlemen
about $3\frac{1}{2}$ million dollars annually. Anything that acts to increase the
number of snails can obviously make this problem an even more serious one.

Over the past decade these problems have cast long shadows, 45
but we have been slow to recognize them. Most of those best fitted
to develop natural controls and assist in putting them into effect
have been too busy laboring in the more exciting vineyards of chemical control. It was reported in 1960 that only 2 per cent of all the
economic entomologists in the country were then working in the
field of biological controls. A substantial number of the remaining
98 per cent were engaged in research on chemical insecticides.

Why should this be? The major chemical companies are pour- 46
ing money into the universities to support research on insecticides.
This creates attractive fellowships for graduate students and attractive staff positions. Biological-control studies, on the other hand, are
never so endowed—for the simple reason that they do not promise
anyone the fortunes that are to be made in the chemical industry.
These are left to state and federal agencies, where the salaries paid
are far less.

This situation also explains the otherwise mystifying fact that 47
certain outstanding entomologists are among the leading advocates
of chemical control. Inquiry into the background of some of these
men reveals that their entire research program is supported by the
chemical industry. Their professional prestige, sometimes their very
jobs depend on the perpetuation of chemical methods. Can we then
expect them to bite the hand that literally feeds them? But knowing
their bias, how much credence can we give to their protests that insecticides are harmless?

Amid the general acclaim for chemicals as the principal method 48
of insect control, minority reports have occasionally been filed by
those few entomologists who have not lost sight of the fact that they
are neither chemists nor engineers, but biologists.

F. H. Jacob in England has declared that "the activities of many 49
so-called economic entomologists would make it appear that they
operate in the belief that salvation lies at the end of a spray nozzle . . .
that when they have created problems of resurgence or resistance or
mammalian toxicity, the chemist will be ready with another pill.

That view is not held here. . . . Ultimately only the biologist will provide the answers to the basic problems of pest control."

"Economic entomologists must realize," wrote A. D. Pickett of 50 Nova Scotia, "that they are dealing with living things . . . their work must be more than simply insecticide testing or a quest for highly destructive chemicals." Dr. Pickett himself was a pioneer in the field of working out sane methods of insect control that take full advantage of the predatory and parasitic species. The method which he and his associates evolved is today a shining model but one too little emulated. Only in the integrated control programs developed by some California entomologists do we find anything comparable in this country.

Dr. Pickett began his work some thirty-five years ago in the 51 apple orchards of the Annapolis Valley in Nova Scotia, once one of the most concentrated fruit-growing areas in Canada. At that time it was believed that insecticides—then inorganic chemicals—would solve the problems of insect control, that the only task was to induce fruit growers to follow the recommended methods. But the rosy picture failed to materialize. Somehow the insects persisted. New chemicals were added, better spraying equipment was devised, and the zeal for spraying increased, but the insect problem did not get any better. Then DDT promised to "obliterate the nightmare" of codling moth outbreaks. What actually resulted from its use was an unprecedented scourge of mites. "We move from crisis to crisis, merely trading one problem for another," said Dr. Pickett.

At this point, however, Dr. Pickett and his associates struck out 52 on a new road instead of going along with other entomologists who continued to pursue the will-o'-the-wisp of the ever more toxic chemical. Recognizing that they had a strong ally in nature, they devised a program that makes maximum use of natural controls and minimum use of insecticides. Whenever insecticides are applied only minimum dosages are used—barely enough to control the pest without avoidable harm to beneficial species. Proper timing also enters in. Thus, if nicotine sulphate is applied before rather than after the apple blossoms turn pink one of the important predators is spared, probably because it is still in the egg stage.

Dr. Pickett uses special care to select chemicals that will do as 53 little harm as possible to insect parasites and predators. "When we reach the point of using DDT, parathion, chlordane, and other new insecticides as routine control measures in the same way we have used the inorganic chemicals in the past, entomologists interested in biological control may as well throw in the sponge," he says. Instead of these highly toxic, broad-spectrum insecticides, he places chief reliance on ryania (derived from ground stems of a tropical plant), nicotine sulphate, and lead arsenate. In certain situations very weak concentrations of DDT or malathion are used (1 or 2 ounces per 100 gallons—in contrast to the usual 1 or 2 pounds per 100 gallons). Although these two are the least toxic of the modern insecticides, Dr. Pickett hopes by further research to replace them with safer and more selective materials.

How well has this program worked? Nova Scotia orchardists who   54
are following Dr. Pickett's modified spray program are producing as high a proportion of first-grade fruit as are those who are using intensive chemical applications. They are also getting as good production. They are getting these results, moreover, at a substantially lower cost. The outlay for insecticides in Nova Scotia apple orchards is only from 10 to 20 per cent of the amount spent in most other apple-growing areas.

More important than even these excellent results is the fact that   55
the modified program worked out by these Nova Scotian entomologists is not doing violence to nature's balance. It is well on the way to realizing the philosophy stated by the Canadian entomologist G. C. Ullyett a decade ago: "We must change our philosophy, abandon our attitude of human superiority and admit that in many cases in natural environments we find ways and means of limiting populations of organisms in a more economical way than we can do it ourselves."

QUESTIONS FOR CRITICAL READING

1. What is the process by which insects are "developing strains resistant to chemicals" (para. 3)?
2. Why do some people dismiss the idea of trying to achieve a balance of nature?
3. What, in general, is the balance of nature?
4. What happens when a major predator is eliminated from an environment in which it formerly thrived?
5. Why is the example of the overpopulation of the Kaibab deer instructive to us?
6. How do insect predators do their job?
7. Which of the predators' behavior seems most extraordinary to you?

SUGGESTIONS FOR WRITING

1. Explain why preservation of the environment is an essential priority for the twenty-first century. Assume you are writing to an audience that does not share your views and may even be threatened by them. Why must chemical companies be encouraged to forgo the sales of

dangerous insecticides (and thereby lose profits) in favor of finding natural ways to protect agriculture?

2. How effective is Carson's argument? Examine the way in which she establishes and defends her position in this essay. Does she convince you? Do you feel she would convince someone in the insecticide business? What might prevent her argument from convincing someone who disagreed with her? Were you to disagree with her, how would you present your counterargument?

3. Take the point of view of the farmer who insists on using sprays to control pests in order to boost crop production. How would the world's food supplies be affected if farmers did not implement widespread spraying? Is the risk of disturbing the environment worth the ultimate outcome of providing adequate food supplies to the world's populations? Given the potential growth of the world population, is it likely that reduced spraying will result in famine?

4. Do some research on a single insect predator, such as the praying mantis or the *Polistes* wasp or the ichneumon wasp. Describe the way in which it goes about its task of controlling insect populations. What is extraordinary about its behavior? How is it affected by insecticide spraying? What are its chances for maintaining its position in the natural order of insect society? If it is threatened, what is being done about it? If it is thriving, how has it done so? What are its prospects for the future?

5. Do a search online to find environmental groups that are concerned about the use of insecticides. Find out their positions on insecticides, and determine whether their stances seem reasonable in light of what Carson has said. You can begin by searching for terms such as *environmentalists* and *insecticides*.

6. **CONNECTIONS** Which of Francis Bacon's idols are at work in the minds of those who approve of the widespread use of insecticides? What makes it difficult for people to believe what Carson has said? What intellectual processes of induction would Bacon have used in order to establish the effectiveness of spraying? Would Bacon have found Carson's argument convincing?

7. **CONNECTIONS** Both Rachel Carson and Stephen Jay Gould describe the behavior of predator wasps. Compare their descriptions and consider their respective concerns regarding these animals. In what way do Gould's issues regarding the wasps affect your interpretation of Carson's argument in favor of letting the wasps do their work?

STEPHEN JAY GOULD
Nonmoral Nature

STEPHEN JAY GOULD (b. 1941) is Alexander Agassiz professor of zoology, professor of geology, and curator of invertebrate
paleontology in the Museum of Comparative Zoology at Harvard
University, where his field of interest centers on the special evolutionary problems related to species of Bahamian snails. He decided
to become a paleontologist when he was five years old, after he visited the American Museum of Natural History in New York City
with his father and first saw reconstructed dinosaurs.

Gould has become well known for essays on science written
with the clarity needed to explain complex concepts to a general audience and also informed by a superb scientific understanding. His
articles for *Natural History* magazine have been widely quoted and
collected in book form. His books have won both praise and prizes;
they include *Ever Since Darwin* (1977), *The Panda's Thumb* (1980),
The Mismeasure of Man (1981), *The Flamingo's Smile* (1985), *Bully
for Brontosaurus* (1991), *Eight Little Piggies* (1993), *Dinosaur in a
Haystack* (1995), *Full House: The Spread of Excellence from Plato to
Darwin* (1996), and *Questioning the Millennium* (1997). In much of
his writing, Gould has pointed to the significance of the work of the
scientist he most frequently cites, Charles Darwin. His books have
been celebrated around the world, and in 1981 Gould won a
MacArthur Fellowship—a stipend of more than $38,000 a year for
five years that permitted him to do any work he wished.

"Nonmoral Nature" examines a highly controversial issue—
the religious "reading" of natural events. Gould opposes the position of creationists who insisted that the Bible's version of creation
be taught in science courses as scientific fact. Moreover, he views
the account of the creation in Genesis as religious, not scientific,

From *Natural History,* vol. 91, no. 2, 1982.

and points out that Darwin (who was trained as a minister) did not see a conflict between his theories and religious beliefs.

Gould's primary point in this selection is that the behavior of animals in nature—with ruthless and efficient predators inflicting pain on essentially helpless prey—has presented theologians with an exacting dilemma: If God is good and if creation reveals his goodness, why do nature's victims suffer?

Gould examines in great detail specific issues that plagued nineteenth-century theologians. One of these, the behavior of the ichneumon wasp, an efficient wasp that plants its egg in a host caterpillar or aphid, is his special concern. Gould describes the behavior of the ichneumon in detail to make it plain that the total mechanism of the predatory, parasitic animal is complex, subtle, and brilliant. The ichneumon paralyzes its host and then eats it from the inside out, taking care not to permit a victim to die until the last morsel is consumed. He also notes that because there are so many species of ichneumons, their behavior cannot be regarded as an isolated phenomenon.

It is almost impossible to read this selection without developing respect for the predator, something that was extremely difficult, if not impossible, for nineteenth-century theologians to do. Their problem, Gould asserts, was that they anthropomorphized the behavior of these insects. That is, they thought of them in human terms. The act of predation was seen as comparable to the acts of human thugs who toy with their victims, or as Gould puts it, the acts of executioners in Renaissance England who inflicted as much pain as possible on traitors before killing them. This model is the kind of lens through which the behavior of predators was interpreted and understood.

Instead of an anthropocentric—human-centered—view, Gould suggests a scientific view that sees the behavior of predators as sympathetically as that of victims. In this way, he asserts, the ichneumon—and nature—will be seen as nonmoral, and the act of predation seen as neither good nor evil. The concept of evil, he says, is limited to human beings. The world of nature is unconcerned with it, and if we apply morality to nature, we see nature as merely a reflection of our own beliefs and values. Instead, he wishes us to conceive of nature as he thinks it is, something apart from strictly human values.

Gould's Rhetoric

Gould's writing is distinguished for its clarity and directness. In this essay, he relies on the testimony of renowned authorities, establishing at once a remarkable breadth of interest and revealing considerably detailed learning about his subject. He explores a number of theories with sympathy and care, demonstrating their limits before offering his own views.

Because his field of interest is advanced biology, he runs the risk of losing the attention of the general reader. To avoid doing this, he could have oversimplified his subject, but he does not: he does not shrink from using Latin classifications to identify his subject matter, but he defines each specialized term when he first uses it. He clarifies each opposing argument and demonstrates, in his analysis, its limitations and potential.

Instead of using a metaphor to convince us of a significant fact or critical opinion, Gould "deconstructs" a metaphor that was once in wide use — that the animal world, like the human world, is ethical. He reveals the metaphor to us, shows how it has affected belief, and then asks us to reject it in favor of seeing the world as it actually is. Although maintaining the metaphor is inviting and can be irresistible, Gould says we must resist it.

Gould also makes widespread use of the rhetorical device of metonymy, in which a part of something stands for the whole. Thus, the details of nature, which is God's creation, are made to reflect the entirety, which is God. Therefore, the behavior of the ichneumon comes to stand for the nature of God; and because the ichneumon's behavior is adjudged evil by those who think that animal behavior is metaphorically like that of people, there is a terrible contradiction that cannot be rationalized by theological arguments.

Gould shows us just how difficult the problem of the theologian is. Then he shows us a way out. But his way out depends on the capacity to think in a new way, a change that some readers may not be able to achieve.

PREREADING QUESTIONS: WHAT TO READ FOR

The following prereading questions may help you anticipate key issues in the discussion on Stephen Jay Gould's "Nonmoral Nature." Keeping them in mind during your first reading of the selection should help focus your reactions.

• What are the consequences of anthropomorphizing nature?

• What does it mean for nature to be nonmoral?

Nonmoral Nature

When the Right Honorable and Reverend Francis Henry, earl of 1
Bridgewater,[1] died in February, 1829, he left £8,000 to support a series of books "on the power, wisdom and goodness of God, as manifested in the creation." William Buckland,[2] England's first official
academic geologist and later dean of Westminster, was invited to
compose one of the nine Bridgewater Treatises. In it he discussed
the most pressing problem of natural theology: If God is benevolent
and the Creation displays his "power, wisdom and goodness," then
why are we surrounded with pain, suffering, and apparently senseless cruelty in the animal world?

Buckland considered the depredation of "carnivorous races" as 2
the primary challenge to an idealized world in which the lion might
dwell with the lamb. He resolved the issue to his satisfaction by arguing that carnivores actually increase "the aggregate of animal enjoyment" and "diminish that of pain." The death of victims, after all, is
swift and relatively painless, victims are spared the ravages of decrepi-
tude and senility, and populations do not outrun their food supply to
the greater sorrow of all. God knew what he was doing when he made
lions. Buckland concluded in hardly concealed rapture:

> The appointment of death by the agency of carnivora, as the ordi-
> nary termination of animal existence, appears therefore in its main
> results to be a dispensation of benevolence; it deducts much from
> the aggregate amount of the pain of universal death; it abridges,
> and almost annihilates, throughout the brute creation, the misery
> of disease, and accidental injuries, and lingering decay; and im-
> poses such salutary restraint upon excessive increase of numbers,
> that the supply of food maintains perpetually a due ratio to the
> demand. The result is, that the surface of the land and depths of
> the waters are ever crowded with myriads of animated beings, the
> pleasures of whose life are co-extensive with its duration; and
> which throughout the little day of existence that is allotted to
> them, fulfill with joy the functions for which they were created.

We may find a certain amusing charm in Buckland's vision 3
today, but such arguments did begin to address "the problem of

---

[1] **Reverend Francis Henry, earl of Bridgewater (1756–1829)** He was the
eighth and last earl of Bridgewater. He was also a naturalist and a Fellow at All Souls
College, Oxford, before he became earl of Bridgewater in 1823. On his death, he left
a fund to be used for the publication of the Bridgewater Treatises, essay discussions
of the moral implications of scientific research and discoveries.

[2] **William Buckland (1784–1856)** An English clergyman and also a geologist. His essay "Geology and Mineralogy" was a Bridgewater Treatise in 1836.

evil" for many of Buckland's contemporaries—how could a benevolent God create such a world of carnage and bloodshed? Yet these claims could not abolish the problem of evil entirely, for nature includes many phenomena far more horrible in our eyes than simple predation. I suspect that nothing evokes greater disgust in most of us than slow destruction of a host by an internal parasite—slow ingestion, bit by bit, from the inside. In no other way can I explain why *Alien,* an uninspired, grade-C, formula horror film, should have won such a following. That single scene of Mr. Alien, popping forth as a baby parasite from the body of a human host, was both sickening and stunning. Our nineteenth-century forebears maintained similar feelings. Their greatest challenge to the concept of a benevolent deity was not simple predation—for one can admire quick and efficient butcheries, especially since we strive to construct them ourselves—but slow death by parasitic ingestion. The classic case, treated at length by all the great naturalists, involved the so-called ichneumon fly. Buckland had sidestepped the major issue.

The ichneumon fly, which provoked such concern among natural theologians, was a composite creature representing the habits of an enormous tribe. The Ichneumonoidea are a group of wasps, not flies, that include more species than all the vertebrates combined (wasps, with ants and bees, constitute the order Hymenoptera; flies, with their two wings—wasps have four—form the order Diptera). In addition, many related wasps of similar habits were often cited for the same grisly details. Thus, the famous story did not merely implicate a single aberrant species (perhaps a perverse leakage from Satan's realm), but perhaps hundreds of thousands of them—a large chunk of what could only be God's creation.

The ichneumons, like most wasps, generally live freely as adults but pass their larval life as parasites feeding on the bodies of other animals, almost invariably members of their own phylum, Arthropoda. The most common victims are caterpillars (butterfly and moth larvae), but some ichneumons prefer aphids and others attack spiders. Most hosts are parasitized as larvae, but some adults are attacked, and many tiny ichneumons inject their brood directly into the egg of their host.

The free-flying females locate an appropriate host and then convert it to a food factory for their own young. Parasitologists speak of ectoparasitism when the uninvited guest lives on the surface of its host, and endoparasitism when the parasite dwells within. Among endoparasitic ichneumons, adult females pierce the host with their ovipositor and deposit eggs within it. (The ovipositor, a thin tube extending backward from the wasp's rear end, may be many times as long as the body itself.) Usually, the host is not otherwise inconvenienced for the moment, at least until the eggs hatch and the ichneumon larvae begin their grim work of interior excavation. Among ectoparasites, however, many females lay their eggs directly upon the host's body. Since an active host would easily dislodge the egg, the ichneumon mother often simultaneously injects a toxin that paralyzes the caterpillar or other victim. The paralysis may be permanent, and the caterpillar lies, alive but immobile, with the agent of its future destruction secure on its belly. The egg hatches, the helpless caterpillar twitches, the wasp larva pierces and begins its grisly feast.

Since a dead and decaying caterpillar will do the wasp larva no good, it eats in a pattern that cannot help but recall, in our inappropriate, anthropocentric interpretation, the ancient English penalty for treason—drawing and quartering, with its explicit object of extracting as much torment as possible by keeping the victim alive and sentient. As the king's executioner drew out and burned his client's entrails, so does the ichneumon larva eat fat bodies and digestive organs first, keeping the caterpillar alive by preserving intact the essential heart and central nervous system. Finally, the larva completes its work and kills its victim, leaving behind the caterpillar's empty shell. Is it any wonder that ichneumons, not snakes or lions, stood as the paramount challenge to God's benevolence during the heyday of natural theology?   7

As I read through the nineteenth- and twentieth-century literature on ichneumons, nothing amused me more than the tension between an intellectual knowledge that wasps should not be described in human terms and a literary or emotional inability to avoid the familiar categories of epic and narrative, pain and destruction, victim and vanquisher. We seem to be caught in the mythic structures of our own cultural sagas, quite unable, even in our basic descriptions, to use any other language than the metaphors of battle and conquest. We cannot render this corner of natural history as anything but story, combining the themes of grim horror and fascination and usually ending not so much with pity for the caterpillar as with admiration for the efficiency of the ichneumon.   8

I detect two basic themes in most epic descriptions: the struggles of prey and the ruthless efficiency of parasites. Although we acknowledge that we witness little more than automatic instinct or physiological reaction, still we describe the defenses of hosts as though they represented conscious struggles. Thus, aphids kick and caterpillars may wriggle violently as wasps attempt to insert their ovipositors. The pupa of the tortoise-shell butterfly (usually considered an inert creature silently awaiting its conversion from duckling to swan) may contort its abdominal region so sharply that attacking   9 wasps are thrown into the air. The caterpillars of *Hapalia,* when attacked by the wasp *Apanteles machaeralis,* drop suddenly from their leaves and suspend themselves in air by a silken thread. But the wasp may run down the thread and insert its eggs nonetheless. Some hosts can encapsulate the injected egg with blood cells that aggregate and harden, thus suffocating the parasite.

J.-H. Fabre,[3] the great nineteenth-century French entomologist, who remains to this day the preeminently literate natural historian of insects, made a special study of parasitic wasps and wrote with an unabashed anthropocentrism about the struggles of paralyzed victims (see his books *Insect Life* and *The Wonders of Instinct*). He describes some imperfectly paralyzed caterpillars that struggle so violently every time a parasite approaches that the wasp larvae must feed with unusual caution. They attach themselves to a silken strand from the roof of their burrow and descend upon a safe and exposed part of the caterpillar:

> The grub is at dinner: head downwards, it is digging into the limp belly of one of the caterpillars. . . . At the least sign of danger in the heap of caterpillars, the larva retreats . . . and climbs back to the ceiling, where the swarming rabble cannot reach it. When peace is restored, it slides down [its silken cord] and returns to table, with its head over the viands and its rear upturned and ready to withdraw in case of need.

In another chapter, he describes the fate of a paralyzed cricket:

> One may see the cricket, bitten to the quick, vainly move its antennae and abdominal styles, open and close its empty jaws, and even move a foot, but the larva is safe and searches its vitals with impunity. What an awful nightmare for the paralyzed cricket!

Fabre even learned to feed some paralyzed victims by placing a syrup of sugar and water on their mouthparts—thus showing that they remained alive, sentient, and (by implication) grateful for any palliation of their inevitable fate. If Jesus, immobile and thirsting on the cross, received only vinegar from his tormentors, Fabre at least could make an ending bittersweet.

The second theme, ruthless efficiency of the parasites, leads to the opposite conclusion—grudging admiration for the victors. We learn of their skill in capturing dangerous hosts often many times larger than themselves. Caterpillars may be easy game, but the

10

11

12

13

---

[3] **Jean-Henri Fabre (1823–1915)** A French entomologist whose patient study of insects earned him the nickname "the Virgil of Insects." His writings are voluminous and, at times, elegant.

psammocharid wasps prefer spiders. They must insert their ovipositors in a safe and precise spot. Some leave a paralyzed spider in its
own burrow. *Planiceps hirsutus,* for example, parasitizes a California
trapdoor spider. It searches for spider tubes on sand dunes, then
digs into nearby sand to disturb the spider's home and drive it out.
When the spider emerges, the wasp attacks, paralyzes its victim,
drags it back into its own tube, shuts and fastens the trapdoor, and
deposits a single egg upon the spider's abdomen. Other psam-
mocharids will drag a heavy spider back to a previously prepared
cluster of clay or mud cells. Some amputate a spider's legs to make
the passage easier. Others fly back over water, skimming a buoyant
spider along the surface.

Some wasps must battle with other parasites over a host's body. 14
Rhyssella curvipes can detect the larvae of wood wasps deep within
alder wood and drill down to its potential victims with its sharply
ridged ovipositor. *Pseudorhyssa alpestris,* a related parasite, cannot
drill directly into wood since its slender ovipositor bears only rudimentary cutting ridges. It locates the holes made by *Rhyssella,* inserts
its ovipositor, and lays an egg on the host (already conveniently paralyzed by *Rhyssella*), right next to the egg deposited by its relative.
The two eggs hatch at about the same time, but the larva of
Pseudorhyssa has a bigger head bearing much larger mandibles.
Pseudorhyssa seizes the smaller *Rhyssella* larva, destroys it, and proceeds to feast upon a banquet already well prepared.

Other praises for the efficiency of mothers invoke the themes of 15
early, quick, and often. Many ichneumons don't even wait for their
hosts to develop into larvae, but parasitize the egg directly (larval
wasps may then either drain the egg itself or enter the developing
host larva). Others simply move fast. *Apanteles militaris* can deposit
up to seventy-two eggs in a single second. Still others are doggedly
persistent. *Aphidius gomezi* females produce up to 1,500 eggs and
can parasitize as many as 600 aphids in a single working day. In a
bizarre twist upon "often," some wasps indulge in polyembryony, a
kind of iterated supertwinning. A single egg divides into cells that
aggregate into as many as 500 individuals. Since some polyembry-
onic wasps parasitize caterpillars much larger than themselves and
may lay up to six eggs in each, as many as 3,000 larvae may develop
within, and feed upon, a single host. These wasps are endoparasites
and do not paralyze their victims. The caterpillars writhe back and
forth, not (one suspects) from pain, but merely in response to the
commotion induced by thousands of wasp larvae feeding within.

The efficiency of mothers is matched by their larval offspring. I 16
have already mentioned the pattern of eating less essential parts first,
thus keeping the host alive and fresh to its final and merciful dis-

patch. After the larva digests every edible morsel of its victim (if only to prevent later fouling of its abode by decaying tissue), it may still use the outer shell of its host. One aphid parasite cuts a hole in the belly of its victim's shell, glues the skeleton to a leaf by sticky secretions from its salivary gland, and then spins a cocoon to pupate within the aphid's shell.

In using inappropriate anthropocentric language in this romp 17 through the natural history of ichneumons, I have tried to emphasize just why these wasps became a preeminent challenge to natural theology—the antiquated doctrine that attempted to infer God's essence from the products of his creation. I have used twentieth-century examples for the most part, but all themes were known and stressed by the great nineteenth-century natural theologians. How then did they square the habits of these wasps with the goodness of God? How did they extract themselves from this dilemma of their own making?

The strategies were as varied as the practitioners; they shared 18 only the theme of special pleading for an a priori doctrine[4]—they knew that God's benevolence was lurking somewhere behind all these tales of apparent horror. Charles Lyell[5] for example, in the first edition of his epochal *Principles of Geology* (1830–1833), decided that caterpillars posed such a threat to vegetation that any natural checks upon them could only reflect well upon a creating deity, for caterpillars would destroy human agriculture "did not Providence put causes in operation to keep them in due bounds."

The Reverend William Kirby,[6] rector of Barham and Britain's 19 foremost entomologist, chose to ignore the plight of caterpillars and focused instead upon the virtue of mother love displayed by wasps in provisioning their young with such care.

> The great object of the female is to discover a proper nidus for her
> eggs. In search of this she is in constant motion. Is the caterpillar
> of a butterfly or moth the appropriate food for her young? You see

---

[4] **an a priori doctrine** *A priori* means "beforehand," and Gould refers to those who approach a scientific situation with a preestablished view in mind. He is suggesting that such an approach prevents the kind of objectivity and fairness that scientific examination is supposed to produce.

[5] **Charles Lyell (1797–1875)** An English geologist who established the glacial layers of the Eocene (dawn of recent), Miocene (less recent), and Pliocene (more recent) epochs during his excavations of Tertiary period strata in Italy. He was influential in urging Darwin to publish his theories. His work is still respected.

[6] **The Reverend William Kirby (1759–1850)** An English specialist in insects. He was the author of a Bridgewater Treatise, *On the power, wisdom, and goodness of God, as manifested in the creation of animals, and in their history, habits, and instincts* (2 vols., 1835).

her alight upon the plants where they are most usually to be met with, run quickly over them, carefully examining every leaf, and, having found the unfortunate object of her search, insert her sting into its flesh, and there deposit an egg. . . . The active Ichneumon braves every danger, and does not desist until her courage and address have insured subsistence for one of her future progeny.

Kirby found this solicitude all the more remarkable because the   20
female wasp will never see her child and enjoy the pleasures of parenthood. Yet her love compels her to danger nonetheless:

> A very large proportion of them are doomed to die before their young come into existence. But in these the passion is not extinguished. . . . When you witness the solicitude with which they provide for the security and sustenance of their future young, you can scarcely deny to them love for a progeny they are never destined to behold.

Kirby also put in a good word for the marauding larvae, praising   21
them for their forbearance in eating selectively to keep their caterpillar prey alive. Would we all husband our resources with such care!

> In this strange and apparently cruel operation one circumstance is truly remarkable. The larva of the Ichneumon, though every day, perhaps for months, it gnaws the inside of the caterpillar, and though at last it has devoured almost every part of it except the skin and intestines, carefully all this time it avoids injuring the vital organs, as if aware that its own existence depends on that of the insect upon which it preys! . . . What would be the impression which a similar instance amongst the race of quadrupeds would make upon us? If, for example, an animal . . . should be found to feed upon the inside of a dog, devouring only those parts not essential to life, while it cautiously left uninjured the heart, arteries, lungs, and intestines — should we not regard such an instance as a perfect prodigy, as an example of instinctive forebearance almost miraculous? [The last three quotes come from the 1856, and last pre-Darwinian, edition of Kirby and Spence's *Introduction to Entomology*.]

This tradition of attempting to read moral meaning from nature   22
did not cease with the triumph of evolutionary theory after Darwin published *On the Origin of Species* in 1859 — for evolution could be read as God's chosen method of peopling our planet, and ethical messages might still populate nature. Thus, St. George Mivart,[7] one

---

[7] **St. George Mivart (1827–1900)** English anatomist and biologist who examined the comparative anatomies of insect-eating and meat-eating animals. A convert to Roman Catholicism in 1844, he was unable to reconcile religious and evolutionary theories and was excommunicated from the Catholic Church in 1900.

of Darwin's most effective evolutionary critics and a devout Catholic, argued that "many amiable and excellent people" had been misled by the apparent suffering of animals for two reasons. First, however much it might hurt, "physical suffering and moral evil are simply incommensurable." Since beasts are not moral agents, their feelings cannot bear any ethical message. But secondly, lest our visceral sensitivities still be aroused, Mivart assures us that animals must feel little, if any, pain. Using a favorite racist argument of the time — that "primitive" people suffer far less than advanced and cultured people — Mivart extrapolated further down the ladder of life into a realm of very limited pain indeed: Physical suffering, he argued,

> depends greatly upon the mental condition of the sufferer. Only during consciousness does it exist, and only in the most highly organized men does it reach its acme. The author has been assured that lower races of men appear less keenly sensitive to physical suffering than do more cultivated and refined human beings. Thus only in man can there really be any intense degree of suffering, because only in him is there that intellectual recollection of past moments and that anticipation of future ones, which constitute in great part the bitterness of suffering. The momentary pang, the present pain, which beasts endure, though real enough, is yet, doubtless, not to be compared as to its intensity with the suffering which is produced in man through his high prerogative of self-consciousness [from *Genesis of Species,* 1871].

It took Darwin himself to derail this ancient tradition — in that gentle way so characteristic of his radical intellectual approach to nearly everything. The ichneumons also troubled Darwin greatly and he wrote of them to Asa Gray[8] in 1860:

> I own that I cannot see as plainly as others do, and as I should wish to do, evidence of design and beneficence on all sides of us. There seems to me too much misery in the world. I cannot persuade myself that a beneficent and omnipotent God would have designedly created the Ichneumonidae with the express intention

---

[8] **Asa Gray (1810–1888)** America's greatest botanist. His works, which are still considered important, are *Structural Botany* (1879; originally published in 1842 as *Botanical Text-Book*), *The Elements of Botany* (1836), *How Plants Grow* (1858), and *How Plants Behave* (1872). Gray was a serious critic of Darwin and wrote a great number of letters to him, but he was also a firm believer in Darwinian evolution. Because he was also a well-known member of an evangelical Protestant faith, he was effective in countering religious attacks on Darwin by showing that there is no conflict between Darwinism and religion.

of their feeding within the living bodies of Caterpillars, or that a cat should play with mice.

Indeed, he had written with more passion to Joseph Hooker[9] in 1856: "What a book a devil's chaplain might write on the clumsy, wasteful, blundering, low, and horribly cruel works of nature!"   24

This honest admission—that nature is often (by our standards) cruel and that all previous attempts to find a lurking goodness behind everything represent just so much absurd special pleading—can lead in two directions. One might retain the principle that nature holds moral messages for humans, but reverse the usual perspective and claim that morality consists in understanding the ways of nature and doing the opposite. Thomas Henry Huxley[10] advanced this argument in his famous essay on *Evolution and Ethics* (1893):   25

> The practice of that which is ethically best—what we call goodness or virtue—involves a course of conduct which, in all respects, is opposed to that which leads to success in the cosmic struggle for existence. In place of ruthless self-assertion it demands self-restraint; in place of thrusting aside, or treading down, all competitors, it requires that the individual shall not merely respect, but shall help his fellows. . . . It repudiates the gladiatorial theory of existence. . . . Laws and moral precepts are directed to the end of curbing the cosmic process.

The other argument, more radical in Darwin's day but common now, holds that nature simply is as we find it. Our failure to discern the universal good we once expected does not record our lack of insight or ingenuity but merely demonstrates that nature contains no moral messages framed in human terms. Morality is a subject for philosophers, theologians, students of the humanities, indeed for all thinking people. The answers will not be read passively from nature; they do not, and cannot, arise from the data of science. The factual state of the world does not teach us how we, with our powers for good and evil, should alter or preserve it in the most ethical manner.   26

---

[9] **Joseph Hooker (1817–1911)** English botanist who studied flowers in exotic locations such as Tasmania, the Antarctic, New Zealand, and India. He was, along with Charles Lyell, a friend of Darwin and one of those who urged him to publish *On the Origin of Species*. He was the director of London's Kew Gardens from 1865 to 1885.

[10] **Thomas Henry Huxley (1825–1895)** An English naturalist who, quite independent of organizations and formal support, became one of the most important scientists of his time. He searched for a theory of evolution that was based on a rigorous examination of the facts and found, in Darwin's work, the theory that he could finally respect. He was a strong champion of Darwin.

Darwin himself tended toward this view, although he could not, 27
as a man of his time, thoroughly abandon the idea that laws of nature might reflect some higher purpose. He clearly recognized that
the specific manifestations of those laws — cats playing with mice,
and ichneumon larvae eating caterpillars — could not embody ethical messages, but he somehow hoped that unknown higher laws
might exist "with the details, whether good or bad, left to the working out of what we may call chance."

Since ichneumons are a detail, and since natural selection is 28
a law regulating details, the answer to the ancient dilemma of
why such cruelty (in our terms) exists in nature can only be that
there isn't any answer — and that the framing of the question "in
our terms" is thoroughly inappropriate in a natural world neither made for us nor ruled by us. It just plain happens. It is a
strategy that works for ichneumons and that natural selection has
programmed into their behavioral repertoire. Caterpillars are not
suffering to teach us something; they have simply been outma-
neuvered, for now, in the evolutionary game. Perhaps they will
evolve a set of adequate defenses sometime in the future, thus
sealing the fate of ichneumons. And perhaps, indeed probably, they
will not.

Another Huxley, Thomas's grandson Julian,[11] spoke for this po- 29
sition, using as an example — yes, you guessed it — the ubiquitous
ichneumons:

> Natural selection, in fact, though like the mills of God in grinding
> slowly and grinding small, has few other attributes that a civilized
> religion would call divine. . . . Its products are just as likely to be
> aesthetically, morally, or intellectually repulsive to us as they are
> to be attractive. We need only think of the ugliness of *Sacculina* or
> a bladderworm, the stupidity of a rhinoceros or a stegosaur, the
> horror of a female mantis devouring its mate or a brood of ichneu-
> mon flies slowly eating out a caterpillar.

It is amusing in this context, or rather ironic since it is too serious to be
amusing, that modern creationists accuse evolutionists of preaching a
specific ethical doctrine called secular humanism and thereby demand
equal time for their unscientific and discredited views. If nature is nonmoral, then evolution cannot teach any ethical theory at all. The assumption that it can has abetted a panoply of social evils that ideologues falsely read into nature from their beliefs — eugenics and
(misnamed) social Darwinism prominently among them. Not only did

---

[11] **Thomas's grandson Julian** Julian Huxley (1887–1975), an English biologist and a brother of the novelist Aldous Huxley.

Darwin eschew any attempt to discover an antireligious ethic in nature, he also expressly stated his personal bewilderment about such deep issues as the problem of evil. Just a few sentences after invoking the ichneumons, and in words that express both the modesty of this splendid man and the compatibility, through lack of contact, between science and true religion, Darwin wrote to Asa Gray,

> I feel most deeply that the whole subject is too profound for the human intellect. A dog might as well speculate on the mind of Newton. Let each man hope and believe what he can.

QUESTIONS FOR CRITICAL READING

1. What does Gould reveal to us about the nature of insect life?
2. What scientific information does Gould provide that is most valuable in explaining how nature works?
3. What does it mean to anthropomorphize nature? What are some concrete results of doing so?
4. Describe the reaction you have to the process by which the ichneumon wasp parasitizes its host.
5. How might the behavior of the ichneumon wasp put at stake any genuine religious questions of today?
6. What counterassertions can you make to Gould's view that nature is nonmoral?

SUGGESTIONS FOR WRITING

1. In a brief essay, try to answer the question Gould examines in paragraph 1: "Why are we surrounded with pain, suffering, and apparently senseless cruelty in the animal world?"
2. Is the fact of such pain, suffering, and apparently senseless cruelty a religious issue? If so, in what way? If not, demonstrate why.
3. In paragraph 17, Gould describes natural theology as "the antiquated doctrine that attempted to infer God's essence from the products of his creation." Is this a reasonable description of natural theology as you understand it? What can a theology that bases its claims in an observation of nature assert about the essence of God? What kind of religion would support a theology that was based on the behavior of natural life, including ichneumons?
4. Gould points out that even after having established his theory of evolution, Darwin could not "thoroughly abandon the idea that laws of nature might reflect some higher purpose" (para. 27). Assuming that you agree with Darwin but also acknowledge the problems that Gould pre-

sents, clarify what the higher purpose of a nature such as Gould describes might be. Does Gould's description of the behavior of the ichneumon (or any other) predator in any way compromise the idea that nature has a higher purpose? Does Gould hold that it has a higher purpose?

5. **CONNECTIONS**   Compare this essay with Francis Bacon's "The Four Idols." What intellectual issues do the two essays share? What common ground do they share regarding attitudes toward science and religion? What might Bacon have decided about the ultimate ethical issues raised by a consideration of the ichneumon? Do you think that Bacon would have held the same views about the ichneumon's predatory powers as did the nineteenth-century theologians? That is, would he have conceived of nature in ethical/moral terms?

6. **CONNECTIONS**   Why would Gould's scientific subject matter involve issues of morality to a greater extent than, say, the subject matter of Francis Bacon, Charles Darwin, or Rachel Carson? Is it possible that the study of physics or chemistry is less fundamentally concerned with moral issues than the study of biology is? One result of Darwin's concerns is the possibility that apes and humans are related. Is this point less worthy of consideration from a moral viewpoint than the behavior of the ichneumon wasp? What are the major moral issues in science that you have observed from examining these writers?

MICHIO KAKU
The Mystery of Dark Matter

MICHIO KAKU (b. 1947) was born and raised in San Jose, California, received his undergraduate degree from Harvard, and returned to California for his Ph.D. in physics at Berkeley in 1972. Since 1973 he has been professor of theoretical physics at the City College and the Graduate Center of the City University of New York, publishing widely on superstring theory, supergravity, and string field theory. He hosts a weekly national radio show on science called *Explorations,* and his other science commentaries on Pacifica National Radio are carried by sixty radio stations in the United States. Kaku is also deeply concerned about the practical ramifications of theoretical physics and has written several books on the dangers of nuclear war. He is active in groups that advocate disarmament.

"The Mystery of Dark Matter" is a chapter in his book entitled *Beyond Einstein* (1987, rev. 1995), written with Jennifer Trainer Thompson. In this work Kaku attempts to explain the circumstances of modern physics, with a special look at efforts to resolve the conflicts between two important theories: quantum theory and the theory of relativity. Quantum theory explains the physics of atoms and small particles. The theory of relativity explains cosmic phenomena such as gravity and the universe. However, neither theory works in the other's sphere of influence. Hence a new theory is needed to resolve the problems: superstring theory, which postulates that instead of hard particles existing at the center of atoms, "tiny strings of energy" vibrate at an infinite number of frequencies. These strings of energy are at the heart of atoms and consist of everything we know of as matter in the universe.

If superstring theory is correct, one of the tests will be a confirmation of the existence of—and perhaps an explanation of—dark

From *Beyond Einstein.*

487

matter. In this essay Kaku describes dark matter as matter that we know exists but that cannot be seen or perceived except in terms of its effect on other bodies, such as stars.

Because physics involves specialized, advanced mathematics, much of what Kaku says is simplified for a general audience. As a result we can understand the theories, but only in general terms. Therefore, without the mathematics, we must accept certain ideas at face value, making an effort to imagine, along with Kaku, how modern theories of physics work. Fortunately his co-author, Jennifer Trainer Thompson, is able to spell out the very complex theories in a fashion that makes them as intelligible as possible for readers who are not experts in mathematics.

Some of the ideas in this essay are also developed in Kaku's best-selling *Hyperspace* (1994), which discusses the so-called crazy theories of contemporary physicists. Kaku tells us that modern research by contemporary physicists has produced a view of the natural world that virtually defies common sense, just as facts such as the earth's roundness (rather than flatness) and its movement around the sun (rather than the reverse) initially contradicted common sense. Unfortunately common sense does not help us understand modern physics or the world of the atom. Because we cannot directly perceive the atom or the molecule, we require sophisticated equipment to make their nature become evident. Interestingly, Francis Bacon insisted in *Novum Organum* that until better tools were developed, people would not be able to perceive the truth about the complexities of nature.

In an early chapter of *Hyperspace*, Kaku tells a story about being a young boy and watching fish in a small pond. He realized that for the carp, it was inconceivable that anything existed outside the water in which they swam. Their perceptions were limited entirely to the watery environment of their home. The same is true for people. Our environment may seem larger and more capacious than a pond, but we, like the carp, are limited in our perceptions. Plato realized this when he postulated his allegory of the cave and theorized that human beings' profoundly limited sensory apparatus prevents us from imagining experiences beyond what we know from our senses.

In "The Mystery of Dark Matter," Kaku discusses a phenomenon that similarly defies common sense. He explains that experiments and observations of a number of important astrophysicists throughout a period of over twenty years have led physicists to conclude that the universe is made up of more than the matter that we can perceive. Indeed, the best observations have suggested that the universe may contain as much as 90 percent dark matter, even though this matter cannot be observed directly. If it were not so, theorists say, the galaxies would spin apart and the stars would drift into distant space, thereby cooling the universe to a temperature that would lead to its death.

Kaku's Rhetoric

Jennifer Trainer Thompson, a nonphysicist, has worked on a number of Kaku's books meant for a general reading public, and she employs techniques common to contemporary journalism. She uses short paragraphs and intriguing subheads, such as "What Is the World Made Of?"; "How Much Does a Galaxy Weigh?"; and "Hot and Cold Dark Matter." These techniques help readers grasp the ideas that the research of Michio Kaku and other modern physicists has developed.

Because the essay offers a general overview of an interesting and elusive subject, Kaku provides a considerable amount of background information. He tells us about the impact of the work of early mathematicians and physicists, some of whom developed theories that were far ahead of their times and who did not benefit from seeing their work validated. This technique is effective rhetorically, because it helps us understand the struggles of scientists on a human level. We feel sympathy for Vera Rubin, for example, who grew up wanting to be an astrophysicist and whose dreams were almost shattered by male scientists who tried to discourage her. Kaku gives insight into her struggles and demonstrates that much of what she thought was true has been borne out in contemporary observations. Kaku describes a number of other scientists who came up with "crazy" early theories, again helping us see the human side of the story.

The most important aspect of this essay's rhetoric involves the explanation of complex theories in terms that readers can grasp easily. Although we will not leave this essay with a full understanding of the complexities of dark matter, we will at least understand the problems that physicists face in trying to both describe how the universe works and postulate the existence of a kind of matter that seems to defy all common sense.

PREREADING QUESTIONS: WHAT TO READ FOR

The following prereading questions may help you anticipate key issues in the discussion on Michio Kaku's "The Mystery of Dark Matter." Keeping them in mind during your first reading of the selection should help focus your reactions.

- Why do physicists call it "dark matter"?
- What evidence tells us dark matter exists?
- What are the primary forces in the universe?

The Mystery of Dark Matter

With the cancellation of the SSC,[1] some commentators have   1
publicly speculated that physics will "come to an end." Promising
ideas such as the superstring theory, no matter how compelling and
elegant, will never be tested and, hence, can never be verified. Physicists, however, are optimists. If evidence for the superstring theory
cannot be found on the earth, then one solution is to leave the earth
and go into outer space. Over the coming years, physicists will rely
increasingly on cosmology to probe the inner secrets of matter and
energy. Their laboratory will be the cosmos and the Big Bang itself.

Already, cosmology has given us several mysteries that may very   2
well provide clues to the ultimate nature of matter. The first is dark
matter, which makes up 90 percent of the universe. And the second
is cosmic strings.

What Is the World Made Of?

One of the greatest achievements of twentieth-century science   3
was the determination of the chemical elements of the universe.
With only a little over one hundred elements, scientists could explain the trillions upon trillions of possible forms of matter, from
DNA to animals to exploding stars. The familiar elements that made
up the earth — such as carbon, oxygen, and iron — were the same as
the elements making up the distant galaxies. Analyzing the light
taken from blazing stars billions of light-years from our galaxy, scientists found precisely the same familiar elements found in our own
backyards, no more, no less.

Indeed, no new mysterious elements were found anywhere in   4
the universe. The universe was made of atoms and their subatomic
constituents. That was the final word in physics.

---

[1] **SSC** An acronym for Superconducting Super Collider, a huge cyclotron designed to test the string theory of matter. It was canceled by the U.S. government in
1993.

But by the late twentieth century, an avalanche of new data has 5
confirmed that over 90 percent of the universe is made of an invisible form of unknown matter, or dark matter. The stars we see in the
heavens, in fact, are now known to make up only a tiny fraction of
the real mass of the universe.

Dark matter is a strange substance, unlike anything ever en- 6
countered before. It has weight but cannot be seen. In theory, if
someone held a clump of dark matter in their hand, it would appear
totally invisible. The existence of dark matter is not an academic
question, because the ultimate fate of the universe, whether it will
die in a fiery Big Crunch or fade away in a Cosmic Whimper or Big
Chill, depends on its precise nature.

High-mass subatomic vibrations predicted by the superstring 7
theory are a leading candidate for dark matter. Thus, dark matter
may give us an experimental clue to probe the nature of the superstring. Even without the SSC, science may be able to explore the
new physics beyond the Standard Model.

How Much Does a Galaxy Weigh?

The scientist who first suspected that there was something 8
wrong about our conception of the universe was Fritz Zwicky,[2] a
Swiss-American astronomer at the California Institute of Technology. In the 1930s, he was studying the Coma cluster of galaxies,
about 300 million light-years away, and was puzzled by the fact that
they were revolving about each other so fast that they should be unstable. To confirm his suspicions, he had to calculate the mass of a
galaxy. Since galaxies can contain hundreds of billion stars, calculat-
ing their weight is a tricky question.

There are two simple ways of making this determination. The 9
fact that these two methods gave startlingly different results has created the present crisis in cosmology.

First, we can count the stars. This may seem like an impossible 10
task, but it's really quite simple. We know the rough average density
of the galaxy, and then we multiply by the total volume of the
galaxy. (That's how, for example, we calculate the number of hairs
on the human head, and how we determine that blondes have fewer
hairs than brunettes.)

Furthermore, we know the average weight of the stars. Of 11
course, no one actually puts a star on a scale. Astronomers instead

---

[2]**Fritz Zwicky (1898–1974)** A Swiss-American astronomer who studied
super novas (huge exploding stars) in distant galaxies.

look for binary star systems, where two stars rotate around each other. Once we know the time it takes for a complete rotation, Newton's laws are then sufficient to determine the mass of each star. By multiplying the number of stars in a galaxy by the average weight of each star, we get a rough number for the weight of the galaxy.

The second method is to apply Newton's laws directly on the   12
galaxy. Distant stars on a spiral arm of the galaxy, for example, orbit around the galactic center at different rates. Furthermore, galaxies and clusters of stars rotate around each other. Once we know the time it takes for these various revolutions, we can then determine the total mass of the galaxy using Newton's laws of motion.

Zwicky calculated the mass necessary to bind this cluster of   13
galaxies by analyzing the rate at which they orbited around each other. He found that this mass was twenty times greater than the actual mass of the luminous stars. In a Swiss journal, Zwicky reported that there was a fundamental discrepancy between these two results. He postulated that there had to be some form of mysterious "dunkle Materie," or dark matter, whose gravitational pull held this galactic cluster together. Without this dark matter, the Coma galaxies should fly apart.

Zwicky was led to postulate the existence of dark matter be-   14
cause of his unshakable belief that Newton's laws were correct out to galactic distances. (This is not the first time that scientists predicted the presence of unseen objects based on faith in Newton's laws. The planets Neptune and Pluto, in fact, were discovered because the orbit of closer planets, such as Saturn, wobbled and deviated from Newton's predictions. Rather than give up Newton's laws, scientists simply predicted the existence of new outer planets.)

However, Zwicky's results were met with indifference, even   15
hostility, by the astronomical community. After all, the very existence of galaxies beyond our own Milky Way galaxy had been determined only nine years before by Edwin Hubble, so most astronomers were convinced that his results were premature, that eventually they would fade away as better, more precise observations were made.

So Zwicky's results were largely ignored. Over the years, as-   16
tronomers accidentally rediscovered them but dismissed them as an aberration. In the 1970s, for example, astronomers using radio telescopes analyzed the hydrogen gas surrounding a galaxy and found that it rotated much faster than it should have, but discounted the result.

In 1973, Jeremiah Ostriker and James Peebles at Princeton Uni-   17
versity resurrected this theory by making rigorous theoretical calculations about the stability of a galaxy. Up to that time, most as-

tronomers thought that a galaxy was very much like our solar system, with the inner planets traveling much faster than the outer planets. Mercury, for example, was named after the Greek god for speed since it raced across the heavens (traveling at 107,000 miles per hour). Pluto, on the other hand, lumbers across the solar system at 10,500 miles per hour. If Pluto traveled around the sun as fast as Mercury, then it would quickly fly into outer space, never to return. The gravitational pull of the sun would not be enough to hold on to Pluto.

However, Ostriker and Peebles showed that the standard picture of a galaxy, based on our solar system, was unstable; by rights, the galaxy should fly apart. The gravitational pull of the stars was not enough to hold the galaxy together. They then showed that a galaxy can become stable if it is surrounded by a massive invisible halo that holds the galaxy together and if 90 percent of its mass was actually in the halo in the form of dark matter. Their paper was also met with indifference. 18

But after decades of skepticism and derision, what finally turned the tide on dark matter was the careful, persistent results of astronomer Vera Rubin and her colleagues at the Carnegie Institution in Washington, D.C. The results of these scientists, who analyzed hundreds of galaxies, verified conclusively that the velocity of the outer stars in a galaxy did not vary much from that of the inner ones, contrary to the planets in our solar system. This meant that the outer stars should fly into space, causing the galaxy to disintegrate into billions of individual stars, unless held together by the gravitational pull of invisible dark matter. 19

Like the history of dark matter itself, it took several decades for Vera Rubin's lifetime of results to be recognized by the skeptical (and overwhelmingly male) astronomical community. 20

One Woman's Challenge

It has never been easy for a female scientist to be accepted by her male peers. In fact, at every step of the way, Dr. Rubin's career came perilously close to being derailed by male hostility. She first became interested in the stars in the 1930s as a ten-year-old child, gazing at the night sky over Washington, D.C., for hours at a time, even making detailed maps of meteor trails across the heavens. 21

Her father, an electrical engineer, encouraged her to pursue her interest in the stars, even helping her build her first telescope at the age of fourteen and taking her to amateur astronomy meetings in Washington. However, the warm encouragement she felt inside her 22 family contrasted sharply with the icy reception she received from the outside world.

When she applied to Swarthmore College, the admissions offi- 23 cer tried to steer her away from astronomy, to a more "ladylike" career of painting astronomical subjects. That became a standard joke around her family. She recalled, "Whenever anything went wrong for me at work, someone would say, 'Have you ever thought of a career in which you paint? . . .'"[3]

When accepted at Vassar, she proudly told her high school 24 physics teacher in the hallway, who replied bluntly, "You'll do all right as long as you stay away from science." (Years later, she recalled, "It takes an enormous amount of self-esteem to listen to things like that and not be demolished.")[4]

After graduating from Vassar, she applied to graduate school at 25 Princeton, which had a world-renowned reputation in astronomy. However, she never even received the school's catalog, since Princeton did not accept female graduate students in astronomy until 1971.

She was accepted at Harvard, but declined the offer because she 26 had just gotten married to Robert Rubin, a physical chemist, and followed him to Cornell University, where the astronomy department consisted of just two faculty members. (After she declined, she got a formal letter back from Harvard, with the handwritten words scrawled on the bottom, "Damn you women. Every time I get a good one ready, she goes off and gets married.")[5]

Going to Cornell, however, was a blessing in disguise, since 27 Rubin took graduate courses in physics from two Nobel laureates in physics, Hans Bethe, who decoded the complex fusion reactions which energize the stars, and Richard Feynman, who renormalized quantum electrodynamics. Her master's thesis met head-on the hostility of a male-dominated world. Her paper, which showed that the faraway galaxies deviated from the uniform expansion of a simplified version of the Big Bang model, was rejected for publication because it was too far-fetched for its time. (Decades later, her paper would be considered prophetic.)

But after receiving her master's degree from Cornell, Rubin 28 found herself an unhappy housewife. "I actually cried every time the *Astrophysical Journal* came into the house . . . nothing in my educa-

[3]Marcia Bartusiak, *Discover* (October 1990): 89. [Kaku's note]
[4]Alan Lightman and Roberta Brawer, *Origins: The Lives and Worlds of Modern Cosmologists* (Cambridge: Harvard University Press, 1990), 305. [Kaku's note]
[5]*Ibid.*, 288. [Kaku's note]

tion had taught me that one year after Cornell my husband would be out doing his science and I would be home changing diapers."[6]

Nonetheless, Rubin struggled to pursue her childhood dream, 29 especially after her husband took a job in Washington. Taking night-time classes, she received her Ph.D. from Georgetown University. In 1954, she published her Ph.D. thesis, a landmark study that showed that the distribution of the galaxies in the heavens was not smooth and uniform, as previously thought, but actually clumpy.

Unfortunately, she was years ahead of her time. Over the years, 30 she gained a reputation of being something of an eccentric, going against the prevailing prejudice of astronomical thought. It would take years for her ideas to gain the recognition they deserved.

Distressed by the controversy her work was generating, Rubin 31 decided to take a respite and study one of the most mundane and unglamorous areas of astronomy, the rotation of galaxies. Innocently enough, Rubin began studying the Andromeda galaxy, our nearest neighbor in space. She and her colleagues expected to find that the gas swirling in the outer fringes of the Andromeda galaxy was travel-ing much slower than the gas near the center. Like our own solar system, the speed of the gas should slow down as one went farther from the galactic nuclei.

Much to their surprise, they found that the velocity of the gas 32 was a constant, whether it was near the center or near the rim of the galaxy. At first, they thought this peculiar result was unique to the Andromeda galaxy. Then they systematically began to analyze hun-dreds of galaxies (two hundred galaxies since 1978) and found the same curious result. Zwicky had been right all along.

The sheer weight of their observational results could not be de- 33 nied. Galaxy after galaxy showed the same, flat curve. Because as-tronomy had become technically much more sophisticated since the time of Zwicky, it was possible for other laboratories to verify Rubin's numbers rapidly. The constancy of velocity of a rotating galaxy was now a universal fact of galactic physics. Dark matter was here to stay.

For her pioneering efforts, Vera Rubin was elected to the presti- 34 gious National Academy of Science in 1981. (Since it was founded in 1863, only 75 women among the 3,508 scientists have been elected to the academy.)

Today, Rubin is still pained by how little progress female scien- 35 tists have made. Her own daughter has a Ph.D. in cosmic ray physics. When she went to Japan for an international conference,

---

[6]Bartusiak, *Discover*, 90. {Kaku's note}

she was the only woman there. "I really couldn't tell that story for a long time without weeping," Rubin recalled, "because certainly in one generation, between her generation and mine, not an awful lot has changed."[7]

Not surprisingly, Rubin is interested in stimulating the interest 36 of young girls to pursue scientific studies. She has even written a children's book, entitled *My Grandmother Is an Astronomer.*

Bending Starlight

Since Rubin's original paper, even more sophisticated analyses of 37 the universe have shown the existence of the dark matter halo, which may be as much as six times the size of the galaxy itself. In 1986, Bodhan Paczynski of Princeton University realized that if the starlight from a distant star traveled by a nearby clump of dark matter, the dark matter might bend the starlight and act as a magnifying lens, making the star appear much brighter. In this way, by looking for dim stars that suddenly got brighter, the presence of dark matter could be detected. In 1994, two groups independently reported photographing such a stellar brightening. Since then, other teams of astronomers have joined in, hoping to find more examples of stellar brightening.

In addition, the bending of starlight by a distant galaxy can be 38 used as another way in which to calculate the galaxy's weight. Anthony Tyson and his colleagues at the AT&T Bell Laboratories have analyzed light rays from dim blue galaxies at the rim of the visible universe. This cluster of galaxies acts like a gravitational lens, bending the light from other galaxies. Photos of distant galaxies have confirmed that the bending is much more than expected, meaning that their weight comes from much more than the sum of their individual stars. Ninety percent of the mass of these galaxies turns out to be dark, as predicted.

Hot and Cold Dark Matter

While the existence of dark matter is no longer in dispute, its 39 composition is a matter of lively controversy. Several schools of thought have emerged, none of them very satisfactory.

First, there is the "hot dark matter" school, which holds that 40 dark matter is made of familiar lightweight subparticles such as

---

[7]Lightman, *Origins,* 305. [Kaku's note]

neutrinos, which are notoriously difficult to detect. Since the total flux of neutrinos filling up the universe is not well known, the universe may be bathed in a flood of neutrinos, making up the dark matter of the universe.

If the electron-neutrino, for example, is found to have a tiny   41 mass, then there is a chance that it may have enough mass to make up the missing mass problem. (In February 1995, physicists at the Los Alamos National Laboratory in New Mexico announced that they had found evidence that the electron-neutrino has a tiny mass: one-millionth the weight of an electron. However, this result must still be verified by other laboratories before it is finally accepted by other physicists.)

Then there is the "cold dark matter" school, which suspects that   42 dark matter is made of heavier, slow-moving, and much more exotic subparticles. For the past decade, physicists have been looking for exotic candidates that might make up cold dark matter. These particles have been given strange, whimsical names, such as "axions," named after a household detergent. Collectively, they are called WIMPs, for "weakly interacting massive particles." (The skeptics have retaliated by pointing out that a significant part of dark matter may consist of familiar but dim forms of ordinary matter, such as red dwarf stars, neutron stars, black holes, and Jupiter-sized planets. Not to be outdone, they have called these objects MACHOs, for "massive astrophysical compact halo objects." However, even the proponents of MACHOs admit that, at best, they can explain only 20 percent of the dark matter problem. In late 1994, however, a version of the MACHO theory was dealt a blow when the Hubble Space Telescope, scanning the Milky Way galaxy for red dwarf stars, found far fewer of these dim stars than expected.)

But perhaps the most promising candidate for WIMPs are the   43 super particles, or "sparticles" for short. Supersymmetry,[8] we remember, was first seen as a symmetry of particle physics in the superstring theory. Indeed, the superstring is probably the only fully consistent theory of superparticles.

According to supersymmetry, every particle must have a super-   44 partner, with differing spin. The leptons (electrons and neutrinos)

---

[8]**Supersymmetry** A mathematical theory that postulates the existence of a "superpartner" for each physical particle discovered. Every particle has a spin and its superparticle has a spin, sometimes the same, sometimes different. All particles are either fermions (electrons, etc.) with a spin of $\frac{1}{2}$ or bosons (photons, etc.) with spins from 0 to 2. Mathematical models match them with superpartners that can sometimes convert bosons into fermions. Fermions are the particles that make up all the material world. Bosons make up gravity and light.

for example, have spin $\frac{1}{2}$. Their superpartners are called "sleptons" and have spin 0. Likewise, the superpartners of the quarks are called "squarks" and also have spin 0.

Furthermore, the superpartner of the spin I photon (which de- 45 scribes light) is called the "photino." And the superpartner of the gluons (which holds the quarks together) is called "gluino."

The main criticism of sparticles is that we have never seen them 46 in the laboratory. At present, there is no evidence that these super-particles exist. However, it is widely believed that this lack of evidence is only because our atom smashers are too feeble to create su-perparticles. In other words, their mass is simply too large for our atom smashers to produce them.

Lack of concrete evidence has not, however, prevented physi- 47 cists from trying to use particle physics to explain the mysteries of dark matter and cosmology. For example, one of the leading candi-dates for the WIMP is the photino.

The cancellation of the SSC, therefore, does not necessarily doom 48 our attempts to verify the correctness of the superstring. Within the next decade, it is hoped that the increased accuracy of our astronomi-cal observations, with the deployment of a new generation of tele-scopes and satellites, may narrow down the candidates for dark matter. If dark matter turns out to be composed, at least in part, of sparticles, belief in the superstring theory would receive an enormous boost.

How Will the Universe Die?

Last, dark matter may prove decisive in understanding the ulti- 49 mate fate of the universe. One persistent controversy has been the fate of an expanding universe. Some believe that there is enough matter and gravity to reverse its expansion. Others believe that the universe is too low in density, so that the galaxies will continue their expansion, until temperatures around the universe approach ab-solute zero.

At present, attempts to calculate the average density of the uni- 50 verse show the latter to be true: The universe will die in a Cosmic Whimper or a Big Chill, expanding forever. However, this theory is open to experimental challenges. Specifically, there might be enough missing matter to boost the average density of the universe.

To determine the fate of the universe, cosmologists use the para- 51 meter called "omega," which measures the matter density of the uni-verse. If omega is greater than one, then there is enough matter in the universe to reverse the cosmic expansion, and the universe will begin to collapse until it reaches the Big Crunch.

However, if omega is less than one, then the gravity of the universe is too weak to change the cosmic expansion, and the universe will expand forever, until it reaches the near-absolute-zero temperatures of the Cosmic Whimper. If omega is equal to one, then the universe is balanced between these two scenarios, and the universe will appear to be perfectly flat, without any curvature. (For omega to equal one, the density of the universe must be approximately three hydrogen atoms per cubic meter.) Current astronomical data favors a value of .1 for omega, which is too small to reverse the cosmic expansion.

The leading modification of the Big Bang theory is the inflationary universe, which predicts a value of omega of precisely 1. However, the visible stars in the heavens only give us 1 percent of the critical density. This is sometimes called the "missing mass" problem. (It is different from the dark matter problem, which was based on purely galactic considerations.) Dust, brown dwarfs, and nonluminous stars may boost this number a bit, but not by much. For example, the results from nucleosynthesis show that the maximum value of the density of this form of nonluminous matter cannot exceed 15 percent of the critical density.

Even if we add in the dark matter halos that surround the galaxies, this only brings us up to 10 percent of the critical value. So the dark matter in halos cannot solve the missing mass problem by itself. . . .

QUESTIONS FOR CRITICAL READING

1. What is the Big Bang?
2. What are the qualities of dark matter? Why is it a "problem"?
3. How will cosmology help physicists understand more about "the inner secrets of matter and energy" (para. 1)?
4. When did scientists begin to notice "that there was something wrong about our conception of the universe" (para. 8)?
5. How do scientists count the stars?
6. What would make a galaxy like ours unstable enough to fly apart? (See paras. 17–18.)
7. Which aspects of Kaku's thinking most defy common sense?

SUGGESTIONS FOR WRITING

1. In two pages, try to explain the nature of dark matter and the problems associated with it to a friend who has not read the Kaku article and who does not have a technical background.

2. Why is it important to know how the universe will end? Which theory is more compelling, the Big Crunch or the Big Chill? Do your best to represent your view as the most likely view.

3. Michio Kaku has written in both *Beyond Einstein* and *Hyperspace* about the superstring theory, which insists that at the heart of the atom is not a hard particle but a vibrating string of energy. Consult either of those books (or other discussions of the theory) and explain it in clear terms so that your classmates will understand it. What is your view of the likelihood of such a theory being accurate?

4. After conducting a search on the Internet for information on black holes, construct an essay that clarifies the nature of the black hole. Try to integrate this information with Kaku's theories about the ways in which a study of the cosmos will contribute to an understanding of the atom's inner workings. How does the behavior of black holes defy common sense? How does it help us understand the nature of the universe?

5. Kaku discusses the decision to abandon the superconducting super collider (SSC) in 1993. Do a search in both popular and scientific journals for a discussion of the promise and purpose of the SSC. Write an essay describing the reasons the SSC was originally planned and its construction begun, as well as the reasons why it was abandoned. Do you think it was a wise decision to give up on the SSC? Are you as optimistic as Kaku regarding the possibility of high-level research continuing despite the SCC's cancellation?

6. **CONNECTIONS**   In his essay "The Relation of Science and Religion," Richard Feynman touches on issues of belief that are very sensitive in contemporary culture. In "The General Nature of Consciousness," Francis Crick talks about the possibility of serious conflicts arising between science and religion. Judging from the two writers' positions, do you feel that the work of Michio Kaku raises serious problems for people who adhere to religious views? What apparent or real sources of conflict do you see as worth examining in depth? How would you resolve the conflict?

7. **CONNECTIONS**   How does Plato's "Allegory of the Cave" prepare us for reading the work of Kaku? What does Plato say about the human mind that has special relevance to Kaku's theories? In what ways would the four idols of Francis Bacon come into play in our efforts to make sense of the theories of physics that Kaku discusses?

RICHARD P. FEYNMAN
The Relation of Science and Religion

RICHARD PHILLIPS FEYNMAN (1918–1988), one of the most impressive and colorful physicists of his age, was generally acknowledged as a genius among geniuses. His research and mathematical formulas thoroughly revised the modern theories of quantum electrodynamics. In fact, he was granted the Nobel Prize in Physics in 1965 for his work in this field.

Born and raised in Far Rockaway, New York, the descendant of Russian and Polish Jews, Feynman received his bachelor's degree at the Massachusetts Institute of Technology in 1939 and his doctorate in theoretical physics at Princeton University in 1942. His work on quantum mechanics at both universities was far-reaching and influential on other researchers. During World War II, Feynman worked on the Manhattan Project, which developed the atomic bomb, and was present at the detonation of the first bomb on July 16, 1945, at Alamogordo, New Mexico. His reaction was mixed; he was thrilled to see that his theories actually worked, but at the same time he was fearful about the bomb's ultimate use.

After the war Feynman worked at Cornell University as associate professor, then moved to the California Institute of Technology in 1950. He remained at Cal Tech for the rest of his career. Because he was a charismatic man with a great sense of adventure and humor, stories of Feynman's brilliance and wit entertained many scientists for years. He wrote two books of interesting personal experiences, *"Surely You're Joking, Mr. Feynman": Adventures of a Curious Character* (1985) and *"What Do You Care What Other People Think?": Further Adventures of a Curious Character* (1988), which both became best-sellers. Another best-seller, *The Pleasure of Finding Things Out* (1999), in which the following essay appears, is a

From *The Pleasure of Finding Things Out.*

collection of his talks and essays that were originally published in magazines. Some of these pieces, especially his essay on miniaturization, "There's Plenty of Room at the Bottom," have proved prophetic.

One of Feynman's most impressive moments came during the investigation of the space shuttle *Challenger*'s explosion in 1986. The *Challenger* was launched in Florida on an unusually cold morning. It exploded moments after liftoff, killing all the astronauts on board. During hearings about the *Challenger* tragedy, Feynman took a piece of the rubber from the O-ring that sealed one of the stages of the booster rocket and dipped it into his ice water. With a flourish, he removed it and showed that the effect of sudden temperature change would have caused the O-ring to crack and fail. By this means, he uncovered the cause of the disaster.

"The Relation of Science and Religion" is an unusual essay for Feynman. Most of his popular writing centers on his adventures in science and his experiences with very colorful scientists and friends. Books of his technical writing (such as *The Feynman Lectures on Physics; Quantum Electrodynamics;* and *Theory of Fundamental Processes*) are demanding, serious texts designed for students of physics. They are also very practical, centering on concrete phenomena and events. By contrast, "The Relation of Science and Religion" is much more abstract and general. In writing about this topic, Feynman cannot point to specific phenomena and analyze them. However, he realizes that the uneasy relationship between science and religion is always relevant to people interested in the way nature works and the way the concept of God should be addressed.

Feynman is careful to make no absolute claims in the essay. Part of his point is that a good scientist is by nature first curious and second skeptical. Skeptics doubt not only what they are told but also what they see. Doubt is at the center of all scientific inquiry, according to Feynman. In the area of religion, faith and belief are at the center of experience. Therefore, there is a natural incompatibility in the way the mind works in scientific and religious areas. However, Feynman also points out that many scientists hold to religion and a belief in God. He does not argue that science and religion are incompatible, nor does he say that scientists are uniformly atheists. Yet he does observe that there have always been conflicts between science and religion. He points to the Middle Ages, for example, when people thought the world was flat, and to the early Renaissance, when the Western church believed the earth was the center of the universe. Both beliefs were proved false, but religion, Feynman reminds us, did not suffer by yielding to science on these issues.

Feynman goes on to mention one of the current conflicts between science and religion: the question of whether human beings are descended from animals. As a scientist, Feynman sides with Darwin and the evolutionists. He also implies that he expects religion to yield on this point at some time in the future without doing harm to the essentials of religious understanding.

Religion promotes specific moral values, and the discoveries of science do not affect moral values or behavior, according to Feynman. Ethics are not disturbed by a change in believing whether the earth is (1) the center of the universe or (2) peripheral to a galaxy that is itself only one of billions. As Feynman says, "there is no scientific evidence bearing on the Golden Rule" (para. 37). Thus, science will not change the basic moral structure of religion. By the same token, the inspirational values of religion, which Feynman sees as deeply important, are not affected by scientific discovery.

Feynman's Rhetoric

This essay was originally written for the California Institute of Technology's magazine, *Engineering and Science*. Feynman's original audience comprised mostly scientists and technicians, which is why he begins by talking about how specialists "who thoroughly know one field are often incompetent to discuss another" (para. 1). Yet his writing style is designed to communicate with the generally literate person, regardless of background. He explains that he has been interested in the relationship between science and religion for some time and manages to give the impression that he, like his audience, is searching for the answers to questions that puzzle most scientists.

He begins with an unusual strategy, imagining that he will "discuss the problem from various sides, like a panel" (para. 2). In an actual panel discussion several participants would take part, usually supporting specific positions on the issue. Not only does Feynman go so far as to play all the parts on his hypothetical panel, but he goes one step further by imagining that "someone has been chosen by lot to be the first to present his views, and I am he so chosen." This strategy puts the audience on a par with the writer. Feynman explains that his job is to go first and to express his views as only one of many.

This rhetorical strategy enables Feynman to avoid posing an argument in favor of either science or religion—an approach that would surely alienate part of his audience. Further, because he knows that most readers will not be moved by an argument, no matter how powerful, he avoids giving the impression that he is arguing. His audience would gladly listen to members of a panel discussing such an interesting subject, even if they did not agree with individual speakers. Thus, he tries to "guarantee" that his audience will at least read what he has to say.

Early in the essay, Feynman poses the problem of the student who studies science and then abandons the religion of his father (para. 3). Feynman asks the rhetorical question "Why does this young man come to disbelieve?" In response to this question, posed to anticipate those of his audience, he suggests one extreme answer: scientists . . . "are all atheists at heart" (para. 5). However, this answer is not offered seriously; Feynman suggests this response only to discount it (in fact, many scientists are strong believers in religion). As Feynman offers a number of other answers, we begin to see his strategy: none of the answers is sufficient to answer the question. Yet all the answers make sense; they are probably the same ones his audience would propose. The ultimate result of this strategy is to defuse any antagonists and open the question, on the basis of its complexity, to a wide range of possibilities.

Like Francis Bacon and other competent rhetoricians, Feynman also uses the technique of enumeration. For instance, he enumerates the answers to his rhetorical question. He then enumerates the attributes of religion that he feels will be unaffected by science: its metaphysical qualities involving knowledge of God, its moral basis, and its power of inspiration. He discusses these characteristics one after another, usually enumerating three items, the most common method among writers.

Because Feynman has a personal position but does not present it as an outright argument, he implies that like his audience, he is searching for answers. This unites Feynman with his audience, helping his readers — regardless of their personal convictions — consider the question of science and religion with an open mind and a curiosity similar to his own.

PREREADING QUESTIONS:
WHAT TO READ FOR

The following prereading questions may help you anticipate key issues in the discussion on Richard Feynman's "The Relation of Science and Religion." Keeping them in mind during your first reading of the selection should help focus your reactions.

- How does the scientific point of view differ from the religious point of view?

- What effect does science have on moral questions?

- In what sense are science and religion two pillars of Western culture?

The Relation of Science and Religion

In this age of specialization, men who thoroughly know one field are often incompetent to discuss another. The great problems of the relations between one and another aspect of human activity have for this reason been discussed less and less in public. When we look at the past great debates on these subjects, we feel jealous of those times, for we should have liked the excitement of such argument. The old problems, such as the relation of science and religion, are still with us, and I believe present as difficult dilemmas as ever, but they are not often publicly discussed because of the limitations of specialization. 1

But I have been interested in this problem for a long time and would like to discuss it. In view of my very evident lack of knowledge and understanding of religion (a lack which will grow more apparent as we proceed), I will organize the discussion in this way: I will suppose that not one man but a group of men are discussing the problem, that the group consists of specialists in many fields—the various sciences, the various religions and so on—and that we are going to discuss the problem from various sides, like a panel. Each is to give his point of view, which may be molded and modified by the later discussion. Further, I imagine that someone has been chosen by lot to be the first to present his views, and I am he so chosen. 2

I would start by presenting the panel with a problem: A young man, brought up in a religious family, studies a science, and as a result he comes to doubt—and perhaps later to disbelieve in—his father's God. Now, this is not an isolated example; it happens time and time again. Although I have no statistics on this, I believe that many scientists—in fact, I actually believe that more than half of the scientists—really disbelieve in their father's God; that is, they don't believe in a God in a conventional sense. 3

Now, since the belief in a God is a central feature of religion, this problem that I have selected points up most strongly the problem of the relation of science and religion. Why does this young man come to disbelieve? 4

The first answer we might hear is very simple: You see, he is 5
taught by scientists, and (as I have just pointed out) they are all
atheists at heart, so the evil is spread from one to another. But if you
can entertain this view, I think you know less of science than I know
of religion.

Another answer may be that a little knowledge is dangerous; 6
this young man has learned a little bit and thinks he knows it all,
but soon he will grow out of this sophomoric sophistication and
come to realize that the world is more complicated, and he will
begin again to understand that there must be a God.

I don't think it is necessary that he come out of it. There are 7
many scientists—men who hope to call themselves mature—who
still don't believe in God. In fact, as I would like to explain later, the
answer is not that the young man thinks he knows it all—it is the
exact opposite.

A third answer you might get is that this young man really 8
doesn't understand science correctly. I do not believe that science
can disprove the existence of God; I think that is impossible. And if
it is impossible, is not a belief in science and in a God—an ordinary
God of religion—a consistent possibility?

Yes, it is consistent. Despite the fact that I said that more than 9
half of the scientists don't believe in God, many scientists *do* believe
in both science and God, in a perfectly consistent way. But this consistency, although possible, is not easy to attain, and I would like to
try to discuss two things: why it is not easy to attain, and whether it
is worth attempting to attain it.

When I say "believe in God," of course, it is always a puzzle— 10
what is God? What I mean is the kind of personal God, characteristic of the Western religions, to whom you pray and who has something to do with creating the universe and guiding you in morals.

For the student, when he learns about science, there are two 11
sources of difficulty in trying to weld science and religion together.
The first source of difficulty is this—that it is imperative in science
to doubt; it is absolutely necessary, for progress in science, to have
uncertainty as a fundamental part of your inner nature. To make
progress in understanding, we must remain modest and allow that
we do not know. Nothing is certain or proved beyond all doubt.
You investigate for curiosity, because it is *unknown,* not because you
know the answer. And as you develop more information in the sciences, it is not that you are finding out the truth, but that you are
finding out that this or that is more or less likely.

That is, if we investigate further, we find that the statements of 12
science are not of what is true and what is not true, but statements
of what is known to different degrees of certainty: "It is very much

more likely that so and so is true than that it is not true"; or "such and such is almost certain but there is still a little bit of doubt"; or— at the other extreme—"well, we really don't know." Every one of the concepts of science is on a scale graduated somewhere between, but at neither end of, absolute falsity or absolute truth.

It is necessary, I believe, to accept this idea, not only for science,   13 but also for other things; it is of great value to acknowledge ignorance. It is a fact that when we make decisions in our life, we don't necessarily know that we are making them correctly; we only think that we are doing the best we can—and that is what we should do.

Attitude of Uncertainty

I think that when we know that we actually do live in uncer-   14 tainty, then we ought to admit it; it is of great value to realize that we do not know the answers to different questions. This attitude of mind—this attitude of uncertainty—is vital to the scientist, and it is this attitude of mind which the student must first acquire. It becomes a habit of thought. Once acquired, one cannot retreat from it anymore.

What happens, then, is that the young man begins to doubt   15 everything because he cannot have it as absolute truth. So the question changes a little bit from "Is there a God?" to "How sure is it that there is a God?" This very subtle change is a great stroke and represents a parting of the ways between science and religion. I do not believe a real scientist can ever believe in the same way again. Although there are scientists who believe in God, I do not believe that they think of God in the same way as religious people do. If they are consistent with their science, I think that they say something like this to themselves: "I am almost certain there is a God. The doubt is very small." That is quite different from saying, "I know that there is a God." I do not believe that a scientist can ever obtain that view— that really religious understanding, that real knowledge that there is a God—that absolute certainty which religious people have.

Of course this process of doubt does not always start by attack-   16 ing the question of the existence of God. Usually special tenets, such as the question of an afterlife, or details of the religious doctrine, such as details of Christ's life, come under scrutiny first. It is more interesting, however, to go right into the central problem in a frank way, and to discuss the more extreme view which doubts the existence of God.

Once the question has been removed from the absolute, and   17 gets to sliding on the scale of uncertainty, it may end up in very different positions. In many cases it comes out very close to being certain. But on the other hand, for some, the net result of close scrutiny of the theory his father held of God may be the claim that it is almost certainly wrong.

Belief in God — and the Facts of Science

That brings us to the second difficulty our student has in trying 18 to weld science and religion: Why does it often end up that the belief in God — at least, the God of the religious type — is considered to be very unreasonable, very unlikely? I think that the answer has to do with the scientific things — the facts or partial facts — that the man learns.

For instance, the size of the universe is very impressive, with us 19 on a tiny particle whirling around the sun, among a hundred thousand million suns in this galaxy, itself among a billion galaxies.

Again, there is the close relation of biological man to the ani- 20 mals, and of one form of life to another. Man is a latecomer in a vast evolving drama; can the rest be but a scaffolding for his creation?

Yet again, there are the atoms of which all appears to be con- 21 structed, following immutable laws. Nothing can escape it; the stars are made of the same stuff, and the animals are made of the same stuff, but in such complexity as to mysteriously appear alive — like man himself.

It is a great adventure to contemplate the universe beyond man, 22 to think of what it means without man — as it was for the great part of its long history, and as it is in the great majority of places. When this objective view is finally attained, and the mystery and majesty of matter are appreciated, to then turn the objective eye back on man viewed as matter, to see life as part of the universal mystery of greatest depth, is to sense an experience which is rarely described. It usually ends in laughter, delight in the futility of trying to understand. These scientific views end in awe and mystery, lost at the edge in uncertainty, but they appear to be so deep and so impressive that the theory that it is all arranged simply as a stage for God to watch man's struggle for good and evil seems to be inadequate.

So let us suppose that this is the case of our particular student, 23 and the conviction grows so that he believes that individual prayer, for example, is not heard. (I am not trying to disprove the reality of God; I am trying to give you some idea of — some sympathy for — the reasons why many come to think that prayer is meaningless.) Of course, as a result of this doubt, the pattern of doubting is turned next to ethical problems, because, in the religion which he learned, moral problems were connected with the word of God, and if the God doesn't exist, what is his word? But rather surprisingly, I think, the moral problems ultimately come out relatively unscathed; at first perhaps the student may decide that a few little things were wrong, but he often reverses his opinion later, and ends with no fundamentally different moral view.

There seems to be a kind of independence in these ideas. In the end, it is possible to doubt the divinity of Christ, and yet to believe firmly that it is a good thing to do unto your neighbor as you would have him do unto you. It is possible to have both these views at the same time; and I would say that I hope you will find that my atheistic scientific colleagues often carry themselves well in society. 24

Communism and the Scientific Viewpoint

I would like to remark, in passing, since the word "atheism" is so closely connected with "communism," that the communist views are the antithesis of the scientific, in the sense that in communism the answers are given to all the questions—political questions as well as moral ones—without discussion and without doubt. The scientific viewpoint is the exact opposite of this; that is, all questions must be doubted and discussed; we must argue everything out—observe things, check them, and so change them. The democratic government is much closer to this idea, because there is discussion and a chance of modification. One doesn't launch the ship in a definite direction. It is true that if you have a tyranny of ideas, so that you know exactly what has to be true, you act very decisively, and it looks good—for a while. But soon the ship is heading in the wrong direction, and no one can modify the direction anymore. So the uncertainties of life in a democracy are, I think, much more consistent with science. 25

Although science makes some impact on many religious ideas, it does not affect the moral content. Religion has many aspects; it answers all kinds of questions. First, for example, it answers questions about what things are, where they come from, what man is, what God is—the properties of God, and so on. Let me call this the metaphysical aspect of religion. It also tells us another thing—how to behave. Leave out of this the idea of how to behave in certain ceremonies, and what rites to perform; I mean it tells us how to behave in life in general, in a moral way. It gives answers to moral questions; it gives a moral and ethical code. Let me call this the ethical aspect of religion. 26

Now, we know that, even with moral values granted, human beings are very weak; they must be reminded of the moral values in 27 order that they may be able to follow their consciences. It is not simply a matter of having a right conscience; it is also a question of maintaining strength to do what you know is right. And it is necessary that religion give strength and comfort and the inspiration to follow these moral views. This is the inspirational aspect of religion. It gives inspiration not only for moral conduct—it gives inspiration for the arts and for all kinds of great thoughts and actions as well.

Interconnections

These three aspects of religion are interconnected, and it is generally felt, in view of this close integration of ideas, that to attack one feature of the system is to attack the whole structure. The three aspects are connected more or less as follows: The moral aspect, the moral code, is the word of God—which involves us in a metaphysical question. Then the inspiration comes because one is working the will of God; one is for God; partly one feels that one is with God. And this is a great inspiration because it brings one's actions in contact with the universe at large.   28

So these three things are very well interconnected. The difficulty is this: that science occasionally conflicts with the first of the three categories—the metaphysical aspect of religion. For instance, in the past there was an argument about whether the earth was the center of the universe—whether the earth moved around the sun or stayed still. The result of all this was a terrible strife and difficulty, but it was finally resolved—with religion retreating in this particular case. More recently there was a conflict over the question of whether man has animal ancestry.   29

The result in many of these situations is a retreat of the religious metaphysical view, but nevertheless, there is no collapse of the religion. And further, there seems to be no appreciable or fundamental change in the moral view.   30

After all, the earth moves around the sun—isn't it best to turn the other cheek? Does it make any difference whether the earth is standing still or moving around the sun? We can expect conflict again. Science is developing and new things will be found out which will be in disagreement with the present-day metaphysical theory of certain religions. In fact, even with all the past retreats of religion, there is still real conflict for particular individuals when they learn about the science and they have heard about the religion. The thing has not been integrated very well; there are real conflicts here—and yet morals are not affected.   31

As a matter of fact, the conflict is doubly difficult in this meta- 32
physical region. Firstly, the facts may be in conflict, but even if the
facts were not in conflict, the attitude is different. The spirit of uncertainty in science is an attitude toward the metaphysical questions
that is quite different from the certainty and faith that is demanded
in religion. There is definitely a conflict, I believe — both in fact and
in spirit — over the metaphysical aspects of religion.

In my opinion, it is not possible for religion to find a set of 33
metaphysical ideas which will be guaranteed not to get into conflicts
with an ever-advancing and always-changing science which is going
into an unknown. We don't know how to answer the questions; it is
impossible to find an answer which someday will not be found to be
wrong. The difficulty arises because science and religion are both
trying to answer questions in the same realm here.

Science and Moral Questions

On the other hand, I don't believe that a real conflict with sci- 34
ence will arise in the ethical aspect, because I believe that moral
questions are outside of the scientific realm.

Let me give three or four arguments to show why I believe this. 35
In the first place, there have been conflicts in the past between the
scientific and the religious view about the metaphysical aspect and,
nevertheless, the older moral views did not collapse, did not change.

Second, there are good men who practice Christian ethics and 36
who do not believe in the divinity of Christ. They find themselves in
no inconsistency here.

Thirdly, although I believe that from time to time scientific evi- 37
dence is found which may be partially interpreted as giving some
evidence of some particular aspect of the life of Christ, for example,
or of other religious metaphysical ideas, it seems to me that there is
no scientific evidence bearing on the Golden Rule. It seems to me
that that is somehow different.

Now, let's see if I can make a little philosophical explanation as 38
to why it is different — how science cannot affect the fundamental
basis of morals.

The typical human problem, and one whose answer religion 39
aims to supply, is always of the following form: Should I do this?
Should we do this? Should the government do this? To answer this
question we can resolve it into two parts: First — If I do this, what
will happen? — and second — Do I want that to happen? What
would come of it of value — of good?

Now a question of the form: If I do this, what will happen? is   40
strictly scientific. As a matter of fact, science can be defined as a
method for, and a body of information obtained by, trying to answer
only questions which can be put into the form: If I do this, what will
happen? The technique of it, fundamentally, is: Try it and see. Then
you put together a large amount of information from such experiences. All scientists will agree that a question—any question, philosophical or other—which cannot be put into the form that can be
tested by experiment (or, in simple terms, that cannot be put into
the form: If I do this, what will happen?) is not a scientific question;
it is outside the realm of science.

I claim that whether you want something to happen or not—   41
what value there is in the result, and how you judge the value of the
result (which is the other end of the question: Should I do this?),
must lie outside of science because it is not a question that you can
answer only by knowing what happens; you still have to *judge* what
happens—in a moral way. So, for this theoretical reason I think that
there is a complete consistency between the moral view—or the
ethical aspect of religion—and scientific information.

Turning to the third aspect of religion—the inspirational as-   42
pect—brings me to the central question that I would like to present
to this imaginary panel. The source of inspiration today—for
strength and for comfort—in any religion is very closely knit with
the metaphysical aspect; that is, the inspiration comes from working
for God, for obeying his will, feeling one with God. Emotional ties
to the moral code—based in this manner—begin to be severely
weakened when doubt, even a small amount of doubt, is expressed
as to the existence of God; so when the belief in God becomes uncertain, this particular method of obtaining inspiration fails.

I don't know the answer to this central problem—the problem   43
of maintaining the real value of religion, as a source of strength and
of courage to most men, while, at the same time, not requiring an
absolute faith in the metaphysical aspects.

The Heritages of Western Civilization

Western civilization, it seems to me, stands by two great her-   44
itages. One is the scientific spirit of adventure—the adventure into
the unknown, an unknown which must be recognized as being unknown in order to be explored; the demand that the unanswerable
mysteries of the universe remain unanswered; the attitude that all is
uncertain; to summarize it—the humility of the intellect. The other
great heritage is Christian ethics—the basis of action on love, the

brotherhood of all men, the value of the individual—the humility
of the spirit.

These two heritages are logically, thoroughly consistent. But 45
logic is not all; one needs one's heart to follow an idea. If people are
going back to religion, what are they going back to? Is the modern
church a place to give comfort to a man who doubts God—more,
one who disbelieves in God? Is the modern church a place to give
comfort and encouragement to the value of such doubts? So far,
have we not drawn strength and comfort to maintain the one or the
other of these consistent heritages in a way which attacks the values
of the other? Is this unavoidable? How can we draw inspiration to
support these two pillars of Western civilization so that they may
stand together in full vigor, mutually unafraid? Is this not the central
problem of our time?

I put it up to the panel for discussion. 46

QUESTIONS FOR CRITICAL READING

1. What is a scientific point of view? As a student, do you share it?
2. Is curiosity a threat to those who hold strong religious beliefs?
3. How well do you think Feynman's strategy of pretending to be part of a panel works?
4. When Feynman says that half of scientists "really disbelieve in their father's God" (para. 3), what does he mean?
5. Do you accept the proposition that a scientific point of view differs from a religious point of view? What are the consequences of accepting such a proposition?
6. Feynman talks of "the kind of personal God [that is] characteristic of the Western religions" (para. 10). What kind of God is that?
7. Feynman says many scientists "believe in both science and God, in a perfectly consistent way" (para. 9). How could that be possible? (See paras. 8–10.) Do you agree with Feynman on this point?

SUGGESTIONS FOR WRITING

1. Imagine that you are the next person on the panel to discuss the question that Feynman has addressed. He has focused our attention on a specific problem: "A young man, brought up in a religious family, studies a science, and as a result he comes to doubt—and perhaps later to disbelieve in—his father's God" (para. 3). Address this problem in your own terms, and discuss what you see to be the relation of science and religion.

2. Feynman says that one source of difficulty for the student of science when approaching religion is "that it is imperative in science to doubt" (para. 11). What is the effect of doubt on religion? Is doubt as healthy in religion as it is in science? Why might those who profess a strong religious belief fear doubt? Why might they welcome it? Is it possible that beginning with an attitude of doubt could produce a stronger religious faith rather than no faith at all?

3. In what ways can you imagine that science can be an aid to religion? If possible, consult newspaper or magazine files and see how often science has come to the aid of religion. (Some of the stories you may find will be concerned with establishing the validity of facts relevant to the Bible, such as the search for Noah's ark or the Ark of the Covenant, or the location of important sites mentioned in the Bible.)

4. Research the inquiry made on the Shroud of Turin, which is purported to be the shroud in which Christ's body was wrapped. It has an image of a crucified man inscribed on it in a manner that has remained a mystery. By searching for "the Shroud of Turin" on the Internet, you will find a number of sites and important bibliographic items that will help you understand the nature of the inquiry and its significance. Write an essay that brings us up-to-date on what is known about the Shroud and what was learned by the panel of experts that examined it.

5. Beginning in paragraph 18, Feynman explores the question of why the "belief in God" is "very unlikely" from a scientific point of view. Do you agree with him? Present a discussion that either confirms his view or suggests a reasonable alternative. Do you think Feynman believes what he says here, or is he offering it as a rhetorical hypothesis to be examined rather than accepted?

6. **CONNECTIONS**   Examine Feynman's views in this essay in relation to the excerpt from the Koran in Part VII. What is the position of the Prophet Muhammad on the question of belief? What is his position on the question of doubt? How might science fit into a belief system that holds to the views of the Prophet Muhammad? Could the revelation of God's signs (see para. 53 of the excerpt from the Koran) be observable in terms of science?

7. **CONNECTIONS**   How compatible are the views of Stephen Jay Gould with those of Feynman? Gould insists that nature is nonmoral. Feynman sees the emphasis on moral issues that confront us as one of religion's most important qualities. Is there a conflict between the two men's views? Would Gould side with Feynman on the question of the relation of science and religion? Would you assume from Gould's essay that he is among the scientists who hold a strong belief in religion?

PART SIX

AMERICAN CULTURE

Álvar Núñez Cabeza de Vaca
J. Hector St. John de Crèvecoeur
Alexis de Tocqueville
Harriet Jacobs (Linda Brent)
Frederick Jackson Turner
James Baldwin

INTRODUCTION

The complexities of American culture have interested thinkers since at least the time of Columbus's explorations in the fifteenth century. The influence of the New World upon the old has been the subject of innumerable books, just as the influence of Old World on the new was a given in the first decades after settlement began. However, the early commentators soon began to meditate on the development of a new kind of person, the American, who seemed quite unlike the original European settler in many ways. As the contact in a new environment with both Native Americans and African Americans transformed the landscape and the people, the concept of a recognizably unique American developed extraordinarily quickly.

One force at work in creating this new kind of person was political. The people who emigrated to America were neither royalty nor aristocracy. Rather, the majority of them felt both dispossessed and adventurous. They were risk takers and often even outcasts who were not always at home in their native countries. The concept of democracy, the seeds of which likely came with some of them, took root once these people reached American shores. Indeed, many settlers viewed each other as equals struggling for opportunity and a new beginning. The metaphor of rebirth has often been applied to the early growth of the American nation, and its appropriateness is apparent in the perception that all the immigrants were more or less in the same condition.

The most obvious exception to this description of the early American was the African slave; for more than three centuries, countless Africans were brought to the shores of America for the sole purpose of serving their owners. Because these slaves were regarded as chattel rather than as human beings, their status in America was the embodiment of inequality and discrimination—especially in comparison to those who came to seek their fortune voluntarily. The slavery issue in American culture haunted the nation for centuries. For example, Henry David Thoreau and other writers recognized the hypocrisy inherent in American ideals of equality during the nineteenth century, just as James Baldwin was aware of the painful inequities of the American dream during the twentieth. However, the interaction of Native American, African, and European transformed all three populations and made the inhabitants of America different forever.

Another force in shaping American culture was the landscape. Most important was the existence of huge tracts of essentially free land. There were no aristocratic landlords, as there had been in Europe, and consequently many Americans could hope to own the land they planted and plowed. The hunter and trapper had huge spaces through which to travel, just as the trader who worked with them covered extensive territory in the effort to sell guns, liquor, food, and other materials to the Native American, who traded with beaver, elk, bobcat, and bear. The mountains shaped their inhabitants much as did the prairies, the plains, and the high desert. Indeed, the expanse of the country and the lure of what might lie beyond the horizon helped shape Americans' imagination and sense of ambition.

Economic opportunity brought immigrants from all over the world. With opportunity relatively limited in Europe, the young and the ambitious crossed the Atlantic looking for the chance to make good. Young people sold themselves as indentured servants, committed to working in a trade for their master for seven years, after which they could go out on their own. For a time, this was one of the most common ways of settling in America. Miners, ranchers, and traders of all kinds found America a responsive environment for those with new ideas and plenty of energy. Some failed, but many succeeded.

Álvar Núñez Cabeza de Vaca came to Florida in the early 1500s, aboard a ship filled with Spanish adventurers anxious to find treasure and make their fortune. However, his fortune was to be shipwrecked and cast ashore, probably on what is now known as Galveston Island off the coast of Texas, where for a time he was made the slave of a Native American tribe called the Avavares. He lived with the Avavares for some eight years before he returned to a Spanish settlement. During that time he learned a great deal about the Avavares and their culture, ultimately earning their respect for his skills as a healer. The tradition of the *curandero* (the person who cures illnesses), may have begun with Cabeza de Vaca, although no one knows for sure. However, he talks about moving around the open country in what is now the state of Texas, trading goods and curing the sick. He was in considerable demand by Native Americans, who brought him to their sick and dying. In one instance he reports having brought a man he thought dead back to life through prayer. As Cabeza de Vaca's testimony in *La Relación* reveals, the earliest Spanish experiences in Texas were marked by hardship and endurance, but also by ingenuity and imagination.

J. Hector St. John de Crèvecoeur (who was also known as Michel-Guillaume Jean de Crèvecoeur) came to America in 1754 with French troops fighting against the English in Canada. After the war was lost, he moved through the Ohio Valley and into the area of present-day New York State and settled down with an American wife to farm fertile land. He became an American citizen in 1765 before the American Revolution. His *Letters from an American Farmer* were philosophical meditations that made him famous in both America and Europe. In one of these letters, Crèvecoeur broached the question "What Is an American?" and, in answering, began a lengthy meditation on the idea that Americans were somehow different from the men and women who had sailed from Europe to follow their dreams. In a sense, most of the later writers who took up the subject of America tried to answer the same question.

Alexis de Tocqueville was a French politician in the early years of the nineteenth century, after France tried to reconstruct its government in the wake of the French Revolution and the destruction of the French Republic under Napoleon Bonaparte. Tocqueville visited America for the express purpose of studying its prisons. However, when he returned to France he not only wrote about its prisons but also wrote *Democracy in America*, one of the most famous books about America's political system and the development of its democracy. Tocqueville has often been praised for the sensitivity of his responses to what he witnessed in America. His description of the conditions that led to the support and shaping of democracy in America have been instructive for future ages. Reflecting careful thought about politics in general, some of his views also proved prophetic of twentieth-century events. All his thought seems to reflect the dynamics of American democracy as he knew it.

The slavery experience in America was recorded eloquently by Frederick Douglass and numerous other former slaves, including Harriet Jacobs (whose pen name was Linda Brent). Even for those who did not face slavery directly, slave narratives like that of Jacobs resonate deep in the heart of the American experience. Decades before the Civil War and the Emancipation Proclamation, Harriet Jacobs ran away from her master. She ultimately became a free woman, but only after a benevolent employer in New York purchased her freedom from a threatening owner and slave hunter. As she tells us in "Free at Last," a chapter from her autobiography, *Incidents in the Life of a Slave Girl*, being treated like a commodity—to be bought and sold—humiliated her. In spite of the obvious benefits of freedom, she pleaded with her employer not to buy her freedom. However, once she had it, Jacobs used it to help relocate former slaves after the Civil War and to establish an organization similar to the NAACP (National Association for the Advancement of Colored People).

In the late nineteenth century, the historian Frederick Jackson Turner developed a thesis that the special qualities regarded as "American" were traceable primarily to the frontier experiences that marked the European move westward. The Frontier Thesis was enormously appealing to a number of historians in the early twentieth century. Even those who disagreed with him credited Turner by taking his thesis seriously enough to construct alternative views to it. For us, Turner's thesis demonstrates the power of cultural interaction during the early contact with Native Americans by trappers, miners, farmers, hunters, and other settlers. The frontier, Turner says, shaped American attitudes toward independence, democracy, and morality. His views have been challenged—especially for his cursory treatment or omission of factors such as the role of women, slavery, immigrants, Native Americans, and other minorities, to name a few—yet they continue to stimulate thinking about the shaping forces of America in the seventeenth, eighteenth, and nineteenth centuries.

Finally, the distinguished American writer James Baldwin, in the 1960s, put forth a prescient warning in his essay "The American Dream and the American Negro." On the eve of the assassinations of Robert Kennedy and Martin Luther King Jr., he reveals the limits of the prosperity and opportunity that were thought to belong to all Americans by right. African Americans, he explains, face several important disadvantages that make it all but impossible for them to thrive in America's atmosphere of racism and inequality. Baldwin's analysis of democracy and equality is at odds with that of other writers who see these ideals in action in very different ways. Baldwin called himself a Jeremiah, meaning a prophet, and his message foreshadowed the race riots of the late 1960s. The place of the African American in America was his subject, and much of what he had to say remains relevant today.

These essays cover a broad range of perspectives. Yet they all treat issues central to America's conception of itself. In one way or another they all ask the question "What Is an American?" Although their answers vary, together they give a complex portrait of an even more complex subject. Their diversity reflects the vitality and the contradictions that have always been part of the American fabric.

ÁLVAR NÚÑEZ CABEZA DE VACA
From *La Relación*

ÁLVAR NÚÑEZ CABEZA DE VACA (c. 1490–c. 1560) was born and died in Spain but is most famous for the years he spent as one of the first Europeans to explore the American Southwest. He was the treasurer for a three-hundred-man expedition that reached Tampa, Florida, in 1528. The party continued overland on foot and then in small boats along the coast. Several boats (including Cabeza de Vaca's) were shipwrecked, probably on what is now known as Galveston Island off of Texas, which he calls the Isle of Ill Fate. Most of the sixty or so survivors were enslaved by the Native Americans and died within a few years, but Cabeza de Vaca—along with his companions Castillo, Dorantes, and Estaban, an African slave—managed to escape inland and survive for eight years. They wandered through southern Texas and Mexico among nomadic groups for some six thousand miles until they eventually met up with Spaniards in a settlement on the Sinalo River in Mexico in 1536. Cabeza de Vaca wrote the story of his adventures shortly afterward, providing us with the earliest European descriptions of the manners of the Native Americans of the Southwest and offering us insights into the ways in which the cultures viewed each other.

The chapters of his *La Relación* (1542) that are included here tell primarily of the months Cabeza de Vaca spent with the Avavares. One of his persistent observations about the Avavares is that they were almost always hungry and gaunt. In a few encampments he visited, the Avavares had a surplus of food: for example, in one community Cabeza de Vaca reports that his companions and he were offered the hearts of six thousand deer. However, in general,

From *The Journey of Álvar Núñez Cabeza De Vaca* (1964). Translated by Fanny Bandelier.

Cabeza de Vaca's descriptions portray most of the Avavares as thin—sometimes to the point of starvation. The Avavares were best fed when the plant they called *tuna*—the prickly pear cactus—was in season. During that period they ate heartily, grinding the fruit for flour and roasting its leaves. But once the season was over, the community went back to a destitute life. Interestingly, some modern commentators have found this description puzzling because the region was known to have had plentiful sources of food.

Some of the most striking features of Cabeza de Vaca's rhetoric are his declarations of religious faith. Given the nature of Spanish culture in the sixteenth century, such declarations may well have been pro forma, a requirement for his audience. However, his faith may also have been as strong as he says it was. Throughout the physical hardships of his journeys—the grueling hikes and the bouts of near starvation—Cabeza de Vaca kept a firm faith in God and the power of prayer to sustain him.

Most surprising, perhaps, are the descriptions Cabeza de Vaca gives of his own role as a shaman, or traditional healer, within the Avavares community. In many Native American societies, the shaman was a highly esteemed figure who was called on to heal the sick or injured through both prayer and herbal medicines. Archaeological research indicates that shamans were usually better fed and housed than ordinary tribe members. Cabeza de Vaca was apparently thrust into this role by the Avavares, who referred to him and his companions as "children of the sun" and ascribed divine powers to them. Ironically, Cabeza de Vaca attributes his Christian faith as the source of the healings he performs. When he offers a remarkable account of raising a man from the dead, he claims that he thinks of Jesus, approaches the man, makes the sign of the cross over him, and later learns that the man has revived.

As with all historical documents, the reader must decide what level of credibility to grant the author; however, it is clear that Cabeza de Vaca's *Relación* offers a look into one of the first interactions between two starkly different cultures that would nonetheless become deeply entwined in the years to come.

Cabeza de Vaca's Rhetoric

One enduring question about *La Relación* concerns its purpose. Some historians have asserted that it was primarily a political document designed to support the official Spanish policy that discouraged taking Native Americans as slaves. Much of the book tells of the kindnesses of the Avavares and their gentleness toward one another. When Cabeza de Vaca does describe the warlike qualities of the Avavares, he highlights their intelligent strategies for protecting themselves, such as the description of setting campfires in their homes and then withdrawing to the forest so that enemies would think that they were "at home" and easy targets. Such a stratagem would have been worthy of advanced European military commanders. His careful descriptions of the ways in which the Avavares conducted warfare would have been relevant for contemporary readers, as warfare was a norm of European life.

Perhaps even more relevant to the Spaniards of the sixteenth century would have been the usefulness of the document to justify the Spanish conquest of the Southwest and Mexico. The Avavares as Cabeza de Vaca portrays them seem a scattered and sometimes helpless group. Their portrait as hungry and sick would make them candidates for colonialization in the name of humanity. Despite his description of their poverty, when Cabeza de Vaca finally found the Spanish settlement and returned to Spain, he reported that he had heard of cities inland that had great wealth in gold. These stories suggest to modern scholars that the Native Americans who told them had already met Europeans and knew what they wanted. By telling them there was gold elsewhere, the Native Americans would ensure that the Europeans moved on. Cabeza de Vaca's reports were directly responsible for Francisco Coronado's later expedition in search of the golden cities of the Americas.

Cabeza de Vaca's primary rhetorical device is the narrative, telling what happened where and when and what the circumstances were like. His descriptions are economical and precise. He tells us a good deal about customs. He notes how the Avavares greeted him and how they were fearful when they first saw a European. He describes the tasks he performed in the community, explaining that he had to take an active role in the Avavares' life or else he would not eat. When he skinned hides, for example, he was allowed to eat the scrapings, a special reward. He not only provides details about Avavares warfare but describes customs of marriage and customs involving the old, the weak, and the dying. He pays special attention to women and the ways that they are treated by men. In some cases, women are peacemakers, as when they arrange a truce after a raid, but in other cases, women are the cause of war.

Cabeza de Vaca remains relevant today because he offers vivid details about the lives of people whose culture is different from ours. The last passage in the selection that follows is perhaps most telling when it states that "all men are curious to know the habits and devices of others" (para. 29), a fact that drives contemporary literature as much as it did the narratives of Cabeza de Vaca's day.

PREREADING QUESTIONS: WHAT TO READ FOR

The following prereading questions may help you anticipate key issues in the discussion on the excerpt that follows from Álvar Núñez Cabeza de Vaca's *La Relación*. Keeping them in mind during your first reading of the selection should help focus your reactions.

- What was Cabeza de Vaca's attitude toward religion?
- How did the Native Americans he encountered treat Cabeza de Vaca?
- How does Cabeza de Vaca regard his extraordinary cures of the sick and dying?

From *La Relación*

Chapter Twenty-two

Early the next day many Indians came and brought five people 1 who were paralyzed and very ill, and they came for Castillo to cure them. Every one of the patients offered him his bow and arrows, which he accepted, and by sunset he made the sign of the cross over each of the sick, recommending them to God, Our Lord, and we all prayed to Him as well as we could to restore them to health. And He, seeing there was no other way of getting those people to help us so that we might be saved from our miserable existence, had mercy upon us, and in the morning all woke up well and hearty and went away in such good health as if they never had had any ailment whatever. This caused them great admiration and moved us to thanks to Our Lord and to greater faith in His goodness and the hope that He would save us, guiding us to where we could serve Him. For myself I may say that I always had full faith in His mercy and in that He would liberate me from captivity, and always told my companions so.

When the Indians had gone and taken along those recently 2 cured, we removed to others that were eating *tunas*[1] also, called *Cultalchuches* and *Maliacones*, which speak a different language, and with them were others, called *Coayos* and *Susolas*, and on another side those called *Atayos*, who were at war with the *Susolas*, and exchanging arrow shots with them every day.

---

[1] *tunas* The Indian name for prickly pear cactus, the fruit of which is edible.

Nothing was talked about in this whole country but of the won- 3
derful cures which God, Our Lord, performed through us, and so they
came from many places to be cured, and after having been with us two
days some Indians of the *Susolas* begged Castillo to go and attend to a
man who had been wounded, as well as to others that were sick and
among whom, they said, was one on the point of death. Castillo was
very timid, especially in difficult and dangerous cases, and always
afraid that his sins might interfere and prevent the cures from being
effective. Therefore the Indians told me to go and perform the cure.
They liked me, remembering that I had relieved them while they were
out gathering nuts, for which they had given us nuts and hides. This
had happened at the time I was coming to join the Christians. So I had
to go, and Dorantes and Estevanico went with me.

When I came close to their ranches I saw that the dying man we 4
had been called to cure was dead, for there were many people
around him weeping and his lodge was torn down, which is a sign
that the owner has died. I found the Indian with eyes upturned,
without pulse and with all the marks of lifelessness. At least so it
seemed to me, and Dorantes said the same. I removed a mat with
which he was covered, and as best I could prayed to Our Lord to restore his health, as well as that of all the others who might be in
need of it, and after having made the sign of the cross and breathed
on him many times they brought his bow and presented it to me,
and a basket of ground *tunas,* and took me to many others who were
suffering from vertigo. They gave me two more baskets of *tunas,*
which I left to the Indians that had come with us. Then we returned
to our quarters.

Our Indians to whom I had given the *tunas* remained there, and 5
at night returned telling that the dead man whom I attended to in
their presence had resuscitated, rising from his bed, had walked
about, eaten and talked to them, and that all those treated by me
were well and in very good spirits. This caused great surprise and
awe, and all over the land nothing else was spoken of. All who heard
it came to us that we might cure them and bless their children, and
when the Indians in our company (who were the *Cultalchulches*) had
to return to their country, before parting they offered us all the *tunas*
they had for their journey, not keeping a single one, and gave us
flint stones as long as one and a half palms, with which they cut and
that are greatly prized among them. They begged us to remember
them and pray to God to keep them always healthy, which we
promised to do, and so they left, the happiest people upon earth,
having given us the very best they had.

We remained with the *Avavares* Indians for eight months, ac- 6
cording to our reckoning of the moons. During that time they came

for us from many places and said that verily we were children of the sun. Until then Dorantes and the Negro had not made any cures, but we found ourselves so pressed by the Indians coming from all sides, that all of us had to become medicine men. I was the most daring and reckless of all in undertaking cures. We never treated anyone that did not afterwards say he was well, and they had such confidence in our skill as to believe that none of them would die as long as we were among them.

These Indians and the ones we left behind told us a very strange tale. From their account it may have occurred fifteen or sixteen years ago. They said there wandered then about the country a man, whom they called "Bad Thing," of small stature and with a beard, although they never could see his features clearly, and whenever he would approach their dwellings their hair would stand on end and they began to tremble. In the doorway of the lodge there would then appear a firebrand. That man thereupon came in and took hold of anyone he chose, and with a sharp knife of flint, as broad as a hand and two palms in length, he cut their side, and, thrusting his hand through the gash, took out the entrails, cutting off a piece one palm long, which he threw into the fire. Afterwards he made three cuts in one of the arms, the second one at the place where people are usually bled,[2] and twisted the arm, but reset it soon afterwards. Then he placed his hands on the wounds, and they told us they closed at once. Many times he appeared among them while they were dancing, sometimes in the dress of a woman and again as a man, and whenever he took a notion to do it he would seize the hut or lodge, take it up into the air and come down with it again with a great crash. They also told us how, many a time, they set food before him, but he never would partake of it, and when they asked him where he came from and where he had his home, he pointed to a rent in the earth and said his house was down below.

We laughed very much at those stories, making fun of them, and then, seeing our incredulity they brought to us many of those whom, they said, he had taken, and we saw the scars of his slashes in the places and as they told. We told them he was a demon and explained as best we could that if they would believe in God, Our Lord, and be Christians like ourselves, they would not have to fear that man, nor would he come and do such things unto them, and they might be sure that as long as we were in this country he would

---

[2] **where people are usually bled** During the sixteenth century and later the practice of blood letting was a recognized medical procedure, usually performed on a vein on the inner arm near the elbow.

not dare to appear again. At this they were greatly pleased and lost much of their apprehension.

The same Indians told us they had seen the Asturian and 9 Figueroa with other Indians further along on the coast, which we had named *of the figs*. All those people had no reckoning by either sun or moon, nor do they count by months and years; they judge of the seasons by the ripening of fruits, by the time when fish die and by the appearance of the stars, in all of which they are very clever and expert. While with them we were always well treated, although our food was never too plentiful, and we had to carry our own water and wood. Their dwellings and their food are like those of the others, but they are much more exposed to starvation, having neither maize nor acorns or nuts. We always went about naked like them and covered ourselves at night with deerskins.

During six of the eighteen months we were with them we suf- 10 fered much from hunger, because they do not have fish either. At the end of that time the *tunas* began to ripen, and without their noticing it we left and went to other Indians further ahead, called *Maliacones,* at a distance of one day's travel. Three days after I and the Negro reached there I sent him back to get Castillo and Dorantes, and after they rejoined me we all departed in company of the Indians, who went to eat a small fruit of some trees. On this fruit they subsist for ten or twelve days until the *tunas* are fully ripe. There they joined other Indians called *Arbadaos,* whom we found to be so sick, emaciated and swollen that we were greatly astonished. The Indians with whom we had come went back on the same trail, and we told them that we wished to remain with the others, at which they showed grief. So we remained with the others in the field near their dwellings.

When the Indians saw us they clustered together, after having 11 talked among themselves, and each one of them took the one of us whom he claimed by the hand and they led us to their homes. While with those we suffered more hunger than among any of the others. In the course of a whole day we did not eat more than two handfuls of the fruit, which was green and contained so much milky juice that our mouths were burnt by it. As water was very scarce, whoever ate of them became very thirsty. And we finally grew so hungry that we purchased two dogs, in exchange for nets and other things, and a hide with which I used to cover myself. I have said already that through all that country we went naked, and not being accustomed to it, like snakes we shed our skin twice a year. Exposure to the sun and air covered our chests and backs with big sores that made it very painful to carry the big and heavy loads, the ropes of which cut into the flesh of our arms.

The country is so rough and overgrown that often after we had   12
gathered firewood in the timber and dragged it out, we would bleed
freely from the thorns and spines which cut and slashed us wherever
they touched. Sometimes it happened that I was unable to carry or
drag out the firewood after I had gathered it with much loss of blood.
In all that trouble my only relief or consolation was to remember the
passion of our Saviour, Jesus Christ, and the blood He shed for me,
and to ponder how much greater His sufferings had been from the
thorns, than those I was then enduring. I made a contract with the Indians to make combs, arrows, bows and nets for them. Also we made
matting of which their lodges are constructed and of which they are in
very great need, for, although they know how to make it, they do not
like to do any work, in order to be able to go in quest of food. Whenever they work they suffer greatly from hunger.

Again, they would make me scrape skins and tan them, and the   13
greatest luxury I enjoyed was on the day they would give me a skin
to scrape, because I scraped it very deep in order to eat the parings,
which would last me two or three days. It also happened to us,
while being with these Indians and those before mentioned, that we
would eat a piece of meat which they gave us, raw, because if we
broiled it the first Indian coming along would snatch and eat it; it
seemed useless to take any pains, in view of what we might expect;
neither were we particular to go to any trouble in order to have it
broiled and might just as well eat it raw. Such was the life we led
there, and even that scanty maintenance we had to earn through the
objects made by our own hands for barter.

Chapter Twenty-three

After we had eaten the dogs it seemed to us that we had enough   14
strength to go further on, so we commended ourselves to the guidance of God, Our Lord, took leave of these Indians, and they put us
on the track of others of their language who were nearby. While on
our way it began to rain and rained the whole day. We lost the trail
and found ourselves in a big forest, where we gathered plenty of
leaves of *tunas* which we roasted that same night in an oven made by
ourselves, and so much heat did we give them that in the morning
they were fit to be eaten. After eating them we recommended ourselves to God again, and left, and struck the trail we had lost.

Issuing from the timber, we met other Indian dwellings, where   15
we saw two women and some boys, who were so frightened at the
sight of us that they fled to the forest to call the men that were in the
woods. When these came they hid behind trees to peep at us. We
called them and they approached in great fear. After we addressed

them they told us they were very hungry and that nearby were many of their own lodges, and they would take us to them. So that night we reached a site where there were fifty dwellings, and the people were stupefied at seeing us and showed much fear. After they had recovered from their astonishment they approached and put their hands to our faces and bodies and afterwards to their faces and bodies also. We stayed there that night, and in the morning they brought their sick people, begging us to cross them, and gave us what they had to eat, which were leaves of *tunas* and green *tunas* baked.

For the sake of this good treatment, giving us all they had, content with being without anything for our sake, we remained with them several days, and during that time others came from further on. When those were about to leave we told the first ones that we intended to accompany them. This made them very sad, and they begged us on their knees not to go. But we went and left them in tears at our departure, as it pained them greatly.   16

Chapter Twenty-four

From the Island of Ill Fate on, all the Indians whom we met as far as to here have the custom of not cohabiting with their wives when these are pregnant, and until the child is two years old.   17

Children are nursed to the age of twelve years, when they are old enough to gather their own food. We asked them why they brought their children up in that way and they replied, it was owing to the great scarcity of food all over that country, since it was common (as we saw) to be without it two or three days, and even four, and for that reason they nursed the little ones so long to preserve them from perishing through hunger. And even if they should survive, they would be very delicate and weak. When one falls sick he is left to die in the field unless he be somebody's child. Other invalids, if unable to travel, are abandoned; but a son or brother is taken along.   18

There is also a custom for husbands to leave their wives if they do not agree, and to remarry whom they please; this applies to the young men, but after they have had children they stay with their women and do not leave them.   19

When, in any village, they quarrel among themselves, they strike and beat each other until worn out, and only then do they separate. Sometimes their women step in and separate them, but men never interfere in these brawls. Nor do they ever use bow and arrow, and after they have fought and settled the question, they take their lodges and women and go out into the field to live apart from the others till their anger is over, and when they are no longer angry   20 and their resentment has passed away they return to the village and are as friendly again as if nothing had happened. There is no need of mediation. When the quarrel is between unmarried people they go to some of the neighbors, who, even if they be enemies, will receive them well, with great festivities and gifts of what they have, so that, when pacified, they return to their village wealthy.

They are all warriors and so astute in guarding themselves from   21 an enemy as if trained in continuous wars and in Italy. When in places where their enemies can offend them, they set their lodges on the edge of the roughest and densest timber and dig a trench close to it in which they sleep. The men at arms are hidden by brushwood and have their loopholes, and are so well covered and concealed that even at close range they cannot be seen.

To the densest part of the forest they open a very narrow trail   22 and there arrange a sleeping place for their women and children. As night sets in they build fires in the lodges, so that if there should be spies about, these would think the people to sleep there. And before sunrise they light the same fires again. Now, if the town is assaulted, they can attack from ditches, without being seen or discovered.

In case there are no forests wherein they can hide thus and pre-   23 pare their ambushes, they settle on the plain wherever it appears most appropriate, surrounding the place with trenches protected by brushwood. In these they open loopholes through which they can reach the enemy with arrows, and those parapets they build for the night. While I was with the *Aguenes* and these not on their guard, their enemies surprised them at midnight, killing three and wounding a number, so that they fled from their houses to the forest. As soon, however, as they noticed that the others had gone they went back, picked up all the arrows the others had spent and left and followed them as stealthily as possible. That same night they reached the others' dwellings unnoticed, and at sunrise attacked, killing five, besides wounding a great many. The rest made their escape, leaving homes and bows behind, with all their other belongings.

A short time after this the women of those calling themselves   24 *Guevenes* came, held a parley and made them friends again, but sometimes women are also the cause of war. All those people when they have personal questions and are not of one family, kill each other in a treacherous way and deal most cruelly with one another.

Chapter Twenty-five

Those Indians are the readiest people with their weapons of all I   25 have seen in the world, for when they suspect the approach of an enemy they lie awake all night with their bows within reach and a dozen of arrows, and before one goes to sleep he tries his bow, and should the string not be to his liking he arranges it until it suits him. Often they crawl out of their dwellings so as not to be seen and look and spy in every direction after danger, and if they detect anything, in less than no time are they all out in the field with their bows and arrows. Thus they remain until daybreak, running hither and thither whenever they see danger or suspect their enemies might approach. When day comes they unstring their bows until they go hunting.

The string of their bows are made of deer sinews. They fight in a   26
crouching posture, and while shooting at each other talk and dart from one side to the other to dodge the arrows of the foe. In this way they receive little damage from our crossbows and muskets. On the contrary, the Indians laugh at those weapons, because they are not dangerous to them on the plains over which they roam. They are only good in narrows and in swamps.

Horses are what the Indians dread most, and by means of which   27
they will be overcome.

Whoever has to fight Indians must take great care not to let   28
them think he is disheartened or that he covets what they own; in war they must be treated very harshly, for should they notice either fear or greed, they are the people who know how to abide their time for revenge and to take courage from the fears of their enemy. After spending all their arrows, they part, going each his own way, and without attempting pursuit, although one side might have more men than the other; such is their custom.

Many times they are shot through and through with arrows, but   29
do not die from the wounds as long as the bowels or heart are not touched; on the contrary, they recover quickly. Their eyesight, hearing and senses in general are better, I believe, than those of any other men upon earth. They can stand, and have to stand, much hunger, thirst and cold, being more accustomed and used to it than others. This I wished to state here, since, besides that all men are curious to know the habits and devices of others, such as might come in contact with those people should be informed of their customs and deeds, which will be of no small profit to them.

QUESTIONS FOR CRITICAL READING

1. What is Cabeza de Vaca's attitude toward his remarkable cures?
2. How does Cabeza de Vaca reveal his feelings about the Avavares? Does he seem to respect them, or is he suspicious of them?

3. How does Cabeza de Vaca know "the dying man" of paragraph 4 is dead? What clues about how he was resuscitated can you derive from Cabeza de Vaca's description?

4. What do the Avavares do when their sick and dying are cured? How does Cabeza de Vaca benefit from praying for the sick?

5. Why did the Avavares feel "that none of them would die as long as we were among them" (para. 6)?

SUGGESTIONS FOR WRITING

1. Try to explain the amazing record of success for the cures performed by Cabeza de Vaca and his companions. To answer this question, you may want to research the practices of shamanism and determine which practices Cabeza de Vaca seems to perform during his cures.

2. Why is it possible for Cabeza de Vaca to establish a trade among the Indians? What kinds of things does he trade? Does he seem to derive satisfaction from his travels?

3. What do you make of the story of the "Bad Thing" who has a beard and carries a flint knife two palms in length (paras. 7 and 8)? There was no source of flint near the Avavares, and even their arrowheads were tiny because the rocks were unsuitable for the purpose of making points. How does Cabeza de Vaca treat the story? Have we such stories in our own culture?

4. Examine this selection for its religious content. Is the religious devotion of Cabeza de Vaca convincing? What seem to be the religious beliefs of the Avavares?

5. What can you tell about the general daily life of the Avavares from this selection? From paragraph 17 onward, Cabeza de Vaca relates interesting details of life that he has witnessed. How much does he sympathize with the specifics of the Avavares' behavior? At what points does he seem impatient with the Avavares' ways?

6. **CONNECTIONS**   Judging from what Cabeza de Vaca says about the ways in which the Avavares' culture functions, what can you tell about its political nature? Jean-Jacques Rousseau spoke often of individuals in a state of nature and may have been thinking of North American Indians. Would Rousseau have praised the political structures that Cabeza de Vaca witnessed?

J. HECTOR ST. JOHN DE CRÈVECOEUR
What Is an American?

CRÈVECOEUR (1735–1813), born in France, near Paris, came to Canada in 1754 with the troops of Montcalm, the French general who subsequently lost Canada to the British in 1759 at the battle of Quebec. After the French and Indian War (1754–1763), as it was known in the colonies, Crèvecoeur explored Ohio and New York and then settled in Orange County, where he took up farming. He became an American citizen in 1765, married an American, Mehitable Tippet, in 1769, and had three children. His time as a farmer in New York was apparently quite satisfying.

He probably wrote *Letters from an American Farmer* (1782), from which "What Is an American?" is taken, during his farming years, from 1765 to 1780. The essay that follows is the third letter in a collection of twelve essays that paints a fascinating picture of America and its people. The book, published under his American name, J. Hector St. John (his French name was Michel-Guillaume Jean de Crèvecoeur), made Crèvecoeur famous. Translated into English and German, it was very widely read and soon went into eight editions. Much later, in 1801, he published *Voyage in Northern Pennsylvania and in the State of New York*. This book, too, was well received.

Unfortunately, Crèvecoeur was in a difficult position when the colonies in America rose against the English monarchy led by King George III. Crèvecoeur had many friends who were part of the rebellion, but his wife's family was staunchly loyalist and opposed to the uprising. Despite his neutral stance, when he went to New York City to embark for France on personal business, he was detained in prison as a spy by the British, who controlled the city in 1780. After three months he was released and went with his older son to

From *Letters from an American Farmer*.

England, where *Letters from an American Farmer* was published. The book's success made Crèvecoeur known to Benjamin Franklin and also gained him membership in the Academy of Sciences in France. In 1783 he was appointed French consul to New York, New Jersey, and Connecticut, and he returned to the United States only to find that his wife had been killed in an Indian raid. He eventually was reunited with his younger son and daughter, who were alive but separated and resettled in Boston. In 1790, during the years of the French Revolution, Crèvecoeur was recalled from New York and returned to Europe. Thereafter he lived in France and Germany as a celebrated man of letters. Interestingly, in 1923 a collection of unpublished English essays was found in an attic in France; attributed to Crèvecoeur, they were published under the title *Sketches of Eighteenth Century America, or More Letters from an American Farmer* (1925).

A careful disquisition on the nature of the colonies that Crèvecoeur had come to love, "What Is an American?" is representative of the rest of *Letters from an American Farmer*. He writes to a distant audience — which is why he fashions his essays as informative letters. He describes the countryside, the regions that can be visited, and the kinds of people the reader might be able to discern, were the reader present with him.

Crèvecoeur claims that Americans are different because they work for themselves and reap the benefits of their own work. There are no aristocrats or landlords in power to stand over them and take their land or their crops. A country that cannot feed a person is not, he says, one's homeland. Instead, he asserts, *"ubi panis ibi patria"*: one's homeland is where one's bread is. In this sense, Crèvecoeur emphasizes economic freedom. This freedom is the most important feature of the colonies. Europeans who emigrate to America can, by dint of hard work, achieve economic independence. Crèvecoeur offers numerous examples of immigrants who came with nothing and who died leaving small fortunes to their heirs.

In his zeal to praise the opportunities of the colonies, he takes a conventional view of his times, similar to that of Thomas Jefferson, and ignores the plight of African slaves. Slavery is not an issue in Crèvecoeur's writing — perhaps because as a Northerner he saw little of it. As a European, he concentrates on the European emigration to America and writes for a European audience.

Crèvecoeur's Rhetoric

Crèvecoeur writes here in the informal mode of the travel letter. His rhetorical purpose is to inform his readers about the nature of a country they have not seen but are likely curious about.

Because this essay is one of twelve letters, it focuses on one aspect of his subject: defining the special condition of being an American. Crèvecoeur's discussion represents one of the first attempts to define the new person who was "created" by the experience of colonizing North America.

His opening paragraphs are an effort at definition by means of comparison. The American is compared with the European, just as the colonies are compared with Europe. By relying on definition as his primary purpose in writing, Crèvecoeur permits himself a wide scope—both in terms of discussing the nature of the Americans whom he has known, and in terms of discussing the political and religious atmosphere in detail. His position is that economic freedom and the resultant economic success of the American, combined with the absence of aristocratic authorities, has created a new kind of person. The American does not hold with the absolute distinctions that are common among Europeans. In America the Dutch marry the English, who marry the French, who marry the Germans, and so on. The result, Crèvecoeur assures us, is increased tolerance and a greater sense of equality than is found in Europe.

The people who emigrate to America are, Crèvecoeur says, from the middle and lower classes. The aristocrats remain in Europe because their wealth and their authority are there. On the other hand, the poor, the improvident, and in some cases the criminal all come eagerly to begin a new life that would have been impossible in Europe.

Crèvecoeur uses a simple pattern of threes to help keep his ideas clear and his views intelligible. For example, beginning in paragraph 7 he discusses three kinds of people likely to be found in America. The first are those who live on the coast and in cities. The sea "renders them more bold and enterprising." They love people, crowds, action. Then there are "those who inhabit the middle settlements." These are farmers, like Crèvecoeur himself. He naturally elevates them in esteem: "the earth purifies them." Their experiences have also transformed them: "Europe has no such class of men." He can say this because most farmers in Europe work on land owned by aristocrats and cannot be said to work for themselves. For Crèvecoeur, this is the class that most inspires him, elevating the soul and promising the greatest gifts of independence and well-being.

The third class are the outliers, those who are found on or near the frontier and live not by farming but by hunting and trapping. This class of people is rough and ready, not as noble as the farmer nor as industrious as the fisherman. Crèvecoeur sees them as lawless, somewhat barbarous and unrefined, like the animals they hunt. He considers these frontier people to be similar to the earliest settlers coping with the forest, and he likens them to the Native Americans who live near them.

Because the essay takes the form of a letter, the prose is informal and informative. Crèvecoeur reports a great many facts, but he also incorporates personal opinions. His detailed writing convinces the reader that he is well informed, which helps the reader accept Crèvecoeur's opinions as valid. To the modern reader, Crèvecoeur may appear to have some cultural biases; for example, he insists that the Irish have not done well in America because they like to drink and fight rather than work. Such a view was common in England at the time, and Crèvecoeur seems to have adopted it. Yet he wisely points out that the way England treated Ireland historically may account for some of the problem. The Irish would not have had the opportunity in Ireland to learn how to cultivate the land to provide the diversity of products that Crèvecoeur marvels over when he speaks of the progress of the Germans, English, and Scots in America.

Like Adam Smith, whose *Wealth of Nations* was published only a few years before *Letters from an American Farmer*, Crèvecoeur places enormous emphasis on the availability of land—not for the wealthy capitalist, but for the industrious farmer. Much of his letter is consumed with his meditations on land. But Crèvecoeur also meditates on the law. In America, government "is derived from the original genius and strong desire of the people ratified and confirmed by the crown" (para. 3), and the laws protect rather than exploit the farmer. In Europe, the laws protect the wealthy. Even with King George III in power, Crèvecoeur feels that the laws benefit the American.

Crèvecoeur's discussion of religion in America resembles his discussion of fishermen, farmers, and hunters. He explains how American Catholics, Presbyterians, Quakers, and Moravians practice their respective religions so as to avoid religious rancor and conflict. Crèvecoeur implies, too, that they may not take their religion as seriously as do Europeans. All these innovations, Crèvecoeur assures us, have made the American unique.

PREREADING QUESTIONS:
WHAT TO READ FOR

The following prereading questions may help you anticipate key issues in the discussion on J. Hector St. John de Crèvecoeur's "What Is an American?" Keeping them in mind during your first reading of the selection should help focus your reactions.

- How does daily life and culture in America contrast with that of Europe, especially in terms of class distinctions?
- What is the effect of available land and gentle laws on the new immigrant?
- How does economic success transform the immigrant?

What Is an American?

I wish I could be acquainted with the feelings and thoughts 1 which must agitate the heart and present themselves to the mind of an enlightened Englishman, when he first lands on this continent. He must greatly rejoice that he lived at a time to see this fair country discovered and settled; he must necessarily feel a share of national pride, when he views the chain of settlements which embellishes these extended shores. When he says to himself, this is the work of my countrymen, who, when convulsed by factions, afflicted by a variety of miseries and wants, restless and impatient, took refuge here. They brought along with them their national genius, to which they principally owe what liberty they enjoy, and what substance they possess. Here he sees the industry of his native country displayed in a new manner, and traces in their works the embryos of all the arts, sciences, and ingenuity which flourish in Europe. Here he beholds fair cities, substantial villages, extensive fields, an immense country filled with decent houses, good roads, orchards, meadows, and bridges, where an hundred years ago all was wild, woody, and uncultivated! What a train of pleasing ideas this fair spectacle must suggest; it is a prospect which must inspire a good citizen with the most heartfelt pleasure. The difficulty consists in the manner of viewing so extensive a scene. He is arrived on a new continent; a modern society offers itself to his contemplation, different from what he had hitherto seen. It is not composed, as in Europe, of great lords who possess everything, and of a herd of people who have nothing. Here are no aristocratical families, no courts, no kings, no bishops, no ecclesiastical dominion, no invisible power giving to a few a very visible one; no great manufacturers employing thousands, no great refinements of luxury. The rich and the poor are not so far removed from each other as they are in Europe. Some few towns excepted, we are all tillers of the earth, from Nova Scotia to West Florida. We are a people of cultivators, scattered over an immense territory, communicating with each other by means of good roads and navigable rivers, united by the silken bands of mild government, all respecting the laws, without dreading their power, because they are equitable. We are all animated with the spirit of an industry which is unfettered and unrestrained, because each person works for himself. If he travels through our rural districts he views not the hostile castle, and the haughty mansion, contrasted with the clay-built hut and miserable cabin, where cattle and men help to keep each other warm, and dwell in meanness, smoke, and indigence. A pleasing uniformity of decent competence appears throughout our habitations. The meanest of our log-houses is a dry and comfortable habitation. Lawyer or merchant are the fairest titles our towns afford; that of a farmer is the only appellation of the rural inhabitants of our country. It must take some time ere he can reconcile himself to our dictionary, which is but short in words of dignity, and names of honour. There, on a Sunday, he sees a congregation of respectable farmers and their wives, all clad in neat homespun, well mounted, or riding in their own humble waggons. There is not among them an esquire, saving the unlettered magistrate. There he sees a parson as simple as his flock, a farmer who does not riot on the labour of others. We have no princes, for whom we toil, starve, and bleed: we are the most perfect society now existing in the world. Here man is free as he ought to be; nor is this pleasing quality so transitory as many others are. Many ages will not see the shores of our great lakes replenished with inland nations, nor the unknown bounds of North America entirely peopled. Who can tell how far it extends? Who can tell the millions of men whom it will feed and contain? for no European foot has as yet travelled half the extent of this mighty continent!

The next wish of this traveller will be to know whence came all 2 these people? they are a mixture of English, Scotch, Irish, French, Dutch, Germans, and Swedes. From this promiscuous breed, that race now called Americans have arisen. The eastern provinces must indeed be excepted, as being the unmixed descendants of Englishmen. I have heard many wish that they had been more intermixed also: for my part, I am no wisher, and think it much better as it has happened. They exhibit a most conspicuous figure in this great and variegated picture; they too enter for a great share in the pleasing perspective displayed in these thirteen provinces. I know it is fashionable to reflect on them, but I respect them for what they have done; for the accuracy and wisdom with which they have settled their territory; for the decency of their manners; for their early love of letters; their ancient college, the first in this hemisphere; for their industry; which to me who am but a farmer, is the criterion of everything. There never was a people, situated as they are, who with so ungrateful a soil have done more in so short a time. Do you think that the monarchical ingredients which are more prevalent in other governments, have purged them from all foul stains? Their histories assert the contrary.

In this great American asylum, the poor of Europe have by some 3 means met together, and in consequence of various causes; to what purpose should they ask one another what countrymen they are? Alas, two thirds of them had no country. Can a wretch who wanders about, who works and starves, whose life is a continual scene of sore affliction or pinching penury; can that man call England or any other kingdom his country? A country that had no bread for him, whose fields procured him no harvest, who met with nothing but the frowns of the rich, the severity of the laws, with jails and punishments; who owned not a single foot of the extensive surface of this planet? No! urged by a variety of motives, here they came. Every thing has tended to regenerate them; new laws, a new mode of living, a new social system; here they are become men: in Europe they were as so many useless plants, wanting vegetative mould, and refreshing showers; they withered, and were mowed down by want, hunger, and war; but now by the power of transplantation, like all other plants they have taken root and flourished! Formerly they were not numbered in any civil lists of their country, except in those of the poor; here they rank as citizens. By what invisible power has this surprising metamorphosis been performed? By that of the laws and that of their industry. The laws, the indulgent laws, protect them as they arrive, stamping on them the symbol of adoption; they receive ample rewards for their labours; these accumulated rewards procure them lands; those lands confer on them the title of freemen, and to that title every benefit is affixed which men can possibly require. This is the great operation daily performed by our laws. From whence proceed these laws? From our government. Whence the government? It is derived from the original genius and strong desire of the people ratified and confirmed by the crown. This is the great chain which links us all, this is the picture which every province exhibits, Nova Scotia excepted. There the crown has done all; either there were no people who had genius, or it was not much attended to: the consequence is, that the province is very thinly inhabited indeed; the power of the crown in conjunction with the musketos has prevented men from settling there. Yet some parts of it flourished once, and it contained a mild-harmless set of people. But for the fault of a few leaders, the whole were banished. The greatest political error the crown ever committed in America, was to cut off men from a country which wanted nothing but men!

What attachment can a poor European emigrant have for a 4 country where he had nothing? The knowledge of the language, the love of a few kindred as poor as himself, were the only cords that tied him: his country is now that which gives him land, bread, protection, and consequence: *Ubi panis ibi patria,*[1] is the motto of all emigrants. What then is the American, this new man? He is either an European, or the descendant of an European, hence that strange mixture of blood, which you will find in no other country. I could point out to you a family whose grandfather was an Englishman, whose wife was Dutch, whose son married a French woman, and whose present four sons have now four wives of different nations. *He* is an American, who, leaving behind him all his ancient prejudices and manners, receives new ones from the new mode of life he has embraced, the new government he obeys, and the new rank he holds. He becomes an American by being received in the broad lap of our great *Alma Mater.* Here individuals of all nations are melted into a new race of men, whose labours and posterity will one day cause great changes in the world. Americans are the western pilgrims, who are carrying along with them that great mass of arts, sciences, vigour, and industry which began long since in the east; they will finish the great circle. The Americans were once scattered all over Europe; here they are incorporated into one of the finest systems of population which has ever appeared, and which will hereafter become distinct by the power of the different climates they inhabit. The American ought therefore to love this country much better than that wherein either he or his forefathers were born. Here the rewards of his industry follow with equal steps the progress of his labour; his labour is founded on the basis of nature, *self-interest;* can it want a stronger allurement? Wives and children, who before in vain demanded of him a morsel of bread, now, fat and frolicsome, gladly help their father to clear those fields whence exuberant crops are to arise to feed and to clothe them all; without any part being claimed, either by a despotic prince, a rich abbot, or a mighty lord. Here religion demands but little of him; a small voluntary salary to the minister, and gratitude to God; can he refuse these? The American is a new man, who acts upon new principles; he must therefore entertain new ideas, and form new opinions. From involuntary idleness, servile dependence, penury, and useless labour, he has passed to toils of a very different nature, rewarded by ample subsistence. — This is an American.

British America is divided into many provinces, forming a large 5 association, scattered along a coast 1500 miles extent and about 200 wide. This society I would fain examine, at least such as it appears in

---

[1] *Ubi panis ibi patria* Where my bread is, there is my home.

the middle provinces; if it does not afford that variety of tinges and gradations which may be observed in Europe, we have colours peculiar to ourselves. For instance, it is natural to conceive that those who live near the sea, must be very different from those who live in the woods; the intermediate space will afford a separate and distinct class.

Men are like plants; the goodness and flavour of the fruit pro- 6 ceeds from the peculiar soil and exposition in which they grow. We are nothing but what we derive from the air we breathe, the climate we inhabit, the government we obey, the system of religion we profess, and the nature of our employment. Here you will find but few crimes; these have acquired as yet no root among us. I wish I was able to trace all my ideas; if my ignorance prevents me from describing them properly, I hope I shall be able to delineate a few of the outlines, which are all I propose.

Those who live near the sea, feed more on fish than on flesh, 7 and often encounter that boisterous element.[2] This renders them more bold and enterprising; this leads them to neglect the confined occupations of the land. They see and converse with a variety of people; their intercourse with mankind becomes extensive. The sea inspires them with a love of traffic, a desire of transporting produce from one place to another; and leads them to a variety of resources which supply the place of labour. Those who inhabit the middle settlements, by far the most numerous, must be very different; the simple cultivation of the earth purifies them, but the indulgences of the government, the soft remonstrances of religion, the rank of independent freeholders, must necessarily inspire them with sentiments, very little known in Europe among people of the same class. What do I say? Europe has no such class of men; the early knowledge they acquire, the early bargains they make, give them a great degree of sagacity. As freemen they will be litigious; pride and obstinacy are often the cause of law suits; the nature of our laws and governments may be another. As citizens it is easy to imagine, that they will carefully read the newspapers, enter into every political disquisition, freely blame or censure governors and others. As farmers they will be careful and anxious to get as much as they can, because what they get is their own. As northern men they will love the cheerful cup. As Christians, religion curbs them not in their opinions; the general indulgence leaves every one to think for themselves in spiritual matters; the laws inspect our actions, our thoughts are left to God. Industry, good living, selfishness, litigiousness, country politics, the pride of freemen, religious indifference, are their characteristics. If

---

[2] **boisterous element** The sea.

you recede still farther from the sea, you will come into more modern settlements; they exhibit the same strong lineaments, in a ruder appearance. Religion seems to have still less influence, and their manners are less improved.

Now we arrive near the great woods, near the last inhabited   8
districts; there men seem to be placed still farther beyond the reach of government, which in some measure leaves them to themselves. How can it pervade every corner; as they were driven there by misfortunes, necessity of beginnings, desire of acquiring large tracts of land, idleness, frequent want of economy, ancient debts; the reunion of such peoples does not afford a very pleasing spectacle. When discord, want of unity and friendship; when either drunkenness or idleness prevail in such remote districts; contention, inactivity, and wretchedness must ensue. There are not the same remedies to these evils as in a long established community. The few magistrates they have, are in general little better than the rest; they are often in a perfect state of war; that of a man against man, sometimes decided by blows, sometimes by means of the law; that of man against every wild inhabitant of these venerable woods, of which they are come to dispossess them. There men appear to be no better than carnivorous animals of a superior rank, living on the flesh of wild animals when they can catch them, and when they are not able, they subsist on grain. He who would wish to see America in its proper light, and have a true idea of its feeble beginnings and barbarous rudiments, must visit our extended line of frontiers where the last settlers dwell, and where he may see the first labours of settlement, the mode of clearing the earth, in all their different appearances; where men are wholly left dependent on their native tempers, and on the spur of uncertain industry, which often fails when not sanctified by the efficacy of a few moral rules. There, remote from the power of example and check of shame, many families exhibit the most hideous parts of our society. They are a kind of forlorn hope, preceding by ten or twelve years the most respectable army of veterans which come after them. In that space, prosperity will polish some, vice and the law will drive off the rest, who uniting again with others like themselves will recede still farther; making room for more industrious people, who will finish their improvements, convert the loghouse into a convenient habitation, and rejoicing that the first heavy labours are finished, will change in a few years that hitherto barbarous country into a fine fertile, well regulated district. Such is our progress, such is the march of the Europeans toward the interior parts of this continent. In all societies there are off-casts; this impure part serves as our precursors or pioneers; my father himself was one of that class, but

he came upon honest principles, and was therefore one of the few who held fast; by good conduct and temperance, he transmitted to me his fair inheritance, when not above one in fourteen of his contemporaries had the same good fortune.

Forty years ago this smiling country was thus inhabited; it is now purged, a general decency of manners prevails throughout, and such has been the fate of our best countries. 9

Exclusive of those general characteristics, each province has its own, founded on the government, climate, mode of husbandry, customs, and peculiarity of circumstances. Europeans submit insensibly to these great powers, and become, in the course of a few generations, not only Americans in general, but either Pennsylvanians, Virginians, or provincials under some other name. Whoever traverses the continent must easily observe those strong differences, which will grow more evident in time. The inhabitants of Canada, Massachusetts, the middle provinces, the southern ones will be as different as their climates; their only points of unity will be those of religion and language. 10

As I have endeavoured to show you how Europeans become Americans; it may not be disagreeable to show you likewise how the various Christian sects introduced, wear out, and how religious indifference becomes prevalent. When any considerable number of a particular sect happen to dwell contiguous to each other, they immediately erect a temple, and there worship the Divinity agreeably to their own peculiar ideas. Nobody disturbs them. If any new sect springs up in Europe it may happen that many of its professors will come and settle in America. As they bring their zeal with them, they are at liberty to make proselytes if they can, and to build a meeting and to follow the dictates of their consciences; for neither the government nor any other power interferes. If they are peaceable subjects, and are industrious, what is it to their neighbours how and in what manner they think fit to address their prayers to the Supreme Being? But if the sectaries are not settled close together, if they are mixed with other denominations, their zeal will cool for want of fuel, and will be extinguished in a little time. Then the Americans become as to religion, what they are as to country, allied to all. In them the name of Englishman, Frenchman, and European is lost, and in like manner, the strict modes of Christianity as practised in Europe are lost also. This effect will extend itself still farther hereafter, and though this may appear to you as a strange idea, yet it is a very true one. I shall be able perhaps hereafter to explain myself better; in the meanwhile, let the following example serve as my first justification. 11

Let us suppose you and I to be travelling; we observe that in this house, to the right, lives a Catholic, who prays to God as he has 12 been taught, and believes in transubstantiation;[3] he works and raises wheat, he has a large family of children, all hale and robust; his belief, his prayers offend nobody. About one mile farther on the same road, his next neighbour may be a good honest plodding German Lutheran, who addresses himself to the same God, the God of all, agreeably to the modes he has been educated in, and believes in con-substantiation;[4] by so doing he scandalises nobody; he also works in his fields, embellishes the earth, clears swamps, etc. What has the world to do with his Lutheran principles? He persecutes nobody, and nobody persecutes him, he visits his neighbours, and his neighbours visit him. Next to him lives a seceder, the most enthusiastic of all sec-taries; his zeal is hot and fiery, but separated as he is from others of the same complexion, he has no congregation of his own to resort to, where he might cabal and mingle religious pride with worldly obsti-nacy. He likewise raises good crops, his house is handsomely painted, his orchard is one of the fairest in the neighbourhood. How does it concern the welfare of the country, or of the province at large, what this man's religious sentiments are, or really whether he has any at all? He is a good farmer, he is a sober, peaceable, good citizen: William Penn himself would not wish for more. This is the visible character, the invisible one is only guessed at, and is nobody's busi-ness. Next again lives a Low Dutchman, who implicitly believes the rules laid down by the synod of Dort. He conceives no other idea of a clergyman than that of an hired man; if he does his work well he will pay him the stipulated sum; if not he will dismiss him, and do with-out his sermons, and let his church be shut up for years. But notwith-standing this coarse idea, you will find his house and farm to be the neatest in all the country; and you will judge by his waggon and fat horses, that he thinks more of the affairs of this world than of those of the next. He is sober and laborious, therefore he is all he ought to be as to the affairs of this life; as for those of the next, he must trust to the great Creator. Each of these people instruct their children as well as they can, but these instructions are feeble compared to those which are given to the youth of the poorest class in Europe. Their children will therefore grow up less zealous and more indifferent in matters of religion than their parents. The foolish vanity, or rather the fury of making Proselytes, is unknown here; they have no time, the seasons

---

[3] **transubstantiation** Catholics believe that the wine and bread of the Eu-charist at their consecration actually become the true blood and body of Christ, while still retaining the appearance of bread and wine.

[4] **consubstantiation** Some Protestants believe the Eucharist is symbolically the blood and body of Christ; others believe the wine and bread are substantially the blood and body of Christ.

call for all their attention, and thus in a few years, this mixed neighbourhood will exhibit a strange religious medley, that will be neither pure Catholicism nor pure Calvinism. A very perceptible indifference even in the first generation, will become apparent; and it may happen that the daughter of the Catholic will marry the son of the seceder, and settle by themselves at a distance from their parents. What religious education will they give their children? A very imperfect one. If there happens to be in the neighbourhood any place of worship, we will suppose a Quaker's meeting; rather than not show their fine clothes, they will go to it, and some of them may perhaps attach themselves to that society. Others will remain in a perfect state of indifference; the children of these zealous parents will not be able to tell what their religious principles are, and their grandchildren still less. The neighbourhood of a place of worship generally leads them to it, and the action of going thither, is the strongest evidence they can give of their attachment to any sect. The Quakers are the only people who retain a fondness for their own mode of worship; for be they ever so far separated from each other, they hold a sort of communion with the society, and seldom depart from its rules, at least in this country. Thus all sects are mixed as well as all nations; thus religious indifference is imperceptibly disseminated from one end of the continent to the other; which is at present one of the strongest characteristics of the Americans. Where this will reach no one can tell, perhaps it may leave a vacuum fit to receive other systems. Persecution, religious pride, the love of contradiction, are the food of what the world commonly calls religion. These motives have ceased here; zeal in Europe is confined; here it evaporates in the great distance it has to travel; there it is a grain of powder inclosed, here it burns away in the open air, and consumes without effect.

But to return to our back-settlers. I must tell you, that there is   13
something in the proximity of the woods, which is very singular. It is with men as it is with the plants and animals that grow and live in the forests; they are entirely different from those that live in the plains. I will candidly tell you all my thoughts but you are not to expect that I shall advance any reasons. By living in or near the woods, their actions are regulated by the wildness of the neighbourhood. The deer often come to eat their grain, the wolves to destroy their sheep, the bears to kill their hogs, the foxes to catch their poultry. This surrounding hostility immediately puts the gun into their hands; they watch these animals, they kill some; and thus by defending their property, they soon become professed hunters; that is the progress; once hunters, farewell to the plough. The chase renders them ferocious, gloomy, and unsociable; a hunter wants no neighbour, he rather hates them, because he dreads the competition.

In a little time their success in the woods makes them neglect their tillage. They trust to the natural fecundity of the earth, and therefore do little; carelessness in fencing often exposes what little they sow to destruction; they are not at home to watch; in order therefore to make up the deficiency, they go oftener to the woods. That new mode of life brings along with it a new set of manners, which I cannot easily describe. These new manners being grafted on the old stock, produce a strange sort of lawless profligacy, the impressions of which are indelible. The manners of the Indian natives are respectable, compared with this European medley. Their wives and children live in sloth and inactivity; and having no proper pursuits, you may judge what education the latter receive. Their tender minds have nothing else to contemplate but the example of their parents; like them they grow up a mongrel breed, half civilised, half savage, except nature stamps on them some constitutional propensities. That rich, that voluptuous sentiment is gone that struck them so forcibly; the possession of their freeholds no longer conveys to their minds the same pleasure and pride. To all these reasons you must add, their lonely situation, and you cannot imagine what an effect on manners the great distances they live from each other has! Consider one of the last settlements in its first view: of what is it composed? Europeans who have not that sufficient share of knowledge they ought to have, in order to prosper; people who have suddenly passed from oppression, dread of government, and fear of laws, into the unlimited freedom of the woods. This sudden change must have a very great effect on most men, and on that class particularly. Eating of wild meat, whatever you may think, tends to alter their temper: though all the proof I can adduce, is, that I have seen it: and having no place of worship to resort to, what little society this might afford is denied them. The Sunday meetings, exclusive of religious benefits, were the only social bonds that might have inspired them with some degree of emulation in neatness. Is it then surprising to see men thus situated, immersed in great and heavy labours, degenerate a little? It is rather a wonder the effect is not more diffusive. The Moravians and the Quakers are the only instances in exception to what I have advanced. The first never settle singly, it is a colony of the society which emigrates; they carry with them their forms, worship, rules, and decency: the others never begin so hard, they are always able to buy improvements, in which there is a great advantage, for by that time the country is recovered from its first barbarity. Thus our bad people are those who are half cultivators and half hunters; and the worst of them are those who have degenerated altogether into the hunting state. As old ploughmen and new men of the woods, as Europeans and new made Indians, they contract the vices of both; they adopt the moroseness and ferocity of a native, without his mildness, or even his industry at home. If manners are not refined, at least they are rendered simple and inoffensive by tilling the earth; all our wants are supplied by it, our time is divided between labour and rest, and leaves none for the commission of great misdeeds. As hunters it is divided between the toil of the chase, the idleness of repose, or the indulgence of inebriation. Hunting is but a licentious idle life, and if it does not always pervert good dispositions; yet, when it is united with bad luck, it leads to want: want stimulates that propensity to rapacity and injustice, too natural to needy men, which is the fatal gradation. After this explanation of the effects which follow by living in the woods, shall we yet vainly flatter ourselves with the hope of converting the Indians? We should rather begin with converting our back-settlers; and now if I dare mention the name of religion, its sweet accents would be lost in the immensity of these woods. Men thus placed are not fit either to receive or remember its mild instructions; they want temples and ministers, but as soon as men cease to remain at home, and begin to lead an erratic life, let them be either tawny or white, they cease to be its disciples.

Thus have I faintly and imperfectly endeavoured to trace our so-   14
ciety from the sea to our woods! yet you must not imagine that every person who moves back, acts upon the same principles, or falls into the same degeneracy. Many families carry with them all their decency of conduct, purity of morals, and respect of religion; but these are scarce, the power of example is sometimes irresistible. Even among these back-settlers, their depravity is greater or less, according to what nation or province they belong. Were I to adduce proofs of this, I might be accused of partiality. If there happens to be some rich intervals, some fertile bottoms, in those remote districts, the people will there prefer tilling the land to hunting, and will attach themselves to it; but even on these fertile spots you may plainly perceive the inhabitants to acquire a great degree of rusticity and selfishness.

It is in consequence of this straggling situation, and the astonish-   15
ing power it has on manners, that the back-settlers of both the Carolinas, Virginia, and many other parts, have been long a set of lawless people; it has been even dangerous to travel among them. Government can do nothing in so extensive a country, better it should wink at these irregularities, than that it should use means inconsistent with its usual mildness. Time will efface those stains: in proportion as the great body of population approaches them they will reform, and be-

come polished and subordinate. Whatever has been said of the four New England provinces, no such degeneracy of manners has ever tarnished their annals; their back-settlers have been kept within the bounds of decency, and government, by means of wise laws, and by the influence of religion. What a detestable idea such people must have given to the natives of the Europeans! They trade with them, the worst of people are permitted to do that which none but persons of the best characters should be employed in. They get drunk with them, and often defraud the Indians. Their avarice, removed from the eyes of their superiors, knows no bounds; and aided by the little superiority of knowledge, these traders deceive them, and even sometimes shed blood. Hence those shocking violations, those sudden devastations which have so often stained our frontiers, when hundreds of innocent people have been sacrificed for the crimes of a few. It was in consequence of such behaviour, that the Indians took the hatchet against the Virginians in 1774. Thus are our first steps trod, thus are our first trees felled, in general, by the most vicious of our people; and thus the path is opened for the arrival of a second and better class, the true American freeholders; the most respectable set of people in this part of the world: respectable for their industry, their happy independence, the great share of freedom they possess, the good regulation of their families, and for extending the trade and the dominion of our mother country.

Europe contains hardly any other distinctions but lords and tenants; this fair country alone is settled by freeholders, the possessors of the soil they cultivate, members of the government they obey, and the framers of their own laws, by means of their representatives. This is a thought which you have taught me to cherish; our difference from Europe, far from diminishing, rather adds to our usefulness and consequence as men and subjects. Had our forefathers remained there, they would only have crowded it, and perhaps prolonged those convulsions which had shook it so long. Every industrious European who transports himself here, may be compared to a sprout growing at the foot of a great tree; it enjoys and draws but a little portion of sap; wrench it from the parent roots, transplant it, and it will become a tree bearing fruit also. Colonists are therefore entitled to the consideration due to the most useful subjects; a hundred families barely existing in some parts of Scotland, will here in six years, cause an annual exportation of 10,000 bushels of wheat: 100 bushels being but a common quantity for an industrious family to sell, if they cultivate good land. It is here then that the idle may be employed, the useless become useful, and the poor become rich; but by riches I do not mean gold and silver, we have but little of those metals; I mean a better sort of wealth, cleared lands, cattle, good houses, good clothes, and an increase of people to enjoy them.

There is no wonder that this country has so many charms, and 17 presents to Europeans so many temptations to remain in it. A traveller in Europe becomes a stranger as soon as he quits his own kingdom; but it is otherwise here. We know, properly speaking, no strangers; this is every person's country; the variety of our soils, situations, climates, governments, and produce, hath something which must please everybody. No sooner does an European arrive, no matter of what condition, than his eyes are opened upon the fair prospect; he hears his language spoke, he retraces many of his own country manners, he perpetually hears the names of families and towns with which he is acquainted; he sees happiness and prosperity in all places disseminated; he meets with hospitality, kindness, and plenty everywhere; he beholds hardly any poor, he seldom hears of punishments and executions; and he wonders at the elegance of our towns, those miracles of industry and freedom. He cannot admire enough our rural districts, our convenient roads, good taverns, and our many accommodations; he involuntarily loves a country where everything is so lovely. When in England, he was a mere Englishman; here he stands on a larger portion of the globe, not less than its fourth part, and may see the productions of the north, in iron and naval stores; the provisions of Ireland, the grain of Egypt, the indigo, the rice of China. He does not find, as in Europe, a crowded society, where every place is over-stocked; he does not feel that perpetual collision of parties, that difficulty of beginning, that contention which oversets so many. There is room for everybody in America; has he any particular talent, or industry? he exerts it in order to procure a livelihood, and it succeeds. Is he a merchant? the avenues of trade are infinite; is he eminent in any respect? he will be employed and respected. Does he love a country life? pleasant farms present themselves; he may purchase what he wants, and thereby become an American farmer. Is he a labourer, sober and industrious? he need not go many miles, nor receive many informations before he will be hired, well fed at the table of his employer, and paid four or five times more than he can get in Europe. Does he want uncultivated lands? thousands of acres present themselves, which he may purchase cheap. Whatever be his talents or inclinations, if they are moderate, he may satisfy them. I do not mean that every one who comes will grow rich in a little time; no, but he may procure an easy, decent maintenance, by his industry. Instead of starving he will be fed, instead of being idle he will have employment; and these are riches enough for such men as come over here. The rich stay in Europe, it is only the middling and the poor that emigrate. Would you wish to travel in independent idleness, from north to south, you will find easy access, and the most cheerful reception at every house; society without ostentation, good cheer without pride, and every decent diversion which the country affords, with little expense. It is no wonder that the European who has lived here a few years, is desirous to remain; Europe with all its pomp, is not to be compared to this continent, for men of middle stations, or labourers.

An European, when he first arrives, seems limited in his intentions, as well as in his views; but he very suddenly alters his scale; two hundred miles formerly appeared a very great distance, it is now but a trifle; he no sooner breathes our air than he forms schemes, and embarks in designs he never would have thought of in his own country. There the plentitude of society confines many useful ideas, and often extinguishes the most laudable schemes which here ripen into maturity. Thus Europeans become Americans. 18

But how is this accomplished in that crowd of low, indigent people, who flock here every year from all parts of Europe? I will tell you; they no sooner arrive than they immediately feel the good effects of that plenty of provisions we possess: they fare on our best food, and they are kindly entertained; their talents, character, and peculiar industry are immediately inquired into; they find countrymen everywhere disseminated, let them come from whatever part of Europe. Let me select one as an epitome of the rest; he is hired, he goes to work, and works moderately; instead of being employed by a haughty person, he finds himself with his equal, placed at the substantial table of the farmer, or else at an inferior one as good; his wages are high, his bed is not like that bed of sorrow on which he used to lie: if he behaves with propriety, and is faithful, he is caressed, and becomes as it were a member of the family. He begins to feel the effects of a sort of resurrection; hitherto he had not lived, but simply vegetated; he now feels himself a man, because he is treated as such; the laws of his own country had overlooked him in his insignificancy; the laws of this cover him with their mantle. Judge what an alteration there must arise in the mind and thoughts of this man; he begins to forget his former servitude and dependence, his heart involuntarily swells and glows; this first swell inspires him with those new thoughts which constitute an American. What love can he entertain for a country where his existence was a burthen to him; if he is a generous good man, the love of this new adoptive parent will sink deep into his heart. He looks around, and sees many a prosperous person, who but a few years before was as poor as himself. This encourages him much, he begins to form some little scheme, the first, alas, he ever formed in his life. If he is wise he 19 thus spends two or three years, in which time he acquires knowledge, the use of tools, the modes of working the lands, felling trees, etc. This prepares the foundation of a good name, the most useful acquisition he can make. He is encouraged, he has gained friends; he is advised and directed, he feels bold, he purchases some land; he gives all the money he has brought over, as well as what he has earned, and trusts to the God of harvests for the discharge of the rest. His good name procures him credit. He is now possessed of the deed, conveying to him and his posterity the fee simple and absolute property of two hundred acres of land, situated on such a river. What an epocha in this man's life! He is become a freeholder, from perhaps a German boor—he is now an American, a Pennsylvanian, an English subject. He is naturalised, his name is enrolled with those of the other citizens of the province. Instead of being a vagrant, he has a place of residence; he is called the inhabitant of such a country, or of such a district, and for the first time in his life counts for something; for hitherto he has been a cypher. I only repeat what I have heard many say, and no wonder their hearts should glow, and he agitated with a multitude of feelings, not easy to describe. From nothing to start into being; from a servant to the rank of a master; from being the slave of some despotic prince, to become a free man, invested with lands, to which every municipal blessing is annexed! What a change indeed! It is in consequence of that change that he becomes an American. This great metamorphosis has a double effect, it extinguishes all his European prejudices, he forgets that mechanism of subordination, that servility of disposition which poverty had taught him; and sometimes he is apt to forget too much, often passing from one extreme to the other. If he is a good man, he forms schemes of future prosperity, he proposes to educate his children better than he has been educated himself; he thinks of future modes of conduct, feels an ardour to labour he never felt before. Pride steps in and leads him to everything that the laws do not forbid: he respects them; with a heart-felt gratitude he looks toward the east, toward that insular government from whose wisdom all his new felicity is derived, and under whose wings and protection he now lives. These reflections constitute him the good man and the good subject. Ye poor Europeans, ye, who sweat, and work for the great—ye, who are obliged to give so many sheaves to the church, so many to your lords, so many to your government, and have hardly any left for yourselves—ye, who are held in less estimation than favourite hunters or useless lap-dogs—ye, who only breathe the air of nature, because it cannot be withheld from you; it is here that ye can conceive the possibility of those feelings I have been describing; it is here the laws of naturalisation invite every one to partake of our great labours and felicity, to till unrented, untaxed lands! Many, corrupted beyond the power of amendment, have brought with them all their vices, and disregarding the advantages held to them, have gone on in their former career of iniquity, until they have been overtaken and punished by our laws. It is not every emigrant who succeeds; no, it is only the sober, the honest, and industrious: happy those to whom this transition has served as a powerful spur to labour, to prosperity, and to the good establishment of children, born in the days of their poverty; and who had no other portion to expect but the rags of their parents, had it not been for their happy emigration. Others again, have been led astray by this enhancing scene; their new pride, instead of leading them to the fields, has kept them in idleness; the idea of possessing lands is all that satisfies them—though surrounded with fertility, they have mouldered away their time in inactivity, misinformed husbandry, and ineffectual endeavours. How much wiser, in general, the honest Germans than almost all other Europeans; they hire themselves to some of their wealthy landsmen, and in that apprenticeship learn everything that is necessary. They attentively consider the prosperous industry of others, which imprints in their minds a strong desire of possessing the same advantages. This forcible idea never quits them, they launch forth, and by dint of sobriety, rigid parsimony, and the most persevering industry, they commonly succeed. Their astonishment at their first arrival from Germany is very great—it is to them a dream; the contrast must be powerful indeed; they observe their countrymen flourishing in every place; they travel through whole counties where not a word of English is spoken; and in the names and the language of the people, they retrace Germany. They have been an useful acquisition to this continent, and to Pennsylvania in particular; to them it owes some share of its prosperity: to their mechanical knowledge and patience it owes the finest mills in all America, the best teams of horses, and many other advantages. The recollection of their former poverty and slavery never quits them as long as they live.

The Scotch and the Irish might have lived in their own country 20 perhaps as poor, but enjoying more civil advantages, the effects of their new situation do not strike them so forcibly, nor has it so lasting an effect. From whence the difference arises I know not, but out of twelve families of emigrants of each country, generally seven Scotch will succeed, nine German, and four Irish. The Scotch are frugal and laborious, but their wives cannot work so hard as German women, who on the contrary vie with their husbands, and often share with them the most severe toils of the field, which they understand better. They have therefore nothing to struggle against, but the common casualties of nature. The Irish do not prosper so well; they love to drink and to quarrel; they are litigious, and soon take to the gun, which is the ruin of everything; they seem beside to labour under a greater degree of ignorance in husbandry than the others; perhaps it is that their industry had less scope, and was less exercised at home. I have heard many relate, how the land was parcelled out in that kingdom; their ancient conquest has been a great detriment to them, by over-setting their landed property. The lands possessed by a few, are leased down *ad infinitum,* and the occupiers often pay five guineas an acre. The poor are worse lodged there than anywhere else in Europe; their potatoes, which are easily raised, are perhaps an inducement to laziness: their wages are too low, and their whisky too cheap.

There is no tracing observations of this kind, without making at the same time very great allowances, as there are everywhere to be found, a great many exceptions. The Irish themselves, from different parts of that kingdom, are very different. It is difficult to account for this surprising locality, one would think on so small an island an Irishman must be an Irishman: yet it is not so, they are different in their aptitude to, and in their love of labour.   21

The Scotch on the contrary are all industrious and saving; they want nothing more than a field to exert themselves in, and they are commonly sure of succeeding. The only difficulty they labour under is, that technical American knowledge which requires some time to obtain; it is not easy for those who seldom saw a tree, to conceive how it is to be felled, cut up, and split into rails and posts.   22

As I am fond of seeing and talking of prosperous families, I intend to finish this letter by relating to you the history of an honest Scotch Hebridean, who came here in 1774, which will show you in epitome what the Scotch can do, wherever they have room for the exertion of their industry. Whenever I hear of any new settlement, I pay it a visit once or twice a year, on purpose to observe the different steps each settler takes, the gradual improvements, the different tempers of each family, on which their prosperity in a great nature depends; their different modifications of industry, their ingenuity, and contrivance; for being all poor, their life requires sagacity and prudence. In the evening I love to hear them tell their stories, they furnish me with new ideas; I sit still and listen to their ancient misfortunes, observing in many of them a strong degree of gratitude to God, and the government. Many a well meant sermon have I preached to some of them. When I found laziness and inattention to prevail, who could refrain from wishing well to these new countrymen, after having undergone so many fatigues? Who could withhold good advice? What a happy change it must be, to descend from the   23 high, sterile, bleak lands of Scotland, where everything is barren and cold, to rest on some fertile farms in these middle provinces! Such a transition must have afforded the most pleasing satisfaction.

The following dialogue passed at an out-settlement, where I 24 lately paid a visit:

Well, friend, how do you do now; I am come fifty odd miles on 25 purpose to see you; how do you go on with your new cutting and slashing? Very well, good Sir, we learn the use of the axe bravely, we shall make it out; we have a belly full of victuals every day, our cows run about, and come home full of milk, our hogs get fat of themselves in the woods: Oh, this is a good country! God bless the king and William Penn; we shall do very well by and by, if we keep our healths. Your loghouse looks neat and light, where did you get these shingles? One of our neighbours is a New-England man, and he showed us how to split them out of chestnut-trees. Now for a barn, but all in good time, here are fine trees to build with. Who is to frame it, sure you don't understand that work yet? A countryman of ours who has been in America these ten years, offers to wait for his money until the second crop is lodged in it. What did you give for your land? Thirty-five shillings per acre, payable in seven years. How many acres have you got? An hundred and fifty. That is enough to begin with; is not your land pretty hard to clear? Yes, Sir, hard enough, but it would be harder still if it were ready cleared, for then we should have no timber, and I love the woods much; the land is nothing without them. Have not you found out any bees yet? No, Sir; and if we had we should not know what to do with them. I will tell you by and by. You are very kind. Farewell, honest man, God prosper you; whenever you travel toward— —, inquire for J.S. He will entertain you kindly, provided you bring him good tidings from your family and farm. In this manner I often visit them, and carefully examine their houses, their modes of ingenuity, their different ways; and make them all relate all they know, and describe all they feel. These are scenes which I believe you would willingly share with me. I well remember your philanthropic turn of mind. Is it not better to contemplate under these humble roofs, the rudiments of future wealth and population, than to behold the accumulated bundles of litigious papers in the office of a lawyer? To examine how the world is gradually settled, how the howling swamp is converted into a pleasing meadow, the rough ridge into a fine field; and to hear the cheerful whistling, the rural song, where there was no sound heard before, save the yell of the savage, the screech of the owl or the hissing of the snake? Here an European, fatigued with luxury, riches, and pleasures, may find a sweet relaxation in a series of interesting scenes, as affecting as they are new. England, which now contains so many domes, so many castles, was once like this; a place woody and marshy; its inhabitants, now the favourite nation for arts and commerce, were once painted like our neighbours. The country will flourish in its turn, and the same observations will be made which I have just delineated. Posterity will look back with avidity and pleasure, to trace, if possible, the era of this or that particular settlement.

Pray, what is the reason that the Scots are in general more reli- 26
gious, more faithful, more honest, and industrious than the Irish? I do not mean to insinuate national reflections, God forbid! It ill becomes any man, and much less an American; but as I know men are nothing of themselves, and that they owe all their different modifications either to government or other local circumstances, there must be some powerful causes which constitute this great national difference.

Agreeable to the account which several Scotchmen have given 27
me of the north of Britain, of the Orkneys, and the Hebride Islands, they seem, on many accounts, to be unfit for the habitation of men; they appear to be calculated only for great sheep pastures. Who then can blame the inhabitants of these countries for transporting themselves hither? This great continent must in time absorb the poorest part of Europe; and this will happen in proportion as it becomes better known; and as war, taxation, oppression, and misery increase there. The Hebrides appear to be fit only for the residence of malefactors, and it would be much better to send felons there than either to Virginia or Maryland. What a strange compliment has our mother country paid to two of the finest provinces in America! England has entertained in that respect very mistaken ideas; what was intended as a punishment, is become the good fortune of several; many of those who have been transported as felons, are now rich, and strangers to the stings of those wants that urged them to violations of the law: they are become industrious, exemplary, and useful citizens. The English government should purchase the most northern and barren of those islands; it should send over to us the honest, primitive Hebrideans, settle them here on good lands, as a reward for their virtue and ancient poverty; and replace them with a colony of her wicked sons. The severity of the climate, the inclemency of the seasons, the sterility of the soil, the tempestuousness of the sea, would afflict and punish enough. Could there be found a spot better adapted to retaliate the injury it had received by their crimes? Some of those islands might be considered as the hell of Great Britain, where all evil spirits should be sent. Two essential ends would be

answered by this simple operation. The good people, by emigration, would be rendered happier; the bad ones would be placed where they ought to be. In a few years the dread of being sent to that wintry region would have a much stronger effect than that of transportation. — This is no place of punishment; were I a poor hopeless, breadless Englishman, and not restrained by the power of shame, I should be very thankful for the passage. It is of very little importance how, and in what manner an indigent man arrives; for if he is but sober, honest, and industrious, he has nothing more to ask of heaven. Let him go to work, he will have opportunities enough to earn a comfortable support, and even the means of procuring some land; which ought to be the utmost wish of every person who has health and hands to work. I knew a man who came to this country, in the literal sense of the expression, stark naked; I think he was a Frenchman, and a sailor on board an English man-of-war. Being discontented, he had stripped himself and swam ashore; where, finding clothes and friends, he settled afterwards at Maraneck, in the county of Chester, in the province of New York: he married and left a good farm to each of his sons. I knew another person who was but twelve years old when he was taken on the frontiers of Canada, by the Indians; at his arrival at Albany he was purchased by a gentleman, who generously bound him apprentice to a tailor. He lived to the age of ninety, and left behind him a fine estate and a numerous family, all well settled; many of them I am acquainted with. — Where is then the industrious European who ought to despair?

After a foreigner from any part of Europe is arrived, and become   28
a citizen; let him devoutly listen to the voice of our great parent, which says to him, "Welcome to my shores, distressed European; bless the hour in which thou didst see my verdant fields, my fair navigable rivers, and my green mountains! — If thou wilt work, I have bread for thee; if thou wilt be honest, sober, and industrious, I have greater rewards to confer on thee — ease and independence. I will give thee fields to feed and clothe thee; a comfortable fireside to sit by, and tell thy children by what means thou hast prospered; and a decent bed to repose on. I shall endow thee beside with the immunities of a freeman. If thou wilt carefully educate thy children, teach them gratitude to God and reverence to that government, that philanthropic government, which has collected here so many men and made them happy. I will also provide for thy progeny; and to every good man this ought to be the most holy, the most powerful, the most earnest wish he can possibly form, as well as the most consolatory prospect when he dies. Go thou and work and till; thou shalt prosper, provided thou be just, grateful, and industrious."

QUESTIONS FOR CRITICAL READING

1. What most impresses Crèvecoeur about the nature of the land in America?
2. What is Crèvecoeur's view of the mixing of different nationalities in America?
3. Why does he call the colonies "this great American asylum" (para. 3)?
4. What are some of the benefits of the fact that there are no aristocrats in America?
5. How does the geography of each region affect the people who settle there?
6. What most pleases Crèvecoeur about the laws in America?
7. How would you describe Crèvecoeur's attitude toward religion?

SUGGESTIONS FOR WRITING

1. In paragraph 4, Crèvecoeur tells us that the American's labor "is founded on the basis of nature, *self-interest*." What does this mean? To what extent is self-interest the basis of human nature? Is Crèvecoeur correct in his analysis in this paragraph?
2. In paragraph 6, Crèvecoeur tells us that "Men are like plants." This simile is crucial to his understanding of what makes the American different from the European. What does the simile imply? Is it true that men are like plants?
3. How much would you agree with Crèvecoeur's view that where the bread is, there is the home? He says this is the motto of all emigrants. Do you think he is correct? To what extent would you modify that motto today? What are the qualities about America that draw emigrants here in the twenty-first century?
4. Of farmers, in paragraph 7, Crèvecoeur says, "Industry, good living, selfishness, litigiousness, country politics, the pride of freemen, religious indifference, are their characteristics." To what extent are these qualities noticeable in the general mass of working people in America today? In what important ways have modern Americans changed?
5. In paragraphs 10 and 11, Crèvecoeur contends that the various provinces of America have produced people with specific qualities and patterns of behavior. What does he mean? Is he correct? Do such differences still exist in America? Describe those that you have noticed, and try to explain what characteristics of the provinces (now states) might have contributed to differences either in Crèvecoeur's time or today.
6. **CONNECTIONS** Examine Thomas Jefferson's Declaration of Independence for issues that relate well to the qualities that Crèvecoeur praises about America. Crèvecoeur was a loyalist, so his attitudes would be contrary to those of Jefferson. In what ways do Jefferson and

Crèvecoeur agree and disagree? Do you think they disagree with each other enough to warrant going to war?

7. **CONNECTIONS**   In 1776, Adam Smith praises land as a source of continuing wealth almost as much as Crèvecoeur does. However, Smith thinks in terms of a landlord with tenant farmers to do the work of tilling the soil. Crèvecoeur thinks of farmers tilling their own soil. Both views are essentially capitalist. To what extent would Crèvecoeur agree with Smith, and to what extent would he disagree concerning the value of land and the importance of opportunity?

ALEXIS DE TOCQUEVILLE
Influence of Democratic Ideas and Feelings on Political Society

ALEXIS DE TOCQUEVILLE (1805–1859) became famous for his best-known book, *Democracy in America*, published in two volumes in 1835 and 1840. In it he described the American system of government in terms of both its strengths and its weaknesses. His close examination of American institutions and his role as an active politician in French governmental affairs rendered him well equipped to make serious comments on America's democracy.

Tocqueville lived in France in the turbulent years following its violent revolution (1789–1799) and the years of Napoleon Bonaparte's spectacular rise to power and his eventual crowning as emperor. The French killed their king, instituted a revolutionary power, and eventually produced the powerful Napoleon—who stands, in the minds of many, as the first of the modern tyrants in whose wake came Mussolini, Hitler, and Stalin. By the time Tocqueville participated in government, however, Napoleon had long since been ousted from power. In his place was a "citizen-king," Louis-Philippe, who came to power in 1830 after the July revolution. His government was unstable and collapsed in a bloody and violent riot in 1848. Following the February revolution of 1848, France reconstituted itself as a republic, but one that was also relatively unstable and that changed forms several times.

During this twenty-year period Tocqueville proved a very popular figure in regional French government, having stood for election and won several times by as much as 80 percent of the vote. He was essentially a liberal, although he carefully observed the excesses of both the conservative and liberal wings of the French government.

From *Democracy in America.*

At one early period during these difficult times, Tocqueville and his close friend, Gustave de Beaumont, got permission to visit the United States to observe its penal system. Tocqueville eventually published *On the Penitentiary System in the United States and Its Application in France* (1833). At the same time, Beaumont published *Marie, or Slavery in the United States* (1835). Clearly, both these men had an opportunity to see America in a way that few others could.

The passage that appears here is from the Fourth Book of the second volume of *Democracy in America*. Although the early sections of the book were highly influential in the United States and elsewhere, this later section contains some of Tocqueville's most instructive thought and philosophy. In these pages he considers the problems of equality and its effects in America and, by extension, in France.

One of Tocqueville's most important points is that equality among individuals eventually produces a strong desire for centralization in government. Why this should be so, when it seems on the surface to be unlikely, depends on the independence that equality produces, especially in the America that Tocqueville grew to know and understand. For example, Tocqueville suggests that in a nation in which people have freedom and independence, their opportunities for action are great. Consequently, they will be extremely busy with their own activities and lives. Although he does not say it directly, he implies that they will be busy making their fortune. As a result, they will expect the government to take care of governing the nation so as to leave them free to pursue their own opportunities.

However, he notes, this condition may also produce governors whose power will be concentrated in such a way as to permit them to exercise it unwisely. In other words, the conditions that produce equality may also produce a despot — especially, Tocqueville says, if the despot desires the same things that the people do. Such an observation is chilling in a document written in the 1830s when one realizes that Adolf Hitler's rise to power in Germany more than one hundred years later followed precisely that pattern, resulting in unbelievable horror and destruction. Partly because of Tocqueville's prescient analysis of equality and its political potential, he was rediscovered as an important thinker in the early twentieth century.

Tocqueville presents a number of other interesting ideas regarding equality. One is that in a democratic state such as America equality produces independence, which in turn produces a society in which the individual is regarded as less important than the larger social order. Although this hypothesis may be difficult to justify in America, it does contain some degree of truth as the ideas of equality were applied in modern communist states, such as the former Soviet Union. Another interesting idea is that equality produces a great hatred for privilege: "This never dying, ever kin-dling hatred which sets a democratic people against the smallest privileges is peculiarly favorable to the gradual concentration of all political rights in the hands of the representative of the state alone" (para. 24). Regardless of Tocqueville's views, they are tempered by his having been raised in a culture in which privilege was still of great importance—despite the fact that many French aristocrats had been killed by or had fled from the revolution.

Certainly, the American democratic experiment looked very exotic to Tocqueville, and as a result it would have been a perfect object of study for one who was himself so politically astute and culturally sensitive. Much of what he had to say about America proved prophetic.

Tocqueville's Rhetoric

Tocqueville wrote for a generally literate audience in Europe, but he also enjoyed a wide readership in America. The structure of his book was meant to command the attention of a serious audi-ence, which would have recognized the book's similarities to im-portant studies of other nations. By dividing his work into four books, he can segment the work into convenient subjects. Then, each chapter within the books covers a limited aspect of the pri-mary subject. One could easily outline the entire project by taking the titles of the books and the individual chapters and organizing them into a conventional outline. Such a structure was familiar to both his European and American audiences in 1840.

The Fourth Book concerns the "Influence of Democratic Ideas and Feelings on Political Society." Its first chapter addresses one concept within that larger framework: "Equality Naturally Gives Men a Taste for Free Institutions." By presenting his material in this fashion—in effect, previewing his conclusion in each chapter heading—Tocqueville avoids the sense that his argument needs support through careful logic and persuasion. The structure gives the reader the impression that the argument has already been won and that the views Tocqueville explores are a given. However, a close examination of any chapter in the book shows that he argues very carefully, expecting his audience to follow and to agree. For example, Tocqueville says that for the American, after the creation of a central power, "uniformity of legislation appears to him to be the first condition of good government" (para. 7). That paragraph establishes certain primary points, then moves to a conclusion that is unavoidable (if the reader accepts the points). In this case

Tocqueville insists that justice implies equality in the eyes of the law. That means fair-handed treatment for all, regardless of their status in the society.

Tocqueville's awareness of his writing strategies sometimes becomes apparent at the end of a chapter, in which he either recapitulates what he has said or establishes what he has tried to do. At the end of Chapter III, for example, he is very direct: "Thus by two separate paths I have reached the same conclusion. I have shown that the principle of equality suggests to men the notion of a sole, uniform and strong government; I have now shown that the principle of equality imparts to them a taste for it" (para. 27).

Because there is little by way of precedent or comparison for discussing the democratic experiment in America, Tocqueville is limited in the ways in which he can press his case and prove his points. He does not use evidence from the experiences of other nations, nor does he refer to other writers on political issues. In other words, he has little or no recourse to authorities that his audience would recognize and respect. He does not cite biblical references any more than he cites political references. Rather, he asserts that Americans are of a specific attitude and then suggests what that attitude is likely to produce.

Tocqueville's style is not always simple, but neither is it convoluted or confusing. The sentences are longer than we are accustomed to today, but the paragraphs are much shorter than Crèvecoeur's. The two writers were both French and relatively close in time (roughly fifty years apart), but Tocqueville's prose is more approachable and accessible; he emphasizes reason, establishing a principle and then developing his ideas from that principle. His evidence begins from his own observations, from which he quickly develops an opinion. He expects us to accept his opinion on important issues because he feels that his logical and rational approach will convince us of his wisdom. Because he is well informed, and especially because he proceeds step by step and with apparent caution, he may indeed convince most of his readers.

PREREADING QUESTIONS:
WHAT TO READ FOR

The following prereading questions may help you anticipate key issues in the discussion on Alexis de Tocqueville's "Influence of Democratic Ideas and Feelings on Political Society." Keeping them in mind during your first reading of the selection should help focus your reactions.

- In a democracy, what does equality produce?
- In what way does a democracy concentrate political power?
- What is the relationship between equality and independence?

Influence of Democratic Ideas and Feelings on Political Society

I should imperfectly fulfill the purpose of this book if, after having shown what ideas and feelings are suggested by the principle of equality, I did not point out, before I conclude, the general influence that these same ideas and feelings may exercise upon the government of human societies. To succeed in this object I shall frequently have to retrace my steps, but I trust the reader will not refuse to follow me through paths already known to him, which may lead to some new truth. 1

Chapter I
Equality Naturally Gives Men a Taste for Free Institutions

The principle of equality, which makes men independent of 2 each other, gives them a habit and a taste for following in their private actions no other guide than their own will. This complete independence, which they constantly enjoy in regard to their equals and in the intercourse of private life, tends to make them look upon all authority with a jealous eye and speedily suggests to them the notion and the love of political freedom. Men living at such times have a natural bias towards free institutions. Take any one of them at a venture and search if you can his most deep-seated instincts, and you will find that, of all governments, he will soonest conceive and most highly value that government whose head he has himself elected and whose administration he may control.

Of all the political effects produced by the equality of conditions, 3 this love of independence is the first to strike the observing and to alarm the timid; nor can it be said that their alarm is wholly misplaced, for anarchy has a more formidable aspect in democratic countries than elsewhere. As the citizens have no direct influence on each other, as soon as the supreme power of the nation fails, which kept them all in their several stations, it would seem that disorder must instantly reach its utmost pitch and that, every man drawing aside in a different direction, the fabric of society must at once crumble away.

I am convinced, however, that anarchy is not the principal evil   4
that democratic ages have to fear, but the least. For the principle of equality begets two tendencies: the one leads men straight to independence and may suddenly drive them into anarchy; the other conducts them by a longer, more secret, but more certain road to servitude. Nations readily discern the former tendency and are prepared to resist it; they are led away by the latter, without perceiving its drift; hence it is peculiarly important to point it out.

Personally, far from finding fault with equality because it inspires a spirit of independence, I praise it primarily for that very reason.   5
son. I admire it because it lodges in the very depths of each man's mind and heart that indefinable feeling, the instinctive inclination for political independence, and thus prepares the remedy for the ill which it engenders. It is precisely for this reason that I cling to it.

Chapter II
That the Opinions of Democratic Nations about Government Are Naturally Favorable to the Concentration of Power

The notion of secondary powers placed between the sovereign   6
and his subjects occurred naturally to the imagination of aristocratic nations, because those communities contained individuals or families raised above the common level and apparently destined to command by their birth, their education, and their wealth. This same notion is naturally wanting in the minds of men in democratic ages, for converse reasons; it can only be introduced artificially, it can only be kept there with difficulty, whereas they conceive, as it were without thinking about the subject, the notion of a single and central power which governs the whole community by its direct influence. Moreover, in politics as well as in philosophy and in religion the intellect of democratic nations is peculiarly open to simple and general notions. Complicated systems are repugnant to it, and its favorite conception is that of a great nation composed of citizens all formed upon one pattern and all governed by a single power.

The very next notion to that of a single and central power which   7
presents itself to the minds of men in the ages of equality is the notion of uniformity of legislation. As every man sees that he differs but little from those about him, he cannot understand why a rule that is applicable to one man should not be equally applicable to all others. Hence the slightest privileges are repugnant to his reason;

the faintest dissimilarities in the political institutions of the same people offend him, and uniformity of legislation appears to him to be the first condition of good government.

I find, on the contrary, that this notion of a uniform rule equally 8 binding on all the members of the community was almost unknown to the human mind in aristocratic ages; either it was never broached, or it was rejected.

These contrary tendencies of opinion ultimately turn on both 9 sides to such blind instincts and ungovernable habits that they still direct the actions of men, in spite of particular exceptions. Notwithstanding the immense variety of conditions in the Middle Ages, a certain number of persons existed at that period in precisely similar circumstances; but this did not prevent the laws then in force from assigning to each of them distinct duties and different rights. On the contrary, at the present time all the powers of government are exerted to impose the same customs and the same laws on populations which have as yet but few points of resemblance.

As the conditions of men become equal among a people, indi- 10 viduals seem of less and society of greater importance; or rather every citizen, being assimilated to all the rest, is lost in the crowd, and nothing stands conspicuous but the great and imposing image of the people at large. This naturally gives the men of democratic periods a lofty opinion of the privileges of society and a very humble notion of the rights of individuals; they are ready to admit that the interests of the former are everything and those of the latter nothing. They are willing to acknowledge that the power which represents the community has far more information and wisdom than any of the members of that community; and that it is the duty, as well as the right, of that power to guide as well as govern each private citizen.

If we closely scrutinize our contemporaries and penetrate to the 11 root of their political opinions, we shall detect some of the notions that I have just pointed out, and we shall perhaps be surprised to find so much accordance between men who are so often at variance.

The Americans hold that in every state the supreme power 12 ought to emanate from the people; but when once that power is constituted, they can conceive, as it were, no limits to it, and they are ready to admit that it has the right to do whatever it pleases. They have not the slightest notion of peculiar privileges granted to cities, families, or persons; their minds appear never to have foreseen that it might be possible not to apply with strict uniformity the same laws to every part of the state and to all its inhabitants.

These same opinions are more and more diffused in Europe; 13 they even insinuate themselves among those nations that most vehemently reject the principle of the sovereignty of the people. Such nations assign a different origin to the supreme power, but they ascribe to that power the same characteristics. Among them all the idea of intermediate powers is weakened and obliterated; the idea of rights inherent in certain individuals is rapidly disappearing from the minds of men; the idea of the omnipotence and sole authority of society at large rises to fill its place. These ideas take root and spread in proportion as social conditions become more equal and men more alike. They are produced by equality, and in turn they hasten the progress of equality.

In France, where the revolution of which I am speaking has   14
gone further than in any other European country, these opinions have got complete hold of the public mind. If we listen attentively to the language of the various parties in France, we find that there is not one which has not adopted them. Most of these parties censure the conduct of the government, but they all hold that the government ought perpetually to act and interfere in everything that is done. Even those which are most at variance are nevertheless agreed on this head. The unity, the ubiquity, the omnipotence of the supreme power, and the uniformity of its rules constitute the principal characteristics of all the political systems that have been put forward in our age. They recur even in the wildest visions of political regeneration; the human mind pursues them in its dreams.

If these notions spontaneously arise in the minds of private indi-   15
viduals, they suggest themselves still more forcibly to the minds of princes. While the ancient fabric of European society is altered and dissolved, sovereigns acquire new conceptions of their opportunities and their duties; they learn for the first time that the central power which they represent may and ought to administer, by its own agency and on a uniform plan, all the concerns of the whole community. This opinion, which, I will venture to say, was never conceived before our time by the monarchs of Europe, now sinks deeply into the minds of kings and abides there amid all the agitation of more unsettled thoughts.

Our contemporaries are therefore much less divided than is   16
commonly supposed; they are constantly disputing as to the hands in which supremacy is to be vested, but they readily agree upon the duties and the rights of that supremacy. The notion they all form of government is that of a sole, simple, providential, and creative power.

All secondary opinions in politics are unsettled; this one re-   17
mains fixed, invariable, and consistent. It is adopted by statesmen and political philosophers; it is eagerly laid hold of by the multitude; those who govern and those who are governed agree to pursue it

with equal ardor; it is the earliest notion of their minds, it seems innate. It originates, therefore, in no caprice of the human intellect, but it is a necessary condition of the present state of mankind.

Chapter III
That the Sentiments of Democratic Nations Accord with Their Opinions in Leading Them to Concentrate Political Power

If it is true that in ages of equality men readily adopt the notion 18 of a great central power, it cannot be doubted, on the other hand, that their habits and sentiments predispose them to recognize such a power and to give it their support. This may be demonstrated in a few words, as the greater part of the reasons to which the fact may be attributed have been previously stated.

As the men who inhabit democratic countries have no superi- 19 ors, no inferiors, and no habitual or necessary partners in their undertakings, they readily fall back upon themselves and consider themselves as beings apart. I had occasion to point this out at considerable length in treating of individualism. Hence such men can never, without an effort, tear themselves from their private affairs to engage in public business; their natural bias leads them to abandon the latter to the sole visible and permanent representative of the interests of the community; that is to say, to the state. Not only are they naturally wanting in a taste for public business, but they have frequently no time to attend to it. Private life in democratic times is so busy, so excited, so full of wishes and of work, that hardly any energy or leisure remains to each individual for public life. I am the last man to contend that these propensities are unconquerable, since my chief object in writing this book has been to combat them. I maintain only that at the present day a secret power is fostering them in the human heart, and that if they are not checked, they will wholly overgrow it.

I have also had occasion to show how the increasing love of 20 well-being and the fluctuating character of property cause democratic nations to dread all violent disturbances. The love of public tranquillity is frequently the only passion which these nations retain, and it becomes more active and powerful among them in proportion as all other passions droop and die. This naturally disposes the members of the community constantly to give or to surrender additional rights to the central power, which alone seems to be interested in defending them by the same means that it uses to defend itself.

As in periods of equality no man is compelled to lend his assis-   21
tance to his fellow men, and none has any right to expect much support from them, everyone is at once independent and powerless.
These two conditions, which must never be either separately considered or confounded together, inspire the citizen of a democratic
country with very contrary propensities. His independence fills him
with self-reliance and pride among his equals; his debility makes
him feel from time to time the want of some outward assistance,
which he cannot expect from any of them, because they are all impotent and unsympathizing. In this predicament he naturally turns
his eyes to that imposing power which alone rises above the level of
universal depression. Of that power his wants and especially his desires continually remind him, until he ultimately views it as the sole
and necessary support of his own weakness.[1]

This may more completely explain what frequently takes place   22
in democratic countries, where the very men who are so impatient
of superiors patiently submit to a master, exhibiting at once their
pride and their servility.

The hatred that men bear to privilege increases in proportion as   23
privileges become fewer and less considerable, so that democratic
passions would seem to burn most fiercely just when they have least
fuel. I have already given the reason for this phenomenon. When all

----

[1]In democratic communities nothing but the central power has any stability in
its position or any permanence in its undertakings. All the citizens are in ceaseless
stir and transformation. Now, it is in the nature of all governments to seek constantly to enlarge their sphere of action; hence it is almost impossible that such a
government should not ultimately succeed, because it acts with a fixed principle and
a constant will upon men whose position, ideas, and desires are constantly
changing.

It frequently happens that the members of the community promote the influence of the central power without intending to. Democratic eras are periods of experiment, innovation, and adventure. There is always a multitude of men engaged in
difficult or novel undertakings, which they follow by themselves without shackling
themselves to their fellows. Such persons will admit, as a general principle, that the
public authority ought not to interfere in private concerns; but, by an exception to
that rule, each of them craves its assistance in the particular concern on which he is
engaged and seeks to draw upon the influence of the government for his own benefit, although he would restrict it on all other occasions. If a large number of men applies this particular exception to a great variety of different purposes, the sphere of
the central power extends itself imperceptibly in all directions, although everyone
wishes it to be circumscribed.

Thus a democratic government increases its power simply by the fact of its permanence. Time is on its side; every incident befriends it; the passions of individuals
unconsciously promote it; and it may be asserted that the older a democratic community is, the more centralized will its government become. [Tocqueville's note]

conditions are unequal, no inequality is so great as to offend the eye, whereas the slightest dissimilarity is odious in the midst of general uniformity; the more complete this uniformity is, the more insupportable the sight of such a difference becomes. Hence it is natural that the love of equality should constantly increase together with equality itself, and that it should grow by what it feeds on.

This never dying, ever kindling hatred which sets a democratic   24
people against the smallest privileges is peculiarly favorable to the gradual concentration of all political rights in the hands of the representative of the state alone. The sovereign, being necessarily and incontestably above all the citizens, does not excite their envy, and each of them thinks that he strips his equals of the prerogative that he concedes to the crown. The man of a democratic age is extremely reluctant to obey his neighbor, who is his equal; he refuses to acknowledge superior ability in such a person; he mistrusts his justice and is jealous of his power; he fears and he despises him; and he loves continually to remind him of the common dependence in which both of them stand to the same master.

Every central power, which follows its natural tendencies,   25
courts and encourages the principle of equality; for equality singularly facilitates, extends, and secures the influence of a central power.

In like manner it may be said that every central government   26
worships uniformity; uniformity relieves it from inquiry into an infinity of details, which must be attended to if rules have to be adapted to different men, instead of indiscriminately subjecting all men to the same rule. Thus the government likes what the citizens like and naturally hates what they hate. These common sentiments, which in democratic nations constantly unite the sovereign and every member of the community in one and the same conviction, establish a secret and lasting sympathy between them. The faults of the government are pardoned for the sake of its inclinations; public confidence is only reluctantly withdrawn in the midst even of its excesses and its errors, and it is restored at the first call. Democratic nations often hate those in whose hands the central power is vested, but they always love that power itself.

Thus by two separate paths I have reached the same conclusion.   27
I have shown that the principle of equality suggests to men the notion of a sole, uniform, and strong government; I have now shown that the principle of equality imparts to them a taste for it. To governments of this kind the nations of our age are therefore tending. They are drawn thither by the natural inclination of mind and heart; and in order to reach that result, it is enough that they do not check themselves in their course.

I am of the opinion that, in the democratic ages which are open- 28
ing upon us, individual independence and local liberties will ever
be the products of art; that centralization will be the natural
government.

Chapter IV
Of Certain Peculiar and Accidental Causes Which
Either Lead a People to Complete the Centralization
of Government or Divert Them from It

If all democratic nations are instinctively led to the centraliza- 29
tion of government, they tend to this result in an unequal manner.
This depends on the particular circumstances which may promote
or prevent the natural consequences of that state of society, circumstances which are exceedingly numerous, but of which I shall mention only a few.

Among men who have lived free long before they became equal, 30
the tendencies derived from free institutions combat, to a certain extent, the propensities superinduced by the principle of equality; and
although the central power may increase its privileges among such a
people, the private members of such a community will never entirely forfeit their independence. But when equality of conditions
grows up among a people who have never known or have long
ceased to know what freedom is (and such is the case on the continent of Europe), as the former habits of the nation are suddenly
combined, by some sort of natural attraction, with the new habits
and principles engendered by the state of society, all powers seem
spontaneously to rush to the center. These powers accumulate there
with astonishing rapidity, and the state instantly attains the utmost
limits of its strength, while private persons allow themselves to sink
as suddenly to the lowest degree of weakness.

The English who emigrated three hundred years ago to found a 31
democratic commonwealth on the shores of the New World had all
learned to take a part in public affairs in their mother country; they
were conversant with trial by jury; they were accustomed to liberty
of speech and of the press, to personal freedom, to the notion of
rights and the practice of asserting them. They carried with them to
America these free institutions and manly customs, and these institutions preserved them against the encroachments of the state. Thus
among the Americans it is freedom that is old; equality is of comparatively modern date. The reverse is occurring in Europe, where
equality, introduced by absolute power and under the rule of kings,

was already infused into the habits of nations long before freedom had entered into their thoughts.

I have said that, among democratic nations the notion of government naturally presents itself to the mind under the form of a sole and central power, and that the notion of intermediate powers is not familiar to them. This is peculiarly applicable to the democratic nations which have witnessed the triumph of the principle of equality by means of a violent revolution. As the classes that managed local affairs have been suddenly swept away by the storm, and as the confused mass that remains has as yet neither the organization nor the habits which fit it to assume the administration of these affairs, the state alone seems capable of taking upon itself all the details of government, and centralization becomes, as it were, the unavoidable state of the country. 32

Napoleon deserves neither praise nor censure for having centered in his own hands almost all the administrative power of France; for after the abrupt disappearance of the nobility and the higher rank of the middle classes, these powers devolved on him of course: it would have been almost as difficult for him to reject as to assume them. But a similar necessity has never been felt by the Americans, who, having passed through no revolution, and having governed themselves from the first, never had to call upon the state to act for a time as their guardian. Thus the progress of centralization among a democratic people depends not only on the progress of equality, but on the manner in which this equality has been established. 33

At the commencement of a great democratic revolution, when hostilities have but just broken out between the different classes of society, the people endeavor to centralize the public administration in the hands of the government, in order to wrest the management of local affairs from the aristocracy. Towards the close of such a revolution, on the contrary, it is usually the conquered aristocracy that endeavors to make over the management of all affairs to the state, because such an aristocracy dreads the tyranny of a people that has become its equal and not infrequently its master. Thus it is not always the same class of the community that strives to increase the prerogative of the government; but as long as the democratic revolution lasts, there is always one class in the nation, powerful in numbers or in wealth, which is induced, by peculiar passions or interests, to centralize the public administration, independently of that hatred of being governed by one's neighbor which is a general and permanent feeling among democratic nations. 34

It may be remarked that at the present day the lower orders in England are striving with all their might to destroy local 35 independence and to transfer the administration from all the points of the circumference to the center; whereas the higher classes are endeavoring to retain this administration within its ancient boundaries. I venture to predict that a time will come when the very reverse will happen.

These observations explain why the supreme power is always stronger, and private individuals weaker, among a democratic people that has passed through a long and arduous struggle to reach a state of equality than among a democratic community in which the citizens have been equal from the first. The example of the Americans completely demonstrates the fact. The inhabitants of the United States were never divided by any privileges; they have never known the mutual relation of master and inferior; and as they neither dread nor hate each other, they have never known the necessity of calling in the supreme power to manage their affairs. The lot of the Americans is singular: they have derived from the aristocracy of England the notion of private rights and the taste for local freedom; and they have been able to retain both because they have had no aristocracy to combat. 36

If education enables men at all times to defend their independence, this is most especially true in democratic times. When all men are alike, it is easy to found a sole and all-powerful government by the aid of mere instinct. But men require much intelligence, knowledge, and art to organize and to maintain secondary powers under similar circumstances and to create, amid the independence and individual weakness of the citizens, such free associations as may be able to struggle against tyranny without destroying public order. 37

Hence the concentration of power and the subjection of individuals will increase among democratic nations, not only in the same proportion as their equality, but in the same proportion as their ignorance. It is true that in ages of imperfect civilization the government is frequently as wanting in the knowledge required to impose a despotism upon the people as the people are wanting in the knowledge required to shake it off; but the effect is not the same on both sides. However rude a democratic people may be, the central power that rules them is never completely devoid of cultivation, because it readily draws to its own uses what little cultivation is to be found in the country, and, if necessary, may seek assistance elsewhere. Hence among a nation which is ignorant as well as democratic an amazing difference cannot fail speedily to arise between the intellectual capacity of the ruler and that of each of his subjects. This completes the easy concentration of all power in his hands: the administrative function of the state is perpetually extended because the state alone is competent to administer the affairs of the country. 38

Aristocratic nations, however unenlightened they may be, never 39 afford the same spectacle, because in them instruction is nearly equally diffused between the monarch and the leading members of the community.

The Pasha who now rules in Egypt found the population of that 40 country composed of men exceedingly ignorant and equal, and he has borrowed the science and ability of Europe to govern that people. As the personal attainments of the sovereign are thus combined with the ignorance and democratic weakness of his subjects, the utmost centralization has been established without impediment, and the Pasha has made the country his factory, and the inhabitants his workmen.

I think that extreme centralization of government ultimately en- 41 ervates society and thus, after a length of time, weakens the government itself; but I do not deny that a centralized social power may be able to execute great undertakings with facility in a given time and on a particular point. This is more especially true of war, in which success depends much more on the means of transferring all the resources of a nation to one single point than on the extent of those resources. Hence it is chiefly in war that nations desire, and frequently need, to increase the powers of the central government. All men of military genius are fond of centralization, which increases their strength; and all men of centralizing genius are fond of war, which compels nations to combine all their powers in the hands of the government. Thus the democratic tendency that leads men unceasingly to multiply the privileges of the state and to circumscribe the rights of private persons is much more rapid and constant among those democratic nations that are exposed by their position to great and frequent wars than among all others.

I have shown how the dread of disturbance and the love of well- 42 being insensibly lead democratic nations to increase the functions of central government as the only power which appears to be intrinsically sufficiently strong, enlightened, and secure to protect them from anarchy. I would now add that all the particular circumstances which tend to make the state of a democratic community agitated and precarious enhance this general propensity and lead private persons more and more to sacrifice their rights to their tranquillity.

A people is therefore never so disposed to increase the functions 43 of central government as at the close of a long and bloody revolution, which, after having wrested property from the hands of its former possessors, has shaken all belief and filled the nation with fierce hatreds, conflicting interests, and contending factions. The love of public tranquillity becomes at such times an indiscriminate passion, and the members of the community are apt to conceive a most inordinate devotion to order.

I have already examined several of the incidents that may con-   44
cur to promote the centralization of power, but the principal cause
still remains to be noticed. The foremost of the incidental causes
which may draw the management of all affairs into the hands of the
ruler in democratic countries is the origin of that ruler himself and
his own propensities. Men who live in the ages of equality are naturally fond of central power and are willing to extend its privileges;
but if it happens that this same power faithfully represents their own
interests and exactly copies their own inclinations, the confidence
they place in it knows no bounds, and they think that whatever they
bestow upon it is bestowed upon themselves.

The attraction of administrative powers to the center will always   45
be less easy and less rapid under the reign of kings who are still in
some way connected with the old aristocratic order than under new
princes, the children of their own achievements, whose birth, prejudices, propensities, and habits appear to bind them indissolubly to
the cause of equality. I do not mean that princes of aristocratic origin
who live in democratic ages do not attempt to centralize; I believe they
apply themselves as diligently as any others to that object. For them
the sole advantages of equality lie in that direction; but their opportunities are less great, because the community, instead of volunteering
compliance with their desires, frequently obey them with reluctance.
In democratic communities the rule is that centralization must increase in proportion as the sovereign is less aristocratic.

When an ancient race of kings stands at the head of an aristoc-   46
racy, as the natural prejudices of the sovereign perfectly accord with
the natural prejudices of the nobility, the vices inherent in aristocratic communities have a free course and meet with no corrective.
The reverse is the case when the scion of a feudal stock is placed at
the head of a democratic people. The sovereign is constantly led, by
his education, his habits, and his associations, to adopt sentiments
suggested by the inequality of conditions, and the people tend as
constantly, by their social condition, to those manners which are engendered by equality. At such times it often happens that the citizens seek to control the central power far less as a tyrannical than as
an aristocratic power, and that they persist in the firm defense of
their independence, not only because they would remain free, but
especially because they are determined to remain equal.

A revolution that overthrows an ancient regal family in order to   47
place new men at the head of a democratic people may temporarily
weaken the central power; but however anarchical such a revolution
may appear at first, we need not hesitate to predict that its final and
certain consequence will be to extend and to secure the prerogatives
of that power.

The foremost or indeed the sole condition required in order to   48
succeed in centralizing the supreme power in a democratic community is to love equality, or to get men to believe you love it. Thus the
science of despotism, which was once so complex, is simplified, and
reduced, as it were, to a single principle.

QUESTIONS FOR CRITICAL READING

1. What is the connection between equality and freedom?
2. How does Tocqueville react to the American "love of independence"?
3. What form of central power does Tocqueville feel appeals to Americans?
4. What is Tocqueville's attitude toward justice in a democracy?
5. Why is privilege such a problem for those who put equality first?
6. How do personal comfort and well-being affect the behavior of those
   in a democracy?
7. Is centralization, as Tocqueville says in paragraph 28, "the natural government"?

SUGGESTIONS FOR WRITING

1. In Chapter III, Tocqueville asserts a number of interesting propositions
   regarding the kind of government that would be preferred by "democratic nations." Examine the principles he outlines, and write a brief
   essay that either defends his views or shows their limitations. In particular, consider what he says about the concentration of political power.
2. How much of what Tocqueville said about nineteenth-century America
   holds true in the twenty-first century? Was Tocqueville correct in his
   analysis of the basic attitudes and aspirations of those living in a
   democracy? Is the idea of equality as important now as it was in his
   time? Does it produce some of the same results in people now as he
   said it did in 1840?
3. Tocqueville says, "Every central power, which follows its natural tendencies, courts and encourages the principle of equality; for equality
   singularly facilitates, extends, and secures the influence of a central
   power" (para. 25). Do you think he is correct in his views of what
   equality "facilitates, extends, and secures"? How would you qualify his
   judgments in relation to what you see happening in American politics
   today?
4. The fact that centralized governments prefer uniformity seems to
   contradict the sense of independence and equality that Tocqueville
   perceives in America. Does government usually prefer uniformity? In
   what ways are equality and uniformity more or less the same thing? In

what ways are they distinct from each other? Does equality imply uniformity? What would it mean for a democracy if that were true?

5. In Chapter IV, Tocqueville examines the different paths by which people can "complete the centralization of government or [be diverted] from it." Comment on the examples he offers in this chapter and decide how convincing he is. Can you think of examples from recent political experience that cast light on his argument? What kinds of centralized governments do you know about that also offer a measure of democratic independence? How accurate are Tocqueville's judgments?

6. S. I. DuPont, founder of the DuPont Chemical Corporation, referred to the corporation as the greatest of modern inventions. The corporation is a business entity that can wield great power and achieve great things. However, it is not a democratic organization. Power in a corporation comes from the top down, not from the bottom up. Many people fear that corporations dominate American politics through contributions to politicians (the contributions help guarantee the election of people who in turn are obliged to favor the corporations that supported them). How serious is this fear? How much of a threat are giant corporations to the freedom and equality of Americans? How might Tocqueville react to their existence?

7. **CONNECTIONS**   Henry David Thoreau, almost a contemporary of Tocqueville, thought deeply about the role of government in his life. How sympathetic would he be with Tocqueville's judgments about the virtues of equality, independence, and democracy? Would he agree with him about the potential for a democracy to produce a very strong central government — perhaps too strong a government?

8. **CONNECTIONS**   Aristotle talks about justice in a democracy, and the Friedmans talk about equality in a democracy. In what ways do these authors intersect with Tocqueville's theories about justice and equality? How does Aristotle's influence on Tocqueville appear in Tocqueville's work? Similarly, in what ways do you see Tocqueville's influence on Rose and Milton Friedman? (Each author would have known the work of the earlier authors.)

HARRIET JACOBS (LINDA BRENT)
Free at Last

HARRIET JACOBS (1813–1897) struggled against enormous odds to achieve freedom from a life of slavery in North Carolina. Until the Emancipation Proclamation of 1863, during the Civil War, the "peculiar institution" of slavery was protected in the United States by harsh laws dating to colonial times. (The Thirteenth Amendment to the U.S. Constitution was passed and ratified in 1865 to ensure the abolishment of slavery from a legal standpoint.) Like many other slave narratives of the time, Jacobs's autobiography, *Incidents in the Life of a Slave Girl* (1861), records a pattern of horror and abuse so egregious as to stun the modern reader. Slaves were beaten with horsehide whips as many as a hundred times for attempted escape. Some were branded with hot irons on their face. Rewards for runaways were common, and in some cases the rewards were increased if the runaway was returned dead. Although the conditions in Edenton, North Carolina, were as harsh as any in the South, Jacobs somehow survived to be witness to some of the most significant changes in American culture: the gradual dismantling of the institution of slavery, and the emergence of a free African American community in the United States during the period of reconstruction following the Civil War.

Jacobs's first mistress, Margaret Horniblow, was unusually gentle and understanding—so much so that Jacobs was unaware she was a slave until she was six years old, when her mother died. Horniblow taught her to read and write, accomplishments rarely accorded to slaves. However, when Jacobs was twelve Margaret Horniblow died, and Jacobs became the property of Dr. James Norcom (named Dr. Flint in the passage reprinted here). Norcom was lecherous and made numerous sexual advances toward Jacobs,

---

From *Incidents in the Life of a Slave Girl.*

which she rebuffed. As a way of keeping Norcom away from her, she had an affair with a nearby white property owner, Mr. Sawyer, by whom she had two children, Joseph and Louisa (their names appear as Benjamin and Ellen in the passage reprinted here).

All this while, Jacobs was a house slave, working closely with the Norcom family and living in relative comfort compared to the slaves who worked in the fields. However, Norcom's wife was suspicious of her husband and frequently took her anger out on innocent slaves. Luckily, because Jacobs's grandmother Molly had been granted her freedom around 1830, she cared for Jacobs's children when they were very young. Jacobs was sometimes sent off by the suspicious Mrs. Norcom to live with Molly, which helped cement their relationship.

In spite of his wife's suspicions about his behavior, Dr. Norcom continued to make advances toward Jacobs. By 1835 he became so angry at her constant refusals that he sent her to work on his nearby plantation. During much of this time she lived with Dr. Norcom's son and his new bride, performing duties similar to those she had had in Dr. Norcom's house. Nevertheless she witnessed the extraordinary brutality the other slaves experienced on the plantation. Men, women, and children were frequently beaten savagely for even minor offenses. Their wounds were often soaked in salt water to make them heal faster and leave less scarring so the slaves would bring more on the auction block.

Jacobs soon became aware that Norcom's son had been given the task of eventually "breaking" her and readying her and her children to be sold. Ultimately he followed his father's pattern of trying to use her sexually, but he never achieved his goal of "breaking" her. As a result of the repeated attempts to sexually abuse her and break up her family, she decided to run away in spite of the terrible risk of getting caught.

In 1835, Jacobs fled the plantation at night and hid in a friend's home. After a search for her turned up nothing, Dr. Norcom put Jacobs's children and several other relatives in prison in an attempt to flush her out of hiding. However, Mr. Sawyer, the (white) father of her children, bought them from a slave trader and sent them to live with their great-grandmother Molly. Jacobs, meanwhile, remained in hiding. The friends who sheltered her eventually became concerned for her safety as well as their own, so Jacobs went into the swamp to hide. After a serious snakebite she was taken at night to Molly's house, where a hiding place beneath the roof rafters was laid out as her "home" for the next seven years. The space was so small that she could not stand or sit and could barely stretch out, but somehow she survived. In 1842, arrangements were made through an uncle's friend to take her to New York. There she was lucky to find a job as a nursemaid for abolitionist Nathaniel Park Willis's family (called the Bruce family in the passage that follows).

While working for the Willises, Jacobs discovered that the Norcoms' daughter, Mary, and her husband, Daniel Messmore, were searching for her to bring her back into slavery. (Dr. Norcom had died in 1850, so his daughter now had legal ownership of all his slaves, including Jacobs and her two children.) Because the Fugitive Slave Law made it a crime to harbor a slave even in Northern territories, Messmore hired a slave hunter to find Jacobs. The threat of this situation pressured Cornelia Willis, Jacobs's employer, to purchase her freedom in 1852, despite the fact that Jacobs protested strongly against her doing so. (She protested because she felt no one had the right to own her, and therefore her freedom should not have to be purchased.) Finally, after seventeen years of flight and hiding, Harriet Jacobs and her children were free.

Jacobs and her daughter, Louisa, worked in the abolitionist movement helping runaway slaves, and after the Civil War ended they returned to Edenton with supplies to relieve the distress of freed slaves. At the same time, Jacobs took possession of the house in which she had hidden for seven years. Soon thereafter, Jacobs went to England to raise support to found an orphanage in Savannah, Georgia. Later, she settled in Cambridge, Massachusetts, to run a boarding house. Her son, Joseph, went to the gold fields of California and then continued on to Australia, where he spent the rest of his life. Louisa continued her work on behalf of freed slaves and participated in organizing the National Association of Colored Women in Washington, D.C.

Jacobs's Rhetoric

"Free at Last" is the forty-first chapter in *Incidents in the Life of a Slave Girl* (1861). In many ways it demonstrates stylistic conventions similar to those of other slave narratives. However, Jacobs also structures the book as a narrative, similar to popular novels of the time. The names of her masters and mistresses are changed. In addition, she changes her own name in the narrative and calls herself Linda Brent. (In the Preface to her autobiography Jacobs claims, "I had no motive for secrecy on my account, but I deemed it kind and considerate towards others to pursue this course.") To some extent, this strategy gives her a measure of freedom and independence: she can be completely candid about the events and behavior of all the people described in the book. This strategy also helps her by involving the emotions of the reader. Rather than limiting herself to factual details, she writes in the manner of the novelist, with the hope of affecting the feelings of the reader. The most celebrated American novel during this period was probably *Uncle Tom's Cabin* (1852) by Harriet Beecher Stowe (1811–1896). Read by millions of Americans, the novel stirred antislavery feelings and probably inspired Jacobs.

Jacobs excels at projecting character. She carefully establishes the goodness of Mrs. Willis (called Mrs. Bruce in the passage) while at the same time clarifying her own nature in statements such as: "Mrs. Bruce, and every member of her family, were exceedingly kind to me. I was thankful for the blessings of my lot, yet I could not always wear a cheerful countenance (para. 1)." Similarly, her "good old grandmother" speaks for herself when she writes a long letter encouraging Jacobs's goodness and emphasizing the love she has for her family — hoping as she does for a reunion in heaven.

When Jacobs receives a letter telling her that Dr. Flint is dead, she honestly cannot grieve, but she does take a moment to marvel at her grandmother's ability to feel any distress at his death. The choice of "Flint" as a pseudonym for Dr. Norcom is a touch of allegory, suggesting the hardness of heart that marked his behavior. As Jacobs says, poignantly, "There are wrongs which even the grave does not bury" (para. 5).

After the introductory passages concerning her grandmother, Jacobs tells her narrative chronologically. She describes how she watched the newspaper for news of arrivals and almost missed the news of the Dodges (the pseudonym she uses for the Messmores) arriving and staying at a "third rate" hotel. The details of their search for her and of her retreat into hiding all read like a suspense novel.

The device of reconstructed dialogue dominates the early portion of the passage, from paragraphs 16 to 22 and later. This strategy makes the experiences Jacobs describes seem all the more immediate. We have the feeling that she narrates things as they actually happened, with the authority of an eyewitness. Of course, in reality she could not have been an eyewitness to every dialogue in the book (in all likelihood, these dialogues were reconstructed on the basis of information from those who were present). For example, the dialogue between Jacobs's "colored friend" and the Dodges took place while Jacobs was hiding in a friend's house. Nevertheless her retelling maintains an authoritative voice throughout the text, and the effect remains powerful and convincing.

The drama of Jacobs's fleeing from the Dodges "in a heavy snow storm" (para. 27) adds to the intensity of the experience.

Clearly she is frightened, and after a period of resistance to the thought of leaving, she is convinced she and her child are in danger. She gives in and heads to New England. Her reprieve comes at the last minute, again in an appropriately dramatic touch, with Mrs. Bruce striking a bargain with the Dodges and paying three hundred dollars for Jacobs's freedom.

Perhaps the most interesting aspect of the passage is that at its end, Jacobs not only comments on her relief and happiness at being free but also puts emphasis on her refusal to think of herself as a commodity, despite the fact that she has just been sold. The injustice of the concept of a human being owning another human being is so overwhelming to her that she can hardly bear to countenance her condition.

The direct address to the "Reader" (para. 36) is also a novelist's convention of the period. Jacobs tells us that the story "ends with freedom; not in the usual way, with marriage." This touch reminds us that Harriet Jacobs has told a story that might qualify as "happy" rather than tragic. Most romantic stories end with a marriage; how much more powerful, however, is this story, which ends in freedom for one who longed all her life to be her own woman.

PREREADING QUESTIONS: WHAT TO READ FOR

The following prereading questions may help you anticipate key issues in the discussion on Harriet Jacobs's "Free at Last." Keeping them in mind during your first reading of the selection should help focus your reactions.

- What is the nature of the claim slaveholders had over their slaves?
- Why did Harriet Jacobs object to having her freedom purchased?
- How did being a woman make Jacobs's plight all the more painful?

Free at Last

Mrs. Bruce, and every member of her family, were exceedingly 1
kind to me. I was thankful for the blessings of my lot, yet I could not always wear a cheerful countenance. I was doing harm to no one; on the contrary, I was doing all the good I could in my small way; yet I could never go out to breathe God's free air without trepidation at

my heart. This seemed hard; and I could not think it was a right state of things in any civilized country.

From time to time I received news from my good old grand- 2 mother. She could not write; but she employed others to write for her. The following is an extract from one of her last letters: —

"Dear Daughter: I cannot hope to see you again on earth; but I 3 pray to God to unite us above, where pain will no more rack this feeble body of mine; where sorrow and parting from my children will be no more. God has promised these things if we are faithful unto the end. My age and feeble health deprive me of going to church now; but God is with me here at home. Thank your brother for his kindness. Give much love to him, and tell him to remember the Creator in the days of his youth, and strive to meet me in the Father's kingdom. Love to Ellen and Benjamin. Don't neglect him. Tell him for me, to be a good boy. Strive, my child; to train them for God's children. May he protect and provide for you, is the prayer of your loving old mother."

These letters both cheered and saddened me. I was always glad 4 to have tidings from the kind, faithful old friend of my unhappy youth; but her messages of love made my heart yearn to see her before she died, and I mourned over the fact that it was impossible. Some months after I returned from my flight to New England, I received a letter from her, in which she wrote, "Dr. Flint is dead. He has left a distressed family. Poor old man! I hope he made his peace with God."

I remembered how he had defrauded my grandmother of the 5 hard earnings she had loaned; how he had tried to cheat her out of the freedom her mistress had promised her, and how he had persecuted her children; and I thought to myself that she was a better Christian than I was, if she could entirely forgive him. I cannot say, with truth, that the news of my old master's death softened my feelings towards him. There are wrongs which even the grave does not bury. The man was odious to me while he lived, and his memory is odious now.

His departure from this world did not diminish my danger. He 6 had threatened my grandmother that his heirs should hold me in slavery after he was gone; that I never should be free so long as a child of his survived. As for Mrs. Flint, I had seen her in deeper afflictions than I supposed the loss of her husband would be, for she had buried several children; yet I never saw any signs of softening in her heart. The doctor had died in embarrassed circumstances, and had little to will to his heirs, except such property as he was unable to grasp. I was well aware what I had to expect from the family of Flints; and my fears were confirmed by a letter from the south, warning me to be on my guard, because Mrs. Flint openly declared that her daughter could not afford to lose so valuable a slave as I was.

I kept close watch of the newspapers for arrivals; but one Satur- 7 day night, being much occupied, I forgot to examine the Evening Express as usual. I went down into the parlor for it, early in the morning, and found the boy about to kindle a fire with it. I took it from him and examined the list of arrivals. Reader, if you have never been a slave, you cannot imagine the acute sensation of suffering at my heart, when I read the names of Mr. and Mrs. Dodge, at a hotel in Courtland Street. It was a third-rate hotel, and that circumstance convinced me of the truth of what I had heard, that they were short of funds and had need of my value, as *they* valued me; and that was by dollars and cents. I hastened with the paper to Mrs. Bruce. Her heart and hand were always open to every one in distress, and she always warmly sympathized with mine. It was impossible to tell how near the enemy was. He might have passed and repassed the house while we were sleeping. He might at that moment be waiting to pounce upon me if I ventured out of doors. I had never seen the husband of my young mistress, and therefore I could not distinguish him from any other stranger. A carriage was hastily ordered; and, closely veiled, I followed Mrs. Bruce, taking the baby again with me into exile. After various turnings and crossings, and returnings, the carriage stopped at the house of one of Mrs. Bruce's friends, where I was kindly received. Mrs. Bruce returned immediately, to instruct the domestics what to say if any one came to inquire for me.

It was lucky for me that the evening paper was not burned up 8 before I had a chance to examine the list of arrivals. It was not long after Mrs. Bruce's return to her house, before several people came to inquire for me. One inquired for me, another asked for my daughter Ellen, and another said he had a letter from my grandmother, which he was requested to deliver in person.

They were told, "She *has* lived here, but she has left." 9

"How long ago?" 10

"I don't know, sir." 11

"Do you know where she went?" 12

"I do not, sir." And the door was closed. 13

This Mr. Dodge, who claimed me as his property, was originally 14 a Yankee peddler in the south; then he became a merchant, and finally a slaveholder. He managed to get introduced into what was called the first society,[1] and married Miss Emily Flint. A quarrel

---

[1] **first society** Upper class, or high society.

arose between him and her brother, and the brother cowhided[2] him. This led to a family feud, and he proposed to remove to Virginia. Dr. Flint left him no property, and his own means had become circumscribed, while a wife and children depended upon him for support. Under these circumstances, it was very natural that he should make an effort to put me into his pocket.

I had a colored friend, a man from my native place, in whom I   15
had the most implicit confidence. I sent for him, and told him that Mr. and Mrs. Dodge had arrived in New York. I proposed that he should call upon them to make inquiries about his friends at the south, with whom Dr. Flint's family were well acquainted. He thought there was no impropriety in his doing so, and he consented. He went to the hotel, and knocked at the door of Mr. Dodge's room, which was opened by the gentleman himself, who gruffly inquired, "What brought you here? How came you to know I was in the city?"

"Your arrival was published in the evening papers, sir; and I   16
called to ask Mrs. Dodge about my friends at home. I didn't suppose it would give any offence."

"Where's that negro girl, that belongs to my wife?"   17

"What girl, sir?"   18

"You know well enough. I mean Linda, that ran away from   19
Dr. Flint's plantation, some years ago. I dare say you've seen her, and know where she is."

"Yes, sir, I've seen her, and know where she is. She is out of   20
your reach, sir."

"Tell me where she is, or bring her to me, and I will give her a   21
chance to buy her freedom."

"I don't think it would be of any use, sir. I have heard her say   22
she would go to the ends of the earth, rather than pay any man or woman for her freedom, because she thinks she has a right to it. Besides, she couldn't do it, if she would, for she has spent her earnings to educate her children."

This made Mr. Dodge very angry, and some high words passed   23
between them. My friend was afraid to come where I was; but in the course of the day I received a note from him. I supposed they had not come from the south, in the winter, for a pleasure excursion; and now the nature of their business was very plain.

Mrs. Bruce came to me and entreated me to leave the city the   24
next morning. She said her house was watched, and it was possible that some clew to me might be obtained. I refused to take her advice. She pleaded with an earnest tenderness, that ought to have

---

[2] **cowhided** Flogged with a cowhide whip.

moved me; but I was in a bitter, disheartened mood. I was weary of flying from pillar to post. I had been chased during half my life, and it seemed as if the chase was never to end. There I sat, in that great city, guiltless of crime, yet not daring to worship God in any of the churches. I heard the bells ringing for afternoon service, and, with contemptuous sarcasm, I said, "Will the preachers take for their text, 'Proclaim liberty to the captive, and the opening of prison doors to them that are bound'? or will they preach from the text, 'Do unto others as ye would they should do unto you'?" Oppressed Poles and Hungarians could find a safe refuge in that city; John Mitchell was free to proclaim in the City Hall his desire for "a plantation well stocked with slaves;" but there I sat, an oppressed American, not daring to show my face. God forgive the black and bitter thoughts I indulged on that Sabbath day! The Scripture says, "Oppression makes even a wise man mad"; and I was not wise.

I had been told that Mr. Dodge said his wife had never signed   25
away her right to my children, and if he could not get me, he would take them. This it was, more than any thing else, that roused such a tempest in my soul. Benjamin was with his uncle William in California, but my innocent young daughter had come to spend a vacation with me. I thought of what I had suffered in slavery at her age, and my heart was like a tiger's when a hunter tries to seize her young.

Dear Mrs. Bruce! I seem to see the expression of her face, as she   26
turned away discouraged by my obstinate mood. Finding her expostulations unavailing, she sent Ellen to entreat me. When ten o'clock in the evening arrived and Ellen had not returned, this watchful and unwearied friend became anxious. She came to us in a carriage, bringing a well-filled trunk for my journey—trusting that by this time I would listen to reason. I yielded to her, as I ought to have done before.

The next day, baby and I set out in a heavy snow storm, bound   27
for New England again. I received letters from the City of Iniquity,[3] addressed to me under an assumed name. In a few days one came from Mrs. Bruce, informing me that my new master was still searching for me, and that she intended to put an end to this persecution by buying my freedom. I felt grateful for the kindness that prompted this offer, but the idea was not so pleasant to me as might have been expected. The more my mind had become enlightened, the more difficult it was for me to consider myself an article of property; and to pay money to those who had so grievously oppressed me seemed like taking from my sufferings the glory of triumph. I wrote

---

[3] **City of Iniquity** New York, in recognition of its liberal attitudes.

to Mrs. Bruce, thanking her, but saying that being sold from one owner to another seemed too much like slavery; that such a great obligation could not be easily cancelled; and that I preferred to go to my brother in California.

Without my knowledge, Mrs. Bruce employed a gentleman in   28
New York to enter into negotiations with Mr. Dodge. He proposed to pay three hundred dollars down, if Mr. Dodge would sell me, and enter into obligations to relinquish all claim to me or my children forever after. He who called himself my master said he scorned so small an offer for such a valuable servant. The gentleman replied, "You can do as you choose, sir. If you reject this offer you will never get any thing; for the woman has friends who will convey her and her children out of the country."

Mr. Dodge concluded that "half a loaf was better than no   29
bread," and he agreed to the proffered terms. By the next mail I received this brief letter from Mrs. Bruce: "I am rejoiced to tell you that the money for your freedom has been paid to Mr. Dodge. Come home to-morrow. I long to see you and my sweet babe."

My brain reeled as I read these lines. A gentleman near me said,   30
"It's true; I have seen the bill of sale." "The bill of sale!" Those words struck me like a blow. So I was *sold* at last! A human being *sold* in the free city of New York! The bill of sale is on record, and future generations will learn from it that women were articles of traffic in New York, late in the nineteenth century of the Christian religion. It may hereafter prove a useful document to antiquaries, who are seeking to measure the progress of civilization in the United States. I well know the value of that bit of paper; but much as I love freedom, I do not like to look upon it. I am deeply grateful to the generous friend who procured it, but I despise the miscreant who demanded payment for what never rightfully belonged to him or his.

I had objected to having my freedom bought, yet I must confess   31
that when it was done I felt as if a heavy load had been lifted from my weary shoulders. When I rode home in the cars I was no longer afraid to unveil my face and look at people as they passed. I should have been glad to have met Daniel Dodge himself; to have had him seen me and known me, that he might have mourned over the untoward circumstances which compelled him to sell me for three hundred dollars.

When I reached home, the arms of my benefactress were   32
thrown round me, and our tears mingled. As soon as she could speak, she said, "O Linda, I'm *so* glad it's all over! You wrote to me as if you thought you were going to be transferred from one owner to another. But I did not buy you for your services. I should have done just the same, if you had been going to sail for California

to-morrow. I should, at least, have the satisfaction of knowing that you left me a free woman."

My heart was exceedingly full. I remembered how my poor father 33 had tried to buy me, when I was a small child, and how he had been disappointed. I hoped his spirit was rejoicing over me now. I remembered how my good old grandmother had laid up her earnings to purchase me in later years, and how often her plans had been frustrated. How that faithful, loving old heart would leap for joy, if she could look on me and my children now that we were free! My relatives had been foiled in all their efforts, but God had raised me up a friend among strangers, who had bestowed on me the precious, long-desired boon. Friend! It is a common word, often lightly used. Like other good and beautiful things, it may be tarnished by careless handling; but when I speak of Mrs. Bruce as my friend, the word is sacred.

My grandmother lived to rejoice in my freedom; but not long 34 after, a letter came with a black seal. She had gone "where the wicked cease from troubling, and the weary are at rest."

Time passed on, and a paper came to me from the south, con- 35 taining an obituary notice of my uncle Phillip. It was the only case I ever knew of such an honor conferred upon a colored person. It was written by one of his friends, and contained these words: "Now that death has laid him low, they call him a good man and a useful citizen; but what are eulogies to the black man, when the world has faded from his vision? It does not require man's praise to obtain rest in God's kingdom." So they called a colored man a *citizen!* Strange words to be uttered in that region!

Reader, my story ends with freedom; not in the usual way, with 36 marriage. I and my children are now free! We are as free from the power of slaveholders as are the white people of the north; and though that, according to my ideas, is not saying a great deal, it is a vast improvement in *my* condition. The dream of my life is not yet realized. I do not sit with my children in a home of my own. I still long for a hearthstone of my own, however humble. I wish it for my children's sake far more than for my own. But God so orders circumstances as to keep me with my friend Mrs. Bruce. Love, duty, gratitude, also bind me to her side. It is a privilege to serve her who pities my oppressed people, and who has bestowed the inestimable boon of freedom on me and my children.

It has been painful to me, in many ways, to recall the dreary 37 years I passed in bondage. I would gladly forget them if I could. Yet the retrospection is not altogether without solace; for with those gloomy recollections come tender memories of my good old grandmother, like light, fleecy clouds floating over a dark and troubled sea.

QUESTIONS FOR CRITICAL READING

1. How effective is Jacobs's method of telling her story?
2. What impression do you get of Jacobs's sense of family?
3. What is the force of religion in this narrative?
4. In what senses were slaves basically property?
5. What was the economic situation of the Bruces?
6. Comment on Harriet Jacobs's sense of history.

SUGGESTIONS FOR WRITING

1. Examine this selection for its comments on religion and its revelation on how religious values satisfy the emotional needs of Jacobs and her grandmother. Comment on the contradictions that are implied in the Christian views that permitted slavery to exist. How important is the church in this piece?
2. Research the Fugitive Slave Law, and comment on the nature of the laws that protected the Dodges' rights to own Harriet Jacobs even though she lived in a non-slavery state when the Dodges found her. How did the laws protect property rights? How did they fail to protect the rights of Harriet Jacobs and her children?
3. One of the most intense moments in Harriet Jacobs's life was her realization that her children could belong to her master, be sold to anyone he chose, and be sent anywhere their new master chose. How do you react to the premise that the laws of the time enslaved not just an individual woman but all her progeny? Imagine yourself to be Harriet Jacobs, and write an essay that clarifies her views on this subject.
4. Because this piece is part of a larger narrative, find a copy of *Incidents in the Life of a Slave Girl* and read the book in its entirety. Jacobs's method is that of the novelist or storyteller; her intention is to involve the reader at the level of both intellect and feeling. How has she affected you on an emotional level? Has she made you feel emotions that are appropriate to her subject matter and appropriate to the magnitude of her experience? What techniques does she use to evoke this response?
5. **CONNECTIONS** To a large extent, Jacobs feels that she and other slaves have been done a terrible injustice by the oppressive system under which they lived. Consult some of the writers in the Justice section, such as Aristotle and Thomas Jefferson. In what ways is Jacobs in agreement with them? In what ways do the circumstances in which she lived contradict the principles that they espouse? Is Jacobs's story ultimately about justice finally being served?
6. **CONNECTIONS** Henry David Thoreau was an active abolitionist. How would he react to this story? What would his views be concerning the laws that determined the fates of Harriet Jacobs and her

children? To what extent did Jacobs live out the principles that Thoreau outlines in "Civil Disobedience"?

7. **CONNECTIONS**   A number of the authors in this collection talk extensively about equality: Aristotle, Tocqueville, the Friedmans, and others. What would they learn about the concept of freedom if they had the opportunity to read Harriet Jacobs's work?

FREDERICK JACKSON TURNER
From *The Significance of the Frontier in American History*

FREDERICK JACKSON TURNER (1861–1932) taught at the University of Wisconsin at Madison when he began his work on the American frontier. Raised in northern Wisconsin in an agricultural area, he observed his surroundings carefully, paying particular attention to the habits and customs of the people in relation to the land. He lived in a time in which scientists felt that the environment—including elements such as geography and weather—strongly influenced behavior and modes of civilization. He credited some of these factors more than contemporary historians do, but he also added to them a number of other important factors: economy, politics, ethnicity, and interaction with other peoples.

Turner was something of a phenomenon in history. In his early thirties he wrote an essay, "The Significance of History" (1891), in which he approvingly suggested that history was rewritten in every age in light of the developments of that age. His first essay on the effect of the frontier on American culture was "Problems in American History" (1892). His landmark work, included here, was his 1893 essay "The Significance of the Frontier in American History," presented at the American Historical Association meeting held at the World's Fair in Chicago. He was known well enough in historical circles to have been invited to give this talk, but once it was delivered and then published in 1894 in the *Annual Report of the American Historical Association for the Year 1893*, Turner suddenly discovered that he was a celebrity. Thereafter known as the Turner Thesis, this essay became the center of a movement in historical studies that influenced the discipline into the late twentieth century.

From *Annual Report of the American Historical Association for the Year 1893* (Washington, D.C.: GPO and American Historical Association, 1894), 199–227.

At the center of the thesis is the view that the great abundance of free land on the frontier created opportunity for immigrants to move westward at a rapid pace. Turner claims this land permitted them to develop themselves economically and consequently produced in them a fierce and commendable independent spirit. Additionally, Turner points out that in many places on the frontier an essential absence of government promoted even greater independence among frontier people, giving them special and recognizable traits. These traits developed in some measure from contact with Native Americans and from the European willingness to assume some Native American patterns of behavior. As Turner puts it, the frontier is "the meeting point between savagery and civilization" (para. 3).

Descriptions like the one above also reveal Turner's biases, which are fairly typical of the period. However, his emphasis is on the fact that the frontier was the place where different cultures converged, changing each irrevocably. For example, he insists that the frontier fostered "Americanization." As he says,

> The wilderness masters the colonist. It finds him a European in dress, industries, tools, modes of travel, and thought. It takes him from the railroad car and puts him in the birch canoe. It strips off the garments of civilization and arrays him in the hunting shirt and the moccasin. It puts him in the log cabin of the Cherokee and Iroquois and runs an Indian palisade around him. Before long he has gone to planting Indian corn and plowing with a sharp stick; he shouts the war cry and takes the scalp in orthodox Indian fashion. In short, at the frontier the environment is at first too strong for the man. (para. 5)

These descriptions underscore Turner's basic point: the process of movement across the western frontier has created a new kind of person, an American. Turner sees Americans not just as transplanted Europeans but as people whose modes of life, thought, and feeling have transformed them through economic, political, and social forces. Turner's emphasis on the influence of these forces helped change the way his contemporaries looked at history.

In this essay, Turner reviews the progress of the nation's move westward, discussing the different kinds of frontiers that Americans faced along the way. One of his key points is that the frontiers change with the westward movement, and in the process they change the people. The early colonists held the Atlantic to be their frontier and consequently looked back to England for influence and support. As colonists moved inland they perceived other frontiers: mountains like the Appalachians, lakes like Lake Ontario, or rivers like the Mississippi. Once past the eastern mountain ranges, those on the frontier looked back to the east less frequently for political or social sustenance. Instead, they looked forward (westward) and learned new skills from the Native Americans they encountered and traded with.

The economic issues, vast as they are, include mining, trapping, hunting, trading, farming, and various industries of manufacture. Turner points out that different cultures approach these in different fashions. The French, for example, were given to trapping and trading weapons with Native Americans for skins and other products of the wilderness. Thus, they left the land undeveloped and perfect for hunting. The English, on the other hand, cleared the land and planted crops, thereby destroying its potential for hunting and trapping. After the acquisition of western lands through the Louisiana Purchase in 1803 — more than eight hundred thousand square miles, doubling the size of the United States — the march westward followed the English pattern.

Turner discusses the effect of the farmer on the land and on westward movement, just as he discusses the effect of the trader on Native American culture and interaction with settlers. He also discusses the cattlemen and sheep herders whose lives depended on the grass on the range. He says, "The unequal rate of advance compels us to distinguish the frontier into the trader's frontier, the rancher's frontier, or the miner's frontier, and the farmer's frontier" (para. 16). Each is distinct, and each produced a recognizable subculture. All contributed to shaping American culture.

It is notable that the significance of the American frontier as an influence on the emerging nation and its people became apparent to Turner at the same time the 1890 Census report became available. Turner quotes from the report in the first paragraph of the essay. The report essentially said that by 1890 there was no longer a recognizable frontier in America. However, that announcement provoked Turner to look back at the frontier movement, establishing his thesis and seeing in it a new way to answer Crèvecoeur's question, "What Is an American?"

Turner's Rhetoric

This essay was originally delivered as a spoken address, with an audience limited to professional historians. As a result, Turner was more interested in being historically complete and accurate than in being emotionally compelling. In other words, his style is that of the historian producing an academic essay with greater emphasis on ideas than on style. Consequently, Turner makes many allusions to American politicians such as John C. Calhoun, Daniel

Webster, and a variety of presidents whose policies affected the frontier. In addition, Turner liberally footnotes the essay with suggestions for further reading—sometimes in languages other than English. This convention was the mode of the time. By following it, Turner guaranteed that what he had to say would be taken seriously by his fellow professionals.

At the time he gave this address, Turner was a historian in a remote university (in Wisconsin) and did not expect to be heard by those in power in universities in the East. However, he was wrong. Because many historians challenged his views, he became the center of controversy and became important almost overnight. Even though he remained at Madison for most of his career, he eventually accepted a professorship at Harvard, where he spent the last fourteen years of his teaching career. To some extent, his celebrity was probably connected to the fact that his writing was not only careful but a bit more stylish than that of the usual academic essays.

Some of Turner's descriptions are colorful and detailed, such as the reference to the European adoption of "the hunting shirt and the moccasin" (para.5). His use of figures of speech also endeared readers to his work; for example, in paragraph 5 he uses glacial patterns as a simile for the development of frontier life. For us, however, one of the most important features of his style is its clear structure. The opening paragraphs are a careful introduction to the frontier topic, but once Turner reveals his assertion that the frontier has shaped the America that we know, he breaks the argument into very carefully structured segments.

Turner's opening section defines the frontier in terms of settlement, "as the margin of that settlement which has a density of two or more to the square mile" (para. 4). He then proceeds to describe the "Stages of Frontier Advance," making distinctions in terms of geography, time, and people. When he comments on the social impact of the frontier, he does so in a carefully identified section. Each major section has subsections clarifying individual points that ultimately add up to a convincing picture. He accounts for the Native American, the rancher, and the farmer and then looks at the larger picture in terms of ethnic demographics in a section he calls "Composite Nationality." (The original essay contained fourteen sections following the introduction. Four of these sections have been omitted here because of space constraints—"Industrial Independence," "The Public Domain," "National Tendencies of the Frontier," and "Missionary Activity." The remaining ten sections appear here in their entirety.)

Turner's thoroughness and attention to detail are designed to convince us of his views. He wants us to accept his interpretation of what makes America recognizably American. Our democracy, he reminds us, is shaped in large measure by the attitudes of those who spent their lives on the frontiers, from colonial times to the early twentieth century. From the time Turner mapped out his Frontier Thesis in 1893 to the latter half of the twentieth century, his views have been challenged again and again, usually because of other factors he either downplays or leaves out (such as the role of women on the frontier). Nevertheless, the provocative nature of his ideas continues to incite critiques and other frontier theories, stimulating current scholarship about the forces that shaped America from the seventeenth to the nineteenth centuries.

PREREADING QUESTIONS: WHAT TO READ FOR

The following prereading questions may help you anticipate key issues in the discussion on the excerpt that follows from Frederick Jackson Turner's "The Significance of the Frontier in American History." Keeping them in mind during your first reading of the selection should help focus your reactions.

- How does Turner define the frontier?
- How does the "existence of an area of free land" (para. 1) explain American development?
- What was the effect of European trade with the Native Americans?

From *"The Significance of the Frontier in American History"*[1]

In a recent bulletin of the Superintendent of the Census for   1
1890 appear these significant words: "Up to and including 1880 the country had a frontier of settlement, but at present the unsettled area has been so broken into by isolated bodies of settlement that

---

[1] Since the meeting of the American Historical Association, this paper has also been given as an address to the State Historical Society of Wisconsin, December 14, 1893. I have to thank the Secretary of the Society, Mr. Reuben G. Thwaites, for securing valuable material for my use in the preparation of the paper. [Turner's note]

there can hardly be said to be a frontier line. In the discussion of its extent, its westward movement, etc., it can not, therefore, any longer have a place in the census reports." This brief official statement marks the closing of a great historic movement. Up to our own day American history has been in a large degree the history of the colonization of the Great West. The existence of an area of free land, its continuous recession, and the advance of American settlement westward, explain American development.

Behind institutions, behind constitutional forms and modifica- 2 tions, lie the vital forces that call these organs into life and shape them to meet changing conditions. The peculiarity of American institutions is, the fact that they have been compelled to adapt themselves to the changes of an expanding people — to the changes involved in crossing a continent, in winning a wilderness, and in developing at each area of this progress out of the primitive economic and political conditions of the frontier into the complexity of city life. Said Calhoun in 1817, "We are great, and rapidly — I was about to say fearfully — growing!"[2] So saying, he touched the distinguishing feature of American life. All peoples show development; the germ theory of politics has been sufficiently emphasized. In the case of most nations, however, the development has occurred in a limited area; and if the nation has expanded, it has met other growing peoples whom it has conquered. But in the case of the United States we have a different phenomenon. Limiting our attention to the Atlantic coast, we have the familiar phenomenon of the evolution of institutions in a limited area, such as the rise of representative government; the differentiation of simple colonial governments into complex organs; the progress from primitive industrial society, without division of labor, up to manufacturing civilization. But we have in addition to this a recurrence of the process of evolution in each western area reached in the process of expansion. Thus American development has exhibited not merely advance along a single line, but a return to primitive conditions on a continually advancing frontier line, and a new development for that area. American social development has been continually beginning over again on the frontier. This perennial rebirth, this fluidity of American life, this expansion westward with its new opportunities, its continuous touch with the simplicity of primitive society, furnish the forces dominating American character. The true point of view in the history of this nation is not the Atlantic coast, it is the great West. Even the slavery struggle, which is made so exclusive an object of attention by writers

---

[2] Abridgment of Debates of Congress, V, p. 706. [Turner's note]

like Prof. von Holst, occupies its important place in American history because of its relation to westward expansion.

In this advance, the frontier is the outer edge of the wave—the 3 meeting point between savagery and civilization. Much has been written about the frontier from the point of view of border warfare and the chase, but as a field for the serious study of the economist and the historian it has been neglected.

The American frontier is sharply distinguished from the Euro- 4 pean frontier—a fortified boundary line running through dense populations. The most significant thing about the American frontier is, that it lies at the hither edge of free land. In the census reports it is treated as the margin of that settlement which has a density of two or more to the square mile. The term is an elastic one, and for our purposes does not need sharp definition. We shall consider the whole frontier belt, including the Indian country and the outer margin of the "settled area" of the census reports. This paper will make no attempt to treat the subject exhaustively; its aim is simply to call attention to the frontier as a fertile field for investigation, and to suggest some of the problems which arise in connection with it.

In the settlement of America we have to observe how European 5 life entered the continent, and how America modified and developed that life and reacted on Europe. Our early history is the study of European germs developing in an American environment. Too exclusive attention has been paid by institutional students to the Germanic origins, too little to the American factors. The frontier is the line of most rapid and effective Americanization. The wilderness masters the colonist. It finds him a European in dress, industries, tools, modes of travel, and thought. It takes him from the railroad car and puts him in the birch canoe. It strips off the garments of civilization and arrays him in the hunting shirt and the moccasin. It puts him in the log cabin of the Cherokee and Iroquois and runs an Indian palisade around him. Before long he has gone to planting Indian corn and plowing with a sharp stick; he shouts the war cry and takes the scalp in orthodox Indian fashion. In short, at the frontier the environment is at first too strong for the man. He must accept the conditions which it furnishes, or perish, and so he fits himself into the Indian clearings and follows the Indian trails. Little by little he transforms the wilderness, but the outcome is not the old Europe, not simply the development of Germanic germs, any more than the first phenomenon was a case of reversion to the Germanic mark. The fact is, that here is a new product that is American. At first, the frontier was the Atlantic coast. It was the frontier of Europe in a very real sense. Moving westward, the frontier became more and more American. As successive terminal moraines result from successive glaciations, so each frontier leaves its traces behind it, and when it becomes a settled area the region still partakes of the frontier characteristics. Thus the advance of the frontier has meant a steady movement away from the influence of Europe, a steady growth of independence on American lines. And to study this advance, the men who grew up under these conditions, and the political, economic, and social results of it, is to study the really American part of our history.

Stages of Frontier Advance

In the course of the seventeenth century the frontier was advanced up the Atlantic river courses, just beyond the "fall line," and the tidewater region became the settled area. In the first half of the eighteenth century another advance occurred. Traders followed the Delaware and Shawnese Indians to the Ohio as early as the end of the first quarter of the century.[3] Gov. Spotswood, of Virginia, made an expedition in 1714 across the Blue Ridge. The end of the first quarter of the century saw the advance of the Scotch-Irish and the Palatine Germans up the Shenandoah Valley into the western part of Virginia, and along the Piedmont region of the Carolinas.[4] The Germans in New York pushed the frontier of settlement up the Mohawk to German Flats.[5] In Pennsylvania the town of Bedford indicates the line of settlement. Settlements had begun on New River, a branch of the Kanawha, and on the sources of the Yadkin and French Broad.[6] The King attempted to arrest the advance by his proclamation of 1763,[7] forbidding settlements beyond the sources of the rivers flowing into the Atlantic; but in vain. In the period of the Revolution the frontier crossed the Alleghanies into Kentucky and Tennessee, and the upper waters of the Ohio were settled.[8] When the first census

6

---

[3] Bancroft (1860 ed.), III, pp. 344, 345, citing Logan MSS.; [Mitchell] Contest in America, etc. (1752), p. 237. [Turner's note]

[4] Kercheval, History of the Valley; Bernheim, German Settlements in the Carolinas; Winsor, Narrative and Critical History of America, V, p. 304; Colonial Records of North Carolina, IV, p. xx; Weston, Documents Connected with the History of South Carolina, p. 82; Ellis and Evans, History of Lancaster County, Pa., chs. III, XXVI. [Turner's note]

[5] Parkman, Pontiac, II; Griffis, Sir William Johnson, p. 6; Simms's Frontiersmen of New York. [Turner's note]

[6] Monette, Mississippi Valley, I, p. 311. [Turner's note]

[7] Wis. Hist. Cols., XI, p. 50; Hinsdale, Old Northwest, p. 121; Burke, "Oration on Conciliation," Works (1872 ed.), I, p. 473. [Turner's note]

[8] Roosevelt, Winning of the West, and citations there given; Cutler's Life of Cutler. [Turner's note]

was taken in 1790, the continuous settled area was bounded by a line which ran near the coast of Maine, and included New England except a portion of Vermont and New Hampshire, New York along the Hudson and up the Mohawk about Schenectady, eastern and southern Pennsylvania, Virginia well across the Shenandoah Valley, and the Carolinas and eastern Georgia.[9] Beyond this region of continuous settlement were the small settled areas of Kentucky and Tennessee, and the Ohio, with the mountains intervening between them and the Atlantic area, thus giving a new and important character to the frontier. The isolation of the region increased its peculiarly American tendencies, and the need of transportation facilities to connect it with the East called out important schemes of internal improvement, which will be noted farther on. The "West," as a self-conscious section, began to evolve.

From decade to decade distinct advances of the frontier occurred.   7
By the census of 1820[10] the settled area included Ohio, southern Indiana and Illinois, southeastern Missouri, and about one-half of Louisiana. This settled area had surrounded Indian areas, and the management of these tribes became an object of political concern. The frontier region of the time lay along the Great Lakes, where Astor's American Fur Company operated in the Indian trade,[11] and beyond the Mississippi, where Indian traders extended their activity even to the Rocky Mountains; Florida also furnished frontier conditions. The Mississippi River region was the scene of typical frontier settlements.[12]

---

[9] Scribner's Statistical Atlas, xxxviii, pl. 13; McMaster, Hist. of People of U.S., I, pp. 4, 60, 61; Imlay and Filson, Western Territory of America (London, 1793); Rochefoucault-Liancourt, Travels Through the United States of North America (London, 1799); Michaux's "Journal," in Proceedings American Philosophical Society, XXVI, No. 129; Forman, Narrative of a Journey Down the Ohio and Mississippi in 1780–'90 (Cincinnati, 1888); Bartram, Travels Through North Carolina, etc. (London, 1792); Pope, Tour Through the Southern and Western Territories, etc. (Richmond, 1792); Weld, Travels Through the States of North America (London, 1799); Baily, Journal of a Tour in the Unsettled States of North America, 1796–'97 (London, 1856); Pennsylvania Magazine of History, July, 1886; Winsor, Narrative and Critical History of America, VII, pp. 491, 492, citations. [Turner's note]

[10] Scribner's Statistical Atlas, xxxix. [Turner's note]

[11] Turner, Character and Influence of the Indian Trade in Wisconsin (Johns Hopkins University Studies, Series IX), pp. 61 ff. [Turner's note]

[12] Monette, History of the Mississippi Valley, II; Flint, Travels and Residence in Mississippi; Flint, Geography and History of the Western States; Abridgment of Debates of Congress, VII, pp. 397, 398, 404; Holmes, Account of the U.S.; Kingdom, America and the British Colonies (London, 1820); Grund, Americans, II, chs. i, iii, vi (although writing in 1836, he treats of conditions that grew out of western advance from the era of 1820 to that time); Peck, Guide for Emigrants (Boston, 1831); Darby, Emigrants' Guide to Western and Southwestern States and Territories; Dana,

The rising steam navigation[13] on western waters, the opening of 8
the Erie Canal, and the westward extension of cotton[14] culture
added five frontier states to the Union in this period. Grund, writing
in 1836, declares: "It appears then that the universal disposition of
Americans to emigrate to the western wilderness, in order to enlarge their dominion over inanimate nature, is the actual result
of an expansive power which is inherent in them, and which by
continually agitating all classes of society is constantly throwing a
large portion of the whole population on the extreme confines of the
State, in order to gain space for its development. Hardly is a new
State or Territory formed before the same principle manifests
itself again and gives rise to a further emigration; and so is it destined to go on until a physical barrier must finally obstruct its
progress."[15]

In the middle of this century the line indicated by the present 9
eastern boundary of Indian Territory, Nebraska, and Kansas marked
the frontier of the Indian country.[16] Minnesota and Wisconsin still
exhibited frontier conditions,[17] but the distinctive frontier of the period is found in California, where the gold discoveries had sent a
sudden tide of adventurous miners, and in Oregon, and the settle-

---

Geographical Sketches in the Western Country; Kinzie, Waubun; Keating, Narrative
of Long's Expedition; Schoolcraft, Discovery of the Sources of the Mississippi River,
Travels in the Central Portions of the Mississippi Valley, and Lead Mines of the Missouri; Andreas, History of Illinois, I, 86–99; Hurlbut, Chicago Antiquities; McKen-
ney, Tour to the Lakes; Thomas, Travels Through the Western Country, etc.
(Auburn, N.Y., 1819). [Turner's note]

[13] Darby, Emigrants' Guide, pp. 272 ff.; Benton, Abridgment of Debates, VII,
p. 397. [Turner's note]

[14] DeBow's Review, IV, p. 254; XVII, p. 428. [Turner's note]

[15] Grund, Americans, II, p. 8. [Turner's note]

[16] Peck, New Guide to the West (Cincinnati, 1848), ch. IV; Parkman, Oregon
Trail; Hall, The West (Cincinnati, 1848); Pierce, Incidents of Western Travel; Mur-
ray, Travels in North America; Lloyd, Steamboat Directory (Cincinnati, 1856);
"Forty Days in a Western Hotel" (Chicago), in Putnam's Magazine, December 1894;
Mackay, The Western World, II, ch. II, III; Meeker, Life in the West; Bogen, German
in America (Boston, 1851); Olmstead, Texas Journey; Greeley, Recollections of a
Busy Life; Schouler, History of the United States, V, 261–67; Peyton, Over the
Alleghanies and Across the Prairies (London, 1870); Loughborough, The Pacific
Telegraph and Railway (St. Louis, 1849); Whitney, Project for a Railroad to the Pa-
cific (New York, 1849); Peyton, Suggestions on Railroad Communication with the
Pacific, and the Trade of China and the Indian Islands; Benton, Highway to the
Pacific (a speech delivered in the U.S. Senate, December 16, 1850). [Turner's note]

[17] A writer in The Home Missionary (1850), p. 239, reporting Wisconsin conditions, exclaims: "Think of this, people of the enlightened East. What an example, to
come from the very frontiers of civilization!" But one of the missionaries writes: "In a
few years Wisconsin will no longer be considered as the West, or as an outpost of civilization, any more than western New York, or the Western Reserve." [Turner's note]

ments in Utah.[18] As the frontier has leaped over the Alleghanies, so now it skipped the Great Plains and the Rocky Mountains; and in the same way that the advance of the frontiersmen beyond the Alleghanies had caused the rise of important questions of transportation and internal improvement, so now the settlers beyond the Rocky Mountains needed means of communication with the East, and in the furnishing of these arose the settlement of the Great Plains and the development of still another kind of frontier life. Railroads, fostered by land grants, sent an increasing tide of immigrants into the far West. The United States Army fought a series of Indian wars in Minnesota, Dakota, and the Indian Territory.

By 1880 the settled area had been pushed into northern Michigan, Wisconsin, and Minnesota, along Dakota rivers, and in the Black Hills region, and was ascending the rivers of Kansas and Nebraska. The development of mines in Colorado had drawn isolated frontier settlements into that region, and Montana and Idaho were receiving settlers. The frontier was found in these mining camps and the ranches of the Great Plains. The superintendent of the census for 1890 reports, as previously stated, that the settlements of the West lie so scattered over the region that there can no longer be said to be a frontier line.   10

In these successive frontiers we find natural boundary lines which have served to mark and to affect the characteristics of the frontiers, namely: The "fall line"; the Alleghany Mountains; the Mississippi; the Missouri, where its direction approximates north and south; the line of the arid lands, approximately the ninety-ninth meridian; and the Rocky Mountains. The fall line marked the frontier of the seventeenth century; the Alleghanies that of the eighteenth; the Mississippi that of the first quarter of the nineteenth; the Missouri that of the middle of this century (omitting the California movement); and the belt of the Rocky Mountains and the arid tract, the present frontier. Each was won by a series of Indian wars.   11

The Frontier Furnishes a Field for
Comparative Study of Social Development

At the Atlantic frontier one can study the germs of processes repeated at each successive frontier. We have the complex European life sharply precipitated by the wilderness into the simplicity of   12

---

[18] Bancroft (H. H.), History of California, History of Oregon, and Popular Tribunals; Shinn, Mining Camps. [Turner's note]

primitive conditions. The first frontier had to meet its Indian question, its question of the disposition of the public domain, of the
means of intercourse with older settlements, of the extension of political organization, of religious and educational activity. And the
settlement of these and similar questions for one frontier served as a
guide for the next. The American student needs not to go to the
"prim little townships of Sleswick" for illustrations of the law of continuity and development. For example, he may study the origin of
our land policies in the colonial land policy; he may see how the
system grew by adapting the statutes to the customs of the successive frontiers.[19] He may see how the mining experience in the lead
regions of Wisconsin, Illinois, and Iowa was applied to the mining
laws of the Rockies,[20] and how our Indian policy has been a series of
experimentations on successive frontiers. Each tier of new States has
found in the older ones material for its constitutions.[21] Each frontier
has made similar contributions to American character, as will be discussed farther on.

   But with all these similarities there are essential differences, due   13
to the place element and the time element. It is evident that the
farming frontier of the Mississippi Valley presents different conditions from the mining frontier of the Rocky Mountains. The frontier
reached by the Pacific Railroad, surveyed into rectangles, guarded by
the United States Army, and recruited by the daily immigrant ship,
moves forward at a swifter pace and in a different way than the frontier reached by the birch canoe or the pack horse. The geologist
traces patiently the shores of ancient seas, maps their areas, and
compares the older and the newer. It would be a work worth the
historian's labors to mark these various frontiers and in detail compare one with another. Not only would there result a more adequate
conception of American development and characteristics, but invaluable additions would be made to the history of society.

   Loria,[22] the Italian economist, has urged the study of colonial   14
life as an aid in understanding the stages of European development,
affirming that colonial settlement is for economic science what the
mountain is for geology, bringing to light primitive stratifications.
"America," he says, "has the key to the historical enigma which

---

[19] See the suggestive paper by Prof. Jesse Macy, The Institutional Beginnings of
a Western State. [Turner's note]

[20] Shinn, Mining Camps. [Turner's note]

[21] Compare Thorpe, in Annals American Academy of Political and Social Science, September, 1891; Bryce, American Commonwealth (1888), II, p. 689.
[Turner's note]

[22] Loria, Analisi della Proprieta Capitalista, II, p. 15. [Turner's note]

Europe has sought for centuries in vain, and the land which has no history reveals luminously the course of universal history." There is much truth in this. The United States lies like a huge page in the history of society. Line by line as we read this continental page from west to east we find the record of social evolution. It begins with the Indian and the hunter; it goes on to tell of the disintegration of savagery by the entrance of the trader, the pathfinder of civilization; we read the annals of the pastoral stage in ranch life; the exploitation of the soil by the raising of unrotated crops of corn and wheat in sparsely settled farming communities; the intensive culture of the denser farm settlement; and finally the manufacturing organization with city and factory system.[23] This page is familiar to the student of census statistics, but how little of it has been used by our historians. Particularly in eastern States this page is a palimpsest. What is now a manufacturing State was in an earlier decade an area of intensive farming. Earlier yet it had been a wheat area, and still earlier the "range" had attracted the cattle-herder. Thus Wisconsin, now developing manufacture, is a State with varied agricultural interests. But earlier it was given over to almost exclusive grain-raising, like North Dakota at the present time.

Each of these areas has had an influence in our economic and political history; the evolution of each into a higher stage has worked political transformations. But what constitutional historian has made any adequate attempt to interpret political facts by the light of these social areas and changes?[24] 15

The Atlantic frontier was compounded of fisherman, fur-trader, miner, cattle-raiser, and farmer. Excepting the fisherman, each type of industry was on the march toward the West, impelled by an irresistible attraction. Each passed in successive waves across the continent. Stand at Cumberland Gap and watch the procession of civilization, marching single file — the buffalo following the trail to the salt springs, the Indian, the fur-trader and hunter, the cattle-raiser, the pioneer farmer — and the frontier has passed by. Stand at South Pass in the Rockies a century later and see the same procession with wider intervals between. The unequal rate of advance compels us to distinguish the frontier into the trader's frontier, the rancher's 16

---

[23] Compare Observations on the North American Land Company, London, 1796, pp. xv, 144; Logan, History of Upper South Carolina, I, pp. 149–51; Turner, Character and Influence of Indian Trade in Wisconsin, p. 18; Peck, New Guide for Emigrants (Boston, 1837), ch. IV; Compendium Eleventh Census, I, p. xl. [Turner's note]

[24] See pages 220, 221, 223, *post,* for illustrations of the political accompaniments of changed industrial conditions. [Turner's note]

frontier, or the miner's frontier, and the farmer's frontier. When the mines and the cow pens were still near the fall line the traders' pack trains were tinkling across the Alleghanies, and the French on the Great Lakes were fortifying their posts, alarmed by the British trader's birch canoe. When the trappers scaled the Rockies, the farmer was still near the mouth of the Missouri.

The Indian Trader's Frontier

Why was it that the Indian trader passed so rapidly across the 17
continent? What effects followed from the trader's frontier? The trade was coeval with American discovery. The Norsemen, Vespuccius, Verrazani, Hudson, John Smith, all trafficked for furs. The Plymouth pilgrims settled in Indian cornfields, and their first return cargo was of beaver and lumber. The records of the various New England colonies show how steadily exploration was carried into the wilderness by this trade. What is true for New England is, as would be expected, even plainer for the rest of the colonies. All along the coast from Maine to Georgia the Indian trade opened up the river courses. Steadily the trader passed westward, utilizing the older lines of French trade. The Ohio, the Great Lakes, the Mississippi, the Missouri, and the Platte, the lines of western advance, were ascended by traders. They found the passes in the Rocky Mountains and guided Lewis and Clark,[25] Fremont, and Bidwell. The explanation of the rapidity of this advance is connected with the effects of the trader on the Indian. The trading post left the unarmed tribes at the mercy of those that had purchased fire-arms — a truth which the Iroquois Indians wrote in blood, and so the remote and unvisited tribes gave eager welcome to the trader. "The savages," wrote La Salle, "take better care of us French than of their own children; from us only can they get guns and goods." This accounts for the trader's power and the rapidity of his advance. Thus the disintegrating forces of civilization entered the wilderness. Every river valley and Indian trail became a fissure in Indian society, and so that society became honeycombed. Long before the pioneer farmer appeared on the scene, primitive Indian life had passed away. The farmers met Indians armed with guns. The trading frontier, while steadily undermining Indian power by making the tribes ultimately dependent on the whites, yet, through its sale of guns, gave to the Indians increased

---

[25] But Lewis and Clark were the first to explore the route from the Missouri to the Columbia. [Turner's note]

power of resistance to the farming frontier. French colonization was dominated by its trading frontier; English colonization by its farming frontier. There was an antagonism between the two frontiers as between the two nations. Said Duquesne to the Iroquois, "Are you ignorant of the difference between the king of England and the king of France? Go see the forts that our king has established and you will see that you can still hunt under their very walls. They have been placed for your advantage in places which you frequent. The English, on the contrary, are no sooner in possession of a place than the game is driven away. The forest falls before them as they advance, and the soil is laid bare so that you can scarce find the wherewithal to erect a shelter for the night."

And yet, in spite of this opposition of the interests of the trader   18
and the farmer, the Indian trade pioneered the way for civilization. The buffalo trail became the Indian trail, and this because the trader's "trace"; the trails widened into roads, and the roads into turnpikes, and these in turn were transformed into railroads. The same origin can be shown for the railroads of the South, the far West, and the Dominion of Canada.[26] The trading posts reached by these trails were on the sites of Indian villages which had been placed in positions suggested by nature; and these trading posts, situated so as to command the water systems of the country, have grown into such cities as Albany, Pittsburgh, Detroit, Chicago, St. Louis, Council Bluffs, and Kansas City. Thus civilization in America has followed the arteries made by geology, pouring an ever richer tide through them, until at last the slender paths of aboriginal intercourse have been broadened and interwoven into the complex mazes of modern commercial lines; the wilderness has been interpenetrated by lines of civilization growing ever more numerous. It is like the steady growth of a complex nervous system for the originally simple, inert continent. If one would understand why we are to-day one nation, rather than a collection of isolated states, he must study this economic and social consolidation of the country. In this progress from savage conditions lie topics for the evolutionist.[27]

The effect of the Indian frontier as a consolidating agent in our   19
history is important. From the close of the seventeenth century

---

[26] Narrative and Critical History of America, VIII, p. 10; Sparks' Washington Works, IX, pp. 303, 327; Logan, History of Upper South Carolina, I; McDonald, Life of Kenton, p. 72; Cong. Record. XXIII, p. 57. [Turner's note]

[27] On the effect of the fur trade in opening the routes of migration, see the author's Character and Influence of the Indian Trade in Wisconsin. [Turner's note]

various intercolonial congresses have been called to treat with Indians and establish common measures of defense. Particularism was strongest in colonies with no Indian frontier. This frontier stretched along the western border like a cord of union. The Indian was a common danger, demanding united action. Most celebrated of these conferences was the Albany congress of 1754, called to treat with the Six Nations, and to consider plans of union. Even a cursory reading of the plan proposed by the congress reveals the importance of the frontier. The powers of the general council and the officers were, chiefly, the determination of peace and war with the Indians, the regulation of Indian trade, the purchase of Indian lands, and the creation and government of new settlements as a security against the Indians. It is evident that the unifying tendencies of the Revolutionary period were facilitated by the previous cooperation in the regulation of the frontier. In this connection may be mentioned the importance of the frontier, from that day to this, as a military training school, keeping alive the power of resistance to aggression, and developing the stalwart and rugged qualities of the frontiersman.

The Rancher's Frontier

It would not be possible in the limits of this paper to trace the   20 other frontiers across the continent. Travelers of the eighteenth century found the "cowpens" among the canebrakes and peavine pastures of the South, and the "cow drivers" took their droves to Charleston, Philadelphia, and New York.[28] Travelers at the close of the War of 1812 met droves of more than a thousand cattle and swine from the interior of Ohio going to Pennsylvania to fatten for the Philadelphia market.[29] The ranges of the Great Plains, with ranch and cowboy and nomadic life, are things of yesterday and of to-day. The experience of the Carolina cowpens guided the ranchers of Texas. One element favoring the rapid extension of the rancher's frontier is the fact that in a remote country lacking transportation facilities the product must be in small bulk, or must be able to transport itself, and the cattle raiser could easily drive this product to market. The effect of these great ranches on the subsequent agrarian history of the localities in which they existed should be studied.

----

[28] Lodge, English Colonies, p. 152 and citations; Logan, Hist. of Upper South Carolina, I, p. 151. [Turner's note]

[29] Flint, Recollections, p. 9. [Turner's note]

The Farmer's Frontier

The maps of the census reports show an uneven advance of the   21
farmer's frontier, with tongues of settlement pushed forward and
with indentations of wilderness. In part this is due to Indian resistance, in part to the location of river valleys and passes, in part to
the unequal force of the centers of frontier attraction. Among the
important centers of attraction may be mentioned the following: fertile and favorably situated soils, salt springs, mines, and army posts.

Army Posts

The frontier army post, serving to protect the settlers from the Indi-   22
ans, has also acted as a wedge to open the Indian country, and has
been a nucleus for settlement.[30] In this connection mention should
also be made of the Government military and exploring expeditions
in determining the lines of settlement. But all the more important
expeditions were greatly indebted to the earliest pathmakers, the Indian guides, the traders and trappers, and the French voyageurs,
who were inevitable parts of governmental expeditions from the
days of Lewis and Clark.[31] Each expedition was an epitome of the
previous factors in western advance.

Salt Springs

In an interesting monograph, Victor Hehn[32] has traced the effect of   23
salt upon early European development, and has pointed out how it
affected the lines of settlement and the form of administration. A
similar study might be made for the salt springs of the United States.
The early settlers were tied to the coast by the need of salt, without
which they could not preserve their meats or live in comfort. Writing in 1752, Bishop Spangenburg says of a colony for which he was
seeking lands in North Carolina, "They will require salt & other necessaries which they can neither manufacture nor raise. Either they
must go to Charleston, which is 300 miles distant . . . Or else they
must go to Boling's Point in V^a on a branch of the James & is also
300 miles from here . . . Or else they must go down the Roanoke—
I know not how many miles—where salt is brought up from the
Cape Fear."[33] This may serve as a typical illustration. An annual

---

[30] See Monette, Mississippi Valley, I, p. 344. {Turner's note]

[31] Coues' Lewis and Clark's Expedition, I, pp. 2, 253–59; Benton, in Cong.
Record, XXIII, p. 57. [Turner's note]

[32] Hehn, Das Salz (Berlin, 1873). [Turner's note]

[33] Col. Records of N.C., V, p. 3. [Turner's note]

pilgrimage to the coast for salt thus became essential. Taking flocks or furs and ginseng root, the early settlers sent their pack trains after seeding time each year to the coast.[34] This proved to be an important educational influence, since it was almost the only way in which the pioneer learned what was going on in the East. But when discovery was made of the salt springs of the Kanawha, and the Holston, and Kentucky, and central New York, the West began to be freed from dependence on the coast. It was in part the effect of finding these salt springs that enabled settlement to cross the mountains.

From the time the mountains rose between the pioneer and the   24
seaboard, a new order of Americanism arose. The West and the East began to get out of touch of each other. The settlements from the sea to the mountains kept connection with the rear and had a certain solidarity. But the over-mountain men grew more and more independent. The East took a narrow view of American advance, and nearly lost these men. Kentucky and Tennessee history bears abundant witness to the truth of this statement. The East began to try to hedge and limit westward expansion. Though Webster could declare that there were no Alleghanies in his politics, yet in politics in general they were a very solid factor.

Land

The exploitation of the beasts took hunter and trader to the west,   25
the exploitation of the grasses took the rancher west, and the exploitation of the virgin soil of the river valleys and prairies attracted the farmer. Good soils have been the most continuous attraction to the farmer's frontier. The land hunger of the Virginians drew them down the rivers into Carolina, in early colonial days; the search for soils took the Massachusetts men to Pennsylvania and to New York. As the eastern lands were taken up migration flowed across them to the west. Daniel Boone, the great backwoodsman, who combined the occupations of hunter, trader, cattle-raiser, farmer, and surveyor — learning, probably from the traders, of the fertility of the lands on the upper Yadkin, where the traders were wont to rest as they took their way to the Indians, left his Pennsylvania home with his father, and passed down the Great Valley road to that stream. Learning from a trader whose posts were on the Red River in Kentucky of its game and rich pastures, he pioneered the way for the farmers to that region. Thence he passed to the frontier of Missouri, where his settlement was long a landmark on the frontier. Here again he helped

---

[34] Findley, History of the Insurrection in the Four Western Counties of Pennsylvania in the Year 1794 (Philadelphia, 1796), p. 35. [Turner's note]

to open the way for civilization, finding salt licks, and trails, and land. His son was among the earliest trappers in the passes of the Rocky Mountains, and his party are said to have been the first to camp on the present site of Denver. His grandson, Col. A. J. Boone, of Colorado, was a power among the Indians of the Rocky Mountains, and was appointed an agent by the Government. Kit Carson's mother was a Boone.[35] Thus this family epitomizes the backwoodsman's advance across the continent.

The farmer's advance came in a distinct series of waves. In Peck's New Guide to the West, published in Boston in 1837, occurs this suggestive passage:

> Generally, in all the western settlements, three classes, like the waves of the ocean, have rolled one after the other. First comes the pioneer, who depends for the subsistence of his family chiefly upon the natural growth of vegetation, called the "range," and the proceeds of hunting. His implements of agriculture are rude, chiefly of his own make, and his efforts directed mainly to a crop of corn and a "truck patch." The last is a rude garden for growing cabbage, beans, corn for roasting ears, cucumbers, and potatoes. A log cabin, and, occasionally, a stable and corn-crib, and a field of a dozen acres, the timber girdled or "deadened," and fenced, are enough for his occupancy. It is quite immaterial whether he ever becomes the owner of the soil. He is the occupant for the time being, pays no rent, and feels as independent as the "lord of the manor." With a horse, cow, and one or two breeders of swine, he strikes into the woods with his family, and becomes the founder of a new county, or perhaps state. He builds his cabin, gathers around him a few other families of similar tastes and habits, and occupies till the range is somewhat subdued, and hunting a little precarious, or, which is more frequently the case, till the neighbors crowd around, roads, bridges, and fields annoy him, and he lacks elbow room. The preemption law enables him to dispose of his cabin and cornfield to the next class of emigrants; and, to employ his own figures, he "breaks for the high timber," "clears out for the New Purchase," or migrates to Arkansas or Texas, to work the same process over.
>
> The next class of emigrants purchase the lands, add field to field, clear out the roads, throw rough bridges over the streams, put up hewn log houses with glass windows and brick or stone chimneys, occasionally plant orchards, build mills, schoolhouses, court-houses, etc., and exhibit the picture and forms of plain, frugal, civilized life.
>
> Another wave rolls on. The men of capital and enterprise come. The settler is ready to sell out and take the advantage of the rise in

---

[35] Hale, Daniel Boone (pamphlet). [Turner's note]

property, push farther into the interior and become, himself, a man of capital and enterprise in turn. The small village rises to a spacious town or city; substantial edifices of brick, extensive fields, orchards, gardens, colleges, and churches are seen. Broadcloths, silks, leghorns, crapes, and all the refinements, luxuries, elegancies, frivolities, and fashions are in vogue. Thus wave after wave is rolling westward; the real Eldorado is still farther on.

A portion of the two first classes remain stationary amidst the general movement, improve their habits and condition, and rise in the scale of society.

The writer has traveled much amongst the first class, the real pioneers. He has lived many years in connection with the second grade; and now the third wave is sweeping over large districts of Indiana, Illinois, and Missouri. Migration has become almost a habit in the West. Hundreds of men can be found, not over 50 years of age, who have settled for the fourth, fifth, or sixth time on a new spot. To sell out and remove only a few hundred miles makes up a portion of the variety of backwoods life and manners.[36]

27 Omitting those of the pioneer farmers who move from the love of adventure, the advance of the more steady farmer is easy to understand. Obviously the immigrant was attracted by the cheap lands of the frontier, and even the native farmer felt their influence strongly. Year by year the farmers who lived on soil whose returns were diminished by unrotated crops were offered the virgin soil of the frontier at nominal prices. Their growing families demanded more lands, and these were dear. The competition of the unexhausted, cheap, and easily tilled prairie lands compelled the farmer either to go west and continue the exhaustion of the soil on a new frontier, or to adopt intensive culture. Thus the census of 1890 shows, in the Northwest, many counties in which there is an absolute or a relative decrease of population. These States have been sending farmers to advance the frontier on the plains, and have themselves begun to turn to intensive farming and to manufacture. A decade before this, Ohio had shown the same transition stage. Thus the demand for land and the love of wilderness freedom drew the frontier ever onward.

28 Having now roughly outlined the various kinds of frontiers, and their modes of advance, chiefly from the point of view of the frontier itself, we may next inquire what were the influences on the East and on the Old World. A rapid enumeration of some of the more noteworthy effects is all that I have time for.

---

[36] Compare Baily, Tour in the Unsettled Parts of North America (London, 1856), pp. 217–19, where a similar analysis is made for 1796. See also Collot, Journey in North America (Paris, 1826), p. 109; Observations on the North American Land Company (London, 1796), pp. xv, 144; Logan, History of Upper South Carolina. [Turner's note]

Composite Nationality

First, we note that the frontier promoted the formation of a com- 29
posite nationality for the American people. The coast was preponder-
antly English, but the later tides of continental immigration flowed
across to the free lands. This was the case from the early colonial days.
The Scotch Irish and the Palatine Germans, or "Pennsylvania Dutch,"
furnished the dominant element in the stock of the colonial frontier.
With these peoples were also the freed indented servants, or redemptioners, who at the expiration of their time of service passed to the
frontier. Governor Spotswood of Virginia writes in 1717, "The inhabitants of our frontiers are composed generally of such as have been
transported hither as servants, and, being out of their time, settle
themselves where land is to be taken up and that will produce the nec-
essarys of life with little labour."[37] Very generally these redemptioners
were of non-English stock. In the crucible of the frontier the immigrants were Americanized, liberated, and fused into a mixed race,
English in neither nationality or characteristics. The process has gone
on from the early days to our own. Burke and other writers in the middle of the eighteenth century believed that Pennsylvania[38] was "threatened with the danger of being wholly foreign in language, manner,
and perhaps even inclinations." The German and Scotch-Irish elements in the frontier of the South were only less great. In the middle
of the present century the German element in Wisconsin was already
so considerable that leading publicists looked to the creation of a German state out of the commonwealth by concentrating their colonization.[39] Such examples teach us to beware of misinterpreting the fact
that there is a common English speech in America into a belief that the
stock is also English.

Effects on National Legislation

The legislation which most developed the powers of the National 30
Government, and played the largest part in its activity, was conditioned on the frontier. Writers have discussed the subjects of tariff,
land, and internal improvement, as subsidiary to the slavery question.
But when American history comes to be rightly viewed it will be seen
that the slavery question is an incident. In the period from the end of
the first half of the present century to the close of the civil war slavery

---

[37] "Spotswood Papers," in Collections of Virginia Historical Society, I, II.
[Turner's note]

[38] [Burke], European Settlements, etc. (1765 ed.), II, p. 200. [Turner's note]

[39] Everest, in Wisconsin Historical Collections, XII, pp. 7 ff. [Turner's quote]

rose to primary, but far from exclusive, importance. But this does not justify Dr. von Holst (to take an example) in treating our constitutional history in its formative period down to 1828 in a single volume, giving six volumes chiefly to the history of slavery from 1828 to 1861, under the title "Constitutional History of the United States." The growth of nationalism and the evolution of American political institutions were dependent on the advance of the frontier. Even so recent a writer as Rhodes, in his History of the United States since the compromise of 1850, has treated the legislation called out by the western advance as incidental to the slavery struggle.

This is a wrong perspective. The pioneer needed the goods of the coast, and so the grand series of internal improvement and railroad legislation began, with potent nationalizing effects. Over internal improvements occurred great debates, in which grave constitutional questions were discussed. Sectional groupings appear in the votes, profoundly significant for the historian. Loose construction increased as the nation marched westward.[40] But the West was not content with bringing the farm to the factory. Under the lead of Clay—"Harry of the West"—protective tariffs were passed, with the cry of bringing the factory to the farm. The disposition of the public lands was a third important subject of national legislation influenced by the frontier.

Growth of Democracy

But the most important effect of the frontier has been in the promotion of democracy here and in Europe. As has been indicated, the frontier is productive of individualism. Complex society is precipitated by the wilderness into a kind of primitive organization based on the family. The tendency is anti-social. It produces antipathy to control, and particularly to any direct control. The tax-gatherer is viewed as a representative of oppression. Prof. Osgood, in an able article,[41] has pointed out that the frontier conditions prevalent in the colonies are important factors in the explanation of the American Revolution, where individual liberty was sometimes confused with absence of all effective government. The same conditions aid in explaining the difficulty of instituting a strong

31

32

---

[40] See, for example, the speech of Clay, in the House of Representatives, January 30, 1824. [Turner's note]

[41] Political Science Quarterly, II, p. 457. Compare Sumner, Alexander Hamilton, chs. II–VII. [Turner's note]

government in the period of the confederacy. The frontier individualism has from the beginning promoted democracy.

The frontier States that came into the Union in the first quarter   33
of a century of its existence came in with democratic suffrage provisions, and had reactive effects of the highest importance upon the older States whose peoples were being attracted there. An extension of the franchise became essential. It was *western* New York that forced an extension of suffrage in the constitutional convention of that State in 1821; and it was *western* Virginia that compelled the tide-water region to put a more liberal suffrage provision in the constitution framed in 1830, and to give to the frontier region a more nearly proportionate representation with the tide-water aristocracy. The rise of democracy as an effective force in the nation came in with western preponderance under Jackson and William Henry Harrison, and it meant the triumph of the frontier—with all of its good and with all of its evil elements.[42] An interesting illustration of the tone of frontier democracy in 1830 comes from the same debates in the Virginia convention already referred to. A representative from western Virginia declared:

> But, sir, it is not the increase of population in the West which this gentleman ought to fear. It is the energy which the mountain breeze and western habits impart to those emigrants. They are regenerated, politically I mean, sir. They soon become *working politicians;* and the difference, sir, between a *talking* and a *working* politician is immense. The Old Dominion has long been celebrated for producing great orators; the ablest metaphysicians in policy; men that can split hairs in all abstruse questions of political economy. But at home, or when they return from Congress, they have negroes to fan them asleep. But a Pennsylvania, a New York, an Ohio, or a western Virginia statesman, though far inferior in logic, metaphysics, and rhetoric to an old Virginia statesman, has this advantage, that when he returns home he takes off his coat and takes hold of the plow. This gives him bone and muscle, sir, and preserves his republican principles pure and uncontaminated.

So long as free land exists, the opportunity for a competency ex-   34
ists, and economic power secures political power. But the democracy born of free land, strong in selfishness and individualism, intolerant of administrative experience and education, and pressing individual liberty beyond its proper bounds, has its dangers as well as its benefits. Individualism in America has allowed a laxity in

[42] Compare Wilson, Division and Reunion, pp. 15, 24. [Turner's note]

regard to governmental affairs which has rendered possible the spoils system and all the manifest evils that follow from the lack of a highly developed civic spirit. In this connection may be noted also the influence of frontier conditions in permitting lax business honor, inflated paper currency and wild-cat banking. The colonial and revolutionary frontier was the region whence emanated many of the worst forms of an evil currency.[43] The West in the war of 1812 repeated the phenomenon on the frontier of that day, while the speculation and wild-cat banking of the period of the crisis of 1837 occurred on the new frontier belt of the next tier of States. Thus each one of the periods of lax financial integrity coincides with periods when a new set of frontier communities had arisen, and coincides in area with these successive frontiers, for the most part. The recent Populist agitation is a case in point. Many a State that now declines any connection with the tenets of the Populists, itself adhered to such ideas in an earlier stage of the development of the State. A primitive society can hardly be expected to show the intelligent appreciation of the complexity of business interests in a developed society. The continual recurrence of these areas of paper-money agitation is another evidence that the frontier can be isolated and studied as a factor in American history of the highest importance.[44]

Attempts to Check and Regulate the Frontier

The East has always feared the result of an unregulated advance   35
of the frontier, and has tried to check and guide it. The English authorities would have checked settlement at the headwaters of the Atlantic tributaries and allowed the "savages to enjoy their deserts in quiet lest the peltry trade should decrease." This called out Burke's splendid protest:

> If you stopped your grants, what would be the consequence? The
> people would occupy without grants. They have already so occu-

---

[43] On the relation of frontier conditions to Revolutionary taxation, see Sumner, Alexander Hamilton, ch. III. [Turner's note]

[44] I have refrained from dwelling on the lawless characteristics of the frontier, because they are sufficiently well known. The gambler and desperado, the regulators of the Carolinas and the vigilantes of California, are types of that line of scum that the waves of advancing civilization bore before them, and of the growth of spontaneous organs of authority where legal authority was absent. Compare Barrows, United States of Yesterday and To-morrow; Shinn, Mining Camps; and Bancroft, Popular Tribunals. The humor, bravery, and rude strength, as well as the vices of the frontier in its worst aspect, have left traces on American character, language, and literature, not soon to be effaced. [Turner's note]

pied in many places. You can not station garrisons in every part of these deserts. If you drive the people from one place, they will carry on their annual tillage and remove with their flocks and herds to another. Many of the people in the back settlements are already little attached to particular situations. Already they have topped the Appalachian mountains. From thence they behold before them an immense plain, one vast, rich, level meadow; a square of five hundred miles. Over this they would wander without a possibility of restraint; they would change their manners with their habits of life; would soon forget a government by which they were disowned; would become hordes of English Tartars; and, pouring down upon your unfortified frontiers a fierce and irresistible cavalry, become masters of your governors and your counselors, your collectors and comptrollers, and of all the slaves that adhered to them. Such would, and in no long time must, be the effect of attempting to forbid as a crime and to suppress as an evil the command and blessing of Providence, "Increase and multiply." Such would be the happy result of an endeavor to keep as a lair of wild beasts that earth which God, by an express charter, has given to the children of men.

But the English Government was not alone in its desire to limit the advance of the frontier and guide its destinies. Tide-water Virginia[45] and South Carolina[46] gerrymandered those colonies to insure the dominance of the coast in their legislatures. Washington desired to settle a State at a time in the Northwest; Jefferson would reserve from settlement the territory of his Louisiana purchase north of the thirty-second parallel, in order to offer it to the Indians in exchange for their settlements east of the Mississippi. "When we shall be full on this side," he writes, "we may lay off a range of States on the Western bank from the head to the mouth, and so range after range, advancing compactly as we multiply." Madison went so far as to argue to the French minister that the United States had no interest in seeing population extend itself on the right bank of the Mississippi, but should rather fear it. When the Oregon question was under debate, in 1824, Smyth, of Virginia, would draw an unchangeable line for the limits of the United States at the outer limit of two tiers of States beyond the Mississippi, complaining that the seaboard States were being drained of the flower of their population by the bringing of too much land into market. Even Thomas Benton, the man of widest views of the destiny of the West, at this stage of his career declared that along the ridge of the Rocky Mountains "the

---

[45] Debates in the Constitutional Convention, 1829–1830. [Turner's note]

[46] [McCrady] Eminent and Representative Men of the Carolinas, I, p. 43; Calhoun's Works, I, pp. 401–06. [Turner's note]

western limits of the Republic should be drawn, and the statue of the fabled god Terminus should be raised upon its highest peak, never to be thrown down."[47] But the attempts to limit the boundaries, to restrict land sales and settlement, and to deprive the West of its share of political power were all in vain. Steadily the frontier of settlement advanced and carried with it individualism, democracy, and nationalism, and powerfully affected the East and the Old World.

Intellectual Traits

From the conditions of frontier life came intellectual traits of profound importance. The works of travelers along each frontier from colonial days onward describe certain common traits, and these traits have, while softening down, still persisted as survivals in the place of their origin, even when a higher social organization succeeded. The result is that to the frontier the American intellect owes its striking characteristics. That coarseness and strength combined with acuteness and inquisitiveness; that practical, inventive turn of mind, quick to find expedients; that masterful grasp of material things, lacking in the artistic but powerful to effect great ends; that restless, nervous energy;[48] that dominant individualism, working for good and for evil, and withal that buoyancy and exuberance which comes with freedom—these are traits of the frontier, or traits called out elsewhere because of the existence of the frontier. Since the days when the fleet of Columbus sailed into the waters of the New World, America has been another name for opportunity, and the people of the United States have taken their tone from the incessant expansion which has not only been open but has even been forced upon them. He would be a rash prophet who should assert that the expansive character of American life has now entirely ceased. Movement has been its dominant fact, and, unless this training has no effect upon a people, the American energy will continually demand a

37

---

[47]Speech in the Senate, March 1, 1825; Register of Debates, I, 721. [Turner's note]

[48]Colonial travelers agree in remarking on the phlegmatic characteristics of the colonists. It has frequently been asked how such a people could have developed that strained nervous energy now characteristic of them. Compare Sumner, Alexander Hamilton, p. 98, and Adams's History of the United States, I, p. 60; IX, pp. 240, 241. The transition appears to become marked at the close of the war of 1812, a period when interest centered upon the development of the West, and the West was noted for restless energy. Grund, Americans, II, ch. I. [Turner's note]

wider field for its exercise. But never again will such gifts of free land offer themselves. For a moment, at the frontier, the bonds of custom are broken and unrestraint is triumphant. There is not *tabula rasa.*[49] The stubborn American environment is there with its imperious summons to accept its conditions; the inherited ways of doing things are also there; and yet, in spite of environment, and in spite of custom, each frontier did indeed furnish a new field of opportunity, a gate of escape from the bondage of the past; and freshness, and confidence, and scorn of older society, impatience of its restraints and its ideas, and indifference to its lessons, have accompanied the frontier. What the Mediterranean Sea was to the Greeks, breaking the bond of custom, offering new experiences, calling out new institutions and activities, that, and more, the ever retreating frontier has been to the United States directly, and to the nations of Europe more remotely. And now, four centuries from the discovery of America, at the end of a hundred years of life under the Constitution, the frontier has gone, and with its going has closed the first period of American history.

QUESTIONS FOR CRITICAL READING

1. In what way is the frontier an American, rather than European, experience?
2. What are the chief characteristics of the frontier?
3. How did the European settlers react to the invitation of the frontier?
4. How did interaction with the Native Americans alter the European outlook?
5. Why did the eastern states wish to limit expansion westward?
6. How was a western attitude and culture formed by frontier experiences?
7. What are the stages of the frontier advance?

SUGGESTIONS FOR WRITING

1. Turner says the frontier was "the meeting point between savagery and civilization" (para. 3). What does this mean? Judging from his comments on the many Native American tribes he refers to, what do you judge to be Turner's attitude toward the Native American? In what ways does he suggest the Native American helped define the American?

---

[49]*tabula rasa* A clean slate.

2. The frontier implied a continuous "rebirth" of opportunities. Each new frontier permitted immigrants to start over, to rebuild, redefine, and reconceive their future. Judging from Turner's views, what do you think was most important in that process: new social opportunities through a mixture of new nationalities; new economic opportunities provided by new geographies; or new political structures provided by greater distance from the original colonies?

3. Research the Louisiana Purchase of 1803, and comment on the extent of the lands acquired from France in that transaction. What kind of land was it, and how did it affect the settlers that moved there? Did it represent a frontier to those who purchased it in the way(s) Turner defines a frontier? What were some of the opinions of those who opposed the purchase? Why did France sell it? How did the Louisiana Purchase change America?

4. Turner talks about "essential differences" in frontiers "due to the place element and the time element" (para. 13). Establish as carefully as you can—based on this Turner essay and, if possible, on further reading in frontier studies—what some of those differences are and how they affect the people who take part in the settlements. How is the trader different from the farmer, and the farmer from the rancher?

5. In "The Indian Trader's Frontier" (paras. 17–19) Turner talks about the Native American in relation to the European trader. What contribution do you think the Native Americans made to characterizing America in its frontier development? How did the Native Americans "Americanize" the Europeans?

6. Among the criticisms of the Turner Thesis is its virtual omission of the contribution of women to the development of a distinctive American culture. When Turner talks about "the trader's frontier, the rancher's frontier, or the miner's frontier, and the farmer's frontier" (para. 16), is he talking only about men—or does he implicitly include women? How would a feminist respond to the views that Turner projects here? How does the absence of his consideration of women affect his basic theories?

7. **CONNECTIONS**   J. Hector St. John de Crèvecoeur defines an American in ways that do not always agree with what Turner ultimately says about the frontier experience. Yet Crèvecoeur lived one of the frontier experiences Turner attempts to describe. Why does Crèvecoeur's emphasis on the role of the farmer shape his views in a different fashion from those of Turner? Do you think these two writers disagree, or do you think that despite their differences they are ultimately in deep agreement about what makes an American?

8. **CONNECTIONS**   How does Adam Smith's attitude toward the possession of land stand in agreement or disagreement with Turner's position on land? Smith writes in a time and place in which land is already owned and in limited supply. Consequently, he sees it as the most important form of wealth. Turner describes frontier people simply living on the land, farming it until it is exhausted, then moving on. Only later does the question of purchase, and therefore value in terms of wealth,

come into play. Turner is aware of Smith's views. Does he seem to respect them?

9. **CONNECTIONS**   Alexis de Tocqueville describes American democracy in terms that do not take into account the frontier experience. What is the relationship between Tocqueville's position on democracy in America and Turner's thesis concerning the ways in which the frontier helped develop and preserve American democracy? Given that when Tocqueville wrote, the frontier was still open and developing rapidly, why do you suppose he neglected to mention it? Is it possible that Turner is overstating his thesis and that Tocqueville's views should have tempered his argument?

•

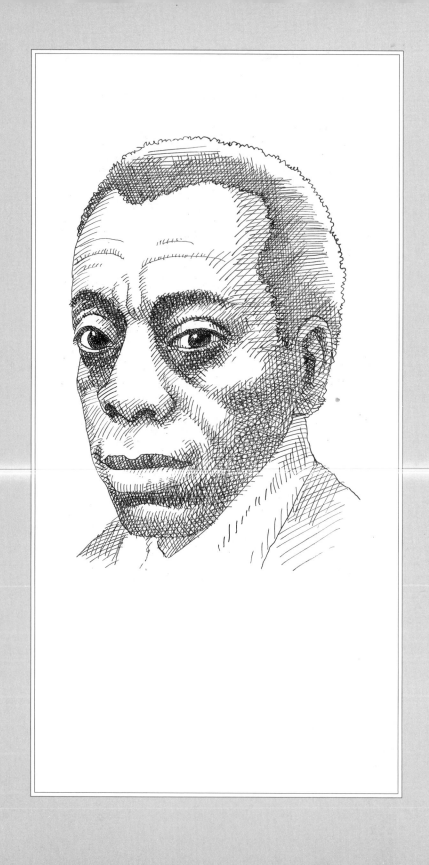

JAMES BALDWIN
The American Dream and the American Negro

BY THE TIME JAMES BALDWIN (1924–1987) wrote this essay in 1965 he was well known as one of America's foremost African American writers, despite the fact that he refused to call himself a black writer. He regarded himself instead as an American writer. He had already become well known for *Go Tell It on the Mountain* (1953), an autobiographical novel about a single day in a church in Harlem. The book drew on Baldwin's personal experiences as a preacher between the ages of fourteen and sixteen. Indeed, he has said that the rhythms of the gospel church were one of his great resources as a writer.

Baldwin's childhood was spent as one of nine children in Harlem. His father was a preacher whose hatred of whites distorted his personality. As a result, Baldwin grew aware of the damage hatred does to the individual, and he credits the efforts of a schoolteacher with making it difficult for him to hate white people. His early essays explore the damage that racism and hatred did to his family. Many of his novels, stories, and essays center on these themes and issues, as well as on the damage done to individuals and to America as a whole. Interestingly, although Baldwin is regarded as a uniquely American writer, he lived primarily in France from 1948 on, returning to the United States on and off to lecture and teach. (He had gone to France in part to avoid American racism and in part to be near Richard Wright [1908–1960], author of *Native Son* [1940].)

From an address at the Cambridge Union Society of Cambridge University, February 1965. Originally published in the *New York Times Magazine*, March 7, 1965.

Baldwin's novel *Giovanni's Room* (1956) moved away from racial subject matter and involved an exploration of gender and romance. The main character was torn between love for a man and love for a woman. Again, the subject matter is somewhat autobiographical; Baldwin refused to identify himself as a gay writer primarily because he felt the important issue was to be able to love whomever he chose, man or woman. In many ways his professional career was spent trying to avoid being labeled as one kind of writer or another.

Baldwin was equally adept at writing in multiple forms—plays, novels, short stories (*Going to Meet the Man,* 1965), and essays—making it all the more difficult for people to categorize him. After writing the play *The Amen Corner* (1955; published 1968), which centers on a woman evangelist married to a jazz musician, he won a Guggenheim Fellowship. His essay collection *Nobody Knows My Name: More Notes of a Native Son* (1961) established him as one of the finest writers of expository prose in America. *Another Country* (1962), addressing interracial and sexual themes, raised his stature as a novelist of distinction. One of his most famous essays, "The Fire Next Time" (1963), long enough to virtually fill an issue of *The New Yorker,* established him as a spokesman for civil rights and black rage. The essay begins with an exploration of his encounter with Black Muslim separatists and then speaks loudly and clearly about the anger and sense of futility experienced by millions of black Americans.

Baldwin was known throughout his adulthood as a sparkling talent, a witty and fascinating person. However, he was also alcoholic and grew increasingly unreliable in his later years. He rarely showed up anywhere on time and often failed to meet publishing deadlines. Some critics have suggested that his personal habits contributed to the falling off of his later work.

In 1965, however, when the essay that follows was written, Baldwin was at the top of his game. He saw America with clear eyes and greeted the civil rights movement with enthusiasm, although without much real hope of significant change in American behavior. "The American Dream and the American Negro" was first delivered orally in a meeting of the Cambridge Union Society in England as his contribution to a subject on which a number of people spoke. It was revised for publication in the *New York Times Magazine* shortly thereafter. Like "The Fire Next Time," this essay explores how racism continues to limit the opportunities of African Americans in the United States. Baldwin warns of the potential for violence and outrage, a warning that was borne out during the inner-city riots of 1967, when troops and tanks were brought into the heart of several cities to quell the disorders.

In the late 1960s Baldwin styled himself as a transatlantic commuter, living part of the time in St. Paul de Vence or other places in southern France, as well as in New York and New England. He had become a citizen of the world, but as "The American Dream and the American Negro" suggests, he always remained an American.

Baldwin's Rhetoric

The essay begins with a reference to Jeremiah, the prophet after whom a book in the Bible is named. Jeremiah was known for handing down harsh verdicts to his people. Baldwin writes in a similar tradition, that of the jeremiad (an extended and angry complaint), alerting us to his tone of seriousness and despair. He does not intend his essay to be entertaining, but rather enlightening. On the one hand he speaks almost like Plato, calling into question our sense of reality. As he says in paragraph 1, how you see yourself in America depends on "what your sense of reality is." He realizes that different people in different situations will have completely different senses of reality: "I have to speak as one of the people who have been most attacked by the western system of reality" (para. 3). The rest of his essay explores this statement.

Beginning with paragraph 5, Baldwin considers the experience of the "American Negro." Living in an essentially white world, Baldwin tells us, he expected that he would have been white when he looked in the mirror. It took him years to realize that was not so. Further, he grew up feeling that not only did the white world of America not value him, it also taught him that he was worthless. As Baldwin learned more about history, he realized that the labor of black Americans had built the country and that cheap—or free—labor was essential to the growth and development of the nation. In other words, his contribution to America was great even when he was only a boy.

The rhythms of the preacher may not be as evident in this essay as they are in others. However, Baldwin writes in such a way that we are always aware of the subtle rhythms of speech beneath the surface of the words. He uses very few unusual rhetorical techniques, switching mostly between the first and third persons (*I* and *he/she/they*, respectively). The sudden use of the second person (*you*) in paragraphs 5 and 6 as well in a few other spots in the essay is the only exception to this pattern, with the appearance of sentences such as, "It comes as a great shock around the age of five, six, or seven to discover that the flag to which you have pledged allegiance, along with everybody else, has not pledged allegiance to you" (para. 5). In that sentence, the balance of *you* and *flag* surprises readers with a sense of reversal, with the direct address forcing us to rethink our notions about American identity, the American dream, and who is really given the opportunity to achieve that dream.

Perhaps one of the most intriguing aspects of the essay is its tone. On the one hand it is conciliatory in that it addresses the audience very politely: "We are sitting in this room and we are all civilized" (para. 17). On the other hand it is challenging, asking "whether one civilization has a right to subjugate—in fact, to destroy—another" (para. 3). The reader should keep in mind that Baldwin's original audience was Englishmen, whose history is one of colonial conquest and whose very university—Cambridge—sent out administrators and military men who subjugated entire subcontinents with ease and profit.

The tone shifts to that of the writer talking about what he has been taught ("that Africa had no history" [para. 15]) and then going on to "teach" the audience before him: "One of the things the white world does not know, but I think I know, is that black people are just like everybody else" (para. 17). Ultimately, the tone he uses is cautionary and is as relevant to the political, social, and economic problems in America today as it was in 1965: "I am not an object of missionary charity, I am one of the people who built the country—until this moment comes [when America accepts that "my ancestors are both black and white"] there is scarcely any hope for the American dream. If the people are denied participation in it, by their very presence they will wreck it" (para. 21).

PREREADING QUESTIONS:
WHAT TO READ FOR

The following prereading questions may help you anticipate key issues in the discussion on James Baldwin's "The American Dream and the American Negro." Keeping them in mind during your first reading of the selection should help focus your reactions.

- What is the American dream?

- In what sense is Baldwin "one of the people who built the country" (para. 21)?

- What changes does Baldwin urge on white society?

The American Dream
and the American Negro

I find myself, not for the first time, in the position of a kind of 1
Jeremiah. It would seem to me that the question before the house is
a proposition horribly loaded, that one's response to that question
depends on where you find yourself in the world, what your sense
of reality is. That is, it depends on assumptions we hold so deeply as
to be scarcely aware of them.

The white South African or Mississippi sharecropper or Al- 2
abama sheriff has at bottom a system of reality which compels them
really to believe when they face the Negro that this woman, this
man, this child must be insane to attack the system to which he
owes his entire identity. For such a person, the proposition which
we are trying to discuss here does not exist.

On the other hand, I have to speak as one of the people who 3
have been most attacked by the western system of reality. It comes
from Europe. That is how it got to America. It raises the question of
whether or not civilizations can be considered equal, or whether one
civilization has a right to subjugate — in fact, to destroy — another.

Now, leaving aside all the physical factors one can quote — leav- 4
ing aside the rape or murder, leaving aside the bloody catalogue of
oppression which we are too familiar with anyway — what the system does to the subjugated is to destroy his sense of reality. It destroys his father's authority over him. His father can no longer tell
him anything because his past has disappeared.

In the case of the American Negro, from the moment you are 5
born every stick and stone, every face, is white. Since you have not
yet seen a mirror, you suppose you are too. It comes as a great shock
around the age of five, six, or seven to discover that the flag to
which you have pledged allegiance, along with everybody else, has
not pledged allegiance to you. It comes as a great shock to see Gary
Cooper killing off the Indians, and, although you are rooting for
Gary Cooper, that the Indians are you.

It comes as a great shock to discover that the country which is 6
your birthplace and to which you owe your life and identity has not,
in its whole system of reality, evolved any place for you. The disaf-
fection and the gap between people, only on the basis of their skins,
begins there and accelerates throughout your whole lifetime. You realize that you are thirty and you are having a terrible time. You have
been through a certain kind of mill and the most serious effect is
again not the catalogue of disaster — the policeman, the taxi driver,

the waiters, the landlady, the banks, the insurance companies, the millions of details twenty-four hours of every day which spell out to you that you are a worthless human being. It is not that. By that time you have begun to see it happening in your daughter, your son or your niece or your nephew. You are thirty by now and nothing you have done has helped you escape the trap. But what is worse is that nothing you have done, and as far as you can tell nothing you *can* do, will save your son or your daughter from having the same disaster and from coming to the same end.

We speak about expense. There are several ways of addressing 7 oneself to some attempt to find out what the word means here. From a very literal point of view, the harbors and the ports and the railroads of the country—the economy, especially in the South— could not conceivably be what they are if it had not been (and this is still so) for cheap labor. I am speaking very seriously, and this is not an overstatement: I picked cotton, I carried it to the market, I built the railroads under someone else's whip for nothing. For nothing.

The Southern oligarchy which has still today so very much 8 power in Washington, and therefore some power in the world, was created by my labor and my sweat and the violation of my women and the murder of my children. This in the land of the free, the home of the brave. None can challenge that statement. It is a matter of historical record.

In the Deep South you are dealing with a sheriff or a landlord or 9 a landlady or the girl at the Western Union desk. She doesn't know quite whom she is dealing with—by which I mean, if you are not part of a town and if you are a northern nigger, it shows in millions of ways. She simply knows that it is an unknown quantity and she wants nothing to do with it. You have to wait a while to get your telegram. We have all been through it. By the time you get to be a man it is fairly easy to deal with.

But what happens to the poor white man's, the poor white 10 woman's mind? It is this: they have been raised to believe, and by now they helplessly believe, that no matter how terrible some of their lives may be and no matter what disaster overtakes them, there is one consolation like a heavenly revelation—at least they are not black. I suggest that of all the terrible things that could happen to a human being that is one of the worst. I suggest that what has happened to the white southerner is in some ways much worse than what has happened to the Negroes there.

Sheriff Clark in Selma, Alabama, cannot be dismissed as a total 11 monster; I am sure he loves his wife and children and likes to get drunk. One has to assume that he is a man like me. But he does not know what drives him to use the club, to menace with the gun and to use the cattle prod. Something awful must have happened to a human being to be able to put a cattle prod against a woman's breasts. What happens to the woman is ghastly. What happens to the man who does it is in some ways much, much worse. Their moral lives have been destroyed by the plague called color.

This is not being done one hundred years ago, but in 1965 and   12
in a country which is pleased with what we call prosperity, with a certain amount of social coherence, which calls itself a civilized nation and which espouses the notion of freedom in the world. If it were white people being murdered, the government would find some way of doing something about it. We have a civil rights bill now. We had the Fifteenth Amendment[1] nearly one hundred years ago. If it was not honored then, I have no reason to believe that the civil rights bill will be honored now.

The American soil is full of the corpses of my ancestors, through   13
four hundred years and at least three wars. Why is my freedom, my citizenship, in question now? What one begs the American people to do, for all our sakes, is simply to accept our history.

It seems to me when I watch Americans in Europe that what   14
they don't know about Europeans is what they don't know about me. They were not trying to be nasty to the French girl, rude to the French waiter. They did not know that they hurt their feelings; they didn't have any sense that this particular man and woman were human beings. They walked over them with the same sort of bland ignorance and condescension, the charm and cheerfulness, with which they had patted me on the head and which made them upset when I was upset.

When I was brought up I was taught in American history books   15
that Africa had no history and that neither had I. I was a savage about whom the least said the better, who had been saved by Europe and who had been brought to America. Of course, I believed it. I didn't have much choice. These were the only books there were. Everyone else seemed to agree. If you went out of Harlem the whole world agreed. What you saw was much bigger, whiter, cleaner, safer. The garbage was collected, the children were happy. You would go back home and it would seem, of course, that this was an act of God. You belonged where white people put you.

It is only since World War II that there has been a counter-   16
image in the world. That image has not come about because of any

---

[1] **Fifteenth Amendment (1870)** Amendment to the Constitution stating that the right to vote cannot be denied "on account of race, color, or previous conditions of servitude."

legislation by any American government, but because Africa was suddenly on the stage of the world and Africans had to be dealt with in a way they had never been dealt with before. This gave the American Negro, for the first time, a sense of himself not as a savage. It has created and will create a great many conundrums.

One of the things the white world does not know, but I think I 17 know, is that black people are just like everybody else. We are also mercenaries, dictators, murderers, liars. We are human, too. Unless we can establish some kind of dialogue between those people who enjoy the American dream and those people who have not achieved it, we will be in terrible trouble. This is what concerns me most. We are sitting in this room and we are all civilized; we can talk to each other, at least on certain levels, so that we can walk out of here assuming that the measure of our politeness has some effect on the world.

I remember when the ex–Attorney General Mr. Robert 18 Kennedy said it was conceivable that in forty years in America we might have a Negro President. That sounded like a very emancipated statement to white people. They were not in Harlem when this statement was first heard. They did not hear the laughter and the bitterness and scorn with which this statement was greeted. From the point of view of the man in the Harlem barber shop, Bobby Kennedy only got here yesterday and now he is already on his way to the Presidency. We were here for four hundred years and now he tells us that maybe in forty years, if you are good, we may let you become President.

Perhaps I can be reasoned with, but I don't know—neither 19 does Martin Luther King—none of us knows how to deal with people whom the white world has so long ignored, who don't believe anything the white world says and don't entirely believe anything I or Martin say. You can't blame them.

It seems to me that the City of New York has had, for example, 20 Negroes in it for a very long time. The City of New York was able in the last fifteen years to reconstruct itself, to tear down buildings and raise great new ones, and has done nothing whatever except build housing projects, mainly in the ghettoes, for the Negroes. And of course the Negroes hate it. The children can't bear it. They want to move out of the ghettoes. If American pretensions were based on more honest assessments of life, it would not mean for Negroes that when someone says "urban renewal" some Negroes are going to be thrown out into the streets, which is what it means now.

It is a terrible thing for an entire people to surrender to the no- 21
tion that one-ninth of its population is beneath them. Until the moment comes when we, the Americans, are able to accept the fact that
my ancestors are both black and white, that on that continent we are
trying to forge a new identity, that we need each other, that I am not
a ward of America, I am not an object of missionary charity, I am
one of the people who built the country—until this moment comes
there is scarcely any hope for the American dream. If the people are
denied participation in it, by their very presence they will wreck it.
And if that happens it is a very grave moment for the West.

QUESTIONS FOR CRITICAL READING

1. What is the American dream, and who is living it?
2. Why did Baldwin take issue with Robert Kennedy's assertion that in
   forty years there might be a black president?
3. What contribution did African American labor make to the building of
   the country?
4. What was Baldwin taught in school about Africa? What were you
   taught?
5. Why did Baldwin as a child feel he was worthless?
6. What kind of violence against blacks does Baldwin refer to?
7. Do you think this is an optimistic or a pessimistic essay?

SUGGESTIONS FOR WRITING

1. Baldwin says, "Unless we can establish some kind of dialogue between
   those people who enjoy the American dream and those people who
   have not achieved it, we will be in terrible trouble" (para. 17). How
   can such a dialogue be established? What would need to change in
   order to do so? Do you see signs of it being established in your personal experience? Do you agree that it is necessary and that it would
   somehow help?
2. Baldwin refers to a "counter-image" (para. 16) of Africa after World
   War II, implying that with Africa's increased importance on the world
   stage, its image improved. What image of Africa do the press and other
   media project now? In what ways does that impact your view of yourself and of African Americans in general? Do images of Europe, such as
   the massacres in Kosovo, reflect similarly on your views of European
   Americans? Why or why not?
3. Research the period in American history from 1965 to 1969, including
   the assassinations of Robert Kennedy, Martin Luther King Jr., and Malcolm X. What were prevailing attitudes toward the American dream

and the American Negro? During this period, civil rights legislation was created and enforced and a great deal of unrest marked the lives of ordinary Americans. To what extent did the words of James Baldwin in this essay prepare you for what you learned?

4. If you find yourself sympathetic to Baldwin's portrait of himself and his feelings about America, write an essay that is your own jeremiad. Describe what you see happening in America and the problems you see facing the country in the future. Establish your own position in the landscape of American society, and suggest what is needed to make the social system more just and equal.

5. In another essay, Baldwin wrote about the projects that were built after World War II, pointing out that the people who lived in them did not like them. What is the general attitude of Americans toward housing projects today? What has changed? Have the projects themselves changed in any significant way? What do politicians say about them? If possible, research the topic in the archives of a major newspaper to determine current opinion.

6. What are some of the realities that Baldwin would like to impart to white America? He says that he is a victim of Western realities. What does he mean? How can someone be the victim of a culture's sense of reality? How can one be critical of one's own sense of reality?

7. **CONNECTIONS**   Examine the views of Alexis de Tocqueville and Milton and Rose Friedman on the question of equality and equality of opportunity. How much do you think Baldwin would agree with them? Are the issues that concern them the same ones that concern Baldwin? Is Tocqueville's sense of democracy of immediate importance to Baldwin? Does Baldwin concern himself with democracy? Is he concerned only with economics?

8. **CONNECTIONS**   Baldwin seems to imply a comparison with Plato when he talks about people not seeing the same reality. To what extent are Plato's concerns about reality evident in Baldwin's views on what reality means to different people? Which reality does Baldwin want his audience to see? Do you think you see it?

PART SEVEN

FAITH

Siddhārtha Gautama, the Buddha
From *The Book of Job*
St. Matthew
The Bhagavad Gītā
The Prophet Muhammad
Friedrich Nietzsche
Simone Weil

INTRODUCTION

Faith is one of the most compelling and enduring ideas that the world has known. Some of the earliest prehistoric artifacts show evidence of belief in a higher power or powers that shape the course of human events, and archaeological digs have revealed the materials of religious practice and of worship of deities spanning thousands of years. Although much of the history of faith is lost in the eons of prehistory, we know that during the last six or seven thousand years of humanity's development, faith has grown and changed as other human ideas and institutions have grown and changed. The earliest evidence suggests that nature worship was common among people all over the globe, often centering on variations of sun worship. Animism, the belief that all things in nature have a spiritual force and must be respected—and in some cases worshiped or deferred to—thrived in ancient times and continues to be practiced to this day. The pantheon of gods that the Egyptians developed and recorded, doubtless from vestiges of their own prehistory, are identified by Herodotus as the precursors of some of the Greek gods that are familiar to us through myth. The Greek and Roman myths center on Zeus and Jupiter but pay tribute to a range of gods with specialized responsibilities.

The rise of monotheism is evident in many cultures, but for Westerners its earliest development centers most prominently in Judaism. The development of monotheism has been seen as evolutionary, but the term *evolution* is a metaphor in this case: there is no objective means of establishing progress in matters of faith. Plato and Aristotle were what modern theologians would call pagans and based their faith—insofar as faith can be identified in either of them—on the polytheism of their time. Later thinkers, such as St. Matthew, absorbed the contemporary revolution of monotheistic thought. Identifying human figures with the godhead occurred relatively late in the development of religious faith. The Buddha, Jesus, and Krishna represent important human figures for the religious systems of which they are part. The idea of their humanity is one of their most important contributions to modern religious faith.

The selections that follow are drawn from several different religions and approaches to the concept of faith. However, the idea that faith transforms the individual is constant across these selections. Some emphasize that change comes from within and that individuals must work at becoming worthy of their faith. Discipline is another common theme among these writers, but it takes several forms and is not always clearly related to moral behavior. In fact, morality—or right action in one's relations with others—is not always central to these writers, although we can infer that it is usually present. Their focus is clearly on making the individual worthy and spiritually unencumbered.

The range of behavior in matters of faith is extraordinary in these selections. The Buddha recommends using self-control and meditation to achieve enlightenment. *The Book of Job,* however, stresses an unshakable faith in God, even in the face of pain and loss, as the key to wisdom and understanding. St. Matthew describes the path that Jesus set out for the disciples, emphasizing mercy and charity. The Lord Krishna tells Arjuna in the *Bhagavad Gītā* that only through discipline and a renouncing of the senses will he know the divinity. The Prophet Muhammad holds a dialogue with Allah concerning the fate of believers and nonbelievers. Friedrich Nietzsche describes aspects of religious faith as practiced by the ancient Greeks and Romans, ranging from cerebral and controlled Apollonian expressions of faith to ecstatic Dionysian effusions. Simone Weil is, in her own way, also ecstatic in her commitment to religious faith.

Siddhārtha Gautama, the Buddha, directs our attention inward to the deepest spiritual resources of the individual. According to the Buddha, meditation is the path to enlightenment, revealing a spiritual life that follows an eightfold path and eventually provides the soul with peace. The Buddha provides instructions in how to control the senses, how to moderate the appetites, and how to control the wandering mind through focus and concentration. Following the eightfold path requires right behavior, which can be achieved only by gaining knowledge of what right behavior is.

The Book of Job, a document from the Hebrew Bible that may date to the sixth century B.C., is especially interesting because it offers a view of a man who led an exemplary life but who nonetheless suffered terrible calamities. Job begins his narrative as a peaceful, upright citizen, respected and honored by all his friends and by citizens of his town of Uz. In a direct challenge to God, Satan sets out to destroy Job's faith by taking all his possessions and wracking his body with painful torments. Job suffers colossal physical and mental pain, and he loses the respect of all his friends and all the citizens of Uz. Yet Job never swerves in his faith. In the end, the ways of God are shown to be more complex and more mysterious than anyone in the narrative could have imagined. The center of religion is shifted from good deeds and a good life to faith in God.

St. Matthew's Gospel can be found in the New Testament of the Bible. It tells the story of Jesus' youth and brief ministry. In the Sermon on the Mount, the selection that appears here, Jesus instructs his disciples beginning with the beatitudes, the blessings that the disciples enjoy as a result of their having faith in Jesus. The Sermon on the Mount focuses on interpretation of the laws, including the subjects of adultery, divorce, vengeance, and charity. It ends with the Lord's Prayer, which Jesus says is the only prayer one needs, because it includes all prayers. The core of the selection focuses on the morality of the individual in daily behavior and an understanding of the spirit of the law.

The *Bhagavad Gītā* presents a portrait of the Hindu divinity Lord Krishna, who, in the guise of Arjuna's charioteer, advises Arjuna on matters of faith. He reveals himself to Arjuna and describes his two selves—the natural self, which is the material of all nature, and the spiritual self, which is the ineffable divinity. Like the Buddha, Lord Krishna emphasizes the role of meditation in seeking enlightenment. For the Hindu, enlightenment involves reaching the end of the indefinite number of incarnations that the individual soul must pass through before achieving nirvana, the point of ultimate oneness with the divine. The path involves self-discipline and a withdrawal from the distractions of the sensory world.

"The Believer," from the Koran, presents a dialogue between Allah and the Prophet Muhammad, a structure similar to that used in the excerpts from St. Matthew and the *Bhagavad Gītā*. The angel Gabriel reveals the word of Allah to Muhammad. In "The Believer" Muhammad compares the fate of those who believe in Allah with that of unbelievers. According to Muhammad, believers will enter into paradise, whereas unbelievers will be lost. "The Believer" moves from discussing the fate of the unfaithful to a review of biblical history to the story of the Egyptian Pharaoh and others who bring destruction upon themselves by refusing to believe in Allah.

Although Friedrich Nietzsche is famous for saying in 1899 that "God is dead," he was nonetheless deeply interested in faith and religion in their many manifestations. In "Apollonianism and Dionysianism" he describes two polarities in religious behavior as they were understood by both the ancients and his contemporaries. Nietzsche seems to have leaned toward approving the divine "madness" of the Dionysian spirit, but he realized that both paths—the thoughtful, restrained Apollonian and the ecstatic, feverish Dionysian—exist and both serve the purposes of faith.

The French philosopher Simone Weil wrote "Spiritual Autobiography" as a letter to a priest during World War II. She was concerned with the ways in which she could establish her own faith and maintain her own integrity. Weil was born a Jew but in her twenties accepted Christ and began to view herself as a Christian. Her religious beliefs were stimulated by her reading of the seventeenth-century English religious poets, such as George Herbert, Richard Crashaw, and John Donne. She felt her faith to be ecstatic and mystical—much as those poets did—and she resisted baptism into the church in part because she wanted her faith to be personal instead of institutional. She felt a deep communion with Christ, which she discusses in "Spiritual Autobiography," explaining herself clearly and patiently. Her beliefs seem to recall those of an earlier time, but she lived during a period of such extraordinary crisis—including the rise of fascism and the eventual outbreak of World War II—that there is no question that intense moments of soul-searching would occur in the lives of intellectuals such as Weil.

These expressions of faith from seven very different points of view demonstrate only a small portion of the variety of experience encompassed by human faith. Religions are complex structures of belief, demanding a special commitment from their members. Some of the attitudes and expressions of faith in this section may seem arbitrary, extreme, or even unbelievable. Yet they are the basic materials of any inquiry into the relationship between human beings and the divine.

SIDDHĀRTHA GAUTAMA, THE BUDDHA
Meditation:
The Path to Enlightenment

SIDDHĀRTHA GAUTAMA (563?–483? B.C.), known as the Buddha (Sanskrit for "enlightened one"), was born in Kapilavastu, the chief town of Kapila in what is now Nepal. His family was petty royalty, and he himself a minor prince. One of his names is Sakyamuni, "sage of the Sakya clan." Early texts state that he was protected from knowledge of the outside world so that when he was twenty-nine, after finally witnessing poverty, illness, and death, he renounced his aristocratic position and his wife and family. He left his home and wandered, living the ascetic religious life, until he reached Bodh Gaya, where he spent his time in meditation until he achieved enlightenment.

His purpose in seeking enlightenment was to show the way to people so they could relieve the misery of their own lives. In most versions of Buddhism, the Buddha is regarded as Lord Buddha. In other versions, he is regarded as a man who reached a level of perfection that is possible for ordinary people to achieve. Some branches of Buddhism describe several Buddhas, or bodhisattvas—those who enter different spiritual stages at different times and may be viewed as either great teachers or heavenly saviors.

In the religion that developed from the Buddha's teachings, the purpose of life is to achieve the enlightenment that will enable the individual to end *samsāra*—the wandering of the soul from one becoming (incarnation) to another—and reach *nirvana*, a peace that

Translated by Edward Conze.

lies beyond human understanding. In the selection that follows, nirvana is referred to as the end of being.

Because Buddhists hope to achieve nirvana, their lives are guided by firm precepts. They believe that the existence they now enjoy was shaped and formed by the soul in a previous existence and that because their present way of life shapes existences to come, they need to make their own *karma*. *Karma* is a Sanskrit word for "making," translated sometimes as "action." Therefore, Buddhists have established eight principles of behavior for creating their karma called the Noble Eightfold Path:

1. Right views — the avoidance of delusion
2. Right aims — purposive intentions to achieve nirvana
3. Right speech — preferring the truth
4. Right conduct — being honest, true, pure in behavior
5. Right living — avoiding hurting all beings and thus preferring a vegetarian diet
6. Self-control — preferring disciplined behavior
7. Right-mindedness — being aware and alert
8. Right meditation — deep contemplation of life and the process of thought

The ethical implications of Buddhism are evident in the eight admonitions of the Noble Eightfold Path.

The Buddhist scriptures, from which the following passage comes, were not written by the Buddha but were gathered from his teachings by disciples such as his personal follower, Ānanda. The scriptures date from the fifth century B.C. and were written down sometime in the seventh century A.D. by monks who were fearful that the teachings might be lost because of intense persecution of Buddhists. Buddhism is rare in India today—its adherents are located mainly in Sri Lanka—but it was transplanted to Tibet, China, and Japan, where it remains influential. Although Southeast Asia today is largely Buddhist, Buddhism coexists with many local religions, some of which reflect dramatically opposing views.

The volume of Buddhist scriptures—hundreds of thousands of pages—resulted from the contribution of many different schools of Buddhism, each with its own interpretation. In Japan, for example, several schools of Buddhism have been prominent. One is the Rinzai sect, a form of Buddhism that meditates on complex and baffling riddles, such as the question "What is the sound of one hand clapping?" Such a riddle, called a *koan,* is especially difficult for the Western mind to comprehend. Another is the Soto sect, which dates from the thirteenth century A.D. and emphasizes quiet sitting—*zazen*—as a means to enlightenment. Both of these sects are still vital in modern Buddhism.

Buddhist meditation, which originated from Zen Buddhism, depends on a willingness to remain quiet and suspend all logical thought, desire, and attachments. It is an extremely difficult discipline but is recognized by all Buddhists as the one true path to enlightenment, demanding the denial of the sensory world, of transitory events and values.

The following passage emphasizes the advantages of meditation as well as the advantages of introversion. The material world is seen as a distraction that incessantly robs people of their peace and their awareness of the truth about existence. Zen meditation is a radical technique for bringing the external world under the control of the spirit. However, it is similar to Greek and Roman advice and fundamental Western views concerning spiritual values in modern times.

Buddhist Rhetoric

The material in this selection is not only translated from a language and a tradition quite foreign to English but is also derived from several sources. "The Advantages of Meditation" comes from a scripture called *Milindapanha* and is rendered in prose. "The Practice of Introversion," however, originates from another text, *Santideva*, and is rendered in poetry. The third section, "The Progressive Steps of Meditation," is from the *Asvaghosa*, yet another important Buddhist text. The fact that these texts differ in age and in approach makes the rhetorical situation unusual.

However, certain qualities are present in all the texts. All are "how-to" texts, offering a step-by-step examination of the nature of meditation, its benefits, characteristics, and results. Typical of many Buddhist texts is the technique of enumeration: listing eight noble paths, twenty-eight advantages to meditation, and so on. Such a technique is especially useful for instruction because of its clear, progressive approach.

However, there is a further problem that the translator must resolve. As Edward Conze, the translator of these texts, explains, "For Buddhists the founder of their religion is the 'Lord Buddha,' a godlike being who has transcended the conditions of ordinary life, and his words are not those of a mere man, but a voice issuing from another world. It is therefore quite inconceivable that the Buddha should speak as ordinary people do." Therefore, the text as translated employs an elevated diction in a tone that is formal and distant. We might consider it priestlike. We usually expect and appreciate conversational, direct prose. But in confronting material that is so serious, dignified, and spiritual, it seems more appropriate that the level of diction be high and the tone formal.

PREREADING QUESTIONS: WHAT TO READ FOR

The following prereading questions may help you anticipate key issues in the discussion on Siddhārtha Gautama's "Meditation: The Path to Enlightenment." Keeping them in mind during your first reading of the selection should help focus your reactions.

- How does one remain mindful?
- How does mindfulness connect to enlightenment?
- What are the benefits of meditation?

Meditation:
The Path to Enlightenment

1. The Advantages of Meditation

Secluded meditation has many virtues. All the Tathagatas[1] have won their all-knowledge in a state of secluded meditation, and, even after their enlightenment, they have continued to cultivate meditation in the recollection of the benefits it brought to them in the past. It is just as a man who has received some boon from a king, and who would, in recollection of the benefits he has had, remain also in the future in attendance on that king.

There are, in fact, twenty-eight advantages to be gained from secluded meditation, and they are the reason why the Tathagatas have devoted themselves to it. They are as follows: secluded meditation guards him who meditates, lengthens his life, gives him strength, and shuts out faults; it removes ill fame, and leads to good repute; it drives out discontent, and makes for contentment; it removes fear, and gives confidence; it removes sloth and generates vigor; it re-

1

2

---

[1] **Tathagata** One of the Buddha's titles. It means "he who has thus come."

moves greed, hate, and delusion; it slays pride, breaks up preoccupations, makes thought one-pointed, softens the mind, generates gladness, makes one venerable, gives rise to much profit, makes one worthy of homage, brings exuberant joy, causes delight, shows the own-being of all conditioned things, abolishes rebirth in the world of becoming, and it bestows all the benefits of an ascetic life. These are the twenty-eight advantages of meditation which induce the Tathagatas to practice it.

And it is because the Tathagatas wish to experience the calm 3
and easeful delight of meditational attainments that they practice meditation with this end in view. Four are the reasons why the Tathagatas tend meditation: so that they may dwell at ease; on account of the manifoldness of its faultless virtues; because it is the road to all holy states without exception; and because it has been praised, lauded, exalted, and commended by all the Buddhas.

2. The Practice of Introversion

With his vigor grown strong, his mind should be placed in samadhi,[2] 4
For if thought be distracted we lie in the fangs of the passions.

No distractions can touch the man who's alone both in his body and 5
    mind.
Therefore renounce you the world, give up all thinking discursive!

Thirsting for gain, and loving the world, the people fail to renounce it. 6
But the wise can discard this love, reflecting as follows:

Through stillness joined to insight true,   7
His passions are annihilated.
Stillness must first of all be found.
That springs from disregarding worldly satisfactions.

Shortlived yourself, how can you think that others, quite as fleeting, 8
    are worthy of your love?
Thousands of births will pass without a sight of him you cherish so.

When unable to see your beloved, discontent disturbs your samadhi; 9
When you have seen, your longing, unsated as ever, returns as before.

Then you forfeit the truth of the Real; your fallen condition shocks 10
    you no longer;
Burning with grief you yearn for reunion with him whom you cherish.

---

[2] **samadhi** Trancelike concentration.

Worries like these consume a brief life — over and over again to no   11
    purpose;
You stray from the Dharma[3] eternal, for the sake of a transient friend.

To share in the life of the foolish will lead to the states of woe;   12
You share not, and they will hate you; what good comes from
    contact with fools?

Good friends at one time, of a sudden they dislike you,   13
You try to please them, quite in vain — the worldly are not easily
    contented!

Advice on their duties stirs anger; your own good deeds they   14
    impede;
When you ignore what they say they are angry, and head for a state
    of woe.

Of his betters he is envious, with his equals there is strife;   15
To inferiors he is haughty, mad for praise and wroth at blame;
Is there ever any goodness in these foolish common men?

Self-applause, belittling others, or encouragement to sin,   16
Some such evil's sure to happen where one fool another meets.

Two evils meet when fools consort together.   17
Alone I'll live, in peace and with unblemished mind.

Far should one flee from fools. When met, they should be won by   18
    kindness,
Not in the hope of intimacy, but so as to preserve an even, holy,
    mind.

Enough for Dharma's work I'll take from him, just as a bee takes   19
    honey from a flower.
Hidden and unknown, like the new moon, I will live my life.

The fools are no one's friends, so have the Buddhas taught us;   20
They cannot love unless their interest in themselves impels them.

Trees do not show disdain, and they demand no toilsome wooing;   21
Fain[4] would I now consort with them as my companions.

---

    [3] **Dharma** Truth, divine law, virtue. This word has numerous meanings, depending on its context.
    [4] **Fain** Gladly.

Fain would I dwell in a deserted sanctuary, beneath a tree, or in a   22
    cave,
In noble disregard for all, and never looking back on what I left.

Fain would I dwell in spacious regions owned by no one,   23
And there, a homeless wanderer, follow my own mind,

A clay bowl as my only wealth, a robe that does not tempt the   24
    robbers,
Dwelling exempt from fear, and careless of my body.

Alone a man is born, and quite alone he also meets his death;   25
This private anguish no one shares; and friends can only bar true
    welfare.

Those who travel through Becoming should regard each incarnation   26
As no more than a passing station on their journey through
    Samsāra.[5]

So will I ever tend delightful and untroubled solitude,   27
Bestowing bliss, and stilling all distractions.

And from all other care released, the mind set on collecting my own   28
    spirit,
To unify and discipline my spirit I will strive.

3. The Progressive Steps of Meditation

The Restraint of the Senses. By taking your stand on mindful-   29
ness you must hold back from the sense-objects your senses, unsteady by nature. Fire, snakes, and lightning are less inimical to us
than our own senses, so much more dangerous. For they assail us all
the time. Even the most vicious enemies can attack only some
people at some times, and not at others, but everybody is always and
everywhere weighed down by his senses. And people do not go to
hell because some enemy has knocked them down and cast them
into it; it is because they have been knocked down by their unsteady
senses that they are helplessly dragged there. Those attacked by external enemies may, or may not, suffer injury to their souls; but
those who are weighed down by the senses suffer in body and soul

---

[5] **Samsāra** The cycle of birth, death, and rebirth.

alike. For the five senses are rather like arrows which have been smeared with the poison of fancies, have cares for their feathers and happiness for their points, and fly about in the space provided by the range of the sense-objects; shot off by Kama, the God of Love, they hit men in their very hearts as a hunter hits a deer, and if men do not know how to ward off these arrows they will be their undoing; when they come near us we should stand firm in self-control, be agile and steadfast, and ward them off with the great armor of mindfulness. As a man who has subdued his enemies can everywhere live and sleep at ease and free from care, so can he who has pacified his senses. For the senses constantly ask for more by way of worldly objects, and normally behave like voracious dogs who can never have enough. This disorderly mob of the senses can never reach satiety, not by any amount of sense-objects; they are rather like the sea, which one can go on indefinitely replenishing with water.

In this world the senses cannot be prevented from being active, 30 each in its own sphere. But they should not be allowed to grasp either the general features of an object, or its particularities. When you have beheld a sight-object with your eyes, you must merely determine the basic element (which it represents, e.g., it is a "sight-object") and should not under any circumstances fancy it as, say, a woman or a man. But if now and then you have inadvertently grasped something as a "woman" or a "man," you should not follow that up by determining the hairs, teeth, etc. as lovely. Nothing should be subtracted from the datum, nothing added to it; it should be seen as it really is, as what it is like in real truth.

If you thus try to look continually for the true reality in that 31 which the senses present to you, covetousness and aversion will soon be left without a foothold. Coveting ruins those living beings who are bent on sensuous enjoyment by means of pleasing forms, like an enemy with a friendly face who speaks loving words, but plans dark deeds. But what is called "aversion" is a kind of anger directed towards certain objects, and anyone who is deluded enough to pursue it is bound to suffer for it either in this or a future life. Afflicted by their likes and dislikes, as by excessive heat or cold, men will never find either happiness or the highest good as long as they put their trust in the unsteady senses.

How the Senses Cause Bondage.   A sense-organ, although it 32 may have begun to react to a sense-object, does not get caught up in it unless the mind conceives imaginary ideas about the object. Both fuel and air must be present for a fire to blaze up; so the fire of the passions is born from a combination of a sense-object with imaginations. For people are tied down by a sense-object when they cover it with unreal imaginations; likewise they are liberated from it when they see it as it really is. The sight of one and the same object may attract one person, repel another, and leave a third indifferent; a fourth may be moved to withdraw gently from it. Hence the sense-object itself is not the decisive cause of either bondage or emancipation. It is the presence or absence of imaginations which determines whether attachment takes place or not. Supreme exertions should therefore be made to bring about a restraint of the senses; for unguarded senses lead to suffering and continued becomings. In all circumstances you should therefore watch out for these enemies which cause so much evil, and you should always control them, i.e., your seeing, hearing, smelling, tasting, and touching. Do not be negligent in this matter even for a moment. The onrush of sense-experiences must be shut out with the sluice-gate of mindfulness.

Moderation in Eating. Moreover you must learn to be moderate in eating, and eat only enough to remain healthy, and fit for trance. For excessive food obstructs the flow of the breath as it goes in and out, induces lassitude and sleepiness, and kills all valor. And as too much food has unfortunate consequences, so also starvation does not lead to efficiency. For starvation drains away the body's volume, luster, firmness, performance, and strength. You should take food in accordance with your individual capacity, neither too much, nor, from pride, too little. As somebody with a running sore puts healing ointment on it, so the man who seeks liberation should use food only to remove his hunger. As the axle of a chariot must be lubricated so that it may work properly, so the wise man employs food only to maintain his life. He takes care of his body, and carries it along with him, not because he has any affection for it, but simply because it enables him to cross the flood of suffering. The spiritual man offers food to his body merely to dispel hunger, and not from greed, or from any love for it.

The Avoidance of Sleep. After he has passed his day in keeping his mind collected, the self-possessed man should shake off his sleepiness and spend also the night in the practice of Yoga.[6] When threatened with sleepiness you should constantly mobilize in your mind the factors of exertion and fortitude, of stamina and courage. You should repeat long passages from the Scriptures which you

33

34

---

[6]**Yoga** Disciplined exercise designed to further self-control. A yogi or yogin is one who practices yoga.

know by heart, expound them to others and reflect on them yourself. In order to keep awake all the time, wet your face with water,
look round in all directions and fix your eyes on the stars. With
your senses turned inwards, unmoved and well-controlled, with
your mind undistracted, you should walk about or sit down at
night. Fear, zest, and grief keep sleepiness away; therefore cultivate
these three when you feel drowsy. Fear is best fostered by the
thought of death coming upon you, zest by thinking of the blessings
of the Dharma, grief by dwelling on the boundless ills which result
from birth. These, and similar steps, my friend, you should take to
keep awake. For what wise man would not regret sleeping away his
life uselessly? In fact a wise man, who wants to be saved from the
great danger, would not want to go to sleep while ignoring his
faults, which are like vicious snakes that have crept into a house.
Who would think of lying down to sleep undisturbed when the
whole living world is like a house on fire, blazing with the flames of
death, disease, and old age? Therefore you should recognize sleep as
a darkening of your mind, and it would be unworthy of you to become absorbed in it while your faults are still with you and threaten
you like enemies with their swords. The first three of the nine hours
of the night you should spend in strenuous activity; then only
should you rest your body, and lie down to sleep, but without relaxing your self-control. With a tranquil mind you should lie on your
right side, you should look forward to the time when you will wake
up and when the sun will shine again. In the third watch you should
get up, and, either walking or sitting, with a pure mind and well-
guarded senses, continue your practice of Yoga.

Full Awareness of the Postures, Etc.   You are further asked to   35
apply mindfulness to your sitting, walking, standing, looking,
speaking, and so on, and to remain fully conscious in all your activities. The man who has imposed strict mindfulness on all he does,
and remains as watchful as a gatekeeper at a city-gate, is safe from
injury by the passions, just as a well-guarded town is safe from its
foes. No defilement can arise in him whose mindfulness is directed
on all that concerns his body. On all occasions he guards his
thought, as a nurse guards a child. Without the armor of mindfulness a man is an easy target for the defilements, just as on a battle-
field someone who has lost his armor is easily shot by his enemies. A
mind which is not protected by mindfulness is as helpless as a sight-
less man walking over uneven ground without a guide. Loss of
mindfulness is the reason why people engage in useless pursuits, do
not care for their own true interests, and remain unalarmed in the
presence of things which actually menace their welfare. And, as a
herdsman runs after his scattered cows, so mindfulness runs after all

the virtues, such as morality, etc., wherever they can be found. The Deathless is beyond the reach of those who disperse their attention, but it is within the grasp of those who direct their mindfulness on all that concerns the body. Without mindfulness no one can have the correct holy method; and in the absence of the holy method he has lost the true Path. By losing the true Path he has lost the road to the Deathless; the Deathless being outside his reach, he cannot win freedom from suffering. Therefore you should superintend your walking by thinking "I am walking," your standing by thinking "I am standing," and so on; that is how you are asked to apply mindfulness to all such activities.

The Advantages of Solitary Meditation. Then, my friend, you 36 should find yourself a living-place which, to be suitable for Yoga, must be without noise and without people. First the body must be placed in seclusion; then detachment of the mind is easy to attain. But those who do not like to live in solitude, because their hearts are not at peace and because they are full of greed, they will hurt themselves there, like someone who walks on very thorny ground because he cannot find the proper road. It is no easier to deny the urges of a man who has not seen the real truth, and who finds himself standing in the fairground of the sensory world, fascinated by its brightness, than it is to deny those of a bull who is eating corn in the middle of a cornfield. A brightly shining fire, when not stirred by the wind, is soon appeased; so the unstimulated heart of those who live in seclusion wins peace without much effort. One who delights in solitude is content with his own company, eats wherever he may be, lodges anywhere, and wears just anything. To shun familiarity with others, as if they were a thorn in the flesh, shows a sound judgment, and helps to accomplish a useful purpose and to know the taste of a happy tranquillity. In a world which takes pleasure in worldly conditions and which is made unrestful by the sense-objects, he dwells in solitude indifferent to worldly conditions, as one who has attained his object, who is tranquil in his heart. The solitary man then drinks the nectar of the Deathless, he becomes content in his heart, and he grieves for the world made wretched by its attachment to sense-objects. If he is satisfied with living alone for a long time in an empty place, if he refrains from dallying with the agents of defilement, regarding them as bitter enemies, and if, content with his own company, he drinks the nectar of spiritual exultation, then he enjoys a happiness greater than that of paradise.

Concentration, and the Forsaking of Idle Thoughts. Sitting 37 cross-legged in some solitary spot, hold your body straight, and for a time keep your attention in front of you, either on the tip of the nose or the space on your forehead between the eyebrows. Then force your wandering mind to become wholly occupied with one object. If that mental fever, the preoccupation with sensuous desires, should dare to attack you, do not give your consent, but shake it off, as if it were dust on your clothes. Although, out of wise consideration, you may habitually eschew sense-desires, you can definitely rid yourself of them only through an antidote which acts on them like sunshine on darkness. There remains a latent tendency towards them, like a fire hidden under the ashes; this, like fire by water, must be put out by systematic meditation. As plants sprout forth from a seed, so sense-desires continue to come forth from that latent tendency; they will cease only when that seed is destroyed. When you consider what sufferings these sense-pleasures entail, by way of their acquisition, and so on, you will be prepared to cut them off at the root, for they are false friends. Sense-pleasures are impermanent, deceptive, trivial, ruinous, and largely in the power of others; avoid them as if they were poisonous vipers! The search for them involves suffering and they are enjoyed in constant disquiet; their loss leads to much grief, and their gain can never result in lasting satisfaction. A man is lost if he expects contentment from great possessions, the fulfilment of all his wishes from entry into heaven, or happiness from the sense-pleasures. These sense-pleasures are not worth paying any attention to, for they are unstable, unreal, hollow, and uncertain, and the happiness they can give is merely imaginary.

But if ill-will or the desire to hurt others should stir your mind, 38 purify it again with its opposite, which will act on it like a wishing jewel on muddied water. Friendliness and compassionateness are, you should know, their antidotes; for they are forever as opposed to hatred as light is to darkness. A man who, although he has learned to abstain from overt immoral acts, still persists in nursing ill-will, harms himself by throwing dirt over himself, like an elephant after his bath. For a holy man forms a tender estimate of the true condition of mortal beings, and how should he want to inflict further suffering on them when they are already suffering enough from disease, death, old age, and so on? With his malevolent mind a man may cause damage to others, or he may not; in any case his own malevolent mind will be forthwith burned up. Therefore you should strive to think of all that lives with friendliness and compassion, and not with ill-will and a desire to hurt. For whatever a man thinks about continually, to that his mind becomes inclined by the force of habit. Abandoning what is unwholesome, you therefore ought to ponder what is wholesome; for that will bring you advantages in this world and help you to win the highest goal. For unwholesome thoughts will grow when nursed in the heart, and breed misfortunes for yourself and others alike. They not only bring calamities to oneself by obstructing the way to supreme beatitude, but they also ruin the affection of others, because one ceases to be worthy of it.

You must also learn to avoid confusion in your mental actions, 39 and you should, my friend, never think even one single unwholesome thought. All the ideas in your mind which are tainted by greed, hate, and delusion deprive you of virtue and fashion your bondage. Delusion injures others, brings hardship to oneself, soils the mind, and may well lead to hell. It is better for you not to hurt yourself with such unwholesome thoughts! Just as an unintelligent person might burn precious aloe wood as if it were a piece of ordinary timber, so by not observing the correct method which leads to emancipation you would waste the rare opportunities offered by a human birth. To neglect the most excellent Dharma, and instead to think demeritorious thoughts, is like neglecting the jewels on a jewel-island and collecting lumps of earth instead. A person who has won existence as a human being, and who would pursue evil rather than good, is like a traveler to the Himalayas who would feed on deadly rather than on health-giving herbs. Having understood this, try to drive out disturbing thoughts by means of their appropriate antidotes, just as one pushes a wedge out of a cleft in a log with the help of a slender counterwedge.

How to Deal with Thoughts Concerning Family and Home- 40 *land.* But if you start worrying about the prosperity or difficulties of your relatives, you should investigate the true nature of the world of the living, and these ideas will disappear again. Among beings whom their Karma drags along in the cycle of Samsāra, who is a stranger, who a relation? Delusion alone ties one person to another. For in the past the person who is now one of your own people happened to be a stranger to you; in the future the stranger of today will be one of your own people. Over a number of lives a person is no more firmly associated with his own people than birds who flock together at the close of day, some here, some there. Relatives are no more closely united than travellers who for a while meet at an inn, and then part again, losing sight of each other. This world is by nature split up into disjointed parts; no one really belongs to anyone else; it is held together by cause and effect, as loose sand by a clenched fist. And yet, a mother will cherish her son because she expects that he will support her, and a son loves his mother because she bore him in her womb. As long as relatives agree with each other, they display affection; but disagreements turn them into enemies. We see relatives behave unkindly, while nonrelatives may show us kindness. Men, indeed, make and break affections according to their interests. As an artist becomes enamored of a woman he has himself painted, so the affection, which a person has for another with whom he feels at one, is entirely of his own making. As for him who in another life was bound to you by ties to kinship, and who was so dear to you then, what is he to you now or you to him? Therefore it is unworthy of you to allow your mind to become preoccupied with thoughts of your relatives. In the Samsaric world there is no fixed division between your own people and other people.

And if you should hit on the idea that this or that country is 41 safe, prosperous, or fortunate, give it up, my friend, and do not entertain it in any way; for you ought to know that the world everywhere is ablaze with the fires of some faults or others. There is certain to be some suffering, either from the cycle of the seasons, or from hunger, thirst, or exhaustion, and a wholly fortunate country does not exist anywhere. Whether it be excessive cold or heat, sickness or danger, something always afflicts people everywhere; no safe refuge can thus be found in the world. And in all countries of the world people are greatly afraid of old age, disease, and death, and there is none where these fears do not arise. Wherever this body may go, there suffering must follow; there is no place in the world where it is not accompanied by afflictions. However delightful, prosperous, and safe a country may appear to be, it should be recognized as a bad country if consumed by the defilements. This world is smitten with countless ills, which affect both body and mind, and we cannot go to any country which is safe from them and where we can expect to live at ease.

Suffering is the lot of everyone, everywhere and all the time; 42 therefore, my friend, do not hanker after the glittering objects of this world! And, once this hankering is extinct in you, then you will clearly see that this entire world of the living can be said to be on fire.

How to Be Mindful of Death.   But if you should make any 43 plans that do not reckon with the inevitability of death, you must make an effort to lay them down again, as if they were an illness which attacks your own self. Not even for a moment should you rely on life going on, for Time, like a hidden tiger, lies in wait to slay the unsuspecting. There is no point in your feeling too strong or too young to die, for death strikes down people whatever their circumstances, and is no respecter of youthful vitality. The body we drag along with us is a fertile soil for all sorts of mishaps, and no sensible person would entertain any firm expectation of well-being or of life. Who could ever be free from cares as long as he has to bear with this body which, as a receptacle of the four great elements, resembles a pot full of snakes at war with each other? Consider how strange and wonderful it is that this man, on drawing in his breath, can immediately afterwards breathe out again; so little can life be trusted! And this is another strange and wonderful thing that, having slept, he wakes up again, and that, having got up, he goes to sleep again; for many are the adversities of those who have a body. How can we ever feel secure from death, when from the womb onwards it follows us like a murderer with his sword raised to kill us? No man born into this world, however pious or strong he be, ever gets the better of the King of Death, either now, or in the past or the future. For when Death in all its ferocity has arrived on the scene, no bargaining can ward him off, no gifts, no attempt at sowing dissension, no force of arms and no restraint. Our hold on life is so uncertain that it is not worth relying on. All the time Death constantly carries people away, and does not wait for them to reach the age of seventy! Who, unless he be quite mad, would make plans which do not reckon with death, when he sees the world so unsubstantial and frail, like a water bubble?

The Four Holy Truths.   Investigating the true nature of reality   44
and directing his mind towards the complete destruction of the Outflows, the Yogin learns to understand correctly the four statements which express the four Truths, i.e., suffering, and the rest. First there is the ubiquitous fact of suffering, which can be defined as oppression; then the cause of suffering, which is the same as its origination; the extinction of suffering, which consists essentially in the definite escape from it; and finally the path which leads to tranquillity, and which has the essential function of saving. And those whose intellect has awakened to these four holy truths, and who have correctly penetrated to their meaning, their meditations shall overcome all the Outflows, they will gain the blessed calm, and no more will they be reborn. It is, on the other hand, through its failure to awaken to these four facts which summarize the essential nature of true reality, and through its inability to penetrate to their meaning, that the Samsaric world whirls round and round, that it goes from one becoming to another, and that it cannot win the blessed calm.

You should therefore, to explain it briefly, know with regard to   45
the fact of ill, that birth is the basis of all the other misfortunes, like old age, and so on; for as all plants grow on the earth, so all calamities grow on the soil of birth. For the birth of a body endowed with sense-organs leads of necessity to manifold ills, and the production of a person's physical existence automatically implies that of death

and sickness. As food, whether good or bad, far from sustaining us becomes merely destructive when mixed with poison, so all birth into this world, whether among animals, or above or below them, tends to ill and not to ease. The numerous afflictions of living beings, such as old age and so on, are unavoidably produced wherever there is Worldly Activity; but even the most frightful gales could not possibly shake trees that have never been planted. Where there is a body, there must also be such sufferings as disease, old age, and so on, and likewise hunger, thirst, wetness, heat, cold, etc. And the mind which is dependent on the body involves us in such ills as grief, discontent, anger, fear, etc. Wherever there is a psychophysical organism, suffering is bound to take place; but for him who is liberated from it there can be no suffering, either now, or in the past, or the future.

And that suffering which we find bound up with Worldly Activity in this world is caused by the multitude of the defilements, such as craving, and the rest; but it is not due to a Creator, or Primordial Matter, or Time, or the Nature of things, or Fate, or Chance. And for that reason, i.e., because all Worldly Activity is a result of the defilements, we can be sure that the passionate and the dull will die, whereas those who are without passion and dullness will not be born again. 46

Therefore, once you have seen, my friend, that craving, etc. are the causes of the manifold ills which follow on birth, remove those causes if you want to be free from suffering; for an effect ceases when its cause has been stopped, and so also suffering becomes extinct when its cause has been quite exhausted. You must therefore come face to face with the holy, calm, and fortunate Dharma, which through dispassion has turned away from craving, which is the supreme place of rest, wherein all Worldly Activity is stopped, a shelter which abides eternally and which nothing can ever take away; that secure place which is final and imperishable, and where there is no birth, old age, death, or disease, no conjunction with unpleasant things, no disappointment over one's wishes, nor separation from what is dear. When the flame of a lamp comes to an end, it does not go anywhere down in the earth or up in the sky, nor into any of the directions of space, but because its oil is exhausted it simply ceases to burn. So, when an accomplished saint comes to the end, he does not go anywhere down in the earth or up in the sky, nor into any of the directions of space, but because his defilements have become extinct he simply ceases to be disturbed. 47

The wise man who wishes to carry out the sacred precepts of tradition should, as a means for the attainment of this Dharma, develop the Eightfold Path—three of its steps, i.e., right speech, right 48 bodily action, and right livelihood concern morality; three, i.e., right views, right intentions, and right effort concern wisdom; two again, i.e., right mindfulness and right concentration promote tranquilizing concentration. As a result of morality the defilements no longer proliferate, as seeds no longer germinate after the right season for them has passed; for when a man's morality is pure, the vices attack his mind but halfheartedly, as if they had become ashamed. Concentration, in its turn, blocks the defilements, as a rock blocks the torrent of a mighty river; for the faults are unable to attack a man who is absorbed in trance, as if they were spellbound snakes immobilized by mantras. Wisdom, finally, completely destroys the defilements, as a river, which in the rainy season overflows its banks, sweeps away the trees that grow on them; consumed by wisdom, the faults cease to thrive and grow, like a tree burnt up by the fire which flares up after it has been struck by a thunderbolt. By entering on this Eightfold Path, which has morality, concentration, and wisdom for its three divisions, and which is holy, incorruptible, and straight, one forsakes those faults which are the causes of suffering, and one attains the state of absolute peace. Ten qualities are required of those who proceed along it: steadfastness, sincerity, self-respect, vigilance, seclusion from the world, contentment with little, simplicity of tastes, nonattachment, aversion to Worldly Activity, and patience. For he who discovers the true nature of ill, its origin and its cessation, can advance on the holy path, in the company of spiritual friends, towards Peace. It is like someone who correctly diagnoses a disease as a disease, and who correctly determines its cause and its cure; when treated by skilful friends he will soon be healthy again. You should therefore regard ill as a disease, the defilements as its cause, their cessation as the state of health, and the path as the remedy. What you must furthermore understand is that suffering is the same as Worldly Activity, and that it is kept going by the defilements; that their stopping is the same as inactivity, and that it is the path which leads to that. As though your turban or your clothes were on fire, so with a sense of urgency should you apply your intellect to the comprehension of the truths. It is because it fails to perceive the guidance given by these truths that the world of the living is being burnt alive. When therefore someone sees that this psychophysical organism is something that ought to be extinguished, then he has the correct vision; in consequence of his correct insight he becomes disgusted with the things of the world; and as he is no longer drawn to them, his greed gradually exhausts itself. Solemnly I assure you that his mind is definitely liberated when passion and the hope of pleasure have become extinct; and that, once his mind is well freed of those two, there is nothing further that he has to do.

For I proclaim it as a fact that the effective extinction of all the Outflows lies in seeing and discerning the own-being of the psychophysical personality, its cause and its disappearance.

QUESTIONS FOR CRITICAL READING

1. What does it mean to restrain the senses?
2. According to the selection, how can restraining the senses produce the results that the Buddha desires?
3. In paragraphs 29 to 31, the Buddha complains about the unsteadiness of the senses. What does he mean? In what ways have you experienced the unsteadiness of the senses?
4. What seem to be the primary advantages of meditation? Which advantages are religious, and which are secular?
5. What is the Buddhist attitude toward the body? How does it seem to differ from Western culture's current attitudes?
6. The Buddha recommends constant mindfulness. What does this entail?
7. Why should meditation be solitary? Are you convinced that solitariness is essential?
8. What does enlightenment seem to mean for the Buddha? Do you feel that it is possible for you to achieve it? How?

SUGGESTIONS FOR WRITING

1. Follow the directions for meditation as closely as possible. Try to spend at least three days meditating for ten minutes a day or longer. Record your experiences and determine the advantages of meditation for you. Reread paragraph 37 closely before beginning this experiment.
2. In paragraph 37, we find the statement "Sense-pleasures are impermanent, deceptive, trivial, ruinous, and largely in the power of others; avoid them as if they were poisonous vipers!" Obviously, this attitude is not generally shared by Westerners. What is your position on the sense-pleasures? Are they as evil as the Buddha suggests? What value do they possess?
3. The Buddha suggests that greed, hate, and delusion lead people into bondage. Refer to specific historical examples or examples from your own experience to explain how this observation is true. How can such ideas potentially damage those who hold them? Does the Buddha recommend ways to avoid holding such ideas? Fashion an essay that examines these questions.
4. In paragraph 44, the Buddha states that suffering is universal. He equates suffering with oppression. Examine his teachings on this question, and relate the question of suffering to modern Western society.

Do you feel that oppression produces suffering today as it did in the Buddha's time? Is there a sense in which the Buddha's suggestions for the relief of suffering—implied in the techniques of meditation—would alleviate the sufferings of oppressed people in our time?

5. The Noble Eightfold Path is discussed in paragraph 48 as well as in the introduction to this selection. Determine its applicability to your life, and take a stand on how your life would improve if you were to follow this path. Be as specific as possible, referring to definitive actions, either actual or potential, and particular relationships, either actual or potential, that would be altered in your life.

6. **CONNECTIONS**   Compare the basic principles of "Meditation: The Path to Enlightenment" with the views of Plato on the trustworthiness of the senses. How closely does the Buddha seem to agree with Plato? What distinctions make their approaches different?

7. **CONNECTIONS**   Are Francis Bacon's four idols related to the Buddha's Eightfold Path? Establish the distinctions and the similarities between the two programs, and decide whether they are basically compatible or incompatible. How can the Buddha's path be adapted to questions of secular knowledge? How can Bacon's four idols be applied to questions of spiritual knowledge?

8. **CONNECTIONS**   To what extent are the philosophies of Lao-tzu and the Buddha parallel in their ultimate intentions regarding the happiness of humankind? What important connections identify them as products of Eastern thought? How can they be contrasted with Western thought?

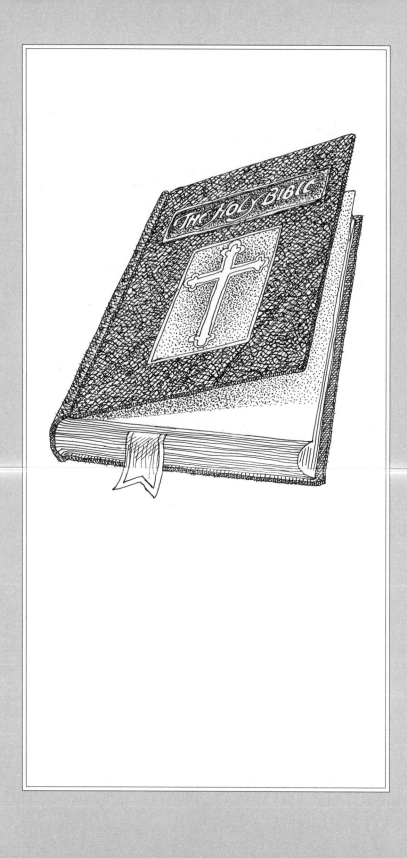

THE BIBLE
From *The Book of Job*

The problem of dating *The Book of Job* has not been entirely settled. The best research to date suggests that the prose Prologue and Epilogue date to the sixth century B.C., whereas the poetic sections may be a bit more recent. However, some scholars believe that the oldest material in the book may date to the eighth century B.C. Others propose that the prose segments may represent an ancient Edomite folktale of a man who endured suffering and kept his faith intact. If so, then the origins of the book may be outside Israel, because Edom was a very early Palestinian settlement.

The author of the text was Jewish, knowledgeable, and well traveled. Internal evidence referring to seafaring suggests an understanding of trade and travel across considerable distances. In addition, certain details seem to imply the influence of Egypt and Egyptian customs. The quality of the poetry demonstrates that the author was exceptionally skilled and widely read. A comparison with classic Greek poetry in the late seventeenth century led some commentators to refer to *The Book of Job* as a brief epic. Similarly, in the eighteenth century certain biblical and literary scholars promoted the idea that the poetry, particularly the dialogue, was influenced by Greek tragedy, although most subsequent scholars have discounted this as unlikely. Nevertheless, the quality of the poetry merits comparison with the greatest of world literature.

The Book of Job appears in a relatively disunited collection of Hebrew writings known as the Ketuvim. The Torah (the first five books of Moses) and the Prophets (twelve prophetic books beginning with Hosea) are other collections of books that make up the Hebrew Bible. Among the many books in the Ketuvim are the Book of Ruth, Song of Solomon, Psalms, Proverbs, Ecclesiastes, I and II

From *The Oxford Study Edition of the New English Bible* (1976).

665

Chronicles, and Lamentations of Jeremiah. Some of the books in the Ketuvim are historical chronicles, some love poetry, some stories (as in the Book of Esther), and some wisdom literature, as is the case with *The Book of Job*. These books were probably gathered together and set in order sometime in the first or second century A.D.

The story of Job is told in three parts. The first is a prologue that describes a meeting of a council in Heaven with Yahweh (an ancient Hebrew name for God) and several angels, including Satan. In the early texts the word for Satan was *the Adversary*. This legalistic term gives a special coloration to the discourse of Yahweh and his councilors, almost implying a meeting of judges who either dispense or withhold justice. The Adversary points to Job as one who keeps his faith with God only because his wealth and power have made him complacent. The Adversary tells Yahweh that if Job's riches were to be taken from him, Job would curse God and reveal his true nature. Yahweh accepts the challenge. Job, whose enormous wealth (including livestock and slaves) is detailed in the beginning of the book, experiences terrible distress. On a single day he loses his livestock, possessions, and land. He then loses his seven sons and three daughters in an apparent earthquake. In spite of these successive tragedies, when Job is reduced to utter poverty he still does not denounce God.

The Adversary then complains to Yahweh that he expected as much, but that he is certain that if Job's health were to be ruined, Job would then show his true character and denounce God. In response, Yahweh permits the Adversary to torment Job but not to take his life. The Adversary makes Job's skin erupt in boils and sores and torments him grievously until he is reduced to sitting on the ground and scraping his skin with shards of pottery. At this point Job's wife asks if he is not ready to denounce God, but Job remains steadfast.

In the second section of *The Book of Job,* Job's friends Eliphaz, Bildad, and Zophar enter into a lengthy dialogue with Job. Some of that dialogue has been omitted in the excerpt that follows, but the tenor of the entire dialogue is consistent with what is included here. (To make it clear to the reader exactly who is speaking in the sections of *The Book of Job* that appear here, labels in brackets have been inserted where appropriate.) Job's friends urge him to confess his sins, because they believe he could only be suffering as he does because of his transgressions. Job, however, refuses to confess to sins that he knows he did not commit. His friends remain convinced of his guilt and continue to urge him to repent. When Job complains to them that he suffers for no reason, they refuse to believe him. Eliphaz tells him that human suffering is a form of discipline meted out by the Lord, yet Job cannot agree.

Job's friends held the common view that those who pleased God prospered, and the more one prospered the more one pleased God. Should an individual be struck with the calamities that afflicted Job, then it was reasonable to assume that the individual had not pleased God and was being punished for falling short. This view was common not only in ancient Israel but also in many later ages, including the early years of Pilgrim settlements (and at other times) in the United States. *The Book of Job* counters this view by suggesting that good people sometimes suffer terrible experiences and that God's will cannot be known with any certainty. The difference between God's wisdom and human wisdom is so great that human beings have no hope of ever understanding God. Therefore, the point is to continue to have faith and believe that what happens is God's will.

Some of the most poignant moments in the narrative involve Job's bafflement at his fate. Indeed, he even wishes he had not been born. In Chapter 10 he gives free rein to his grief: "Why didst thou bring me out of the womb? O that I had ended there and no eye had seen me, / that I had been carried from the womb to the grave" (10:18–19). In his "final survey of his case" in Chapter 29, he reviews his life and the good deeds he has done, certain that he has been a good man and thus still perplexed at his terrible fate.

Throughout the text, Job is quizzed with questions he cannot answer. Only after he is convinced of his ignorance and the need for wisdom does he find that he is to be rewarded for his faith. As Yahweh says, "The fear of the Lord is wisdom, and to turn from evil is understanding" (28:28). In Chapter 37 Elihu, a mysterious character, asks, "Do you know how God assigns them [God's works] their tasks, how he sends light flashing from his clouds?" (37:15). Job cannot answer. In the third part of *The Book of Job*, beginning with Chapter 38, Job hears Yahweh, as in a whirlwind ("out of the tempest"), essentially dress him down for his ignorance: "Who is this whose ignorant words cloud my design in darkness?" (38:2).

When Job finally says, "I repent in dust and ashes" (42:6), his possessions are not only restored but are substantially increased so that he is even more wealthy than he was before the tragedies befell him. He is given the same number of children and experiences even more joy. (Whether these are the same children he had before is unclear in the text; some interpreters maintain that Yahweh restored the same children after having them spirited away rather than having them killed.) In the Epilogue, Job's friends are rebuked by Yahweh for having misunderstood Job's nature. With Job as intercessor, however, they are forgiven.

The Rhetoric of *The Book of Job*

Because *The Book of Job* is a narrative, it follows the traditional pattern of beginning, middle, and end,—with a prologue, a series of dialogues and reflections, and an epilogue. The main parts of the narrative are in verse, suggesting that the author may have wanted to heighten their significance; the author may even have reworked the original material evident in the prose sections of the book.

As in much poetry, the text employs dependable rhythmic patterns, precise imagery, and careful figures of speech, such as similes and metaphors. In addition, following the tradition of wisdom literature of the time, it also uses repetition to excellent effect. Apart from the prayer-like repetition of words and phrases, a number of interesting key terms reappear in different sections, sometimes hinting at parallels in the action. In the prose Prologue, repetition of phrases (such as Job "feared God and set his face against wrongdoing") helps emphasize a basic point of great importance.

The prose Prologue, which also includes the dialogue between the Adversary (Satan) and Yahweh (the Lord), uses the term *hedged* in the Adversary's complaint about how God has protected Job: "Have you not hedged him round on every side with your protection . . . ?" (1:10). Ironically, in the first poetic passage, when Job complains to God in Chapter 3, he uses the same term to convey the opposite meaning: "Why should a man be born to wander blindly, hedged in by God on every side?" (3:23). Similarly, when Job answers Eliphaz in Chapter 19, he complains, "If I cry 'Murder!' no one answers; if I appeal for help, I get no justice. / He has walled in my path so that I cannot break away, and he has hedged in the road before me" (19:7–8). The hedge, a metaphorically limiting fence, takes on great significance, implying that Job's will is ineffective, that his chosen course is irrelevant when his fate seems determined by a force beyond him. The significant repetition of a key metaphor leads us to meditate on the concept of free will and its relation to fate and God's will.

The similes and metaphors in the poetry abound with a vivid richness that stimulates the imagination: "I put on righteousness as a garment and it clothed me; justice, like a cloak or a turban, wrapped me round. / I was eyes to the blind and feet to the lame" (29:14–15). Later, when Job feels even more desolate, he says of himself, "The wolf is now my brother" (30:29). In a particularly powerful combination of simile and imagery we are told, "Yet as a falling mountain-side is swept away, and a rock is dislodged from its place, as water wears away stones, and a rain-storm scours the soil from the land, so thou hast wiped out the hope of frail man" (14:18–19).

The literary form of *The Book of Job* has long produced admirers who see the work as a powerful story reflecting deeply significant truths about the human condition. When bad things happen to good people, we need to ask serious questions about the nature of life. *The Book of Job* impresses us with the pain of Job, the glory of his steadfastness in the face of wrongdoing, and his refusal to curse God for his circumstances. The wisdom in this piece of wisdom literature is to accept that we know nothing and that we cannot understand the will of God; we can only experience it.

PREREADING QUESTIONS: WHAT TO READ FOR

The following prereading questions may help you anticipate key issues in the discussion on the excerpt that follows from *The Book of Job*. Keeping them in mind during your first reading of the selection should help focus your reactions.

- What is the nature of the challenge Satan offers to the Lord?
- In what ways does Job seem blessed at the beginning of the story?
- Why does Job resist the advice given by his friends?

From *The Book of Job*

Prologue
1

There lived in the land of Uz a man of blameless and upright life named Job, who feared God and set his face against wrongdoing.

2 He had seven sons and three daughters;

Note: Some of the verses in the excerpt that follows may appear to be missing or out of numerical order. These rearrangements have been made intentionally by the book's translators.

3 and he owned seven thousand sheep and three thousand camels, five hundred yoke of oxen and five hundred asses, with a large number of slaves. Thus Job was the greatest man in all the East.

4 Now his sons used to foregather and give, each in turn, a feast in his own house; and they used to send and invite their three sisters to eat and drink with them.

5 Then, when a round of feasts was finished, Job sent for his children and sanctified them, rising early in the morning and sacrificing a whole-offering for each of them; for he thought that they might somehow have sinned against God and committed blasphemy in their hearts. This he always did.

6 The day came when the members of the court of heaven took their places in the presence of the LORD, and Satan was there among them.

7 The LORD asked him where he had been. 'Ranging over the earth', he said, 'from end to end.'

8 Then the LORD asked Satan, 'Have you considered my servant Job? You will find no one like him on earth, a man of blameless and upright life, who fears God and sets his face against wrongdoing.'

9 Satan answered the LORD, 'Has not Job good reason to be God-fearing?

10 Have you not hedged him round on every side with your protection, him and his family and all his possessions? Whatever he does you have blessed, and his herds have increased beyond measure.

11 But stretch out your hand and touch all that he has, and then he will curse you to your face.'

12 Then the LORD said to Satan, 'So be it. All that he has is in your hands; only Job himself you must not touch.' And Satan left the LORD's presence.

13 When the day came that Job's sons and daughters were eating and drinking in the eldest brother's house,

14 a messenger came running to Job and said, 'The oxen were ploughing and the asses were grazing near them,

15 when the Sabaeans swooped down and carried them off, after putting the herdsmen to the sword; and I am the only one to escape and tell the tale.'

16 While he was still speaking, another messenger arrived and said, 'God's fire flashed from heaven. It struck the sheep and the shepherds and burnt them up; and I am the only one to escape and tell the tale.'

17 While he was still speaking, another arrived and said, 'The Chaldaeans, three bands of them, have made a raid on the camels

and carried them off, after putting the drivers to the sword; and I am the only one to escape and tell the tale.'

18 While this man was speaking, yet another arrived and said, 'Your sons and daughters were eating and drinking in the eldest brother's house,

19 when suddenly a whirlwind swept across from the desert and struck the four corners of the house, and it fell on the young people and killed them; and I am the only one to escape and tell the tale.'

20 At this Job stood up and rent his cloak; then he shaved his head and fell prostrate on the ground,

21 saying:

> Naked I came from the womb,
> naked I shall return whence I came.
> The LORD gives and the LORD takes away;
> blessed be the name of the LORD.

22 Throughout all this Job did not sin; he did not charge God with unreason.

2

Once again the day came when the members of the court of heaven took their places in the presence of the LORD, and Satan was there among them.

2 The LORD asked him where he had been. 'Ranging over the earth', he said, 'from end to end.'

3 Then the LORD asked Satan, 'Have you considered my servant Job? You will find no one like him on earth, a man of blameless and upright life, who fears God and sets his face against wrongdoing. You incited me to ruin him without a cause, but his integrity is still unshaken.'

4 Satan answered the LORD, 'Skin for skin! There is nothing the man will grudge to save himself.

5 But stretch out your hand and touch his bone and his flesh, and see if he will not curse you to your face.'

6 Then the LORD said to Satan, 'So be it. He is in your hands; but spare his life.'

7 And Satan left the LORD's presence, and he smote Job with running sores from head to foot,

8 so that he took a piece of a broken pot to scratch himself as he sat among the ashes.

9 Then his wife said to him, 'Are you still unshaken in your integrity? Curse God and die!'

10 But he answered, 'You talk as any wicked fool of a woman might talk. If we accept good from God, shall we not accept evil?' Throughout all this, Job did not utter one sinful word.

11 When Job's three friends, Eliphaz of Teman, Bildad of Shuah, and Zophar of Naamah, heard of all these calamities which had overtaken him, they left their homes and arranged to come and condole with him and comfort him.

12 But when they first saw him from a distance, they did not recognize him; and they wept aloud, rent their cloaks and tossed dust into the air over their heads.

13 For seven days and seven nights they sat beside him on the ground, and none of them said a word to him; for they saw that his suffering was very great.

Job's Complaint to God
3

1–2 After this Job broke silence and cursed the day of his birth:

3 Perish the day when I was born and the night which said, 'A man is conceived'!

4 May that day turn to darkness; may God above not look for it, nor light of dawn shine on it.

5 May blackness sully it, and murk and gloom, cloud smother that day, swift darkness eclipse its sun.

6 Blind darkness swallow up that night; count it not among the days of the year, reckon it not in the cycle of the months.

7 That night, may it be barren for ever, no cry of joy be heard in it.

8 Cursed be it by those whose magic binds even the monster of the deep, who are ready to tame Leviathan[1] himself with spells.

9 May no star shine out in its twilight; may it wait for a dawn that never comes, nor ever see the eyelids of the morning,

10 because it did not shut the doors of the womb that bore me and keep trouble away from my sight.

11 Why was I not still-born, why did I not die when I came out of the womb?

12 Why was I ever laid on my mother's knees or put to suck at her breasts?

---

[1] **Leviathan** Whale.

16 Why was I not hidden like an untimely birth, like an infant that has not lived to see the light?

13 For then I should be lying in the quiet grave, asleep in death, at rest,

14 with kings and their ministers who built themselves palaces,

15 with princes rich in gold who filled their houses with silver.

17 There the wicked man chafes no more, there the tired labourer rests;

18 the captive too finds peace there and hears no taskmaster's voice;

19 high and low are there, even the slave, free from his master.

20 Why should the sufferer be born to see the light? Why is life given to men who find it so bitter?

21 They wait for death but it does not come, they seek it more eagerly than hidden treasure.

22 They are glad when they reach the tomb, and when they come to the grave they exult.

23 Why should a man be born to wander blindly, hedged in by God on every side?

24 My sighing is all my food, and groans pour from me in a torrent.

25 Every terror that haunted me has caught up with me, and all that I feared has come upon me.

26 There is no peace of mind nor quiet for me; I chafe in torment and have no rest.

[Speech of Eliphaz the Temanite]
5

Call if you will; is there any to answer you? To which of the holy ones will you turn?

2 The fool is destroyed by his own angry passions, and the end of childish resentment is death.

3 I have seen it for myself: a fool uprooted, his home in sudden ruin about him,

4 his children past help, browbeaten in court with none to save them.

5 Their rich possessions are snatched from them; what they have harvested others hungrily devour; the stronger man seizes it from the panniers, panting, thirsting for their wealth.

6 Mischief does not grow out of the soil nor trouble spring from the earth;

7 man is born to trouble, as surely as birds fly upwards.

8 For my part, I would make my petition to God and lay my cause before him,
9 who does great and unsearchable things, marvels without number.
10 He gives rain to the earth and sends water on the fields;
11 he raises the lowly to the heights, the mourners are uplifted by victory;
12 he frustrates the plots of the crafty, and they win no success,
13 he traps the cunning in their craftiness, and the schemers' plans are thrown into confusion.
14 In the daylight they run into darkness, and grope at midday as though it were night.
15 He saves the destitute from their greed, and the needy from the grip of the strong;
16 so the poor hope again, and the unjust are sickened.

17 Happy the man whom God rebukes! therefore do not reject the discipline of the Almighty.
18 For, though he wounds, he will bind up; the hands that smite will heal.
19 You may meet disaster six times, and he will save you; seven times, and no harm shall touch you.
20 In time of famine he will save you from death, in battle from the sword.
21 You will be shielded from the lash of slander, and when violence comes you need not fear.
22 You will laugh at violence and starvation and have no need to fear wild beasts;.
23 for you have a covenant with the stones to spare your fields, and the weeds have been constrained to leave you at peace.
24 You will know that all is well with your household, you will look round your home and find nothing amiss;
25 you will know, too, that your descendants will be many and your offspring like grass, thick upon the earth.
26 You will come in sturdy old age to the grave as sheaves come in due season to the threshing-floor.

27 We have inquired into all this, and so it is; this we have heard, and you may know it for the truth.

[Job Speaks]
10

I am sickened of life; I will give free rein to my griefs, I will speak out in bitterness of soul.

2 I will say to God, 'Do not condemn me, but tell me the ground of thy complaint against me.

3 Dost thou find any advantage in oppression, in spurning the fruit of all thy labour and smiling on the policy of wicked men?

4 Hast thou eyes of flesh or dost thou see as mortal man sees?

5 Are thy days as those of a mortal or thy years as the life of a man,

6 that thou lookest for guilt in me and dost seek in me for sin,

7 though thou knowest that I am guiltless and have none to save me from thee?

8 'Thy hands gave me shape and made me; and dost thou at once turn and destroy me?

9 Remember that thou didst knead me like clay; and wouldst thou turn me back into dust?

10 Didst thou not pour me out like milk and curdle me like cheese,

11 clothe me with skin and flesh and knit me together with bones and sinews?

12 Thou has given me life and continuing favour, and thy providence has watched over my spirit.

13 Yet this was the secret purpose of thy heart, and I know that this was thy intent:

14 that, if I sinned, thou wouldst be watching me and wouldst not acquit me of my guilt.

15 If I indeed am wicked, the worse for me! If I am righteous, even so I may lift up my head;

16 if I am proud as a lion, thou dost hunt me down and dost confront me again with marvellous power;

17 thou dost renew thy onslaught upon me, and with mounting anger against me bringest fresh forces to the attack.

18 Why didst thou bring me out of the womb? O that I had ended there and no eye had seen me,

19 that I had been carried from the womb to the grave and were as though I had not been born.

20 Is not my life short and fleeting? Let me be, that I may be happy for a moment,

21 before I depart to a land of gloom, a land of deep darkness, never to return,

22 a land of gathering shadows, of deepening darkness, lit by no ray of light, dark upon dark.'

[Job Answers Zophar the Naamathite]
14

Man born of woman is short-lived and full of disquiet.

2 He blossoms like a flower and then he withers; he slips away like a shadow and does not stay; he is like a wine-skin that perishes or a garment that moths have eaten.

3 Dost thou fix thine eyes on such a creature, and wilt thou bring him into court to confront thee?

5 The days of his life are determined, and the number of his months is known to thee; thou hast laid down a limit, which he cannot pass.

6 Look away from him therefore and leave him alone counting the hours day by day like a hired labourer.

7 If a tree is cut down, there is hope that it will sprout again and fresh shoots will not fail.

8 Though its roots grow old in the earth, and its stump is dying in the ground,

9 if it scents water it may break into bud and make new growth like a young plant.

10 But a man dies, and he disappears; man comes to his end, and where is he?

11 As the waters of a lake dwindle, or as a river shrinks and runs dry,

12 so mortal man lies down, never to rise until the very sky splits open. If a man dies, can he live again? He shall never be roused from his sleep.

13 If only thou wouldst hide me in Sheol[2] and conceal me till thy anger turns aside, if thou wouldst fix a limit for my time there, and then remember me!

14 Then I would not lose hope, however long my service, waiting for my relief to come.

15 Thou wouldst summon me, and I would answer thee; thou wouldst long to see the creature thou hast made.

---

[2] **Sheol** A locale in which God is not present.

16 But now thou dost count every step I take, watching all my course.

17 Every offence of mine is stored in thy bag; thou dost keep my iniquity under seal.

18 Yet as a falling mountain-side is swept away, and a rock is dislodged from its place,

19 as water wears away stones, and a rain-storm scours the soil from the land, so thou hast wiped out the hope of frail man;

20 thou dost overpower him finally, and he is gone; his face is changed, and he is banished from thy sight.

22 His flesh upon him becomes black, and his life-blood dries up within him.

21 His sons rise to honour, and he sees nothing of it; they sink into obscurity, and he knows it not.

19

Then Job answered [Eliphaz]:

2 How long will you exhaust me and pulverize me with words?

3 Time and time again you have insulted me and shamelessly done me wrong.

4 If in fact I had erred, the error would still be mine.

5 But if indeed you lord it over me and try to justify the reproaches levelled at me,

6 I tell you, God himself has put me in the wrong, he has drawn the net round me.

7 If I cry 'Murder!' no one answers; if I appeal for help, I get no justice.

8 He has walled in my path so that I cannot break away, and he has hedged in the road before me.

9 He has stripped me of all honour and has taken the crown from my head.

10 On every side he beats me down and I am gone; he has pulled up my tent-rope like a tree.

11 His anger is hot against me and he counts me his enemy.

12 His raiders gather in force and encamp about my tent.

13 My brothers hold aloof from me, my friends are utterly estranged from me;

14–15 my kinsmen and intimates fall away, my retainers have forgotten me; my slave-girls treat me as a stranger, I have become an alien in their eyes.

16 I summon my slave, but he does not answer, though I entreat him as a favour,

17 My breath is noisome to my wife, and I stink in the nostrils of my own family.

18 Mere children despise me and, when I rise, turn their backs on me;

19 my intimate companions loathe me, and those whom I love have turned against me.

20 My bones stick out through my skin, and I gnaw my underlip with my teeth.

21 Pity me, pity me, you that are my friends; for the hand of God has touched me.

22 Why do you pursue me as God pursues me? Have you not had your teeth in me long enough?

23 O that my words might be inscribed, O that they might be engraved in an inscription,

24 cut with an iron tool and filled with lead to be a witness in hard rock!

25 But in my heart I know that my vindicator lives and that he will rise last to speak in court;

26 and I shall discern my witness standing at my side and see my defending counsel, even God himself,

27 whom I shall see with my own eyes, I myself and no other.

28 My heart failed me when you said, 'What a train of disaster he has brought on himself! The root of the trouble lies in him.'

29 Beware of the sword that points at you, the sword that sweeps away all iniquity; then you will know that there is a judge.

God's Unfathomable Wisdom
28

There are mines for silver and places where men refine gold;

2 where iron is won from the earth and copper smelted from the ore;

3 the end of the seam lies in darkness, and it is followed to its farthest limit.

4 Strangers cut the galleries; they are forgotten as they drive forward far from men.

5 While corn is springing from the earth above, what lies beneath is raked over like a fire,

6 and out of its rocks comes lapis lazuli, dusted with flecks of gold.

7 No bird of prey knows the way there, and the falcon's keen eye cannot descry[3] it;

8 proud beasts do not set foot on it, and no serpent comes that way.

9 Man sets his hand to the granite rock and lays bare the roots of the mountains;

10 he cuts galleries in the rocks, and gems of every kind meet his eye;

11 he dams up the sources of the streams and brings the hidden riches of the earth to light.

12 But where can wisdom be found? And where is the source of understanding?

13 No man knows the way to it; it is not found in the land of living men.

14 The depths of ocean say, 'It is not in us', and the sea says, 'It is not with me.'

15 Red gold cannot buy it, nor can its price be weighed out in silver;

16 it cannot be set in the scales against gold of Ophir, against precious cornelian or lapis lazuli;

17 gold and crystal are not to be matched with it, no work in fine gold can be bartered for it;

18 black coral and alabaster are not worth mention, and a parcel of wisdom fetches more than red coral;

19 topaz from Ethiopia is not to be matched with it, it cannot be set in the scales against pure gold.

20 Where then does wisdom come from, and where is the source of understanding?

21 No creature on earth can see it, and it is hidden from the birds of the air.

22 Destruction and death say, 'We know of it only by report.'

23 But God understands the way to it, he alone knows its source;

24 for he can see to the ends of the earth and he surveys everything under heaven.

25 When he made a counterpoise[4] for the wind and measured out the waters in proportion,

26 when he laid down a limit for the rain and a path for the thunderstorm,

27 even then he saw wisdom and took stock of it, he considered it and fathomed its very depths.

---

[3] **descry** See.
[4] **counterpoise** A counteracting force.

28 And he said to man: The fear of the Lord is wisdom, and to turn from evil is understanding.

Job's Final Survey of His Case
29

Then Job resumed his discourse:

2 If I could only go back to the old days, to the time when God was watching over me,

3 when his lamp shone above my head, and by its light I walked through the darkness!

4 If I could be as in the days of my prime, when God protected my home,

5 while the Almighty was still there at my side, and my servants stood round me,

6 while my path flowed with milk, and the rocks streamed oil!

7 If I went through the gate out of the town to take my seat in the public square,

8 young men saw me and kept out of sight; old men rose to their feet,

9 men in authority broke off their talk and put their hands to their lips;

10 the voices of the nobles died away, and every man held his tongue.

21 They listened to me expectantly and waited in silence for my opinion.

22 When I had spoken, no one spoke again; my words fell gently on them;

23 they waited for them as for rain and drank them in like showers in spring.

24 When I smiled on them, they took heart; when my face lit up, they lost their gloomy looks.

25 I presided over them, planning their course, like a king encamped with his troops.

11 Whoever heard of me spoke in my favour, and those who saw me bore witness to my merit,

12 how I saved the poor man when he called for help and the orphan who had no protector.

13 The man threatened with ruin blessed me, and I made the widow's heart sing for joy.

14 I put on righteousness as a garment and it clothed me; justice, like a cloak or a turban, wrapped me round.

15 I was eyes to the blind and feet to the lame;

16 I was a father to the needy, and I took up the stranger's cause.

17 I broke the fangs of the miscreant and rescued the prey from his teeth.

18 I thought, 'I shall die with my powers unimpaired and my days uncounted as the grains of sand,

19 with my roots spreading out to the water and the dew lying on my branches,

20 with the bow always new in my grasp and the arrow ever ready to my hand.'

30

But now I am laughed to scorn by men of a younger generation, men whose fathers I would have disdained to put with the dogs who kept my flock.

2 What use were their strong arms to me, since their sturdy vigour had wasted away?

3 They gnawed roots in the desert, gaunt with want and hunger,

4 they plucked saltwort and wormwood and root of broom for their food.

5 Driven out from the society of men, pursued like thieves with hue and cry,

6 they lived in gullies and ravines, holes in the earth and rocky clefts;

7 they howled like beasts among the bushes, huddled together beneath the scrub,

8 vile base-born wretches, hounded from the haunts of men.

9 Now I have become the target of their taunts, my name is a byword among them.

10 They loathe me, they shrink from me, they dare to spit in my face.

11 They run wild and savage me; at sight of me they throw off all restraint.

12 On my right flank they attack in a mob; they raise their siege-ramps against me,

13 they tear down my crumbling defences to my undoing, and scramble up against me unhindered;

14 they burst in through the gaping breach; at the moment of the crash they come rolling in.

15 Terror upon terror overwhelms me, it sweeps away my resolution like the wind, and my hope of victory vanishes like a cloud.

16 So now my soul is in turmoil within me, and misery has me daily in its grip.

17 By night pain pierces my very bones, and there is ceaseless throbbing in my veins;

18 my garments are all bespattered with my phlegm, which chokes me like the collar of a shirt.

19 God himself has flung me down in the mud, no better than dust or ashes.

20 I call for thy help, but thou dost not answer; I stand up to plead, but thou sittest aloof;

21 thou hast turned cruelly against me and with thy strong hand pursuest me in hatred;

22 thou dost snatch me up and set me astride the wind, and the tempest tosses me up and down.

23 I know that thou wilt hand me over to death, to the place appointed for all mortal men.

24 Yet no beggar held out his hand but was relieved by me in his distress.

25 Did I not weep for the man whose life was hard? Did not my heart grieve for the poor?

26 Evil has come though I expected good; I looked for light but there came darkness.

27 My bowels are in ferment and know no peace; days of misery stretch out before me.

28 I go about dejected and friendless; I rise in the assembly, only to appeal for help.

29 The wolf is now my brother, the owls of the desert have become my companions.

30 My blackened skin peels off, and my body is scorched by the heat.

31 My harp has been tuned for a dirge, my flute to the voice of those who weep.

[Speeches of Elihu Continue]
37

This too makes my heart beat wildly and start from its place.

2 Listen, listen to the thunder of God's voice and the rumbling of his utterance.

3 Under the vault of heaven he lets it roll, and his lightning reaches the ends of the earth;

4 there follows a sound of roaring as he thunders with the voice of majesty.

5 God's voice is marvellous in its working; he does great deeds that pass our knowledge.

6 For he says to the snow, 'Fall to earth', and to the rainstorms, 'Be fierce.' And when his voice is heard, the floods of rain pour down unchecked.

7 He shuts every man fast indoors, and all men whom he has made must stand idle;

8 the beasts withdraw into their lairs and take refuge in their dens.

9 The hurricane bursts from its prison, and the rain-winds bring bitter cold;

10 at the breath of God the ice-sheet is formed, and the wide waters are frozen hard as iron.

11 He gives the dense clouds their load of moisture, and the clouds spread his mist abroad,

12 as they travel round in their courses, steered by his guiding hand to do his bidding all over the habitable world.

14 Listen, Job, to this argument; stand still, and consider God's wonderful works.

15 Do you know how God assigns them their tasks, how he sends light flashing from his clouds?

16 Do you know why the clouds hang poised overhead, a wonderful work of his consummate skill,

17 sweating there in your stifling clothes, when the earth lies sultry under the south wind?

18 Can you beat out the vault of the skies, as he does, hard as a mirror of cast metal?

19 Teach us then what to say to him; for all is dark, and we cannot marshal our thoughts.

20 Can any man dictate to God when he is to speak? or command him to make proclamation?

21 At one moment the light is not seen, it is overcast with clouds and rain; then the wind passes by and clears them away,

22 and a golden glow comes from the north.

23 But the Almighty we cannot find; his power is beyond our ken, and his righteousness not slow to do justice.

24 Therefore mortal men pay him reverence, and all who are wise look to him.

God's Answer and Job's Submission
38

Then the LORD answered Job out of the tempest:

2 Who is this whose ignorant words cloud my design in darkness?

3 Brace yourself and stand up like a man; I will ask questions, and you shall answer.

4 Where were you when I laid the earth's foundations? Tell me, if you know and understand.

5 Who settled its dimensions? Surely you should know. Who stretched his measuring-line over it?

6 On what do its supporting pillars rest? Who set its corner-stone in place,

7 when the morning stars sang together and all the sons of God shouted aloud?

8 Who watched over the birth of the sea, when it burst in flood from the womb? —

9 when I wrapped it in a blanket of cloud and cradled it in fog,

10 when I established its bounds, fixing its doors and bars in place,

11 and said, 'Thus far shall you come and no farther, and here your surging waves shall halt.'

12 In all your life have you ever called up the dawn or shown the morning its place?

13 Have you taught it to grasp the fringes of the earth and shake the Dog-star[5] from its place;

14 to bring up the horizon in relief as clay under a seal, until all things stand out like the folds of a cloak,

15 when the light of the Dog-star is dimmed and the stars of the Navigator's Line[6] go out one by one?

16 Have you descended to the springs of the sea or walked in the unfathomable deep?

17 Have the gates of death been revealed to you? Have you ever seen the door-keepers of the place of darkness?

18 Have you comprehended the vast expanse of the world? Come, tell me all this, if you know.

19 Which is the way to the home of light and where does darkness dwell?

20 And can you then take each to its appointed bound and escort it on its homeward path?

21 Doubtless you know all this; for you were born already, so long is the span of your life!

22 Have you visited the storehouse of the snow or seen the arsenal where hail is stored,

---

[5] **Dog-star** The star Sirius.
[6] **Navigator's Line** A course set by observing the stars.

23 which I have kept ready for the day of calamity, for war and for the hour of battle?

24 By what paths is the heat spread abroad or the east wind carried far and wide over the earth?

25 Who has cut channels for the downpour and cleared a passage for the thunderstorm,

26 for rain to fall on land where no man lives and on the deserted wilderness,

27 clothing lands waste and derelict with green and making grass grow on thirsty ground?

28 Has the rain a father? Who sired the drops of dew?

29 Whose womb gave birth to the ice, and who was the mother of the frost from heaven,

30 which lays a stony cover over the waters and freezes the expanse of ocean?

31 Can you bind the cluster of the Pleiades[7] or loose Orion's belt?

32 Can you bring out the signs of the zodiac in their season or guide Aldebaran and its train?

33 Did you proclaim the rules that govern the heavens, or determine the laws of nature on earth?

34 Can you command the dense clouds to cover you with their weight of waters?

35 If you bid lightning speed on its way, will it say to you, 'I am ready'?

36 Who put wisdom in depths of darkness and veiled understanding in secrecy?

37 Who is wise enough to marshal the rain-clouds and empty the cisterns of heaven,

38 when the dusty soil sets hard as iron, and the clods of earth cling together?

39 Do you hunt her prey for the lioness and satisfy the hunger of young lions,

40 as they crouch in the lair or lie in wait in the covert?

41 Who provides the raven with its quarry when its fledglings croak for lack of food?

42

Then Job answered the LORD:

---

[7] **Pleiades . . . Orion's belt . . . Aldebaran** Constellations and stars used by navigators at sea.

2 I know that thou canst do all things and that no purpose is beyond thee.

3 But I have spoken of great things which I have not understood, things too wonderful for me to know.

5 I knew of thee then only by report but now I see thee with my own eyes.

6 Therefore I melt away, I repent in dust and ashes.

Epilogue

7 When the LORD had finished speaking to Job, he said to Eliphaz the Temanite, 'I am angry with you and your two friends, because you have not spoken as you ought about me, as my servant Job has done.

8 So now take seven bulls and seven rams, go to my servant Job and offer a whole-offering for yourselves, and he will intercede for you; I will surely show him favour by not being harsh with you because you have not spoken as you ought about me, as he has done.'

9 Then Eliphaz the Temanite and Bildad the Shuhite and Zophar the Naamathite went and carried out the LORD's command, and the LORD showed favour to Job when he had interceded for his friends.

10 So the LORD restored Job's fortunes and doubled all his possessions.

11 Then all Job's brothers and sisters and his former acquaintance came and feasted with him in his home, and they consoled and comforted him for all the misfortunes which the LORD had brought on him; and each of them gave him a sheep and a gold ring.

12 Furthermore, the LORD blessed the end of Job's life more than the beginning; and he had fourteen thousand head of small cattle and six thousand camels, a thousand yoke of oxen and as many she-asses.

13 He had seven sons and three daughters;

14 and he named his eldest daughter Jemimah, the second Keziah and the third Keren-happuch.

15 There were no women in all the world so beautiful as Job's daughters; and their father gave them an inheritance with their brothers.

16 Thereafter Job lived another hundred and forty years, he saw his sons and his grandsons to four generations,

17 and died at a very great age.

QUESTIONS FOR CRITICAL READING

1. What is Job's condition at the beginning of the story?
2. Job's sons used to put on successive feasts in their houses. What does this fact imply about their position in life?
3. The Lord mentions Job to Satan in the "court of heaven." Why do you suppose he does this?
4. What is the message in Eliphaz's speech in Chapter 5?
5. Do you think Job complains prematurely when he says he is "sickened of life" in Chapter 10?
6. Does Job's wish that he had never been born seem like a childish reaction, or is it justified?
7. What wisdom does Job receive at the end of the narrative?
8. Do you think Job is treated fairly in this piece?

SUGGESTIONS FOR WRITING

1. Describe the "court of heaven" as you imagine the author intended it to be. The Lord is there and so is Satan, his Adversary. Is this a law court, or is it the kind of court that was maintained by kings and queens? Why would Satan be present in a calm conversation with God? What does Satan's presence imply about his nature? What does it imply about his relation to God? What is implied by the fact that a challenge is given to God and that God accepts it?
2. What does Job's answer in Chapter 19 reveal about his character and personality? Consider the significance of all the complaints he makes. What kinds of losses most alarm him and make him regretful? Of all his "possessions," what does he find most painfully absent? Would you say that this extended speech represents the lamentation of a materialistic person?
3. Some commentators on *The Book of Job* have questioned the "fairness" of God's choosing Job to be tried so severely by Satan. Others have said that human beings are most revealed to themselves by the instrument of trial, and thus it is especially fair to try someone whose faith is unusually strong. Do you think God has treated Job fairly?
4. This work is part of a collection of books intended to impart wisdom and to give readers some insight into the mysterious ways in which God works. The text may be at least 2,600 years old. How pertinent is the wisdom imparted in this book for modern society and the ways we now live? If possible, try to illustrate your answer with examples from experience, either yours or someone else's.
5. Examine the entirety of *The Book of Job* for metaphors relating to law and legality. You may wish to consult the entirety of the work in the Bible to supplement the excerpts you have here. Apart from the references to a court and to the Adversary (Satan), Job refers to a "defending counsel" and says, "Beware of the sword that points at you, the

sword that sweeps away all iniquity; then you will know that there is a judge" (19:29). Why are all these (and other) references so legalistic? Is it possible the author conceives of God as a judge and each person as being called before God for judgment?

6. To the best of your ability, spell out what you think is "God's unfathomable wisdom," detailed in Chapter 28. Why can't we fathom the wisdom of God? How inclusive is this wisdom? How effective are the verses of Chapter 28 in convincing you of your limitations in understanding the wisdom of God?

7. **CONNECTIONS**   Contrast the portrait of God in *The Book of Job* with that of the portrait in "The Believer" from the Koran. In what ways are they similar? In what ways different? Comment, too, on the comparison of the portraits of human beings in relation to God. Are these two works in agreement or disagreement? *The Book of Job* was probably written around 1,200 years before the Koran. Does the more modern document sound more modern to you?

8. **CONNECTIONS**   Compare the dialogue between The Blessed One and Arjuna in the selection from the *Bhagavad Gītā* with the dialogue in *The Book of Job*. In the *Bhagavad Gītā* Arjuna rarely speaks, and when he does, it is usually only to explain the difficulty of acting out Krishna's demands. In *The Book of Job* both Yahweh (the Lord) and Job speak. How similar in attitude is The Blessed One to Yahweh, and how distinct and different are the purposes of the dialogues in each case? How much respect does Arjuna get from The Blessed One? How much respect does Job get from Yahweh? How important is humanity in God's perspective in each of these holy texts?

ST. MATTHEW
The Sermon on the Mount

MATTHEW, believed to be the author of the Gospel of St. Matthew, was also known as Levi, one of the twelve disciples of Jesus. He was a Jewish tax collector working for the Roman governors in Galilee, a region of what was then known as Palestine. His dates are uncertain, but he lived in the period of A.D. 10 to 80, and the best modern sources suggest that his gospel was composed sometime after A.D. 70 and probably written in Greek. Although some early church historians say this gospel was written originally in Hebrew, there is no evidence that a Hebrew text existed. This detail is important only because of the reputation of the Gospel of St. Matthew: it is said to be the most Jewish of the gospels. Even though it originally was addressed not to Jewish Christians but to Gentile Christians, it frequently quotes from and refers to Jewish law and the teachings and text of the Old Testament. Because the Romans repressed the Jews after their uprising in A.D. 66 to 70, few if any Jews were thought to remain in Palestine.

The Gospels of St. Matthew, St. Mark, and St. Luke are called synoptic, because they contain a great deal of the same material: the story of the ministry of Jesus. The Gospel of St. Matthew may not have been written first, as it seems to rely in part on the Gospel of St. Mark. However, it has special authority because Matthew (and not Mark or Luke) was one of Jesus' twelve disciples. Despite his importance to the early church, very little is known about Matthew, and it is uncertain whether he wrote the Gospel that bears his name or whether he was the sole author. The strongest evidence in favor of his authorship is tradition, particularly the attribution of Papias, a second-century bishop of the church.

From the King James version, 1611.

Matthew's plan in the gospel seems to have been to structure his observations in five parts, possibly emulating the Pentateuch (five books) of Moses, who is known as the lawgiver. Matthew is very knowledgeable about Jewish law and interprets that law through the teachings of Jesus. His focus, on at least one level, is on the details, or letter, of the law. Jesus felt the scribes and Pharisees — two groups of "righteous" citizens — concerned themselves with the details of following legal prescripts and not with the spirit of the law. For example, because it was against the law to work on the Sabbath, pulling a donkey out of a hole on the Sabbath, thereby relieving its misery, was a crime according to the Pharisees — but not to Jesus.

The Gospel of St. Matthew tells of the early life of Jesus; his activity in Galilee, including the Sermon on the Mount, which appears here; his activity in Jerusalem; and his eventual crucifixion. Matthew emphasizes Jesus' powers as a healer and the spiritual value of his message. Part of the Sermon on the Mount includes the beatitudes (5:1–13), nine blessings that Jesus offers the multitude. The Gospel of St. Luke (6:20–23) includes four more beatitudes:

> Blessed are you poor, for yours is the kingdom of God.
> Blessed are you that hunger now, for you shall be satisfied.
> Blessed are you that weep now, for you shall laugh.
> Blessed are you when men hate you, and when they exclude you and revile you, and cast out your name as evil, on account of the Son of man! Rejoice in that day, and leap for joy, for behold, your reward is great in heaven; for so their fathers did to the prophets.

These blessings indicate the spiritual comfort that Matthew and the disciples received from the teachings of Jesus.

The Sermon on the Mount goes beyond spiritual comfort, however, by offering a guide for living as a Christian. In it, Jesus discourses on the law itself, the power of anger, adultery, lawsuits, loving one's enemies, charity, prayer, fasting, heaven, and God, as well as many other subjects. Some of this guidance is similar to the guidance that the Buddha gives in his efforts to point the way to enlightenment. Thus, the Sermon on the Mount offers the followers of Jesus a pattern for faith and a prescription for moral behavior.

St. Matthew's Rhetoric

The Gospel of St. Matthew is by far the most quoted of the four gospels. Matthew's style is crisp, sharpened, and pared to a remarkable economy of expression. By fashioning statements to make them memorable, he hopes to make the sayings of Jesus available to a multitude. Expressions such as "an eye for an eye" (5:38), "whosoever shall smite thee on thy right cheek, turn to him the other also" (5:39), "judge not, that ye be not judged" (7:1), "wide is the gate, and broad is the way, that leadeth to destruction" (7:13), "false prophets ... in sheep's clothing" (7:15), and many more are found in the selection that is presented here. Even though he borrows or modifies expressions from the Old Testament, Matthew's Gospel shows him to be a gifted literary man as well as a spiritual guide.

The structure of the selection presented here is a narration of the story of Jesus' ministry, beginning with Jesus preaching to the multitude in Galilee (4:23–25). Chapter 5 contains the Sermon on the Mount ("he went up into a mountain," 5:1) and first examines the blessings — the beatitudes — that Jesus taught to the disciples. The Sermon on the Mount is an oral presentation of important teachings delivered directly to the disciples who have been chosen to carry out Jesus' work. The teachings continue in Chapters 6 and 7, which cover many of the important issues that concerned people who desired to learn how to live by proper precepts. Interestingly, when Jesus came down from the mount, one of his first acts was to cleanse a leper.

Most of the following selection records what Jesus said more than what he did, and part of Matthew's skill centers on getting Jesus' words, including his tone, "right." One reason for comparing the Gospel of St. Matthew with the Gospels of St. Mark and St. Luke is to see the nuances they each perceived in Jesus' tone and manner.

Partly because Matthew is economical in his recording of Jesus' sayings, later generations have pored over them carefully in an effort to decide exactly what they mean. Matthew is able to freight expressions with a considerable range of significance. An expression such as "an eye for an eye, and a tooth for a tooth" (5:38) needs careful examination, both in the context in which Jesus uses it and in the context of the entire Bible, because it also appears in the Old Testament in Exodus (21:23–24). The amplification that Jesus offers the expression effectively alters its meaning to help accomplish the reinterpretation of the law that is central to Matthew's understanding of Jesus' mission. Therefore, one of the rewards of reading St. Matthew lies in the invitation to read carefully and in depth.

PREREADING QUESTIONS: WHAT TO READ FOR

The following prereading questions may help you anticipate key issues in the discussion on St. Matthew's "The Sermon on the Mount." Keeping them in mind during your first reading of the selection should help focus your reactions.

• How do the beatitudes help one learn to live a good life?

• What is Jesus' attitude toward the law?

• Which infractions of the law seem most serious?

The Sermon on the Mount

23 And Jesus went about all Galilee, teaching in their synagogues, and preaching the gospel of the kingdom, and healing all manner of sickness and all manner of disease among the people.

24 And his fame went throughout all Syria: and they brought unto him all sick people that were taken with divers diseases and torments, and those which were possessed with devils, and those which were lunatic, and those that had the palsy; and he healed them.

25 And there followed him great multitudes of people from Galilee, and *from* Decapolis, and *from* Jerusalem, and *from* Judea, and *from* beyond Jordan.

5

And seeing the multitudes, he went up into a mountain: and when he was set, his disciples came unto him:

2 And he opened his mouth, and taught them, saying,

3 Blessed *are* the poor in spirit: for theirs is the kingdom of heaven.

4 Blessed *are* they that mourn: for they shall be comforted.

5 Blessed *are* the meek: for they shall inherit the earth.

6 Blessed *are* they which do hunger and thirst after righteousness: for they shall be filled.

7 Blessed *are* the merciful: for they shall obtain mercy.

8 Blessed *are* the pure in heart: for they shall see God.

9 Blessed *are* the peacemakers: for they shall be called the children of God.

10 Blessed *are* they which are persecuted for righteousness' sake: for theirs is the kingdom of heaven.

11 Blessed are ye, when *men* shall revile you, and persecute *you,* and shall say all manner of evil against you falsely, for my sake.

12 Rejoice, and be exceeding glad: for great *is* your reward in heaven: for so persecuted they the prophets which were before you.

13 Ye are the salt of the earth: but if the salt have lost his savor, wherewith shall it be salted? It is thenceforth good for nothing, but to be cast out, and to be trodden under foot of men.

14 Ye are the light of the world. A city that is set on a hill cannot be hid.

15 Neither do men light a candle, and put it under a bushel, but on a candlestick; and it giveth light unto all that are in the house.

16 Let your light so shine before men, that they may see your good works, and glorify your Father which is in heaven.

17 Think not that I am come to destroy the law, or the prophets: I am not come to destroy, but to fulfil.

18 For verily I say unto you, Till heaven and earth pass, one jot or one tittle shall in no wise pass from the law, till all be fulfilled.

19 Whosoever therefore shall break one of these least commandments, and shall teach men so, he shall be called the least in the kingdom of heaven: but whosoever shall do and teach *them,* the same shall be called great in the kingdom of heaven.

20 For I say unto you, That except your righteousness shall exceed *the righteousness* of the scribes and Pharisees, ye shall in no case enter into the kingdom of heaven.

21 Ye have heard that it was said by them of old time, Thou shalt not kill; and whosoever shall kill shall be in danger of the judgment:

22 But I say unto you, That whosoever is angry with his brother without a cause shall be in danger of the judgment: and whosoever shall say to his brother, Raca, shall be in danger of the council: but whosoever shall say, Thou fool, shall be in danger of hell fire.

23 Therefore if thou bring thy gift to the altar, and there rememberest that thy brother hath aught against thee;

24 Leave there thy gift before the altar, and go thy way; first be reconciled to thy brother, and then come and offer thy gift.

25 Agree with thine adversary quickly, while thou art in the way with him; lest at any time the adversary deliver thee to the judge, and the judge deliver thee to the officer, and thou be cast into prison.

26 Verily I say unto thee, Thou shalt by no means come out thence, till thou hast paid the uttermost farthing.

27 Ye have heard that it was said by them of old time, Thou shalt not commit adultery:

28 But I say unto you, That whosoever looketh on a woman to lust after her hath committed adultery with her already in his heart.

29 And if thy right eye offend thee, pluck it out, and cast *it* from thee: for it is profitable for thee that one of thy members should perish, and not *that* thy whole body should be cast into hell.

30 And if thy right hand offend thee, cut it off, and cast *it* from thee: for it is profitable for thee that one of thy members should perish, and not *that* thy whole body should be cast into hell.

31 It hath been said, Whosoever shall put away his wife, let him give her a writing of divorcement:

32 But I say unto you, That whosoever shall put away his wife, saving for the cause of fornication, causeth her to commit adultery: and whosoever shall marry her that is divorced committeth adultery.

33 Again, ye have heard that it hath been said by them of old time, Thou shalt not forswear thyself, but shalt perform unto the Lord thine oaths:

34 But I say unto you, Swear not at all; neither by heaven; for it is God's throne:

35 Nor by the earth; for it is his footstool: neither by Jerusalem; for it is the city of the great King.

36 Neither shalt thou swear by thy head, because thou canst not make one hair white or black.

37 But let your communication be, Yea, yea; Nay, nay: for whatsoever is more than these cometh of evil.

38 Ye have heard that it hath been said, An eye for an eye, and a tooth for a tooth:

39 But I say unto you, That ye resist not evil: but whosoever shall smite thee on thy right cheek, turn to him the other also.

40 And if any man will sue thee at the law, and take away thy coat, let him have *thy* cloak also.

41 And whosoever shall compel thee to go a mile, go with him twain.

42 Give to him that asketh thee, and from him that would borrow of thee turn not thou away.

43 Ye have heard that it hath been said, Thou shalt love thy neighbor, and hate thine enemy.

44 But I say unto you, Love your enemies, bless them that curse you, do good to them that hate you, and pray for them which despitefully use you, and persecute you;

45 That ye may be the children of your Father which is in heaven: for he maketh his sun to rise on the evil and on the good, and sendeth rain on the just and on the unjust.

46 For if ye love them which love you, what reward have ye? do not even the publicans[1] the same?

47 And if ye salute your brethren only, what do ye more *than others*? do not even the publicans so?

---

[1] **publicans** Tax collectors for the Roman Empire.

48 Be ye therefore perfect, even as your Father which is in heaven is perfect.

6

Take heed that ye do not your alms before men, to be seen of them: otherwise ye have no reward of your Father which is in heaven.

2 Therefore when thou doest *thine* alms, do not sound a trumpet before thee, as the hypocrites do in the synagogues and in the streets, that they may have glory of men. Verily I say unto you, They have their reward.

3 But when thou doest alms, let not thy left hand know what thy right hand doeth:

4 That thine alms may be in secret: and thy Father which seeth in secret himself shall reward thee openly.

5 And when thou prayest, thou shalt not be as the hypocrites *are:* for they love to pray standing in the synagogues and in the corners of the streets, that they may be seen of men. Verily I say unto you, They have their reward.

6 But thou, when thou prayest, enter into thy closet, and when thou hast shut thy door, pray to thy Father which is in secret; and thy Father which seeth in secret shall reward thee openly.

7 But when ye pray, use not vain repetitions, as the heathen *do:* for they think that they shall be heard for their much speaking.

8 Be not ye therefore like unto them: for your Father knoweth what things ye have need of, before ye ask him.

9 After this manner therefore pray ye: Our father which art in heaven, Hallowed be thy name.

10 Thy kingdom come. Thy will be done in earth, as *it is* in heaven.

11 Give us this day our daily bread.

12 And forgive us our debts, as we forgive our debtors.

13 And lead us not into temptation, but deliver us from evil: For thine is the kingdom, and the power, and the glory, for ever. Amen.

14 For if ye forgive men their trespasses, your heavenly Father will also forgive you:

15 But if ye forgive not men their trespasses, neither will your Father forgive your trespasses.

16 Moreover when ye fast, be not, as the hypocrites, of a sad countenance: for they disfigure their faces, that they may appear unto men to fast. Verily I say unto you, They have their reward.

17 But thou, when thou fastest, anoint thine head, and wash thy face;

18 That thou appear not unto men to fast, but unto thy Father which is in secret: and thy Father which seeth in secret shall reward thee openly.

19 Lay not up for yourselves treasures upon earth, where moth and rust doth corrupt, and where thieves break through and steal:

20 But lay up for yourselves treasures in heaven, where neither moth nor rust doth corrupt, and where thieves do not break through nor steal:

21 For where your treasure is, there will your heart be also.

22 The light of the body is the eye: if therefore thine eye be single,[2] thy whole body shall be full of light.

23 But if thine eye be evil, thy whole body shall be full of darkness. If therefore the light that is in thee be darkness, how great *is* that darkness!

24 No man can serve two masters: for either he will hate the one, and love the other; or else he will hold to the one, and despise the other. Ye cannot serve God and mammon.[3]

25 Therefore I say unto you, Take no thought for your life, what ye shall eat, or what ye shall drink; nor yet for your body, what ye shall put on. Is not the life more than meat, and the body than raiment?[4]

26 Behold the fowls of the air: for they sow not, neither do they reap, nor gather into barns; yet your heavenly Father feedeth them. Are ye not much better than they?

27 Which of you by taking thought can add one cubit unto his stature?

28 And why take ye thought for raiment? Consider the lilies of the field, how they grow; they toil not, neither do they spin:

29 And yet I say unto you, That even Solomon in all his glory was not arrayed like one of these.

30 Wherefore, if God so clothe the grass of the field, which today is, and tomorrow is cast into the oven, *shall he* not much more *clothe* you, O ye of little faith?

31 Therefore take no thought, saying, What shall we eat? or, What shall we drink? or, Wherewithal shall we be clothed?

32 (For after all these things do the Gentiles seek:) for your heavenly Father knoweth that ye have need of all these things.

33 But seek ye first the kingdom of God, and his righteousness; and all these things shall be added unto you.

---

[2] **single** Focused on proper things.
[3] **mammon** Pagan god, associated with materialism.
[4] **raiment** Clothing.

34 Take therefore no thought for the morrow: for the morrow shall take thought for the things of itself. Sufficient unto the day is the evil thereof.

7

Judge not, that ye be not judged.

2 For with what judgment ye judge, ye shall be judged: and with what measure ye mete, it shall be measured to you again.

3 And why beholdest thou the mote that is in thy brother's eye, but considerest not the beam that is in thine own eye?

4 Or how wilt thou say to thy brother, Let me pull out the mote out of thine eye; and, behold, a beam is in thine own eye?

5 Thou hypocrite, first cast out the beam out of thine own eye; and then shalt thou see clearly to cast out the mote out of thy brother's eye.

6 Give not that which is holy unto the dogs, neither cast ye your pearls before swine, lest they trample them under their feet, and turn again and rend you.

7 Ask, and it shall be given you; seek, and ye shall find; knock, and it shall be opened unto you:

8 For every one that asketh receiveth; and he that seeketh findeth; and to him that knocketh it shall be opened.

9 Or what man is there of you, whom if his son ask bread, will he give him a stone?

10 Or if he ask a fish, will he give him a serpent?

11 If ye then, being evil, know how to give good gifts unto your children, how much more shall your Father which is in heaven give good things to them that ask him?

12 Therefore all things whatsoever ye would that men should do to you, do ye even so to them: for this is the law and the prophets.

13 Enter ye in at the strait gate: for wide is the gate, and broad is the way, that leadeth to destruction, and many there be which go in thereat:

14 Because strait is the gate, and narrow is the way, which leadeth unto life, and few there be that find it.

15 Beware of false prophets, which come to you in sheep's clothing, but inwardly they are ravening wolves.

16 Ye shall know them by their fruits. Do men gather grapes of thorns, or figs of thistles?

17 Even so every good tree bringeth forth good fruit; but a corrupt tree bringeth forth evil fruit.

18 A good tree cannot bring forth evil fruit, neither *can* a corrupt tree bring forth good fruit.

19 Every tree that bringeth not forth good fruit is hewn down, and cast into the fire.

20 Wherefore by their fruits ye shall know them.

21 Not every one that saith unto me, Lord, Lord, shall enter into the kingdom of heaven; but he that doeth the will of my Father which is in heaven.

22 Many will say to me in that day, Lord, Lord, have we not prophesied in thy name? and in thy name have cast out devils? and in thy name done many wonderful works?

23 And then will I profess unto them, I never knew you: depart from me, ye that work iniquity.

24 Therefore whosoever heareth these sayings of mine, and doeth them, I will liken him unto a wise man, which built his house upon a rock:

25 And the rain descended, and the floods came, and the winds blew, and beat upon that house; and it fell not: for it was founded upon a rock.

26 And every one that heareth these sayings of mine, and doeth them not, shall be likened unto a foolish man, which built his house upon the sand:

27 And the rain descended, and the floods came, and the winds blew, and beat upon that house; and it fell: and great was the fall of it.

28 And it came to pass, when Jesus had ended these sayings, the people were astonished at his doctrine:

29 For he taught them as *one* having authority, and not as the scribes.

QUESTIONS FOR CRITICAL READING

1. What is a beatitude?
2. What is Jesus' attitude toward adultery?
3. What is the connection between "an eye for an eye" (5:38) and turning the other cheek?
4. What is Jesus' teaching on charity?
5. What is of importance in Jesus' references to the "lilies of the field" (6:28)?

SUGGESTIONS FOR WRITING

1. Describe what you feel is the central spiritual message of the selection. What prescription for living does the Sermon on the Mount offer the individual? What basis of faith does Jesus seem to require of his followers? Is faith a moral issue in this selection?

2. Why should a person's faith demand a specific manner of behavior? What is the connection between actions and beliefs as St. Matthew sees it?

3. Which of the teachings of Jesus is most difficult to follow? Why? Does the emphasis that Matthew gives that teaching imply its difficulty? Which of Jesus' teachings seem problematic for Matthew?

4. Apart from the fact that the Lord's Prayer begins with "Our father" (6:9), which of Jesus' teachings are patriarchal in implication? Would following his teachings produce a patriarchal society in which women are devalued? What implications for the modern world do you derive from your analysis of this issue?

5. The expression "eye for an eye" (5:38) appears in Exodus (21:23–24) as well as in the Sermon on the Mount. How does Jesus modify this expression? Read both versions to make your comparison. Analyze the text carefully in this selection (5:38–39) for the significance of the saying.

6. What are Jesus' teachings about lawbreakers? He speaks both of a higher law to which we are to adhere and also of the ordinary laws of the land. What distinctions does he make between those laws? And what are his directives regarding our responsibility to these laws? What contemporary legal cases can you think of that reveal important distinctions that would be of interest to St. Matthew or Jesus?

7. **CONNECTIONS** How compatible are the teachings of Jesus with the teachings of the Buddha? Are both equally moral in nature? Is the question of faith more important in one than in the other? How do the ultimate goals of each text differ? How are they similar? In what ways would the path of the disciples also be the path to enlightenment?

8. **CONNECTIONS** Consider the views of those who comment on government. How would this selection be interpreted by Jefferson? By Rousseau? By Machiavelli? Which commentators on government could be considered in general alignment with the teachings of Jesus as imparted by St. Matthew?

THE BHAGAVAD GĪTĀ
Meditation and Knowledge

THE *BHAGAVAD GĪTĀ* — song (gītā) of the Lord (Bhagavat) —
is a religious poem embedded within a vastly larger epic called the
Mahabharata. Its author or authors remain unknown, as do the authors of most early Indian religious and philosophical literature.
Most estimates date the work from the first or second century A.D.
For most Hindus, the *Bhagavad Gītā* serves the same purpose as
the New Testament does for Christians. The poem is essentially a
long dialogue, with most of the speaking done by Lord Krishna to
his disciple Arjuna. (The portrait on the facing page is based on religious depictions of Lord Krishna.)

For modern thinkers concerned with Hindu philosophy and religion, an important aspect of the *Bhagavad Gītā* is its tendency toward monotheism. Although this point is still controversial, some
commentators suggest that the cult of the Bhagavata was specifically monotheistic and promoted a single god with several names:
Vishnu (the old name for the Vedic god found in the Rig Veda, one
of the most ancient of Indian religious documents), Vāsudeva (a
name used in the following text), Krishna, Hari, and Nārāyana. All
these names refer to the same person, although, as in the case of
Lord Krishna, an individual name implies a specific incarnation of
the deity. The important point is that the deity is personal. In the
Bhagavad Gītā the Lord Krishna is a strong personality, and the
monotheistic practice of establishing a personal god is clearly
present.

The *Mahabharata* is loosely translated as the "Great Epic of the
Bharata Dynasty." It tells of an epic battle between two great families, the Kauravas and the Pandavas. Pandu is the father of the Pan-
dava brothers, and in the *Bhagavad Gītā* one of the five brothers,

Translated by Franklin Edgerton, 1944.

Arjuna, is often referred to as "son of Pandu." The sole survivors of the great battle are the Pandova brothers and Krishna, who acts as Arjuna's charioteer. In the epic Krishna overcomes Arjuna's reluctance to fight the Kauravas (he is related to both families) by explaining that those who are slain only seem to be slain, and those who slay only seem to slay. These actions are illusions. By freeing the soul from illusions and imparting the truth, the teachings of the *Bhagavad Gītā* aim to help readers set free their souls.

In his introduction, Franklin Edgerton, the translator and interpreter of the passages selected here, explains some of the basic beliefs of Hinduism in this fashion: "First, *pessimism:* all empiric existence is evil. Second, *transmigration,* with the doctrine of *karma:* all living beings are subject to an indefinite series of reincarnations, and the conditions of each incarnation are determined by the moral quality of acts performed in previous incarnations. Third, *salvation* lies in release from this chain of existences; it is to be gained primarily by knowledge of the supreme truth." The world of the senses—empiric existence—is beguiling and potentially destructive because it generates desires and desires entangle the soul and condemn it to further incarnations. The goal of the individual is to gain the knowledge of the truth necessary to put an end to the soul's transmigration—movement from being to being—and reunite it with the great oversoul, sometimes referred to as the Brahman.

The *Bhagavad Gītā* is divided into eighteen chapters that in some versions and translations are called Yogas. Thus, for the two chapters that appear here, Chapter 6 is sometimes called The Yoga of Meditation, and Chapter 7 is sometimes called The Yoga of Spirit and Nature. Calling each chapter a Yoga identifies the text as a meditation leading to wisdom. Although the materials of meditation offered in specific verses will sometimes appear to introduce contradictions, it is important to keep in mind that the text as we have it is not concerned with a logical consistency and will sometimes appear to move in several directions simultaneously.

Chapter 6 focuses on the "Discipline of Meditation" and the way to knowledge of Krishna through discipline. As Krishna says in verse 46, "The man of discipline is higher than men of austerities, / Also than men of knowledge he is held to be higher; / And the man of discipline is higher than men of ritual action; / Therefore be a man of discipline, Arjuna." In this, Krishna offers advice that parallels both that of the Buddha and that of Jesus in St. Matthew's Gospel. The first verse of Chapter 6 recommends action ("action that is required") and the "renunciation and discipline (of action)." Thus, according to Krishna, some action is necessary, but action ultimately must give way to discipline and knowledge of the truth.

The discourse on the self is meaningful especially in relation to the invitation to Arjuna to be disciplined. When Lord Krishna says, "the self is the self's only friend, / And the self is the self's only enemy" (6:5), he reminds Arjuna that the important thing is what happens within him. The disciplined person retires to meditation, fixing the mind on a "single object" as a means to "practice / Discipline unto self-purification" (6:12). Lord Krishna offers some advice about temperate eating habits, temperate behavior, and a path toward freeing one from "all desires" (6:18). These are preliminary to becoming disciplined, which is preliminary to gaining knowledge.

Chapter 7, called "Discipline of Theoretical and Practical Knowledge," continues the message of Krishna. It begins with the invitation to focus on Krishna and to know "Me in very truth" (7:3). He reminds Arjuna that many begin the struggle toward truth but only a few have the endurance to continue the way. Lord Krishna reveals in the early verses that he has two natures: the lower nature being the things of the world that may be perceived, such as the basic natural elements of verse 4, and the higher nature being the invisible self (Spirit). Thus, Krishna can say, "I am taste in water," "I am light in the moon and sun, / The sacred syllable (*om*) in all the Vedas, / Sound in ether, manliness in men" (verse 8). Krishna says "On Me all this (universe) is strung, / Like heaps of pearls on a string" (verse 7), echoing in a remarkable way the theories of Michio Kaku in Part Five of this book.

The chapter ends with a concern for knowledge. In verse 26 Krishna says, "I know those that are past, / And that are present, Arjuna, / And beings that are yet to be, / But no one knows Me." And in the last verse, after having praised knowledge and "the possessor of knowledge, constantly disciplined" (7:17), Lord Krishna says, "And (who know) Me even at the hour of death, / They (truly) know (Me), with disciplined hearts" (7:30).

The Rhetoric
of the *Bhagavad Gītā*

The *Bhagavad Gītā* is written in very high quality verse within a poem whose own standards of poetic excellence are high. Some English translations render the text in prose, and this translation is essentially prose that is set up to look like poetry and that tries to maintain the poetic nature of the original by supplying some of the prayer-like repetition of the original. As with all texts that are scriptural in nature, the text does not present an argument but rather a system of recommended behavior. Such texts make no effort to convince readers why the proper behavior should be followed but simply tell them what that behavior is.

Although it is found within a long narrative poem, the *Bhagavad Gītā* does not tell a story. The most important and obvious rhetorical device the text uses is the dialogue. In this sense, it shares the same rhetorical structure Plato uses in most of his writings. However, the *Bhagavad Gītā* does not invite response from Arjuna. In Chapter 7, Arjuna does not speak at all. In Chapter 6, when he does speak, he explains how difficult it is for anyone to do the things Krishna demands. When Lord Krishna explains that the mind must be disciplined thoroughly, Arjuna replies, "fickle is the thought-organ, Krishna, / Impetuous, mighty, and hard; / The restraining of it, I conceive, / Is very difficult, as of the wind" (6:34). Lord Krishna is gentle with Arjuna and reassures him that by means of "practice" (6:35) it is possible to bring the "impetuous" organ under control.

The use of careful comparisons helps illuminate specific teachings of Lord Krishna, as when he compares the disciplined person to "a lamp stationed in a windless place / [that] Flickers not" (6:19). But the text relies on only a few such comparisons, choosing to be more direct and specific. Careful repetition is one strategy of the text; another is the variety achieved by using different names to address Arjuna. "Son of Kuntī," "son of Kuru," and "son of Pṛthā" are all used to address Arjuna and remind the reader of Arjuna's ancestors. This is similar to the lists of ancestors sometimes provided in the Bible.

Ultimately, the *Bhagavad Gītā* is a text that is intended to be examined in detail and depth. It is compressed, as we expect of all poetry, and needs expansion. Many modern editions of the *Bhagavad Gītā* offer extensive interpretations between most of the verses, and most of them do not print merely the verses as they appear in this book. For most modern editors the interlineated commentary is as important as the verses themselves. For us, part of the pleasure of the text is meditating on its possible meanings.

PREREADING QUESTIONS: WHAT TO READ FOR

The following prereading questions may help you anticipate key issues in the discussion on "Meditation and Knowledge" from the *Bhagavad Gītā*. Keeping them in mind during your first reading of the selection should help focus your reactions.

• How does meditation aid discipline?

• What theoretical and practical knowledge does meditation impart?

Meditation and Knowledge

Chapter 6
Discipline of Meditation

The Blessed One said:

Not interested in the fruit of action,   1
    Who does action that is required (by religion),
He is the possessor of both renunciation and discipline (of action);
    Not he who builds no sacred fires and does no (ritual) acts.

What they call renunciation,   2
    Know that that is discipline (of action), son of Paṇḍu.
For not without renouncing purpose
    Does any one become possessed of discipline.

For the sage that desires to mount to discipline   3
    Action is called the means;
For the same man when he has mounted to discipline
    Quiescence is called the means.

For when not to the objects of sense   4
    Nor to actions is he attached,
Renouncing all purpose,
    Then he is said to have mounted to discipline.

One should lift up the self by the self,   5
    And should not let the self down;
For the self is the self's only friend,
    And the self is the self's only enemy.

The self is a friend to that self   6
    By which self the very self is subdued;
But to him that does not possess the self, in enmity
    Will abide his very self, like an enemy.

Of the self-subdued, pacified man,   7
    The supreme self remains concentrated (in absorption),
In cold and heat, pleasure and pain,
    Likewise in honor and disgrace.

His self satiated with theoretical and practical knowledge,   8
    Immovable, with subdued senses,

The possessor of discipline is called (truly) disciplined,
    To whom clods, stones, and gold are all one.

To friend, ally, foe, remote neutral,   9
    Holder of middle ground, object of enmity, and kinsman,
To good and evil men alike,
    Who has the same mental attitude, is superior.

Let the disciplined man ever discipline   10
    Himself, abiding in a secret place,
Solitary, restraining his thoughts and soul,
    Free from aspirations and without possessions.

In a clean place establishing   11
    A steady seat for himself,
That is neither too high nor too low,
    Covered with a cloth, a skin, and kuśa-grass,

There fixing the thought-organ on a single object,   12
    Restraining the activity of his mind and senses,
Sitting on the seat, let him practice
    Discipline unto self-purification.

Even body, head, and neck   13
    Holding motionless, (keeping himself) steady,
Gazing at the tip of his own nose,
    And not looking in any direction,

With tranquil soul, rid of fear,   14
    Abiding in the vow of chastity,
Controlling the mind, his thoughts on Me,
    Let him sit disciplined, absorbed in Me.

Thus ever disciplining himself,   15
    The man of discipline, with controlled mind,
To peace that culminates in nirvāṇa,[1]
    And rests in Me, attains.

But he who eats too much has no discipline,   16
    Nor he who eats not at all;
Neither he who is over-given to sleep,
    Nor yet he who is (ever) wakeful, Arjuna.

---

[1] **nirvāṇa** Enlightenment; the end of material existence.

Who is disciplined (moderate) in food and recreation,　　　17
　　　And has disciplined activity in works,
And is disciplined in both sleep and wakefulness,
　　　To him belongs discipline that bans misery.

When the thought, controlled,　　　18
　　　Settles on the self alone,
The man free from longing for all desires
　　　Is then called disciplined.

As a lamp stationed in a windless place　　　19
　　　Flickers not, this image is recorded
Of the disciplined man controlled in thought,
　　　Practicing discipline of the self.

When the thought comes to rest,　　　20
　　　Checked by the practice of discipline,
And when, the self by the self
　　　Contemplating, he finds satisfaction in the self;

That supernal bliss which　　　21
　　　Is to be grasped by the consciousness and is beyond the senses,
When he knows this, and not in the least
　　　Swerves from the truth, abiding fixed (in it);

And which having gained, other gain　　　22
　　　He counts none higher than it;
In which established, by no misery,
　　　However grievous, is he moved;

This (state), let him know, — from conjunction with misery　　　23
　　　The disjunction, — is known as discipline;
With determination must be practiced this
　　　Discipline, with heart undismayed.

The desires that spring from purposes　　　24
　　　Abandoning, all without remainder,
With the thought-organ alone the throng of senses
　　　Restraining altogether,

Little by little let him come to rest　　　25
　　　Through the consciousness, held with firmness;
Keeping the thought-organ fixed in the self,
　　　He should think on nothing at all.

Because of whatsoever thing strays   26
    The thought-organ, fickle and unstable,
From every such thing holding it back,
    He shall bring it into control in the self alone.

For to him when his thought-organ is tranquil,   27
    To the disciplined one, supreme bliss
Approaches, his passion stilled,
    Become (one with) Brahman, stainless.

Thus ever disciplining himself,   28
    The disciplined man, free from stain,
Easily to contact with Brahman,
    To endless bliss, attains.

Himself as in all beings,   29
    And all beings in himself,
Sees he whose self is disciplined in discipline,
    Who sees the same in all things.

Who sees Me in all,   30
    And sees all in Me,
For him I am not lost,
    And he is not lost for Me.

Me as abiding in all beings whoso   31
    Reveres, adopting (the belief in) one-ness,
Though abiding in any possible condition,
    That disciplined man abides in Me.

By comparison with himself, in all (beings)   32
    Whoso sees the same, Arjuna,
Whether it be pleasure or pain,
    He is deemed the supreme disciplined man.

    Arjuna said:

This discipline which by Thee has been explained   33
    As indifference, Slayer of Madhu,
Thereof I do not see
    Any permanent establishment, because of (man's) fickleness.

For fickle is the thought-organ, Kṛṣṇa,   34
    Impetuous, mighty, and hard;

The restraining of it, I conceive,
    Is very difficult, as of the wind.

    The Blessed One said:

Without doubt, great-armed one,   35
    The thought-organ is hard to control, and fickle;
But by practice, son of Kuntī,
    And by ascetic aversion, it may be controlled.

For one not self-controlled, discipline   36
    Is hard to reach, I believe;
But by the self-controlled man who strives
    It may be attained through the proper method.

    Arjuna said:

An unsuccessful striver who is endowed with faith,   37
    Whose mind falls away from discipline
Without attaining perfection of discipline,
    To what goal does he go, Kṛṣṇa?

Fallen from both, does he not   38
    Perish like a cloven cloud,
Having no (religious) foundation, great-armed one,
    Gone astray on Brahman's path?

This matter, my doubt, O Kṛṣṇa,   39
    Be pleased to cleave without remainder;
Other than Thee, of this doubt
    No cleaver, surely, can be found.

    The Blessed One said:

Son of Pṛthā, neither in this world nor in the next   40
    Does any destruction of him occur.
For no doer of the right
    Comes to a bad end, my friend.

Attaining the heavenly worlds of the doers of right,   41
    Dwelling there for endless years,
In the house of pure and illustrious folk
    One that has fallen from discipline is born.

Or else of possessors of discipline, rather,   42
     Enlightened folk, in their family he comes into existence;
For this is yet harder to attain,
     Such a birth as that in the world.

There that association of mentality   43
     He obtains, which was his in his former body;
And he strives from that point onward
     Unto perfection, son of Kuru.

For by that same former practice   44
     He is carried on even without his wish.
Even one who (merely) wishes to know discipline
     Transcends the word-Brahman (the Vedic religion).

But striving zealously,   45
     With sins cleansed, the disciplined man,
Perfected through many rebirths,
     Then (finally) goes to the highest goal.

The man of discipline is higher than men of austerities,   46
     Also than men of knowledge he is held to be higher;
And the man of discipline is higher than men of ritual action;
     Therefore be a man of discipline, Arjuna.

Of all men of discipline, moreover,   47
     With inner soul gone to Me
Whoso reveres Me with faith,
     Him I hold the most disciplined.

     Here ends the Sixth Chapter, called Discipline of Meditation.

Chapter 7
Discipline of Theoretical and
Practical Knowledge

The Blessed One said:

With mind attached to Me, son of Pṛthā,   1
     Practicing discipline with reliance on Me,
Without doubt Me entirely
     How thou shalt know, that hear!

Theoretical knowledge to thee along with practical   2
     I shall now expound completely;

Having known which, in this world no other further
    Thing to be known is left.

Among thousands of men   3
    Perchance one strives for perfection;
Even of those that strive and are perfected,
    Perchance one knows Me in very truth.

Earth, water, fire, wind,   4
    Ether, thought-organ, and consciousness,
And I-faculty: thus My
    Nature is divided eight-fold.

This is My lower (nature). But other than this,   5
    My higher nature know:
It is the Life (soul), great-armed one,
    By which this world is maintained.

Beings spring from it,   6
    All of them, be assured.
Of the whole world I am
    The origin and the dissolution too.

Than Me no other higher thing   7
    Whatsoever exists, Dhanaṃjaya;[2]
On Me all this (universe) is strung,
    Like heaps of pearls on a string.

I am taste in water, son of Kuntī,   8
    I am light in the moon and sun,
The sacred syllable (*om*) in all the Vedas,
    Sound in ether, manliness in men.

Both the goodly odor in earth,   9
    And brilliance in fire am I,
Life in all beings,
    And austerity in ascetics am I.

The seed of all beings am I,   10
    The eternal, be assured, son of Pṛthā;
I am intelligence of the intelligent,
    Majesty of the majestic am I.

---

[2] **Dhanaṃjaya** Winner of good fortune.

Might of the mighty am I, too,   11
    (Such as is) free from desire and passion;
(So far as it is) not inconsistent with right, in creatures
    I am desire, O best of Bharatas.

Both whatsoever states are of (the Strand) goodness,   12
    And those of (the Strands) passion and darkness too,
Know that they are from Me alone;
    But I am not in them; they are in Me.

By the three states[3] (of being), composed of the Strands,   13
    These (just named), all this world,
Deluded, does not recognize
    Me that am higher than they and eternal.

For this is My divine strand-composed   14
    Trick-of-illusion, hard to get past;
Those who resort to Me alone
    Penetrate beyond this trick-of-illusion.

Not to Me do deluded evil-doers   15
    Resort, base men,
Whom this illusion robs of knowledge,
    Who cleave to demoniac estate.

Fourfold are those that worship Me,   16
    (All) virtuous folk, Arjuna:
The afflicted, the knowledge-seeker, he who seeks personal ends,
    And the possessor of knowledge, bull of Bharatas.

Of these the possessor of knowledge, constantly disciplined,   17
    Of single devotion, is the best;
For extremely dear to the possessor of knowledge
    Am I, and he is dear to Me.

All these are noble;   18
    But the man of knowledge is My very self, so I hold.
For he with disciplined soul has resorted
    To Me alone as the highest goal.

---

[3] **states** Goodness, passion, and darkness. These are known as the *gunas* (primal qualities) of nature.

At the end of many births   19
    The man of knowledge resorts to Me;
Who thinks 'Vāsudeva (Kṛṣṇa) is all,'
    That noble soul is hard to find.

Deprived of knowledge by this or that desire,   20
    Men resort to other deities,
Taking to this or that (religious) rule,
    Constrained by their own nature.

Whatsoever (divine) form any devotee   21
    With faith seeks to worship,
For every such (devotee), faith unswerving
    I ordain that same to be.

He, disciplined with that faith,   22
    Seeks to propitiate that (divine being),
And obtains therefrom his desires,
    Because I myself ordain them.

But finite fruition for them   23
    That becomes, (since) they are of scant intelligence;
The worshipers of the gods go to the gods,
    My devotees go to Me also.

Unmanifest, as having come into manifestation   24
    Fools conceive Me,
Not knowing the higher essence
    Of Me, which is imperishable, supreme.

I am not revealed to every one,   25
    Being veiled by My magic trick-of-illusion;
'Tis deluded and does not recognize
    Me the unborn, imperishable, — this world.

I know those that are past,   26
    And that are present, Arjuna,
And beings that are yet to be,
    But no one knows Me.

It arises from desire and loathing,   27
    The delusion of the pairs (of opposites), son of Bharata;
Because of it all beings to confusion
    Are subject at their birth, scorcher of the foe.

But those whose sin is ended,   28
    Men of virtuous deeds,
Freed from the delusion of the pairs,
    Revere Me with firm resolve.

Unto freedom from old age and death   29
    Those who strive, relying on Me,
They know that Brahman entire,
    And the over-soul, and action altogether.

Me together with the over-being and the over-divinity,   30
    And with the over-worship, whoso know,
And (who know) Me even at the hour of death,
    They (truly) know (Me), with disciplined hearts.

Here ends the Seventh Chapter, called Discipline of Theoretical
and Practical Knowledge.

QUESTIONS FOR CRITICAL READING

1. What is the connection between renouncing purpose and possessing discipline (see Chapter 6, verses 1 and 2)?
2. How does one renounce purpose? Does it mean renouncing action?
3. What action does the sage use to "mount to discipline" (6:3)?
4. What does Lord Krishna tell us about the senses and their role in coming to know him?
5. What is the "supernal bliss" that Lord Krishna describes (6:21)?
6. Is it possible to tell what kinds of sins a person must be "cleansed" of before achieving the "highest goal" (6:45)?
7. What is the knowledge Lord Krishna refers to in Chapter 7, verse 2?
8. Explain the role devotion has in the discipline Lord Krishna describes.

SUGGESTIONS FOR WRITING

1. In this selection, Lord Krishna is in the form of Arjuna's charioteer on the field of battle and is speaking directly to Arjuna. What constitutes the issues of faith in this dialogue? What faith does Lord Krishna demand of Arjuna? Lord Krishna explains his nature in Chapter 7. What about his explanation would test the faith of Arjuna? Why is faith important to Lord Krishna? He says, "Whoso reveres Me with faith, / Him I hold the most disciplined" (6:47). What, then, is the relationship between faith and discipline?

2. Is it true that "the self is the self's only friend, / And the self is the self's only enemy" (6:5)? In what ways is this verse generally true for all people? Cite examples that can validate or invalidate the insight of that verse.

3. Beginning with verse 10 in Chapter 6, describe the method the Lord Krishna recommends for achieving discipline. Is such discipline possible? How could you achieve it in today's world? What obstacles would you face? What would be your chances of success?

4. Lord Krishna constantly refers to the "disciplined man." Do you feel these chapters are patriarchal in their message? Does Lord Krishna mean to exclude women from his teachings, or does the term *man* include all people? What aspects of the message in these chapters convinces you that it either is inclusive of feminist values or ignores them?

5. In a brief essay, explain the relation that Lord Krishna sees between the body and the soul, between nature and spirit.

6. **CONNECTIONS**   Compare the discipline described by Lord Krishna with the disciplines recommended by the Buddha and Jesus in the Gospel of St. Matthew. In what ways are they similar, and in what ways are they dissimilar? Is it possible to isolate important differences among these three writings?

In deference to Muslim sensitivities about representations of human beings — religious figures in particular — a portrait of the prophet Muhammad does not appear in *A World of Ideas*. Instead, we have included the Arabic inscription above, which appears in every chapter in the Koran, and reads, "In the name of God, the merciful, the compassionate."

THE PROPHET MUHAMMAD
From the Koran

THE PROPHET MUHAMMAD (A.D. c. 570–c. 632) was born in Mecca in what is now Saudi Arabia. Mecca is the holiest city in Islam in part for that reason. He was born a few months after his father died and became an orphan six years later when his mother died. For health reasons he spent part of his early life with nomadic tribes outside Mecca. Families in Mecca belonged to tight-knit clans, some of which held great power. His family, led by an uncle, Abu Talib, was part of the Hashim, a strong clan involved in trading with Syria. In around 595, while in his middle twenties and on a trading journey with his uncle, Muhammad managed the merchandise of a wealthy older woman, Khadijah, who was so impressed with him that she agreed to marriage. The marriage was successful and produced a number of children, two boys who died at a young age and four daughters who survived. When Khadijah died in 619, Muhammad inherited her fortune and achieved independence.

Muhammad was a deeply religious man in early life. In Mecca during his youth, religion was marked by idol worship and paganism centering on a sacred site called the Ka'bah. Sometime around 610 Muhammad began having visions and revelations, which he believed were given to him by the Archangel Gabriel. He was much shaken by these revelations, but his wife, Khadijah, reassured him and encouraged him to welcome them. Gabriel told him, "You are the messenger of God." The word *messenger* may also be translated as "apostle." In Arabic, it is *rasūl,* and Muhammad was described as *rasūl Allah* (messenger of God). As far as is known, because Muhammad was illiterate, he memorized these revelations, which the Archangel Gabriel told him came directly from God. They were

Translated by N. J. Dawood, 1956.

written down by others early in the period during which the revelations occurred. They were gathered together in written form around 650.

In 613, Muhammad began preaching in response to his revelations and became known as the Prophet. He faced derision at first. Meccans claimed he was possessed by spirits and that he was a shaman, not a true prophet, or a mere poet—because the Koran is in rhymed Arabic prose. In response he claimed this as proof that the Koran was a miracle, which his followers accepted. Nonetheless, he was generally ridiculed and rejected by people in his own clan and by others who denied him their business.

He eventually drew followers—about thirty-nine at first but growing soon to seventy. At the time of Muhammad, Mecca had no powerful central religion. The idols in the Ka'bah and the place itself were important, but most citizens were involved in mercantile activities and devoted little energy to religion. Muhammad, on the other hand, was fervent in his beliefs and seems to have represented a threat to the order of Mecca as early as 620, when he took the famous "night journey" to Jerusalem and envisioned heaven. In 622 he began the *Hejira*, the emigration from Mecca to Medina with his followers, sending them off in small groups and taking a circuitous route to avoid assassination. Muhammad's religion was known as Islam, meaning something close to "surrender to God's will," and his followers were known as Muslims—those who have surrendered. It is from this year, 622, that the Muslims begin their modern era.

The following years were filled with struggle as the number of Muslims increased. Raids on trading parties of both Meccans and Muslims led to battles between relatively large armies. Most of the struggles were won by Muhammad and his followers, but in 625 at the battle of Uhud the Muslims were defeated. Because Muhammad firmly believed that the will of God determines victory, the experience of defeat shook the faith of his followers. His opponents were unable to take advantage of their victory, however, and Muhammad soon restored faith in his followers and pressed forward.

In the year 627 Muhammad defeated a large Meccan army that attacked his party at Medina. In the same year he expelled a Jewish clan, al-Nadīr, from Medina on the grounds that it was conspiring against him, and he attacked and dispersed the Jewish clan of the Qurayzah on the same grounds. Although by 628 Muhammad and his followers were strong enough to enforce a truce with Mecca, his men soon were attacked by groups associated with Mecca, and as a result Muhammad gathered ten thousand men to attack Mecca.

When he arrived in 630, however, the city essentially gave up without a fight, and Muhammad triumphed. Most Meccans converted to Islam even though Muhammad did not make that a condition of surrender. Thereafter he sent messengers to other parts of the Middle East to encourage other nations to convert to Islam and to recognize the Muslims as a formidable power in the Arab world.

By the time he died, his movement had grown enormously. Islam was destined to spread throughout the entire Arab world and beyond, rapidly becoming one of the world's largest religions.

The Rhetoric of the Koran

The Koran was composed in prose but with rhymes that were sometimes very close and sometimes rather distant. According to Arab scholars, there is no adequate way to translate the Koran, and therefore the English version that follows, like all non-Arabic versions, must be regarded as a paraphrase rather than a strict translation. The beauty of the original Arabic often depends on the sounds of words and their association with the words' meaning. But it also depends on the subtlety of possible interpretations resulting from purposeful ambiguities designed to produce a richly significant text. Many of these qualities are lost in English.

On the other hand, the sense that this is a text from a holy book is plain in terms of its resemblance to the Bible. Muhammad was aware of the Jewish Bible and the Christian New Testament. He also was aware that in the Koran the Muslims now had their own holy book. The Koran consists of 114 surahs, or chapters. The names of the surahs usually relate to a detail in the surah or to the subject of the surah. Examples are "The Ant," surah 27; "Smoke," surah 44; "The Hypocrites," surah 63; "The Soul-Snatchers," surah 79. "The Believer" is surah 40 and is also sometimes called "The Forgiving One." The order of the surahs is not chronological but traditional. The order of composition is uncertain, although surah 93, "Daylight," is sometimes cited as the first.

"The Believer" begins with an untranslatable Arabic letter: *Hā' mīm*. The Koran contains several such expressions that are undefinable. N. J. Dawood, the translator, says that "Traditional commentators dismiss them by saying 'God alone knows what He means by these letters.'" The surah opens by telling us that it is "revealed by God" and then goes on to explain the fate of unbelievers.

God speaks directly to Muhammad, usually speaking as "we" but sometimes shifting to "I" or "he." The shifting point of view may imply the all-inclusive nature of God. The use of dialogue is characteristic of the text, but narrative is also introduced early on. The story of Moses (paras. 13–32) demonstrates how God sends his messages to the world and how believers will respond to those messages. Noah (para. 3) was a believer who built the ark in response to the word he received from God. The willingness of unbelievers to be violent toward him is an important detail, just as is Pharaoh's willingness to slay infants and children in order to "slay Moses" (para. 15).

For religious purposes, the most important rhetorical quality of the text is its use of declarations such as "He reveals to you His signs" (para. 53), coupled with questions to the listener such as "Which of God's signs do you deny?" (para. 53). This method involves the listener in an active role while also imparting the truth. Jewish and Christian wisdom books also used these techniques, in particular interspersing rhetorical questions to keep the listener alert to the need to eventually answer to his God.

"The Believer" is especially important because it contrasts those who believe in Allah with those who believe in idols. It is said that when Muhammad returned triumphantly to Mecca, he entered the Ka'bah, approached each of the more than one hundred idols, and reached from his camel with his stick to knock over each idol as he said, "The truth has come." "The Believer" is about the truth that has come; it describes the necessity of faith in a God who supplants all idols and all others.

PREREADING QUESTIONS:
WHAT TO READ FOR

The following prereading questions may help you anticipate key issues in the discussion on the excerpt that follows from the Koran. Keeping them in mind during your first reading of the selection should help focus your reactions.

- What are some of the characteristics of the believer?
- What does the believer believe in?
- What are the qualities of God?

From the Koran

The Believer

In the Name of God, the Compassionate, the Merciful

Hā' mīm. This Book is revealed by God, the Mighty One, the 1
All-knowing, who forgives sin and accepts repentance.

His punishment is stern, and His bounty infinite. There is no 2
god but Him. All shall return to Him.

None but the unbelievers dispute the revelations of God. Do not 3
be deceived by their prosperous dealings in the land. Long before
them the people of Noah denied Our revelations, and so did the factions after them. Every nation strove to slay their apostle, seeking
with false arguments to refute the truth; but I smote them, and how
stern was My punishment! Thus shall the word of your Lord be fulfilled concerning the unbelievers: they are the heirs of the Fire.

Those who bear the Throne and those who stand around it give 4
glory to their Lord and believe in Him. They implore forgiveness for
the faithful, saying: "Lord, you embrace all things with Your mercy
and Your knowledge. Forgive those that repent and follow Your
path. Shield them from the scourge of Hell. Admit them, Lord, to
the gardens of Eden which You have promised them, together with
all the righteous among their fathers, their spouses, and their descendants. You are the Almighty, the Wise One. Deliver them from
all evil. He whom You will deliver from evil on that day will surely
earn Your mercy. That is the supreme triumph."

But to the unbelievers a voice will cry: "God's abhorrence of you 5
is greater than your hatred of yourselves. You were called to the
Faith, but you denied it."

They shall say: "Lord, twice have You made us die, and twice have 6
You given us life. We now confess our sins. Is there no way out?"

They shall be answered: "This is because when God was in- 7
voked alone, you disbelieved; but when you were bidden to serve
other gods besides Him you believed in them. Today judgement
rests with God, the Most High, the Supreme One."

It is He who reveals His signs to you, and sends down suste- 8
nance from the sky for you. Yet none takes heed except the repen-
tant. Pray, then, to God and worship none but Him, however much
the unbelievers may dislike it.

Exalted and throned on high, He lets the Spirit descend at His 9
behest on those of His servants whom He chooses, that He may
warn them of the day when they shall meet Him; the day when they

shall rise up from their graves with nothing hidden from God. And who shall reign supreme on that day? God, the One, the Almighty.

On that day every soul shall be paid back according to what it did. On that day none shall be wronged. Swift is God's reckoning. 10

Forewarn them of the approaching day, when men's hearts will leap up to their throats and choke them; when the wrongdoers will have neither friend nor intercessor to be heard. He knows the furtive look and the secret thought. God will judge with fairness, but the idols to which they pray besides Him can judge nothing. God alone hears all and observes all. 11

Have they never journeyed through the land and seen what was the end of those who have gone before them, nations far greater in prowess and in splendour? God scourged them for their sins, and from God they had none to protect them. That was because their apostles had come to them with clear revelations and they denied them. So God smote them. Mighty is God, and stern His retribution. 12

We sent forth Moses with Our signs and with clear authority to Pharaoh, Haman, and Korah. But they said: "A sorcerer, a teller of lies." 13

And when he brought them the Truth from Ourself, they said: "Put to death the sons of those who share his faith, and spare only their daughters." Futile were the schemes of the unbelievers. 14

Pharaoh said: "Let me slay Moses, and then let him invoke his god! I fear that he will change your religion and spread disorder in the land." 15

Moses said: "I take refuge in my Lord and in your Lord from every tyrant who denies the Day of Reckoning." 16

But one of Pharaoh's kinsmen, who in secret was a true believer, said: "Would you slay a man merely because he says: 'My Lord is God'? He has brought you evident signs from your Lord. If he is lying, may his lie be on his head; but if he is speaking the truth, a part at least of what he threatens will smite you. God does not guide the lying transgressor. Today you are the masters, my people, illustrious throughout the earth. But who will save us from the might of God when it bears down upon us?" 17

Pharaoh said: "I have told you what I think. I will surely guide you to the right path." 18

He who was a true believer said: "I warn you, my people, against the fate which overtook the factions: the people of Noah, 'Ād, and Thamūd, and those that came after them. God does not seek to wrong His servants. 19

"I warn you, my people, against the day when men will cry out to one another, when you will turn and flee, with none to defend 20 you against God. He whom God confounds shall have none to guide him. Long before this, Joseph came to you with veritable signs, but you never ceased to doubt them; and when he died you said: 'After him God will never send another apostle.' Thus God confounds the doubting transgressor. Those who dispute God's revelations, with no authority vouchsafed to them, are held in deep abhorrence by God and by the faithful. Thus God seals up the heart of every scornful tyrant."

Pharaoh said to Haman: "Build me a tower that I may reach the 21 highways—the very highways—of the heavens, and look upon the god of Moses. I am convinced that he is lying."

Thus was Pharaoh seduced by his foul deeds, and he was turned 22 away from the right path. Pharaoh's cunning led to nothing but perdition.

He who was a true believer said: "Follow me, my people, that I 23 may guide you to the right path. My people, the life of this world is a fleeting comfort, but the life to come is an everlasting mansion. Those that do evil shall be rewarded with like evil; but those that have faith and do good works, both men and women, shall enter the gardens of Paradise and therein receive blessings without number.

"My people, how is it that I call you to salvation, while you call 24 me to the Fire? You bid me deny God and serve other gods I know nothing of; while I exhort you to serve the Almighty, the Benignant One. Indeed, the gods to whom you call me can be invoked neither in this world nor in the hereafter. To God we shall return. The transgressors are the heirs of the Fire.

"Bear in mind what I have told you. To God I commend myself. 25 God is cognizant of all His servants."

God delivered him from the evils which they planned, and a 26 grievous scourge encompassed Pharaoh's people. They shall be brought before the Fire morning and evening, and on the day the Hour strikes, a voice will cry: "Mete out to the people of Pharaoh the sternest punishment!"

And when they argue in the Fire, the humble will say to those 27 who deemed themselves mighty: "We have been your followers: will you now ward off from us some of these flames?" But those who deemed themselves mighty will reply: "Here are all of us now. God has judged His servants."

And those in the Fire will say to the keepers of Hell: "Implore 28 your Lord to relieve our torment for one day!"

"But did your apostles not come to you with undoubted signs?" 29 they will ask.

"Yes," they will answer. And their keepers will say: "Then offer 30 your prayers." But vain shall be the prayers of the unbelievers.

We shall help Our apostles and the true believers both in this 31
world and on the day when the witnesses rise to testify. On that day
no excuse will avail the guilty. The Curse shall be their lot, and the
scourge of the hereafter.

We gave Moses Our guidance and the Israelites the Book[1] to in- 32
herit: a guide and an admonition to men of understanding. Therefore have patience; God's promise is surely true. Implore forgiveness
for your sins, and celebrate the praise of your Lord evening and
morning.

As for those who dispute the revelations of God, with no au- 33
thority vouchsafed to them, they nurture in their hearts ambitions
they shall never attain. Therefore seek refuge in God; it is He that
hears all and observes all.

Surely, the creation of the heavens and the earth is greater than 34
the creation of man; yet most men have no knowledge.

The blind and the seeing are not equal, nor are the wicked the 35
equal of those that have faith and do good works. Yet do you seldom
give thought.

The Hour of Doom is sure to come: of this there is no doubt; 36
and yet most men do not believe.

Your Lord has said: "Call on me and I will answer you. Those 37
that disdain My service shall enter Hell with all humility."

It was God who made for you the night to rest in and the day to 38
give you light. God is bountiful to men, yet most men do not give
thanks.

Such is God your Lord, the Creator of all things. There is no 39
god but Him. How then can you turn away from Him? Yet even thus
the men who deny God's revelations turn away from Him.

It is God who has made the earth a dwelling-place for you, and 40
the sky a ceiling. He has moulded your bodies into a comely shape
and provided you with good things.

Such is God, your Lord. Blessed be God, Lord of the Universe.   41

He is the Living One; there is no god but Him. Pray to Him, 42
then, and worship none besides Him. Praise be to God, Lord of the
Universe!

Say: "I am forbidden to serve your idols, now that clear proofs 43
have been given me from my Lord. I am commanded to surrender
myself to the Lord of the Universe."

It was He who created you from dust, then from a little germ, 44
and then from a clot of blood. He brings you infants into the world;
you reach manhood, then decline into old age (though some of you

---

[1] **The Book** The Bible.

die young), so that you may complete your appointed term and grow in wisdom.

It is He who ordains life and death. If He decrees a thing, He 45 need only say: "Be," and it is.

Do you not see how those who dispute the revelations of God 46 turn away from the right path? Those who have denied the Book and the message We sent through Our apostles shall realize the truth hereafter: when, with chains and shackles round their necks, they shall be dragged through scalding water and burnt in the fire of Hell.

They will be asked: "Where are the gods whom you have served 47 besides God?"

"They have forsaken us," they will reply. "Indeed, they were 48 nothing, those gods to whom we prayed." Thus God confounds the unbelievers.

And they will be told: "That is because on earth you took de- 49 light in falsehoods, and led a wanton life. Enter the gates of Hell and stay therein for ever. Evil is the home of the arrogant."

Therefore have patience: God's promise is surely true. Whether 50 We let you[2] glimpse in some measure the scourge We threaten them with, or call you back to Us before We smite them, to Us they shall return.

We sent forth other apostles before your time; of some We have 51 already told you, of others We have not yet told you. None of those apostles could bring a sign except by God's leave. And when God's will was done, justice prevailed and there and then the disbelievers lost.

It is God who has provided you with beasts, that you may ride 52 on some and eat the flesh of others. You put them to many uses; they take you where you wish to go, carrying you by land as ships carry you by sea.

He reveals to you His signs. Which of God's signs do you deny? 53

Have they never journeyed through the land and seen what was 54 the end of those who have gone before them? More numerous were they in the land, and far greater in prowess and in splendour; yet all their labours proved of no avail to them.

When their apostles brought them veritable signs they proudly 55 boasted of their own knowledge; but soon the scourge at which they scoffed encompassed them. And when they beheld Our might they said: "We now believe in God alone. We deny the idols which We served besides Him."

---

[2] Muḥammad. [Translator's note]

But their new faith was of no use to them, when they beheld   56
Our might: such being the way of God with His creatures; and there
and then the unbelievers lost.

QUESTIONS FOR CRITICAL READING

1. What are the characteristics of a believer?
2. To what extent are faith and belief the same? To what extent are they different?
3. What does the believer believe?
4. What does God promise to the believer?
5. How might one describe the tone of God's words in this surah?
6. Why is punishment meted out to people? What behavior deserves punishment?
7. What signs does God reveal to humanity?
8. What is the meaning of the sentence "Mighty is God, and stern his retribution" (para. 12)?

SUGGESTIONS FOR WRITING

1. According to this surah, what are the qualities of God? Choose specific passages that help you understand the qualities of God. See especially paragraphs 8 to 12. What are God's concerns? What are God's views about the world and the history that he describes?
2. What does God expect of men and women? Why does he speak so earnestly to Muhammad? What are God's views of humanity? Find passages that establish these concerns.
3. When Muhammad experienced these revelations, idol worship was common in Mecca. Is idol worship common in modern life? What might be considered our modern idols? Write an essay clarifying the nature of modern idol worship and contrasting that kind of worship with the belief that is promoted in this surah.
4. For Muhammad, what is the fate of unbelievers? Does their fate differ widely from the fate of unbelievers in your own religion? If you are not religious, compare the fate of the unbeliever in this surah with the fate of unbelievers in any religion that you know enough about to speak confidently on.
5. **CONNECTIONS** In paragraphs 23 to 25, "He who was a true believer" is described in action. In what ways does this description compare with Matthew's description of Jesus? The Koran refers often to Joseph and Mary as well as to Jesus, who is considered a prophet. Compare the portraits of Matthew's Jesus with the "true believer" in "The Believer."

6. **CONNECTIONS**   In the *Bhagavad Gītā* Lord Krishna reveals himself to Arjuna, and in "The Believer" Allah reveals himself to Muhammad. How are these portrayals of the Lord similar and different? What are his concerns for humanity? How does he view the nature of men and women?

FRIEDRICH NIETZSCHE
Apollonianism and Dionysianism

FRIEDRICH NIETZSCHE (1844–1900), one of the most influential modern thinkers, was concerned that the rise of science in the modern world and the changes in attitudes toward religion and the nature of God would leave people with a loss of purpose. Like many historians and philosophers of the day, he feared that modern civilization itself was somehow hanging in the balance, and that unless people struggled to reclaim the spiritual energy that brought progress and prosperity, the foundations of society would collapse.

His solution for the malaise that he felt was settling on modern society involved a search for meaning through a form of introspection and self-understanding that might well have been intelligible to Buddha, Plato, or St. Matthew. For Nietzsche, self-mastery was the key to transcending the confusion of modern thought. Realizing that self-domination was not an easy state to achieve, he called the man who succeeded in mastering himself "superman"—a man who could create his own values instead of blindly following conventional or societal standards.

Nietzsche's own personal life was difficult. His minister-father died when he was four years old, leaving Nietzsche to be raised in a household of women. Some critics have felt that the antifemale tone in certain of his writings is a result of his upbringing, but it also may be related to the syphilis that he may have contracted from a prostitute when he was a young man.

From *The Birth of Tragedy and the Genealogy of Morals.* Translated by Francis Golffing, 1956.

He was a brilliant student, particularly of the classics, and he became a professor at the University of Basel at a young age. His first book, *The Birth of Tragedy from the Spirit of Music* (1872), is the result of his effort to clarify certain aspects of the music of Richard Wagner, the contemporary composer who created a mythology depicting Scandinavian gods for his Ring Cycle of operas. Nietzsche eventually broke with Wagner on philosophical matters, but his regard for Wagner's music remained strong. The insight on which *The Birth of Tragedy* rests, presented in the selection reprinted here, is an attempt to clarify the two basic religious forces in humankind: Apollonian intellectuality and Dionysian passion. The first reflects the god Apollo, whose symbols were the bow and the lyre, implying his fierceness as a god of conscience combined with his love of the arts and music. The second reflects the god Dionysus, a deity associated with vegetation, plentifulness, passion, and especially wine. Both were sons of Zeus, and each represented extremes in behavior, whether religious or secular.

Both forces were present in ancient Greek society, which Nietzsche takes as a standard of high civilization, particularly in its Doric phase—a phase of clear, calm, beautiful works of religious expression, such as the Parthenon in Athens. Although Apollonian qualities appear to oppose Dionysian qualities, Nietzsche notes that the Greeks discovered the need for both forces to be present in their culture. Greek tragedy, he says, was the ground on which these forces were able to meet in ancient Greece. In Nietzsche's time—as he points out in a section not included here—they meet in the music of Richard Wagner.

The kinds of personal behavior countenanced by these two gods are quite different, but each god represents an aspect of the larger divinity. The rational qualities of Apollonianism approximate the ideals of Plato and Aristotle, whereas the ecstatic qualities of Dionysianism come closer to the views of some saints. The distinction between these two states of mind is considerable, but both are associated with artistic expression and religious practice throughout the world.

Nietzsche relies on art to help him clarify the distinction between each of these Greek gods. Apollo dominates intellectually. He demands clarity, order, reason, and calm. He is also the god of the individual. Dionysus, on the other hand, is the god of ecstasy and passion. Obscurity, disorder, irrational behavior, even hysteria are encouraged by Dionysus. He is the god of throngs and mobs. After reading this excerpt, we can realize that most of us have both capacities within us and that one of life's challenges is learning how to balance them.

Nietzsche's Rhetoric

The most obvious rhetorical device Nietzsche uses is comparison and contrast. The Apollonian contrasts with the Dionysian, the Greek with the barbarian, the dream with the illusion, the god with the human, the individual with the group, the one with the many, even life with death. In this sense, the subject at hand has governed the basic shape of the work.

Nietzsche's task was to explain the polarities, their form of expression, and their effect. Because these terms were quite new to most contemporary readers, he took time to clarify the nature of the *Apollonian* and the *Dionysian*. In a sense, the first paragraphs are spent in the task of definition. Once each polarity is defined, Nietzsche goes on to explain its sphere of influence, its nature, and its implications. Insofar as those qualities are present in the rhetoric, this essay is itself Apollonian.

There is a surprise in Nietzsche's use of rhetoric here, however. Through rhetorical techniques, he also illustrates some aspects of the Dionysian nature. There are passages in the selection, such as the discussion of Dionysus in paragraph 5, that can best be described as ecstatic, poetic, and if not irrational, certainly obscure and difficult to grasp. The Dionysian aspects of the passage are based on feeling. We all know that some poems cannot be broken down into other words—or even explained to others. What we extract from such poems is not an understanding but a complex feeling or impression. The same is true of the passages we confront in this essay. They challenge us because we know that the general character of any essay must be Apollonian. When we are greeted by Dionysian verbal excursions, we are thrown off. Yet that is part of Nietzsche's point: verbal artifacts (such as Greek tragedy) can combine both forces.

Nietzsche's most important point may be that the original religious forces implied by both gods are expressed in the modern world in terms of art. It has become something of a commonplace for contemporary people to assert that the emotion that went into religion in the time of the Greeks or in the great age of the cathedrals in Europe is now expressed in art. The power of Wagnerian music and Wagnerian opera, whose shape borrows some aspects from Greek tragedy, would have been as much a religious experience as an aesthetic experience for many people. Apollo was the god around whom the muses gathered, and therefore he was a caretaker of music, poetry, and dance. Dionysus was the god to whom the citizens of Athens sacrificed when they put on their great tragic competitions. The City Dionysia was the most important of the celebrations involving Greek drama, and its god was Dionysus.

If it can be said that religious faith can be embodied in dramatic art, then it might be said that for the ancients it was present in the work of the Greek tragedians, for the Elizabethans it was present in Shakespeare, and for Nietzsche's contemporaries it was in Wagner's Ring Cycle. The ultimate effect of using the rhetorical device of comparison and contrast is to emphasize the need for these two forces to be unified in the highest cultures. Diversity is everywhere in nature, as Nietzsche implies throughout, but that diversity has one deep longing: to be one with the One. As he explains (para. 14), the eternal goal of the original Oneness is its redemption through illusion. Illusion is art, not just dream. Great artists of all ages understood that dream and illusion are the means of art and make accessible the inner nature of humanity.

PREREADING QUESTIONS: WHAT TO READ FOR

The following prereading questions may help you anticipate key issues in the discussion on Friedrich Nietzsche's "Apollonianism and Dionysianism." Keeping them in mind during your first reading of the selection should help focus your reactions.

• How does Apollonianism differ from Dionysianism?
• How is Apollonian or Dionysian behavior related to religion?

Apollonianism and Dionysianism

Much will have been gained for esthetics once we have succeeded   1
in apprehending directly—rather than merely *ascertaining*—that art owes its continuous evolution to the Apollonian-Dionysiac duality, even as the propagation of the species depends on the duality of the sexes, their constant conflicts and periodic acts of reconciliation. I have borrowed my adjectives from the Greeks, who developed their mystical doctrines of art through plausible *embodiments*, not through purely conceptual means. It is by those two art-sponsoring deities,

Apollo and Dionysos,[1] that we are made to recognize the tremendous split, as regards both origins and objectives, between the plastic, Apollonian arts and the non-visual art of music inspired by Dionysos. The two creative tendencies developed alongside one another, usually in fierce opposition, each by its taunts forcing the other to more energetic production, both perpetuating in a discordant concord that agon[2] which the term *art* but feebly denominates: until at last, by the thaumaturgy[3] of an Hellenic art of will, the pair accepted the yoke of marriage and, in this condition, begot Attic tragedy,[4] which exhibits the salient features of both parents.

To reach a closer understanding of both these tendencies, let us 2 begin by viewing them as the separate art realms of *dream* and *intoxication,* two physiological phenomena standing toward one another in much the same relationship as the Apollonian and Dionysiac. It was in a dream, according to Lucretius,[5] that the marvelous gods and goddesses first presented themselves to the minds of men. That great healing sculptor, Phidias,[6] beheld in a dream the entrancing bodies of more-than-human beings, and likewise, if anyone had asked the Greek poets about the mystery of poetic creation, they too would have referred him to dreams and instructed him much as Hans Sachs[7] instructs us in *Die Meistersinger:*

> My friend, it is the poet's work
> Dreams to interpret and to mark.
> Believe me that man's true conceit
> In a dream becomes complete:
> All poetry we ever read
> Is but true dreams interpreted.

The fair illusion of the dream sphere, in the production of 3 which every man proves himself an accomplished artist, is a

---

[1] **Apollo and Dionysos (Dionysus)** Apollo is the god of music, healing, and archery, and, as Phoebus Apollo, is also regarded as the god of light. Dionysus is the god of wine and drunkenness.

[2] **agon** A contest or opposition of forces.

[3] **thaumaturgy** A magical change. Nietzsche means that a powerful transformation was needed for Apollo and Dionysus to be able to join together.

[4] **Attic tragedy** Greek tragedy performed in Athens, in the Greek region of Attica, sixth century to fourth century B.C.

[5] **Lucretius (100?–55 B.C.)** A Roman philosopher whose book on natural science was standard for more than a millennium.

[6] **Phidias (fl. 430 B.C.)** Greek sculptor who carved the figures of the gods and goddesses on the Parthenon.

[7] **Hans Sachs** The legendary singer-hero of Richard Wagner's opera *Die Meistersinger von Nürnberg;* the lines quoted are from that opera.

precondition not only of all plastic art, but even, as we shall see presently, of a wide range of poetry. Here we enjoy an immediate apprehension of form, all shapes speak to us directly, nothing seems indifferent or redundant. Despite the high intensity with which these dream realities exist for us, we still have a residual sensation that they are illusions; at least such has been my experience—and the frequency, not to say normality, of the experience is borne out in many passages of the poets. Men of philosophical disposition are known for their constant premonition that our everyday reality, too, is an illusion, hiding another, totally different kind of reality. It was Schopenhauer[8] who considered the ability to view at certain times all men and things as mere phantoms or dream images to be the true mark of philosophic talent. The person who is responsive to the stimuli of art behaves toward the reality of dream much the way the philosopher behaves toward the reality of existence: he observes exactly and enjoys his observations, for it is by these images that he interprets life, by these processes that he rehearses it. Nor is it by pleasant images only that such plausible connections are made: the whole divine comedy of life, including its somber aspects, its sudden balkings, impish accidents, anxious expectations, moves past him, not quite like a shadow play—for it is he himself, after all, who lives and suffers through these scenes—yet never without giving a fleeting sense of illusion; and I imagine that many persons have reassured themselves amidst the perils of dream by calling out, "It is a dream! I want it to go on." I have even heard of people spinning out the causality of one and the same dream over three or more successive nights. All these facts clearly bear witness that our innermost being, the common substratum of humanity, experiences dreams with deep delight and a sense of real necessity. This deep and happy sense of the necessity of dream experiences was expressed by the Greeks in the image of Apollo. Apollo is at once the god of all plastic powers[9] and the soothsaying god. He who is etymologically the "lucent" one, the god of light, reigns also over the fair illusions of our inner world of fantasy. The perfection of these conditions in contrast to our imperfectly understood waking reality, as well as our profound awareness of nature's healing powers during the interval of sleep and dream, furnishes a symbolic analogue to the soothsaying faculty and quite generally to the arts, which make life possible and

---

[8] **Arthur Schopenhauer (1788–1860)** German philosopher who influenced Nietzsche. His books, *The World as Will and Idea* (1819) and *On the Will in Nature* (1836; tr. 1889), emphasized the power of free will as a chief force in the world.

[9] **plastic powers** Apollo is associated with the arts, which are plastic in that they reshape reality and foster imagination.

worth living. But the image of Apollo must incorporate that thin line which the dream image may not cross, under penalty of becoming pathological, of imposing itself on us as crass reality: a discreet limitation, a freedom from all extravagant urges, the sapient tranquility of the plastic god. His eye must be sunlike, in keeping with his origin. Even at those moments when he is angry and ill-tempered there lies upon him the consecration of fair illusion. In an eccentric way one might say of Apollo what Schopenhauer says, in the first part of *The World as Will and Idea,* of man caught in the veil of Maya:[10] "Even as on an immense, raging sea, assailed by huge wave crests, a man sits in a little rowboat trusting his frail craft, so, amidst the furious torments of this world, the individual sits tranquilly, supported by the *principium individuationis*[11] and relying on it." One might say that the unshakable confidence in that principle has received its most magnificent expression in Apollo, and that Apollo himself may be regarded as the marvelous divine image of the *principium individuationis,* whose looks and gestures radiate the full delight, wisdom, and beauty of "illusion."

In the same context Schopenhauer has described for us the tremendous awe which seizes man when he suddenly begins to doubt the cognitive modes of experience, in other words, when in a given instance the law of causation seems to suspend itself. If we add to this awe the glorious transport which arises in man, even from the very depths of nature, at the shattering of the *principium individuationis,* then we are in a position to apprehend the essence of Dionysiac rapture, whose closest analogy is furnished by physical intoxication. Dionysiac stirrings arise either through the influence of those narcotic potions of which all primitive races speak in their hymns, or through the powerful approach of spring, which penetrates with joy the whole frame of nature. So stirred, the individual forgets himself completely. It is the same Dionysiac power which in medieval Germany drove ever increasing crowds of people singing and dancing from place to place; we recognize in these St. John's and St. Vitus' dancers the bacchic choruses[12] of the Greeks, who had their precursors in Asia Minor and as far back as Babylon and the

---

[10] **Maya** A Hindu term for the delusion of the senses by the material world. The veil of Maya is the illusion hiding the reality that lies beneath material surfaces.

[11] *principium individuationis* The principle of the individual, as apart from the crowd.

[12] **bacchic choruses** Bacchus was the god of wine and ecstasy (a variant of Dionysus); thus, this term means ecstatic choruses. The St. John's and St. Vitus's dancers were ecstatic Christian dancers of the Middle Ages. Their dance was a mania that spread to a number of major religious centers.

orgiastic Sacaea.[13] There are people who, either from lack of experience or out of sheer stupidity, turn away from such phenomena, and, strong in the sense of their own sanity, label them either mockingly or pityingly "endemic diseases." These benighted souls have no idea how cadaverous and ghostly their "sanity" appears as the intense throng of Dionysiac revelers sweeps past them.

Not only does the bond between man and man come to be forged   5
once more by the magic of the Dionysiac rite, but nature itself, long alienated or subjugated, rises again to celebrate the reconciliation with her prodigal son, man. The earth offers its gifts voluntarily, and the savage beasts of mountain and desert approach in peace. The chariot of Dionysos is bedecked with flowers and garlands; panthers and tigers stride beneath his yoke. If one were to convert Beethoven's "Paean to Joy"[14] into a painting and refuse to curb the imagination when that multitude prostrates itself reverently in the dust, one might form some apprehension of Dionysiac ritual. Now the slave emerges as a freeman; all the rigid, hostile walls which either necessity or despotism has erected between men are shattered. Now that the gospel or universal harmony is sounded, each individual becomes not only reconciled to his fellow but actually at one with him — as though the veil of Maya had been torn apart and there remained only shreds floating before the vision of mystical Oneness. Man now expresses himself through song and dance as the member of a higher community; he has forgotten how to walk, how to speak, and is on the brink of taking wing as he dances. Each of his gestures betokens enchantment; through him sounds a supernatural power, the same power which makes the animals speak and the earth render up milk and honey. He feels himself to be godlike and strides with the same elation and ecstasy as the gods he has seen in his dreams. No longer the *artist,* he has himself become a *work of art:* the productive power of the whole universe is now manifest in his transport, to the glorious satisfaction of the primordial One. The finest clay, the most precious marble — man — is here kneaded and hewn, and the chisel blows of the Dionysiac world artist are accompanied by the cry of the Eleusinian mystagogues:[15] "Do you fall on your knees, multitudes, do you divine your creator?"

---

[13] **Sacaea** A Babylonian summer festival for the god Ishtar. The point is that such religious orgies are ancient.

[14] **"Paean to Joy"** This is Friedrich von Schiller's (1759–1805) poem, *Ode to Joy,* which Ludwig van Beethoven (1770–1827) set to music in the last movement of his Symphony no. 9 (*Choral*).

[15] **Eleusinian mystagogues** Those who participate in the ancient Greek Eleusinian secret ceremonies celebrating life after death.

So far we have examined the Apollonian and Dionysiac states as the product of formative forces arising directly from nature without the mediation of the human artist. At this stage artistic urges are satisfied directly, on the one hand through the imagery of dreams, whose perfection is quite independent of the intellectual rank, the artistic development of the individual; on the other hand, through an ecstatic reality which once again takes no account of the individual and may even destroy him, or else redeem him through a mystical experience of the collective. In relation to these immediate creative conditions of nature every artist must appear as "imitator," either as the Apollonian dream artist or the Dionysiac ecstatic artist, or, finally (as in Greek tragedy, for example) as dream and ecstatic artist in one. We might picture to ourselves how the last of these, in a state of Dionysiac intoxication and mystical self-abrogation,[16] wandering apart from the reveling throng, sinks upon the ground, and how there is then revealed to him his own condition — complete oneness with the essence of the universe — in a dream similitude.

Having set down these general premises and distinctions, we now turn to the Greeks in order to realize to what degree the formative forces of nature were developed in them. Such an inquiry will enable us to assess properly the relation of the Greek artist to his prototypes or, to use Aristotle's expression, his "imitation of nature."[17] Of the dreams the Greeks dreamed it is not possible to speak with any certainty, despite the extant dream literature and the large number of dream anecdotes. But considering the incredible accuracy of their eyes, their keen and unabashed delight in colors, one can hardly be wrong in assuming that their dreams too showed a strict consequence of lines and contours, hues and groupings, a progression of scenes similar to their best bas-reliefs.[18] The perfection of these dream scenes might almost tempt us to consider the dreaming Greek as a Homer and Homer as a dreaming Greek; which would be as though the modern man were to compare himself in his dreaming to Shakespeare.

Yet there is another point about which we do not have to conjecture at all: I mean the profound gap separating the Dionysiac

[16] **self-abrogation** The reveler "loses" his self, his sense of being an individual apart from the throng.

[17] **"imitation of nature"** A key term in Aristotle's theory of *mimesis*, the doctrine that art imitates nature and that the artist must observe nature carefully. Nietzsche emphasizes dreams as a part of nature and something to be closely observed by the artist.

[18] **bas-reliefs** Sculptures projecting only slightly from a flat surface; they usually tell a story in a series of scenes.

Greeks from the Dionysiac barbarians. Throughout the range of ancient civilization (leaving the newer civilizations out of account for the moment) we find evidence of Dionysiac celebrations which stand to the Greek type in much the same relation as the bearded satyr,[19] whose name and attributes are derived from the he-goat, stands to the god Dionysos. The central concern of such celebrations was, almost universally, a complete sexual promiscuity overriding every form of established tribal law; all the savage urges of the mind were unleashed on those occasions until they reached that paroxysm of lust and cruelty which has always struck me as the "witches' cauldron" *par excellence*. It would appear that the Greeks were for a while quite immune from these feverish excesses which must have reached them by every known land or sea route. What kept Greece safe was the proud, imposing image of Apollo, who in holding up the head of the Gorgon[20] to those brutal and grotesque Dionysiac forces subdued them. Doric art has immortalized Apollo's majestic rejection of all license. But resistance became difficult, even impossible, as soon as similar urges began to break forth from the deep substratum of Hellenism itself. Soon the function of the Delphic god[21] developed into something quite different and much more limited: all he could hope to accomplish now was to wrest the destructive weapon, by a timely gesture of pacification, from his opponent's hand. That act of pacification represents the most important event in the history of Greek ritual, every department of life now shows symptoms of a revolutionary change. The two great antagonists have been reconciled. Each feels obliged henceforth to keep to his bounds, each will honor the other by the bestowal of periodic gifts, while the cleavage remains fundamentally the same. And yet, if we examine what happened to the Dionysiac powers under the pressure of that treaty we notice a great difference: in the place of the Babylonian Sacaea, with their throwback of men to the condition of apes and tigers, we now see entirely new rites celebrated: rites of universal redemption, of glorious transfiguration. Only now has it become possible to speak of nature's celebrating an *esthetic* triumph; only

---

[19] **satyr** Greek god, half man, half goat; a symbol of lechery.

[20] **Gorgon** Powerful monster in Greek mythology with serpents for hair. There were three Gorgons, all sisters, but only Medusa was not immortal. With the help of the goddess Athena, Perseus beheaded Medusa, whose very glance was supposed to turn men to stone. Later Perseus vanquished his enemies by exposing the head to them and turning them to stone.

[21] **Delphic god** Apollo. The oracle at the temple to Apollo at Delphi, in Greece, was for more than one thousand years a source of prophecies of the future. It was among the most sacred places in Greece.

now has the abrogation of the *principium individuationis* become an esthetic event. That terrible witches' brew concocted of lust and cruelty has lost all power under the new conditions. Yet the peculiar blending of emotions in the heart of the Dionysiac reveler—his ambiguity if you will—seems still to hark back (as the medicinal drug harks back to the deadly poison) to the days when the infliction of pain was experienced as joy while a sense of supreme triumph elicited cries of anguish from the heart. For now in every exuberant joy there is heard an undertone of terror, or else a wistful lament over an irrecoverable loss. It is as though in these Greek festivals a sentimental trait of nature were coming to the fore, as though nature were bemoaning the fact of her fragmentation, her decomposition into separate individuals. The chants and gestures of these revelers, so ambiguous in their motivation, represented an absolute *novum*[22] in the world of the Homeric Greeks; their Dionysiac music, in especial, spread abroad terror and a deep shudder. It is true: music had long been familiar to the Greeks as an Apollonian art, as a regular beat like that of waves lapping the shore, a plastic rhythm[23] expressly developed for the portrayal of Apollonian conditions. Apollo's music was a Doric architecture of sound—of barely hinted sounds such as are proper to the cithara.[24] Those very elements which characterize Dionysiac music and, after it, music quite generally: the heart-shaking power of tone, the uniform stream of melody, the incomparable resources of harmony—all those elements had been carefully kept at a distance as being inconsonant with the Apollonian norm. In the Dionysiac dithyramb[25] man is incited to strain his symbolic faculties to the utmost; something quite unheard of is now clamoring to be heard: the desire to tear asunder the veil of Maya, to sink back into the original oneness of nature; the desire to express the very essence of nature symbolically. Thus an entirely new set of symbols springs into being. First, all the symbols pertaining to physical features: mouth, face, the spoken word, the dance movement which coordinates the limbs and bends them to its rhythm. Then suddenly all the rest of the symbolic forces—music and rhythm as such, dynamics, harmony—assert themselves with great energy. In order to comprehend this total emancipation of all

---

[22] **an absolute *novum*** A genuine novelty.

[23] **plastic rhythm** Plastic in this sense means capable of being shaped, responsive to slight changes—not rigid.

[24] **cithara** An ancient stringed instrument, similar to the lyre, used to accompany songs and recitations.

[25] **Dionysiac dithyramb** A passionate hymn to Dionysus, usually delivered by a chorus.

the symbolic powers one must have reached the same measure of inner freedom those powers themselves were making manifest; which is to say that the votary of Dionysos[26] could not be understood except by his own kind. It is not difficult to imagine the awed surprise with which the Apollonian Greek must have looked on him. And that surprise would be further increased as the latter realized, with a shudder, that all this was not so alien to him after all, that his Apollonian consciousness was but a thin veil hiding from him the whole Dionysiac realm.

In order to comprehend this we must take down the elaborate   9
edifice of Apollonian culture stone by stone until we discover its foundations. At first the eye is struck by the marvelous shapes of the Olympian gods who stand upon its pediments, and whose exploits, in shining bas-relief, adorn its friezes. The fact that among them we find Apollo as one god among many, making no claim to a privileged position, should not mislead us. The same drive that found its most complete representation in Apollo generated the whole Olympian world, and in this sense we may consider Apollo the father of that world. But what was the radical need out of which that illustrious society of Olympian beings sprang?

Whoever approaches the Olympians with a different religion in   10
his heart, seeking moral elevation, sanctity, spirituality, loving-kindness, will presently be forced to turn away from them in ill-humored disappointment. Nothing in these deities reminds us of asceticism, high intellect, or duty: we are confronted by luxuriant, triumphant *existence,* which defies the good and the bad indifferently. And the beholder may find himself dismayed in the presence of such overflowing life and ask himself what potion these heady people must have drunk in order to behold, in whatever direction they looked, Helen[27] laughing back at them, the beguiling image of their own existence. But we shall call out to this beholder, who has already turned his back: Don't go! Listen first to what the Greeks themselves have to say of this life, which spreads itself before you with such puzzling serenity. An old legend has it that King Midas[28]

---

[26] **votary of Dionysos** A follower of Dionysus; one devoted to Dionysian ecstasy.

[27] **Helen** The runaway wife of Menelaus, immortalized in Homer's *Iliad* as the cause of the ten-year Trojan War. She was not "good" or ascetic, but her intensity of living secured her a permanent place in history and myth.

[28] **King Midas** Midas was a foolish king who kidnapped Silenus, a satyr (half man, half goat) who was a companion of Dionysus. Silenus, a daemon or spirit, granted Midas his wish to have everything he touched turn to gold. Because his food turned to gold, he almost died. Dionysus eventually saved him by bathing him in a sacred river.

hunted a long time in the woods for the wise Silenus, companion of Dionysos, without being able to catch him. When he had finally caught him the king asked him what he considered man's greatest good. The daemon remained sullen and uncommunicative until finally, forced by the king, he broke into a shrill laugh and spoke: "Ephemeral wretch, begotten by accident and toil, why do you force me to tell you what it would be your greatest boon not to hear? What would be best for you is quite beyond your reach: not to have been born, not to *be,* to be *nothing.* But the second best is to die soon."

What is the relation of the Olympian gods to this popular wisdom? It is that of the entranced vision of the martyr to his torment.   11

Now the Olympian magic mountain opens itself before us,   12 showing us its very roots. The Greeks were keenly aware of the terrors and horrors of existence; in order to be able to live at all they had to place before them the shining fantasy of the Olympians. Their tremendous distrust of the titanic forces of nature: *Moira,*[29] mercilessly enthroned beyond the knowable world; the vulture which fed upon the great philanthropist Prometheus;[30] the terrible lot drawn by wise Oedipus; the curse on the house of Atreus which brought Orestes to the murder of his mother: that whole Panic philosophy,[31] in short, with its mythic examples, by which the gloomy Etruscans perished, the Greeks conquered—or at least hid from view—again and again by means of this artificial Olympus. In order to live at all the Greeks had to construct these deities. The Apollonian need for beauty had to develop the Olympian hierarchy of joy by slow degrees from the original titanic hierarchy of terror, as roses are seen to break from a thorny thicket. How else could life have been borne by a race so hypersensitive, so emotionally intense, so equipped for suffering? The same drive which called art into being as a completion and consummation of existence, and as a guarantee of further existence, gave rise also to that Olympian realm which acted as a transfiguring mirror to the Hellenic will. The gods justified human life by living it themselves—the only satisfactory theodicy[32] ever invented. To exist in the clear sunlight of such deities was now felt to be the highest good, and the only real grief suffered by

---

[29] **Moira** Fate personified; the figure who gives each person his or her fate.

[30] **Prometheus** The god who gave men fire—thus, his generosity is philanthropy, the love of man. He was punished by the gods.

[31] **Panic philosophy** Belief in fate. Oedipus's fate was to murder his father and marry his mother. He tried to escape it but could not. Orestes murdered his mother, Clytemnestra, because she had murdered his father, Agamemnon. All of these were members of the cursed house of Atreus and provide examples of how fate works.

[32] **theodicy** Examination of the question of whether the gods are just. Because the gods shared human life, they ennobled it; they suffered evil as well.

Homeric man was inspired by the thought of leaving that sunlight, especially when the departure seemed imminent. Now it became possible to stand the wisdom of Silenus on its head and proclaim that it was the worst evil for man to die soon, and second worst for him to die at all. Such laments as arise now arise over short-lived Achilles,[33] over the generations ephemeral as leaves, the decline of the heroic age. It is not unbecoming to even the greatest hero to yearn for an afterlife, though it be as a day laborer. So impetuously, during the Apollonian phase, does man's will desire to remain on earth, so identified does he become with existence, that even his lament turns to a song of praise.

It should have become apparent by now that the harmony with   13
nature which we late-comers regard with such nostalgia, and for which Schiller has coined the cant term naïve,[34] is by no means a simple and inevitable condition to be found at the gateway to every culture, a kind of paradise. Such a belief could have been endorsed only by a period for which Rousseau's Émile was an artist and Homer just such an artist nurtured in the bosom of nature. Whenever we encounter "naïveté" in art, we are face to face with the ripest fruit of Apollonian culture—which must always triumph first over titans, kill monsters, and overcome the somber contemplation of actuality, the intense susceptibility to suffering, by means of illusions strenuously and zestfully entertained. But how rare are the instances of true naïveté, of that complete identification with the beauty of appearance! It is this achievement which makes Homer so magnificent—Homer, who, as a single individual, stood to Apollonian popular culture in the same relation as the individual dream artist to the oneiric[35] capacity of a race and of nature generally. The naïveté of Homer must be viewed as a complete victory of Apollonian illusion. Nature often uses illusions of this sort in order to accomplish its secret purposes. The true goal is covered over by a phantasm. We stretch out our hands to the latter, while nature, aided by our deception, attains the former. In the case of the Greeks it was the will wishing to behold itself in the work of art, in the transcendence of

---

[33] **short-lived Achilles** Achilles' fate was to lead the Greeks to victory at Troy but to die by an arrow shot by Paris, who had taken Helen to Troy. Apollo guided the arrow so that it hit Achilles in the heel, his one vulnerable spot. Achilles, like many heroes, lived a brief but intense life.

[34] **naïve** Friedrich Schiller's (1759–1805) *On the Naïve and the Sentimental in Poetry* (1795–1796) contrasted the classic (naïve) with the romantic (sentimental) in art. It is not the same as Nietzsche's distinction, but it is similar. Nietzsche uses naïve to refer to a kind of classical purity and temper.

[35] **oneiric** Pertaining to dreams.

genius; but in order so to behold itself its creatures had first to view themselves as glorious, to transpose themselves to a higher sphere, without having that sphere of pure contemplation either challenge them or upbraid them with insufficiency. It was in that sphere of beauty that the Greeks saw the Olympians as their mirror images; it was by means of that esthetic mirror that the Greek will opposed suffering and the somber wisdom of suffering which always accompanies artistic talent. As a monument to its victory stands Homer, the naïve artist.

We can learn something about that naïve artist through the analogy of dream. We can imagine the dreamer as he calls out to himself, still caught in the illusion of his dream and without disturbing it, "This is a dream, and I want to go on dreaming," and we can infer, on the one hand, that he takes deep delight in the contemplation of his dream, and, on the other, that he must have forgotten the day, with its horrible importunity, so to enjoy his dream. Apollo, the interpreter of dreams, will furnish the clue to what is happening here. Although of the two halves of life—the waking and the dreaming—the former is generally considered not only the more important but the only one which is truly lived, I would, at the risk of sounding paradoxical, propose the opposite view. The more I have come to realize in nature those omnipotent formative tendencies and, with them, an intense longing for illusion, the more I feel inclined to the hypothesis that the original Oneness, the ground of Being, ever-suffering and contradictory, time and again has need of rapt vision and delightful illusion to redeem itself. Since we ourselves are the very stuff of such illusions, we must view ourselves as the truly non-existent, that is to say, as a perpetual unfolding in time, space, and causality—what we label "empiric reality."[36] But if, for the moment, we abstract from our own reality, viewing our empiric existence, as well as the existence of the world at large, as the *idea* of the original Oneness, produced anew each instant, then our dreams will appear to us as illusions of illusions, hence as a still higher form of satisfaction of the original desire for illusion. It is for this reason that the very core of nature takes such a deep delight in the naïve artist and the naïve work of art, which likewise is merely the illusion of an illusion. Raphael,[37] himself one of those immortal "naïve" artists, in a symbolic canvas has illustrated that reduction of illusion to further illusion which is the original act of the

14

---

[36] **"empiric reality"** The reality we can test by experience.

[37] **Raphael (1483–1520)** A Renaissance artist. Raphael was influenced by classical forms, but his work became progressively more humanistic, in some cases tending to Schiller's "sentimental." *Transfiguration* (1517–1520), his last painting, points to the new age of Baroque painting: an intense, emotional, ecstatic style.

naïve artist and at the same time of all Apollonian culture. In the lower half of his "Transfiguration," through the figures of the possessed boy, the despairing bearers, the helpless, terrified disciples, we see a reflection of original pain, the sole ground of being: "illusion" here is a reflection of eternal contradiction, begetter of all things. From this illusion there rises, like the fragrance of ambrosia, a new illusory world, invisible to those enmeshed in the first: a radiant vision of pure delight, a rapt seeing through wide-open eyes. Here we have, in a great symbol of art, both the fair world of Apollo and its substratum, the terrible wisdom of Silenus, and we can comprehend intuitively how they mutually require one another. But Apollo appears to us once again as the apotheosis[38] of the *principium individuationis,* in whom the eternal goal of the original Oneness, namely its redemption through illusion, accomplishes itself. With august gesture the god shows us how there is need for a whole world of torment in order for the individual to produce the redemptive vision and to sit quietly in his rocking rowboat in mid-sea, absorbed in contemplation.

If this apotheosis of individuation is to be read in nominative   15 terms, we may infer that there is one norm only: the individual — or, more precisely, the observance of the limits of the individual: *sophrosyne.*[39] As a moral deity Apollo demands self-control from his people and, in order to observe such self-control, a knowledge of self. And so we find that the esthetic necessity of beauty is accompanied by the imperatives, "Know thyself," and "Nothing too much." Conversely, excess and *hubris*[40] come to be regarded as the hostile spirits of the non-Apollonian sphere, hence as properties of the pre-Apollonian era — the age of Titans[41] — and the extra-Apollonian world, that is to say the world of the barbarians. It was because of his Titanic love of man that Prometheus had to be devoured by vultures; it was because of his extravagant wisdom which succeeded in solving the riddle of the Sphinx[42] that Oedipus had to be cast into a whirlpool of crime: in this fashion does the Delphic god interpret the Greek past.

---

[38] **apotheosis** Godlike embodiment. Nietzsche is saying that Apollo is the god in whom the concept of the individual is best expressed.

[39] *sophrosyne* Greek word for wisdom, moderation.

[40] *hubris* Greek word for pride, especially dangerous, defiant pride.

[41] **age of Titans** A reference to the gods who reigned before Zeus; an unenlightened, violent age.

[42] **riddle of the Sphinx** The sphinx, part woman and part beast, waited outside Thebes for years, killing all who tried to pass by but could not solve its riddle. Oedipus (see note 31) answered the riddle: "What walks on four legs in the morning, two legs in the day, and three legs in the evening?" The answer: man, who crawls in infancy, walks upright in his prime, and uses a cane in old age. The solution freed Thebes from its bondage to the Sphinx, but it brought Oedipus closer to his awful fate.

The effects of the Dionysiac spirit struck the Apollonian Greeks as titanic and barbaric; yet they could not disguise from themselves the fact that they were essentially akin to those deposed Titans and heroes. They felt more than that: their whole existence, with its temperate beauty, rested upon a base of suffering and *knowledge* which had been hidden from them until the reinstatement of Dionysos uncovered it once more. And lo and behold! Apollo found it impossible to live without Dionysos. The elements of titanism and barbarism turned out to be quite as fundamental as the Apollonian element. And now let us imagine how the ecstatic sounds of the Dionysiac rites penetrated ever more enticingly into that artificially restrained and discreet world of illusion, how this clamor expressed the whole outrageous gamut of nature—delight, grief, knowledge—even to the most piercing cry; and then let us imagine how the Apollonian artist with his thin, monotonous harp music must have sounded beside the demoniac chant of the multitude! The muses presiding over the illusory arts paled before an art which enthusiastically told the truth, and the wisdom of Silenus cried "Woe!" against the serene Olympians. The individual, with his limits and moderations, forgot himself in the Dionysiac vortex and became oblivious to the laws of Apollo. Indiscreet extravagance revealed itself as truth, and contradiction, a delight born of pain, spoke out of the bosom of nature. Wherever the Dionysiac voice was heard, the Apollonian norm seemed suspended or destroyed. Yet it is equally true that, in those places where the first assault was withstood, the prestige and majesty of the Delphic god appeared more rigid and threatening than before. The only way I am able to view Doric art and the Doric[43] state is as a perpetual military encampment of the Apollonian forces. An art so defiantly austere, so ringed about with fortifications—an education so military and exacting—a polity so ruthlessly cruel—could endure only in a continual state of resistance against the titanic and barbaric menace of Dionysos. 16

Up to this point I have developed at some length a theme which was sounded at the beginning of this essay: how the Dionysiac and Apollonian elements, in a continuous chain of creations, each enhancing the other, dominated the Hellenic mind: how from the Iron Age,[44] with its battles of Titans and its austere popular philosophy, there developed under the aegis of Apollo the Homeric world of beauty; how this "naïve" splendor was then absorbed once more by the Dionysiac torrent, and how, face to face with this new power, the Apollonian code rigidified into the majesty of Doric art and 17

---

[43] **Doric** The Doric styles were unadorned, clear, and intellectual rather than sensual. They represent purity and uprightness.

[44] **Iron Age** An earlier age, ruled by sterner, less humane gods, the Titans.

contemplation. If the earlier phase of Greek history may justly be broken down into four major artistic epochs dramatizing the battle between the two hostile principles, then we must inquire further (lest Doric art appear to us as the acme and final goal of all these striving tendencies) what was the true end toward which that evolution moved. And our eyes will come to rest on the sublime and much lauded achievement of the dramatic dithyramb and Attic tragedy, as the common goal of both urges; whose mysterious marriage, after long discord, ennobled itself with such a child, at once Antigone and Cassandra.[45]

QUESTIONS FOR CRITICAL READING

1. Define *Apollonianism* and *Dionysianism*. What kind of behavior does each word stand for?
2. What are the important distinctions between the self and the mob? Between dream and illusion?
3. In paragraph 6, Nietzsche speaks of the "mystical experience of the collective." What does he mean by this phrase? Is there such an experience?
4. Which paragraphs in the selection are most obscure and difficult to understand? How do they seem to show Dionysian qualities?
5. What contemporary art unifies the Apollonian and the Dionysian? Would Nietzsche have thought a modern film could do so?
6. Do the distinctions Nietzsche makes give you useful insights into religion or faith? If so, how?
7. What moral issues might the Apollonian person and the Dionysian person interpret differently?
8. For which of these polarities of behavior is self-control more likely a virtue?

SUGGESTIONS FOR WRITING

1. Examine paragraph 6 carefully. How valid are Nietzsche's insights concerning the self and the "reveling throng"? Drawing on personal experience, contrast the behavior of yourself or a friend—first as an indi-

---

[45] **Antigone and Cassandra** Children in Greek tragedies; Antigone, daughter of Oedipus, defied the authorities in *Antigone* by Sophocles (496?–406 B.C.) and suffered death; Cassandra, daughter of Priam, king of Troy, appears in Homer's *Iliad* and several tragedies by Aeschylus (525–456 B.C.) and Euripides (484?–406 B.C.). She had the gift of prophecy but was doomed never to be believed. She foresaw the destruction of Troy, and after its fall she was taken prisoner by Agamemnon and was killed with him. She and Antigone were both heroic in their suffering.

vidual and then as a member of a large gathering of people. Are you (or your friend) "possessed" when you are a member of such an assemblage? Be as specific as possible in writing about this contrast.

2. Establish a principle of moral behavior by which you feel the Apollonian can live. Then establish one for the Dionysian. Compare the two personalities to determine their differences and their similarities. How would the mental states represented by these polarities make their moral behavior different? On what would they agree? Is either of these polarities in danger of appearing immoral to people in general?

3. Music is the inspiration for this essay. Choose a piece of music that is important to you. Consider it as an artifact, and describe the qualities it has that you feel are Apollonian and Dionysian, respectively. Is the range of the music—in terms of exciting or sustaining emotional response—narrow or great? Describe your emotional and intellectual reactions to the music, and ask others about their responses to the same music. Is music an appropriate source for finding the conjunction of these two forces?

4. Examine aspects of our culture that reveal whether it is basically Apollonian or basically Dionysian. Be sure to consider matters of religion, literature, music, faith, and art and any aspects of personal life in your immediate environment. In considering these features of our culture, use Nietzsche's technique of comparison and contrast. For instance, you may find the Apollonian and Dionysian sides of, say, the modern film as interesting contrasts, just as you may wish to contrast rock music and Muzak, or any other related pairs.

5. Which of these two polarities of behavior most resembles your own behavior? Are you Apollonian or Dionysian? Define your behavior with reference to Nietzsche. Ask others who have read this selection to comment on your character in terms of the Apollonian-Dionysian distinction. Do you think that you achieve the kind of control that enables you to realize yourself fully in terms of these polarities, or do you feel that control is not an issue? Is inspiration an issue?

6. **CONNECTIONS** How would the Buddha critique Nietzsche's proposals? What ethical issues might he find in Nietzsche's suggestions that the Apollonian and Dionysian extremes are desirable? What fault might Plato find with Nietzsche's views? Do you find yourself convinced more by Plato and the Buddha or by Nietzsche?

7. **CONNECTIONS** Decide which of the other selections in the Faith section reveal an Apollonian attitude toward religion and religious behavior. Establish their Apollonian credentials by making reference to the characteristics that Nietzsche elaborates in this essay. How well do these other selections "fit" Nietzsche's pattern? Is it possible that some of these selections also reveal the Dionysian side of religious expression? If so, establish clearly how they do so; explain the ways in which they agree with Nietzsche's description and the ways in which they differ from it.

SIMONE WEIL
Spiritual Autobiography

SIMONE WEIL (1909–1943) was born in Paris and died in Kent, England. Weil (pronounced Vay) was a highly controversial figure in modern thought, ranking in some people's estimation as among the most important thinkers of her generation. She has been praised by Jean-Paul Sartre, Albert Camus, and T. S. Eliot for the spiritual intensity of her life and her writing. She has been described in terms that are usually reserved for saints. She was, however, a remarkably contradictory person. Born a Jew yet feeling herself to be a Christian, she also resisted baptism into the Christian faith. Her struggles with Judaism parallel her struggles with the authoritative aspects of the Roman Catholic Church. Always, her sympathies were with the weak. The tenets and practices of institutional religions were often at odds with her thinking.

She was an intellectual who demanded of herself that she bring her life into accord with her beliefs. She was influenced by Marxist thought when she was at the Sorbonne, and in 1931 she began teaching philosophy at a girls' school near Lyon. Her activities as a supporter of unemployed workers caused a scandal and cost her her job. It was not the last time such activism caused her to lose a teaching post. In 1934 she began to feel that physical labor is an essential part of the spiritual life, and thus she took time off from teaching to become a worker. She eventually worked at the Renault plant. It was after she left her factory job that she began to think of herself as a Christian.

During the Spanish civil war in 1936 she took part on the side of the anti-Fascist Republicans, posing as a journalist. Her health, which had always been frail, was dealt a serious blow when, early in her stay in Spain, she spilled a pot of boiling oil on her leg. She

From *The Simone Weil Reader*, 1976.

was invalided out of the war and returned to France after only two months. During her convalescence she traveled to Switzerland and then went to Italy, where she found herself in the chapel of Santa Maria degli Angeli where St. Francis of Assisi had often prayed. She found herself kneeling for the first time in her life—impressed, as she said, by a spiritual force that was greater than herself.

She was on extended sick leave from teaching in 1938 when the headaches that she had suffered from the age of twelve became almost unbearable. In the abbey of Solesmes that Easter she experienced a mystical revelation, as she informs us in her "Spiritual Autobiography." As she mentions, too, she became influenced by English metaphysical poetry of the seventeenth century, a spiritual, often mystical poetry that moved her deeply.

In 1939, at the beginning of World War II, Weil began writing extensively about religious matters and reading and studying Greek and Hindu philosophy. When France fell to the Nazis, she lived and worked on a farm in the unoccupied zone, called Vichy, and left some important writings with spiritual advisers. Among the most influential of the spiritual guides of this period was Father J.-M. Perrin, to whom the letter "Spiritual Autobiography" is addressed.

In May 1942 Weil and her parents left France for Casablanca, then eventually worked their way to New York. While she was in New York, she attended mass daily. After only a short time she decided that she had to help the French Resistance in England, and she managed to find passage to Liverpool. However, both her earlier pacifist views and the fact that she had fought for the Spanish Republicans—essentially supported by Communists—made the authorities suspicious of her.

Eventually, she attached herself to a Free French ministry, but in response to the fact that some French were dying of starvation in the German-occupied area of France, she began to cut her food to match the rations of her compatriots on the Continent. During this period, she wrote extensively about politics and philosophy. Eventually, she fell ill and refused to eat. In her final illness she also refused baptism into the church, though she accepted the ministrations of a priest. She died in 1943 of starvation and tuberculosis at the age of thirty-four.

"Spiritual Autobiography" tells Father Perrin a great deal about Weil's development as a Christian thinker. It also helps to explain why she felt herself to be Christian but refused to be baptized. She seems to have felt the need to remain an outsider, somewhat like Christ himself. Her religion was personal, mystical, outside the institutional church. Her writings are subtle and complex, and they constantly probe the spiritual meaning of life.

Her "Spiritual Autobiography" reads more like the memoir of a seventeenth-century mystic than it does of a twentieth-century philosopher. A document by a very unusual modern intellectual, it is unabashed, unashamed in describing events that are, to say the least, quite startling and, perhaps, difficult to believe. Yet we cannot doubt that she believed what she said and that she expected Father Perrin to believe it too.

Weil's Rhetoric

This is a very straightforward work. Because it is a letter, it has a specific audience in mind: a priest who had been both Weil's spiritual guide and friend. Undoubtedly, Weil expected that the letter would be published, and therefore it is not typical of intimate correspondence. It is more like Martin Luther King Jr.'s, "Letter from Birmingham Jail," and like King's letter, it is written in full awareness of the tradition of the epistles of the New Testament.

Interestingly, unlike King, she expected no reply, as she says at the outset. She wrote the letter on May 15, and she left France forever on May 17. She implies that she and Father Perrin may have time for correspondence later, but her purposes are as explicit as are those stated in King's letter. She is trying to explain her indebtedness to Father Perrin and to convince him that she was not wrong to avoid baptism. Baptism would have brought her into the spiritual fold of Roman Catholicism — it would have made her officially a Christian.

Her letter is detailed, simple, and sometimes startling. She explains that although she did not seek God, God found her. She tells us almost matter-of-factly that "Christ himself came down and took possession of me" (para. 21). Her reading had not prepared her for this event, and she is all the more grateful that this was so. It happened in a way that admitted no resistance; her experience was that of a mystic, of a modern St. Teresa of Avila (1515–1582), who described her visions of Christ in her journals.

When one reads this letter, it must be kept in mind that Weil was by no means an impressionable young woman. When she took a nationwide examination for college, she placed first in France; the great French intellectual Simone de Beauvoir placed second. Weil's writings are deep, brilliant, and extensive in scope. They reveal a stunningly capacious mind. Thus, this record of a modern mystical experience cannot be simply dismissed. Rather, we must pay close attention to try to understand exactly what Weil experienced and to discover what that experience meant to her.

PREREADING QUESTIONS:
WHAT TO READ FOR

The following prereading questions may help you anticipate key issues in the discussion on Simone Weil's "Spiritual Autobiography." Keeping them in mind during your first reading of the selection should help focus your reactions.

- What does Weil's spiritual autobiography reveal about her?
- Why does she not want to be baptized?
- What is Weil's attitude toward Christianity?

Spiritual Autobiography

P.S. TO BE READ FIRST

This letter is fearfully long—but as there is no question of an answer—especially as I shall doubtless have gone[1] before it reaches you—you have years ahead of you in which to read it if you care to. Read it all the same, one day or another.   1

From Marseilles, about May 15

FATHER,

Before leaving I want to speak to you again, it may be the last time perhaps, for over there I shall probably send you only my news from time to time just so as to have yours.   2

I told you that I owed you an enormous debt. I want to try to tell you exactly what it consists of. I think that if you could really understand what my spiritual state is you would not be at all sorry that you did not lead me to baptism. But I do not know if it is possible for you to understand this.   3

You neither brought me the Christian inspiration nor did you bring me to Christ; for when I met you there was no longer any need; it had been done without the intervention of any human   4

---

[1] **have gone** Weil was leaving France because of its occupation by the Nazis. She left eventually for the United States.

being. If it had been otherwise, if I had not already been won, not only implicitly but consciously, you would have given me nothing, because I should have received nothing from you. My friendship for you would have been a reason for me to refuse your message, for I should have been afraid of the possibilities of error and illusion which human influence in the divine order is likely to involve.

I may say that never at any moment in my life have I "sought for God." For this reason, which is probably too subjective, I do not like this expression and it strikes me as false. As soon as I reached adolescence, I saw the problem of God as a problem the data of which could not be obtained here below, and I decided that the only way of being sure not to reach a wrong solution, which seemed to me the greatest possible evil, was to leave it alone. So I left it alone. I neither affirmed nor denied anything. It seemed to me useless to solve the problem, for I thought that, being in this world, our business was to adopt the best attitude with regard to the problems of this world, and that such an attitude did not depend upon the solution of the problem of God.

This held good as far as I was concerned at any rate, for I never hesitated in my choice of an attitude; I always adopted the Christian attitude as the only possible one. I might say that I was born, I grew up, and I always remained within the Christian inspiration. While the very name of God had no part in my thoughts, with regard to the problems of this world and this life I shared the Christian conception in an explicit and rigorous manner, with the most specific notions it involves. Some of these notions have been part of my outlook for as far back as I can remember. With others I know the time and manner of their coming and the form under which they imposed themselves upon me.

For instance I never allowed myself to think of a future state, but I always believed that the instant of death is the center and object of life. I used to think that, for those who live as they should, it is the instant when, for an infinitesimal fraction of time, pure truth, naked, certain, and eternal, enters the soul. I may say that I never desired any other good for myself. I thought that the life leading to this good is not only defined by a code of morals common to all, but that for each one it consists of a succession of acts and events strictly personal to him, and so essential that he who leaves them on one side never reaches the goal. The notion of vocation was like this for me. I saw that the carrying out of a vocation differed from the actions dictated by reason or inclination in that it was due to an impulse of an essentially and manifestly different order; and not to follow such an impulse when it made itself felt, even if it demanded impossibilities, seemed to me the greatest of all ills. Hence my conception of obedience; and I put this conception to the test when I entered the factory and stayed on there, even when I was in that state of intense and uninterrupted misery about which I recently told you. The most beautiful life possible has always seemed to me to be one where everything is determined, either by the pressure of circumstances or by impulses such as I have just mentioned and where there is never any room for choice.

At fourteen I fell into one of those fits of bottomless despair that 8
come with adolescence, and I seriously thought of dying because of the mediocrity of my natural faculties. The exceptional gifts of my brother, who had a childhood and youth comparable to those of Pascal,[2] brought my own inferiority home to me. I did not mind having no visible successes, but what did grieve me was the idea of being excluded from that transcendent kingdom to which only the truly great have access and wherein truth abides. I preferred to die rather than live without that truth. After months of inward darkness, I suddenly had the everlasting conviction that any human being, even though practically devoid of natural faculties, can penetrate to the kingdom of truth reserved for genius, if only he longs for truth and perpetually concentrates all his attention upon its attainment. He thus becomes a genius too, even though for lack of talent his genius cannot be visible from outside. Later on, when the strain of headaches caused the feeble faculties I possess to be invaded by a paralysis, which I was quick to imagine as probably incurable, the same conviction led me to persevere for ten years in an effort of concentrated attention that was practically unsupported by any hope of results.

Under the name of truth I also included beauty, virtue, and 9
every kind of goodness, so that for me it was a question of a conception of the relationship between grace and desire. The conviction that had come to me was that when one hungers for bread one does not receive stones. But at that time I had not read the Gospel.

Just as I was certain that desire has in itself an efficacy in the 10
realm of spiritual goodness whatever its form, I thought it was also possible that it might not be effective in any other realm.

As for the spirit of poverty, I do not remember any moment 11
when it was not in me, although only to that unhappily small extent

---

[2] **Blaise Pascal (1623–1662)** French philosopher and mathematician whose most important work, *Pensées* [Thoughts], was published posthumously in 1670 in a version that was totally garbled. It was published again in 1844 in a restored version. He is famous for having pointed out that it is better to believe in God than not: there is everything to lose if God exists but nothing to lose if God does not exist. This has been condemned as a cynical and theologically useless argument.

compatible with my imperfection. I fell in love with Saint Francis of Assisi[3] as soon as I came to know about him. I always believed and hoped that one day Fate would force upon me the condition of a vagabond and a Beggar which he embraced freely. Actually I felt the same way about prison.

From my earliest childhood I always had also the Christian idea 12
of love for one's neighbor, to which I gave the name of justice—a name it bears in many passages of the gospel and which is so beautiful. You know that on this point I have failed seriously several times.

The duty of acceptance in all that concerns the will of God, 13
whatever it may be, was impressed upon my mind as the first and most necessary of all duties from the time when I found it set down in Marcus Aurelius[4] under the form of the *amor fati* of the Stoics. I saw it as a duty we cannot fail in without dishonoring ourselves.

The idea of purity, with all that this word can imply for a Chris- 14
tian, took possession of me at the age of sixteen, after a period of several months during which I had been going through the emotional unrest natural in adolescence. This idea came to me when I was contemplating a mountain landscape and little by little it was imposed upon me in an irresistible manner.

Of course I knew quite well that my conception of life was 15
Christian. That is why it never occurred to me that I could enter the Christian community. I had the idea that I was born inside. But to add dogma[5] to this conception of life, without being forced to do so by indisputable evidence, would have seemed to me like a lack of honesty. I should even have thought I was lacking in honesty had I considered the question of the truth of dogma as a problem for myself or even had I simply desired to reach a conclusion on this subject. I have an extremely severe standard for intellectual honesty, so severe that I never met anyone who did not seem to fall short of it in more than one respect; and I am always afraid of failing in it myself.

Keeping away from dogma in this way, I was prevented by a 16
sort of shame from going into churches, though all the same I like

---

[3] **Saint Francis of Assisi (1182?–1226)** Founder of the Franciscan order of Roman Catholic monks. He committed himself to poverty and a simple life and was a model of pious devotion. In 1224 he fasted on a mountaintop for forty days and nights and experienced the stigmata, an appearance on his body of the wounds of Christ on the cross.

[4] **Marcus Aurelius (121–180)** Roman emperor and an important Stoic philosopher. Stoicism praised self-sacrifice to the state and praised one who could suffer his fate with dignity and in silence. His *Meditations* is his most important work; *amor fati* means love of (one's) fate or contentment with one's lot.

[5] **dogma** The tenets of the Roman Catholic faith.

being in them. Nevertheless, I had three contacts with Catholicism that really counted.

After my year in the factory, before going back to teaching, I   17
had been taken by my parents to Portugal, and while there I left them to go alone to a little village. I was, as it were, in pieces, soul and body. That contact with affliction had killed my youth. Until then I had not had any experience of affliction, unless we count my own, which, as it was my own, seemed to me, to have little importance, and which moreover was only a partial affliction, being biological and not social. I knew quite well that there was a great deal of affliction in the world, I was obsessed with the idea, but I had not had prolonged and first-hand experience of it. As I worked in the factory, indistinguishable to all eyes, including my own, from the anonymous mass, the affliction of others entered into my flesh and my soul. Nothing separated me from it, for I had really forgotten my past and I looked forward to no future, finding it difficult to imagine the possibility of surviving all the fatigue. What I went through there marked me in so lasting a manner that still today when any human being, whoever he may be and in whatever circumstances, speaks to me without brutality, I cannot help having the impression that there must be a mistake and that unfortunately the mistake will in all probability disappear. There I received forever the mark of a slave, like the branding of the red-hot iron the Romans put on the foreheads of their most despised slaves. Since then I have always regarded myself as a slave.

In this state of mind then, and in a wretched condition physi-   18
cally, I entered the little Portuguese village, which, alas, was very wretched too, on the very day of the festival of its patron saint. I was alone. It was the evening and there was a full moon over the sea. The wives of the fishermen were, in procession, making a tour of all the ships, carrying candles and singing what must certainly be very ancient hymns of a heart-rending sadness. Nothing can give any idea of it. I have never heard anything so poignant unless it were the song of the boatmen on the Volga. There the conviction was suddenly borne in upon me that Christianity is pre-eminently the religion of slaves, that slaves cannot help belonging to it, and I among others.

In 1937 I had two marvelous days at Assisi. There, alone in the   19
little twelfth-century Romanesque chapel of Santa Maria degli Angeli,[6] an incomparable marvel of purity where Saint Francis often

---

[6] **Santa Maria degli Angeli** Saint Mary of the Angels, a church in which St. Francis prayed and received enlightenment.

used to pray, something stronger than I was compelled me for the first time in my life to go down on my knees.

In 1938 I spent ten days at Solesmes, from Palm Sunday to 20 Easter Tuesday, following all the liturgical services. I was suffering from splitting headaches; each sound hurt me like a blow; by an extreme effort of concentration I was able to rise above this wretched flesh, to leave it to suffer by itself, heaped up in a corner, and to find a pure and perfect joy in the unimaginable beauty of the chanting and the words. This experience enabled me by analogy to get a better understanding of the possibility of loving divine love in the midst of affliction. It goes without saying that in the course of these services the thought of the Passion of Christ entered into my being once and for all.

There was a young English Catholic there from whom I gained 21 my first idea of the supernatural power of the sacraments because of the truly angelic radiance with which he seemed to be clothed after going to communion. Chance—for I always prefer saying chance rather than Providence—made of him a messenger to me. For he told me of the existence of those English poets of the seventeenth century who are named metaphysical. In reading them later on, I discovered the poem of which I read you what is unfortunately a very inadequate translation. It is called "Love."[7] I learned it by heart. Often, at the culminating point of a violent headache, I make myself say it over, concentrating all my attention upon it and clinging with all my soul to the tenderness it enshrines. I used to think I was merely reciting it as a beautiful poem, but without my knowing it the recitation had the virtue of a prayer. It was during one of these recitations that, as I told you, Christ himself came down and took possession of me.

In my arguments about the insolubility of the problem of God, I 22 had never foreseen the possibility of that, of a real contact, person to person, here below, between a human being and God. I had vaguely heard tell of things of this kind, but I had never believed in them. In the *Fioretti*[8] the accounts of apparitions rather put me off if anything, like the miracles in the Gospel. Moreover, in this sudden possession of me by Christ, neither my senses nor my imagination had any part; I only felt in the midst of my suffering the presence of a love, like that which one can read in the smile on a beloved face.

---

[7]**"Love"** A poem by the English metaphysical poet George Herbert (1593–1633). He was a clergyman whose poems were often profoundly religious. His *The Temple* is a cycle of poems based on the architecture of the church.

[8]**Fioretti** Literally, little flowers. These were important writings of St. Francis.

I had never read any mystical works because I had never felt any 23
call to read them. In reading as in other things I have always striven
to practice obedience. There is nothing more favorable to intellectual progress, for as far as possible I only read what I am hungry for
at the moment when I have an appetite for it, and then I do not
read, I *eat*. God in his mercy had prevented me from reading the
mystics, so that it should be evident to me that I had not invented
this absolutely unexpected contact.

Yet I still half refused, not my love but my intelligence. For it 24
seemed to me certain, and I still think so today, that one can never
wrestle enough with God if one does so out of pure regard for the
truth. Christ likes us to prefer truth to him because, before being
Christ, he is truth. If one turns aside from him to go toward the
truth, one will not go far before falling into his arms.

After this I came to feel that Plato was a mystic, that all the *Iliad* 25
is bathed in Christian light, and that Dionysus and Osiris[9] are in a
certain sense Christ himself; and my love was thereby redoubled.

I never wondered whether Jesus was or was not the Incarnation 26
of God; but in fact I was incapable of thinking of him without thinking of him as God.

In the spring of 1940 I read the *Bhagavad Gītā*.[10] Strange to say 27
it was in reading those marvelous words, words with such a Christian sound, put into the mouth of an incarnation of God, that I came
to feel strongly that we owe an allegiance to religious truth which is
quite different from the admiration we accord to a beautiful poem; it
is something far more categorical.

Yet I did not believe it to be possible for me to consider the 28
question of baptism. I felt that I could not honestly give up my opinions concerning the non-Christian religions and concerning Israel —
and as a matter of fact time and meditation have only served to
strengthen them — and I thought that this constituted an absolute
obstacle. I did not imagine it as possible that a priest could even
dream of granting me baptism. If I had not met you, I should never
have considered the problem of baptism as a practical problem.

During all this time of spiritual progress I had never prayed. I 29
was afraid of the power of suggestion that is in prayer — the very

---

[9] **the *Iliad* . . . Dionysus . . . Osiris** Homer's epic *Iliad* tells the story of the
destruction of Troy and establishes the role of the Greek gods in human affairs.
Dionysus was, in ancient Greek religion, a god of fertility and was associated with
ecstatic rites and rituals. Osiris was the center of an important early cult originating
in Egypt and was associated with the god of the underworld.
[10] **Bhagavad Gītā** Song of The Blessed One; an Indian Sanskrit poem, part of
the larger *Mahabharata*. It is a sacred text explaining the relation of God to his loved
one.

power for which Pascal recommends it. Pascal's method seems to me one of the worst for attaining faith.

Contact with you was not able to persuade me to pray. On the contrary I thought the danger was all the greater, since I also had to beware of the power of suggestion in my friendship with you. At the same time I found it very difficult not to pray and not to tell you so. Moreover I knew I could not tell you without completely misleading you about myself. At that time I should not have been able to make you understand.

Until last September I had never once prayed in all my life, at least not in the literal sense of the word. I had never said any words to God, either out loud or mentally. I had never pronounced a liturgical prayer. I had occasionally recited the *Salve Regina*,[11] but only as a beautiful poem.

Last summer, doing Greek with T___, I went through the Our Father word for word in Greek. We promised each other to learn it by heart. I do not think he ever did so, but some weeks later, as I was turning over the pages of the Gospel, I said to myself that since I had promised to do this thing and it was good, I ought to do it. I did it. The infinite sweetness of this Greek text so took hold of me that for several days I could not stop myself from saying it over all the time. A week afterward I began the vine harvest.[12] I recited the Our Father in Greek every day before work, and I repeated it very often in the vineyard.

Since that time I have made a practice of saying it through once each morning with absolute attention. If during the recitation my attention wanders or goes to sleep, in the minutest degree, I begin again until I have once succeeded in going through it with absolutely pure attention. Sometimes it comes about that I say it again out of sheer pleasure, but I only do it if I really feel the impulse.

The effect of this practice is extraordinary and surprises me every time, for although I experience it each day, it exceeds my expectation at each repetition.

At times the very first words tear my thoughts from my body and transport it to a place outside space where there is neither perspective nor point of view. The infinity of the ordinary expanses of perception is replaced by an infinity to the second or sometimes the third degree. At the same time, filling every part of this infinity of infinity, there is silence, a silence which is not an absence of sound but which is the

---

[11] **Salve Regina** Hail Mary, a prayer or hymn to the Virgin Mary.

[12] **vine harvest** At the time, Weil was working in the fields as a farm laborer in an effort to simplify her life and to get in closer touch with the soil.

object of a positive sensation, more positive than that of sound. Noises, if there are any, only reach me after crossing this silence.

Sometimes, also during this recitation or at other moments, 36 Christ is present with me in person, but his presence is infinitely more real, more moving, more clear than on that first occasion when he took possession of me.

I should never have been able to take it upon myself to tell you 37 all this had it not been for the fact that I am going away. And as I am going more or less with the idea of probable death, I do not believe that I have the right to keep it to myself. For after all, the whole of this matter is not a question concerning me myself. It concerns God. I am really nothing in it all. If one could imagine any possibility of error in God, I should think that it had all happened to me by mistake. But perhaps God likes to use castaway objects, waste, rejects. After all, should the bread of the host be moldy, it would become the Body of Christ[13] just the same after the priest had consecrated it. Only it cannot refuse, while we can disobey. It sometimes seems to me that when I am treated in so merciful a way, every sin on my part must be a mortal sin. And I am constantly committing them.

I have told you that you are like a father and brother at the same 38 time to me. But these words only express an analogy. Perhaps at bottom they only correspond to a feeling of affection, of gratitude and admiration. For as to the spiritual direction of my soul, I think that God himself has taken it in hand from the start and still looks after it.

That does not prevent me from owing you the greatest debt of 39 gratitude that I could ever have incurred toward any human being. This is exactly what it consists of.

First you once said to me at the beginning of our relationship 40 some words that went to the bottom of my soul. You said: "Be very careful, because if you should pass over something important through your own fault it would be a pity."

That made me see intellectual honesty in a new light. Till then I 41 had only thought of it as opposed to faith; your words made me think that perhaps, without my knowing it, there were in me obstacles to the faith, impure obstacles, such as prejudices, habits. I felt that after having said to myself for so many years simply: "Perhaps all that is not true," I ought, without ceasing to say it—I still take care to say it very often now—to join it to the opposite formula, namely: "Perhaps all that is true," and to make them alternate.

---

[13] **bread of the host . . . Body of Christ** The doctrine of transubstantiation, part of the sacrament of the Mass, establishes that when the priest consecrates the bread (the host) it becomes the body of Christ, which is then partaken by the communicant.

At the same time, in making the problem of baptism a practical 42 problem for me, you have forced me to face the whole question of the faith, dogma, and the sacraments, obliging me to consider them closely and at length with the fullest possible attention, making me see them as things toward which I have obligations that I have to discern and perform. I should never have done this otherwise and it is indispensible for me to do it.

But the greatest blessing you have brought me is of another 43 order. In gaining my friendship by your charity (which I have never met anything to equal), you have provided me with a source of the most compelling and pure inspiration that is to be found among human things. For nothing among human things has such power to keep our gaze fixed ever more intensely upon God, than friendship for the friends of God.

Nothing better enables me to measure the breadth of your char- 44 ity than the fact that you bore with me for so long and with such gentleness. I may seem to be joking, but that is not the case. It is true that you have not the same motives as I have myself (those about which I wrote to you the other day), for feeling hatred and re-pulsion toward me. But all the same I feel that your patience with me can only spring from a supernatural generosity.

I have not been able to avoid causing you the greatest disap- 45 pointment it was in my power to cause you. But up to now, al-though I have often asked myself the question during prayer, during Mass, or in the light of the radiancy that remains in the soul after Mass, I have never once had, even for a moment, the feeling that God wants me to be in the Church. I have never even once had a feeling of uncertainty. I think that at the present time we can finally conclude that he does not want me in the Church. Do not have any regrets about it.

He does not want it so far at least. But unless I am mistaken I 46 should say that it is his will that I should stay outside for the future too, except perhaps at the moment of death. Yet I am always ready to obey an order, whatever it may be. I should joyfully obey the order to go to the very center of hell and to remain there eternally. I do not mean, of course, that I have a preference for orders of this nature. I am not perverse like that.

Christianity should contain all vocations without exception 47 since it is catholic.[14] In consequence the Church should also. But in my eyes Christianity is catholic by right but not in fact. So many things are outside it, so many things that I love and do not want to

---

[14]**catholic** All inclusive.

give up, so many things that God loves, otherwise they would not be in existence. All the immense stretches of past centuries, except the last twenty are among them; all the countries inhabited by colored races; all secular life in the white peoples' countries; in the history of these countries, all the traditions banned as heretical, those of the Manicheans and Albigenses[15] for instance; all those things resulting from the Renaissance, too often degraded but not quite without value.

Christianity being catholic by right but not in fact, I regard it as   48
legitimate on my part to be a member of the Church by right but not in fact, not only for a time, but for my whole life if need be.

But it is not merely legitimate. So long as God does not give me   49
the certainty that he is ordering me to do anything else, I think it is my duty.

I think, and so do you, that our obligation for the next two or   50
three years, an obligation so strict that we can scarcely fail in it without treason, is to show the public the possibility of a truly incarnated Christianity. In all the history now known there has never been a period in which souls have been in such peril as they are today in every part of the globe. The bronze serpent must be lifted up again so that whoever raises his eyes to it may be saved.

But everything is so closely bound up together that Christianity   51
cannot be really incarnated unless it is catholic in the sense that I have just defined. How could it circulate through the flesh of all the nations of Europe if it did not contain absolutely everything in itself? Except of course falsehood. But in everything that exists there is most of the time more truth than falsehood.

Having so intense and so painful a sense of this urgency, I   52
should betray the truth, that is to say the aspect of truth that I see, if I left the point, where I have been since my birth, at the intersection of Christianity and everything that is not Christianity.

I have always remained at this exact point, on the threshold of   53
the Church, without moving, quite still, ἐν ὑπομονῇ[16] (it is so much more beautiful a word than *patientia*!); only now my heart has been

---

[15] **Manicheans and Albigenses** The Manicheans were a cult that developed before the time of Christ; they believed that good and evil were in a constant struggle for the possession of the world and that the fate of the world was in doubt. This belief was declared heretical because it did not demonstrate faith in the providence of God. Albigensians were a thirteenth-century sect of Christians in southern France; they were Manicheans who believed that all matter was evil, and they practiced a form of birth control in order to prevent the soul—the human spirit—from being entrapped in a material fleshly body.

[16] ἐν ὑπομονῇ In patient endurance.

transported, forever, I hope, into the Blessed Sacrament exposed on the altar.

You see that I am very far from the thoughts that H ____, with the best of intentions, attributed to me. I am far also from being worried in any way.

If I am sad, it comes primarily from the permanent sadness that destiny has imprinted forever upon my emotions, where the greatest and purest joys can only be superimposed and that at the price of a great effort of attention. It comes also from my miserable and continual sins; and from all the calamities of our time and of all those of all the past centuries.

I think that you should understand why I have always resisted you, if in spite of being a priest you can admit that a genuine vocation might prevent anyone from entering the Church.

Otherwise a barrier of incomprehension will remain between us, whether the error is on my part or on yours. This would grieve me from the point of view of my friendship for you, because in that case the result of all these efforts and desires, called forth by your charity toward me, would be a disappointment for you. Moreover, although it is not my fault, I should not be able to help feeling guilty of ingratitude. For, I repeat, my debt to you is beyond all measure.

I should like to draw your attention to one point. It is that there is an absolutely insurmountable obstacle to the Incarnation of Christianity. It is the use of the two little words *anathema sit.*[17] It is not their existence, but the way they have been employed up till now. It is that also which prevents me from crossing the threshold of the Church. I remain beside all those things that cannot enter the Church, the universal repository, on account of those two little words. I remain beside them all the more because my own intelligence is numbered among them.

The Incarnation of Christianity implies a harmonious solution of the problem of the relations between the individual and the collective. Harmony in the Pythagorean[18] sense; the just balance of contraries. This solution is precisely what men are thirsting for today.

The position of the intelligence is the key to this harmony, because the intelligence is a specifically and rigorously individual

54

55

56

57

58

59

60

---

[17] **anathema sit** "It is evil"—the Church's powerful curse; it is pronounced during excommunication. It was first pronounced during the excommunication of Martin Luther in 1520.

[18] **Pythagorean** This refers to Pythagoras (sixth century B.C.), a Greek philosopher who according to legend developed the tuned string and worked out the relationships between the notes of the musical scale.

thing. This harmony exists wherever the intelligence, remaining in its place, can be exercised without hindrance and can reach the complete fulfillment of its function. That is what Saint Thomas[19] says admirably of all the parts of the soul of Christ, with reference to his sensitiveness to pain during the crucifixion.

The special function of the intelligence requires total liberty, im-   61 plying the right to deny everything, and allowing of no domination. Wherever it usurps control there is an excess of individualism. Wherever it is hampered or uneasy there is an oppressive collectivism, or several of them.

The Church and the State should punish it, each one in its   62 own way, when it advocates actions of which they disapprove. When it remains in the region of purely theoretical speculation they still have the duty, should occasion arise, to put the public on their guard, by every effective means, against the danger of the practical influence certain speculations might have upon the conduct of life. But whatever these theoretical speculations may be, the Church and the State have no right either to try to stifle them or to inflict any penalty material or moral upon their authors. Notably, they should not be deprived of the sacraments if they desire them. For, whatever they may have said, even if they have publicly denied the existence of God, they may not have committed any sin. In such a case the Church should declare that they are in error, but it should not demand of them anything whatever in the way of a disavowal of what they have said, nor should it deprive them of the Bread of Life.

A collective body is the guardian of dogma; and dogma is an ob-   63 ject of contemplation for love, faith, and intelligence, three strictly individual faculties. Hence, almost since the beginning, the individual has been ill at ease in Christianity, and this uneasiness has been notably one of the intelligence. This cannot be denied.

Christ himself who is Truth itself, when he was speaking before   64 an assembly such as a council, did not address it in the same language as he used in an intimate conversation with his well-beloved friend, and no doubt before the Pharisees[20] he might easily have been accused of contradiction and error. For by one of those laws of

---

[19] **Saint Thomas** St. Thomas Aquinas (1225?–1274) was among the most powerful philosophers of the Catholic Church. His *Summa Theologica* is still studied by modern theologians.

[20] **Pharisees** Members of a Jewish group concerned with the law, in both its written and oral forms. Jesus spoke with them concerning the law and its interpretations. See Luke 7. Paul said, "After the most straitest sect of our religion I lived a Pharisee," Acts 26:5.

nature, which God himself respects, since he has willed them from all eternity, there are two languages that are quite distinct although made up of the same words; there is the collective language and there is the individual one. The Comforter whom Christ sends us, the Spirit of truth, speaks one or other of these languages, whichever circumstances demand, and by a necessity of their nature there is not agreement between them.

When genuine friends of God—such as was Eckhart[21] to my way of thinking—repeat words they have heard in secret amidst the silence of the union of love, and these words are in disagreement with the teaching of the Church, it is simply that the language of the market place is not that of the nuptial chamber. — 65

Everybody knows that really intimate conversation is only possible between two or three. As soon as there are six or seven, collective language begins to dominate. That is why it is a complete misinterpretation to apply to the Church the words "Wheresoever two or three are gathered together in my name, there am I in the midst of them." Christ did not say two hundred, or fifty, or ten. He said two or three. He said precisely that he always forms the third in the intimacy of the tête-à-tête.[22] — 66

Christ made promises to the Church, but none of these promises has the force of the expression "Thy Father who seeth in secret."[23] The word of God is the secret word. He who has not heard this word, even if he adheres to all the dogmas taught by the Church, has no contact with truth. — 67

The function of the Church as the collective keeper of dogma is indispensable. She has the right and the duty to punish those who make a clear attack upon her within the specific range of this function, by depriving them of the sacraments. — 68

---

[21] **Meister Johannes Eckhart (1260?–1327)** An important early German mystic and theologian. The Church found it difficult to accept some of his teachings, and some things he said were condemned after his death. He believed that God was everything—that everything had its own essence but that its existence was only in God. His ideas have sometimes been thought to be pantheistic—seeing God in everything.

[22] **tête-à-tête** Literally, head to head; an intimate conversation.

[23] **"Thy Father who seeth in secret."** Matthew 6:1–4: "Take heed that ye do not your alms before men, to be seen of them: otherwise ye have no reward of your Father which is in heaven. Therefore when thou doest thine alms, do not sound a trumpet before thee, as the hypocrites do in the synagogues and in the streets, that they may have glory of men. Verily I say unto you, They have their reward. But when thou doest alms, let not thy left hand know what thy right hand doeth: that thine alms may be in secret: and thy Father which seeth in secret himself shall reward thee openly."

Thus, although I know practically nothing of this business, I in-   69
cline to think provisionally that she was right to punish Luther.[24]

But she is guilty of an abuse of power when she claims to force   70
love and intelligence to model their language upon her own. This
abuse of power is not of God. It comes from the natural tendency of
every form of collectivism, without exception, to abuse power.

The image of the Mystical Body of Christ is very attractive. But I   71
consider the importance given to this image today as one of the most
serious signs of our degeneration. For our true dignity is not to be
parts of a body, even though it be a mystical one, even though it be
that of Christ. It consists in this, that in the state of perfection,
which is the vocation of each one of us, we no longer live in ourselves, but Christ lives in us; so that through our perfection Christ in
his integrity and in his indivisible unity, becomes in a sense each
one of us, as he is completely in each host. The hosts are not a *part*
of his body.

This present-day importance of the image of the Mystical Body   72
shows how wretchedly susceptible Christians are to outside influences. Undoubtedly there is real intoxication in being a member of
the Mystical Body of Christ. But today a great many other mystical
bodies, which have not Christ for their head, produce an intoxication in their members that to my way of thinking is of the same
order.

As long as it is through obedience, I find sweetness in my depri-   73
vation of the joy of membership in the Mystical Body of Christ. For if
God is willing to help me, I may thus bear witness that without this
joy one can nevertheless be faithful to Christ unto death. Social en-
thusiasms have such power today, they raise people so effectively to
the supreme degree of heroism in suffering and death, that I think it is
as well that a few sheep should remain outside the fold in order to
bear witness that the love of Christ is essentially something different.

The Church today defends the cause of the indefeasible rights[25]   74
of the individual against collective oppression, of liberty of thought
against tyranny. But these are causes readily embraced by those
who find themselves momentarily to be the least strong. It is their

---

[24] **Martin Luther (1483–1546)** German theologian whose ninety-five theses
in 1517 began the Protestant Reformation. He was excommunicated from the
Roman Catholic Church for refusing to change his stand on the question of whether
good deeds contributed to salvation; he insisted that only faith mattered: doing good
deeds was irrelevant to one's salvation.
[25] **indefeasible rights** Rights that cannot be made otherwise or cannot be re-
pealed. They are absolute rights.

only way of perhaps one day becoming the strongest. That is well known.

You may perhaps be offended by this idea. You are not the 75 Church. During the periods of the most atrocious abuse of power committed by the Church, there must have been some priests like you among the others. Your good faith is not a guarantee, even were it shared by all your Order. You cannot foresee what turn things may take.

In order that the present attitude of the Church should be effec- 76 tive and that she should really penetrate like a wedge into social existence, she would have to say openly that she had changed or wished to change. Otherwise who could take her seriously when they remembered the Inquisition?[26] My friendship for you, which I extend through you to all your Order, makes it very painful for me to bring this up. But it existed. After the fall of the Roman Empire, which had been totalitarian, it was the Church that was the first to establish a rough sort of totalitarianism in Europe in the thirteenth century, after the war with the Albigenses. This tree bore much fruit.

And the motive power of this totalitarianism was the use of 77 those two little words: *anathema sit.*

It was moreover by a judicious transposition of this use that all 78 the parties which in our own day have founded totalitarian régimes were shaped. This is a point of history I have specially studied.

I must give you the impression of a Luciferian pride in speaking 79 thus of a great many matters that are too high for me and about which I have no right to understand anything. It is not my fault. Ideas come and settle in my mind by mistake, then, realizing their mistake, they absolutely insist on coming out. I do not know where they come from, or what they are worth, but, whatever the risk, I do not think I have the right to prevent this operation.

Good-by, I wish you all possible good things except the cross; 80 for I do not love my neighbor as myself, you particularly, as you have noticed. But Christ granted to his well-beloved disciple, and probably to all that disciple's spiritual lineage, to come to him not through degradation, defilement, and distress, but in uninterrupted joy, purity, and sweetness. That is why I can allow myself to wish that even if one day you have the honor of dying a violent death for

---

[26] **the Inquisition** An organization founded by the Church in the thirteenth century to root out heresy. It became a tyrannical court of inquiry that often tortured and executed its victims and expressed its power whimsically and viciously. It has become a symbol of the excesses to which even benign powerful institutions such as the Church sometimes can resort.

Our Lord, it may be with joy and without any anguish; also that only three of the beatitudes[27] (*mites, mundo corde, pacifici*) will apply to you. All the others involve more or less of suffering.

This wish is not due only to the frailty of human friendship. For 81 with any human being taken individually, I always find reasons for concluding that sorrow and misfortune do not suit him, either because he seems too mediocre for anything so great or, on the contrary, too precious to be destroyed. One cannot fail more seriously in the second of the two essential commandments. And as to the first, I fail to observe that, in a still more horrible manner, for every time I think of the crucifixion of Christ I commit the sin of envy.

Believe more than ever and forever in my filial and tenderly 82 grateful friendship.

Simone Weil

QUESTIONS FOR CRITICAL READING

1. What does Weil mean when she tells Father Perrin that she was not brought to Christianity by any human intervention?
2. What does the relationship between Father Perrin and Weil seem to have been like? What kind of an audience did she expect him to be for this letter?
3. Weil describes herself as an adolescent. What was she like?
4. The relationship of God to the truth is detailed in paragraph 24. What does Weil seem to mean in this paragraph? Do you agree with her?
5. What kind of religious experience is Weil describing? Is it what you think of when you contemplate religion and religious experience?

SUGGESTIONS FOR WRITING

1. Write a letter in response to Weil's. You needn't imagine yourself to be Father Perrin (although you may do so if you wish). In any case, simply respond to Simone Weil in your own voice and rely on your own attitudes toward religious experience. In the course of your letter, offer her your own "spiritual autobiography."
2. Relying on Weil's letter, describe her religious views. Remember that she avoided joining a specific religion; however, she felt herself to be genuinely religious. What does it mean to be religious but not be a

---

[27] **three of the beatitudes** A reference to Christ's Sermon on the Mount, which begins, "Blessed are the poor in spirit." *Mites, mundo corde, pacifici* are the humble, the pure of heart, and the peacemakers.

member of a church? What does it mean to consider yourself a Christian but not permit yourself to be baptized into that faith? Remember that Weil addresses a man who is a priest — who has, in other words, the vocation that she says she lacks.

3. What is Weil's attitude toward God? Consider all that she says about God and try to imagine how she conceptualizes God. What would God want of her? What would God want of anyone? What does she feel she can give God? What, if anything, would she hold back?

4. Starting in paragraph 47, Weil expresses her reservations about the Catholic Church. What are they? What is her attitude toward institutionalized religion? Does she include Father Perrin in the institution of the church?

5. What does Weil mean when she says that since her youth she has been "at the intersection of Christianity and everything that is not Christianity" (para. 52)? She says she feels that Christianity must include all that is not Christianity. What does she mean by this statement? What things would she consider as being part of Christianity today? What things would not be part of Christianity? Do you find yourself agreeing with her or not?

6. Throughout the letter, Weil worries that she may somehow be committing a sin of pride by seeming so self-centered in her quest. Decide whether Weil demonstrates qualities of pride or of humility. Which ones will serve her best in her spiritual journey? How do you interpret her tone in this letter? Are you convinced that she has found a true religion for herself and that she is motivated by her love of God?

7. **CONNECTIONS** In paragraph 27, Weil tells us that she read the *Bhagavad Gītā* and that she found the words put in the mouth of Krishna sounding very Christian. Examine the *Bhagavad Gītā* and decide how Weil must have viewed the "incarnation of God." She says she felt that she owed "an allegiance to religious truth." What does she mean? In reading both these works, can you explain what Weil might mean by a "religious truth"?

8. **CONNECTIONS** In his essay "The Relation of Science and Religion," Richard P. Feynman seems to take a view that is quite different from that of Weil. Compare their views on religion, and establish what makes Weil's views different from Feynman's. If you feel their views are close on specific issues, establish what those issues are and explain how Weil and Feynman have similar viewpoints. Which of the two writers' views on religion means the most to you? Which one convinces you more completely?

PART EIGHT

FEMINISM

Mary Wollstonecraft
Virginia Woolf
Simone de Beauvoir
Carol Gilligan
bell hooks

INTRODUCTION

Feminism is an issue that has long been important to the modern intellectual. Although it was only in the twentieth century that many basic feminist ideas became accepted within the mainstream of most societies, the history of feminist thought spans more than three hundred years. Feminists were at work long before anarchist and political idealist William Godwin (1756–1836) wrote about the rights of women during the Romantic period in English literature. Feminist writing has also traditionally extended into scholarly disciplines, from politics to philosophy to psychology to literature. For example, in the nineteenth century, intense activity in Scandinavian feminism produced a number of important literary artifacts, not the least of which was Henrik Ibsen's play *A Doll's House,* which figures in one of these essays. In our time, we associate feminism with important mid-twentieth-century writings by a diverse array of writers, as well as with feminist groups organized in the 1960s and 1970s such as the National Organization for Women. The essays included here depict some of the most important eras in feminist thought. Readers should keep in mind, however, that these five essays represent only a fraction of the feminist works that have been written and published over the centuries. Like most feminist writers, the authors excerpted here echo some of the issues raised by Aristotle and Alexis de Tocqueville concerning equality. However, because the feminist writers take issues of gender, race, and class into account, they address the question of equality in more complex and concrete ways.

Mary Wollstonecraft wrote in a time of extreme political change: when revolution was erupting in the American colonies in 1776 and in France in 1789. Kings and aristocrats were losing their heads, literally. Monarchies were giving way to republics. During this period democracy in its modern forms began to grace the lives of some, whereas tyranny oppressed others. Even though radical changes took place in some areas, a conservative backlash in England and elsewhere threatened to heighten oppression rather than expand freedom. Although Wollstonecraft is known today chiefly for her feminist works, she was also engaged in the radical political thought of the time. For example, her defense of the ideals of the French Revolution in *A Vindication of the Rights of Men* (1790) brought her work to the attention of other radical thinkers such as William Godwin (whom she later married), Thomas Paine, William Blake, and William Wordsworth.

Still, Wollstonecraft's name remains a keystone in the history of feminism. She went on to write one of the most important books of the late eighteenth century, *Vindication of the Rights of Woman*

(1792), and is remembered most for her careful analysis of a society that did not value the gifts and talents of women. Her complaint is based on a theory of efficiency and economics: it is a waste to limit the opportunities of women. By making her appeal in this fashion she may have expected to gain the attention of the men who held power in late eighteenth-century England. Some of them did listen. By the 1830s, at the height of the industrial revolution, women were often employed outside the home. However, they were frequently given the most wretched jobs (such as in mining) and were not accorded the kind of respect and opportunity that Wollstonecraft envisioned. They often became drudges in a process of industrial development that demeaned their humanity.

In 1929, the novelist and essayist Virginia Woolf considered the question of how gifted women could hope to achieve important works if the current and historical patterns of oppression were to continue. Her book *A Room of One's Own* was addressed originally to a group of women studying at Cambridge in the two colleges reserved for them at the time. Woolf regarded these women appropriately as gifted, but she worried for their future because their opportunities in postwar England were quite limited. In a stroke of brilliance, Woolf demonstrates the pattern that oppresses gifted women by imagining for William Shakespeare an equally gifted sister named Judith and then tracing her probable development in sixteenth-century England. What chance would Judith have had to be a world-famous figure like her brother? Woolf's discussion is so lifelike and so well realized that it stands as a classic in modern feminist literature.

After the publication of her remarkable book *The Second Sex* (1949; 1953 in English), the French writer and philosopher Simone de Beauvoir was credited with inaugurating the modern feminist movement. Of course, the movement had been developing already in the work of countless women who fought for the right to vote (Russia, 1917; United States, 1920; Great Britain, 1928; France, 1945). Many years before Beauvoir began writing, numerous women had also sought better employment opportunities, improved wages and benefits, and better working conditions. Yet Beauvoir's book hit a nerve because it was one of the most scholarly and comprehensive works on the subject. *The Second Sex* was clearly the work of a gifted mind, brilliant in areas of philosophy, psychology, economics, and history. As a result, the book drew admiration from men as well as women. The essay included here considers one aspect of psychology: the negative effect of society's reliance on seemingly innocent cultural myths about women.

In her landmark work, *In a Different Voice* (1982), distinguished psychologist Carol Gilligan analyzes the basic male texts in psychology that explain the development of children into adults. She concludes that because the data came from studies of boys, "half the world was excluded." Experts in psychology insisted that these studies produced conclusions that were as true of women as they were of men. However, Gilligan felt they were wrong and went on to secure fresh data drawn from women and girls. When analyzed, her data gave new answers to old questions. The original studies of boys emphasized competitiveness and "liberal independence," whereas Gilligan's data showed that women often rejected these values in favor of communalism and a need for intimacy and cooperation. Gilligan shows how these qualities were interpreted to imply that women are somehow inferior to men—but only when one depends on data collected from men.

Gilligan has become a champion of feminists even though a number of respected critics disagree with her. Ultimately, much of what she has discovered about women's development has been shown to be true of men as well. Her work shows that a new model of human growth and development no longer supports a view that women are morally deficient in relation to men.

One of the most scathing (and common) critiques of modern feminism comes from bell hooks, whose *Black Women: Shaping Feminist Theory*, from her 1984 book *Feminist Theory: From Margin to Center* (revised 2000), focuses on the limitations of white feminists. hooks maintains that women who write from a privileged position do not take into account the issues that affect the "masses of women," especially black and third world women. In a powerful examination of the limits of influential feminists such as Betty Friedan, author of *The Feminine Mystique* (1963), hooks calls white feminists to task, describing as racist, sexist, and classist their inability to account for the needs of black women.

In a most interesting strategy, hooks includes a section discussing her own experience in early university classes on feminist theory: other students were condescending toward her because they had such different perspectives. Whereas her fellow students were thrilled by the opportunity to become part of a community of women for the first time, hooks had spent most of her childhood in a community of women who gave each other immense support and love. It was nothing new to her. Neither, however, was patriarchal tyranny. hooks knew it firsthand.

Working out her personal difficulties with fellow students gave hooks the insight to clarify her belief that feminism need not be merely a white bourgeois movement. hooks also acknowledges how difficult it is to create an inclusive feminism and how unimportant that goal has been, even for very ardent early feminists.

Nevertheless, she urges a communal approach that crosses lines of class and color.

These essays represent a wide variety of stances and cover a broad range of disciplines. Although they hardly cover the entire territory of feminism, they offer insights from diverse historical periods and from several important intellectual angles. Further, they reveal the resilience and the dynamic of the feminist movement, which continues today.

MARY WOLLSTONECRAFT

*Pernicious Effects Which
Arise from the
Unnatural Distinctions
Established in Society*

MARY WOLLSTONECRAFT (1759–1797) was born into relatively simple circumstances, with a father whose heavy drinking
and spending eventually ruined the family and left her and her sisters to support themselves. She became a governess, a teacher, and
eventually a writer. Her views were among the most enlightened of
her day, particularly regarding women and women's rights, giving
her the reputation of being a very forward-looking feminist, even
for our time. Her thinking, however, is comprehensive and not limited to a single issue.

She was known to the American patriot Thomas Paine (1737–
1809), to Dr. Samuel Johnson (1709–1783), and to the English
philosopher William Godwin (1756–1836), whom she eventually
married. Her views on marriage were remarkable for her time;
among other beliefs, she felt it unnecessary to marry a man in
order to live happily with him. Her first liaison, with an American,
Gilbert Imlay, gave her the opportunity to travel and learn something about commerce and capitalism at first hand. Her second liaison, with Godwin, brought her into the intellectual circles of her
day. She married Godwin when she was pregnant and died in
childbirth. Her daughter, Mary, married the poet Percy Bysshe
Shelley and wrote the novel *Frankenstein* (1818).

From *Vindication of the Rights of Woman.*

The excitement generated by the French Revolution (1789–1799) caused Wollstonecraft to react against the very conservative view put forward by the philosopher Edmund Burke. Her pamphlet *A Vindication of the Rights of Men* (1790) was well received. She followed it with *Vindication of the Rights of Woman* (1792), which was translated into French.

She saw feminism in political terms. The chapter reprinted here concentrates on questions of property, class, and law. As a person committed to the revolutionary principles of liberty, equality, and fraternity, Wollstonecraft linked the condition of women to the political and social structure of her society. Her aim was to point out the inequities in treatment of women—which her society simply did not perceive—and to attempt to rectify them.

Wollstonecraft's Rhetoric

Mary Wollstonecraft wrote for an audience that did not necessarily appreciate brief, exact expression. Rather, they appreciated a more luxuriant and leisurely style than we do today. As a result, her prose can sometimes seem wordy to a modern audience. However, she handles imagery carefully (especially in the first paragraph) without overburdening her prose. She uses an approach that she calls "episodical observations" (para. 12). These are anecdotes—personal stories—and apparently casual cataloguings of thoughts on a number of related issues. She was aware that her structure was not tight, that it did not develop a specific argument, and that it did not force the reader to accept or reject her position. She also considered this a wise approach, because it was obvious to her that her audience was completely prejudiced against her view. To attempt to convince them of her views was to invite total defeat.

Instead, she simply puts forward several observations that stand by themselves as examples of the evils she condemns. Even those who stand against her will see that there is validity to her claims; and they will not be so threatened by her argument as to become defensive before they have learned something new. She appeals always to the higher intellectual capacities of both men and women, directing her complaints, too, against both men and women. This balance of opinion, coupled with a range of thought-provoking examples, makes her views clear and convincing.

Also distinctive in this passage is the use of metaphor. The second sentence of paragraph 1 is particularly heavy with metaphor: "For it is in the most polished society that noisome reptiles and venomous serpents lurk under the rank herbage; and there is voluptuousness pampered by the still sultry air, which relaxes every good disposition before it ripens into virtue." The metaphor presents society as a garden in which the grass is decaying and dangerous serpents are lurking. Good disposition—character—is a plant that might ripen, but—continuing the metaphor—it ripens into virtue, not just a fruit. A favorite source of metaphors for Wollstonecraft is drapery (dressmaking). When she uses one of these metaphors she is usually reminding the reader that drapery gives a new shape to things, that it sometimes hides the truth, and that it ought not to put a false appearance on what it covers.

One of her rhetorical techniques is that of literary allusion. By alluding to important literary works and writers—such as Greek mythology, William Shakespeare, Jean-Jacques Rousseau, and Samuel Johnson—she not only demonstrates her knowledge but also shows that she respects her audience, which she presumes shares that same knowledge. She does not show off by overquoting or by referring to very obscure writers. She balances it perfectly, even by transforming folk aphorisms into "homely proverbs" such as, "whoever the devil finds idle he will employ."

Wollstonecraft's experiences with her difficult father gave her knowledge of gambling tables and card games, another source of allusions. She draws further on personal experience—shared by some of her audience—when she talks about the degradation felt by a woman of intelligence forced to act as a governess—a glorified servant—in a well-to-do family. Wollstonecraft makes excellent uses of these allusions, never overdoing them, always giving them just the right touch.

PREREADING QUESTIONS: WHAT TO READ FOR

The following prereading questions may help you anticipate key issues in the discussion on Mary Wollstonecraft's "Pernicious Effects Which Arise from the Unnatural Distinctions Established in Society." Keeping them in mind during your first reading of the selection should help focus your reactions.

- What are some of the pernicious effects that Wollstonecraft decries?
- What kinds of work are women fit for, in Wollstonecraft's view?
- What happens to people who are born to wealth and have nothing to do?

Pernicious Effects Which Arise from the Unnatural Distinctions Established in Society

From the respect paid to property flow, as from a poisoned 1
fountain, most of the evils and vices which render this world such a
dreary scene to the contemplative mind. For it is in the most polished society that noisome reptiles and venomous serpents lurk
under the rank herbage; and there is voluptuousness pampered by
the still sultry air, which relaxes every good disposition before it
ripens into virtue.

One class presses on another; for all are aiming to procure re- 2
spect on account of their property: and property, once gained, will
procure the respect due only to talents and virtue. Men neglect the
duties incumbent on man, yet are treated like demi-gods; religion is
also separated from morality by a ceremonial veil, yet men wonder
that the world is almost, literally speaking, a den of sharpers or
oppressors.

There is a homely proverb, which speaks a shrewd truth, that 3
whoever the devil finds idle he will employ. And what but habitual
idleness can hereditary wealth and titles produce? For man is so
constituted that he can only attain a proper use of his faculties by
exercising them, and will not exercise them unless necessity of some
kind first set the wheels in motion. Virtue likewise can only be acquired by the discharge of relative duties; but the importance of
these sacred duties will scarcely be felt by the being who is cajoled
out of his humanity by the flattery of sycophants.[1] There must be
more equality established in society, or morality will never gain
ground, and this virtuous equality will not rest firmly even when
founded on a rock, if one half of mankind be chained to its bottom
by fate, for they will be continually undermining it through ignorance or pride.

It is vain to expect virtue from women till they are in some de- 4
gree independent of men; nay, it is vain to expect that strength of
natural affection which would make them good wives and mothers.
Whilst they are absolutely dependent on their husbands they will be
cunning, mean, and selfish, and the men who can be gratified by the

---

[1] **sycophants** Toadies or false flatterers.

fawning fondness of spaniel-like affection have not much delicacy, for love is not to be bought, in any sense of the words; its silken wings are instantly shrivelled up when anything beside a return in kind is sought. Yet whilst wealth enervates men, and women live, as it were, by their personal charms, how can we expect them to discharge those ennobling duties which equally require exertion and self-denial? Hereditary property sophisticates[2] the mind, and the unfortunate victims to it, if I may so express myself, swathed from their birth, seldom exert the locomotive faculty of body or mind; and, thus viewing everything through one medium, and that a false one, they are unable to discern in what true merit and happiness consist. False, indeed, must be the light when the drapery of situation hides the man, and makes him stalk in masquerade, dragging from one scene of dissipation to another the nerveless limbs that hang with stupid listlessness, and rolling round the vacant eye which plainly tells us that there is no mind at home.

I mean, therefore, to infer[3] that the society is not properly organized which does not compel men and women to discharge their respective duties, by making it the only way to acquire that countenance from their fellow-creatures which every human being wishes some way to attain. The respect, consequently, which is paid to wealth and mere personal charms, is a true north-east blast that blights the tender blossoms of affection and virtue. Nature has wisely attached affections to duties to sweeten toil, and to give that vigour to the exertions of reason which only the heart can give. But the affection which is put on merely because it is the appropriated insignia of a certain character, when its duties are not fulfilled, is one of the empty compliments which vice and folly are obliged to pay to virtue and the real nature of things.

To illustrate my opinion, I need only observe that when a woman is admired for her beauty, and suffers herself to be so far intoxicated by the admiration she receives as to neglect to discharge the indispensable duty of a mother, she sins against herself by neglecting to cultivate an affection that would equally tend to make her useful and happy. True happiness, I mean all the contentment and virtuous satisfaction that can be snatched in this imperfect state, must arise from well regulated affections; and an affection includes a duty. Men are not aware of the misery they cause and the vicious weakness they cherish by only inciting women to render themselves pleasing; they do not consider that they thus make natural and

---

[2] **sophisticates** Ruins or corrupts.
[3] **infer** Imply.

artificial duties clash by sacrificing the comfort and respectability of a woman's life to voluptuous notions of beauty when in nature they all harmonize.

Cold would be the heart of a husband, were he not rendered 7 unnatural by early debauchery, who did not feel more delight at seeing his child suckled by its mother, than the most artful wanton tricks could ever raise; yet this natural way of cementing the matrimonial tie and twisting esteem with fonder recollections, wealth leads women to spurn. To preserve their beauty and wear the flowery crown of the day, which gives them a kind of right to reign for a short time over the sex, they neglect to stamp impressions on their husbands' hearts that would be remembered with more tenderness when the snow on the head began to chill the bosom than even their virgin charms. The maternal solicitude of a reasonable affectionate woman is very interesting, and the chastened dignity with which a mother returns the caresses that she and her child receive from a father who has been fulfilling the serious duties of his station, is not only a respectable but a beautiful sight. So singular indeed are my feelings, and I have endeavored not to catch factitious[4] ones, that after having been fatigued with the sight of insipid grandeur and the slavish ceremonies that with cumbrous pomp supplied the place of domestic affections, I have turned to some other scene to relieve my eye by resting it on the refreshing green everywhere scattered by nature. I have then viewed with pleasure a woman nursing her children, and discharging the duties of her station with, perhaps, merely a servant maid to take off her hands the servile part of the household business. I have seen her prepare herself and children, with only the luxury of cleanliness, to receive her husband, who returning weary home in the evening found smiling babes and a clean hearth. My heart has loitered in the midst of the group, and has even throbbed with sympathetic emotion, when the scraping of the well known foot has raised a pleasing tumult.

Whilst my benevolence has been gratified by contemplating this 8 artless picture, I have thought that a couple of this description, equally necessary and independent of each other, because each fulfilled the respective duties of their station, possessed all that life could give. Raised sufficiently above abject poverty not to be obliged to weigh the consequence of every farthing they spend, and having sufficient to prevent their attending to a frigid system of economy, which narrows both heart and mind, I declare, so vulgar[5] are my

---

[4] **factitious** False.
[5] **vulgar** Common.

conceptions, that I know not what is wanted to render this the happiest as well as the most respectable situation in the world, but a taste for literature, to throw a little variety and interest into social converse, and some superfluous money to give to the needy and to buy books. For it is not pleasant when the heart is opened by compassion and the head active in arranging plans of usefulness, to have a prim urchin continually twitching back the elbow to prevent the hand from drawing out an almost empty purse, whispering at the same time some prudential maxim about the priority of justice.

Destructive, however, as riches and inherited honours are to the human character, women are more debased and cramped, if possible, by them than men, because men may still, in some degree, unfold their faculties by becoming soldiers and statesmen. 9

As soldiers, I grant, they can now only gather, for the most part, vainglorious laurels, whilst they adjust to a hair the European balance, taking especial care that no bleak northern nook or sound incline the beam.[6] But the days of true heroism are over, when a citizen fought for his country like a Fabricius[7] or a Washington, and then returned to his farm to let his virtuous fervour run in a more placid, but not a less salutary, stream. No, our British heroes are oftener sent from the gaming table than from the plough[8] and their passions have been rather inflamed by hanging with dumb suspense on the turn of a die, than sublimated by panting after the adventurous march of virtue in the historic page. 10

The statesman, it is true, might with more propriety quit the faro bank, or card table, to guide the helm, for he has still but to shuffle and trick.[9] The whole system of British politics, if system it may courteously be called, consisting in multiplying dependents and contriving taxes which grind the poor to pamper the rich; thus a war, or any wild goose chase, is, as the vulgar use the phrase, a lucky turn-up of 11

---

[6] **incline the beam** The metaphor is of the balance — the scale that representations of blind justice hold up. Wollstonecraft's point is that in her time soldiers fought to prevent the slightest changes in a balance of power that grew ever more delicate, not in heroic wars with heroic consequences.

[7] **Fabricius (fl. 282 B.C.)** Gaius Fabricius, a worthy Roman general and statesman known for resistance to corruption.

[8] **from the plough** Worthy Roman heroes were humble farmers, not gamblers.

[9] **shuffle and trick** The upper class spent much of its time gambling: faro is a high-stakes card game. Wollstonecraft is ironic when she says the statesman has "still but to shuffle and trick," but she connects the "training" of faro with the practice of politics in a deft, sardonic fashion. She is punning on the multiple meanings of *shuffle* — to mix up a deck of cards and to move oneself or one's papers about slowly and aimlessly — and *trick* — to win one turn of a card game and to do a devious deed.

patronage for the minister, whose chief merit is the art of keeping himself in place. It is not necessary then that he should have bowels for[10] the poor, so he can secure for his family the odd trick. Or should some show of respect, for what is termed with ignorant ostentation an Englishman's birthright, be expedient to bubble the gruff mastiff[11] that he has to lead by the nose, he can make an empty show very safely by giving his single voice and suffering his light squadron to file off to the other side. And when a question of humanity is agitated he may dip a sop in the milk of human kindness to silence Cerberus,[12] and talk of the interest which his heart takes in an attempt to make the earth no longer cry for vengeance as it sucks in its children's blood, though his cold hand may at the very moment rivet their chains by sanctioning the abominable traffic. A minister is no longer a minister than while he can carry a point which he is determined to carry. Yet it is not necessary that a minister should feel like a man, when a bold push might shake his seat.

But, to have done with these episodical observations, let me re-   12
turn to the more specious slavery which chains the very soul of woman, keeping her for ever under the bondage of ignorance.

The preposterous distinctions of rank, which render civilization   13
a curse by dividing the world between voluptuous tyrants and cunning envious dependents, corrupt, almost equally, every class of people, because respectability is not attached to the discharge of the relative duties of life, but to the station, and when the duties are not fulfilled the affections cannot gain sufficient strength to fortify the virtue of which they are the natural reward. Still there are some loopholes out of which a man may creep, and dare to think and act for himself; but for a woman it is a herculean task, because she has difficulties peculiar to her sex to overcome which require almost superhuman powers.

A truly benevolent legislator always endeavors to make it the in-   14
terest of each individual to be virtuous; and thus private virtue becoming the cement of public happiness, an orderly whole is consolidated by the tendency of all the parts towards a common centre. But, the private or public virtue of woman is very problematical; for Rousseau, and a numerous list of male writers, insist that she should all her life be subjected to a severe restraint, that of propriety. Why subject her to propriety—blind propriety, if she be capable of acting from a nobler spring, if she be an heir of immortality? Is sugar always to be produced by vital blood? Is one half of the human

---

[10] **bowels for** Feelings for; sense of pity.
[11] **to bubble the gruff mastiff** To fool even a guard dog.
[12] **Cerberus** The guard dog of Hades, the Greek hell or underworld.

species, like the poor African slaves, to be subject to prejudices that brutalize them, when principles would be a surer guard, only to sweeten the cup of man? Is not this indirectly to deny woman reason? for a gift is a mockery, if it be unfit for use.

Women are, in common with men, rendered weak and luxurious by the relaxing pleasures which wealth procures; but added to this they are made slaves to their persons, and must render them alluring that man may lend them his reason to guide their tottering steps aright. Or should they be ambitious, they must govern their tyrants by sinister tricks, for without rights there cannot be any incumbent duties. The laws respecting woman, which I mean to discuss in a future part, make an absurd unit of a man and his wife,[13] and then, by the easy transition of only considering him as responsible, she is reduced to a mere cypher.[14]

The being who discharges the duties of its station is independent; and, speaking of women at large, their first duty is to themselves as rational creatures, and the next in point of importance, as citizens, is that which includes so many, of a mother. The rank in life which dispenses with their fulfilling this duty necessarily degrades them by making them mere dolls. Or, should they turn to something more important than merely fitting drapery upon a smooth block, their minds are only occupied by some soft platonic attachment; or, the actual management of an intrigue may keep their thoughts in motion; for when they neglect domestic duties, they have it not in their own power to take the field and march and counter-march like soldiers, or wrangle in the senate to keep their faculties from rusting.

I know that, as a proof of the inferiority of the sex, Rousseau has exultingly exclaimed, How can they leave the nursery for the camp![15] And the camp has by some moralists been termed the school of the most heroic virtues; though, I think, it would puzzle a keen casuist[16] to prove the reasonableness of the greater number of wars that have dubbed heroes. I do not mean to consider this question critically; because, having frequently viewed these freaks of ambition as the first natural mode of civilization, when the ground must be torn up, and the woods cleared by fire and sword, I do not choose to call them pests; but surely the present system of war has

15

16

17

---

[13] **absurd unit of a man and his wife** In English law man and wife were legally one; the man spoke for both.

[14] **cypher** Zero.

[15] **leave the nursery for the camp!** Rousseau's Émile complains that women cannot leave a nursery to go to war.

[16] **casuist** One who argues closely, persistently, and sometimes unfairly.

little connection with virtue of any denomination, being rather the school of *finesse* and effeminacy than of fortitude.

Yet if defensive war, the only justifiable war, in the present ad- 18 vanced state of society, where virtue can show its face and ripen amidst the rigours which purify the air on the mountain's top, were alone to be adopted as just and glorious, the true heroism of antiquity might again animate female bosoms. But fair and softly, gentle reader, male or female, do not alarm thyself, for though I have compared the character of a modern soldier with that of a civilized woman, I am not going to advise them to turn their distaff[17] into a musket, though I sincerely wish to see the bayonet converted into a pruning-hook. I only recreated an imagination, fatigue by contemplating the vices and follies which all proceed from a feculent[18] stream of wealth that has muddied the pure rills of natural affection, by supposing that society will some time or other be so constituted, that man must necessarily fulfill the duties of a citizen or be despised, and that while he was employed in any of the departments of civil life, his wife, also an active citizen, should be equally intent to manage her family, educate her children, and assist her neighbours.

But, to render her really virtuous and useful, she must not, if she 19 discharge her civil duties, want, individually, the protection of civil laws; she must not be dependent on her husband's bounty for her subsistence during his life or support after his death — for how can a being be generous who has nothing of its own? or virtuous, who is not free?

The wife, in the present state of things, who is faithful to her 20 husband, and neither suckles nor educates her children, scarcely deserves the name of a wife, and has no right to that of a citizen. But take away natural rights, and duties become null.

Women then must be considered as only the wanton solace of 21 men when they become so weak in mind and body that they cannot exert themselves, unless to pursue some frothy pleasure or to invent some frivolous fashion. What can be a more melancholy sight to a thinking mind than to look into the numerous carriages that drive helter-skelter about this metropolis in a morning full of pale-faced creatures who are flying from themselves. I have often wished, with Dr. Johnson,[19] to place some of them in a little shop with half a

---

[17] **distaff** Instrument to wind wool in the act of spinning, notoriously a job only "fit for women."

[18] **feculent** Filthy, polluted; related to *feces.*

[19] **Dr. Samuel Johnson (1709–1784)** The greatest lexicographer and one of the most respected authors of England's eighteenth century. He was known to Mary Wollstonecraft and to her sister, Eliza, a teacher. The reference is to an item published in his *Rambler,* essay 85.

dozen children looking up to their languid countenances for support. I am much mistaken if some latent vigour would not soon give health and spirit to their eyes, and some lines drawn by the exercise of reason the blank cheeks, which before were only undulated by dimples, might restore lost dignity to the character, or rather enable it to attain the true dignity of its nature. Virtue is not to be acquired even by speculation, much less by the negative supineness that wealth naturally generates.

Besides, when poverty is more disgraceful than even vice, is not   22
morality cut to the quick? Still to avoid misconstruction, though I consider that women in the common walks of life are called to fulfill the duties of wives and mothers, by religion and reason, I cannot help lamenting that women of a superior cast have not a road open by which they can pursue more extensive plans of usefulness and independence. I may excite laughter by dropping a hint which I mean to pursue some future time, for I really think that women ought to have representatives, instead of being arbitrarily governed without having any direct share allowed them in the deliberations of government.

But, as the whole system of representation is now in this coun-   23
try only a convenient handle for despotism, they need not complain, for they are as well represented as a numerous class of hard-working mechanics, who pay for the support of royalty when they can scarcely stop their children's mouths with bread. How are they represented whose very sweat supports the splendid stud of an heir apparent, or varnishes the chariot of some female favourite who looks down on shame? Taxes on the very necessaries of life enable an endless tribe of idle princes and princesses to pass with stupid pomp before a gaping crowd, who almost worship the very parade which costs them so dear. This is mere gothic grandeur, something like the barbarous useless parade of having sentinels on horseback at Whitehall,[20] which I could never view without a mixture of contempt and indignation.

How strangely must the mind be sophisticated when this sort of   24
state impresses it! But, till these monuments of folly are levelled by virtue, similar follies will leaven the whole mass. For the same character, in some degree, will prevail in the aggregate of society; and the refinements of luxury, or the vicious repinings,[21] of envious

---

[20] **sentinels on horseback at Whitehall** This is a reference to the expensive demonstration of showmanship that continues to our day: the changing of the guard at Whitehall.

[21] **repinings** Discontent, fretting.

poverty, will equally banish virtue from society, considered as the characteristic of that society, or only allow it to appear as one of the stripes of the harlequin coat worn by the civilized man.

In the superior ranks of life every duty is done by deputies, as if   25 duties could ever be waived, and the vain pleasures which consequent idleness forces the rich to pursue appear so enticing to the next rank that the numerous scramblers for wealth sacrifice everything to tread on their heels. The most sacred trusts are then considered as sinecures,[22] because they were procured by interest, and only sought to enable a man to keep *good company*. Women in particular, all want to be ladies. Which is simply to have nothing to do, but listlessly to go they scarcely care where, for they cannot tell what.

But what have women to do in society? I may be asked, but to   26 loiter with easy grace; surely you would not condemn them all to suckle fools and chronicle small beer![23] No. Women might certainly study the art of healing, and be physicians as well as nurses. And midwifery, decency seems to allot to them, though I am afraid the word midwife in our dictionaries will soon give place to *accoucheur,*[24] and one proof of the former delicacy of the sex be effaced from the language.

They might also study politics, and settle their benevolence on   27 the broadest basis; for the reading of history will scarcely be more useful than the perusal of romances, if read as mere biography; if the character of the times, the political improvements, arts, &c., be not observed. In short, if it be not considered as the history of man; and not of particular men, who filled a niche in the temple of fame, and dropped into the black rolling stream of time, that silently sweeps· all before it, into the shapeless void called—eternity. For shape, can it be called, "that shape hath none"?[25]

Business of various kinds they might likewise pursue, if they   28 were educated in a more orderly manner, which might save many from common and legal prostitution. Women would not then marry for a support, as men accept of places under government, and neglect the implied duties; nor would an attempt to earn their own subsistence—a most laudable one!—sink them almost to the level of those poor abandoned creatures who live by prostitution. For are

---

[22] **sinecures** Jobs with few duties but good pay.

[23] **chronicle small beer!** *Othello* (II.i. 158). This means to keep the household accounts.

[24] *accoucheur* Male version of the female midwife.

[25] **"that shape hath none"** The reference is to *Paradise Lost* (II.667) by John Milton (1608–1674); it is an allusion to death.

not milliners and mantua-makers[26] reckoned the next class? The few employments open to women, so far from being liberal, are menial; and when a superior education enables them to take charge of the education of children as governesses, they are not treated like the tutors of sons, though even clerical tutors are not always treated in a manner calculated to render them respectable in the eyes of their pupils, to say nothing of the private comfort of the individual. But as women educated like gentlewomen are never designed for the humiliating situation which necessity sometimes forces them to fill, these situations are considered in the light of a degradation; and they know little of the human heart, who need to be told that nothing so painfully sharpens sensibility as such a fall in life.

Some of these women might be restrained from marrying by a 29 proper spirit or delicacy, and others may not have had it in their power to escape in this pitiful way from servitude; is not that government then very defective, and very unmindful of the happiness of one half of its members, that does not provide for honest, independent women, by encouraging them to fill respectable stations? But in order to render their private virtue a public benefit, they must have a civil existence in the state, married or single; else we shall continually see some worthy woman, whose sensibility has been rendered painfully acute by undeserved contempt, droop like "the lily broken down by a plowshare."

It is a melancholy truth—yet such is the blessed effect of civiliza- 30 tion!—the most respectable women are the most oppressed; and, unless they have understandings far superior to the common run of understandings, taking in both sexes, they must, from being treated like contemptible beings, become contemptible. How many women thus waste life away the prey of discontent, who might have practiced as physicians, regulated a farm, managed a shop, and stood erect, supported by their own industry, instead of hanging their heads surcharged with the dew of sensibility, that consumes the beauty to which it at first gave lustre; nay, I doubt whether pity and love are so near akin as poets feign, for I have seldom seen much compassion excited by the helplessness of females, unless they were fair; then, perhaps pity was the soft handmaid of love, or the harbinger of lust.

How much more respectable is the woman who earns her own 31 bread by fulfilling any duty, than the most accomplished beauty!— beauty did I say?—so sensible am I of the beauty of moral loveliness, or the harmonious propriety that attunes the passions of a well

---

[26]**milliners and mantua-makers** Dressmakers, usually women (whereas tailors were usually men).

regulated mind, that I blush at making the comparison; yet I sigh to think how few women aim at attaining this respectability by withdrawing from the giddy whirl of pleasure, or the indolent calm that stupefies the good sort of women it sucks in.

Proud of their weakness, however, they must always be pro- 32
tected, guarded from care, and all the rough toils that dignify the mind. If this be the fiat of fate, if they will make themselves insignificant and contemptible, sweetly to waste "life away," let them not expect to be valued when their beauty fades, for it is the fate of the fairest flowers to be admired and pulled to pieces by the careless hand that plucked them. In how many ways do I wish, from the purest benevolence, to impress this truth on my sex; yet I fear that they will not listen to a truth that dear-bought experience has brought home to many an agitated bosom, nor willingly resign the privileges of rank and sex for the privileges of humanity, to which those have no claim who do not discharge its duties.

Those writers are particularly useful, in my opinion, who make 33
man feel for man, independent of the station he fills, or the drapery of factitious sentiments. I then would fain[27] convince reasonable men of the importance of some of my remarks; and prevail on them to weigh dispassionately the whole tenor of my observations. I appeal to their understandings; and, as a fellow-creature, claim, in the name of my sex, some interest in their hearts. I entreat them to assist to emancipate their companion, to make her a *help meet*[28] for them!

Would men but generously snap our chains, and be content 34
with rational fellowship instead of slavish obedience, they would find us more observant daughters, more affectionate sisters, more faithful wives, more reasonable mothers—in a word, better citizens. We should then love them with true affection, because we should learn to respect ourselves; and, the peace of mind of a worthy man would not be interrupted by the idle vanity of his wife, not the babes sent to nestle in a strange bosom, having never found a home in their mother's.

QUESTIONS FOR CRITICAL READING

1. Who is the audience for Wollstonecraft's writing? Is she writing more for men than for women? Is it clear from what she says that she addresses an explicit audience with specific qualities?

---

[27] **fain** Happily, gladly.
[28] ***help meet*** Helper, helpmate.

2. Analyze paragraph 1 carefully for the use of imagery, especially metaphor. What are the effects of these images? Are they overdone?

3. Wollstonecraft begins by attacking property, or the respect paid to it. What does she mean? Does she sustain that line of thought throughout the piece?

4. In paragraph 12, Wollstonecraft speaks of the "bondage of ignorance" in which women are held. Clarify precisely what she means by that expression.

5. In paragraph 30, Wollstonecraft says that people who are treated as if they were contemptible will become contemptible. Is this a political or a psychological judgment?

6. What is the substance of Wollstonecraft's complaint concerning the admiration of women for their beauty?

SUGGESTIONS FOR WRITING

1. Throughout the piece Wollstonecraft attacks the unnatural distinctions made between men and women. Establish carefully what those unnatural distinctions are, why they are unnatural, and whether such distinctions persist to the present day. By contrast, establish what some natural distinctions between men and women are and whether Wollstonecraft has taken them into consideration.

2. References are made throughout the piece to prostitution and to the debaucheries of men. Paragraph 7 specifically refers to the "wanton tricks" of prostitutes. What is Wollstonecraft's attitude toward men in regard to sexuality and their attitudes toward women—both the women of the brothels and the women with whom men live? Find passages in the piece that you can quote and analyze in an effort to examine her views.

3. In paragraph 2, Wollstonecraft complains that "the respect due only to talents and virtue" is instead being given to people on account of their property. Further, she says in paragraph 9 that riches are "destructive . . . to the human character." Determine carefully, by means of reference to and analysis of specific passages, just what Wollstonecraft means by such statements. Then, use your own anecdotes or "episodical observations" to take a stand on whether these are views you yourself can hold for our time. Are riches destructive to character? Is too much respect paid to those who possess property? If possible, use metaphor or allusion—literary or personal.

4. In paragraph 4, Wollstonecraft speaks of "men who can be gratified by the fawning fondness of spaniel-like affection" from their women. Search through the essay for other instances of similar views and analyze them carefully. Establish exactly what the men she describes want their women to be like. Have today's men changed very much in their expectations? Why? Why not? Use personal observations where possible in answering this question.

5. The question of what roles women ought to have in society is addressed in paragraphs 26, 27, and 28. What are those roles? Why are they defined in terms of work? Do you agree that they are, indeed, the roles that women should assume? Would you include more roles? Do women in our time have greater access to those roles? Consider what women actually did in Wollstonecraft's time and what they do today.

6. **CONNECTIONS** Compare Wollstonecraft's views on the ways in which women are victims of prejudice with the views of Martin Luther King Jr. How much do women of Wollstonecraft's time have in common with the conditions of African Americans as described by King? What political issues are central to the efforts of both groups to achieve justice and equal opportunity? Might Wollstonecraft see herself in the same kind of struggle as King, or would she draw sharp distinctions?

VIRGINIA WOOLF
Shakespeare's Sister

VIRGINIA WOOLF (1882–1941), one of the most gifted of the modernist writers, was a prolific essayist and novelist in what came to be known as the Bloomsbury group, named after a section of London near the British Museum. Most members of the group were writers, such as E. M. Forster, Lytton Strachey, and the critic Clive Bell, and some were artists, such as Duncan Grant and Virginia Woolf's sister, Vanessa Bell. The eminent economist John Maynard Keynes was part of the group as well, along with a variety of other accomplished intellectuals.

Virginia Woolf published some of the most important works of the early twentieth century, including the novels *Jacob's Room* (1922), *Mrs. Dalloway* (1925), *To the Lighthouse* (1927), *Orlando* (1928), and *The Waves* (1931). Among her many volumes of nonfiction prose is *A Room of One's Own* (1929). In this book Woolf speculates on what life would have been like for an imaginary gifted sister of William Shakespeare.

In discussing the imaginary Judith Shakespeare, Woolf examines the circumstances common to women's lives during the Renaissance. For example, women had little or no say in their future. Unlike their male counterparts, they were not educated in grammar schools and did not learn trades that would enable them to make a living for themselves. Instead, they were expected to marry as soon as possible, even as young as thirteen or fourteen years of age, and begin raising a family of their own. When they did marry, their husbands were men selected by their parents; the wives essentially became the property of those men. Under English law a married couple was regarded as one entity, and that entity was spoken for

From *A Room of One's Own*.

only by the man. Similarly, the women of the period had few civil rights. As Woolf points out, the history books do not mention women very often, and when they do, it is usually to relate that wife beating was common and generally approved in all classes of society.

As Woolf comments on the opportunities that women were denied during the Renaissance, she agrees with an unnamed bishop who said that no woman could have written Shakespeare's plays. Woolf explains that no woman could have had enough contact with the theater in those days to be received with anything but disdain and discourtesy. Women could not even act on stage in Shakespeare's time, much less write for it.

It would be all but impossible in a society of this sort to imagine a woman as a successful literary figure, much less as a popular playwright. After all, society excluded women, marginalizing them as insignificant—at least in the eyes of historians. Certainly women were mothers; as such, they bore the male children who went on to become accomplished and famous. However, without a trade or an education, women in Shakespeare's time were all but chattel slaves in a household.

In this setting, Woolf places a brilliant girl named Judith Shakespeare, a fictional character who, in Woolf's imaginative construction, had the same literary fire as her famous brother. How would she have tried to express herself? How would she have followed her talent? Woolf suggests the results would be depressing, and with good reason. No one would have listened to Judith; in all likelihood her life would have ended badly.

The women of Shakespeare's time mentioned in the history books are generally Elizabeths and Marys, queens and princesses whose power was inherent in their positions. Little is known, Woolf says, about the lives of ordinary middle-class women. In Woolf's time, historians were uninterested in such information. However, the feminist movement of the mid twentieth century promoted deeper research into women's society. As a result, many recent books have included detailed research into the lives of people in the Elizabethan period. Studying journals, day-books (including budgets and planning), and family records, modern historians have found much more information than English historian George Trevelyan (to whom Woolf refers in her essay) drew on. In fact, it is now known that women's lives were more varied than even Woolf implies, but women still had precious few opportunities compared to men of the period.

Woolf's Rhetoric

This selection is the third chapter from *A Room of One's Own*; thus, it begins with a sentence that implies continuity with an earlier section. The context for the essay's opening is as follows: a male dinner guest has said something insulting to women at a dinner party, and Woolf wishes she could come back with some hard fact to contradict the insult. However, she has no hard fact, so her strategy is to construct a situation that is as plausible and as accurate as her knowledge of history permits. Lacking fact, the novelist Virginia Woolf relies on imagination.

As it turned out, Woolf's portrait of Judith Shakespeare is so vivid that many readers actually believed William Shakespeare had such a sister. Judith Shakespeare did not exist, however. Her fictional character enables Woolf to speculate on how the life of any talented woman would have developed given the circumstances and limitations imposed on all women at the time. In the process, Woolf tries to reconstruct the world of Elizabethan England and place Judith in it.

Woolf goes about this act of imagination with extraordinary deliberateness. Her tone is cool and detached, almost as if she were a historian herself. She rarely reveals contempt for the opinions of men who are dismissive of women, such as the unnamed bishop. Yet, we catch an edgy tone when she discusses his views on women in literature. On the other hand, when she turns to Mr. Oscar Browning, a professor who believed the best women in Oxford were inferior to the worst men, we see another side of Woolf. She reveals that after making his high-minded pronouncements, Mr. Browning returned to his quarters for an assignation with an illiterate stable boy. This detail is meant to reveal the true intellectual level of Mr. Browning, as well as his attitude toward women.

Woolf makes careful use of simile in such statements as, "for fiction, imaginative work that is, is not dropped like a pebble upon the ground, as science may be; fiction is like a spider's web, attached ever so lightly perhaps, but still attached to life at all four corners" (para. 2). Later, she shows a highly efficient use of language: "to write a work of genius is almost always a feat of prodigious difficulty. . . . Dogs will bark; people will interrupt; money must be made; health will break down" (para. 11). For a woman—who would not even have had a room of her own in an Elizabethan household—the impediments to creating "a work of genius" were insurmountable.

One reason for Woolf's controlled and cool tone is that she wrote with the knowledge that most men were very conservative on matters of feminism. In 1929, people would not read what she wrote if she became enraged on paper. They would turn the page and ignore her argument. Thus, her tone seems inviting and cautious, almost as if Woolf is portraying herself as conservative on women's issues and in agreement with men like the historian Trevelyan and the unnamed bishop. However, nothing could be further from the truth. Woolf's anger may seethe and rage beneath the surface, but she keeps the surface smooth enough for those who disagree with her to be lured on to read.

One of the interesting details of Woolf's style is her allusiveness. She alludes to the work of many modern writers, such as John Keats, Alfred, Lord Tennyson, Robert Burns, and women writers such as Jane Austen, Emily Brontë, and George Eliot. Woolf's range of reference is that of the highly literary person—which she was; yet the way in which she makes reference to other important writers is designed not to offend the reader. If the reader knows the references, then Woolf will communicate on a special shared level of understanding. If the reader does not know the references, there is nothing in Woolf's manner that makes it difficult for the reader to continue and understand her main points.

Woolf's rhetoric in this piece is singularly polite. She makes her points without rancor and alarm. They are detailed, specific, and in many ways irrefutable. What she feels she has done is nothing less than telling the truth.

PREREADING QUESTIONS: WHAT TO READ FOR

The following prereading questions may help you anticipate key issues in the discussion on Virginia Woolf's "Shakespeare's Sister." Keeping them in mind during your first reading of the selection should help focus your reactions.

- What was the expected role of women in Shakespeare's time?
- By what means could Shakespeare's imaginary sister have become a dramatist?

Shakespeare's Sister

It was disappointing not to have brought back in the evening 1
some important statement, some authentic fact. Women are poorer
than men because—this or that. Perhaps now it would be better to
give up seeking for the truth, and receiving on one's head an
avalanche of opinion hot as lava, discolored as dish-water. It would
be better to draw the curtains; to shut out distractions; to light the
lamp; to narrow the enquiry and to ask the historian, who records
not opinions but facts, to describe under what conditions women
lived, not throughout the ages, but in England, say in the time of
Elizabeth.

For it is a perennial puzzle why no woman wrote a word of that 2
extraordinary literature when every other man, it seemed, was capable of song or sonnet. What were the conditions in which women
lived, I asked myself; for fiction, imaginative work that is, is not
dropped like a pebble upon the ground, as science may be; fiction is
like a spider's web, attached ever so lightly perhaps, but still attached to life at all four corners. Often the attachment is scarcely
perceptible; Shakespeare's plays, for instance, seem to hang there
complete by themselves. But when the web is pulled askew, hooked
up at the edge, torn in the middle, one remembers that these webs
are not spun in midair by incorporeal creatures, but are the work of
suffering human beings, and are attached to grossly material things,
like health and money and the houses we live in.

I went, therefore, to the shelf where the histories stand and took 3
down one of the latest, Professor Trevelyan's[1] *History of England.*
Once more I looked up Women, found "position of," and turned to
the pages indicated. "Wife-beating," I read, "was a recognised right
of man, and was practised without shame by high as well as low. . . .
Similarly," the historian goes on, "the daughter who refused to
marry the gentleman of her parents' choice was liable to be locked
up, beaten and flung about the room, without any shock being inflicted on public opinion. Marriage was not an affair of personal affection, but of family avarice, particularly in the 'chivalrous' upper
classes. . . . Betrothal often took place while one or both of the parties was in the cradle, and marriage when they were scarcely out of
the nurses' charge." That was about 1470, soon after Chaucer's time.
The next reference to the position of women is some two hundred
years later, in the time of the Stuarts. "It was still the exception for

---

[1] **Trevelyan: George Macaulay (1876–1962)** One of England's great historians. [Woolf's note]

women of the upper and middle class to choose their own husbands, and when the husband had been assigned, he was lord and master, so far at least as law and custom could make him. Yet even so," Professor Trevelyan concludes, "neither Shakespeare's women nor those of authentic seventeenth-century memoirs, like the Verneys and the Hutchinsons, seem wanting in personality and character." Certainly, if we consider it, Cleopatra must have had a way with her; Lady Macbeth, one would suppose, had a will of her own; Rosalind, one might conclude, was an attractive girl. Professor Trevelyan is speaking no more than the truth when he remarks that Shakespeare's women do not seem wanting in personality and character. Not being a historian, one might go even further and say that women have burnt like beacons in all the works of all the poets from the beginning of time—Clytemnestra, Antigone, Cleopatra, Lady Macbeth, Phèdre, Cressida, Rosalind, Desdemona, the Duchess of Malfi, among the dramatists; then among the prose writers: Millamant, Clarissa, Becky Sharp, Anna Karenina, Emma Bovary, Madame de Guermantes—the names flock to mind, nor do they recall women "lacking in personality and character." Indeed, if woman had no existence save in the fiction written by men, one would imagine her a person of the utmost importance; very various; heroic and mean; splendid and sordid; infinitely beautiful and hideous in the extreme; as great as a man, some think even greater.[2] But this is woman in fiction. In fact, as Professor Trevelyan points out, she was locked up, beaten and flung about the room.

A very queer, composite being thus emerges. Imaginatively she is of the highest importance; practically she is completely insignificant. She pervades poetry from cover to cover; she is all but absent from history. She dominates the lives of kings and conquerors in

[2]**even greater** "It remains a strange and almost inexplicable fact that in Athena's city, where women were kept in almost Oriental suppression as odalisques or drudges, the stage should yet have produced figures like Clytemnestra and Cassandra, Atossa and Antigone, Phèdre and Medea, and all the other heroines who dominate play after play of the 'misogynist' Euripides. But the paradox of this world where in real life a respectable woman could hardly show her face alone in the street, and yet on the stage a woman equals or surpasses a man, has never been satisfactorily explained. In modern tragedy the same predominance exists. At all events, a very cursory survey of Shakespeare's work (similarly with Webster, though not with Marlowe or Jonson) suffices to reveal how this dominance, this initiative of women, persists from Rosalind to Lady Macbeth. So too in Racine; six of his tragedies bear their heroines' names; and what male characters of his shall we set against Hermione and Andromaque, Bérénice and Roxane, Phèdre and Athalie? So again with Ibsen; what men shall we match with Solveig and Nora, Hedda and Hilda Wangel and Rebecca West?"—F. L. Lucas, *Tragedy*, pp. 114–15. [Woolf's note]

fiction; in fact she was the slave of any boy whose parents forced a ring upon her finger. Some of the most inspired words, some of the most profound thoughts in literature fall from her lips; in real life she could hardly read, could scarcely spell, and was the property of her husband.

It was certainly an odd monster that one made up by reading 5 the historians first and the poets afterwards—a worm winged like an eagle; the spirit of life and beauty in a kitchen chopping up suet. But these monsters, however amusing to the imagination, have no existence in fact. What one must do to bring her to life was to think poetically and prosaically at one and the same moment, thus keeping in touch with fact—that she is Mrs. Martin, aged thirty-six, dressed in blue, wearing a black hat and brown shoes; but not losing sight of fiction either—that she is a vessel in which all sorts of spirits and forces are coursing and flashing perpetually. The moment, however, that one tries this method with the Elizabethan woman, one branch of illumination fails; one is held up by the scarcity of facts. One knows nothing detailed, nothing perfectly true and substantial about her. History scarcely mentions her. And I turned to Professor Trevelyan again to see what history meant to him. I found by looking at his chapter headings that it meant—

"The Manor Court and the Methods of Open-field Agricul- 6 ture . . . The Cistercians and Sheep-farming . . . The Crusades . . . The University . . . The House of Commons . . . The Hundred Years' War . . . The Wars of the Roses . . . The Renaissance Scholars . . . The Dissolution of the Monasteries . . . Agrarian and Religious Strife . . . The Origin of English Sea-power . . . The Armada . . . and so on. Occasionally an individual woman is mentioned, an Elizabeth, or a Mary; a queen or a great lady. But by no possible means could middle-class women with nothing but brains and character at their command have taken part in any one of the great movements which, brought together, constitute the historian's view of the past. Nor shall we find her in any collection of anecdotes. Aubrey[3] hardly mentions her. She never writes her own life and scarcely keeps a diary; there are only a handful of her letters in existence. She left no plays or poems by which we can judge her. What one wants, I thought—and why does not some brilliant student at Newnham or Girton[4] supply it?—is a mass

---

[3] **John Aubrey (1626–1697)** English antiquarian noted for his *Brief Lives,* biographical sketches of famous men.

[4] **Newnham and Girton** Two women's colleges founded at Cambridge in the 1870s. [Woolf's note] Newnham (1871) and Girton (1869) were the first women's colleges at Cambridge University.

of information; at what age did she marry; how many children had she
as a rule; what was her house like; had she a room to herself; did she
do the cooking; would she be likely to have a servant? All these facts
lie somewhere, presumably, in parish registers and account books;
the life of the average Elizabethan woman must be scattered about
somewhere, could one collect it and make a book of it. It would be
ambitious beyond my daring, I thought, looking about the shelves for
books that were not there, to suggest to the students of those famous
colleges that they should rewrite history, though I own that it often
seems a little queer as it is, unreal, lopsided; but why should they not
add a supplement to history? calling it, of course, by some inconspicuous name so that women might figure there without impropriety?
For one often catches a glimpse of them in the lives of the great,
whisking away into the background, concealing, I sometimes think, a
wink, a laugh, perhaps a tear. And, after all, we have lives enough of
Jane Austen; it scarcely seems necessary to consider again the influence of the tragedies of Joanna Baillie upon the poetry of Edgar Allan
Poe; as for myself, I should not mind if the homes and haunts of Mary
Russell Mitford were closed to the public for a century at least. But
what I find deplorable, I continued, looking about the bookshelves
again, is that nothing is known about women before the eighteenth
century. I have no model in my mind to turn about this way and that.
Here am I asking why women did not write poetry in the Elizabethan
age, and I am not sure how they were educated; whether they were
taught to write; whether they had sitting-rooms to themselves; how
many women had children before they were twenty-one; what, in
short, they did from eight in the morning till eight at night. They had
no money evidently; according to Professor Trevelyan they were married whether they liked it or not before they were out of the nursery, at
fifteen or sixteen very likely. It would have been extremely odd, even
upon this showing, had one of them suddenly written the plays of
Shakespeare, I concluded, and I thought of that old gentleman, who is
dead now, but was a bishop, I think, who declared that it was impossible for any woman, past, present, or to come, to have the genius of
Shakespeare. He wrote to the papers about it. He also told a lady who
applied to him for information that cats do not as a matter of fact go to
heaven, though they have, he added, souls of a sort. How much thinking those old gentlemen used to save one! How the borders of ignorance shrank back at their approach! Cats do not go to heaven.
Women cannot write the plays of Shakespeare.

Be that as it may, I could not help thinking, as I looked at the   7
works of Shakespeare on the shelf, that the bishop was right at least
in this; it would have been impossible, completely and entirely, for
any woman to have written the plays of Shakespeare in the age of

Shakespeare. Let me imagine, since facts are so hard to come by, what would have happened had Shakespeare had a wonderfully gifted sister, called Judith, let us say. Shakespeare himself went, very probably—his mother was an heiress—to the grammar school, where he may have learnt Latin—Ovid, Virgil and Horace—and the elements of grammar and logic. He was, it is well known, a wild boy who poached rabbits, perhaps shot a deer, and had, rather sooner than he should have done, to marry a woman in the neighborhood, who bore him a child rather quicker than was right. That escapade sent him to seek his fortune in London. He had, it seemed, a taste for the theatre; he began by holding horses at the stage door. Very soon he got work in the theatre, became a successful actor, and lived at the hub of the universe, meeting everybody, knowing everybody, practicing his art on the boards, exercising his wits in the streets, and even getting access to the palace of the queen. Meanwhile his extraordinarily gifted sister, let us suppose, remained at home. She was as adventurous, as imaginative, as agog to see the world as he was. But she was not sent to school. She had no chance of learning grammar and logic, let alone of reading Horace and Virgil. She picked up a book now and then, one of her brother's perhaps, and read a few pages. But then her parents came in and told her to mend the stockings or mind the stew and not moon about with books and papers. They would have spoken sharply but kindly, for they were substantial people who knew the conditions of life for a woman and loved their daughter—indeed, more likely than not she was the apple of her father's eye. Perhaps she scribbled some pages up in an apple loft on the sly, but was careful to hide them or set fire to them. Soon, however, before she was out of her teens, she was to be betrothed to the son of a neighboring wool-stapler. She cried out that marriage was hateful to her, and for that she was severely beaten by her father. Then he ceased to scold her. He begged her instead not to hurt him, not to shame him in this matter of her marriage. He would give her a chain of beads or a fine petticoat, he said; and there were tears in his eyes. How could she disobey him? How could she break his heart? The force of her own gift alone drove her to it. She made up a small parcel of her belongings, let herself down by a rope one summer's night and took the road to London. She was not seventeen. The birds that sang in the hedge were not more musical than she was. She had the quickest fancy, a gift like her brother's, for the tune of words. Like him, she had a taste for the theatre. She stood at the stage door; she wanted to act, she said. Men laughed in her face. The manager—a fat, loose-lipped man—guffawed. He bellowed something about poodles dancing and women acting—no woman, he said, could possibly be an actress. He hinted—you can imagine what. She could get no training in her craft. Could she even seek her dinner in a tavern or roam the streets at midnight? Yet her genius was for fiction and lusted to feed abundantly upon the lives of men and women and the study of their ways. At last—for she was very young, oddly like Shakespeare the poet in her face, with the same grey eyes and rounded brows—at last Nick Greene, the actor-manager took pity on her; she found herself with child by that gentleman and so— who shall measure the heat and violence of the poet's heart when caught and tangled in a woman's body?—killed herself one winter's night and lies buried at some cross-roads where the omnibuses now stop outside the Elephant and Castle.[5]

    That, more or less, is how the story would run, I think, if a   8 woman in Shakespeare's day had had Shakespeare's genius. But for my part, I agree with the deceased bishop, if such he was—it is un-thinkable that any woman in Shakespeare's day should have had Shakespeare's genius. For genius like Shakespeare's is not born among laboring, uneducated, servile people. It was not born in En-gland among the Saxons and the Britons. It is not born today among the working classes. How, then, could it have been born among women whose work began, according to Professor Trevelyan, almost before they were out of the nursery, who were forced to it by their parents and held to it by all the power of law and custom? Yet genius of a sort must have existed among women as it must have ex-isted among the working classes. Now and again an Emily Brontë or a Robert Burns[6] blazes out and proves its presence. But certainly it never got itself on to paper. When, however, one reads of a witch being ducked, of a woman possessed by devils, of a wise woman selling herbs, or even of a very remarkable man who had a mother, then, I think we are on the track of a lost novelist, a suppressed poet, of some mute and inglorious Jane Austen, some Emily Brontë who dashed her brains out on the moor or mopped and mowed about the highways crazed with the torture that her gift had put her to. Indeed, I would venture to guess that Anon, who wrote so many poems without signing them, was often a woman. It was a woman Edward Fitzgerald,[7] I think, suggested who made the ballads and

---

    [5] **Elephant and Castle** A bus stop in London. The name came from a local pub.

    [6] **Emily Brontë (1818–1848)** wrote *Wuthering Heights;* **Robert Burns (1759–1796)** was a Scots poet; **Jane Austen (1775–1817)** wrote *Pride and Prejudice* and many other novels. All three wrote against very great odds.

    [7] **Edward Fitzgerald (1809–1883)** British scholar, poet, and translator who wrote *The Rubaiyat of Omar Khayyam.*

the folk-songs, crooning them to her children, beguiling her spinning with them, or the length of the winter's night.

This may be true or it may be false—who can say?—but what 9
is true in it, so it seemed to me, reviewing the story of Shakespeare's
sister as I had made it, is that any woman born with a great gift in
the sixteenth century would certainly have gone crazed, shot herself,
or ended her days in some lonely cottage outside the village, half
witch, half wizard, feared and mocked at. For it needs little skill in
psychology to be sure that a highly gifted girl who had tried to use
her gift for poetry would have been so thwarted and hindered by
other people, so tortured and pulled asunder by her own contrary
instincts, that she must have lost her health and sanity to a certainty.
No girl could have walked to London and stood at a stage door and
forced her way into the presence of actor-managers without doing
herself a violence and suffering an anguish which may have been irrational—for chastity may be a fetish invented by certain societies
for unknown reasons—but were none the less inevitable. Chastity
had then, it has even now, a religious importance in a woman's life,
and has so wrapped itself round with nerves and instincts that to cut
it free and bring it to the light of day demands courage of the rarest.
To have lived a free life in London in the sixteenth century would
have meant for a woman who was poet and playwright a nervous
stress and dilemma which might well have killed her. Had she survived, whatever she had written would have been twisted and de-
formed, issuing from a strained and morbid imagination. And undoubtedly, I thought, looking at the shelf where there are no plays
by women, her work would have gone unsigned. That refuge she
would have sought certainly. It was the relic of the sense of chastity
that dictated anonymity to women even so late as the nineteenth
century. Currer Bell, George Eliot, George Sand,[8] all the victims of
inner strife as their writings prove, sought ineffectively to veil themselves by using the name of a man. Thus they did homage to the
convention, which if not implanted by the other sex was liberally
encouraged by them (the chief glory of a woman is not to be talked
of, said Pericles, himself a much-talked-of man), that publicity in
women is detestable. Anonymity runs in their blood. The desire to
be veiled still possesses them. They are not even now as concerned
about the health of their fame as men are, and, speaking generally,
will pass a tombstone or a signpost without feeling an irresistible

---

[8] **Currer Bell (1816–1855), George Eliot (1819–1880), George Sand
(1804–1876)** Masculine pen names for Charlotte Brontë, Mary Ann Evans, and
Amandine-Aurore-Lucille Dudevant, three major novelists of the nineteenth century.

desire to cut their names on it, as Alf, Bert or Chas. must do in obedience to their instinct, which murmurs if it sees a fine woman go
by, or even a dog, Ce chien est à moi.[9] And, of course, it may not be
a dog, I thought, remembering Parliament Square, the Sieges Allee
and other avenues; it may be a piece of land or a man with curly
black hair. It is one of the great advantages of being a woman that
one can pass even a very fine negress without wishing to make an
Englishwoman of her.

That woman, then, who was born with a gift of poetry in the   10
sixteenth century, was an unhappy woman, a woman at strife
against herself. All the conditions of her life, all her own instincts,
were hostile to the state of mind which is needed to set free whatever is in the brain. But what is the state of mind that is most propitious to the act of creation, I asked. Can one come by any notion of
the state that furthers and makes possible that strange activity? Here
I opened the volume containing the Tragedies of Shakespeare. What
was Shakespeare's state of mind, for instance, when he wrote *Lear*
and *Antony and Cleopatra*? It was certainly the state of mind most favorable to poetry that there has ever existed. But Shakespeare himself said nothing about it. We only know casually and by chance
that he "never blotted a line." Nothing indeed was ever said by the
artist himself about his state of mind until the eighteenth century
perhaps. Rousseau perhaps began it. At any rate, by the nineteenth
century self-consciousness had developed so far that it was the habit
for men of letters to describe their minds in confessions and auto-
biographies. Their lives also were written, and their letters were
printed after their deaths. Thus, though we do not know what
Shakespeare went through when he wrote *Lear,* we do know
what Carlyle went through when he wrote the *French Revolution;*
what Flaubert went through when he wrote *Madame Bovary;* what
Keats[10] was going through when he tried to write poetry against the
coming of death and the indifference of the world.

And one gathers from this enormous modern literature of con-   11
fession and self-analysis that to write a work of genius is almost always a feat of prodigious difficulty. Everything is against the likelihood that it will come from the writer's mind whole and entire.
Generally material circumstances are against it. Dogs will bark;
people will interrupt; money must be made; health will break down.
Further, accentuating all these difficulties and making them harder

[9] **Ce chien est à moi** That's my dog.
[10] **Thomas Carlyle (1795–1881), Gustave Flaubert (1821–1880), and John Keats (1795–1821)** Important nineteenth-century writers, all men.

to bear is the world's notorious indifference. It does not ask people to write poems and novels and histories; it does not need them. It does not care whether Flaubert finds the right word or whether Carlyle scrupulously verifies this or that fact. Naturally, it will not pay for what it does not want. And so the writer, Keats, Flaubert, Carlyle, suffers, especially in the creative years of youth, every form of distraction and discouragement. A curse, a cry of agony, rises from those books of analysis and confession. "Mighty poets in their misery dead"—that is the burden of their song. If anything comes through in spite of all this, it is a miracle, and probably no book is born entire and uncrippled as it was conceived.

But for women, I thought, looking at the empty shelves, these 12 difficulties were infinitely more formidable. In the first place, to have a room of her own, let alone a quiet room or a sound-proof room, was out of the question, unless her parents were exceptionally rich or very noble, even up to the beginning of the nineteenth century. Since her pin money, which depended on the good will of her father, was only enough to keep her clothed, she was debarred from such alleviations as came even to Keats or Tennyson or Carlyle, all poor men, from a walking tour, a little journey to France, from the separate lodging which, even if it were miserable enough, sheltered them from the claims and tyrannies of their families. Such material difficulties were formidable; but much worse were the immaterial. The indifference of the world which Keats and Flaubert and other men of genius have found so hard to bear was in her case not indifference but hostility. The world did not say to her as it said to them, Write if you choose; it makes no difference to me. The world said with a guffaw, Write? What's the good of your writing? Here the psychologists of Newnham and Girton might come to our help, I thought, looking again at the blank spaces on the shelves. For surely it is time that the effect of discouragement upon the mind of the artist should be measured, as I have seen a dairy company measure the effect of ordinary milk and Grade A milk upon the body of the rat. They set two rats in cages side by side, and of the two one was furtive, timid and small, and the other was glossy, bold and big. Now what food do we feed women as artists upon? I asked, remembering, I suppose, that dinner of prunes and custard. To answer that question I had only to open the evening paper and to read that Lord Birkenhead is of opinion—but really I am not going to trouble to copy our Lord Birkenhead's opinion upon the writing of women. What Dean Inge says I will leave in peace. The Harley Street specialist may be allowed to rouse the echoes of Harley Street with his vociferations without raising a hair on my head. I will quote, however, Mr. Oscar Browning, because Mr. Oscar Browning was a great figure in Cambridge at one time, and used to examine the students at Girton and Newnham. Mr. Oscar Browning was wont to declare "that the impression left on his mind, after looking over any set of examination papers, was that, irrespective of the marks he might give, the best woman was intellectually the inferior of the worst man." After saying that Mr. Browning went back to his rooms—and it is this sequel that endears him and makes him a human figure of some bulk and majesty—he went back to his rooms and found a stable-boy lying on the sofa—"a mere skeleton, his cheeks were cavernous and sallow, his teeth were black, and he did not appear to have the full use of his limbs. . . . 'That's Arthur' [said Mr. Browning]. 'He's a dear boy really and most high-minded.'" The two pictures always seem to me to complete each other. And happily in this age of biography the two pictures often do complete each other, so that we are able to interpret the opinions of great men not only by what they say, but by what they do.

But though this is possible now, such opinions coming from the   13 lips of important people must have been formidable enough even fifty years ago. Let us suppose that a father from the highest motives did not wish his daughter to leave home and become writer, painter or scholar. "See what Mr. Oscar Browning says," he would say; and there was not only Mr. Oscar Browning; there was the *Saturday Review;* there was Mr. Greg—the "essentials of a woman's being," said Mr. Greg emphatically, "are that *they are supported by, and they minister to, men*"—there was an enormous body of masculine opinion to the effect that nothing could be expected of women intellectually. Even if her father did not read out loud these opinions, any girl could read them for herself; and the reading, even in the nineteenth century, must have lowered her vitality, and told profoundly upon her work. There would always have been that assertion—you cannot do this, you are incapable of doing that—to protest against, to overcome. Probably for a novelist this germ is no longer of much effect; for there have been women novelists of merit. But for painters it must still have some sting in it; and for musicians, I imagine, is even now active and poisonous in the extreme. The woman composer stands where the actress stood in the time of Shakespeare. Nick Greene, I thought, remembering the story I had made about Shakespeare's sister, said that a woman acting put him in mind of a dog dancing. Johnson repeated the phrase two hundred years later of women preaching. And here, I said, opening a book about music, we have the very words used again in this year of grace, 1928, of women who try to write music. "Of Mlle. Germaine Tailleferre one can only repeat Dr. Johnson's dictum concerning a woman preacher, transposed into terms of music. 'Sir, a woman's composing is like a dog's walking on his hind legs. It is not done well, but you are surprised to find it done at all.'"[11] So accurately does history repeat itself.

Thus, I concluded, shutting Mr. Oscar Browning's life and pushing away the rest, it is fairly evident that even in the nineteenth century a woman was not encouraged to be an artist. On the contrary, she was snubbed, slapped, lectured and exhorted. Her mind must have been strained and her vitality lowered by the need of opposing this, of disproving that. For here again we come within range of that very interesting and obscure masculine complex which has had so much influence upon the woman's movement; that deep-seated desire, not so much that *she* shall be inferior as that *he* shall be superior, which plants him wherever one looks, not only in front of the arts, but barring the way to politics too, even when the risk to himself seems infinitesimal and the suppliant humble and devoted. Even Lady Bessborough, I remembered, with all her passion for politics, must humbly bow herself and write to Lord Granville Leveson-Gower: ". . . notwithstanding all my violence in politics and talking so much on that subject, I perfectly agree with you that no woman has any business to meddle with that or any other serious business, farther than giving her opinion (if she is ask'd)." And so she goes on to spend her enthusiasm where it meets with no obstacle whatsoever upon that immensely important subject, Lord Granville's maiden speech in the House of Commons. The spectacle is certainly a strange one, I thought. The history of men's opposition to women's emancipation is more interesting perhaps than the story of that emancipation itself. An amusing book might be made of it if some young student at Girton or Newnham would collect examples and deduce a theory—but she would need thick gloves on her hands, and bars to protect her of solid gold.

But what is amusing now, I recollected, shutting Lady Bessborough, had to be taken in desperate earnest once. Opinions that one now pastes in a book labelled cock-a-doodle-dum and keeps for reading to select audiences on summer nights once drew tears, I can assure you. Among your grandmothers and great-grandmothers there were many that wept their eyes out. Florence Nightingale shrieked aloud in her agony.[12] Moreover, it is all very well for you, who have got yourselves to college and enjoy sitting-rooms—or is it only bed-sitting-rooms?—of your own to say that genius should disregard such

14

15

---

[11] *A Survey of Contemporary Music*, Cecil Gray, p. 246. [Woolf's note]

[12] *See Cassandra* by Florence Nightingale, printed in *The Cause*, by R. Strachey. [Woolf's note]

opinions; that genius should be above caring what is said of it. Unfortunately, it is precisely the men or women of genius who mind most what is said of them. Remember Keats. Remember the words he had cut on his tombstone.[13] Think of Tennyson; think—but I need hardly multiply instances of the undeniable, if very unfortunate, fact that it is the nature of the artist to mind excessively what is said about him. Literature is strewn with the wreckage of men who have minded beyond reason the opinions of others.

And this susceptibility of theirs is doubly unfortunate, I   16 thought, returning again to my original enquiry into what state of mind is most propitious for creative work, because the mind of an artist, in order to achieve the prodigious effort of freeing whole and entire the work that is in him, must be incandescent, like Shakespeare's mind, I conjectured, looking at the book which lay open at *Antony and Cleopatra*. There must be no obstacle in it, no foreign matter unconsumed.

For though we say that we know nothing about Shakespeare's   17 state of mind, even as we say that, we are saying something about Shakespeare's state of mind. The reason perhaps why we know so little of Shakespeare—compared with Donne or Ben Jonson or Milton[14]—is that his grudges and spites and antipathies are hidden from us. We are not held up by some "revelation" which reminds us of the writer. All desire to protest, to preach, to proclaim an injury, to pay off a score, to make the world the witness of some hardship or grievance was fired out of him and consumed. Therefore his poetry flows from him free and unimpeded. If ever a human being got his work expressed completely, it was Shakespeare. If ever a mind was incandescent, unimpeded, I thought, turning again to the bookcase, it was Shakespeare's mind.

QUESTIONS FOR CRITICAL READING

1. How did Elizabethan gender roles limit opportunities in literature?
2. Why does Woolf begin by referring to an eminent historian?
3. Why does history treat sixteenth- and seventeenth-century women with so little notice?
4. What is Woolf's point regarding the behavior of Oscar Browning?

---

[13]**words . . . tombstone** "Here lies one whose name is writ on water." [Woolf's note]

[14]**John Donne (1572–1631), Ben Jonson (1572/3–1694), and John Milton (1608–1674)** Three of the most important seventeenth-century poets.

5. Why does Woolf worry over the relation of opinions to facts?

6. What is the difference between the way women are represented in history and the way they are depicted in fiction?

7. Why does Woolf have Judith Shakespeare become pregnant?

SUGGESTIONS FOR WRITING

1. Woolf says that a woman "born with a gift of poetry in the sixteenth century, was an unhappy woman, a woman at strife against herself" (para. 10). What does it mean for a woman to be "at strife against herself"? What are the characteristics of such a strife, and what are its implications for the woman? In what ways would she be aware of such inner strife?

2. Look up brief biographies of the women writers who took a man's name. Woolf lists three together: Currer Bell, George Eliot, and George Sand. What did they have in common? Why did they feel the need to use a man's name for their pseudonym? What did they do to avoid being stigmatized as women writers? Were they equally successful? Are they now considered feminist writers?

3. Despite the calmness of her tone, it is clear that Woolf feels very deeply about the issues that she discusses in this piece. In what ways can you justify this as a formative piece of feminist writing? What elements establish it as either feminist or not? If you feel it is not a feminist piece, explain why, and try to show what changes would help it to qualify as a feminist essay.

4. Read the book from which this essay comes, *A Room of One's Own*. The last chapter discusses androgyny, the quality of possessing characteristics of both sexes. Woolf argues that perhaps a writer should not be exclusively male or female in outlook, but should combine both. How effective is her argument in that chapter? How much of an impact did the book have on your own views of feminism?

5. Explain why it is so important for a woman to have "a room of one's own." Obviously, the use of the word *room* stands for much more than a simple room with four walls and a door. What is implied in the way Woolf uses this term? Do you think this point is still valid for women in the twenty-first century? Why are so many women in any age denied the right to have "a room of one's own"?

6. Woolf says that "even in the nineteenth century a woman was not encouraged to be an artist. On the contrary, she was snubbed, slapped, lectured and exhorted. Her mind must have been strained and her vitality lowered by the need of opposing this, of disproving that" (para. 14). Explain the implications of this statement, and decide whether it still describes the situation of many or most women. Use your personal experience where relevant, but consider the situations of any women you find interesting.

7. **CONNECTIONS** In what ways are Mary Wollstonecraft and Virginia Woolf in agreement about the waste of women's talents in any age? As you comment on this, consider, too, the ways in which these writers differ in their approach to discussing women and the ways in which women sometimes cooperate in accepting their own restrictions. Which of these writers is more obviously a modern feminist in your mind? Which of them is more convincing? Why?

8. **CONNECTIONS** Based on Woolf's attitudes in this essay, which of the male writers in this collection comes closest to supporting feminist views? Consider especially the work of Karl Marx, Martin Luther King Jr., Henry David Thoreau, and James Baldwin. Which of their views seems most sympathetic to the problems Woolf considers here?

9. **CONNECTIONS** Judging from Woolf's views in this essay, would she consider the works of Elizabeth Cady Stanton and Harriet Jacobs to be feminist essays? What would attract her to either or both of these writers? Which of the two had feminist ideals that sympathized most closely with those of Woolf? Woolf spoke of women in the sixteenth century. Stanton and Jacobs spoke of them in the nineteenth century. Had women's condition changed significantly by then?

SIMONE DE BEAUVOIR
Woman: Myth and Reality

Simone de Beauvoir (1908–1986) was one of the most important post–World War II French intellectuals. Her work was primarily philosophical, and she herself taught philosophy and lived for a time with one of France's preeminent existentialist philosophers, Jean-Paul Sartre (1905–1980). These two independent and brilliant leftist thinkers represented the ideal couple to many intellectuals, although recent biographical studies have demonstrated that in their relationship Beauvoir's ambitions were subjugated to those of Sartre.

Beauvoir prepared for a career as a teacher at the École Normale Superieure and taught in Marseilles, Rouen, and Paris, all the while writing novels, memoirs, and essays. Her best-known book is *Le Deuxième Sexe* (1949), published in English in 1953 as *The Second Sex*, a book now regarded as a beacon for the modern feminist movement. When Beauvoir began work on this book, French women were not permitted to vote (they did not win suffrage until 1945). In *The Second Sex* Beauvoir discusses how women are cast as the Other, the alienated of society. She explores the implications of defining women in relation to men—as *what men are not* rather than as *what women are*, as a category in and of themselves.

According to Beauvoir, a person is not born a woman but makes herself a woman. This suggestion implies, for Beauvoir, that the individual is shaped and formed by social convention, especially by conventions associated with gender. Certain conventions maintain a social fiction that pleases the "ruling caste," which in Beauvoir's view is exclusively masculine. She compares the myth of the Eternal Feminine with a Platonic idea. For Plato, the reality of the world is inferior to the pure ideas that exist in heaven. These

---

From *The Second Sex*. Translated and edited by H. M. Parshley.

ideas are fixed and unaltered by experience. In that sense, Beauvoir regards the myth of the Eternal Feminine as an idea that does not change, even in the face of human experience that contradicts it.

Part of the idea of the Eternal Feminine involves the myth that women are mysterious and incomprehensible to men; they are completely unlike men and, therefore, the Other. Beauvoir complains that no amount of personal experience seems to shatter the myth of women's mystery. She also states that mysteriousness does not serve women well, nor does it serve men; nevertheless, the concept of mystery lingers. She explains that in the relationship of master to slave, it is always the slave who is mysterious and difficult to understand. The slave is always the Other. Through this logic Beauvoir leads us to understand that as long as the mystery of woman defines her, woman will always be in a subordinate relationship to men.

One important consequence of accepting the myth of woman is that men will fail to understand women as they are—as friends, as equals. Even worse, women who accept the myth will constantly distort their personalities in order to please the "master." Beauvoir asks, which is it that a woman loves: her husband or her marriage? Women who accept the myth will manipulate men for their own purposes by trading on that myth, but in the process they will lose their individual nature, surrendering it to some imagined "immanence." *Immanence* is one of the most frequently repeated words in the essay (see para. 5); by this term, Beauvoir usually means an imagined essential quality, associated here with a myth.

The problem is that the myth of the Eternal Feminine, however it is expressed, contradicts the essential nature of individuals. It is an archetype that cannot be altered even when we see individuals contradicting the archetype. When that happens, Beauvoir says, we assume the individual is aberrant in some way. Beauvoir encourages us to reject the myth of the Eternal Feminine and to accept the reality that presents itself before our eyes. Thus, Beauvoir does not subscribe to the Platonic view; instead she follows the Aristotelian view that prefers examination of a scientific sort, one that accepts perceived facts.

Beauvoir's Rhetoric

This essay makes a plea for equality between men and women on several levels. As society is structured, Beauvoir knows, the concept of equality is impossible. The social order, she tells us, is essentially patriarchal. As a result, women have a subordinate and restricted role that is maintained in part by the persistence of the myth of the Eternal Feminine. Therefore, the general structure of the essay is as an argument decrying the persistence of the myth and revealing the damage that it does to members of society, both men and women.

At the time she wrote this piece, Beauvoir was not known as a feminist. Indeed, in the late 1940s and early 1950s, few modern feminists were known in the United States or in France. Long before Beauvoir aligned herself with certain militant feminists in the 1970s, *The Second Sex* provided a rallying cry because it was a treatise that examined with great authority the representation of women in many different intellectual and cultural arenas. For that reason, the book became a memorable document of great political power. Its rhetoric is not patterned or self-conscious but simple and straightforward. The calm, reasonable, direct style enforces the author's persuasiveness.

Beauvoir's method in this piece is careful analysis of a circumstance that she defines at the outset: the myth of the Eternal Feminine. Once she has described and defined this myth—and in the process established its persistence—she analyzes its character and its implications. Her analysis of the myth's uses in society reveals how it guarantees a woman's subordination. Beauvoir also calls women to task for accepting a myth that ultimately imprisons them. She urges change, suggesting that certain basic transformations may make it possible for men and women to achieve a form of equality that preserves their respective masculinity and femininity without demanding that one become the Other.

Beauvoir has drawn criticism for the tone of her description of women's behavior. Writers such as the poet Stevie Smith have accused Beauvoir of standing aside from the mass of women as if she herself were in a separate category. Some readers and close friends felt that her relationship with Sartre, in which they saw her treated as an absolute equal intellectually, led her to develop a distorted view of the nature of women's subjection and gave her writing a cool, overly reserved, academic quality.

In fact, it is true that this piece is reserved. It is also true, however, that Beauvoir strikes at a given in the social order of mid-century Europe and America. And it is true that she generally talks about women who are in a comfortable social class, women that bell hooks would refer to as bourgeois and privileged. Nonetheless, Beauvoir maintains that as long as women are seen as mysterious and different in a male-dominated world, they will remain subordinate. The myths associated with women may be several, contradictory, and seemingly harmless, but Beauvoir insists they are ultimately damaging to women and to the relationship between the sexes.

One of the most distinctive qualities of *The Second Sex* is its learnedness. Beauvoir avoids giving the impression that she is merely stating opinion by pausing occasionally to make references to important writers such as Auguste Comte, Søren Kierkegaard, André Gide, and Maurice Maeterlinck. Most of the writers she refers to are men, and most are longstanding philosophers and classic authors. By citing such authorities she reveals a capacious mind, one that is not ignorant of the role of male writers and the problems of a society dominated by males.

The power of the piece lies in its clarity and depth of thought. Beauvoir was a consummate intellectual in an environment that nurtured such types of thinkers, and what she has to say demands our attention and respect.

PREREADING QUESTIONS: WHAT TO READ FOR

The following prereading questions may help you anticipate key issues in the discussion on Simone de Beauvoir's "Woman: Myth and Reality." Keeping them in mind during your first reading of the selection should help focus your reactions.

- What is the myth of the Eternal Feminine?
- Why do men prefer the myth of the Eternal Feminine to the reality of women?
- How does men's power benefit from the myth(s) of women?

Woman: Myth and Reality

The myth of woman plays a considerable part in literature; but what is its importance in daily life? To what extent does it affect the customs and conduct of individuals? In replying to this question it will be necessary to state precisely the relations this myth bears to reality.

There are different kinds of myths. This one, the myth of woman, sublimating an immutable aspect of the human condition — namely, the 'division' of humanity into two classes of individuals — is a static myth. It projects into the realm of Platonic ideas a reality that is directly experienced or is conceptualized on a basis of experience; in place of fact, value, significance, knowledge, empirical law, it substitutes a transcendental Idea, timeless, unchangeable, necessary. This idea is indisputable because it is beyond the given: it is endowed with absolute truth. Thus, as against the dispersed, contingent, and multiple existences of actual women, mythical thought opposes the Eternal Feminine, unique and changeless. If the definition provided for this concept is contradicted by the behavior of flesh-and-blood women, it is the latter who are wrong: we are told not that Femininity is a false entity, but that the women concerned are not feminine. The contrary facts of experience are impotent against the myth. In a way, however, its source is in experience. Thus it is quite true that woman is other than man, and this alterity is directly felt in desire, the embrace, love; but the real relation is one of reciprocity; as such it gives rise to authentic drama. Through eroticism, love, friendship, and their alternatives, deception, hate, rivalry, the relation is a struggle between conscious beings each of whom wishes to be essential, it is the mutual recognition of free beings who confirm one another's freedom, it is the vague transition from aversion to participation. To pose Woman is to pose the absolute Other, without reciprocity, denying against all experience that she is a subject, a fellow human being.

In actuality, of course, women appear under various aspects; 3 but each of the myths built up around the subject of woman is intended to sum her up *in toto;* each aspires to be unique. In consequence, a number of incompatible myths exist, and men tarry musing before the strange incoherencies manifested by the idea of Femininity. As every woman has a share in a majority of these archetypes—each of which lays claim to containing the sole Truth of woman—men of today also are moved again in the presence of their female companions to an astonishment like that of the old sophists who failed to understand how man could be blond and dark at the same time! Transition toward the absolute was indicated long ago in social phenomena: relations are easily congealed in classes, functions in types, just as relations, to the childish mentality, are fixed in things. Patriarchal society, for example, being centered upon the conservation of the patrimony, implies necessarily, along with those who own and transmit wealth, the existence of men and women who take property away from its owners and put it into circulation. The men—adventurers, swindlers, thieves, speculators—are generally repudiated by the group; the women, employing their erotic attraction, can induce young men and even fathers of families to scatter their patrimonies, without ceasing to be within the law. Some of these women appropriate their victims' fortunes or obtain legacies by using undue influence; this role being regarded as evil, those who play it are called 'bad women.' But the fact is that quite to the contrary they are able to appear in some other setting— at home with their fathers, brothers, husbands, or lovers—as guardian angels; and the courtesan who 'plucks' rich financiers is, for painters and writers, a generous patroness. It is easy to understand in actual experience the ambiguous personality of Aspasia or Mme de Pompadour.[1] But if woman is depicted as the Praying Mantis, the Mandrake, the Demon, then it is most confusing to find in woman also the Muse, the Goddess Mother, Beatrice.

As group symbols and social types are generally defined by   4
means of antonyms in pairs, ambivalence will seem to be an intrinsic quality of the Eternal Feminine. The saintly mother has for correlative the cruel stepmother, the angelic young girl has the perverse virgin: thus it will be said sometimes that Mother equals Life, sometimes that Mother equals Death, that every virgin is pure spirit or flesh dedicated to the devil.

Evidently it is not reality that dictates to society or to individuals   5
their choice between the two opposed basic categories; in every period, in each case, society and the individual decide in accordance with their needs. Very often they project into the myth adopted the institutions and values to which they adhere. Thus the paternalism that claims woman for hearth and home defines her as sentiment, inwardness, immanence. In fact every existent is at once immanence and transcendence; when one offers the existent no aim, or prevents him from attaining any, or robs him of his victory, then his transcendence falls vainly into the past—that is to say, falls back into immanence. This is the lot assigned to woman in the patriarchate; but it is in no way a vocation, any more than slavery is the vocation of the slave. The development of this mythology is to be clearly seen in Auguste Comte.[2] To identify Woman with Altruism is to guarantee to man absolute rights in her devotion, it is to impose on women a categorical imperative.

The myth must not be confused with the recognition of signifi-   6
cance; significance is immanent in the object; it is revealed to the mind through a living experience; whereas the myth is a transcendent Idea that escapes the mental grasp entirely. When in *L'Age*

---

[1] **Aspasia . . . Mme de Pompadour** Aspasia (5th century B.C.) was mistress to the great Greek statesman, Pericles; Mme. de Pompadour (1721–1764) was mistress to France's Louis XV. Both were powerful women and both were sometimes the object of popular scorn.

[2] **Auguste Comte (1798–1857)** Comte is credited with having founded the study of sociology.

d'homme Michel Leiris[3] describes his vision of the feminine organs, he tells us things of significance and elaborates no myth. Wonder at the feminine body, dislike for menstrual blood, come from perceptions of a concrete reality. There is nothing mythical in the experience that reveals the voluptuous qualities of feminine flesh, and it is not an excursion into myth if one attempts to describe them through comparisons with flowers or pebbles. But to say that Woman is Flesh, to say that the Flesh is Night and Death, or that it is the splendor of the Cosmos, is to abandon terrestrial truth and soar into an empty sky. For man also is flesh for woman; and woman is not merely a carnal object; and the flesh is clothed in special significance for each person and in each experience. And likewise it is quite true that woman—like man—is a being rooted in nature; she is more enslaved to the species than is the male, her animality is more manifest; but in her as in him the given traits are taken on through the fact of existence, she belongs also to the human realm. To assimilate her to Nature is simply to act from prejudice.

Few myths have been more advantageous to the ruling caste 7 than the myth of woman: it justifies all privileges and even authorizes their abuse. Men need not bother themselves with alleviating the pains and the burdens that physiologically are women's lot, since these are 'intended by Nature'; men use them as a pretext for increasing the misery of the feminine lot still further, for instance by refusing to grant to woman any right to sexual pleasure, by making her work like a beast of burden.[4]

Of all these myths, none is more firmly anchored in masculine 8 hearts than that of the feminine 'mystery.' It has numerous advantages. And first of all it permits an easy explanation of all that appears inexplicable; the man who 'does not understand' a woman is happy to substitute an objective resistance for a subjective deficiency of mind; instead of admitting his ignorance, he perceives the presence of a 'mystery' outside himself: an alibi, indeed, that flatters laziness and vanity at once. A heart smitten with love thus avoids many disappointments: if the loved one's behavior is capricious, her remarks stupid, then the mystery serves to excuse it all. And finally, thanks again to the mystery, that negative relation is perpetuated

---

[3] **Michel Leiris (1901–1990)** A popular French writer and art critic.

[4] Cf. Balzac: *Physiology of Marriage*: 'Pay no attention to her murmurs, her cries, her pains; *nature has made her for our use* and for bearing everything: children, sorrows, blows and pains inflicted by man. Do not accuse yourself of hardness. In all the codes of so-called civilized nations, man has written the laws that ranged woman's destiny under this bloody epigraph: "*Væ victis!* Woe to the weak!" [Beauvoir's note]

which seemed to Kierkegaard[5] infinitely preferable to positive possession; in the company of a living enigma man remains alone —
alone with his dreams, his hopes, his fears, his love, his vanity. This
subjective game, which can go all the way from vice to mystical ecstasy, is for many a more attractive experience than an authentic relation with a human being. What foundations exist for such a profitable illusion?

Surely woman is, in a sense, mysterious, 'mysterious as is all the   9
world,' according to Maeterlinck.[6] Each is *subject* only for himself;
each can grasp in immanence only himself, alone: from this point of
view the *other* is always a mystery. To men's eyes the opacity of the
self-knowing self, of the *pour-soi*, is denser in the *other* who is feminine; men are unable to penetrate her special experience through
any working of sympathy: they are condemned to ignorance of the
quality of woman's erotic pleasure, the discomfort of menstruation,
and the pains of childbirth. The truth is that there is mystery on
both sides: as the *other* who is of masculine sex, every man, also, has
within him a presence, an inner self impenetrable to woman; she in
turn is in ignorance of the male's erotic feeling. But in accordance
with the universal rule I have stated, the categories in which men
think of the world are established *from their point of view, as absolute:*
they misconceive reciprocity, here as everywhere. A mystery for
man, woman is considered to be mysterious in essence.

To tell the truth, her situation makes woman very liable to such   10
a view. Her physiological nature is very complex; she herself submits to it as to some rigmarole from outside; her body does not seem
to her to be a clear expression of herself; within it she feels herself a
stranger. Indeed, the bond that in every individual connects the
physiological life and the psychic life — or better the relation existing between the contingence of an individual and the free spirit that
assumes it — is the deepest enigma implied in the condition of being
human, and this enigma is presented in its most disturbing form in
woman.

But what is commonly referred to as the mystery is not the sub-   11
jective solitude of the conscious self, nor the secret organic life. It is
on the level of communication that the word has its true meaning: it
is not a reduction to pure silence, to darkness, to absence; it implies

---

[5] **Søren Kierkegaard (1813–1855)** A major Danish philosopher, often credited with having founded the school of philosophy known as existentialism, to
which Beauvoir was sympathetic.
[6] **Maurice Maeterlinck (1862–1949)** A Belgian playwright whose *Pelleas
and Melisande* (1892) was one of the greatest of the symbolist dramas of the late
nineteenth century.

a stammering presence that fails to make itself manifest and clear. To say that woman is mystery is to say, not that she is silent, but that her language is not understood; she is there, but hidden behind veils; she exists beyond these uncertain appearances. What is she? Angel, demon, one inspired, an actress? It may be supposed either that there are answers to these questions which are impossible to discover, or, rather, that no answer is adequate because a fundamental ambiguity marks the feminine being; and perhaps in her heart she is even for herself quite indefinable: a sphinx.

The fact is that she would be quite embarrassed to decide *what*   12 she *is*; but this not because the hidden truth is too vague to be discerned: it is because in this domain there is no truth. An existent is nothing other than what he does; the possible does not extend beyond the real, essence does not precede existence: in pure subjectivity, the human being *is not anything*. He is to be measured by his acts. Of a peasant woman one can say that she is a good or a bad worker, of an actress that she has or does not have talent; but if one considers a woman in her immanent presence, her inward self, one can say absolutely nothing about her, she falls short of having any qualifications. Now, in amorous or conjugal relations, in all relations where the woman is the vassal, the other, she is being dealt with in her immanence. It is noteworthy that the feminine comrade, colleague, and associate are without mystery; on the other hand, if the vassal is male, if, in the eyes of a man or a woman who is older, or richer, a young fellow, for example, plays the role of the inessential object, then he too becomes shrouded in mystery. And this uncovers for us a substructure under the feminine mystery which is economic in nature.

A sentiment cannot be supposed to *be* anything. 'In the domain   13 of sentiments,' writes Gide,[7] 'the real is not distinguished from the imaginary. And if to imagine one loves is enough to be in love, then also to tell oneself that one imagines oneself to be in love when one is in love is enough to make one forthwith love a little less.' Discrimination between the imaginary and the real can be made only through behavior. Since man occupies a privileged situation in this world, he is in a position to show his love actively; very often he supports the woman or at least helps her; in marrying her he gives her social standing; he makes her presents; his independent economic and social position allows him to take the initiative and think up contrivances: it was M. de Norpois who, when separated from

---

[7] **André Gide (1869–1951)** Gide won the Nobel Prize for Literature in 1947. He was an influential French philosopher, writer, and art critic.

Mme de Villeparisis, made twenty-four-hour trips to visit her. Very often the man is busy, the woman idle: he *gives* her the time he passes with her; she takes it: is it with pleasure, passionately, or only for amusement? Does she accept these benefits through love or through self-interest? Does she love her husband or her marriage? Of course, even the man's evidence is ambiguous: is such and such a gift granted through love or out of pity? But while normally a woman finds numerous advantages in her relations with a man, his relations with a woman are profitable to a man only in so far as he loves her. And so one can almost judge the degree of his affection by the total picture of his attitude.

But a woman hardly has means for sounding her own heart; according to her moods she will view her own sentiments in different lights, and as she submits to them passively, one interpretation will be no truer than another. In those rare instances in which she holds the position of economic and social privilege, the mystery is reversed, showing that it does not pertain to *one* sex rather than the other, but to the situation. For a great many women the roads to transcendence are blocked: because they *do* nothing, they fail to *make themselves* anything. They wonder indefinitely what they *could have* become, which sets them to asking about what they *are*. It is a vain question. If man fails to discover that secret essence of femininity, it is simply because it does not exist. Kept on the fringe of the world, woman cannot be objectively defined through this world, and her mystery conceals nothing but emptiness. 14

Furthermore, like all the oppressed, woman deliberately dissembles her objective actuality; the slave, the servant, the indigent, all who depend upon the caprices of a master, have learned to turn toward him a changeless smile or an enigmatic impassivity; their real sentiments, their actual behavior, are carefully hidden. And moreover woman is taught from adolescence to lie to men, to scheme, to be wily. In speaking to them she wears an artificial expression on her face; she is cautious, hypocritical, play-acting. 15

But the Feminine Mystery as recognized in mythical thought is a more profound matter. In fact, it is immediately implied in the mythology of the absolute Other. If it be admitted that the inessential conscious being, too, is a clear subjectivity, capable of performing the *Cogito*,[8] then it is also admitted that this being is in truth sovereign and returns to being essential; in order that all reciprocity may appear quite impossible, it is necessary for the Other to be for 16

---

[8]***Cogito*** Reference to René Descartes (1596–1650), who "proved" his existence with the Latin phrase, "Cogito, ergo sum" — I think, therefore I am.

itself an other, for its very subjectivity to be affected by its otherness; this consciousness which would be alienated as a consciousness, in its pure immanent presence, would evidently be Mystery. It would be Mystery in itself from the fact that it would be Mystery for itself; it would be absolute Mystery.

In the same way it is true that, beyond the secrecy created by their 17 dissembling, there is mystery in the Black, the Yellow, in so far as they are considered absolutely as the inessential Other. It should be noted that the American citizen, who profoundly baffles the average European, is not, however, considered as being 'mysterious': one states more modestly that one does not understand him. And similarly woman does not always 'understand' man; but there is no such thing as a masculine mystery. The point is that rich America, and the male, are on the Master side and that Mystery belongs to the slave.

To be sure, we can only muse in the twilight byways of bad faith 18 upon the positive reality of the Mystery; like certain marginal hallucinations, it dissolves under the attempt to view it fixedly. Literature always fails in attempting to portray 'mysterious' women; they can appear only at the beginning of a novel as strange, enigmatic figures; but unless the story remains unfinished they give up their secret in the end and they are then simply consistent and transparent persons. The heroes in Peter Cheyney's books, for example, never cease to be astonished at the unpredictable caprices of women: no one can ever guess how they will act, they upset all calculations. The fact is that once the springs of their action are revealed to the reader, they are seen to be very simple mechanisms: this woman was a spy, that one a thief; however clever the plot, there is always a key; and it could not be otherwise, had the author all the talent and imagination in the world. Mystery is never more than a mirage that vanishes as we draw near to look at it.

We can see now that the myth is in large part explained by its 19 usefulness to man. The myth of woman is a luxury. It can appear only if man escapes from the urgent demands of his needs; the more relationships are concretely lived, the less they are idealized. The fellah of ancient Egypt, the Bedouin peasant, the artisan of the Middle Ages, the worker of today has in the requirements of work and poverty relations with his particular woman companion which are too definite for her to be embellished with an aura either auspicious or inauspicious. The epochs and the social classes that have been marked by the leisure to dream have been the ones to set up the images, black and white, of femininity. But along with luxury there was utility; these dreams were irresistibly guided by interests. Surely most of the myths had roots in the spontaneous attitude of man toward his own existence and toward the world around him. But going beyond experience toward the transcendent Idea was deliberately used by patriarchal society for purposes of self-justification; through the myths this society imposed its laws and customs upon individuals in a picturesque, effective manner; it is under a mythical form that the group-imperative is indoctrinated into each conscience. Through such intermediaries as religions, traditions, language, tales, songs, movies, the myths penetrate even into such existences as are most harshly enslaved to material realities. Here everyone can find sublimation of his drab experiences: deceived by the woman he loves, one declares that she is a Crazy Womb; another, obsessed by his impotence, calls her a Praying Mantis; still another enjoys his wife's company: behold, she is Harmony, Rest, the Good Earth! The taste for eternity at a bargain, for a pocket-sized absolute, which is shared by a majority of men, is satisfied by myths. The smallest emotion, a slight annoyance, becomes the reflection of a timeless Idea—an illusion agreeably flattering to the vanity.

The myth is one of those snares of false objectivity into which   20
the man who depends on ready-made valuations rushes headlong. Here again we have to do with the substitution of a set idol for actual experience and the free judgments it requires. For an authentic relation with an autonomous existent, the myth of Woman substitutes the fixed contemplation of a mirage. 'Mirage! Mirage!' cries Laforgue.[9] 'We should kill them since we cannot comprehend them; or better tranquilize them, instruct them, make them give up their taste for jewels, make them our genuinely equal comrades, our intimate friends, real associates here below, dress them differently, cut their hair short, say anything and everything to them.' Man would have nothing to lose, quite the contrary, if he gave up disguising woman as a symbol. When dreams are official community affairs, clichés, they are poor and monotonous indeed beside the living reality; for the true dreamer, for the poet, woman is a more generous fount than is any down-at-heel marvel. The times that have most sincerely treasured women are not the period of feudal chivalry nor yet the gallant nineteenth century. They are the times—like the eighteenth century—when men have regarded women as fellow creatures; then it is that women seem truly romantic, as the reading of *Liaisons dangereuses, Le Rouge et le noir, Farewell to Arms,* is sufficient to show. The heroines of Laclos, Stendhal, Hemingway[10] are

---

[9] **Jules Laforgue (1860–1887)** A French symbolist poet.
[10] **Pierre Choderlos de Laclos (1741–1803), Stendhal (1783–1842), Ernest Hemingway (1899–1961)** Laclos was a French novelist who wrote *Dangerous Liaisons* and *On the Education of Women*; Stendhal was the pen name of Marie-Henri Beyle, a French novelist who wrote *The Red and the Black* and *The Charterhouse of Parma*; Ernest Hemingway an important twentieth-century American novelist, who wrote *The Sun Also Rises* and *Farewell to Arms.*

without mystery, and they are not the less engaging for that. To recognize in woman a human being is not to impoverish man's experience: this would lose none of its diversity, its richness, or its intensity if it were to occur between two subjectivities. To discard the myths is not to destroy all dramatic relation between the sexes, it is not to deny the significance authentically revealed to man through feminine reality; it is not to do away with poetry, love, adventure, happiness, dreaming. It is simply to ask that behavior, sentiment, passion be founded upon the truth.[11]

'Woman is lost. Where are the women? The women of today are 21 not women at all!' We have seen what these mysterious slogans mean. In men's eyes—and for the legion of women who see through men's eyes—it is not enough to have a woman's body nor to assume the female function as mistress or mother in order to be a 'true woman.' In sexuality and maternity woman as subject can claim autonomy; but to be a 'true woman' she must accept herself as the Other. The men of today show a certain duplicity of attitude which is painfully lacerating to women; they are willing on the whole to accept woman as a fellow being, an equal; but they still require her to remain the inessential. For her these two destinies are incompatible; she hesitates between one and the other without being exactly adapted to either, and from this comes her lack of equilibrium. With man there is no break between public and private life: the more he confirms his grasp on the world in action and in work, the more virile he seems to be; human and vital values are combined in him. Whereas woman's independent successes are in contradiction with her femininity, since the 'true woman' is required to make herself object, to be the Other.

It is quite possible that in this matter man's sensibility and sexu- 22 ality are being modified. A new æsthetics has already been born. If the fashion of flat chests and narrow hips—the boyish form—has had its brief season, at least the overopulent ideal of past centuries has not returned. The feminine body is asked to be flesh, but with discretion; it is to be slender and not loaded with fat; muscular, supple, strong, it is bound to suggest transcendence; it must not be pale like a too shaded hothouse plant, but preferably tanned like a workman's torso from being bared to the open sun. Woman's dress

---

[11] Laforgue goes on to say regarding woman: 'Since she has been left in slavery, idleness, without occupation or weapon other than her sex, she has over-developed this aspect and has become the Feminine. . . . We have permitted this hypertrophy; she is here in the world for our benefit. . . . Well! that is all wrong. . . . Up to now we have played with woman as if she were a doll. This has lasted altogether too long! . . .' [Beauvoir's note]

in becoming practical need not make her appear sexless: on the contrary, short skirts made the most of legs and thighs as never before. There is no reason why working should take away woman's sex appeal.[12] It may be disturbing to contemplate woman as at once a social personage and carnal prey: in a recent series of drawings by Peynet (1948), we see a young man break his engagement because he was seduced by the pretty mayoress who was getting ready to officiate at his marriage. For a woman to hold some 'man's position' and be desirable at the same time has long been a subject for more or less ribald joking; but gradually the impropriety and the irony have become blunted, and it would seem that a new form of eroticism is coming into being — perhaps it will give rise to new myths.

What is certain is that today it is very difficult for women to accept at the same time their status as autonomous individuals and their womanly destiny; this is the source of the blundering and restlessness which sometimes cause them to be considered a 'lost sex.' And no doubt it is more comfortable to submit to a blind enslavement than to work for liberation: the dead, for that matter, are better adapted to the earth than are the living. In all respects a return to the past is no more possible than it is desirable. What must be hoped for is that the men for their part will unreservedly accept the situation that is coming into existence; only then will women be able to live in that situation without anguish. Then Laforgue's prayer will be answered: 'Ah, young women, when will you be our brothers, our brothers in intimacy without ulterior thought of exploitation? When shall we clasp hands truly?' Then Breton's 'Mélusine, no longer under the weight of the calamity let loose upon her by man alone, Mélusine set free . . .' will regain 'her place in humanity.' Then she will be a full human being, 'when,' to quote a letter of Rimbaud,[13] the infinite bondage of woman is broken, when she will live in and for herself, man — hitherto detestable — having let her go free.'

23

QUESTIONS FOR CRITICAL READING

1. What do you understand to be the myth of the Eternal Feminine?
2. In what literary works or films have you seen the myth of woman illustrated?

---

[12] A point that hardly needs to be made in America, where even cursory acquaintance with any well-staffed business office will afford confirmatory evidence. [Translator's note]

[13] **Arthur Rimbaud (1854–1891)** A French symbolist poet of great imaginative power.

3. What role does mystery play in the relationship of men to women?
4. Does a myth of the Eternal Masculine exist?
5. What are some of the contradictory aspects of myths about women?
6. What is the patrimony that Beauvoir refers to in paragraph 3, and how does it shape social experience?
7. Do you think people actually maintain the myth of the Eternal Feminine today?
8. What is Beauvoir's strongest argument for eliminating the myth of the Eternal Feminine?

SUGGESTIONS FOR WRITING

1. Beauvoir points out that whatever the myth of woman might be, it "is intended to sum her up *in toto*" (para. 3). Therefore, she says, there will be necessary contradictions in myths that disagree with each other. Give some examples of what Beauvoir means, and show how they might affect the behavior of those who accept such myths. If possible, draw on experiences of your own to demonstrate how people who accept the myths behave.

2. Explain the very important concept that Beauvoir outlines in paragraph 3 concerning the role of patrimony in "patriarchal society." She refers to moneyed families that pass down their wealth to their sons and expect that those sons will in turn pass it to their own sons. The role of women in this system is obviously restricted. How does Beauvoir treat this issue? How important do you think it is? Why do you think the words *patrimony* and *matrimony* have such distinct meanings for men and women?

3. Beauvoir says, "group symbols and social types are generally defined by means of antonyms in pairs" (para. 4). What symbols can you define that exist in contradictory types? How do they work? What effect are they likely to have on people's behavior? One obvious contradiction is to see woman as either virgin or whore, but nothing in between. Do such contradictions exist in your own social circle? Do such contradictions surprise you? Has your social group made progress in dealing with social symbols of this type?

4. Beauvoir says again and again that reality and experience do not seem to affect the way people think about women. The myths, in other words, stand for reality and seem more powerful than reality. Do you agree with this assertion? Can you see evidence of that behavior at work in your own social experience? Do you know people who seem to ignore reality and prefer the myth?

5. Beauvoir says that woman's "animality is more manifest" than man's (para. 6). Examine this statement, and decide first what she means. Then decide if she is convincing. Take a stand yourself, and treat the issue with some thoroughness. Avoid oversimplifying your position; try to impart an understanding of the complexity of Beauvoir's statement.

6. Why has the "myth of woman" been advantageous for the "ruling caste"? Beauvoir says that no feminine myth "is more firmly anchored

in masculine hearts than that of the feminine 'mystery'" (para. 8). How true is this statement? Why is belief in such a myth of advantage for men? How does it "justify all privileges" and authorize their "abuse" (para. 7)?

7. **CONNECTIONS**   How do the views of Karen Horney on the relationship between men and women compare with Beauvoir's analysis of the myths of women? Beauvoir has also written material that is psychological in scope; she understands the principles that Horney discusses. Are both writers talking about some form of basic psychology and how it controls our thinking and attitudes? Would Horney agree with Beauvoir?

8. **CONNECTIONS**   bell hooks believes white feminists are limited in their understanding of the role of black women in the feminist movement. How would hooks critique Beauvoir's essay, and how would Beauvoir defend her views? Consider their respective arguments, and offer an analysis that takes into account at least one major argumentative position from each author.

CAROL GILLIGAN
Woman's Place in Man's Life Cycle

CAROL GILLIGAN (b. 1936) is professor of education at Harvard University. She concentrates on issues in psychology and has made important contributions to theories concerning the ways in which women develop differently from men, from childhood to adulthood. In 1997, she received the Heinz Award in the Human Condition. Her work has involved various aspects of psychological development, but one important focus has been the development of the individual's moral nature. In talking about these issues, she has examined the work of some of the world's most important psychologists, such as Sigmund Freud (1856–1939), Jean Piaget (1896–1980), Erik Erikson (1902–1994) and her own teacher, Lawrence Kohlberg (1927–1987). As she demonstrates in her discussion, the work of these men in establishing parameters of social and moral development depended almost entirely on studying boys, not girls. Gilligan suggests that the differences in early development between boys and girls makes those observations of limited value.

Gilligan's book *In a Different Voice: Psychological Theory and Women's Development* (1982) was the result of many years of research on the ways in which women treat the relational aspects of life differently from men—in part because of the different ways in which girls and boys are raised. "Woman's Place in Man's Life Cycle" is the first chapter in that book; it establishes the need to account appropriately for women's development by examining how women are socialized in school and at home.

Some of the factors that appear to impede women's success, Gilligan finds, actually confer strength on them. For example, the nature of boys' games differs from that of girls' because boys accept competition—including the need for one party to lose while

From *In a Different Voice: Psychological Theory and Women's Development.*

another wins — as a natural course, provided the rules are followed
carefully. Girls tend to treat rules as more elastic if they interfere
with the pleasure of the games. This pattern, according to some
male psychologists, tends to make it difficult for women to achieve
success in later life. Gilligan, however, explains that this pattern
actually helps women succeed on a deeper personal level in ways
that men do not normally achieve, especially in mid-life when both
sexes better understand the need for intimacy and closeness.

Gilligan's efforts to move psychologists away from using only
male-based data for establishing norms of behavior and development seems like common sense. Why, then, did people not consider this previously? One reason is that when Gilligan was formulating her ideas in the 1970s, many feminists felt that establishing
key differences between men and women would only fuel the controversy about whether women and men should be treated equally.
If there were to be complete fairness in gender relations, they
reasoned, the false distinctions that Mary Wollstonecraft and her
twentieth-century counterparts felt were holding women back
would only be accentuated. Fair treatment of the sexes, they
thought, demanded that the sexes be considered as more alike than
different.

Gilligan fought against this tide at some risk, but her psychological model eventually won out by helping to promote the view
that Simone de Beauvoir supported: avoiding the judging of women
by men's standards. In Beauvoir's view, men tend to judge women
as the Other, or as not-men, rather than as women with their own
natures and identities. Gilligan's efforts moved this discourse on
gender to a new level by doing what seems natural and reasonable
in retrospect: studying the way girls interact and seeing how that
interaction is different from that of boys. As she points out in this
piece, children have a very powerful gender sense by age three, and
their development along gender lines begins no later than that.

Gilligan's work has pointed out the ways in which boys need to
break away from their mothers early on in an effort to model themselves on their fathers or other masculine figures, thereby achieving independence. Girls, on the other hand, see themselves as more
like their mothers. In girls' socialization there is greater emphasis
on familial continuity, and as a result women develop a sense of
connectedness, intimacy, and interdependence that men are less
aware of because of their own individual needs.

In addition, by examining these qualities in girls, Gilligan
finds that intimacy, concern for others, empathy, and a need for
interdependence are not exclusively characteristics of women. Indeed, such qualities are essential to the human condition and have

probably aided our biological survival. Although they are sometimes masked by social pressures in early child development, men possess these qualities as well. As one commentator observed, Gilligan "began by posing a deceptively simple question: What are we missing by not listening to half the population?" The answer was a great deal.

Gilligan's Rhetoric

By opening her essay with a reference to *The Cherry Orchard* by Anton Chekhov, Gilligan establishes herself as a literate analyst, taking the conversation from Chekhov's play and revealing its deeper significance. In a way, this is a model for psychoanalysis as well as a model for interpretation that would serve in any given study. Gilligan's conclusions about the distinctions in women's development actually arise from extensive interviews analyzed in similar ways. According to some critics, not everyone would come to the same conclusions that Gilligan reaches. But the point is that "reading" implies interpretation, and Gilligan's interpretation of the texts she gathered has convinced her that earlier psychologists were wrong in thinking that women had limited moral development compared to men.

"Woman's Place in Man's Life Cycle" has been praised as the foundation of Gilligan's argument in *In a Different Voice*. This opening chapter establishes not only her views but those of earlier academics as well. Therefore, the essay has the flavor of an academic study, revealing Gilligan's extensive reading and research while at the same time offering her the opportunity to analyze each important figure she treats. What this establishes rhetorically is thoroughness. Gilligan presents the authorities that are important to consider and thus offers us the opportunity to read them on our own.

Some of the authorities to which she refers are giants in the field: Freud, Piaget, and Erikson certainly, but also psychologist Bruno Bettelheim (1903–1990) and novelists Maxine Hong Kingston (b. 1940) and Virginia Woolf (1882–1941). Some are current researchers, such as Nancy Chodorow and Janet Lever, whose works Gilligan examines and then builds upon. This rhetorical method is basic to academic research and imparts to the reader a sense of completion. The early part of the essay reviews the current intellectual discussion on women's development and the differences in the ways in which women observe and analyze events, especially moral events. The later part of the essay clarifies Gilligan's own position on these issues.

Gilligan worked with Lawrence Kohlberg, her teacher at Harvard. To the moral development of the child, Kohlberg applied a theory of Jean Piaget concerning the stages of intellectual development of the child. Piaget conceived of three stages of development, and so did Kohlberg, although he broke each stage into two substages. Kohlberg titled his three stages as follows: preconventional (up to age nine); conventional (to age twenty); and postconventional (age twenty and above, but possibly never achieved). He regarded the earliest stage of moral development as being dominated by the avoidance of punishment. The second stage was dominated by gaining approval and avoiding disapproval. The third stage involved recognizing the rights of others and establishing personal moral values on the basis of a sense of justice. Some people, Kohlberg felt, might never achieve the last stage of establishing personal moral values

In paragraph 39, Gilligan presents a man's response to one of Kohlberg's interviews. In paragraph 40, she offers a response from a woman in one of her own interviews to demonstrate some of the gender differences that she has been discussing. This strategy permits the reader to participate in the study in a genuine way, because the reader can validate Gilligan's views directly from the data.

Just as Gilligan opens the passage with a literary reference, she closes it with another. This time she refers to the classical myth of Demeter and Persephone, complete with a moral for the story. The final paragraph of the essay, a careful analysis of the Persephone myth, shows that the principles of female behavior are timeless. Moreover, in the final paragraph Gilligan makes a plea that "the continuing importance of attachment in the human life cycle" be recognized for its potential to maintain life and to sustain a healthy relationship between men and women.

PREREADING QUESTIONS:
WHAT TO READ FOR

The following prereading questions may help you anticipate key issues in the discussion on Carol Gilligan's "Woman's Place in Man's Life Cycle." Keeping them in mind during your first reading of the selection should help focus your reactions.

• What are the differences between men and women in terms of the way they regard relationships?

- What is the result of basing theories of human development on studies that include only boys?
- How do boys and girls differ in their regard for rules?

Woman's Place in Man's Life Cycle

In the second act of *The Cherry Orchard,* Lopahin, a young merchant, describes his life of hard work and success. Failing to convince Madame Ranevskaya to cut down the cherry orchard to save her estate, he will go on in the next act to buy it himself. He is the self-made man who, in purchasing the estate where his father and grandfather were slaves, seeks to eradicate the "awkward, unhappy life" of the past, replacing the cherry orchard with summer cottages where coming generations "will see a new life." In elaborating this developmental vision, he reveals the image of man that underlies and supports his activity: "At times when I can't go to sleep, I think: Lord, thou gavest us immense forests, unbounded fields and the widest horizons, and living in the midst of them we should indeed be giants"—at which point, Madame Ranevskaya interrupts him, saying, "You feel the need for giants—They are good only in fairy tales, anywhere else they only frighten us."

Conceptions of the human life cycle represent attempts to order and make coherent the unfolding experiences and perceptions, the changing wishes and realities of everyday life. But the nature of such conceptions depends in part on the position of the observer. The brief excerpt from Chekhov's play suggest that when the observer is a woman, the perspective may be of a different sort. Different judgments of the image of man as giant imply different ideas about human development, different ways of imagining the human condition, different notions of what is of value in life.

At a time when efforts are being made to eradicate discrimination between the sexes in the search for social equality and justice, the differences between the sexes are being rediscovered in the social sciences. This discovery occurs when theories formerly considered to be sexually neutral in their scientific objectivity are found instead to reflect a consistent observational and evaluative bias. Then the presumed neutrality of science, like that of language itself, gives way to the recognition that the categories of knowledge are human constructions. The fascination with point of view that has informed the fiction of the twentieth century and the corresponding recognition of the relativity of judgment infuse our scientific understanding as well when we begin to notice how accustomed we have become to seeing life through men's eyes.

A recent discovery of this sort pertains to the apparently innocent classic *The Elements of Style* by William Strunk and E. B. White. A Supreme Court ruling on the subject of sex discrimination led one teacher of English to notice that the elementary rules of English usage were being taught through examples which counterposed the birth of Napoleon, the writings of Coleridge, and statements such as "He was an interesting talker. A man who had traveled all over the world and lived in half a dozen countries," with "Well, Susan, this is a fine mess you are in" or, less drastically, "He saw a woman, accompanied by two children, walking slowly down the road."   4

Psychological theorists have fallen as innocently as Strunk and White into the same observational bias. Implicitly adopting the male life as the norm, they have tried to fashion women out of a masculine cloth. It all goes back, of course, to Adam and Eve—a story which shows, among other things, that if you make a woman out of a man, you are bound to get into trouble. In the life cycle, as in the Garden of Eden, the woman has been the deviant.   5

The penchant of developmental theorists to project a masculine image, and one that appears frightening to women, goes back at least to Freud (1905), who built his theory of psychosexual development around the experiences of the male child that culminate in the Oedipus complex. In the 1920s, Freud struggled to resolve the contradictions posed for his theory by the differences in female anatomy and the different configuration of the young girl's early family relationships. After trying to fit women into his masculine conception, seeing them as envying that which they missed, he came instead to acknowledge, in the strength and persistence of women's pre-Oedipal attachments to their mothers, a developmental difference. He considered this difference in women's development to be responsible for what he saw as women's developmental failure.   6

Having tied the formation of the superego or conscience to castration anxiety, Freud considered women to be deprived by nature of the impetus for a clear-cut Oedipal resolution. Consequently, women's superego—the heir to the Oedipus complex—was compromised: it was never "so inexorable, so impersonal, so independent of its emotional origins as we require it to be in men." From this observation of difference, that "for women the level of what is ethically normal is different from what it is in men," Freud concluded that women "show less sense of justice than men, that they are less ready to submit to the great exigencies of life, that they are   7 more often influenced in their judgements by feelings of affection or hostility" (1925, pp. 257–258).

Thus a problem in theory became cast as a problem in women's development, and the problem in women's development was located in their experience of relationships. Nancy Chodorow (1974), attempting to account for "the reproduction within each generation of certain general and nearly universal differences that characterize masculine and feminine personality and roles," attributes these differences between the sexes not to anatomy but rather to "the fact that women, universally, are largely responsible for early child care." Because this early social environment differs for and is experienced differently by male and female children, basic sex differences recur in personality development. As a result, "in any given society, feminine personality comes to define itself in relation and connection to other people more than masculine personality does" (pp. 43–44). 8

In her analysis, Chodorow relies primarily on Robert Stoller's studies which indicate that gender identity, the unchanging core of personality formation, is "with rare exception firmly and irreversibly established for both sexes by the time a child is around three." Given that for both sexes the primary caretaker in the first three years of life is typically female, the interpersonal dynamics of gender identity formation are different for boys and girls. Female identity formation takes place in a context of ongoing relationship since "mothers tend to experience their daughters as more like, and continuous with, themselves." Correspondingly, girls, in identifying themselves as female, experience themselves as like their mothers, thus fusing the experience of attachment with the process of identity formation. In contrast, "mothers experience their sons as a male opposite," and boys, in defining themselves as masculine, separate their mothers from themselves, thus curtailing "their primary love and sense of empathic tie." Consequently, male development entails a "more emphatic individuation and a more defensive firming of experienced ego boundaries." For boys, but not girls, "issues of differentiation have become iintertwined with sexual issues" (1978, pp. 150, 166–167). 9

Writing against the masculine bias of psychoanalytic theory, Chodorow argues that the existence of sex differences in the early experiences of individuation and relationship "does not mean that women have 'weaker' ego boundaries than men or are more prone to psychosis." It means instead that "girls emerge from this period with a basis for 'empathy' built into their primary definition of self in a way that boys do not." Chodorow thus replaces Freud's negative and derivative description of female psychology with a positive and 10 direct account of her own: "Girls emerge with a stronger basis for experiencing another's needs or feelings as one's own (or of thinking that one is so experiencing another's needs and feelings). Furthermore, girls do not define themselves in terms of the denial of pre-Oedipal relational modes to the same extent as do boys. Therefore, regression to these modes tends not to feel as much a basic threat to their ego. From very early, then, because they are parented by a person of the same gender . . . girls come to experience themselves as less differentiated than boys, as more continuous with and related to the external object-world, and as differently oriented to their inner object-world as well" (p. 167).

Consequently, relationships, and particularly issues of dependency, are experienced differently by women and men. For boys and men, separation and individuation are critically tied to gender identity since separation from the mother is essential for the development of masculinity. For girls and women, issues of femininity or feminine identity do not depend on the achievement of separation from the mother or on the progress of individuation. Since masculinity is defined through separation while femininity is defined through attachment, male gender identity is threatened by intimacy while female gender identity is threatened by separation. Thus males tend to have difficulty with relationships, while females tend to have problems with individuation. The quality of embeddedness in social interaction and personal relationships that characterizes women's lives in contrast to men's, however, becomes not only a descriptive difference but also a developmental liability when the milestones of childhood and adolescent development in the psychological literature are markers of increasing separation. Women's failure to separate then becomes by definition a failure to develop. 11

The sex differences in personality formation that Chodorow describes in early childhood appear during the middle childhood years in studies of children's games. Children's games are considered by George Herbert Mead (1934) and Jean Piaget (1932) as the crucible of social development during the school years. In games, children learn to take the role of the other and come to see themselves through another's eyes. In games, they learn respect for rules and come to understand the ways rules can be made and changed. 12

Janet Lever (1976), considering the peer group to be the agent of socialization during the elementary school years and play to be a major activity of socialization at that time, set out to discover whether there are sex differences in the games that children play. Studying 181 fifth-grade, white, middle-class children, ages ten and eleven, she observed the organization and structure of their playtime activities. She watched the children as they played at school during 13 recess and in physical education class, and in addition kept diaries of their accounts as to how they spent their out-of-school time. From this study, Lever reports sex differences: boys play out of doors more often than girls do; boys play more often in large and age-heterogeneous groups; they play competitive games more often, and their games last longer than girls' games. The last is in some ways the most interesting finding. Boys' games appeared to last longer not only because they required a higher level of skill and were thus less likely to become boring, but also because, when disputes arose in the course of a game, boys were able to resolve the disputes more effectively than girls: "During the course of this study, boys were seen quarrelling all the time, but not once was a game terminated because of a quarrel and no game was interrupted for more than seven minutes. In the gravest debates, the final word was always, to 'repeat the play,' generally followed by a chorus of 'cheater's proof'" (p. 482). In fact, it seemed that the boys enjoyed the legal debates as much as they did the game itself, and even marginal players of lesser size or skill participated equally in these recurrent squabbles. In contrast, the eruption of disputes among girls tended to end the game.

Thus Lever extends and corroborates the observations of Piaget 14 in his study of the rules of the game, where he finds boys becoming through childhood increasingly fascinated with the legal elaboration of rules and the development of fair procedures for adjudicating conflicts, a fascination that, he notes, does not hold for girls. Girls, Piaget observes, have a more "pragmatic" attitude toward rules, "regarding a rule as good as long as the game repaid it" (p. 83). Girls are more tolerant in their attitudes toward rules, more willing to make exceptions, and more easily reconciled to innovations. As a result, the legal sense, which Piaget considers essential to moral development, "is far less developed in little girls than in boys" (p. 77).

The bias that leads Piaget to equate male development with 15 child development also colors Lever's work. The assumption that shapes her discussion of results is that the male model is the better one since it fits the requirements for modern corporate success. In contrast, the sensitivity and care for the feelings of others that girls develop through their play have little market value and can even impede professional success. Lever implies that, given the realities of adult life, if a girl does not want to be left dependent on men, she will have to learn to play like a boy.

To Piaget's argument that children learn the respect for rules 16 necessary for moral development by playing rule-bound games, Lawrence Kohlberg (1969) adds that these lessons are most effectively learned through the opportunities for role-taking that arise in the course of resolving disputes. Consequently, the moral lessons inherent in girls' play appear to be fewer than in boys'. Traditional girls' games like jump rope and hopscotch are turn-taking games, where competition is indirect since one person's success does not necessarily signify another's failure. Consequently, disputes requiring adjudication are less likely to occur. In fact, most of the girls whom Lever interviewed claimed that when a quarrel broke out, they ended the game. Rather than elaborating a system of rules for resolving disputes, girls subordinated the continuation of the game to the continuation of relationships.

Lever concludes that from the games they play, boys learn both   17
the independence and the organizational skills necessary for coordinating the activities of large and diverse groups of people. By participating in controlled and socially approved competitive situations, they learn to deal with competition in a relatively forthright manner—to play with their enemies and to compete with their friends—all in accordance with the rules of the game. In contrast, girls' play tends to occur in smaller, more intimate groups, often the best-friend dyad, and in private places. This play replicates the social pattern of primary human relationships in that its organization is more cooperative. Thus, it points less, in Mead's terms, toward learning to take the role of "the generalized other," less toward the abstraction of human relationships. But it fosters the development of the empathy and sensitivity necessary for taking the role of "the particular other" and points more toward knowing the other as different from the self.

The sex differences in personality formation in early childhood   18
that Chodorow derives from her analysis of the mother-child relationship are thus extended by Lever's observations of sex differences in the play activities of middle childhood. Together these accounts suggest that boys and girls arrive at puberty with a different interpersonal orientation and a different range of social experiences. Yet, since adolescence is considered a crucial time for separation, the period of "the second individuation process" (Blos, 1967), female development has appeared most divergent and thus most problematic at this time.

"Puberty," Freud says, "which brings about so great an accession   19
of libido in boys, is marked in girls by a fresh wave of *repression*," necessary for the transformation of the young girl's "masculine sexuality" into the specifically feminine sexuality of her adulthood (1905, pp. 220–221). Freud posits this transformation on the girl's acknowledgment and acceptance of "the fact of her castration" (1931, p. 229). To the girl, Freud explains, puberty brings a new awareness of "the wound to her narcissism" and leads her to develop, "like a scar, a sense of inferiority" (1925, p. 253). Since in Erik Erikson's

expansion of Freud's psychoanalytic account, adolescence is the time when development hinges on identity, the girl arrives at this juncture either psychologically at risk or with a different agenda.

The problem that female adolescence presents for theorists of human development is apparent in Erikson's scheme. Erikson (1950) charts eight stages of psychosocial development, of which adolescence is the fifth. The task at this stage is to forge a coherent sense of self, to verify an identity that can span the discontinuity of puberty and make possible the adult capacity to love and work. The preparation for the successful resolution of the adolescent identity crisis is delineated in Erikson's description of the crises that characterize the preceding four stages. Although the initial crisis in infancy of "trust versus mistrust" anchors development in the experience of relationship, the task then clearly becomes one of individuation. Erikson's second stage centers on the crisis of "autonomy versus shame and doubt," which marks the walking child's emerging sense of separateness and agency. From there, development goes on through the crisis of "initiative versus guilt," successful resolution of which represents a further move in the direction of autonomy. Next, following the inevitable disappointment of the magical wishes of the Oedipal period, children realize that to compete with their parents, they must first join them and learn to do what they do so well. Thus in the middle childhood years, development turns on the crisis of "industry versus inferiority," as the demonstration of competence becomes critical to the child's developing self-esteem. This is the time when children strive to learn and master the technology of their culture, in order to recognize themselves and to be recognized by others as capable of becoming adults. Next comes adolescence, the celebration of the autonomous, initiating, industrious self through the forging of an identity based on an ideology that can support and justify adult commitments. But about whom is Erikson talking? 20

Once again it turns out to be the male child. For the female, Erikson (1968) says, the sequence is a bit different. She holds her identity in abeyance as she prepares to attract the man by whose name she will be known, by whose status she will be defined, the man who will rescue her from emptiness and loneliness by filling "the inner space." While for men, identity precedes intimacy and generativity in the optimal cycle of human separation and attachment, for women these tasks seem instead to be fused. Intimacy goes along with identity, as the female comes to know herself as she is known, through her relationships with others. 21

Yet despite Erikson's observation of sex differences, his chart of life-cycle stages remains unchanged: identity continues to precede 22 intimacy as male experience continues to define his life-cycle conception. But in this male life cycle there is little preparation for the intimacy of the first adult stage. Only the initial stage of trust versus mistrust suggests the type of mutuality that Erikson means by intimacy and generativity and Freud means by genitality. The rest is separateness, with the result that development itself comes to be identified with separation, and attachments appear to be developmental impediments, as is repeatedly the case in the assessment of women.

Erikson's description of male identity as forged in relation to the   23
world and of female identity as awakened in a relationship of intimacy with another person is hardly new. In the fairy tales that Bruno Bettelheim (1976) describes an identical portrayal appears. The dynamics of male adolescence are illustrated archetypically by the conflict between father and son in "The Three Languages." Here a son, considered hopelessly stupid by his father, is given one last chance at education and sent for a year to study with a master. But when he returns, all he has learned is "what the dogs bark." After two further attempts of this sort, the father gives up in disgust and orders his servants to take the child into the forest and kill him. But the servants, those perpetual rescuers of disowned and abandoned children, take pity on the child and decide simply to leave him in the forest. From there, his wanderings take him to a land beset by furious dogs whose barking permits nobody to rest and who periodically devour one of the inhabitants. Now it turns out that our hero has learned just the right thing: he can talk with the dogs and is able to quiet them, thus restoring peace to the land. Since the other knowledge he acquires serves him equally well, he emerges triumphant from his adolescent confrontation with his father, a giant of the life-cycle conception.

In contrast, the dynamics of female adolescence are depicted   24
through the telling of a very different story. In the world of the fairy tale, the girl's first bleeding is followed by a period of intense passivity in which nothing seems to be happening. Yet in the deep sleeps of Snow White and Sleeping Beauty, Bettelheim sees that inner concentration which he considers to be the necessary counterpart to the activity of adventure. Since the adolescent heroines awake from their sleep, not to conquer the world, but to marry the prince, their identity is inwardly and interpersonally defined. For women, in Bettelheim's as in Erikson's account, identity and intimacy are intricately conjoined. The sex differences depicted in the world of fairy tales, like the fantasy of the woman warrior in Maxine Hong Kingston's (1977) recent autobiographical novel which echoes the old stories of Troilus and Cressida and Tancred and Chlorinda, indicate repeat-

edly that active adventure is a male activity, and that if a woman is to embark on such endeavors, she must at least dress like a man.

These observations about sex difference support the conclusion reached by David McClelland (1975) that "sex role turns out to be one of the most important determinants of human behavior; psychologists have found sex differences in their studies from the moment they started doing empirical research." But since it is difficult to say "different" without saying "better" or "worse," since there is a tendency to construct a single scale of measurement, and since that scale has generally been derived from and standardized on the basis of men's interpretations of research data drawn predominantly or exclusively from studies of males, psychologists "have tended to regard male behavior as the 'norm' and female behavior as some kind of deviation from that norm" (p. 81). Thus, when women do not conform to the standards of psychological expectation, the conclusion has generally been that something is wrong with the women.

What Matina Horner (1972) found to be wrong with women was the anxiety they showed about competitive achievement. From the beginning, research on human motivation using the Thematic Apperception Test (TAT) was plagued by evidence of sex differences which appeared to confuse and complicate data analysis. The TAT presents for interpretation an ambiguous cue—a picture about which a story is to be written or a segment of a story that is to be completed. Such stories, in reflecting projective imagination, are considered by psychologists to reveal the ways in which people construe what they perceive, that is, the concepts and interpretations they bring to their experience and thus presumably the kind of sense that they make of their lives. Prior to Horner's work it was clear that women made a different kind of sense than men of situations of competitive achievement, that in some way they saw the situations differently or the situations aroused in them some different response.

On the basis of his studies of men, McClelland divided the concept of achievement motivation into what appeared to be its two logical components, a motive to approach success ("hope success") and a motive to avoid failure ("fear failure"). From her studies of women, Horner identified as a third category the unlikely motivation to avoid success ("fear success"). Women appeared to have a problem with competitive achievement, and that problem seemed to emanate from a perceived conflict between femininity and success, the dilemma of the female adolescent who struggles to integrate her feminine aspirations and the identifications of her early childhood with the more masculine competence she has acquired at school. From her analysis of women's completions of a story that began,

25

26

27

"after first term finals, Anne finds herself at the top of her medical school class," and from her observation of women's performance in competitive achievement situations, Horner reports that, "when success is likely or possible, threatened by the negative consequences they expect to follow success, young women become anxious and their positive achievement strivings become thwarted" (p. 171). She concludes that this fear "exists because for most women, the anticipation of success in competitive achievement activity, especially against men, produces anticipation of certain negative consequences, for example, threat of social rejection and loss of femininity" (1968, p. 125).

Such conflicts about success, however, may be viewed in a different light. Georgia Sassen (1980) suggests that the conflicts expressed by the women might instead indicate "a heightened perception of the 'other side' of competitive success, that is, the great emotional costs at which success achieved through competition is often gained—an understanding which, though confused, indicates some underlying sense that something is rotten in the state in which success is defined as having better grades than everyone else" (p. 15). Sassen points out that Horner found success anxiety to be present in women only when achievement was directly competitive, that is, when one person's success was at the expense of another's failure. 28

In his elaboration of the identity crisis, Erikson (1968) cites the life of George Bernard Shaw to illustrate the young person's sense of being co-opted prematurely by success in a career he cannot wholeheartedly endorse. Shaw at seventy, reflecting upon his life, described his crisis at the age of twenty as having been caused not by the lack of success or the absence of recognition, but by too much of both: "I made good in spite of myself, and found, to my dismay, that Business, instead of expelling me as the worthless imposter I was, was fastening upon me with no intention of letting me go. Behold me, therefore, in my twentieth year, with a business training, in an occupation which I detested as cordially as any sane person lets himself detest anything he cannot escape from. In March 1876 I broke loose" (p. 143). At this point Shaw settled down to study and write as he pleased. Hardly interpreted as evidence of neurotic anxiety about achievement and competition, Shaw's refusal suggests to Erikson "the extraordinary workings of an extraordinary personality [coming] to the fore" (p. 144). 29

We might on these grounds begin to ask, not why women have conflicts about competitive success, but why men show such readiness to adopt and celebrate a rather narrow vision of success. Remembering Piaget's observation, corroborated by Lever, that boys in 30 their games are more concerned with rules while girls are more concerned with relationships, often at the expense of the game itself—and given Chodorow's conclusion that men's social orientation is positional while women's is personal—we begin to understand why, when "Anne" becomes "John" in Horner's tale of competitive success and the story is completed by men, fear of success tends to disappear. John is considered to have played by the rules and won. He has the *right* to feel good about his success. Confirmed in the sense of his own identity as separate from those who, compared to him, are less competent, his positional sense of self is affirmed. For Anne, it is possible that the position she could obtain by being at the top of her medical school class may not, in fact, be what she wants.

    "It is obvious," Virginia Woolf says, "that the values of women   31 differ very often from the values which have been made by the other sex" (1929, p.76). Yet, she adds, "it is the masculine values that prevail." As a result, women come to question the normality of their feelings and to alter their judgments in deference to the opinion of others. In the nineteenth century novels written by women, Woolf sees at work "a mind which was slightly pulled from the straight and made to alter its clear vision in deference to external authority." The same deference to the values and opinions of others can be seen in the judgments of twentieth century women. The difficulty women experience in finding or speaking publicly in their own voices emerges repeatedly in the form of qualification and self-doubt, but also in intimations of a divided judgment, a public assessment and private assessment which are fundamentally at odds.

    Yet the deference and confusion that Woolf criticizes in women   32 derive from the values she sees as their strength. Women's deference is rooted not only in their social subordination but also in the substance of their moral concern. Sensitivity to the needs of others and the assumption of responsibility for taking care lead women to attend to voices other than their own and to include in their judgment other points of view. Women's moral weakness, manifest in an apparent diffusion and confusion of judgment, is thus inseparable from women's moral strength, an overriding concern with relationships and responsibilities. The reluctance to judge may itself be indicative of the care and concern for others that infuse the psychology of women's development and are responsible for what is generally seen as problematic in its nature.

    Thus women not only define themselves in a context of human   33 relationship but also judge themselves in terms of their ability to care. Women's place in man's life cycle has been that of nurturer, caretaker, and helpmate, the weaver of those networks of relationships on which she in turn relies. But while women have thus taken care of men, men have, in their theories of psychological development, as in their economic arrangements, tended to assume or devalue that care. When the focus on individuation and individual achievement extends into adulthood and maturity is equated with personal autonomy, concern with relationships appears as a weakness of women rather than as a human strength (Miller, 1976).

The discrepancy between womanhood and adulthood is nowhere 34 more evident than in the studies on sex-role stereotypes reported by Broverman, Vogel, Broverman, Clarkson, and Rosenkrantz (1972). The repeated finding of these studies is that the qualities deemed necessary for adulthood—the capacity for autonomous thinking, clear decision-making, and responsible action—are those associated with masculinity and considered undesirable as attributes of the feminine self. The stereotypes suggest a splitting of love and work that relegates expressive capacities to women while placing instrumental abilities in the masculine domain. Yet looked at from a different perspective, these stereotypes reflect a conception of adulthood that is itself out of balance, favoring the separateness of the individual self over connection to others, and leaning more toward an autonomous life of work than toward the interdependence of love and care.

The discovery now being celebrated by men in mid-life of the 35 importance of intimacy, relationships, and care is something that women have known from the beginning. However, because that knowledge in women has been considered "intuitive" or "instinctive," a function of anatomy coupled with destiny, psychologists have neglected to describe its development. In my research, I have found that women's moral development centers on the elaboration of that knowledge and thus delineates a critical line of psychological development in the lives of both of the sexes. The subject of moral development not only provides the final illustration of the reiterative pattern in the observation and assessment of sex differences in the literature on human development, but also indicates more particularly why the nature and significance of women's development has been for so long obscured and shrouded in mystery.

The criticism that Freud makes of women's sense of justice, see- 36 ing it as compromised in its refusal of blind impartiality, reappears not only in the work of Piaget but also in that of Kohlberg. While in Piaget's account (1932) of the moral judgment of the child, girls are an aside, a curiosity to whom he devotes four brief entries in an index that omits "boys" altogether because "the child" is assumed to be male, in the research from which Kohlberg derives his theory, females simply do not exist. Kohlberg's (1958, 1981) six stages that describe the development of moral judgment from childhood to adulthood are based empirically on a study of eighty-four boys whose development Kohlberg has followed for a period of over twenty years. Although Kohlberg claims universality for his stage sequence, those groups not included in his original sample rarely reach his higher stages (Edwards, 1975; Holstein, 1976; Simpson, 1974). Prominent among those who thus appear to be deficient in moral development when measured by Kohlberg's scale are women, whose judgments seem to exemplify the third stage of his six-stage sequence. At this stage morality is conceived in interpersonal terms and goodness is equated with helping and pleasing others. This conception of goodness is considered by Kohlberg and Kramer (1969) to be functional in the lives of mature women insofar as their lives take place in the home. Kohlberg and Kramer imply that only if women enter the traditional arena of male activity will they recognize the inadequacy of this moral perspective and progress like men toward higher stages where relationships are subordinated to rules (stage four) and rules to universal principles of justice (stages five and six).

37   Yet herein lies a paradox, for the very traits that traditionally have defined the "goodness" of women, their care for and sensitivity to the needs of others, are those that mark them as deficient in moral development. In this version of moral development, however, the conception of maturity is derived from the study of men's lives and reflects the importance of individuation in their development. Piaget (1970), challenging the common impression that a developmental theory is built like a pyramid from its base in infancy, points out that a conception of development instead hangs from its vertex of maturity, the point toward which progress is traced. Thus, a change in the definition of maturity does not simply alter the description of the highest stage but recasts the understanding of development, changing the entire account.

38   When one begins with the study of women and derives developmental constructs from their lives, the outline of a moral conception different from that described by Freud, Piaget, or Kohlberg begins to emerge and informs a different description of development. In this conception, the moral problem arises from conflicting responsibilities rather than from competing rights and requires for its resolution a mode of thinking that is contextual and narrative rather than formal and abstract. This conception of morality as concerned with the activity of care centers moral development around the understanding of responsibility and relationships, just as the conception of morality as fairness ties moral development to the understanding of rights and rules.

39   This different construction of the moral problem by women may be seen as the critical reason for their failure to develop within

the constraints of Kohlberg's system. Regarding all constructions of responsibility as evidence of a conventional moral understanding, Kohlberg defines the highest stages of moral development as deriving from a reflective understanding of human rights. That the morality of rights differs from the morality of responsibility in its emphasis on separation rather than connection, in its consideration of the individual rather than the relationship as primary, is illustrated by two responses to interview questions about the nature of morality. The first comes from a twenty-five-year-old man, one of the participants in Kohlberg's study:

> [*What does the word morality mean to you?*] Nobody in the world knows the answer. I think it is recognizing the right of the individual, the rights of other individuals, not interfering with those rights. Act as fairly as you would have them treat you. I think it is basically to preserve the human being's right to existence. I think that is the most important. Secondly, the human being's right to do as he pleases, again without interfering with somebody's else's rights.
>
> [*How have your views on morality changed since the last interview?*] I think I am more aware of an individual's rights now. I used to be looking at it strictly from my point of view, just for me. Now I think I am more aware of what the individual has a right to.

Kohlberg (1973) cites this man's response as illustrative of the principled conception of human rights that exemplifies his fifth and sixth stages. Commenting on the response, Kohlberg says: "Moving to a perspective outside of that of his society, he identifies morality with justice (fairness, rights, the Golden Rule), with recognition of the rights of others as these are defined naturally or intrinsically. The human's being right to do as he pleases without interfering with somebody else's rights is a formula defining rights prior to social legislation" (pp. 29–30).

The second response comes from a woman who participated in   40
the rights and responsibilities study. She also was twenty-five and, at the time, a third-year law student:

> [*Is there really some correct solution to moral problems, or is everybody's opinion equally right?*] No, I don't think everybody's opinion is equally right. I think that in some situations there may be opinions that are equally valid, and one could conscientiously adopt one of several courses of action. But there are other situations in which I think there are right and wrong answers, that sort of inhere in the nature of existence, of all individuals here who need to live with each other to live. We need to depend on each other, and hopefully it is not only a physical need but a need of fulfillment in ourselves, that a person's life is enriched by cooperating

with other people and striving to live in harmony with everybody else, and to that end, there are right and wrong, there are things which promote that end and that move away from it, and in that way it is possible to choose in certain cases among different courses of action that obviously promote or harm that goal.

[*Is there a time in the past when you would have thought about these things differently?*] Oh, yeah, I think that I went through a time when I thought that things were pretty relative, that I can't tell you what to do and you can't tell me what to do, because you've got your conscience and I've got mine.

[*When was that?*] When I was in high school. I guess that it just sort of dawned on me that my own ideas changed, and because my own judgment changed, I felt I couldn't judge another person's judgment. But now I think even when it is only the person himself who is going to be affected, I say it is wrong to the extent it doesn't cohere with what I know about human nature and what I know about you, and just from what I think is true about the operation of the universe, I could say I think you are making a mistake.

[*What led you to change, do you think?*] Just seeing more of life, just recognizing that there are an awful lot of things that are common among people. There are certain things that you come to learn promote a better life and better relationships and more personal fulfillment than other things that in general tend to do the opposite, and the things that promote these things, you would call morally right.

This response also represents a personal reconstruction of 41 morality following a period of questioning and doubt, but the reconstruction of moral understanding is based not on the primacy and universality of individual rights, but rather on what she describes as a "very strong sense of being responsible to the world." Within this construction, the moral dilemma changes from how to exercise one's rights without interfering with the rights of others to how "to lead a moral life which includes obligations to myself and my family and people in general." The problem then becomes one of limiting responsibilities without abandoning moral concern. When asked to describe herself, this woman says that she values "having other people that I am tied to, and also having people that I am responsible to. I have a very strong sense of being responsible to the world, that I can't just live for my enjoyment, but just the fact of being in the world gives me an obligation to do what I can to make the world a better place to live in, no matter how small a scale that may be on." Thus while Kohlberg's subject worries about people interfering with each other's rights, this woman worries about "the possibility of omission, of your not helping others when you could help them."

The issue that this woman raises is addressed by Jane Loe- 42
vinger's fifth "autonomous" stage of ego development, where
autonomy, placed in a context of relationships, is defined as modu-
lating an excessive sense of responsibility through the recognition
that other people have responsibility for their own destiny. The autonomous stage in Loevinger's account (1970) witnesses a relin-
quishing of moral dichotomies and their replacement with "a feeling
for the complexity and multifaceted character of real people and real
situations" (p. 6). Whereas the rights conception of morality that informs Kohlberg's principled level (stages five and six) is geared to arriving at an objectively fair or just resolution to moral dilemmas
upon which all rational persons could agree, the responsibility conception focuses instead on the limitations of any particular resolution and describes the conflicts that remain.

Thus it becomes clear why a morality of rights and noninterfer- 43
ence may appear frightening to women in its potential justification of
indifference and unconcern. At the same time, it becomes clear why,
from a male perspective, a morality of responsibility appears incon-
clusive and diffuse, given its insistent contextual relativism. Women's
moral judgments thus elucidate the pattern observed in the description of the developmental differences between the sexes, but they also
provide an alternative conception of maturity by which these differences can be assessed and their implications traced. The psychology
of women that has consistently been described as distinctive in its
greater orientation toward relationships and interdependence implies
a more contextual mode of judgment and a different moral understanding. Given the differences in women's conceptions of self and
morality, women bring to the life cycle a different point of view and
order human experience in terms of different priorities.

The myth of Demeter and Persephone, which McClelland 44
(1975) cites as exemplifying the feminine attitude toward power,
was associated with the Eleusinian Mysteries celebrated in ancient
Greece for over two thousand years. As told in the Homeric *Hymn to
Demeter,* the story of Persephone indicates the strengths of interdependence, building up resources and giving, that McClelland found
in his research on power motivation to characterize the mature feminine style. Although, McClelland says, "it is fashionable to conclude
that no one knows what went on in the Mysteries, it is known that
they were probably the most important religious ceremonies, even
partly on the historical record, which were organized by and for
women, especially at the onset before men by means of the cult of
Dionysos began to take them over." Thus McClelland regards the
myth as "a special presentation of feminine psychology" (p. 96). It
is, as well, a life-cycle story par excellence.

Persephone, the daughter of Demeter, while playing in a   45
meadow with her girlfriends, sees a beautiful narcissus which she
runs to pick. As she does so, the earth opens and she is snatched
away by Hades, who takes her to his underworld kingdom. Demeter, goddess of the earth, so mourns the loss of her daughter that she
refuses to allow anything to grow. The crops that sustain life on
earth shrivel up, killing men and animals alike, until Zeus takes pity
on man's suffering and persuades his brother to return Persephone
to her mother. But before she leaves, Persephone eats some pome-
granate seeds, which ensures that she will spend part of every year
with Hades in the underworld.

The elusive mystery of women's development lies in its recogni-   46
tion of the continuing importance of attachment in the human life
cycle. Woman's place in man's life cycle is to protect this recognition
while the developmental litany intones the celebration of separation,
autonomy, individuation, and natural rights. The myth of Persephone
speaks directly to the distortion in this view by reminding us that narcissism leads to death, that the fertility of the earth is in some mysterious way tied to the continuation of the mother-daughter relationship,
and that the life cycle itself arises from an alternation between the
world of women and that of men. Only when life-cycle theorists divide their attention and begin to live with women as they have lived
with men will their vision encompass the experience of both sexes and
their theories become correspondingly more fertile.

SELECTED BIBLIOGRAPHY
FOR GILLIGAN'S "WOMAN'S PLACE
IN MAN'S LIFE CYCLE"

Carol Gilligan mentions a number of important authorities in psychology in
"Woman's Place in Man's Life Cycle." Here are some of the books to which
she refers:

Bruno Bettelheim. *The Uses of Enchantment.* New York: Knopf, 1976.

Nancy Chodorow. *The Reproduction of Mothering.* Berkeley: University of
California Press, 1978.

Erik H. Erikson. *Childhood and Society.* New York: W. W. Norton, 1950.

Lawrence Kohlberg. *The Philosophy of Moral Development.* San Francisco:
Harper and Row, 1981.

Janet Lever. "Sex Differences in the Games Children Play." *Social Problems*
23 (1976): 478–487.

Jane Loevinger and Ruth Wessler. *Measuring Ego Development.* San Francisco: Jossey-Bass, 1970.

David C. McClelland. *Power: The Inner Experience*. New York: Irvington, 1975.

George Herbert Mead. *Mind, Self, and Society*. Chicago: University of Chicago Press, 1934.

Jean Piaget. *The Moral Judgment of the Child* (1932). New York: The Free Press, 1965.

QUESTIONS FOR CRITICAL READING

1. Do you agree that men and women observe things differently?
2. What is the importance of Gilligan's observations about *Elements of Style* (see para. 4)?
3. What does it mean that "developmental theorists . . . project a masculine image" (para. 6)?
4. Why did Freud think women "show less sense of justice than men" (para. 7)?
5. Do you agree that "mothers tend to experience their daughters as more like, and continuous with, themselves" (para. 9)?
6. Does your experience validate the conclusion that women express more empathy than men?
7. What differences do you see between the games boys play and the games girls play?

SUGGESTIONS FOR WRITING

1. Psychologists place great importance on the ways in which boys and girls play games. Judging from your own experience playing games as a child, can you validate that there is an important socializing difference in the games that boys and girls play and how they play them? Establish the values that you gained from the socialization that is implied in playing games. How much of what you learned in playing games still operates in your behavior?
2. One of the chief theories of psychologists concerns the link between boys and their mothers and girls and their mothers. One theory is that because mothers see their daughters as like themselves they tend to treat them as continuous with themselves, thus making it difficult for women later to break away. Boys, however, because of the gender distinction, find it easier as adults to break away and pursue successful careers. How true do you think this hypothesis is? Find examples to use in your argument.
3. Judging from your own experiences, what kinds of quarrels do boys have among themselves? How do they differ from the quarrels that girls have among themselves? What do the differences imply for the

development of boys into men and girls into women? Try to be as specific as possible in recalling or describing quarrels of your own. You may wish to interview a member of the opposite sex to get a different perspective.

4. Read Sigmund Freud on the Oedipus Complex and comment on his observations about the development of boys and girls. Is it clear that as Gilligan suggests, he worked entirely from observation of the male gender and did not take into account differences in anatomy or in social development between boys and girls? What claims by Freud seem most unlikely to you?

5. The term *narcissism* is mentioned in the text (paras. 19, 46). Look up the term in a psychological dictionary or psychological handbook. What is narcissism? Why do we think of it as a problem? Look up the myth of Narcissus and see what has been said about it. Is narcissism more likely to be a problem of men or of women? What kind of problems does it produce in individuals?

6. Erik Erikson suggests that "the female comes to know herself as she is known, through her relationships with others" (para. 21). To what extent do you think is this true? How differently does self-knowledge come to men? Do you feel there is a distinction between the ways in which men and women define themselves? Which sex is most affected by social identification, accepting the definitions of friends and acquaintances?

7. **CONNECTIONS**   Life is full of rules. Do you observe a distinction in the ways in which men and women regard rules? What are some of the rules by which you live? How do you regard them? Is it essential to learn how to abide by rules in order to be a fully moral person? Was Henry David Thoreau typical of the male who understands and respects the rules? Is his sense of justice typically male?

8. **CONNECTIONS**   Virginia Woolf addressed "Shakespeare's Sister" to an audience of young women in college. To what extent does her essay reflect the views that Gilligan develops in her essay? Would Woolf consider Gilligan to be a feminist? What aspects of Woolf's comments on Shakespeare's hypothetical sister do you think most support the views that Gilligan presents in her essay?

9. **CONNECTIONS**   What are the important points of agreement and disagreement between Gilligan's essay and Karen Horney's "Distrust between the Sexes"? Is Horney's essay in agreement with the theories and conclusions that Gilligan draws, or does it contradict them? Both Gilligan and Horney are psychologists. Which one offers you the most insights into the distinctions between the sexes? Which one offers you the best insights into the qualities that link the sexes?

BELL HOOKS

Black Women:
Shaping Feminist Theory

BELL HOOKS (b. 1952) is the pen name of Gloria Jean Watkins, who was born in Hopkinsville, Kentucky, and received her B.A. at Stanford University and her Ph.D. from the University of California at Santa Cruz. She eventually took the name of her great-grandmother and uses the lower-case initials as a way of taking the spotlight off herself as author and putting it on her works instead. hooks began her first book at age nineteen, and after eight years of research and writing she published *Ain't I a Woman: Black Women and Feminism* (1981) while she was still in graduate school. Her works have focused on black feminism, third world issues, and her own personal experiences. She is known as a memoirist as well as a keen social critic.

Recently hooks was distinguished professor of English at City College, City University of New York. She is one of the most visible of America's black intellectuals, but she has steadfastly asserted, despite her own academic connections, that intellectual achievements are not limited to universities. Much of her critical work is devoted to analyzing popular culture, such as contemporary films and rap music. Among her works are *Talking Back: Thinking Feminist, Thinking Black* (1989); *Teaching to Transgress: Education as the Practice of Freedom* (1994); *Outlaw Culture: Resisting Representation* (1994); *Feminism Is for Everybody* (2000); and two personal memoirs, *Bone Black: Memoirs of a Girlhood* (1996) and *Wounds of Passion: The Writing Life* (1997).

The book from which the following essay is taken, *Feminist Theory: From Margin to Center,* was published first in 1984 and

From *Feminist Theory: From Margin to Center.*

then in a new, revised edition in 2000. This selection offers one of the most forceful and clearest critiques of the limits of the feminist movement, while at the same time honoring the underlying radicalism that presses feminism forward. The primary point hooks makes is that the standard feminist treatises of the 1960s and 1970s, such as Betty Friedan's *The Feminine Mystique* (1963), were limited by their failure to understand and represent the circumstances of black women in America. Friedan ultimately founded the National Organization for Women (NOW) and influenced the modern feminist movement in much the way hooks suggests.

According to hooks, the vision that Friedan brought to the struggle for equal rights for women was fashioned from a middle-class, white perspective. When Friedan complained about the limitations of women in the modern world, she was referring to the limitations of a woman compelled to stay at home while her husband worked. In addition, she addressed the limitations of a woman who was prevented from holding the same jobs men held or getting the same pay that men got. hooks asserts that this vision is not representative of the "mass of women" who are currently oppressed by male dominance.

hooks is very much a radical thinker: she goes to the foundation of the problems she addresses rather than simply discussing the observable symptoms. Therefore, hooks talks about racism and classism as the proper targets of an effective feminist movement. However, she goes even further in placing the blame on capitalism itself, which in her view promotes the exploitation of women and protects the "ruling class" of white men. In her review of the mechanism of exploitation, she points out that white men can exploit white women, who in turn can exploit black men and women, and black men can exploit black women—but black women can only exploit each other. They are, hooks reminds us, the end of the line of exploitation.

In comparison to some of the earlier essays in this book on the subject of equality—such as Aristotle's and Tocqueville's discussions of democracy and Rose and Milton Friedman's discussion of equality of opportunity—hooks offers a vastly less optimistic vision. For her, the problems women face are marked by a social structure that maintains patriarchal control over most cultural institutions. Some of her thinking reflects the views of Karl Marx, although hooks does not advocate communism as much as communalism. She reflects on personal experiences that benefited from the communal spirit of the women in her family, who clung together in mutual support. Her critique of "liberal independence" is fascinating, especially in contrast to Frederick Jackson Turner's praise of the kind of liberal independence promoted by the American frontier. Obviously, hooks is not convinced that "liberal independence" will produce as much happiness and personal satisfaction as would a more communal approach to living. In this sense she is an idealist, but her ideals are clear and concrete—and for some people, doubtless achievable.

hooks's Rhetoric

"Black Women: Shaping Feminist Theory" is the first chapter in a book that develops important ideas constituting a theory of black feminism. Thus, this chapter must establish the basic principles of feminism, including its current problems, and clarify the concerns that are central to hooks's thinking. This foundational chapter succeeds through the use of several important and effective techniques.

hooks structures the chapter in three distinct sections. The first section focuses on one of the primary texts of modern feminism, Betty Friedan's *The Feminine Mystique*. As a result of hooks's strategy—in which she acts as a literary critic and offers up a careful, close reading—she takes the average feminist off guard by criticizing the limitations of what, for some, is almost a sacred text. By focusing on Friedan in her opening paragraphs, hooks has the advantage of speaking concretely about a problem that might become vague and ill-defined if there were no text to use as a reference.

In the second section, from paragraph 5 to paragraph 15, hooks consults a number of other authors, much as Carol Gilligan does: Rita Mae Brown, Leah Fritz, Benjamin Barber, Christine Delphy, Sookie Stambler, Antoinette Fouque, Carol Ehrlich, Zillah Eisenstein, and Susan Griffin. In each case, hooks quotes liberally and then comments on the significance of the quotation. In some cases, the writer verifies hooks's position; in others, hooks uses the passage to establish the limitations of feminism as it is interpreted by specific theorists. In every case, however, the technique is one of quotation and analysis, all in the interest of pushing forward her argument that contemporary feminism is a white, bourgeois movement and that it needs to free itself of racist and classist limitations if it is to make progress.

The third section of the essay, beginning with paragraph 16, uses a strategy similar to those employed in sections one and two in that it presents a text to analyze, but different in that the text is not someone's book or essay. Rather, it is the text of bell hooks's own life. She begins by describing her experiences growing up in a black family with women who bonded together. She explains that she grew up "in a Southern, black, father-dominated, working-class household" (para. 16). In other words, she experienced the sting of patriarchal power firsthand (so did her mother, sisters, and brother). In this environment the very term *feminism* was not used or referred to. As she says, "I had not known a life where women had not been together, where women had not helped, protected, and loved one another deeply" (para. 18). In light of this background she comments on her first experiences with feminist discourse, at which she was surprised by the condescension of white feminists who had not had similar experiences.

In graduate school, especially in a class on feminist theory (para. 21), hooks found resistance from other women who failed to understand her perspective. She describes the antagonism between herself and other students, devoting the last part of the passage to her personal experiences with feminists who could not understand her position on feminism.

The personal ending of the essay provides some of the information that her fellow students did not have regarding hooks's background. Obviously there was antagonism and misunderstanding, but hooks continues her critique of "privileged feminists" to the end of the discussion, hoping that the reader will by then have a fuller understanding of her as a black woman interested in resisting oppression of any kind.

Rhetorically, hooks's strategies achieve several things. First, the concrete opening begins a process of textual analysis that is essential to a real understanding of her views. Second, the introduction of texts by representative authorities demonstrates hooks's considerable research into her subject. Third, her personal observations humanize the essay, giving a personal touch that may help us achieve a sense of warmth toward bell hooks as a person concerned with true equality.

PREREADING QUESTIONS: WHAT TO READ FOR

The following prereading questions may help you anticipate key issues in the discussion on bell hooks's "Black Women: Shaping Feminist Theory." Keeping them in mind during your first reading of the selection should help focus your reactions.

- How does racism express itself in feminist groups?

- What social classes are represented in feminist texts of the 1960s?

- What can black women contribute to the feminist movement?

Black Women:
Shaping Feminist Theory

Feminism in the United States has never emerged from the 1
women who are most victimized by sexist oppression; women who
are daily beaten down, mentally, physically, and spiritually—
women who are powerless to change their condition in life. They are
a silent majority. A mark of their victimization is that they accept
their lot in life without visible question, without organized protest,
without collective anger or rage. Betty Friedan's *The Feminine Mystique* is still heralded as having paved the way for contemporary feminist movement—it was written as if these women did not exist.
(Although *The Feminine Mystique* has been criticized and even attacked from various fronts, I call attention to it again because certain
biased premises about the nature of women's social status put forth
initially in this text continue to shape the tenor and direction of feminist movement.)

Friedan's famous phrase, "the problem that has no name," often 2
quoted to describe the condition of women in this society, actually
referred to the plight of a select group of college-educated, middle-
and upper-class, married white women—housewives bored with
leisure, with the home, with children, with buying products, who
wanted more out of life. Friedan concludes her first chapter by stating: "We can no longer ignore that voice within women that says: 'I
want something more than my husband and my children and my
house.'" That "more" she defined as careers. She did not discuss
who would be called in to take care of the children and maintain the
home if more women like herself were freed from their house labor
and given equal access with white men to the professions. She did
not speak of the needs of women without men, without children,
without homes. She ignored the existence of all non-white women
and poor white women. She did not tell readers whether it was more
fulfilling to be a maid, a babysitter, a factory worker, a clerk, or a
prostitute than to be a leisure-class housewife.

She made her plight and the plight of white women like herself 3
synonymous with a condition affecting all American women. In so
doing, she deflected attention away from her classism, her racism, her
sexist attitudes towards the masses of American women. In the context
of her book, Friedan makes clear that the women she saw as victimized
by sexism were college-educated white women who were compelled
by sexist conditioning to remain in the home. She contends:

> It is urgent to understand how the very condition of being a
> housewife can create a sense of emptiness, non-existence,

nothingness in women. There are aspects of the housewife role that make it almost impossible for a woman of adult intelligence to retain a sense of human identity, the firm core of self or "I" without which a human being, man or woman, is not truly alive. For women of ability in America today, I am convinced that there is something about the housewife state itself that is dangerous.

Specific problems and dilemmas of leisure-class white housewives were real concerns that merited consideration and change, but they were not the pressing political concerns of masses of women. Masses of women were concerned about economic survival, ethnic and racial discrimination, etc. When Friedan wrote *The Feminine Mystique,* more than one-third of all women were in the work force. Although many women longed to be housewives, only women with leisure time and money could actually shape their identities on the model of the feminine mystique. They were women who, in Friedan's words, were "told by the most advanced thinkers of our time to go back and live their lives as if they were Noras,[1] restricted to the doll's house by Victorian prejudices."

From her early writing, it appears that Friedan never wondered   4 whether or not the plight of college-educated white housewives was an adequate reference point by which to gauge the impact of sexism or sexist oppression on the lives of women in American society. Nor did she move beyond her own life experience to acquire an expanded perspective on the lives of women in the United States. I say this not to discredit her work. It remains a useful discussion of the impact of sexist discrimination on a select group of women. Examined from a different perspective, it can also be seen as a case study of narcissism, insensitivity, sentimentality, and self-indulgence, which reaches its peak when Friedan, in a chapter titled "Progressive Dehumanization," makes a comparison between the psychological effects of isolation on white housewives and the impact of confinement on the self-concept of prisoners in Nazi concentration camps.

Friedan was a principal shaper of contemporary feminist thought.   5 Significantly, the one-dimensional perspective on women's reality presented in her book became a marked feature of the contemporary feminist movement. Like Friedan before them, white women who dominate feminist discourse today rarely question whether or not their perspective on women's reality is true to the lived experiences of women as a collective group. Nor are they aware of the extent to which their perspectives reflect race and class biases, although there has been

---

[1] **Nora** Chief character in Henrik Ibsen's *A Doll's House* (1879), an important feminist play.

a greater awareness of biases in recent years. Racism abounds in the writings of white feminists, reinforcing white supremacy and negating the possibility that women will bond politically across ethnic and racial boundaries. Past feminist refusal to draw attention to and attack racial hierarchies suppressed the link between race and class. Yet class structure in American society has been shaped by the racial politic of white supremacy; it is only by analyzing racism and its function in capitalist society that a thorough understanding of class relationships can emerge. Class struggle is inextricably bound to the struggle to end racism. Urging women to explore the full implication of class in an early essay, "The Last Straw," Rita Mae Brown[2] explained:

> Class is much more than Marx's definition of relationship to the means of production. Class involves your behavior, your basic assumptions about life. Your experience (determined by your class) validates those assumptions, how you are taught to behave, what you expect from yourself and from others, your concept of a future, how you understand problems and solve them, how you think, feel, act. It is these behavioral patterns that middle-class women resist recognizing although they may be perfectly willing to accept class in Marxist terms, a neat trick that helps them avoid really dealing with class behavior and changing that behavior in themselves. It is these behavioral patterns which must be recognized, understood, and changed.

White women who dominate feminist discourse, who for the most part make and articulate feminist theory, have little or no understanding of white supremacy as a racial politic, of the psychological impact of class, of their political status within a racist, sexist, capitalist state.

It is this lack of awareness that, for example, leads Leah Fritz to write in *Dreamers and Dealers,* a discussion of the current women's movement published in 1979:

> Women's suffering under sexist tyranny is a common bond among all women, transcending the particulars of the different forms that tyranny takes. *Suffering cannot be measured and compared quantitatively.* Is the enforced idleness and vacuity of a "rich" woman, which leads her to madness and/or suicide, greater or less than the suffering of a poor woman who barely survives on welfare but retains somehow her spirit? There is no way to measure such difference, but should these two women survey each other without the screen of patriarchal class, they may find a commonality in the fact that they are both oppressed, both miserable.

---

[2] **Rita Mae Brown (b. 1944)** Author of an important lesbian novel, *Rubyfruit Jungle* (1973).

Fritz's statement is another example of wishful thinking, as well as the conscious mystification of social divisions between women that has characterized much feminist expression. While it is evident that many women suffer from sexist tyranny, there is little indication that this forges "a common bond among all women." There is much evidence substantiating the reality that race and class identity creates differences in quality of life, social status, and lifestyle that take precedence over the common experience women share—differences that are rarely transcended. The motives of materially privileged, educated white women with a variety of career and lifestyle options available to them must be questioned when they insist that "suffering cannot be measured." Fritz is by no means the first white feminist to make this statement. It is a statement that I have never heard a poor woman of any race make. Although there is much I would take issue with in Benjamin Barber's critique of the women's movement, *Liberating Feminism,* I agree with his assertion:

> Suffering is not necessarily a fixed and universal experience that can be measured by a single rod: it is related to situations, needs, and aspirations. But there must be some historical and political parameters for the use of the term so that political priorities can be established and different forms and degrees of suffering can be given the most attention.

A central tenet of modern feminist thought has been the assertion [7] that "all women are oppressed." This assertion implies that women share a common lot, that factors like class, race, religion, sexual preference, etc. do not create a diversity of experience that determines the extent to which sexism will be an oppressive force in the lives of individual women. Sexism as a system of domination is institutionalized, but it has never determined in an absolute way the fare of all women in this society. Being oppressed means the *absence of choices.* It is the primary point of contact between the oppressed and the oppressor. Many women in this society do have choices (as inadequate as they are); therefore exploitation and discrimination are words that more accurately describe the lot of women collectively in the United States. Many women do not join organized resistance against sexism precisely because sexism has not meant an absolute lack of choices. They may know they are discriminated against on the basis of sex, but they do not equate this with oppression. Under capitalism, patriarchy is structured so that sexism restricts women's behavior in some realms even as freedom from limitations is allowed in other spheres. The absence of extreme restrictions leads many women to ignore the areas in which they are exploited or discriminated against; it may even lead them to imagine that no women are oppressed.

There are oppressed women in the United States, and it is both 8
appropriate and necessary that we speak against such oppression.
French feminist Christine Delphy makes the point in her essay
"For a Materialist Feminism" that the use of the term "oppression"
is important because it places feminist struggle in a radical political framework (a fuller discussion of Christine Delphy's perspective may be found in the collected essays of her work, *Close to
Home*):

> The rebirth of feminism coincided with the use of the term "op-
> pression." The ruling ideology, i.e. common sense, daily speech,
> does not speak about oppression but about a "feminine condi-
> tion." It refers back to a naturalist explanation: to a constraint of
> nature, exterior reality out of reach and not modifiable by human
> action. The term "oppression," on the contrary, refers back to a
> choice, an explanation, a situation that is political. "Oppression"
> and "social oppression" are therefore synonyms, or rather social
> oppression is a redundance: the notion of a political origin, i.e. so-
> cial, is an integral part of the concept of oppression.

However, feminist emphasis on "common oppression" in the United
States was less a strategy for politicization than an appropriation by
conservative and liberal women of a radical political vocabulary that
masked the extent to which they shaped the movement so that it addressed and promoted their class interests.

Although the impulse towards unity and empathy that informed 9
the notion of common oppression was directed at building solidarity,
slogans like "organize around your own oppression" provided the excuse many privileged women needed to ignore the differences between their social status and the status of masses of women. It was a
mark of race and class privilege, as well as the expression of freedom
from the many constraints sexism places on working-class women,
that middle-class white women were able to make their interests the
primary focus of feminist movement and employ a rhetoric of com-
monality that made their condition synonymous with "oppression."
Who was there to demand a change in vocabulary? What other group
of women in the United States had the same access to universities,
publishing houses, mass media, money? Had middle-class black
women begun a movement in which they had labeled themselves "oppressed," no one would have taken them seriously. Had they established public forums and given speeches about their "oppression,"
they would have been criticized and attacked from all sides. This was
not the case with white bourgeois feminists, for they could appeal to a
large audience of women like themselves who were eager to change
their lot in life. Their isolation from women of other class and race

groups provided no immediate comparative base by which to test their assumptions of common oppression.

Initially, radical participants in women's movement demanded 10 that women penetrate that isolation and create a space for contact. Anthologies like *Liberation Now!, Women's Liberation: Blueprint for the Future, Class and Feminism, Radical Feminism,* and *Sisterhood Is Powerful,* all published in the early 1970s, contain articles that attempted to address a wide audience of women, an audience that was not exclusively white, middle-class, college-educated, and adult (many have articles on teenagers). Sookie Stambler articulated this radical spirit in her introduction to *Women's Liberation: Blueprint for the Future:*

> Movement women have always been turned off by the media's necessity to create celebrities and superstars. This goes against our basic philosophy. We cannot relate to women in our ranks towering over us with prestige and fame. We are not struggling for the benefit of the one woman or for one group of women. We are dealing with issues that concern all women.

These sentiments, shared by many feminists early in the move- 11 ment, were not sustained. As more and more women acquired prestige, fame, or money from feminist writings or from gains from feminist movement for equality in the work force, individual opportunism undermined appeals for collective struggle. Women who were not opposed to patriarchy, capitalism, classism, or racism labeled themselves "feminist." Their expectations were varied. Privileged women wanted social equality with men of their class; some women wanted equal pay for equal work; others wanted an alternative lifestyle. Many of these legitimate concerns were easily co-opted by the ruling capitalist patriarchy. French feminist Antoinette Fouque states:

> The actions proposed by the feminist groups are spectacular, provoking. But provocation only brings to light a certain number of social contradictions. It does not reveal radical contradictions within society. The feminists claim that they do not seek equality with men, but their practice proves the contrary to be true. Feminists are a bourgeois avant-garde that maintains, in an inverted form, the dominant values. Inversion does not facilitate the passage to another kind of structure. Reformism suits everyone! Bourgeois order, capitalism, phallocentrism are ready to integrate as many feminists as will be necessary. Since these women are becoming men, in the end it will only mean a few more men. The difference between the sexes is not whether one does or doesn't have a penis, it is whether or not one is an integral part of a phallic masculine economy.

Feminists in the United States are aware of the contradictions.   12
Carol Ehrlich makes the point in her essay "The Unhappy Marriage
of Marxism and Feminism: Can It Be Saved?" that "feminism seems
more and more to have taken on a blind, safe, nonrevolutionary outlook" as "feminist radicalism loses ground to bourgeois feminism,"
stressing that "we cannot let this continue":

> Women need to know (and are increasingly prevented from finding
> out) that feminism is *not* about dressing for success, or becoming a
> corporate executive, or gaining elective office; it is *not* being able to
> share a two-career marriage and take skiing vacations and spend
> huge amounts of time with your husband and two lovely children
> because you have a domestic worker who makes all this possible for
> you, but who hasn't the time or money to do it for herself; it is *not*
> opening a Women's Bank, or spending a weekend in an expensive
> workshop that guarantees to teach you how to become assertive
> (but not aggressive); it is most emphatically *not* about becoming a
> police detective or CIA agent or marine corps general.
>
> But if these distorted images of feminism have more reality than
> ours do, it is partly our own fault. We have not worked as hard as
> we should have at providing clear and meaningful alternative
> analyses which relate to people's lives, and at providing active, ac-
> cessible groups in which to work.

It is no accident that feminist struggle has been so easily co-   13
opted to serve the interests of conservative and liberal feminists,
since feminism in the United States has so far been a bourgeois
ideology. Zillah Eisenstein discusses the liberal roots of North American feminism in *The Radical Future of Liberal Feminism*, explaining
in the introduction:

> One of the major contributions to be found in this study is the
> role of the ideology of liberal individualism in the construction of
> feminist theory. Today's feminists either do not discuss a theory of
> individuality or they unself-consciously adopt the competitive,
> atomistic ideology of liberal individualism. There is much confu-
> sion on this issue in the feminist theory we discuss here. Until a
> conscious differentiation is made between a theory of individual-
> ity that recognizes the importance of the individual within the
> social collectivity and the ideology of individualism that assumes a
> competitive view of the individual, there will not be a full ac-
> counting of what a feminist theory of liberation must look like in
> our Western society.

The ideology of "competitive, atomistic . . . liberal individual-   14
ism" has permeated feminist thought to such an extent that it undermines the potential radicalism of feminist struggle. The usurpation

of feminism by bourgeois women to support their class interests has been to a very grave extent justified by feminist theory as it has so far been conceived (for example, the ideology of "common oppression"). Any movement to resist the co-optation of feminist struggle must begin by introducing a different feminist perspective—a new theory—one that is not informed by the ideology of liberal individualism.

The exclusionary practices of women who dominate feminist discourse have made it practically impossible for new and varied theories to emerge. Feminism has its party line, and women who feel a need for a different strategy, a different foundation, often find themselves ostracized and silenced. Criticisms of or alternatives to established feminist ideas are not encouraged, e.g. recent controversies about expanding feminist discussions of sexuality. Yet groups of women who feel excluded from feminist discourse and praxis[3] can make a place for themselves only if they first create, via critiques, an awareness of the factors that alienate them. Many individual white women found in the women's movement a liberatory solution to personal dilemmas. Having directly benefited from the movement, they are less inclined to criticize it or to engage in rigorous examination of its structure than those who feel it has not had a revolutionary impact on their lives or the lives of masses of women in our society. Non-white women who feel affirmed within the current structure of feminist movement (even though they may form autonomous groups) seem also to feel that their definitions of the party line, whether on the issue of black feminism or on other issues, are the only legitimate discourse. Rather than encourage a diversity of voices, critical dialogue, and controversy, they, like some white women, seek to stifle dissent. As activists and writers whose work is widely known, they act as if they are best able to judge whether other women's voices should be heard. Susan Griffin warns against this overall tendency towards dogmatism in her essay "The Way of All Ideology":

> When a theory is transformed into an ideology, it begins to destroy the self and self-knowledge. Originally born of feeling, it pretends to float above and around feeling. Above sensation. It organizes experience according to itself, without touching experience. By virtue of being itself, it is supposed to know. To invoke the name of this ideology is to confer truthfulness. No one can tell it anything new. Experience ceases to surprise it, inform it, transform it. It is annoyed by any detail which does not fit into its

---

[3]**praxis** Practice, action.

world view. Begun as a cry against the denial of truth, now it denies any truth which does not fit into its scheme. Begun as a way to restore one's sense of reality, now it attempts to discipline real people, to remake natural beings after its own image. All that it fails to explain it records as its enemy. Begun as a theory of liberation, it is threatened by new theories of liberation; it builds a prison for the mind.

We resist hegemonic dominance of feminist thought by insisting   16 that it is a theory in the making, that we must necessarily criticize, question, re-examine, and explore new possibilities. My persistent critique has been informed by my status as a member of an oppressed group, my experience of sexist exploitation and discrimination, and the sense that prevailing feminist analysis has not been the force shaping my feminist consciousness. This is true for many women. There are white women who had never considered resisting male dominance until the feminist movement created an awareness that they could and should. My awareness of feminist struggle was stimulated by social circumstance. Growing up in a Southern, black, father-dominated, working-class household, I experienced (as did my mother, my sisters, and my brother) varying degrees of patriarchal tyranny, and it made me angry—it made us all angry. Anger led me to question the politics of male dominance and enabled me to resist sexist socialization. Frequently, white feminists act as if black women did not know sexist oppression existed until they voiced feminist sentiment. They believe they are providing black women with "the" analysis and "the" program for liberation. They do not understand, cannot even imagine, that black women, as well as other groups of women who live daily in oppressive situations, often acquire an awareness of patriarchal politics from their lived experience, just as they develop strategies of resistance (even though they may not resist on a sustained or organized basis).

These black women observed white feminist focus on male   17 tyranny and women's oppression as if it were a "new" revelation, and felt such a focus had little impact on their lives. To them it was just another indication of the privileged living conditions of middle- and upper-class white women that they would need a theory to "inform them that they were oppressed." The implication being that people who are truly oppressed know it even though they may not be engaged in organized resistance or are unable to articulate in written form the nature of their oppression. These black women saw nothing liberatory in party-line analyses of women's oppression. Neither the fact that black women have not organized collectively in huge numbers around the issues of "feminism" (many of us do not know or use the term) nor the fact that we have not had access to the machinery of power that would allow us to share our analyses or theories about gender with the American public negates its presence in our lives or places us in a position of dependency in relationship to those white and non-white feminists who address a larger audience.

The understanding I had by age thirteen of patriarchal politics 18 created in me expectations of the feminist movement that were quite different from those of young, middle-class white women. When I entered my first women's studies class at Stanford University in the early 1970s, white women were reveling in the joy of being together—to them it was an important, momentous occasion. I had not known a life where women had not been together, where women had not helped, protected, and loved one another deeply. I had not known white women who were ignorant of the impact of race and class on their social status and consciousness. (Southern white women often have a more realistic perspective on racism and classism than white women in other areas of the United States.) I did not feel sympathetic to white peers who maintained that I could not expect them to have knowledge of or understand the life experiences of black women. Despite my background (living in racially segregated communities) I knew about the lives of white women, and certainly no white women lived in our neighborhood, attended our schools, or worked in our homes.

When I participated in feminist groups, I found that white 19 women adopted a condescending attitude towards me and other non-white participants. The condescension they directed at black women was one of the means they employed to remind us that the women's movement was "theirs"—that we were able to participate because they allowed it, even encouraged it; after all, we were needed to legitimate the process. They did not see us as equals. They did not treat us as equals. And though they expected us to provide first-hand accounts of black experience, they felt it was their role to decide if these experiences were authentic. Frequently, college-educated black women (even those from poor and working-class backgrounds) were dismissed as mere imitators. Our presence in movement activities did not count, as white women were convinced that "real" blackness meant speaking the patois of poor black people, being uneducated, streetwise, and a variety of other stereotypes. If we dared to criticize the movement or to assume responsibility for reshaping feminist ideas and introducing new ideas, our voices were tuned out, dismissed, silenced. We could be heard only if our statements echoed the sentiments of the dominant discourse.

Attempts by white feminists to silence black women are rarely 20 written about. All too often they have taken place in conference rooms, classrooms, or the privacy of cozy living-room settings, where one lone black woman faces the racist hostility of a group of white women. From the time the women's liberation movement began, individual black women went to groups. Many never returned after a first meeting. Anita Cornwell is correct in "Three for the Price of One: Notes from a Gay Black Feminist" when she states, "Sadly enough, fear of encountering racism seems to be one of the main reasons that so many black women refuse to join the women's movement." Recent focus on the issue of racism has generated discourse but has had little impact on the behavior of white feminists towards black women. Often the white women who are busy publishing papers and books on "unlearning racism" remain patronizing and condescending when they relate to black women. This is not surprising given that frequently their discourse is aimed solely in the direction of a white audience and the focus solely on changing attitudes rather than addressing racism in a historical and political context. They make us the "objects" of their privileged discourse on race. As "objects," we remain unequals, inferiors. Even though they may be sincerely concerned about racism, their methodology suggests they are not yet free of the type of paternalism endemic to white supremacist ideology. Some of these women place themselves in the position of "authorities" who must mediate communication between racist white women (naturally they see themselves as having come to terms with their racism) and angry black women whom they believe are incapable of rational discourse. Of course, the system of racism, classism, and educational elitism must remain intact if they are to maintain their authoritative positions.

In 1981, I enrolled in a graduate class on feminist theory where 21 we were given a course reading list that had writings by white women and men and one black man, but no material by or about black, Native American Indian, Hispanic, or Asian women. When I criticized this oversight, white women directed an anger and hostility at me that was so intense I found it difficult to attend the class. When I suggested that the purpose of this collective anger was to create an atmosphere in which it would be psychologically unbearable for me to speak in class discussions or even attend class, I was told that they were not angry. *I* was the one who was angry. Weeks after class ended, I received an open letter from one white female student acknowledging her anger and expressing regret for her attacks. She wrote:

> I didn't know you. You were black. In class after a while I noticed myself, that I would always be the one to respond to whatever you said. And usually it was to contradict. Not that the argument was always about racism by any means. But I think the hidden logic was that if I could prove you wrong about one thing, then you might not be right about anything at all.

And in another paragraph:

> I said in class one day that there were some people less entrapped
> than others by Plato's picture of the world. I said I thought we,
> after fifteen years of education, courtesy of the ruling class, might
> be more entrapped than others who had not received a start in life
> so close to the heart of the monster. My classmate, once a close
> friend, sister, colleague, has not spoken to me since then. I think
> the possibility that we were not the best spokespeople for all
> women made her fear for her self-worth and for her Ph.D.

Often in situations where white feminists aggressively attacked 22
individual black women, they saw themselves as the ones who were
under attack, who were the victims. During a heated discussion with
another white female student in a racially mixed women's group I
had organized, I was told that she had heard how I had "wiped out"
people in the feminist theory class, that she was afraid of being
"wiped out," too. I reminded her that I was one person speaking to a
large group of angry, aggressive people; I was hardly dominating the
situation. It was I who left the class in tears, not any of the people I
had supposedly "wiped out."

Racist stereotypes of the strong, superhuman black woman are 23
operative myths in the minds of many white women, allowing them
to ignore the extent to which black women are likely to be victimized in this society, and the role white women may play in the maintenance and perpetuation of that victimization. In Lillian Hellman's
autobiographical work *Pentimento,* she writes, "All my life, beginning
at birth, I have taken orders from black women, wanting them and
resenting them, being superstitious the few times I disobeyed." The
black women Hellman describes worked in her household as family
servants, and their status was never that of an equal. Even as a child,
she was always in the dominant position as they questioned, advised, or guided her; they were free to exercise these rights because
she or another white authority figure allowed it. Hellman places
power in the hands of these black women rather than acknowledge
her own power over them; hence she mystifies the true nature of
their relationship. By projecting onto black women a mythical
power and strength, white women both promote a false image of
themselves as powerless, passive victims and deflect attention away
from their aggressiveness, their power (however limited in a white
supremacist, male-dominated state), their willingness to dominate
and control others. These unacknowledged aspects of the social
status of many white women prevent them from transcending racism
and limit the scope of their understanding of women's overall social
status in the United States.

Privileged feminists have largely been unable to speak to, with,   24
and for diverse groups of women because they either do not understand fully the interrelatedness of sex, race, and class oppression or
refuse to take this interrelatedness seriously. Feminist analyses of
woman's lot tend to focus exclusively on gender and do not provide
a solid foundation on which to construct feminist theory. They reflect the dominant tendency in Western patriarchal minds to mystify
woman's reality by insisting that gender is the sole determinant of
woman's fate. Certainly it has been easier for women who do not experience race or class oppression to focus exclusively on gender. Although socialist feminists focus on class and gender, they tend to
dismiss race, or they make a point of acknowledging that race is important and then proceed to offer an analysis in which race is not
considered.

As a group, black women are in an unusual position in this soci-   25
ety, for not only are we collectively at the bottom of the occupa-
tional ladder, but our overall social status is lower than that of any
other group. Occupying such a position, we bear the brunt of sexist,
racist, and classist oppression. At the same time, we are the group
that has not been socialized to assume the role of exploiter/
oppressor in that we are allowed no institutionalized "other" that we
can exploit or oppress. (Children do not represent an institutionalized other even though they may be oppressed by parents.) White
women and black men have it both ways. They can act as oppressor
or be oppressed. Black men may be victimized by racism, but sexism allows them to act as exploiters and oppressors of women.
White women may be victimized by sexism, but racism enables
them to act as exploiters and oppressors of black people. Both
groups have led liberation movements that favor their interests and
support the continued oppression of other groups. Black male sexism has undermined struggles to eradicate racism just as white female racism undermines feminist struggle. As long as these two
groups, or any group, defines liberation as gaining social equality
with ruling-class white men, they have a vested interest in the continued exploitation and oppression of others.

Black women with no institutionalized "other" that we may dis-   26
criminate against, exploit, or oppress often have a lived experience
that directly challenges the prevailing classist, sexist, racist social
structure and its concomitant ideology. This lived experience may
shape our consciousness in such a way that our world view differs
from those who have a degree of privilege (however relative within
the existing system). It is essential for continued feminist struggle
that black women recognize the special vantage point our marginal-
ity gives us and makes use of this perspective to criticize the

dominant racist, classist, sexist hegemony as well as to envision and create a counter-hegemony. I am suggesting that we have a central role to play in the making of feminist theory and a contribution to offer that is unique and valuable. The formation of a liberatory feminist theory and praxis is a collective responsibility, one that must be shared. Though I criticize aspects of feminist movement as we have known it so far, a critique which is sometimes harsh and unrelenting, I do so not in an attempt to diminish feminist struggle but to enrich, to share in the work of making a liberatory ideology and a liberatory movement.

QUESTIONS FOR CRITICAL READING

1. What problems did hooks see in Betty Friedan's *The Feminist Mystique?*
2. What did feminist housewives want, according to Friedan?
3. Do you agree that the women's movement in America is sexist, racist, and classist?
4. Why doesn't "sexist tyranny" forge "a common bond between all women"?
5. What distinctions does hooks make about the suffering of the oppressed (see para. 7)?
6. What were hooks's personal experiences with women as she grew up?
7. In what ways does hooks describe herself as an oppressed woman?

SUGGESTIONS FOR WRITING

1. Judging from your experience, how open is the feminist movement to the needs of black women and other women of color? If you have participated in a women's studies program or in feminist organizations, use both your reading and your personal observations to describe the nature of the movement and its sensitivity to the needs of a broad spectrum of social classes. How effective is hooks's essay in helping feminists reshape their goals?
2. In much of her discussion, hooks refers to "a racist, sexist, capitalist state." To what extent do you think she is correct in describing America in these terms? Do you think that men would be as likely to agree with her as women? Would the women you know be likely to agree with her? Are the needs of feminists shaped by issues of sexism, racism, and capitalism? Try to qualify the extent to which you feel hooks is either being accurate or exaggerating the situation.
3. In paragraph 6, hooks says, "There is much evidence substantiating the reality that race and class identity creates differences in quality of life, social status, and lifestyle that take precedence over the common expe-

rience women share." What are the common experiences that women share? To what extent is hooks right in saying that race and class make it difficult or impossible for women to share common ground, even in terms of the feminist movement? Have you had any personal experience that might validate or invalidate hooks's view?

4. Read Betty Friedan's *The Feminine Mystique,* especially Chapter 3, "The Happy Housewife Heroine." Examine Friedan's views in this chapter and establish the extent to which hooks's analysis of the book is accurate. hooks is careful to criticize Friedan without declaring her work to be invalid or useless, but she is very direct in claiming that Friedan distorts women's issues. Is hooks right?

5. In paragraph 7, hooks says, "Being oppressed means the *absence of choices.*" How would you define the oppression of women? Be detailed and refer as much as possible to the experiences of individual women (or collective women, where appropriate). Is oppression only a matter of restricting choices? Would you say you yourself have felt oppressed because of a restriction of choices? If so, what can you do about your circumstances in order to improve them? How can you fight oppression?

6. About the desires of feminists in the 1970s, hooks says, "Their expectations were varied. Privileged women wanted social equality with men of their class; some women wanted equal pay for equal work; others wanted an alternative lifestyle" (para. 11). Consult with women you know and gather some data through interviews, in the manner of Carol Gilligan. Write down what they feel women need now in the first decade of the twenty-first century. How much have women's desires changed? What has altered to make women's needs different?

7. **CONNECTIONS** In what ways do the selections by Mary Wollstonecraft and Virginia Woolf reveal the problems that hooks describes? What would the importance of social class be to Wollstonecraft and Woolf? Would they be open to the problems of black women? Would they be open to the problems of women of the servant classes of their own time? How might bell hooks critique their work? For whom do Wollstonecraft and Woolf write? How do those audiences compare with the audience hooks addresses?

8. **CONNECTIONS** To what extent are Simone de Beauvoir's concerns about the myth of women relevant to hooks's statement, "By projecting onto black women a mythical power and strength, white women both promote a false image of themselves as powerless, passive victims and deflect attention away from their aggressiveness, their power (however limited in a white supremacist, male-dominated state), their willingness to dominate and control others" (para. 23)? How does the act of mythicizing women—regardless of color—affect them negatively? To what extent does hooks think that white women retain considerable power even while experiencing oppression? Do you find yourself in agreement with Beauvoir and hooks on the effect of myth on women?

9. **CONNECTIONS** In what ways do the experiences of Harriet Jacobs authenticate the concerns of bell hooks? Jacobs is not only black, but also first a slave, then a servant. How do her issues differ from those of

Mary Wollstonecraft? How do Jacobs's issues inform the reader of the extent to which oppression is a problem for women? How does reading Jacobs help us expand the limits of Virginia Woolf's focus on the "gifted" woman? Is Harriet Jacobs gifted? Are Wollstonecraft and Jacobs sensitive to the question hooks raises concerning the extent and depth of suffering experienced by women in different social circumstances (see paras. 13–14)?

WRITING ABOUT IDEAS
An Introduction to Rhetoric

Writing about ideas has several functions. First, it helps make our thinking available to others for examination. The writers whose works are presented in this book benefited from their first readers' examinations and at times revised their work considerably as a result of such criticism. Writing about ideas also helps us to refine what we think—even without criticism from others—because writing is a self-instructional experience. We learn by writing in part because writing clarifies our thinking. When we think silently, we construct phrases and then reflect on them; when we speak, we both utter these phrases and sort them out in order to give our audience a tidier version of our thoughts. But spoken thought is difficult to sustain because we cannot review or revise what we said an hour earlier. Writing has the advantage of permitting us to expand our ideas, to work them through completely, and possibly to revise in the light of later discoveries. It is by writing that we truly gain control over our ideas.

GENERATING TOPICS FOR WRITING

Filled with sophisticated discussions of important ideas, the selections in this volume endlessly stimulate our responses and our writing. Reading the works of great thinkers can also be chastening to the point of making us feel sometimes that they have said it all and there is no room for our own thoughts. However, the suggestions that follow will assist you in writing your response to the ideas of an important thinker.

Thinking Critically: Asking a Question. One of the most reliable ways to start writing is to ask a question and then to answer it. In many ways, that is what the writers in this book have done again and again. Karen Horney asked whether what Freud said about female psychology was true. Adam Smith asked what the principles of accumulating wealth really were and proceeded to examine the economic system of his time in such detail that his views are still valued. He is associated with the capitalist system as firmly as Marx is with the communist system. John Kenneth Galbraith asked questions about why poverty existed in a prosperous nation such as the United States. Richard P. Feynman asked whether scientists could be religious. Michio Kaku asked whether the theory of dark matter constituting 90 percent of the universe can be true. Such questioning is at the center of all critical thinking.

As a writer stimulated by other thinkers, you can use the same technique. For example, turn back to the Machiavelli excerpt annotated in "Evaluating Ideas: An Introduction to Critical Reading" (pp. 5–8). All the annotations can easily be turned into questions. Any of the following questions, based on the annotations and our brief summary of the passage, could be the basis of an essay:

- Should a leader be armed?
- Is it true that an unarmed leader is despised?
- Will those leaders who are always good come to ruin among those who are not good?
- To remain in power, must a leader learn how not to be good?

One technique is to structure an essay around the answer to such a question. Another is to develop a series of questions and to answer each of them in various parts of an essay. Yet another technique is to use the question indirectly—by answering it, but not in an obvious way. In "Why the Rich Are Getting Richer and the Poor, Poorer," for example, Robert B. Reich answers a question we may not have asked. In the process he examines the nature of our current economy to see what it promises for different sectors of the population. His answer to the question concerns the shift in labor from manufacturing to information, revealing that what he calls "symbolic analysts" have the best opportunities in the future to amass wealth.

Many kinds of questions can be asked of a passage even as brief as the sample from Machiavelli. For one thing, we can limit ourselves to our annotations and go no further. But we also can reflect on larger issues and ask a series of questions that constitute a fuller inquiry. Out of that inquiry we can generate ideas for our own writing.

Two important ideas were isolated in our annotations. The first was that the prince must devote himself to war. In modern times, this implies that a president or other national leader must put matters of defense first—that a leader's knowledge, training, and concerns must revolve around warfare. Taking that idea in general, we can develop other questions that, stimulated by Machiavelli's selection, can be used to generate essays:

- Which modern leaders would Machiavelli support?
- Would Machiavelli approve of our current president?
- Do military personnel make the best leaders?
- Should our president have a military background?
- Could a modern state survive with no army or military weapons?
- What kind of a nation would we have if we did not stockpile nuclear weapons?

These questions derive from "The prince's profession should be war," the first idea that we isolated in the annotations. The next group of questions comes from the second idea, the issue of whether a leader can afford to be moral:

- Can virtues cause a leader to lose power?
- Is Machiavelli being cynical about morality, or is he being realistic (as he claims he is)? (We might also ask if Machiavelli uses the word *realistic* as a synonym for *cynical*.)
- Do most American leaders behave morally?
- Do most leaders believe that they should behave morally?
- Should our leaders be moral all the time?
- Which vices can we permit our leaders to have?
- Are there any vices we want our leaders to have?
- Which world leaders behave most morally? Are they the ones we most respect?
- Could a modern government govern well or at all if it were to behave morally in the face of immoral adversaries?

One reason for reading Machiavelli is to help us confront broad and serious questions. One reason for writing about these ideas is to help clarify our own positions on such important issues.

Using Suggestions for Writing. Every selection in this book is followed by a number of questions and a number of writing assignments. The questions are designed to help clarify the most important issues raised in the piece. Unlike the questions derived from annotation, their purpose is to stimulate a classroom discussion so that you can benefit from hearing others' thoughts on these issues. Naturally, subjects for essays can arise from such discussion, but the discussion is most important for refining and focusing your ideas. The writing assignments, on the other hand, are explicitly meant to provide a useful starting point for producing an essay of five hundred to one thousand words.

A sample suggestion for writing about Machiavelli follows:

> Machiavelli advises the prince to study history and reflect on the actions of great men. Do you support such advice? Machiavelli mentions a number of great leaders in his essay. Which leaders would you recommend a prince should study? How do you think Machiavelli would agree or disagree with your recommendations?

Like most of the suggestions for writing, this one can be approached in several ways. It can be broken down into three parts. The first question is whether it is useful to study, as Machiavelli does, the performance of past leaders. If you agree, then the second question asks you to name some leaders whose behavior you would recommend studying. If you do not agree, you can point to the performance of some past leaders and explain why their study would be pointless today. Finally, the third question asks how you think Machiavelli would agree or disagree with your choices.

To deal successfully with this suggestion for writing, you could begin by giving your reasons for recommending that a political leader study "the actions of great men." George Santayana once said, "Those who cannot remember the past are condemned to repeat it." That is, we study history in order not to have to live it over again. If you believe that a study of the past is important, the first part of an essay can answer the question of why such study could make a politician more successful.

The second part of the suggestion focuses on examples. In the sample from Machiavelli above, we omitted the examples, but in the complete essay they are very important for bringing Machiavelli's point home. Few things can convince as completely as examples, so the first thing to do is to choose several leaders to work with. If you have studied a world leader, such as Indira Gandhi, Winston Churchill, Franklin Delano Roosevelt, or Margaret Thatcher, you could use that figure as one of your examples. If you have not done so, then use the research library's sections on history and politics to find books or articles on one or two leaders and read them with an eye to establishing their usefulness for your argument. An Internet search can help you gather information efficiently. Consult the Internet resources created specially for this book at: www .bedfordstmartins.com/worldofideas. The central question you would seek to answer is how a specific world leader could benefit from studying the behavior and conduct of a modern leader.

The third part of the suggestion for writing—how Machiavelli would agree or disagree with you—is highly speculative. It invites you to look through the selection to find quotes or comments that indicate probable agreement or disagreement on Machiavelli's part. You can base your argument only on what Machiavelli says or implies, and this means that you will have to reread his essay to find evidence that will support your view.

In a sense, this part of the suggestion establishes a procedure for working with the writing assignments. Once you clarify the parts of the assignment and have some useful questions to guide you, and once you determine what research, if any, is necessary, the next step is to reread the selection to find the most appropriate information to help you write your own essay. One of the most important activities in learning how to write from these selections is to reread while paying close attention to the annotations that you've made in the margins of the essays. It is one way in which reading about significant ideas differs from reading for entertainment. Important ideas demand reflection and reconsideration. Rereading provides both.

DEVELOPING IDEAS IN WRITING

Every selection in this book—whether by Francis Bacon or Simone de Beauvoir, Frederick Douglass or Karl Marx—employs specific rhetorical techniques that help the author communicate important ideas. Each introduction identifies the special rhetorical techniques used by the writer, partly to introduce you to the way in which such techniques are used. For example, Richard P. Feynman uses several instances of enumeration. He enumerates three interconnected aspects of religion and discusses them. Then, in the section titled "Science and Moral Questions" he says, "I believe that moral questions are outside of the scientific realm." Then he continues by enumerating the reasons why he believes this assertion is true:

> Let me give three or four arguments to show why I believe this. In the first place, there have been conflicts in the past between the scientific and the religious view about the metaphysical aspect and, nevertheless, the older moral views did not collapse, did not change.
>
> Second, there are good men who practice Christian ethics and who do not believe in the divinity of Christ. They find themselves in no inconsistency here.

Thirdly, although I believe that from time to time scientific evidence is found which may be partially interpreted as giving some evidence of some particular aspect of the life of Christ, for example, or of other religious metaphysical ideas, it seems to me that there is no scientific evidence bearing on the Golden Rule. It seems to me that that is somehow different. (paras. 35–37)

This structure helps us follow the argument and maintain clarity. Feynman makes his point, and enumeration helps cement it in our minds.

Rhetoric is a general term used to discuss effective writing techniques. For example, an interesting rhetorical technique that Machiavelli uses is illustration by example, usually to prove his points. Francis Bacon uses the technique of enumeration by partitioning his essay into four sections. Enumeration is especially useful when the writer wishes to be very clear or to cover a subject point by point, using each point to accumulate more authority in the discussion. Martin Luther King Jr. uses the technique of allusion, reminding the religious leaders who were his readers that St. Paul wrote similar letters to help early Christians better understand the nature of their faith. By alluding to the Bible and St. Paul, King effectively reminded his audience that they all were serving God.

A great many more rhetorical techniques may be found in these readings. Some of the techniques are familiar because many of us already use them, but we study them to understand their value and to use them more effectively. After all, rhetorical techniques make it possible for us to communicate the significance of important ideas. Many of the authors in this book would surely admit that the effect of their ideas actually depends on the way they are expressed, which is a way of saying that they depend on the rhetorical methods used to express them.

Methods of Development

Most of the rhetorical methods used in these essays are discussed in the introductions to the individual selections. Several represent exceptionally useful general techniques. These are methods of development and represent approaches to developing ideas that contribute to the fullness and completeness of an essay. You may think of them as techniques that can be applied to any idea in almost any situation. They can enlarge on the idea, clarify it, express it, and demonstrate its truth or effectiveness. Sometimes a technique may be direct, sometimes indirect. Sometimes it calls attention to itself, sometimes it works behind the scenes. Sometimes it is used alone, sometimes in conjunction with other methods. The most important techniques are explained and then illustrated with examples from the selections in the book.

Development by Definition. Definition is essential for two purposes: to make certain that you have a clear grasp of your concepts and that you communicate a clear understanding to your reader. Definition goes far beyond the use of the dictionary in the manner of "According to Webster's, ..." Such an approach is facile because complex ideas are not easily reduced to dictionary definitions. A more useful strategy is to offer an explanation followed by an example. Because some of the suggestions for writing that follow the selections require you to use definition as a means of writing about ideas, the following tips should be kept in mind:

- Definition can be used to develop a paragraph, a section, or an entire essay.
- It considers questions of function, purpose, circumstance, origin, and implications for different groups.
- Explanations and examples make all definitions more complete and effective.

Many of the selections are devoted almost entirely to the act of definition. For example, in "The Position of Poverty," John Kenneth Galbraith begins by defining the two kinds of poverty that he feels characterize the economic situation of the poor—case poverty and insular poverty. He defines case poverty in this paragraph:

> Case poverty is commonly and properly related to some characteristic of the individuals so afflicted. Nearly everyone else has mastered his environment; this proves that it is not intractable. But some quality peculiar to the individual or family involved—mental deficiency, bad health, inability to adapt to the discipline of industrial life, uncontrollable procreation, alcohol, discrimination involving a very limited minority, some educational handicap unrelated to community shortcoming, or perhaps a combination of several of these handicaps—has kept these individuals from participating in the general well-being. (para. 7)

When he begins defining insular poverty, however, he is unable to produce a neat single-paragraph definition. He first establishes that insular poverty describes a group of people alienated from the majority for any of many reasons. Next, he spends five paragraphs discussing what can produce such poverty—migration, racial prejudice, and lack of education. When working at the level of seriousness that characterizes his work, Galbraith shows us that definition works best when it employs full description and complex, detailed discussion.

An essay on the annotated selection from Machiavelli might define a number of key ideas. For example, to argue that Machiavelli is cynical in suggesting that his prince would not retain power if he acted morally, we would need to define what it means to be cynical and what moral behavior means in political terms. When we argue any point, it is important to spend time defining key ideas.

Martin Luther King Jr., in "Letter from Birmingham Jail," takes time to establish some key definitions so that he can speak forcefully to his audience:

> Let us consider a more concrete example of just and unjust laws. An unjust law is a code that a numerical or power majority group compels a minority group to obey but does not make binding on itself. This is *difference* made legal. By the same token, a just law is a code that a majority compels a minority to follow and that it is willing to follow itself. This is *sameness* made legal. (para. 17)

This is an adequate definition as far as it goes, but most serious ideas need more extensive definition than this passage gives us. And King does go further, providing what Machiavelli does in his essay: examples and explanations. Every full definition will profit from the extension of understanding that an explanation and example will provide. Consider this paragraph from King:

> Let me give another explanation. A law is unjust if it is inflicted on a minority that, as a result of being denied the right to vote, had no part in enacting or devising the law. Who can say that the legislature of Alabama which set up that state's segregation laws was democratically elected? Throughout Alabama all sorts of devious methods are used to prevent Negroes from becoming registered voters, and there are some counties in which, even though Negroes constitute a majority of the population, not a single Negro is registered. Can any law enacted under such circumstances be considered democratically structured? (para. 18)

King makes us aware of the fact that definition is complex and capable of great subtlety. It is an approach that can be used to develop a paragraph or an essay.

Development by Comparison. Comparison is a natural operation of the mind. We rarely talk for long about any topic without comparing it with something else. We are fascinated with comparisons between ourselves and others and come to know ourselves better as a result of such comparisons. Machiavelli, for example, compares the armed with the unarmed prince and shows us, by means of examples, the results of being unarmed.

Comparison usually includes the following:

- A definition of two or more elements to be compared (by example, explanation, description, or any combination of these),
- Discussion of shared qualities,
- Discussion of unique qualities,
- A clear reason for making the comparison.

Virginia Woolf's primary rhetorical strategy in "Shakespeare's Sister" is to invent a comparison between William Shakespeare and a fictional sister that he never had. Woolf's point is that if indeed Shakespeare had had a sister who was as brilliant and gifted as he was, she could not have become famous like her brother. The Elizabethan environment would have expected her to remain uneducated and to serve merely as a wife and mother. In the sixteenth century, men like William Shakespeare could go to London and make their fortune. Women, in comparison, were prisoners of social attitudes regarding their sex. As Woolf tells us,

> He was, it is well known, a wild boy who poached rabbits, perhaps shot a deer, and had, rather sooner than he should have done, to marry a woman in the neighborhood, who bore him a child rather quicker than was right. That escapade sent him to seek his fortune in London. He had, it seemed, a taste for the theatre; he began by holding horses at the stage door. Very soon he got work in the theatre, became a successful actor, and lived at the hub of the universe, meeting everybody, knowing everybody, practicing his art on the boards, exercising his wits in the streets, and even getting access to the palace of the queen. Meanwhile his extraordinarily gifted sister, let us suppose, remained at home. She was as adventurous, as imaginative, as agog to see the world as he was. But she was not sent to school. She had no chance of learning grammar and logic, let alone of reading Horace and Virgil. She picked up a book now and then, one of her brother's perhaps, and read a few pages. But then her parents came in and told her to mend the stockings or mind the stew and not moon about with books and papers. (para. 7)

Woolf's comparison makes it clear that the social circumstances of the life of a woman in Shakespeare's time worked so much against her personal desires and ambitions that it would be all but impossible for her to achieve anything of distinction on the London stage — or in any other venue in which men dominated. Even though a woman was monarch in England, it was a man's world.

Development by Example. Examples make abstract ideas concrete. When Machiavelli talks about looking at history to learn political lessons, he cites specific cases and brings them to the attention of his audience, the prince. Thomas Jefferson in the Declaration of Independence devotes most of his text to examples of the unacceptable behavior of the English king toward the colonies. Elizabeth Cady Stanton follows his lead and does the same, beginning her list of examples of gender discrimination with the assertion that "The history of mankind is a history of repeated injuries and usurpations on the part of man toward woman, having in direct object the establishment of an absolute tyranny over her. To prove this, let facts be submitted to a candid world" (para. 3). Then she lists the facts just as did Jefferson. Every selection in this book offers examples either to convince us of the truth of a proposition or to deepen our understanding of a statement.

Examples need to be chosen carefully because the burden of proof and of explanation and clarity often depends on them. When the sample suggestion given earlier for writing on Machiavelli's essay asks who among modern world leaders Machiavelli would approve, it is asking for carefully chosen examples. When doing research for an essay, it is important to be sure that your example or examples really suit your purposes.

Examples can be used in several ways. One is to do as Darwin does and present a large number of examples that force readers to a given conclusion. This indirect method is sometimes time-consuming, but the weight of numerous examples can be effective. A second method, such as Machiavelli's, also can be effective. By making a statement that is controversial or questionable and that can be tested by example, you can lead your audience to draw a reasonable conclusion.

When using examples, keep these points in mind:

- Choose a few strong examples that support your point.
- Be concrete and specific — naming names, citing events, and giving details where necessary.
- Develop each example as fully as possible, and point out its relevance to your position.

In some selections, such as Charles Darwin's discussion of natural selection, the argument hinges entirely on examples, and Darwin cites one example after another. Stephen Jay Gould shows how a particular example, that of the parasitical ichneumon fly, causes certain philosophical difficulties for theologians studying biology and therefore for anyone who looks closely at nature. The ichneumon, which people find ugly, attacks caterpillars, which people find sympathetic. As Gould tells us, we tend to dislike the parasite and sympathize with its victim. But there is another side to this, a second theme:

> The second theme, ruthless efficiency of the parasites, leads to the opposite conclusion—grudging admiration for the victors. We learn of their skill in capturing dangerous hosts often many times larger than themselves. Caterpillars may be easy game, but the psammocharid wasps prefer spiders. They must insert their ovipositors in a safe and precise spot. Some leave a paralyzed spider in its own burrow. *Planiceps hirsutus,* for example, parasitizes a California trapdoor spider. It searches for spider tubes on sand dunes, then digs into nearby sand to disturb the spider's home and drive it out. When the spider emerges, the wasp attacks, paralyzes its victim, drags it back into its own tube, shuts and fastens the trapdoor, and deposits a single egg upon the spider's abdomen. Other psammocharids will drag a heavy spider back to a previously prepared cluster of clay or mud cells. Some amputate a spider's legs to make the passage easier. Others fly back over water, skimming a buoyant spider along the surface. (para. 13)

Gould's example demonstrates that there are two ways of thinking about the effectiveness of the parasitic psammocharid. The wasp does not always make its life easier by attacking defenseless prey; instead, it goes after big game spiders. Gould's description technique, emphasizing the wasp's risk of danger, forces readers to respect the daring and ingenuity of the parasite even if at first we would not think to do so.

Development by Analysis of Cause and Effect.

People are interested in causes. We often ask what causes something, as if understanding the cause will somehow help us accept the result. Yet cause and effect can be subtle. With definition, comparison, and example, we can feel that the connections between a specific topic and our main points are reasonable. With cause and effect, however, we need to reason out the cause. Be warned that development by analysis of cause and effect requires you to pay close attention to the terms and situations you write about. Because it is easy to be wrong about causes and effects, their relationship must be examined thoughtfully. After an event has occurred, only a hypothesis about its cause may be possible. In the same sense, if no effect has been observed, only speculation about outcomes with various plans of action may be possible. In both cases, reasoning and imagination must be employed to establish a relationship between cause and effect.

The power of the rhetorical method of development through cause and effect is such that you will find it in every section of this book, in the work of virtually every author. Keep in mind these suggestions for using it to develop your own thinking:

- Clearly establish in your own mind the cause and the effect you wish to discuss.

- Develop a good line of reasoning that demonstrates the relationship between the cause and the effect.

- Be sure that the cause-effect relationship is real and not merely apparent.

In studying nature, scientists often examine effects in an effort to discover causes. Darwin, for instance, sees the comparable structure of the skeletons of many animals of different species and makes every effort to find the cause of such similarity. His answer is a theory: evolution. Another theorist, Michio Kaku, informs us that 90 percent of the universe is composed of dark matter: "Dark matter is a strange substance, unlike anything ever encountered before. It has weight but cannot be seen. In theory, if someone held a clump of dark matter in their hand, it would appear totally invisible. The existence of dark matter is not an academic question, because the ultimate fate of the universe, whether it will die in a fiery Big Crunch or fade away in a Cosmic Whimper of Big Chill, depends on its precise nature" (para. 6). Having said that, he goes on to explain the cause and effect equation:

> However, Ostriker and Peebles showed that the standard picture of a galaxy, based on our solar system, was unstable; by rights, the galaxy should fly apart. The gravitational pull of the stars was not enough to hold the galaxy together. They then showed that a galaxy can become stable if it is surrounded by a massive invisible halo that holds the galaxy together and if 90 percent of its mass was actually in the halo in the form of dark matter. (para. 18)

In this case, Kaku reveals that on the basis of the observed effect — that the universe does not fall apart even though it seems that it should — a theory must be constructed to explain the cause of its remaining held together. That theory produces the very puzzling concept of dark matter.

Everywhere in this collection authors rely on cause and effect to develop their thoughts. Thomas Jefferson establishes the relationship between abuses by the British and America's need to sever its colonial ties. Karl Marx establishes the capitalist economic system as the cause of the oppression of the workers who produce the wealth enjoyed by the rich. The Buddha regards spiritual fulfillment as the result of the practice of meditation. John Kenneth Galbraith is concerned with the causes of poverty, which he feels is an anomaly in modern society. Henry David Thoreau establishes the causes that demand civil disobedience as an effect.

Development by Analysis of Circumstances.   Everything we discuss exists as certain circumstances. Traditionally, the discussion of circumstances has had two parts. The first examines what is possible or impossible in a given situation. Whenever you try to convince your audience to take a specific course of action, it is helpful to show that given the circumstances, no other action is possible. If you disagree with a course of action that people may intend to follow because none other seems possible, however, you may have to demonstrate that another is indeed possible.

The second part of this method of development analyzes what has been done in the past: if something was done in the past, then it may be possible to do it again in the future. A historical survey of a situation often examines circumstances.

When using the method of examination of circumstances to develop an idea, keep in mind the following tips:

- Clarify the question of possibility and impossibility.

- Review past circumstances so that future ones can be determined.

- Suggest a course of action based on an analysis of possibility and past circumstances.

- Establish the present circumstances, listing them if necessary. Be detailed, and concentrate on facts.

Martin Luther King Jr. examines the circumstances that led to his imprisonment and the writing of "Letter from Birmingham Jail." He explains that "racial injustice engulfs this community," and he reviews the "hard brutal facts of the case." His course of action is clearly stated and reviewed. He explains why some demonstrations were postponed and why his organization and others have been moderate in demands and actions. But he also examines the possibility of using nonviolent action to help change the inequitable social circumstances that existed in Birmingham. His examination of past action goes back to the Bible and the actions of the Apostle Paul. His examination of contemporary action is based on the facts of the situation, which he carefully enumerates. He concludes his letter by inviting the religious leaders to whom he addresses himself to join him in a righteous movement for social change.

Machiavelli is also interested in the question of possibility, because he is trying to encourage his ideal prince to follow a prescribed pattern of behavior. As he constantly reminds us, if the prince does not do so, it is possible that he will be deposed or killed. Taken as a whole, "The Qualities of the Prince" is a recitation of the circumstances that are necessary for success in politics. Machiavelli establishes this in a single paragraph:

> Therefore, it is not necessary for a prince to have all of the above-mentioned qualities, but it is very necessary for him to appear to have them. Furthermore, I shall be so bold as to assert this: that having them and practicing them at all times is harmful; and appearing to have them is useful; for instance, to seem merciful, faithful, humane, forthright, religious, and to be so; but his mind should be disposed in such a way that should it become necessary not to be so, he will be able and know how to change to the contrary. And it is essential to understand this: that a prince, and especially a new prince, cannot observe all those things by which men are considered good, for in order to maintain the state he is often obliged to act against his promise, against charity, against humanity, and against religion. And therefore, it is necessary that he have a mind ready to turn itself according to the way the winds of Fortune and the changeability of affairs require him; and, as I said above, as long as it is possible, he should not stray from the good, but he should know how to enter into evil when necessity commands. (para. 23)

This is the essential Machiavelli, the Machiavelli who is often thought of as a cynic. He advises his prince to be virtuous but says that it is not always possible to be so. Therefore, the prince must learn how not to be good when "necessity commands." The circumstances, he tells us, always determine whether it is possible to be virtuous. A charitable reading of this passage must conclude that his advice is at best amoral.

Many of the essays in this collection rely on an analysis of circumstances. Frederick Douglass examines the circumstances of slavery and freedom. When Karl Marx reviews the changes in economic history in *The Communist Manifesto,* he examines the circumstances under which labor functions:

> The feudal system of industry, under which industrial production was monopolized by closed guilds, now no longer sufficed for the growing wants of the new market. The manufacturing sys-

tem took its place. The guild-masters were pushed on one side by the manufacturing middle-class: division of labor between the different corporate guilds vanished in the face of division of labor in each single workshop. (para. 14)

Robert B. Reich examines the circumstances of our contemporary economy. He determines, among other things, that the wages of in-person servers—bank tellers, retail salespeople, restaurant employees, and others—will continue to be low despite the great demand for such workers. Not only are these workers easily replaced, but automation has led to the elimination of jobs—including bank teller jobs made redundant by automatic tellers and by banking with personal computers and routine factory jobs replaced by automation. Under current circumstances, these workers will lose out to the "symbolic analysts" who know how to make their specialized knowledge work for them and who cannot be easily replaced.

Development by Analysis of Quotations. Not all the essays in this collection rely on quotations from other writers, but many do. "Letter from Birmingham Jail," for example, relies on quotations from the Bible. In that piece, Martin Luther King Jr. implies his analysis of the quotations because the religious leaders to whom he writes know the quotations well. By invoking the quotations, King gently chides the clergy, who ought to be aware of their relevance. In a variant on using quotations, Robert B. Reich relies on information taken from various government reports. He includes the information in his text and supplies numerous footnotes indicating the sources, which are usually authoritative and convincing.

When you use quotations, remember these pointers:

- Quote accurately, and avoid distorting the original context.
- Unless the quotation is absolutely self-evident, offer your own clarifying comments.
- To help your audience understand why you have chosen a specific quotation, establish its function in your essay.

The feminist bell hooks, in "Black Women: Shaping Feminist Theory," structures her essay in three parts. The first responds to a single book, with liberal quotation and analysis. The second discusses quotations from nine different feminist writers to demonstrate hooks's contention that mainstream feminists of the 1960s and 1970s ignored issues relevant to black women. In some cases hooks examines the limitations of the author quoted, and in some cases the quoted author reinforces hooks's position by showing how feminists have limited the discussion. The overall effect of this rhetorical strategy is to demonstrate that hooks knows the literature of feminism and that her method of analysis reinforces her basic position. The quotations help the reader assess hooks's views because they represent evidence that the reader can evaluate. Keeping in mind that bell hooks is an English professor, we can see that her method of textual analysis is accepted practice among scholars and helps her convince the reader of her argument.

In his examination of our tendency to anthropomorphize nature, Stephen Jay Gould uses quotations to show that there is a considerable literature on his subject. He quotes from J. H. Fabre, a French entomologist, to show how Fabre "humanized" caterpillars and demonstrated sympathy for the paralyzed victims of the parasitic wasps that fed off them. On the other hand, Gould points out that an equally interesting group of thinkers was impressed by the wasps' capacity to provide for their offspring. To support the viewpoint that admires the wasp, Gould quotes extensively from the writing of the Reverend William Kirby and other scientists, including Darwin (see paras.19–29). Although Gould interprets these paragraphs, they speak clearly for themselves and fit into his argument perfectly. He ends his essay with a quotation from Darwin about the relation of religion and evolution: "I feel most deeply that the whole subject is too profound for the human intellect. A dog might as well speculate on the mind of Newton. Let each man hope and believe what he can."

In your own writing you will find plenty of opportunity to cite passages from an author whose ideas have engaged your attention. In writing an essay in response to Machiavelli, Carl Jung, Carol Gilligan, or any other author in the book, you may find yourself quoting and commenting in some detail on specific lines or passages. This is especially true if you find yourself disagreeing with a point. Your first job, then, is to establish what you disagree with—and usually it helps to quote, which is essentially a way of producing evidence.

Finally, it must be noted that only a few aspects of the rhetorical methods used by the authors in this book have been discussed here. Rhetoric is a complex art that needs fuller study. But the points raised here are important because they are illustrated in many of the texts you will read, and by watching them at work you can begin to learn to use them yourself. By using them you will be able to achieve in your writing the fullness and purposiveness that mark mature prose.

A SAMPLE ESSAY

The following sample essay is based on the first several paragraphs of Machiavelli's "The Qualities of the Prince" that were annotated in "Evaluating Ideas: An Introduction to Critical Reading" (pp. 5–8). The essay is based on the annotations and the questions that were developed from them:

- Should a leader be armed?
- Is it true that an unarmed leader is despised?
- Will those leaders who are always good come to ruin among those who are not good?
- To remain in power, must a leader learn how not to be good?

Not all these questions are addressed in the essay, but they serve as a starting point and a focus for writing. The methods of development that are discussed above form the primary rhetorical techniques of the essay, and each method that is used is labeled in the margin. The sample essay does two things simultaneously: it attempts to clarify the meaning of Machiavelli's advice, and then it attempts to apply that advice to a contemporary circumstance. Naturally, the essay could have chosen to discuss only the Renaissance situation that Machiavelli described, but to do so would have required specialized knowledge of that period. In this sample essay the questions prompted by the annotations serve as the basis of the discussion.

The Qualities of the President

Introduction Machiavelli's essay, "The Qualities of the Prince," has a number of very worrisome points. The ones that worry me most have to do with the question of whether it is reasonable to expect a leader to behave virtuously. I think this is connected to the question of whether the leader should be armed. Machiavelli emphasizes that the prince must be armed or else face the possibility that someone will take over the government. When I think about how that advice applies to modern times, particularly in terms of how our president should behave, I find Machiavelli's position very different from my own.

Circumstance First, I want to discuss the question of being armed. That is where Machiavelli starts, and it is an important concern. In Machiavelli's time, the late fifteenth and early sixteenth centuries, it was common for men to walk in the streets of Florence wearing a rapier for protection. The possibility of robbery or even attack by rival political groups was great in those days. Even if he had a bodyguard, it was still important for a prince to know how to fight and to be able to defend himself. Machiavelli seems to be talking only about self-defense when he recommends that the prince be armed. In our time, sadly, it too is important to think about protecting the president and other leaders.

Examples   In recent years there have been many assassination attempts on world leaders, and our president, John F. Kennedy, was killed in Dallas in 1963. His brother Robert was killed when he was campaigning for the presidency in 1968. Also in 1968 Martin Luther King Jr. was killed in Memphis because of his beliefs in racial equality. In the 1980s Pope John Paul II was shot by a would-be assassin, as was President Ronald Reagan. They both lived, but Indira Gandhi, the leader of India, was shot and killed in 1984. This is a frightening record. Probably even Machiavelli would have been appalled. But would his solution--being armed--have helped? I do not think so.

Cause/Effect   For one thing, I cannot believe that if the pope had a gun he would have shot his would-be assassin, Ali Acga. The thought of it is almost silly. Martin Luther King Jr., who constantly preached the value of nonviolence, logically could not have shot at an assailant. How could John F. Kennedy have returned fire at a sniper? Robert Kennedy had bodyguards, and both President Reagan and Indira Gandhi were protected by armed guards. The presence of arms obviously does not produce the desired effect: security. The only thing that can produce that is to reduce the visibility of a leader. The president could speak on television or, when he must appear in public, use a bulletproof screen. The opportunities for would-be assassins can be reduced. But the thought of an American president carrying arms is unacceptable.

Comparison   The question of whether a president should be armed is to some extent symbolic. Our president stands for America, and if he were to appear in press conferences or state meetings wearing a gun, he would give a symbolic message to the world: look out, we're dangerous. Cuba's Fidel Castro usually appears in a military uniform with a gun, and when he spoke at the United Nations in 1960, he was the first, and I think the only, world leader to wear a pistol there. I have seen pictures of Benito Mussolini and Adolf Hitler appearing in public in military uniform, but never in a business suit. The same is true of Libyan leader Muammar al-Qaddafi and Iraq's Saddam Hussein. Today when a president or a head of state is armed there is often reason to worry. The current leaders of Russia usually wear suits, but Joseph Stalin always wore a military uniform. His rule in Russia was marked by the extermination of whole groups of people and the imprisonment of many more. We do not want an armed president.

Use of   Yet Machiavelli plainly says, "among the other
quotations bad effects it causes, being disarmed makes you despised . . . for between an armed and an unarmed man
also there is no comparison whatsoever" (para. 2). The problem with this statement is that it is more
Comparison relevant to the sixteenth century than the twentieth. In our time the threat of assassination is so great that being armed would be no sure protection, as we have seen in the case of the assassination of President Sadat of Egypt, winner of the Nobel Peace Prize. On the other hand, the pope, like Martin Luther King Jr., would never have appeared with a weapon, and yet it can hardly be said they were despised. If anything, the world's respect for them is enormous. America's president also commands the world's respect, as does the prime minister of Great Britain. Yet neither would ever

think of being armed. If what Machiavelli said was true in the early 1500s, it is pretty clear that it is not true today.

Definition   All this basically translates into a question of whether a leader should be virtuous. I suppose the definition of <u>virtuous</u> would differ with different people, but I think of it as holding a moral philosophy that you try to live by. No one is ever completely virtuous, but I think a president ought to try to be so. That means the president ought to tell the truth, since that is one of the basic virtues. The cardinal virtues--which were the same in Machiavelli's time as in ours--are justice, prudence, fortitude, and temperance. In a president, the virtue of justice is absolutely a must, or else what America stands for is lost. We definitely want our president to be prudent, to use good judgment, particularly in this nuclear age, when acts of imprudence could get us blown up. Fortitude, the ability to stand up for what is right, is a must for our president. Temperance is also important; we do not want a drunk for a president, nor do we want anyone with excessive bad habits.

Conclusion   It seems to me that a president who was armed or who emphasized arms in the way Machiavelli appears to mean would be threatening injustice (the way Stalin did) and implying intemperance, like many armed world leaders. When I consider this issue, I cannot think of any vice that our president ought to possess at any time. Injustice, imprudence, cowardice, and intemperance are, for me, unacceptable. Maybe Machiavelli was thinking of deception and lying as necessary evils, but they are a form of injustice, and no competent president--no president who was truly virtuous--would need them. Prudence and fortitude are the two virtues most essential for diplomacy. The president who has those virtues will govern well and uphold our basic values.

The range of this essay is controlled and expresses a viewpoint that is focused and coherent. This essay of about one thousand words illustrates each method of development discussed in the text and uses each one to further the argument. The writer disagrees with one of Machiavelli's positions and presents an argument based on personal opinion that is bolstered by example and by analysis of current political conditions as they compare with those of Machiavelli's time. A longer essay could have gone more deeply into issues raised in any single paragraph and could have studied more closely the views of a specific president, such as President Ronald Reagan, who opposed stricter gun control laws even after he was shot.

The range of the selections in this volume is great, constituting a significant introduction to important ideas in many areas. They are especially useful for stimulating our own thoughts and ideas. There is an infinite number of ways to approach a subject, but observing how writers apply rhetorical methods in their work is one way to begin our own development as writers. Careful analysis of each selection can guide our exploration of these writers, who encourage our learning and reward our study.

Acknowledgments

Hannah Arendt, "Ideology and Terror: A Novel Form." Excerpt from *The Origins of Totalitarianism* by Hannah Arendt. Copyright © 1951 and renewed 1979 by Mary McCarthy West. Reprinted by permission of Harcourt, Inc.

Aristotle, "A Definition of Justice." From *Poetics*, translated by Gerald F. Else. Copyright © 1967 by the University of Michigan. Used by permission of the University of Michigan Press.

James Baldwin, "The American Dream and the American Negro." Originally published in *The New York Times Magazine*. Collected in *The Price of the Ticket* by James Baldwin. Copyright © 1985, published by St. Martin's Press. Reprinted by arrangement with the James Baldwin Estate.

Simone De Beauvoir, "Women, Myth and Reality." From *The Second Sex* by Simone De Beauvoir, translated by H. M. Parshley. Copyright © 1942 and renewed 1980 by Alfred A. Knopf, Inc. Reprinted by permission of the publisher.

Rachel Carson, "Nature Fights Back." From *Silent Spring* by Rachel Carson. Copyright © 1962 by Rachel L. Carson. Renewed 1990 by Roger Christie. Reprinted by permission of Houghton Mifflin Company. All rights reserved.

Francis Crick, "The General Nature of Consciousness." From *The Astonishing Hypothesis: The Scientific Search for the Soul*. Copyright © 1995 by Francis Crick. Reprinted by permission of Simon & Schuster.

Richard P. Feynman, "The Relation of Science and Religion." From *The Pleasure of Finding Things Out: The Best Short Works of Richard P. Feynman*. Copyright © 1999 by Richard P. Feynman. Reprinted by permission of Perseus Books.

Sigmund Freud, "The Interpretation of Dreams." Originally titled "A Dream is the Fulfillment of a Wish" from *The Interpretation of Dreams* by Sigmund Freud, translated and edited by Dr. A.A. Brill and originally published by George Allen and Unwin Ltd. Reprinted by permission.

Milton and Rose Friedman, "Created Equal." From *Free to Choose: A Personal Statement*. Copyright © 1980 by Milton Friedman and Rose D. Friedman. Reprinted by permission of Harcourt, Inc.

John Kenneth Galbraith, "The Position of Poverty." Excerpt from *The Affluent Society*, 4th ed. Copyright © 1958, 1969, 1976, and 1984 by John Kenneth Galbraith. Reprinted by permission of Houghton Mifflin Company. All rights reserved.

Howard Gardner, "A Rounded Version: The Theory of Multiple Intelligences." From *Multiple Intelligences*. Copyright © 1993 by Howard Gardner. Reprinted by permission of Perseus Books.

Carol Gilligan, "Woman's Place in Man's Life Cycle." From *In A Different Voice* by Carol Gilligan. Copyright © 1982, 1993 by Carol Gilligan. Reprinted by permission of Harvard University Press.

Stephen Jay Gould, "Nonmoral Nature." From *Natural History*, February 1982. Copyright © 1982 by the Museum of Natural History. Reprinted with permission.

bell hooks, "Black Women: Shaping Feminist Theory." From *Feminist Theory* by bell hooks. Copyright © 2000. Reprinted by permission of South End Press.

Karen Horney, "The Distrust Between the Sexes." Speech read before the Berlin-Brandenburg Branch of the German Women's Medical Association on November 20, 1930, as "Das Misstrauen zwischen den Geschlechtern." *Die Artzin*, VII (1931), pp. 5–12. Reprinted in translation with the permission of the Karen Horney Estate.

Carl Jung, "The Personal and the Collective Unconscious." From *The Basic Writings of C. G. Jung* edited by Violet deLaszlo. Copyright © 1990 Princeton University Press. Reprinted by permission.

Michio Kaku, "The Mystery of Dark Matter." From *Beyond Einstein: The Cosmic Quest for the Theory of the Universe*. Copyright © 1987, 1995 by Michio Kaku and Jennifer Trainer Thompson. Reprinted by permission of the Stuart Krichevsky Literary Agency, Inc.

Martin Luther King, Jr., "Letter from Birmingham Jail." Copyright © 1963 by Martin Luther King Jr., copyright renewed 1991 by Coretta Scott King. Reprinted by arrangement with The Heirs to the Estate of Martin Luther King, Jr., c/o Writers House Inc., as agent for the proprietor.

Lao-tzu, from the *Tao-te Ching*. Excerpts as submitted from *Tao Te Ching* by Lao-tzu, A New English Version, with Foreword and Notes by Stephen Mitchell. Translation copyright © 1988 by Stephen Mitchell. Reprinted by permission of HarperCollins Publishers, Inc.

Niccolò Machiavelli, excerpts from "The Prince," by Niccolò di Bernardo Machiavelli, Peter Bondanella and Mark Musa, translated from *Portable Machiavelli* by Peter Bondanella and Mark Musa. Copyright © 1979 by Viking Penguin, Inc. Used by permission of Viking Penguin, and a division of Penguin Books USA, Inc.

The Prophet Muhammad, "The Believer." From the Koran, translated by N.J. Dawood (Penguin Classics 1956, Fifth revised edition 1990). Copyright © N. J. Dawood 1956, 1959, 1966, 1968, 1990. Reprinted by permission of Penguin Books Ltd.

Friedrich Nietzsche, "Apollonianism and Dionysianism." From *The Birth of Tragedy and the Genealogy of Morals* by Friedrich Nietzsche. Copyright © 1956 by Doubleday, a division of Bantam, Doubleday, Dell Publishing Group, Inc. Used by permission of Doubleday, a division of Random House, Inc.

Robert Reich, "Why the Rich Are Getting Richer and the Poor, Poorer." From *The Work of Nations* by Robert Reich. Copyright © 1991 by Robert B. Reich. Reprinted by permission of Alfred A. Knopf, Inc.

Jean-Jacques Rousseau, "The Origin of Civil Society." Translated by Gerard Hopkins, from *Social Contract: Essays by Locke, Hume and Rousseau* edited by Sir Ernest Barker (1947). Reprinted by permission of Oxford University Press.

Siddhartha Gautama, The Buddha, "Meditation: The Path to Enlightenment." Excerpted from *The Buddhist Scriptures*, translated by Edward Conze (Penguin Classics, 1959). Copyright © 1959 by Edward Conze. Reprinted by permission of Penguin Books Ltd.

Alexis de Tocqueville, "Influence of Democratic Ideas and Feelings on Political Society." From *Democracy in America* by Alexis de Tocqueville, translated by Henry Reeve. Copyright © 1945 and renewed 1973 by Alfred A. Knopf, a division of Random House, Inc. Used by permission of Alfred A. Knopf, a division of Random House.

Simone Weil, "Spiritual Autobiography." From *Waiting for God* by Simone Weil, translated by Emma Craufurd. Copyright © 1951, renewed 1979 by G.P. Putnam's Sons. Used by permission of G.P. Putnam's Sons, a division of Penguin Putnam, Inc.

Virginia Woolf, "Shakespeare's Sister." From *A Room of One's Own* by Virginia Woolf. Copyright © 1929 by Harcourt, Inc. and renewed 1957 by Leonard Woolf. Reprinted by permission of the publisher.

INDEX OF
RHETORICAL TERMS

allegory, 314
allusion, 781, 800, 884
ambiguity, 19, 825
analogy, 55, 114, 144. *See also*
    comparison and contrast
analysis, 21, 55, 76, 86–87,
    144, 181, 248, 327, 328,
    342, 343, 359, 819, 861–862
anaphora, 77
anecdotes, 780
annotations, 1, 4–5, 880–881
antagonist, 221, 506
aphorism, 3, 21, 37, 55. *See also*
    testimony
archetype, 309, 341, 342–343,
    818
argument, 36, 55, 113–114,
    171–172, 181, 210,
    263–264, 314, 328, 343,
    376, 455, 473, 505–506,
    567, 780, 800, 819, 899
asking questions. *See* questions;
    rhetorical questions
assumptions, 10, 11
audience, 77, 143, 144, 359,
    376, 454–455, 505–506,
    538, 567, 568, 780

authorities. *See* reference to
    authorities; testimony

balance, 76–77, 143–144, 171,
    418, 780, 781
beginning. *See* introduction
brevity, 36

cause and effect, 76–77, 358,
    359, 889–891. *See also*
    relationship
chiasmus, 144
chronological narrative. *See*
    narrative
circumstances, 87, 144, 797,
    819, 891–893
clarity, 143, 144, 249, 263, 376,
    418, 419, 472
comparison and contrast, 37,
    220, 264, 437, 455, 539,
    706, 733, 734, 887–888
complaint, 181, 221, 631
conclusion, 55, 143, 249, 397,
    567–568
contradiction, 704
contrast. *See* comparison and
    contrast

definition, 263, 419, 437, 539,
    733, 885–886
demonstration, 86, 437, 473
description, 86–87, 127, 455
details, 55, 114, 289, 455, 525,
    602–603, 692
development by analysis, 4,
    313, 314–315, 588, 642,
    665, 666, 668, 703, 706,
    722. *See also* analysis; cause
    and effect; circumstances;
    quotation
dialogue, 86–87, 127, 314–315,
    588, 665, 666, 668, 703,
    706, 722
diction, 647–648
division, 249

effect. *See* cause and effect
end. *See* conclusion; summary
enumeration, 76–77, 375, 376,
    397–398, 418, 506, 647
epistle. *See* letter
essay, 142, 143, 733, 894–899
evidence, 328, 358, 437, 568
example, 125, 127, 264, 289,
    328–329, 343, 376, 419,
    437, 455, 538, 780, 888–889
experience, 36, 341, 342, 504
exposition, 358–359

facts, 113, 289, 540. *See also* cir-
    cumstances
first person, 126–127, 143,
    631–632
folk aphorism. *See* aphorism

generalization, 209

hypothesis, 114, 358, 418, 437,
    566, 890

illustration. *See* example
imagery, 20, 359, 668, 669, 780

induction, 417–418, 437
introduction, 2, 602

jeremiad, 631
journal, 141–144

key terms, 144, 668

lecture, 143, 359
letter, 179–180, 520, 537–539,
    692, 753–754
list (listing), 76–77. *See also*
    enumeration
literary allusion. *See* allusion
logic, 86, 181, 375, 417, 567

meditation, 77, 540, 645–647,
    704
memorable phrase, 75,
    143–144, 692–693
metaphor, 20, 288–289, 314,
    329, 455, 473, 668–669,
    780–781
metonymy, 341, 473
myths, 20, 341, 342–343, 732,
    817–819, 838

narrative, 126–127, 343–344,
    525, 587–588, 667, 668,
    706, 722

observation, 328, 374, 412,
    417–419, 436, 437, 488,
    489, 523, 568, 780, 862
opposition, 36, 87
organization, 263, 418
organon, 417

paradox, 19, 21
parallelism, 76–77, 171, 376
pedantic tone. *See* tone
periodic sentence, 76–77, 171
personification, 412
poetics, 668, 705, 733

point of view, 55, 180, 721–722
premise, 86, 249
process, 87

questions (question asking),
    4–5, 21, 56, 114, 221, 287,
    375, 396, 398, 418–419,
    879–881. *See also* rhetorical
    questions
quotation, 76–77, 358, 359,
    889–891. *See also* reference to
    authorities; testimony

readers. *See* audience
reasoning, 54, 181, 374, 417,
    419, 568. *See also* induction;
    logic
reference to authorities, 249,
    568, 691, 820, 837, 873. *See
    also* quotation; testimony
relationship, 104, 202, 203,
    262, 358, 359, 455, 504,
    505, 818, 819–820. *See also*
    cause and effect;
    circumstances
repetition, 76–77, 143–144,
    668, 706
rhetoric, 20–21, 36–37, 54–56,
    76–77, 86–87, 113–114,
    126–127, 142–144, 171–172,
    180–181, 209–210, 220–221,
    249, 263–264, 288–289,
    314–315, 328–329, 343–344,
    358–359, 375–376, 397–398,
    418–419, 437, 454–455,
    472–473, 489, 505–506,

524–525, 538–540, 567–568,
    587–589, 601–603, 631–632,
    647–648, 668–669, 692–693,
    705–706, 721–722, 733–734,
    753–754, 780–781, 799–800,
    818–820, 837–838, 861–862
rhetorical questions, 314–315,
    375, 506, 722
rhyme, 143, 720, 721

second person, 631–632
simile, 602, 668–669, 799
Socratic method, 314–315
speech. *See* lecture
statistics, 249
structure, 77, 113, 126, 171,
    220–221, 288, 567, 587,
    602, 693, 819, 861
style, 126, 127, 220, 249, 315,
    328, 454–455, 505, 568,
    601, 602, 692, 800
subject, 249, 473, 630
summary, 210, 221, 419
symbol, 289, 342–343
synopsis, 691

testimony, 55, 437, 455,
    472–473. *See also* aphorism;
    quotation; reference to
    authorities
theory, 86, 328, 373, 398, 436,
    487–488, 838, 861
thesis, 437, 599–600
third person, 631–632
tone, 144, 180, 631, 632,
    647–648, 693, 799–800

Research and Writing Online

Whether you want to investigate the ideas behind a thought-provoking essay or conduct in-depth research for a paper, the Web resources for *A World of Ideas* can help you find what you need on the Web—and then use it once you find it.

The English Research Room for Navigating the Web

www.bedfordstmartins.com/english_research

The Web brings a flood of information to your screen, but it still takes skill to track down the best sources. Not only does *The English Research Room* point you to some reliable starting places for Web investigations, but it also lets you tune up your skills with interactive tutorials.

•Do you want to improve your skill at searching electronic databases, online catalogs, and the Web? Try the *Interactive Tutorials* for some hands-on practice.

•Do you need quick access to online search engines, reference sources, and research sites? Explore *Research Links* for some good starting places.

•Do you have questions on evaluating the sources you find, navigating the Web, or conducting research in general? Consult one of our *Reference Units* for authoritative advice.

Research and Documentation Online for Including Sources in Your Writing

www.bedfordstmartins.com/resdoc

Including sources correctly in a paper is often a challenge, and the Web has made it even more complex. This online version of the popular booklet *Research and Documentation in the Electronic Age*, by Diana Hacker, provides clear advice for the humanities, social sciences, history, and the sciences on—

•Which Web and library sources are relevant to your topic (with links to Web sources)

•How to integrate outside material into your paper

•How to cite sources correctly, using the appropriate documentation style

•What the format for the final paper should be